Gower Handbook of Programme Management

In the ten years since this Gower Handbook was first published, Programme Management has been transformed to become the vehicle of choice for realising the objectives of large scale, complicated, business, government and social investment.

The Second Edition of this Gower Handbook is a completely new text; designed as a definitive guide to the current state of Programme Management. To that end the text offers foundation theory and knowledge around key issues such as, managing programme contracts, people and know-how, complexity and uncertainty, benefits and success measures, as well as every stage of the programme life cycle. The main central section of the book provides theory, tools, advice and examples of practical application from an industry context and covers sectors including construction, energy, aerospace and defence, IT, automotive and the public sector. The Handbook also includes a section with chapters on assessing and improving programme competences and developing maturity. Discrete chapters relate programme management to the international baselines and standards.

Collectively, the Gower Handbook of Programme Management is most comprehensive guide to the subject that you can buy.

Dennis Lock has written or edited some of the defining books on project management, including *Project Management* (now in its Tenth Edition) and *Gower Handbook of People in Project Management*. Following a career in engineering and management, Dennis has lectured on project management at Masters level.

Reinhard Wagner is President of IPMA, Past President and Honorary Fellow of GPM (the German Project Management Association), and founder and CEO of Projectivists, a PM Consultancy.

Gower Handbook of Programme Management

Second Edition

Edited by

Dennis Lock and Reinhard Wagner

 Routledge
Taylor & Francis Group

LONDON AND NEW YORK

Second edition published 2016
by Routledge
2 Park Square, Milton Park, Abingdon, Oxon OX14 4RN

and by Routledge
711 Third Avenue, New York, NY 10017

Routledge is an imprint of the Taylor & Francis Group, an informa business

First edition published by Gower Publishing 2006

British Library Cataloguing in Publication Data
A catalogue record for this book is available from the British Library

Library of Congress Cataloguing in Publication Data
A catalog record for this title has been requested.

ISBN: 978-1-4724-4577-3 (hbk)
ISBN: 978-1-3155-8573-4 (ebk)

Typeset in Baskerville
by Out of House Publishing

Printed in the United Kingdom
by Henry Ling Limited

Contents

List of Figures   xvii
Notes on the Contributors   xxii
Preface   xxxv

PART I
Foundations of Programme Management   I

1   **Introduction to Programme Management**   3
     REINHARD WAGNER AND DENNIS LOCK

     The roads we have travelled 3
     The roads we shall follow in the future 6
     Challenges and concepts for programme management 8
     Jargon and the language of programme management 13
     Conclusion 13
     Organizations representing the profession of project management 14
     References and further reading 16

2   **International Standards for Programme Management and**
     Their Application   18
     REINHARD WAGNER

     Introduction 18
     Programme management standards in the aerospace and defence industry 18
     Competence standards for programme management 18
     Practice standards for programme management 21
     Other related standards for programme management 24
     Conclusion 27
     References and further reading 28

3   **The Nature of Programmes and their Interrelation with Projects,**
    Portfolios and Operations   29
    RODNEY TURNER

    Introduction 29
    History of multiprojects 30
    Definitions 31
    The cascade 34
    Three organizations 34
    The nature of programmes 35
    Relationship of programmes with projects, portfolios and operations 38
    References and further reading 39

PART II
Good Practice in Programme Management   41

4   **Distinguishing Different Types of Programmes**   43
    ALAN STRETTON

    Introduction 43
    Categorizations for organizations that manage programmes 44
    Attributes used by organizations in categorizing projects and programmes 48
    Programme categorizations used by external entities 49
    Initial collation of programme types from the literature 51
    Summary and conclusions 56
    References and further reading 57

5   **Programme Management in the Space Sector**   58
    SÉVERIN DROGOUL

    Main characteristics of the space sector 58
    Brief history of programmes in the space sector 60
    Programme management specifications 62
    Programme governance, organization and communication 63
    Work breakdown structure (WBS) 68
    Development process: phasing and planning management 72
    Relationships between phases and technical states 74
    Configuration management 76
    Dependability, risk and quality assurance 76
    Cost and schedule control 79
    Conclusion 80
    References and further reading 81

6   **Programme Management in the Aircraft Industry**   82
    SIMON HENLEY

    The market 82
    Governance 84
    Organization 84
    Programme management impacts 85
    Risk management 85
    Engineering development 86
    Certification 87
    Fitness for purpose 87
    Configuration management 87
    Supply chain management 89
    Aftermarket management 90
    Summary and conclusion 90
    References and further reading 91

7   **Programme Management in the Automotive Industry**   92
    HANS-HENRICH ALTFELD

    Introduction 92
    Evolution of programme management in the automotive industry 94
    Programme management applications 94
    Classical programme management for the automotive industry 96
    Quality management standards and tools 97
    The APQP-based product development process 98
    Managing programme risks 104
    Managing parallel programmes 105
    Effects of globalization 108
    Supply chain management 108
    Programme governance 109
    Conclusion 113
    References and further reading 115

8   **Programme Management in the Aviation Industry**   117
    BERNHARD DIETRICH

    Characteristics of the aviation industry 117
    Case study: a holistic business programme in the aviation industry 118
    Programme management 121
    Results of the case study programme 129
    Outlook and conclusion 130

9   **Programme Management in Construction and Engineering**   132
    JOSÉ REYES

    Introduction 132
    Definitions and characteristics of C&E programmes 132
    Role of government in C&E programmes 134
    Governance and organization of C&E programmes 135
    Summary of best practices in C&E programmes 137
    Developing a high performance programme management team 140
    Quality in C&E programmes 141
    Completing functional elements of programme deliverables 143
    Managing contextual environmental requirements 146
    Outlook and conclusions 147
    References and further reading 148

10 **Programme Management in Mining**   149
    MICHIEL C. BEKKER

    Introduction 149
    Definition and main characteristics of the mining sector 149
    Programme management 155
    Programme management in the mining industry 156
    Summary 160
    Acknowledgements 162
    References and further reading 162

11 **Programme Management in the Pharmaceutical Sector**   163
    LYNNE HUGHES AND SUSIE BOYCE

    Introduction 163
    Background 163
    Drug development stages 165
    Programme management 168
    Outsourcing 172
    Conclusion 172
    References and further reading 172

12 **Programme Management for Humanitarian and Development Projects**   174
    RICARDO VIANA VARGAS, FARHAD ABDOLLAHYAN, CARLOS
    ALBERTO PEREIRA SOARES AND ANDRÉ BITTENCOURT DO VALLE

    Introduction 174
    Characteristics of humanitarian and development projects 175
    Design, monitoring and evaluation frameworks 178
    Case example: LIFT 181

The 16/6 Haiti Programme 188
Conclusion 192
References and further reading 192

13   **Programme Management in the Police**   194
DAVID STEWART

Definition and main characteristics of the sector 194
Relevance of programme management to policing 195
The national police reform programme in Scotland 195
Programme methodology 197
Programme analysis and review 199
Programme control 200
Implementation 201
Result 203
Lessons 204
References and further reading 204

14   **Programme Management in the Transport Sector**   205
BEN GANNEY AND ARNAB BANERJEE

Introduction and a profile of Transport for London 205
TfL's programme delivery in context 206
What TfL delivers 208
The structure of delivery 208
The product matrix: underpinning the lifecycles 209
Roles, responsibilities and core functions 213
Conclusions 220
References and further reading 220

15   **Programme Management in the ICT Sector**   221
BURKHARD GÖRTZ AND SILKE SCHÖNERT

Introduction 221
The initial situation 221
Challenges 223
The solution and factors for success 224
Concluding summary 227

16   **Managing Change Programmes**   229
OLIVER MACK

Organizational change management: continuously needed and
  still challenging 229
Change programmes: a special type of programme 232

Managing change programmes: some aspects from a systemic perspective 234
Conclusion and outlook 243
References and further reading 243

17 **Programmes and Collaborative Working**   245
DAVID E. HAWKINS

Introduction 245
The best practice principles of BS 11000 250
Conclusion 257
References and further reading 258

18 **Managing Strategic Initiatives**   259
TERRY COOKE-DAVIES

Introduction 259
Outcome, process and control 260
Engaging people in changes 261
Complexity 263
Leadership 264
Pulling it all together: managing strategic initiatives for success 265
References and further reading 265

PART III
Programme Governance, Organization and Culture   **269**

19 **Programme Governance**   271
MARTIN SAMPHIRE

Introduction 271
Importance of project and programme governance 272
The governance landscape 272
Established guidelines 275
Key enablers 276
Ten golden rules 277
The key players in governance 283
How much governance is enough? 283
Case study 1: transformation programme in a global services company 284
Case study 2: project management capability improvement 286
Summary 288
References and further reading 289

20 **Mastering Integration in Programme Management**   290
MARTIN SEDLMAYER

Introduction and background 290
The challenge 293
Contextual dimensions 295
The programme approach 298
Lessons learned 310
References and further reading 311

21 **Programme Management Offices**   312
EILEEN RODEN, LINDSAY SCOTT AND DENNIS LOCK

Introduction 312
PMO functions and services 313
Specific PMO functions and services 314
Skills within the PMO 318
Strategic and operational PMO functions and services 319
Tools 319
PMO structures 320
The PMO lifecycle 322
Managing the PMO 324
Closing down a PMO 325
Challenges and trends for the PMO of the future 326
References and further reading 328

22 **Programme Culture**   330
STEVEN RAUE AND LOUIS KLEIN

Programme culture: winning or losing the benefits 330
Understanding programme culture 331
The organizational perspective 334
Mastering culture 336
Summary 337
References and further reading 337

PART IV
Programme Lifecycles, Processes, Methods and Tools   **339**

23 **Programme Lifecycles**   341
ANDREA DEMARIA AND JOSEPH SOPKO

Introduction 341
Benefit lifecycle: from opportunity to full benefit delivery 341

The programme business case 344
Programme lifecycle boundaries and phases 345
Interaction between programme components 352
Interactions between project and programme portfolios 354
References and further reading 354

24   An Overview of the Programme Management Process   355
ROBERT BUTTRICK

Programme management: process or method? 355
Programme management processes and methods: context is key 357
Formal, informal, light or tight? 357
Ensuring an architecture for programme management processes 359
Management processes 363
Managing a programme 364
Supporting processes 368
Specialist or 'other' processes 368
The importance of change management 370
Tailoring 372
Documenting processes 372
References and further reading 374

25   Programme Identification and Initiation   375
COLIN BAILEY

Introduction 375
Part 1: where are we going? 376
Part 2: are we there yet? 379
Part 3: putting the support in place 382
Conclusion 383
References and further reading 384

26   Programme Planning   385
JOEL CROOK

Introduction 385
Case study 386
Programme management plan 387
Integration 390
Scope management 391
Work breakdown structure 392
Benefits realization plan 393
Integrated master plan 393

Programme schedule 395
Stakeholders 398
Communications management plan 399
Risk management plan 399
Supply chain management plan 403
Financial management plan 404
Quality management plan 404
Other plans 405
References and further reading 405

27 **Controlling Programmes for IT and Business Change**   406
GERRIT KOCH AND DENNIS LOCK

A few golden rules 406
The business case for a change programme 407
Programmes in an organization 411
Project, programme and portfolio management controls 413
Defining roles 418
Cost control 419
Benefits realization and measurement 420
Closing a programme 421
Fast systems development 422
The bigger picture 423
References and further reading 423

28 **Using Modern Technologies for Programme Management**   424
MARK PHILLIPS

Introduction 424
Case 1 424
Case 2 426
Concluding case 428

29 **Managing Programme Benefits**   430
ANDREW HUDSON

Introduction 430
The nature of programme benefits management 432
Programme benefits management roles 437
Programme benefits management practices 439
Benefit measures 441
Conclusion 443
References and further reading 443

30 **Managing Complexity in Programmes**   444
STEPHEN HAYES

Introduction 444
Characteristics of complexity 445
Failures in complex programmes 445
Assessing complexity in programmes 447
Tools for complex programmes 452
Conclusion 457
References and further reading 457

31 **Managing Uncertainties in Programmes**   459
MOTOH SHIMIZU

Introduction 459
Explanation of programme uncertainty 459
Strategy and uncertainty 460
Uncertainty management processes 461
Categorized causal elements of programme uncertainties 464
Conclusion 471
References and further reading 472

32 **Managing Programme Resources**   473
DENNIS LOCK

Introduction 473
Resource categories 473
Managing the resource of time 474
Scheduling resources 475
Risk management and programme resources 480
Managing supplies and materials 481
Managing cash as a resource 481
Managing office accommodation space 486
References and further reading 487

33 **Managing People in Programmes**   488
DENNIS LOCK AND ALAN FOWLER, WITH KEIKO MOEBUS

Introduction 488
*The contribution of early management theorists towards our understanding
    of people in the workplace 489*
Understanding how people can react to change 491
Communicating for programme success 495
Managing the mindsets 496
Experience-related performance 496

Ways of making change happen 498
Conclusion 501
Acknowledgement 501
References and further reading 501

34 **Managing Partners in Programmes**   502
    HUBERTUS C. TUCZEK AND JÜRGEN FRANK

    Introduction 502
    Strategic level 503
    Relationship level 505
    Cooperation level 511
    Programme closure 518
    References and further reading 519

35 **Managing Contracts in Programmes**   520
    TIM CUMMINS

    Introduction 520
    Things that can go wrong 521
    Achieving better results 530
    Conclusion 531
    References and further reading 532

36 **Creating Knowledge Services for Modern Technical Project
    Organizations: The REAL Knowledge Approach**   533
    EDWARD J. HOFFMAN AND JON BOYLE

    Introduction 533
    The project knowledge environment 534
    Knowledge services governance 536
    Strategic imperatives in the modern project knowledge environment 540
    The REAL model 542
    REAL knowledge services examples at NASA 548
    Summary and future research 553
    References and further reading 555

PART V
Developing Maturity in Programme Management   **557**

37 **Introducing Programme Management into an Organization**   559
    MARCUS PAULUS

    Introduction: the nature of programmes 559
    *Programme governance in the context of portfolio, programme and project
        management 561*

Creating clarity in the terminology 562
Roles, responsibilities and duties 566
Programme initiation, planning, control and closing 567
Integration of programmes in the total portfolio 570
Revising existing project management reporting and communication structures 572
Training and recruitment 573
References and further reading 574

38 **Assessing and Improving Programme Management Maturity**   575
    MATTI HAUKKA AND MIRKKA LYYTIKÄINEN

Introduction 575
Prerequisites for programme management maturity 575
Assessing programme management maturity in a single programme 581
Summary and conclusions 583
References and further reading 583

39 **Developing Competencies of People in Programmes**   584
    MICHAEL YOUNG

Introduction 584
Defining competence 584
Current and emerging competence standards for programme managers 585
Competence assessment 588
Other uses of competence standards 588
Developing competence 589
Barriers to competence development 591
Conclusion 592
References and further reading 592

Index   595

List of Figures

1.1	Organization chart of officers in a Chinese military battalion for bridge building (Ming Dynasty)	4
1.2	Projects, portfolios and programmes in an organization	9
1.3	Linking projects through programmes with strategy	10
1.4	A few common examples of project and programme management jargon	14
2.1	The 'eye of competence' of IPMA ICB	19
2.2	Organizational competence elements	26
3.1	An investment portfolio	33
3.2	The normal (dominant) cascade	34
3.3	Three organizations involved in the management of projects	35
3.4	Portfolio, programme, operation, projects	38
4.1	Map of attributes for building project categorization systems	49
4.2	Initial collation of project and programme types from the literature	51
4.3	Types of programmes with case examples	53
4.4	Proposed grouping to provide a skeleton on which to develop further a robust classification of technological projects/programmes	54
4.5	Model relating to 'technological' programmes with programme application sectors	55
5.1	Space launcher programmes are high risk	59
5.2	Management requirements structure	62
5.3	Typical programme organization within a dedicated actor (customer or supplier)	65
5.4	Key rules for actor interrelationships	67
5.5	Part of a typical work breakdown structure	71
5.6	Typical programme lifecycle (simplified)	73
5.7	Flow chart of programme development showing milestones and phase reviews	75
5.8	Key activities and reviews at constituent product level	76
5.9	Key activities for risk analysis and mitigation	77
5.10	Risk identification, assessment and mitigation (RAMS)	77
7.1	Examples of quality management tools and standards used in the automotive industry	97

7.2   The APQP product development process   99
7.3   Skills and competencies required for programme managers in
       the automotive industry   112
8.1   Return on capital employed averaged over five years   118
8.2   Overall programme organization   122
8.3   Overview of programme phases and status   124
8.4   Overview of project types   125
8.5   Controlling the programme   126
8.6   Format of monthly development forecasts   127
9.1   Typical organization of a construction and engineering programme   136
9.2   Typical construction and engineering programme scheme   139
9.3   Construction and engineering programme quality documentation   142
9.4   Using milestones in construction and engineering
       programme management   144
9.5   Phase 3 of construction and engineering programme controls   145
10.1   Stages of mining   151
10.2   Sequenced production profile of a mining complex   152
10.3   Lifecycle of a mine project   154
10.4   Programme value path   155
10.5   Programme plan   158
10.6   Benefit measurement   161
11.1   The pharmaceutical research and development process   167
11.2   Success rates across drug development phases   167
11.3   Success rates of NDAs, NMEs approvals since 2010   172
12.1   Disaster risk and its relation to resilience   176
12.2   LogFrame matrix   180
12.3   LIFT programme governance source   184
12.4   Organization of the programme management office   185
12.5   Managing the tranches   187
12.6   Activities, reach and impact   188
13.1   Comparison of senior management numbers before and
       after the reforms   203
14.1   The Transport for London story, showing the importance of
       infrastructure delivery   206
14.2   The delivery environment in the context of the TfL
       organizational environment   207
14.3   The project lifecycle   208
14.4   The delivery portfolio lifecycle   209
14.5   The programme lifecycle   210
14.6   A typical TfL Pathway product   211
14.7   Product matrix   212
14.8   The sponsor in context   214
14.9   Sponsor involvement (characteristic)   215
15.1   First implementation plan   222
15.2   HERKULES meets reality   224
15.3   Overall implementation plan   226
16.1   Change types   230

16.2	Different objectives of change projects	231
16.3	Project types	233
16.4	Change role set-up in a transformation programme	235
17.1	CRAFT/BS 11000 eight-step model	247
17.2	Skills and organizational enablers	248
17.3	High performing organizations	249
17.4	Interpreting communications	249
17.5	Understanding Maslow's hierarchy of motivational needs	250
19.1	Generic organizational governance linkages	273
19.2	Key governance players and accountability lines	283
20.1	The business architecture	294
20.2	The relevant stakeholders	300
20.3	Programme mission	301
20.4	The Virtual Centre programme as a sketch	302
20.5	The seven building blocks	303
20.6	The governance structure	305
20.7	Programme organization	306
20.8	Roadmap of the Virtual Centre programme	307
21.1	The full range of PMO types within organizations	313
21.2	The three segments resulting from the relationship between the scope and the approach relationship	314
21.3	Programme management office stakeholders	315
21.4	Value of the programme management office	315
21.5	The programme management office as an overarching entity	315
21.6	The programme management office hub	318
22.1	In Tichy's TPC matrix social complexity evolves in the political and cultural dimensions	332
22.2	Scott's three principles of observation	335
23.1	Realization of benefits from deliverables	343
23.2	Programme lifecycle phases	346
23.3	Relationships between enabling projects and programme waves	350
23.4	Relationship between transition projects and programme waves	351
24.1	Efficient programme management requires more than process or methods, culture (values and mindsets)	356
24.2	Management support and specialist programmes: high-level architecture	359
24.3	Decomposition of a programme into components	360
24.4	Starting to build detail into the architecture: choosing the activities which are key for the programme	362
24.5	Programme management architecture in the context of organization, portfolio, programme, project and portfolio management	363
24.6	Information flow and activities for directing and managing a programme	365
24.7	Typical processes and control methods	369
24.8	Typical quality related processes	370
24.9	Typical commercial processes or methods	371

24.10 Project scope encompassing both outcomes and benefits,
      as used in an extended project lifecycle   371
24.11 Cascade for tailoring   373
25.1   The process of programme identification   377
25.2   The process of programme initiation   381
26.1   Programme documents arranged by subject matter and priority   389
26.2   Project 'stove-pipe' organization compared with an integrated
      programme organization   391
26.3   Probability-impact matrix showing the 'area of interest'   401
26.4   Risk category examples   401
26.5   Example using a tornado diagram to show the risk position
      for a project   402
27.1   Initial task check-list for a management change project   408
27.2   The missing link   413
27.3   Programme control loops   415
27.4   Elaborated control model   417
29.1   Connecting strategy with change and operations   431
29.2   Programme benefits lifecycle   433
29.3   Programme benefits management challenges and mitigations   436
29.4   A strategic alignment matrix   439
29.5   Example of a benefit dependency map   440
29.6   Example of a cash flow profile   441
30.1   Complex programme maturity model and variability index   449
30.2   Remington and Pollack's four types of complexity   451
30.3   Relationship between the ELLab and the Think2Impact platforms   455
31.1   Basic processes of programme uncertainty management   462
31.2   Causal elements and corresponding phases   464
31.3   Causal elements by category, and major examples of countermeasures   465
31.4   Some causes and effects of programme change   471
32.1   Rate variable and rate constant resource patterns for a single task   477
32.2   Resource-limited and time-limited resource usage plans   479
32.3   The PMO as guardian of the programme resource schedule model   480
32.4   Possible cash flow for the contractor of a construction project   483
32.5   Possible cash flow for a change programme (office relocation)   484
33.1   Abraham Maslow's hierarchy of human needs   490
33.2   Typical human responses to a controllable change   492
33.3   Typical human responses to uncontrollable change   493
33.4   Understanding where people are coming from (the iceberg)   498
34.1   Three-level concept for the management of partners in programmes   504
34.2   Concept for stakeholder analysis   506
34.3   Cooperation matrix with meeting planner   507
34.4   An escalation and decision template   508
34.5   The process of contract management   509
34.6   Explicit and implicit culture: Trompenaars' culture model   510
34.7   Linked programmes along the supply chain   512
34.8   Example of an activity interface matrix   513
34.9   Integrated view of programme control over time   514

34.10 Interface matrix for deliverables and work packages   517
34.11 An issue list   518
35.1 Major causes of value erosion   522
35.2 A framework for stakeholder analysis   524
35.3 The most frequently negotiated terms and conditions   526
35.4 Benefits typically achieved moving towards more collaborative,
       outcome-based contracts   530
35.5 Challenges expected when moving towards more collaborative,
       outcome-based contracts   531
36.1 Knowledge services strategic framework   537
36.2 Example NASA knowledge map   539
36.3 The REAL knowledge model   543
36.4 The 4A word cloud   547
36.5 The NASA knowledge referee process   550
37.1 Development roadmap of programme management in
       an organization   560
37.2 Internal and external environment for analysing usage of
       the term 'programme'   563
37.3 Principles of a hierarchical project portfolio   571
38.1 Prerequisites related to organization management and structures   577
38.2 Prerequisites related to project and portfolio management (PPM)
       capability   578
38.3 Indicators of readiness for change programme implementation   582

Notes on the Contributors

Farhad Abdollahyan is consultant, researcher and teacher, in São Paulo, Brazil, with a solid academic background in business administration and finance, as well as project management. He holds several professional certifications and has more than 30 years of diversified experience in multinational companies, government and NGOs. Mr Abdollahyan participated in developing PMI's OPM3 and portfolio management standards and is portfolio, programme and project management practice adviser at UNOPS. He also has hands-on experience in post-disaster reconstruction programmes.

Hans-Henrich Altfeld is Global VP for Program Management with Johnson Controls, one of the largest first-tier suppliers to the automotive industry. His responsibilities include the development, delivery and continuous improvement of the program management-driven product development culture for the company's seating products. Some of Dr Altfeld's previous executive roles included setting up and leading the Center of Competence 'Project and Program Management' at Airbus Toulouse, France, as well as the Project Management Office for the development of the A380 wing at Bristol, UK. He also served as VP Production at Airbus' plant at Hamburg, Germany. He received his PhD in 1989 and has since held positions with several aerospace industry organizations, among them Messerschmitt-Bölkow-Blohm, DASA, Dornier Satellite Systems, the European Aerospace Industries Association. In 1999 he joined Airbus as Director for A380 Strategic Issues and Organisation Development, where he was in charge of developing the 'design-built team'-based organization for the 5,000 employees involved in the development of the Airbus A380. Dr Altfeld is a member of the German Engineers Society, Honorary Chairman of the Royal Aeronautical Society Hamburg Branch and during the term 2007/2008 was also a member of the RAeS President's Council. He is the author of the book *Commercial Aircraft Projects: Managing Complex Product Developments*, which has been published in English and Chinese.

Colin Bailey is a strategist level programme director within Hewlett Packard Enterprise, responsible for all transformations, programmes and projects for the United Kingdom and Ireland Infrastructure Outsourcing business. With 29 years of project and programme management experience, he works with client board members to define transition and transformation strategies, and leads large, complex, global implementation programmes and an organization of over 700 project and programme management professionals. Colin has supported commercial sector customers including financial services, manufacturing, leisure and retail, in addition to UK Government (national and local). He attended the University of Warwick gaining a BSc in Mathematics, and earned an MBA in International Business from the University of Birmingham.

Arnab Banerjee has spent his career in the infrastructure industry, starting in the Power field (ALSTOM Power) and then in Transport (Transport for London). He has worked in various functions ranging from engineering to sales, strategy, commercial, corporate, programme management and a PMO. His focus and passion now is for change management and transformation from inception to embedment. Arnab holds an MBA from the University of Warwick, is a Fellow of the Institution of Mechanical Engineers (UK) and began his working life with a Masters degree in Mechanical Engineering from Imperial College, London.

Michiel C. Bekker has more than 25 years' experience in project and programme management in industries such as petrochemical, mining, telecommunications and infrastructure development. A professional mechanical engineer by trade, he also holds an MBA and PhD. He currently teaches project management at postgraduate level and has developed numerous in-house training programmes and methodologies for private and public organizations. His work has been published in various journals and he regularly presents at international conferences. He participated in the development of ISO 21500 and 21503. In practice Michiel founded the consulting firm ProjectWay, serves as Director of the Construction Industry Institute South African Chapter and is a recipient of the Excellence Award for Project Execution from PMSA.

Susie Boyce has over 20 years' experience in project management; leading multi-disciplinary teams to deliver large, complex clinical trials across a range of therapeutic areas (cardiovascular, oncology, respiratory, central nervous system, endocrinology, musculo-skeletal osteoporosis and post-surgical pain) across all phases of drug development and managing budgets of many millions of dollars to non-negotiable timelines. She started her career as a scientist and worked in two UK National Health Service centres of excellence, The Royal Brompton National Heart and Lung Hospital and subsequently as Deputy Clinical Physiologist at Harefield Hospital. She moved to the pharmaceutical industry and progressed to project management. She is PMP certified and a Chartered Scientist. She is now Senior Director in Project Leadership, Central Nervous System EMEA at Quintiles, a clinical research organization. She is currently responsible for leading a team of project and programme directors and overseeing a portfolio of projects and programmes across the globe. Susie is a Trustee and Non-Executive Director of the UK Association of Project Management (APM) and a former joint co-chair of their Women in Project Management Specific Interest Group.

Jon Boyle has served in several capacities in public and private sector organizations, from industrial production lines and overseas military combat units to multinational corporations, NASA flight facilities and academia. He has expertise in cognitive neurosciences, industrial/organizational psychology, knowledge management, group processes, human resources and workforce development, business strategy, technology-enabled learning, research and development and process improvement. Jon currently serves as the NASA Agency Deputy Chief Knowledge Officer (InuTeq), where he contributes to the development of the overall NASA technical workforce through knowledge services. He earned a BA degee in Psychology and Biology from the University of Southern Maine; an M.Ed. from Boston University; an MA in Industrial and Organizational Psychology from George Mason University; and a PhD in Human Development from Virginia Tech, as well as participating in diverse training and certifications in technology, project management, quality-related topics, acquisition and procurement, leadership and coaching. He currently teaches several undergraduate and graduate programmes and maintains an active research and publication agenda.

Robert Buttrick is an international authority on business-led, programme and project management with a successful track record in a wide variety of blue-chip companies, most recently as BT's PPM Method Director. Prior to this he was with the PA Consulting Group, and specialized in business-led project management, advising across a range of sectors. His early career was as a civil engineer working in Africa, the Middle East and at the World Bank in the USA. He is a published author (*The Project Workout*) and an active contributor to project management handbooks, methods, professional journals and conferences. Robert received a Distinguished Service Certificate from BSI for services to national and international project management standards; he is a member of the Chartered Institute of Marketing, is Chartered Engineer and an Honorary Fellow of the Association for Project Management. Robert currently works as an independent consultant and is a Visiting Teaching Fellow at the University of Warwick.

Terry Cooke-Davies was the founder and Group Chairman of Human Systems International (HSI), a project management assessment and benchmarking firm that was acquired by the Project Management Institute (PMI) in September 2013. With a PhD in Project Management, a Bachelor's degree in Theology, and qualifications in electrical engineering, management accounting and counselling, Terry has worked alongside senior leaders and managers in both the public and the private sectors, to ensure the delivery of business critical change programmes and enhance the quality of leadership. In October 2006, the Association for Project Management awarded Terry the Sir Monty Finneston Award for his outstanding contribution to the development of project management as a vehicle for effective change, and in 2009 it appointed him an Honorary Fellow.

Joel Crook is Director of Enterprise Risk Management for Consolidated Nuclear Security, LLC. Prior to this assignment, Mr Crook was a Program Director for ATK Aerospace Systems, responsible for a system-level space launch vehicle programme. He is a graduate of Texas A&M – Texarkana, where he earned an MS in Business Administration, and the University of Wyoming where he graduated with a BS in Mechanical Engineering. He has several published works. Mr Crook has over 25 years of project, programme and portfolio management experience in the aerospace and defence industry. He has led highly successful teams in the development of 'first-of-their-kind' products and services. He is a member of the US

Technical Advisory Group to the American National Standards Institute (ANSI), and an elected US delegate to ISO, for development of the International Project Portfolio Management Standard and Program Management Standard.

Tim Cummins is founder and Chief Executive Officer for the International Association for Contract and Commercial Management, a global, non-profit professional association. His career included management and executive positions within banking, automotive, aerospace and technology sectors, in finance, marketing and commercial management. Tim's work has involved extensive international experience, negotiating contracts up to $1.5 billion in value in more than 40 countries and having lived in France (for four years) and the United States (15 years). He led re-engineering of IBM Corporation's global contracting process and has provided support and advisory services to both private and public sector agencies, including the United Nations, World Bank and governments in Australia, Canada, the UK, United States, Japan, Denmark and Malaysia.

Andrea Demaria is project manager (PMI PMP, IPMA B), programme management coach (Axelos MSP) and assessor for project management maturity (Siemens MPM) based in Munich, Germany. With more than 10 years of experience in the area of programme management, he is currently responsible for the development and implementation of programme management at Siemens and has been actively contributing to the definition of international project, programme and portfolio management standards (PMI, ISO, DIN). Author of several publications on programme and portfolio management, Andrea holds a degree as 'Ingegnere Elettronico' form Politecnico di Torino, Italy, and has a strong IT background.

Bernhard Dietrich is Vice President Optimization and Process Efficiency at LSG Sky Chefs, a Lufthansa company, and currently head of the Project Office for overhead optimization. He holds degrees as Dipl.-Ing. agr. and Dipl.-Wirtsch.-Ing. from the Technical University of Munich. He has 20 years' experience in the aviation industry with a focus on project management and programme management for strategy and process optimization.

Séverin Drogoul is in charge of Programme Assessments in Airbus Group Corporate as Vice President. Since the 1980s he has acquired a strong background in programme management and technical experience in the aerospace sector and a large experience of aerospace industry and agencies (ESA-CNES-ARIANESPACE-Airbus Group and Subcontractors) including large knowledge on launchers and space technical fields (more than 25 years); quality assurance, programme and control management (more than 20 years) and system engineering, risk management, quality management system, product assurance and safety management (more than 20 years).

Alan Fowler is a director of Isochron, a UK company specializing in designing and delivering futures for organizations. He developed the D4 method that the company owns, having originated the core concepts with colleagues in 1987–91. Alan set up Isochron in 2002 and has engaged services applying D4 in both private and public sector organizations. Alan spent one third of his career working in UK central government, one third with Ernst Young UK and one third in SME business.

Besides 28 years' experience in businesses large and small, Alan is passionately interested in how time and change is managed in organizations. He has carried out original research into the subject and presented papers at international conferences. Alan is the author with Dennis Lock of *Accelerating Business and IT Change.* He has lectured in many organizations including the British Computer Society, IBM and PMI. Now semi-retired, he lives in Edinburgh and enjoys mentoring, working with a select number of people to accelerate their careers. He is continuing to support organizations that are making use of the techniques and approaches from D4 and is a partner in Outcome Delivery Network Ltd.

Jürgen Frank is Head of Project Office at Dräxlmaier Group, Vilsbiburg. He holds a degree as Dipl.-Ing. (FH) from OTH Regensburg and he has an MBA in Systems Engineering of UAS Landshut and University of Texas at Dallas. His experience is based on 20 years in the automotive industry, with a focus on international project and programme management. During his career he spent seven years working in North America, managing engineering, sales and supplier quality. He is a member of various focus groups of GPM, the German Project Management Association and DGQ, the German Association for Quality Management. He also teaches programme management at the UAS in Landshut. Consequently his expertise lies in both the methodological and operational aspects of programme management.

Ben Ganney, Benefits and Value Functional Lead, TfL. Ben is the 'professional head' of project and programme benefits management across TfL. He is responsible for developing and promoting consistent and best practice benefits management, assessing maturity and subsequent competency development and providing support and advice to sponsors and project staff in developing scalable and appropriate strategies to ensure successful benefits realization. He has also developed the project, programme and portfolio benefits management policy and processes, as part of the single TfL Pathway PPM methodology, in line with external best practice and internal lessons learnt. Prior to joining TfL in 2012 Ben was Head of Demand, Benefits and Capital Programming for the Metropolitan Police's Directorate of Information. He was responsible for driving forward operational efficiency through comprehensive management of benefits from ICT investment, robust and consultative capital investment planning and prioritization and the management of value delivered ensuring that opportunities and outcomes from change were optimized. He has a BA Hons degree in Business Studies from the University of Kent and an MSc in Information Technology from Kingston University.

Burkhard Görtz is Head of Program Management Department at BWI Informationstechnik GmbH – a joint venture of Siemens AG, the Federal Republic of Germany represented by the Federal Ministry of Defence and IBM Deutschland GmbH. Before this engagement he was project manager for several projects at Siemens and finally project manager responsible for the contract negotiations of the large-scale ICT-project HERKULES, Europe's largest public–private partnership at that time with a total budget of €7.2 billion and a duration of 10 years, resulting in the foundation of BWI IT in 2006. With his accumulated experience in programme management, he and his co-authors wrote one of the first

German books on the management of programmes in 2012. He is now responsible particularly for strategic programmes, project governance and enterprise risk management.

Matti Haukka has provided tailored project management training for various companies and worked as a consultant for several organizations of different fields since 1989. At Project Institute Finland he has been in charge of developing the ABC Project model™ and held numerous presentations about the topic in international project management conferences. Also he has been the main instructor of the training course 'Managing Corporate Project Portfolios' in IPMA Advanced Courses since 2006. Today he mainly trains experienced project managers, members of steering groups and boards of directors and provides consulting services for clients who want to develop their project management culture. His specialities are earned value management, strategic PMOs and project portfolio management.

David E. Hawkins is Knowledge Architect and Operations Director of the Institute for Collaborative Working. He has an extensive career in projects and procurement within the construction industry. For over 40 years he has been associated with the development and implementation of major projects in many parts of the world, which has provided an insight into the many organizational and cultural challenges that projects and global operations can generate. He has been an active promoter of collaborative concepts and the development of extended enterprises through the building of alliances. He is the architect of the CRAFT programme and was the technical author of the British Standards Institution's PAS 11000 collaborative business relationship standard (world first published in 2006); also chairman of the BSI committee that developed BS 11000 (published in October 2010). He is now leading the development of ISO 11000 (targeted to be published in 2016).

Stephen Hayes MBE is the Managing Partner of Gravity Consulting and Managing Director of Complexity Solutions. Stephen is internationally recognized as the founding Managing Director and Chief Executive of the International Centre for Complex Project Management. He is also Chair of the International Task Force that developed the internationally acclaimed report 'Complex Project Management – Global Perspectives and the Strategic Agenda to 2025' and the founding Chair of the International Complex Project Management Research Council. Building on his extensive industry expertise, Stephen leads Gravity Consulting's consulting practice to support government and industry in the successful delivery of complex endeavours, including the practical use of innovations in systems sciences as well as capacity building for the delivery of complex projects and programmes.

Simon Henley MBE has 40 years' experience in aerospace and defence, the last 20 years of which has been in hands-on roles delivering major aerospace projects. He had a 32-year career in the Royal Navy, retiring with the rank of Rear Admiral, with roles including Engineering Sponsor for the introduction to service of the Lynx Mk8 and Merlin helicopters and the Sea Harrier FRS2, and nine years on the Joint Strike Fighter Programme, including four years with overall responsibility for the UK's participation in JSF. He subsequently worked for six years for Rolls-Royce, initially as Programme Director for a portfolio of development and in-service projects in defence, and was then seconded as President of Europrop International in Madrid, developing and introducing to service the TP400 engine for the Airbus A400M Military Airlifter. He is currently Director, Major Development Programmes for Marshall Aerospace and Defence Group in Cambridge, and also the Deputy Chair of the International Centre for Complex Project Management (ICCPM). He is a Fellow of the Royal Aeronautical Society, a Chartered Engineer, and is a Registered Project Professional and Assessor for that standard. He was made an Honorary Fellow of the APM in 2015.

Edward J. Hoffman is NASA's Chief Knowledge Officer. He works within NASA as well as with leaders of industry, academia, professional associations and other government agencies to develop the agency's capabilities in programme and project management and engineering. Dr Hoffman has written numerous journal articles, co-authored *Shared Voyage: Learning and Unlearning from Remarkable Projects* (NASA, 2005) and *Project Management Success Stories: Lessons of Project Leaders* (Wiley, 2000), and speaks frequently at conferences and associations. He serves as adjunct faculty at The George Washington University. He holds a Doctorate, as well as MA and MSc degrees from Columbia University in the area of social and organizational psychology. He received a BSc degree in Psychology from Brooklyn College in 1981.

Andrew Hudson is the managing director of ChangeDirector. He is an experienced practitioner of management disciplines including strategy, change, benefits, project portfolio, business process and performance measurement. He has implemented management and governance systems for many organizations in a number of sectors and geographies. His current innovation focus is working with teams to drive operational performance improvement through more effective process management, measurement and change.

Lynne Hughes has in excess of 30 years' experience in project management, leading large global clinical trials in neurology and oncology and managing budgets of many millions of dollars to non-negotiable timelines. She has been involved in the development of every neurology drug on the world market. She is PMP certified and has lived and worked both in the US and in the UK. She has worked in pharmaceutical industries from large pharmas to biotechnology companies and is now Vice President and Head of the Centre of Excellence, Neurology at Quintiles, a clinical research organization. She currently is involved in determining the most efficient and regulatory-acceptable route of drug development for potential new products in neurological indications, spending much time in the design and planning of trials using evidence-based data.

Louis Klein is an internationally recognized expert on change management and systems thinking. He is founder and president of the Systemic Excellence Group and Managing Director of Systemic Projects GmbH. Holding a PhD in Sociology Louis Klein is Director of the World Organisation of Systems and Cybernetics (WOSC) and currently Vice President at the International Society for the Systems Sciences. He is recipient of the first research award of the International Centre for Complex Project Management, where he is also chairman of the Focus Group on Social and Cultural Complexity.

Gerrit Koch has a background in mathematics, psychology, ICT and business administration. He holds an IPMA level A certificate. From 1990 on he has worked as project/programme manager. In 1997 he became responsible for the competence project management within PinkRoccade, a large ICT-company. As such, he was responsible for the business team management services of some 40 project, programme and interim managers (IPMA level B and A). After this he worked as principal adviser for Berenschot and in 2010 he switched to Van Aetsveld, a consultancy firm with passion for people in projects and change. He now combines doing complex and challenging programmes with giving board-level advice on competence development of project managers and their organizations. Gerrit is lead trainer for IPMA's advanced workshop on programme management. He validates PM certification in various countries, assesses IPMA level A and B candidates and classifies organizations in their ability to organize and perform projects and programmes. He is co-author of the International Competence Baseline, writes and speaks with passion about his profession and is a member of the editorial board of the *International Journal for Project Management.*

Dennis Lock began his career as an electronics engineer in a research laboratory but has subsequently served many successful years in project and administration management. His industrial experience is extraordinarily wide, ranging from guided weapons electronics to heavy special machine tool systems and mining engineering. Dennis has carried out consultancy assignments in Europe, and was for eight years an external lecturer in project management to Masters degree students at two British universities. He is a best-selling author and has written or edited over 60 books, many published in multiple languages, most for Gower. He is a Fellow of the APM, Member of the Chartered Management Institute and is now a freelance writer.

Mirkka Lyytikäinen has ten years of experience in developing and assessing project, portfolio and programme management practices in companies and public organizations. She has been involved especially in project management assessment and in developing and tailoring project management models and guidelines for different organizations. Through her experience Ms Lyytikäinen has a good understanding of the development needs and project management maturity in different types of organizations.

Oliver Mack is a researcher, entrepreneur and consultant located in Salzburg and Vienna. He studied business administration and law at the University of Mannheim and gained his PhD in Political Science at Johannes Gutenberg University of Mainz, Germany. He is the author of several publications, speaker at international conferences and meetings, and is academic teacher at international business schools. Oliver Mack is founder of mack:consulting, a consulting company that helps companies and organizations in the '3rd mode of consulting', combining traditional top management consulting and systemic change consulting in the main areas of project-orientated enterprise, organizational design/change and complexity management. He is also founder and Lead Researcher at the xm:institute, an innovative organization doing applied research and application of 'Ideas for

Management and Leadership in the Next Society'. He is active in various associations and research groups.

Keiko Moebus is an experienced aviation professional, strategist and entrepreneur who is internationally recognized as an expert in safety and business process improvement and human factors research and implementation. Besides her 20 years of solid work experience in the aviation/aerospace sector, she has often been involved in projects and programmes at Swiss national and European level. She is a truly global person who has lived and worked in Japan, the US and Europe. She has also served as an in-house entrepreneur at a large Swiss aerospace company as well as operating her own international aviation consultancy in the past. She currently works at a Swiss air navigation service provider and leads organizational-wide efforts in promoting more systematic and active human factors implementation in the company's daily business and technical operations.

Marcus Paulus is Head of Enterprise PMO at Wien Energie GmbH, Austria's largest energy provider. In this role he is an internal consultant to the C-level management and responsible for the consistency in the management of the company's portfolio and all its components, projects and programmes. Before this, Marcus worked as a consultant in real estate management in private and public sectors for nearly 20 years. He has conducted client projects in a number of different fields (for example technical, organizational and IT in Central and Eastern Europe). Marcus holds an MBA from the Vienna University of Economics and is certified as PMP and Prince2 Practitioner. He is a member of Austrian Standards Institute (ASI) and an Austrian delegate to ISO TC258, for development of the International Project, Programme, and Portfolio Management Standard.

Mark Phillips is an accomplished business leader and author. For over 17 years he helped to build a project management software company and consultancy, serving clients including multinational automotive companies, defence contractors, web start-ups and financial service providers. In 2014 he wrote *Reinventing Communication*, the ground-breaking book on programme management, communication and uncertainty. Mark is a member of the Board of Advisers and Adjunct Professor in the College of Management at Lawrence Technological University. You can follow Mark at www.reinventingcommunication.com.

Steven Raue is an expert for change and project management. Since 2011 he has been member of the Systemic Excellence Group, and is part of the management board. Steve is a researcher in the area of organizational ethnography and wrote his dissertation with a focus on implications for a future project management on the basis of conventional, agile and systemic project perspectives. As founding member of the Agile Management Group at the German Project Management Association he explores integrated management approaches.

José Reyes is a civil engineer with geotechnical expertise. He graduated from Universidad Santa Maria (1985) and has an MBA from Universidad Interamericana and Program Management at George Washington University. He has received training at INCAE and US and European universities and has attended workshops and technical seminars in diverse countries of America and Europe. Author of more than 50 articles, papers and a project management textbook, he is Chairman of the Panamanian Association of Project Management and Director of LATNET (IPMA networks of Latin Associations). Currently engaged in his doctorate degree, Mr Reyes has 30 years' experience working in different managerial and programme/project management positions at the Panama Canal Authority and is currently directing the Third Set of Locks Project of the Panama Canal Expansion Programme. He is also a part-time consultant with 10 years as a university professor in project management curricula.

Eileen Roden focuses on the practical application of project and programme management to help organizations improve their PPM delivery capability. Her expertise is founded in 15 years' practitioner experience in a variety of project management roles (predominantly PMO management) along with functional IT and HR management in national and global organizations. She holds a first degree in Business Studies and a Masters in Applied Project Management. She has contributed to many APM standards and publications, including the RPP, Body of Knowledge and Competency Framework. She was also the lead author on the refresh of the P3O® Best Management Practice. She is currently an active member of the APM PMOSIG and PMO Flashmob and a frequent speaker at various conferences.

Martin Samphire is the owner and Managing Director of 3pmxl Ltd, a consultancy that specializes in transformation using structured PPPM approaches. He has over 40 years' management consulting, change, project, programme and portfolio implementation experience in the private and public sectors, in the UK and internationally. He has directed and contributed to a number of complex business change and transformation programmes. He holds a first degree in mechanical engineering and a Masters in Project Management from Cranfield. He started his career in capital project contracting in the petrochemical sector with Foster Wheeler and subsequently worked for The Nichols Group, Impact Plus and Hitachi Consulting before starting 3pmxl. He is Chairman of the Association for Project Management SIG on Governance which has developed guidelines for governance including 'Directing Change', 'Co-Directing Change' and 'Sponsoring Change'.

Silke Schönert has been a Professor for Business Information Systems and Project Management at the University of Applied Science in Cologne since 2013. Before that she was Head of Strategic Planning and Controlling of the Program Management Department at BWI Informationstechnik GmbH – a joint venture of Siemens AG and the Federal Republic of Germany represented by the Federal Ministry of Defence and IBM Deutschland GmbH. With her experience in programme management, she and her co-authors wrote one of the first German books on the management of programmes in 2012. She has 20 years' experience in several industries and academic organizations, with a focus on project management and programme management for strategy and process optimization.

Lindsay Scott is a director of Arras People, a programme and project management recruitment organization. She is the founder of the PMO Conference and the PMO Flashmob. Lindsay regularly speaks on the topic of PMOs and was previously PMO Manager at Hewlett-Packard in the UK. With Dennis Lock she co-edited Gower's *Handbook of People in Programme Management*.

Martin Sedlmayer has gained deep experience in project, programme and portfolio management in various sectors including process manufacturing, insurance, transportation and different services industries. He successfully realized complex change programmes, worked both as line manager and spent a long period as a consultant. He holds an MBA in International Management, a CMA/CFA diploma and is certified Projects Director IPMA since 2002. He is a board member of the Swiss project management association and acts for IPMA as an assessor Level A in various countries. He recently developed for IPMA in the role of project manager and lead editor of the Individual Competence Baseline version 4.

Joseph Sopko is an independent organizational project management consultant in the Lehigh Valley in eastern Pennsylvania. Joe is a joint recipient of the 2013 Shingo Prize Research Award as a contributing author to *The Guide to Lean Enablers for Managing Engineering Programs.* Joe is also a frequent author of papers regarding the practical use of programme management, PMO development and value delivery with impacts on improving organizational excellence. Joe has served in a wide range of operational and project leadership roles in defence as well as commercial industries in both government and the private sector. He has also been an active contributor to global standards in project and programme management. Most recently, Joe served as a corporate senior staff consultant with Siemens Corporate Technologies in the US.

David Stewart spent 30 years as a police officer in Scotland, rising to senior management levels. During the last five years of his police service he undertook numerous project and programme roles including property- and IT-related programmes. In 2012 he was appointed as Programme Manager for the Scottish National Police Reform programme, which was the largest public sector reform programme in the UK that saw the merger of 10 organizations into a new single police service. He then became the first Head of Business Change for the new organization. He left the police in 2013 and set up his own company, Taynuilt Associates Ltd, providing consultancy and contracting services in project, programme, risk and benefit management. David is a Chartered Fellow of the Chartered Management Institute, a Member of the Association for Project Management and a Professional Member of the Institute of Operational Risk.

Alan Stretton graduated in Civil Engineering (BE, Tasmania) and Mathematics (MA, Oxford), and then worked in the building and construction industries in Australia, New Zealand and the US for some 38 years. His responsibilities included management of construction and R&D projects, the introduction of information and control systems, internal management education programmes and organizational change projects. In 1988 he was appointed by the University of Technology, Sydney, Australia to develop and deliver a Master of Project Management programme in the Faculty of Design, Architecture and Building, from whence he retired in 2006. In the previous year he was awarded an honorary PhD in Strategy, Programme and Project Management (ESC, Lille). He is currently a member of the Faculty Corps of the University of Management and Technology, Arlington, VA. Alan was Chairman of the Standards (PMBOK)

Committee of the Project Management Institute from late 1989 to early 1992. He held a similar position with the Australian Institute of Project Management (AIPM), and was elected a Life Fellow of AIPM in 1996. He has published over 150 professional articles, mainly on project management, and continues to contribute in that area.

Hubertus C. Tuczek has gained more than 30 years' experience in project management in the machinery and equipment, aerospace and automotive industries. During the last 17 years he held the position of a vice president on the board of the Draexlmaier Group, an automotive supplier operating worldwide. Besides other responsibilities he was in charge of international business development and project management. At the beginning of 2015 he was appointed as a Professor for Project Management and Leadership at the University of Applied Sciences at Landshut near Munich.

Rodney Turner is Professor of Project Management at SKEMA Business School, in Lille where he is Scientific Director for the PhD in Project and Programme Management and is the SAIPEM Professor of Project Management at the Politecnico di Milano. He is also Adjunct Professor at the University of Technology Sydney. Rodney is the author or editor of 18 books, and editor of *The International Journal of Project Management*. His research areas cover project management in small to medium-sized enterprises, the management of complex projects, the governance of project management (including ethics and trust), project leadership and human resource management in the project-orientated firm. Rodney is Vice President, Honorary Fellow of the UK's Association for Project Management and Honorary Fellow and former President and Chairman of the International Project Management Association. He received a life-time research achievement award from PMI in 2004 and IPMA in 2012.

Ricardo Viana Vargas is an accredited project, portfolio and risk management specialist. Over the past 20 years, he has been responsible for over 80 major projects in various countries within the petroleum, energy, infrastructure, telecommunications, information technology and finance industries; covering an investment portfolio of over $20 billion. He is currently Director of the Infrastructure and Project Management Group with the United Nations Office for Project Services (UNOPS) in Copenhagen. His work is focused on improving the design, infrastructure and management of humanitarian, peace-building and infrastructure development projects in countries across the world, including (but not limited to) Haiti, Afghanistan, Syria, Myanmar, Iraq and South Sudan. He is the first Latin American person to be elected Chairman of the Board for PMI and has written 14 books on project management, published in Portuguese, English and Spanish, which have sold over 300,000 copies globally. Ricardo is a chemical engineer by trade, holds a Masters degree in Industrial Engineering from UFMG (Federal University of Minas Gerais) and is a doctoral student in Civil Engineering at the Universidade Federal Fluminense (UFF). He became a Professional Member of the Royal Institution of Chartered Surveyors (MRICS) in 2015 and has been accredited with the most prestigious certifications in the project, portfolio and risk management fields. He has also attended the Program on Negotiation for Executives at Harvard Law School, the Advanced Project Management Program at Stanford University and has an executive formation in Strategy and Innovation from Massachusetts Institute of Technology (MIT).

Reinhard Wagner has gained more than 30 years of project-related leadership experience in sectors such as air defence, automotive engineering, machinery and not-for-profit organizations. As Certified Projects Director (IPMA Level A), he proved to be experienced in managing projects, programmes and project portfolios in a complex and dynamic context. For more than 15 years he has been actively involved in the development of project, programme and portfolio management standards (for example as convenor of a working group for the development of ISO 21500 *Guidance on Project Management* as well as ISO 21503 *Guidance on Programme Management*). Reinhard is President of IPMA, Honorary Fellow of GPM (the German Project Management Association) as well as founder and CEO of the Projectivists.

Adjunct Associate Professor Michael Young is an innovator and entrepreneur with a passion for sustainable change and the implementation of strategy. He plays an active leadership role in the project management profession both within Australia and internationally. Michael is a board member of the Australian Institute of Project Management (AIPM) and is also a member of the International Project Management Association (IPMA) Research Management Board. Michael has actively contributed to standards development internationally including numerous ISO standards, IPMA Individual Competency Baseline (ICB4) as well as numerous professional standards in Australia. Michael is a Fellow of the Australian Institute of Project Management, Fellow of the Association of Project Management, Fellow of the Australian Institute of Management, a Certified Practicing Project Director, and a Certified Projects Director (IPMA Level A). Michael speaks regularly at international events and has written over 50 academic and industry papers, book chapters and edited books.

Preface

Although projects and their management have been around since civilization began, project management did not come into its own as a separate management discipline until after 1950. Then project management became a recognized profession, personified with the emergence of its own institutions (notably IPMA and PMI). The first books treating project management holistically (rather than books on single topics such as critical path scheduling) appeared around 1960. Peter Morris chronicles the history of our profession well in his 1997 book *The Management of Projects* (London, Thomas Telford).

At first our profession was concerned principally with industries such as construction, manufacturing and defence. We became expert in scheduling tasks, costs and resources using critical path methods, batch processed on mainframe computers. Then, those of us who were more adventurous became adept at scheduling several simultaneous or overlapping projects as one model. We called that *multiproject scheduling*, which was probably the beginning of today's programme management.

With the emergence of the IT industry, which mushroomed in the 1970s, another quite separate branch of project management evolved. These project managers were systems engineers who worked only with IT and had little or no interest in the traditional so-called 'hard' projects. As time went on, companies realized that organization change (such as mergers and acquisitions or relocations) could also be managed as projects, using the same tools and techniques already developed for hard projects.

So projects and programmes come in all shapes and sizes. Some 'experts' refer to projects as endeavours that 'create change', and their world contains only IT and organization change projects and programmes. Others of us, through our industrial experience, are more familiar with projects and programmes that produce more tangible results, such as a new motorway, shopping mall, aircraft or international airport. Unsurprisingly, many of us have our own ingrained notions about what a project or a programme actually is. Those differences will become apparent when you read the chapters in this handbook, which include examples from many industries and range from disaster relief to organization change programmes.

This second edition is all new. It has been compiled to give a varied and comprehensive account of programme management as experienced by people (many holding very senior positions) from a wide variety of industries and professions. Our earlier comment about people regarding projects and programmes differently, as either vehicles for creating change or as something more concrete, becomes apparent when reading and comparing our contributors' chapters. Here is a rich mix of experience with something for everyone working in projects and programme management, providing a valuable source of knowledge from 50 contributors spread over different organizations, industries and nations. Most chapters end with references and further reading lists for those who wish to follow specific subjects in greater depth.

Handbooks such as this are intended to be works of reference – not as 'story books' to be read from beginning to end. To help you navigate this large text we have, of course, provided an index. Also, the chapters are logically grouped within five main sections named: Foundations of Programme Management; Good Practice in Programme Management; Programme Governance, Organization and Culture; Programme Lifecycle, Processes, Methods and Tools; and (finally) Developing Maturity in Programme Management.

We gratefully acknowledge the way in which all our contributors have responded to our 'call for papers' by enthusiastically providing chapters of a very high standard. We must also mention the early contribution of Merv Wyeth, who helped us to formulate the handbook content and introduced us to some of the contributors. Finally, we gratefully acknowledge the unfailing, highly professional support and encouragement from Jonathan Norman of Gower Publishing throughout the many months taken to compile this handbook.

Dennis Lock
Chesham, United Kingdom
Reinhard Wagner
Friedberg, Germany

Part I

Foundations of Programme Management

Chapter 1

Introduction to Programme Management

Reinhard Wagner and Dennis Lock

This chapter gives an outline description of programmes and programme management, includes some of the accepted definitions, predicts future trends and explains how the following chapters are arranged.

The roads we have travelled

Project management has been applied as a recognized discipline since the 1950s but the increasing volume and complexity of project-based work (as well as the change aspects of multiple projects) require more than a simple project management methodology. Hence the emergence of programme management as a new approach in recent years.

History is full of examples that could be perceived as large projects (or even programmes). Familiar instances include the Pyramids of Giza, the Colosseum in Rome, the Great Wall of China, the Taj Mahal and many, many more. Those endeavours were organized in a systematic way, with many organizational and management characteristics similar to today's project and programme management. Formal management organization structures owe their origins principally to the church and the military (Figure 1.1). But our ancestors did not have the technological advantages of communications, modern materials and design aids that we enjoy today, which makes those early achievements even more remarkable.

As long ago as 1697, Daniel Defoe wrote *An Essay upon Projects*, a stunning book about changing society through 'projects'. Our current notion of 'management' did not exist at that time; thus a person doing projects was called 'projector'. An honest projector 'is he who, having by fair and plain principles of sense, honesty, and ingenuity brought any contrivance to a suitable perfection, makes out what he pretends to, picks nobody's pocket, puts his project in execution, and contents himself with the real produce as the profit of his invention' (Defoe, 1697). Defoe concluded, 'for indeed the true definition of a project, according to modern acceptation, is, as is said before, a vast undertaking, too big to be managed, and therefore likely enough to come to nothing.'

Interestingly, Defoe claimed the seventeenth century to be a 'projectized' century. Nearly a hundred years before industrialization, the endeavours called 'projects' helped to shape society. It was simply about 'getting things done' and to 'project'

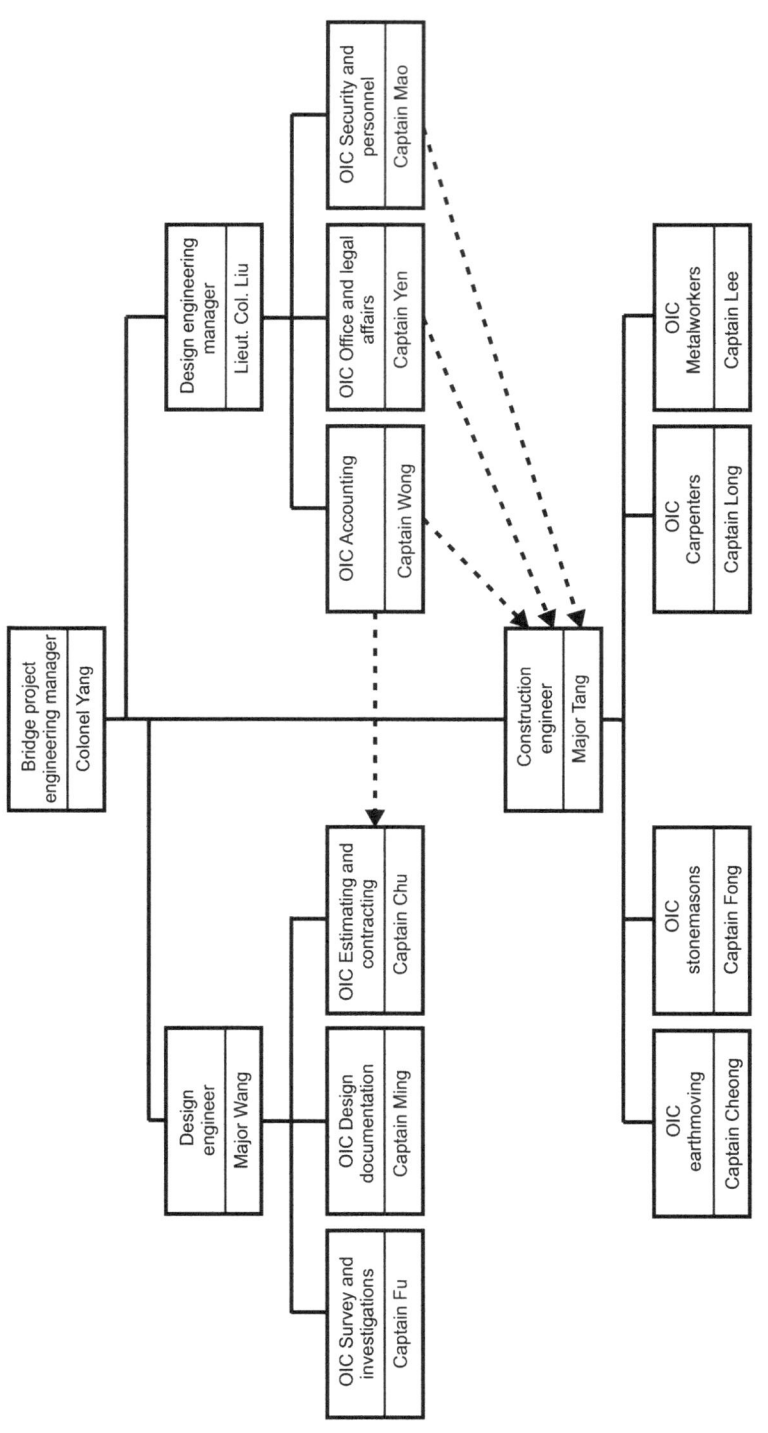

Figure 1.1 Organization chart of officers in a Chinese military battalion for bridge building (Ming Dynasty)
By kind permission of the Chinese Association of South Australia.

OIC = officer in charge

ideas into reality. Peter Morris mentions another example of that time, the founding Fellow of the British Royal Society, Sir Christopher Wren, who changed the traditional approach to building: 'The huge amount of materials and personnel necessary called for careful management of the work and control of costs. The beginnings of modern construction management can be seen in the way Wren's office was organized. The complementary roles of architect, engineer, surveyor and contractor emerged' (Morris, 2013, p. 15).

The focus of projects changed after the start of the Industrial Revolution in the 1760s. It was mainly industrialization that shaped societies in Europe, and the need for efficient usage of resources for the manufacturing processes. Projects were performed in the context of technological and economic progress to turn small-scale workshops into large-scale manufacturing facilities that could produce the machine tools and other machinery needed to equip steam-powered factories. On the one hand, the division of labour helped to gain efficiency, but on the other hand it required better coordination or integration of the activities performed.

The late nineteenth and early twentieth centuries saw the emergence of the first management scientists. Some of their stories are summarized in Chapter 31 of Lock and Scott (2013). Frederick Winslow Taylor and his colleagues tried to improve productivity by analysing and synthesizing workflows in a process that became known as 'Taylorism'. Their objective was to improve efficiency, especially labour productivity, and to apply scientific insights to the design of processes and to management (Kanigel, 1997).

The disciplines of project and programme management emerged during the early 1950s in the USA. The aerospace and defence sectors were called upon to perform large and complex undertakings, such as the development of missiles and (later) the Apollo programme. The US Airforce and Department of Defense (DoD) wanted to manage those endeavours in the best way. Both organizations were influenced by operations research (OR) as the predominant contemporary management science (applying advanced analytical methods to help people make better decisions). That began the widespread use of critical path network planning with techniques such as the 'Programme Evaluation and Review Technique' (PERT) and several others. Interestingly, during this period the words 'project' and 'programme' were used interchangeably in this sector.

At that time the first manuals on programme management were developed, such as the DoD manual on 'Systems Programme Management'. Support units emerged in the organizations, with names such as 'Special Projects Office' (SPO), which we would now call Programme or Programme Management Offices (Morris, 2013, p. 33). This sector was also influential in developing the methodology for programme scheduling (NASA, 2011) and is currently developing international standards for the planning and control of large and complex programmes (see the next chapter of this Handbook).

Starting from the early 1960s, other industries followed the approach of the aerospace and defence sector. These included, for example, the nuclear industry, construction, process industry and more recently the telecommunication and information technology (IT) sectors. One of us (DL) was involved in complex network-based multiproject scheduling of resources and costs for the special heavy machine tool industry in the late 1960s. However, none of these 'latecomers' was as influential in developing the methodologies as the aerospace and defence industries.

The first professional associations in the fields of project, programme and portfolio management were founded during the 1960s. In 1965, the International Project Management Association (IPMA) started in Europe; 1969 saw the foundation of the Project Management Institute (PMI) in the USA; the Association for Project Management (APM) dates from 1972. All started to formalize the expertise in project and programme management. They published either a Body of Knowledge (APM) or a Competence Baseline (IPMA) covering project and programme management.

These standards proliferated into many sectors and organizations, which adopted and applied the contained expertise. Industry experts helped to spread the word by becoming university lecturers. Now many academic institutions offer training programmes or even masters degree courses in project or programme management (such as Oxford University's MSc in Major Programme Management). Professional associations and/or their accredited partners offer qualification and certification schemes in programme management. Even large organizations provide specific training for their employees involved in programmes and programme management. Now the practice of programme management is widespread.

Different types of programmes require their own specific approaches. The roles of people involved in (or affected) by programmes are increasingly recognized and that influences the way in which programmes are managed. For example, the engagement of stakeholders, leadership aspects and the management of change are influencing programme management beyond the very basic planning and control approaches of the early days.

The roads we shall follow in the future

What are the emerging trends for programme management? A survey by the Technical University Berlin together with the German Project Management Association (GPM) reveals interesting details (Gemünden and Schoper, 2014). Four trends will be highlighted here:

- projectification;
- coping with complexity;
- professionalization;
- project-orientated organization.

Projectification is about the significantly increasing number of projects throughout our societies. Projects occur in all sectors and types of organizations, including (but not limited to) industry, public administration, leisure activities and schools. The sheer number of projects requires coordination (in the form of programme, portfolio or multiproject management). It also raises awareness of the competencies needed for the professional conduct of those projects and the involvement of all sorts of stakeholders (such as top management for taking decisions). Because of the interrelations between projects, coordination is needed at a higher level to manage the projects in an integrated manner. That will call for more programme management in the future.

Complexity is a perception that we all have today. The complexity of projects and programmes is increasing significantly. Certainly, information technology is a main driver for this complexity. We are able to retrieve large amounts of data ('big data') via laptop computers and share that with our colleagues (who can be in remote places). People from various cultural backgrounds collaborate. Team dynamics and conflicts are perceived as complexities that project or programme managers need to deal with. Complex systems require programme managers to manage such endeavours from a systems viewpoint, understanding the interdependencies and system dynamics from a programme and/or systems manager perspective. Context factors, like market dynamics, a changing political situation, the environment, societal dynamics and other factors can impose additional 'stress' on the situation. It is clear that all these complexity factors need to be respected and managed by the people responsible for a programme.

The third trend of the survey, *professionalization*, deals with the need for all individuals, teams and organizations to develop their competencies in managing programmes. It might not be enough for an individual to 'learn by doing' as most of the 'accidental' programme managers have done in the past. Professionalism in programme management begins with learning the foundations of the discipline, applying them in real life, and improving personal competencies on a continuous basis. This applies not only to the manager of a programme, but to all team members and managers serving on steering committees or decision-making bodies. It also includes the people of line functions, who might be only partly involved in programmes. They need to understand the basis of programme management and contribute accordingly. Teams must understand the social dynamics awaiting them throughout the lifecycle of a programme. Finally, an organization needs to set the scene for its programme management, developing situation-specific standards, providing training and steering the application of programme management towards the benefits of the organization and its vision, mission and strategy. Sustainable success requires the organization's top management to allow for an in-depth analysis of the situation and an organizational learning process.

Project orientation, the fourth and last-mentioned trend, recognizes the impact that all the other trends would have on an organization. Organizations that were previously organized functionally would become matrix-type organizations, in which project or programme functions overlap the line functions. In the beginning, the power to influence is still with the traditional line functions and their managers. However, things change. The more an organization becomes projectized, the more the power transfers from the line managers to the project or programme managers. Specific organizational units, such as a programme management office (PMO), will take over tasks to standardize, support the programmes, and monitor and control performance for the managers in charge. Steering committees are gaining more importance, perhaps on two or more levels of the organization. The organization cares for organizational development and its maturity in project, programme and portfolio management and begins initiatives to develop consciously on an evolutionary path.

There are certainly many other trends out there, which might influence programme management in the future. For example, globalization is driving complexity by involving people from different geographical areas, time zones and cultures. This is why this Handbook displays so many different perspectives of programme manage-ment and provides insights in the actual situation and emerging trends.

Challenges and concepts for programme management

There are many challenges to be overcome in practice which could be tackled by pro-gramme management. The ideas in the following paragraphs build up the concep-tual framework sequentially for what we believe programme management is about. It helps us to understand what differentiates programmes and their management from other endeavours, such as operations management, projects and portfolios.

The increasing number of projects and their interrelationships

The sheer number of projects often overwhelms organizations. Often some (if not all) of those projects are interdependent regarding strategic intent, content, time-lines, resources and organizational settings. It is a conscious decision of the respect-ive management to group some of the projects together and thus form a programme. By grouping them together, management is looking from a higher level to these projects. That provides an opportunity for synergies, managing them jointly instead of independently from each other.

The question then becomes how to group the interrelated projects together? One approach is to look into the interdependencies and, based on that, decide which pro-jects should be bundled together. For example, all projects related to a complex sys-tems development during its lifecycle could be grouped. However, different types of interdependent projects can also often be grouped together, such as change projects, process improvement projects and projects for the development and implementation of new software systems. It is even possible to group projects within a programme into a subprogramme, to coordinate them better towards the overall goals (Figure 1.2). Coordinated management of all constituent parts of the programme facilitates realiz-ing benefits for the organization, such as higher efficiency and effectiveness.

Long-term outcomes instead of short-term deliverables

Projects focus on deliverables. Often it is not in the interest or scope of projects to manage actively how the deliverables will be used throughout their lifecycles. For example, the buildings for the 2012 London Olympic Games were designed and built principally only for four weeks of usage. But why not think beyond the games and design and build them for a much longer period of time? The local community could use them for many other purposes, which allows realizing sustainability and ever-increasing benefits.

Thus programme management focuses on benefits realization – utilizing projects for building certain capabilities that allow the organization to harvest benefits over the longer term. Those benefits need to be defined upfront and agreed upon by the programme manager and all stakeholders. It is the main task of programme manage-ment to identify, evaluate, plan, manage and realize benefits. The benefits should be closely aligned to the organization's overall vision, mission and strategy. Whether the programme is chartered to realize all benefits throughout the programme, or

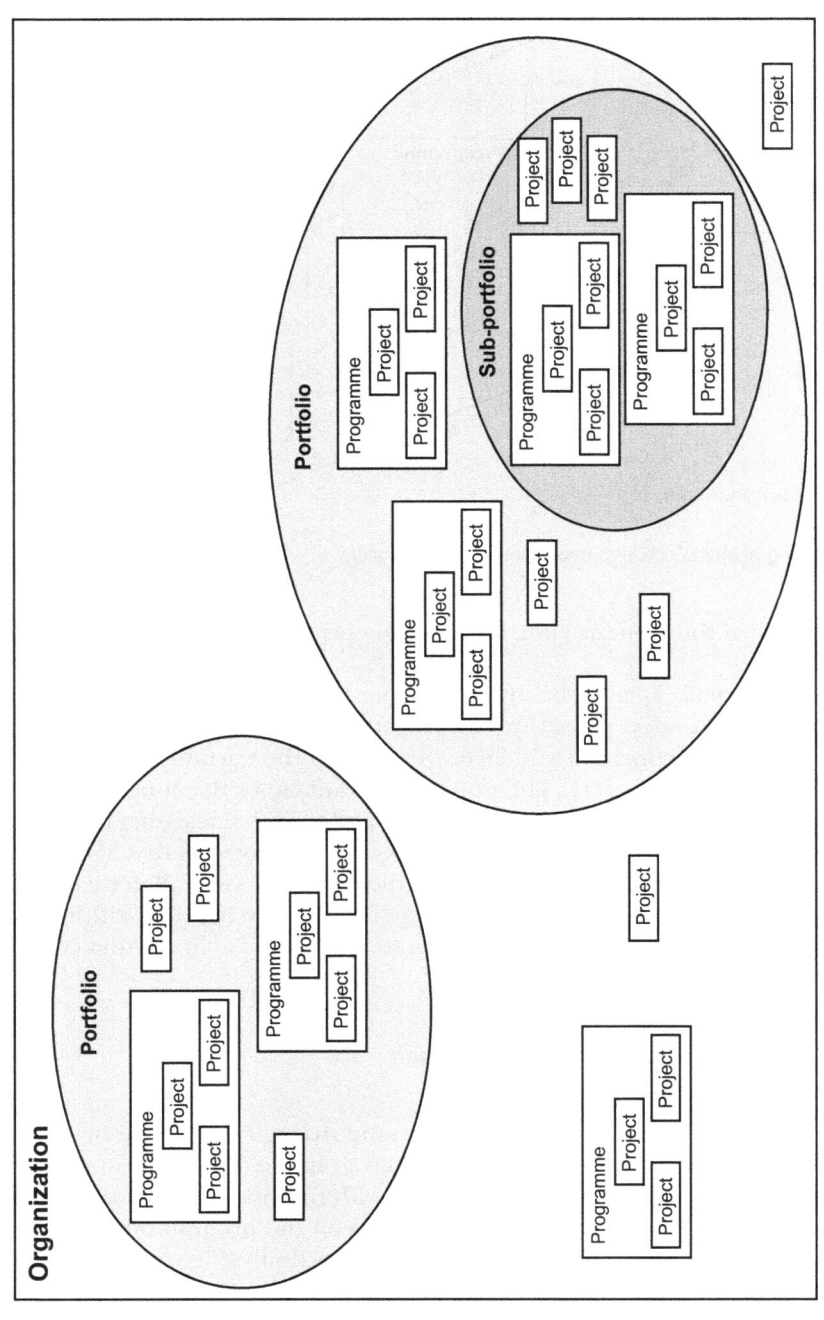

Figure 1.2 Projects, portfolios and programmes in an organization

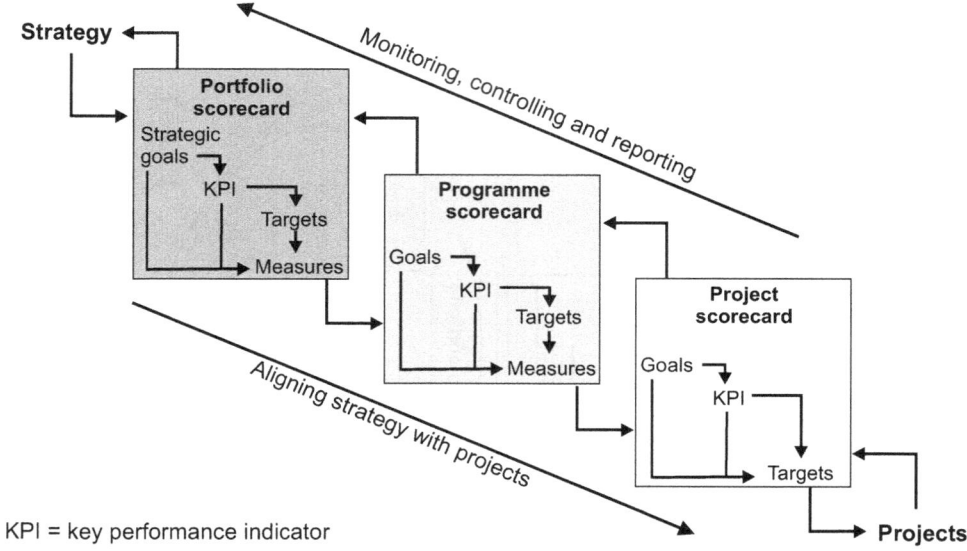

KPI = key performance indicator

Figure 1.3 Linking projects through programmes with strategy

to achieve some of the benefits later, is one of the prior clarifications necessary for a new programme.

Programmes usually span a much longer time than projects. They typically progress towards an extended phase for realizing the intended benefits (for example during the mass production of a vehicle or throughout the warranty period of a complex system sold to a customer). The potential advantage of this longer timespan is to learn during the period of benefits realization and feed that learning back into the next projects or programmes. Another advantage over a project is that a programme plans for the handover of the deliverables and the period of usage. Potential conflicts or risks are reduced to a minimum. Late change requests are handled within the programme setting, and not by a different organizational unit. All in all, that equates to synergies.

Improved alignment of project goals through a programme with strategic goals

We can often observe a significant gap between the strategic level of an organization and the level of its execution through projects. Programme management is intended to bridge that gap and align the projects better with the vision, mission and strategy of the organization. If there is a portfolio in between the programme and the strategic level, the programme needs to align with the portfolio (Figure 1.3).

Alignment means a two-way approach. Programme goals are broken down from the strategic level, but the programme shows how the strategic goals could be reached, perhaps also refined and developed by learning from the implementation. Key performance indicators (KPIs) are important means for clarifying the management's expectations at strategic level. The programme manager plans, monitors and controls the programme through KPIs, and reports to the strategic level. In addition the KPIs are a learning tool, and any deviations (also called variances or exceptions) indicate possibilities for improving the management system and/or the competencies of all people involved.

Managing change in a dynamic context

Like projects, programmes are unique, different from routine work, and are intended to create something new. That is why change is an important part of programmes. Change may affect the way organizations work and how they are structured into processes and functions. A programme might have an impact on the culture of the organization with its values and beliefs, and require a change in the behaviour of people.

Standards of the UK focus on change aspects of programme management. They see programmes as a means of effective change. The programme manager thus needs to combine traditional planning and control methodology with change management approaches. The aforementioned approach of programme management (based on scientific management and OR) comes to its limits when attempting to deal with people's behaviours, conflicts and potential resistance to change. Programme management needs to be seen as a holistic approach, combining hard and soft skills to deal with all the challenges.

Managing risk and the unforeseen

Risks and uncertainties are inherent characteristics of programmes. Risks (and opportunities) are something that we can predict; we can estimate the probability and the impact based on previous experiences. In a programme, all project managers need to perform a risk analysis and report the results to the programme manager. Nevertheless, the risk of a programme is much more than the sum of the individual risks. The interrelations between the constituent projects may cause a risk, or bundling projects may lead to a concentration risk. Therefore, programme management needs to consider all these risks and manage them from a higher-level perspective. Through the reporting system, a programme manager needs to link the project and programme level risks with the portfolio or the strategic risk management. Unfortunately, in many organizations we observe that those levels operate independently from each other, and certain risks might be hidden and cause avoidable damage.

Because of the longer duration of programmes in comparison with projects, development in the future is difficult to predict. During ten years of a systems development programme, the technology available for the system will almost certainly change significantly. That could cause the programme management to decide either to switch to the new technology or to stop the programme. Thus, in addition to the customary methods for risk assessment and management (with their probability of occurrence, potential impact and measures for avoidance or mitigation), programme managers need also to anticipate the future using scenario techniques, wild cards or other methods. They need to analyse the context of the programme carefully and sense the weak signals heralding events that could cause trouble for the programme over its lifecycle. These signals could come from the programme environment (such as stakeholders, legislation or politics), from the team involved in the programme or directly from the work being performed within the programme. All this requires an attitude of openness, a holistic view of the programme with all its diverse perspectives and an entrepreneurial type of personality, to balance opportunities and threats.

Establishing temporary organizational structures for a programme

A programme is a temporary endeavour, which means that its organizational structure is also temporary. This organization structure might comprise a programme manager and a programme management team, working in a matrix organization together with all related line functions. Alternatively, the whole programme could be separated and performed as autonomous organization, with resources from the line functions deployed to the programme and put under the leadership of the programme manager. Some programmes might even work as independent organizations (an example would be a consortium or joint enterprise in the construction sector).

We have already said that programmes have much longer lifespans than projects. Therefore, more line functions tend to be included into the programme setting (such as operations or service units). Additionally, the client organization and organizational interfaces to main suppliers have to be integrated into the programme structure. Those are the reasons why many programmes have a programme office, with support functions to:

- organize communications;
- plan and control the projects as well as the programme;
- be instrumental in the consulting, coaching and training of all the stakeholders involved.

The programme manager needs to clarify the interfaces and requirements of relevant governance bodies, such as steering committees or decision-making bodies.

In addition, a portfolio and/or project management office may require the programme manager to report and cooperate in certain issues, but might also offer support for the programme in matters that concern aligning the programme with strategy and a higher-level portfolio. The organizational structure will clearly be dependent on the situation, the governance established in the embedding organization and the requirements of stakeholders such as clients, suppliers or partners.

In the final analysis the goal is to find the right balance between the temporary organizational structure of the programme and the permanent structures of the organization.

Essential foundations for programme management

Running through the following chapters, all written by experts in their fields, one finds a common thread of good advice on the principles for effective and successful programme management. Here are the salient points:

- Realize that every programme needs the active support of top management.
- Base the programme on a sound business case that aligns with corporate vision and strategy.
- Where cash outflows and inflows are forecast far ahead into the future, ensure that all figures are suitably discounted to their net present values.
- Identify, know, respect and involve the stakeholders.
- Predict and manage risks.
- Prevent unauthorized changes to the approved programme and do not allow scope creep.
- Staff the key programme management roles with suitably qualified and experienced people.
- Put planning and control in the hands of a programme management office.
- Establish regular monitoring, measuring and reporting against schedules, budgets and financial forecasts.
- Always remember that the expected programme benefits depend on people, so the people in the organization who will have to accept and implement change must be suitably informed, managed, motivated and, where necessary, trained in new working methods.
- Appreciate that the full benefits might not be realized until some considerable time after the initial programme work has finished and the programme management organization has been disbanded.

We add one cautionary piece of advice ourselves here. That is to avoid having two or more programmes running in an organization at the same time, where these might cause conflict and consternation among the staff who will be expected to work with new systems. In such cases one programme must be allowed to 'bed down' and become accepted before additional change is introduced.

Jargon and the language of programme management

Every specialized branch of industry, science and management has its own vocabulary and programme management is no exception to this rule. Many of the terms used in programme management will be familiar to those involved in project management. Terms and abbreviations that are specific to programme management are generally explained where they occur in the following chapters.

However, most information is best communicated in plain English that could be understood by the average person in the street. Unfortunately our beautiful English language is occasionally distorted by some people who use the jargon that is commonly known as 'management speak'. Programme management has not escaped this infection. So, we have encouraged all our contributors to avoid unnecessary jargon and the text has been edited with that objective in mind. Figure 1.4 explains a few examples of the jargon that we have tried to avoid.

Conclusion

Any organization that runs several projects at the same time, or wishes to change its working methods or organization structure, can find itself having to manage one or

The word or phrase	Comment
Addressing issues	A much over-used expression meaning dealing with real or potential problems. How would one 'address an issue'? Write it a letter addressed 'Dear Issue?'.
Escalating issues	In plain English this means referring potential or real problems higher up the chain of command.
Issues	Issues are real or potential problems, but the word 'issue' is over-used in management speak. There are many words used in management for naming things or events that do not go to plan. The most common examples are: - exception (meaning any variation from the intended result); - noncomformance (used particularly in quality management); - variation (another word for exception, favoured particularly by cost and management accountants).
Leverage	In English this word is a noun, not a verb. One cannot 'leverage' anything. The appropriate English verbs are to 'use' or 'exploit'.
Measures	The average well-educated English person would understand this to mean actions taken to deal with potential or real problems. In programme management parlance it is sometimes a substitute for measurements, such as those relating to quantifying realized benefits.
Program or programme	Program is the US spelling of programme. Program has long been the internationally accepted spelling relating to computer applications but in this Handbook, published in England, we have used the UK spelling 'programme' throughout except when the word appears in a quotation or the title of a publication.

Figure 1.4 A few common examples of project and programme management jargon

more programmes. Acquisitions and mergers, company relocations, development of new product ranges, and installation of new IT systems are some of the cases where programme management skills will be required.

This and the next three chapters are about the nature of programmes and their place in organizations. Chapters 5 to 19 document the experiences of experts from a wide range of industry and other sectors. We, as editors, found these different accounts fascinating, as they describe the problems encountered and methods for overcoming them, and offer expert advice.

Each of the remaining chapters gives expert advice on the management of programmes so that the intended benefits will be realized. All are written by very experienced people and, together, they represent a valuable fund of knowledge. We hope that you, our readers, will gain as much from them as we have.

Organizations representing the profession of project management

The International Project Management Association (IPMA)

Spread across more than 60 countries, the IPMA is a vigorous network of project management associations, supporting organizations, people, suppliers and sponsors moving the profession forward. The idea of a network fits more than ever to the current situation of the world. A network can adjust flexibly to changes in the context, exploit the diversity of cultures involved and support collaboration between members (such as regional networks). A network needs a powerful vision as orientation for joint activities. 'Promoting competence throughout society to enable a world in which all projects succeed' is the aspirational vision of IPMA.

Competence is what differentiates IPMA from other associations. Competence is much more than knowledge. It is the demonstrated ability to apply knowledge and/or skills and, where relevant, demonstrated personal attributes. IPMA standards cover the most important success factors. Besides the technical competencies (project, programme and portfolio management) there are personal and social competencies as well as the competencies of dealing with relevant contextual factors. In an increasingly complex world, technical competencies alone are no longer sufficient. IPMA also addresses social dynamics and intercultural settings – communication, cooperation and coordination are the key words for success in projects, programmes and portfolios. Contact details for IPMA are as follows:

PO Box 7905,
1008 AC Amsterdam,
The Netherlands.
Telephone: +31 33 247 34 30
Email: info@ipma.world
Website: www.ipma.world

The Association for Project Management (APM)

The corporate member of the IPMA in the UK is the Association for Project Management (APM) and further information is available from their secretariat at:

The Association for Project Management
Ibis House,
Regent Park,
Summerleys Road,
Princess Risborough,
Buckinghamshire, HP27 9LE,
UK.
Telephone: 0845 458 1944
Email: info@apm.org.uk
Website: www.apm.org.uk

The Association arranges seminars and meetings through its network of local branches. Its numerous publications include the periodical journal *Project* and the *APM Body of Knowledge*. Personal or corporate membership of the Association enables project managers and others involved in project management to meet and to maintain current awareness of all aspects of project management. Membership starts at student level and rises through various grades to full member (MAPM) and fellow (FAPM).

The Association has a well-established certification procedure for project managers, who must already be full members. To quote from the Association's own literature, 'the certificated project manager is at the pinnacle of the profession, possessing extensive knowledge and having carried responsibility for the delivery of at least one significant project'. As evidence of competence, certification has obvious advantages for the project manager, and will increasingly be demanded as mandatory by some project purchasers. Certification provides employers with a useful measure when recruiting or assessing staff and the company that can claim to employ certificated project managers will benefit from an enhanced professional image. Certification has relevance also for project clients. It helps them to assess a project manager's competence by providing clear proof that the individual concerned has gained peer recognition of his or her ability to manage projects.

The Project Management Institute (PMI)

Founded in the USA in 1969, the PMI is the world's leading not-for-profit organization for individuals around the globe who work in, or are interested in, project management. PMI develops recognized standards, not least of which is the widely respected project management body of knowledge guide, commonly known by its abbreviated title the *PMBOK Guide*.

PMI publications include the monthly professional magazine *PM Network*, the monthly newsletter *PMI Today* and the quarterly *Project Management Journal* as well as many project management books. In addition to its research and education activities, PMI is dedicated to developing and maintaining a rigorous, examination-based professional certification programme to advance the project management profession and recognize the achievements of individual professionals. PMI's Project Management Professional (PMP) certification is the world's most recognized professional credential for project management practitioners and others in the profession. For more information, contact PMI at:

PMI Headquarters,
Four Campus Boulevard,
Newtown Square,
PA 19073-3299,
USA.
Telephone: +610 356 4600
Email: pmihq@pmi.org
Website: www.pmi.org

References and further reading

Defoe, D. (1697), *An Essay upon Projects*, London (available from Amazon in modern reprints).
Gemünden, H. G. and Schoper, Y. (2014), 'Future Trends in Project Management', in *PM Aktuell*, 05/2014, Nuremberg: Deutsche Gesellschaft für Projektmanagement.
IPMA (2013), *IPMA Organisational Competence Baseline*, Version 1.0, Nijkerk: International Project Management Association.

Kanigel, R. (1997), *The One Best Way: Frederick Winslow Taylor and the Enigma of Efficiency*, London: Little, Brown and Co.

Lock, D. and Scott, L. (eds.) (2013), *Gower Handbook of People in Project Management*, Farnham: Gower.

Morris, P. W. G. (1994), *The Management of Projects*, London: Thomas Telford.

Morris, P. W. G. (2013), *Reconstructing Project Management*, Chichester: John Wiley.

NASA (2011), *Schedule Management Handbook*, Washington, DC: National Aeronautics and Space Administration.

Chapter 2

International Standards for Programme Management and Their Application

Reinhard Wagner

This chapter explains the most important standards for programme management and how various target audiences can use them.

Introduction

There are many standards for programme management. There are national, international, generic and sector-specific, process- and competence-orientated standards. It is difficult for the users to understand the commonalities of these standards and the differences between them, and apply them adequately in a specific context. For the sake of simplicity, in this chapter I shall focus on international standards.

Programme management standards in the aerospace and defence industry

Programme management can be traced back to the early 1950s in the USA. The Department of Defense (DoD) developed several handbooks for the design of complex aerospace and defence systems, which formed the basis for today's project and programme management. The concept of programme management is still very popular in the sector. A working group of the ISO/TC 20 Aircraft and Space Vehicles is developing international standards on programme and quality management. More than ten ISO standards are available that address programmes and their respective management, such as ISO 14300, 'Space systems – Programme management' and ISO 27026, 'Space systems – Programme management – Breakdown of project management structures'.

Interestingly, the terms 'project' and 'programme' are used interchangeably. These standards are used in organizations which are involved in respective programmes as guidelines for developing their own organization-specific standards or for collaborating with other organizations. The standards support a common understanding of programme management. They help to align the varying concepts of programme management in joint activities and thus increase efficiency. Many national standards bodies have adopted the ISO standards or have used them for developing their own standards.

Competence standards for programme management

It is *people* who perform programme management. Thus the competence of people is at the core of competence-orientated standards. From those standards

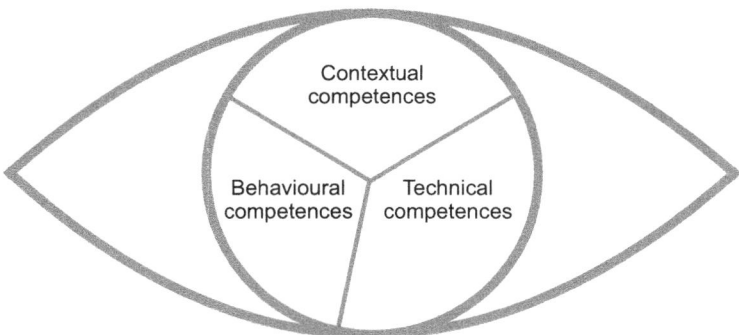

Figure 2.1 The 'eye of competence' of IPMA ICB

practitioners can learn about the competence requirements. Training and other ways of competence development can provide relevant knowledge of such standards and enable the participants in gaining experience (for example through learning by doing). Certification bodies can use competence-orientated standards for programme management as their baseline for assessing and certifying personnel. Competence-orientated standards typically are not intended to be used as process models or methodologies. They do not describe detailed input/output relationships and activities for all process steps of programme management.

The IPMA Individual Competence Baseline (IPMA ICB)

The International Project Management Association (IPMA) was the world's first international project management association, founded in 1965 in Europe. The approach of IPMA was mainly to improve the competencies of individuals involved in projects, programmes and portfolios through a standard, and to offer education and training as well as certification schemes through its National Certification Bodies in more than 60 countries worldwide. The first version of the IPMA ICB was published in 1999, based on the approaches of four European project management associations (including France, Germany, Switzerland and the UK). Programme management was one of the 28 competence elements described in this standard.

The current version of IPMA ICB (Version 3.0) was published seven years later (see IPMA, 2006). It describes a range of competencies, split into 'technical competencies', 'behavioural competencies' and 'contextual competencies' (Figure 2.1). In total, 47 competence elements describe the demonstrated ability to apply knowledge, skills and personal attributes. A related certification scheme contains the specific requirements for particular categories of people. Training providers could help people to attain the necessary competencies for a specific role and/or job level, such as certified project director (IPMA Level A). The certifications bodies of IPMA use ICB 3.0 as a baseline for their assessments.

IPMA recently published the fourth edition of its ICB. This goes a step further and separates the three domains of:

- project management;
- programme management;
- portfolio management.

A set of competence elements is described with Key Competence Indicators (KCIs) for each of these three domains. These KCIs provide definitive indicators of successful project, programme and portfolio management for one, two or all three domains. Based on IPMA ICB Version 4.0, the certification bodies will offer certification in the domain of programme management on two levels: 'certified programme manager' and 'certified programme director'.

GAPPS programme manager framework

The Global Alliance of Project Performance Standards (GAPPS) was formed in 2003 as a unique alliance of government, industry, professional associations, national qualification bodies, training and academic institutions to help practitioners and organizations make sense of the many standards and certifications available globally. GAPPS offers 'A Framework for Performance Based Competency Standards for Program Managers', which is intended to support the development and recognition of local standards and to provide a sound basis for mutual recognition and transferability of project and programme management qualifications (GAPPS, 2011). Based on their own framework, GAPPS maps other programme management standards (such as the IPMA ICB) to show how well each of these standards covers the core and to identify the extent to which each standard goes beyond the core.

Furthermore, GAPPS has developed a tool for categorizing programmes based on their complexity. The Aitken-Carnegie-Duncan Complexity (ACDC) table is used to differentiate programme manager roles according to the management complexity of the respective programmes. The table includes 29 detail factors arranged into the following five groups:

- governance complexity;
- stakeholder relationship complexity;
- programme definition complexity;
- benefits delivery complexity;
- resource complexity.

Each of these factors can be rated from 1 to 4, using a qualitative points scale. Altogether, the factors provide a management complexity rating for the programme in scope, and a mechanism for matching competencies needed by the programme manager.

GAPPS also provides a typology for programmes. Taking into account the wide range of applications for programmes, including but not limited to systems development, change initiatives or construction, a typology may provide a means for understanding the requirements and dealing with the challenges appropriately. The GAPPS programme typology distinguishes between a strategic programme, an operational programme, a multiproject programme and megaprojects. One of the conclusions drawn from the analysis of the different programme types is that the role of the programme manager is fundamentally the same for strategic, operational and multi-project programmes. However, the role of the manager of a megaproject is substantially different from that of a manager of one of the other three programme types.

Practice standards for programme management

Management standards typically build on what is called 'good practice'. They try to capture this practice and extract key concepts, principles, processes, methodologies and tools for any type of organization, and for any type of programme, irrespective of complexity, volume or duration. There are three internationally acknowledged standards available for programme management:

1. ISO 21503 Guidance on programme management.
2. The best management practice standard 'Managing Successful Programmes' of AXELOS.
3. PMI's Standard for Program Management.

ISO 21503 Guidance on programme management

In 2007, ISO chartered a project to develop an international project management standard, the ISO 21500 'Guidance on project management'. It is a process-orientated standard for the management of a single project. In a conceptual part, it mentions programmes and programme management as follows: 'A programme is generally a group of related projects and other activities aligned with strategic goals. Programme management consists of centralized and coordinated activities to achieve the goals' (ISO, 2012, p. 6). Shortly before finishing the ISO 21500, a new technical committee was established (the ISO/TC 258 Project, Programme and Portfolio Management).

In 2014, development of an ISO standard for programme management started. The future ISO 21503 'Guidance on programme management' is presently available as a committee draft (CD).

Unlike ISO 21500, the programme management standard does not follow a process-orientated approach. The upcoming standard defines terms and concepts for programmes and programme management; it elaborates on programme management practices and how to introduce programme management to an organization. A programme is defined as 'a temporary structure of interrelated programme components managed in a coordinated way to enable the realization of benefits' (ISO, 2015a). Programme components could be projects, programmes and other related work. The main purpose of setting up a programme is to achieve synergies between the interrelated components. Programme management is defined as 'coordinated activities to direct and control the achievement of programme objectives'. Main practices mentioned are programme planning, programme controls, programme integration and benefits management. The section on introducing programme management covers aspects such as governance, roles and responsibilities, and the alignment of programme management within the organization. The programme management standard of ISO is a guidance standard, which means that its intent is neither to be certified against nor to replace other (national or sector-specific) standards.

The AXELOS standard on 'Managing Successful Programmes'

There is a long tradition of programme management in the UK. The Association for Project Management (APM), some universities and many industry experts made specific expertise available for the *APM Body of Knowledge*, 6th edition. This Body of Knowledge defines programme management as follows (APM, 2012, p. 14): 'Programme management is the coordinated management of projects and change management activities to achieve beneficial change.'

Programme management aims at making change happen. This demonstrates a different focus in the UK regarding programme management than in the rest of the world. Programmes are performed to achieve change. This is also the case with the Best Management Practice Standard 'Managing Successful Programmes (MSP)'. The Office of Government Commerce (OGC) published the first edition of MSP in 1999. The OGC function later moved into the Cabinet Office as part of HM Government, which merged the function with a private organization into a joint venture, called 'AXELOS', which now owns all Best Management Practice Standards.

MSP claims to provide 'proven good practice in programme management in successfully delivering transformational change, drawn from the experiences of both public and private sector organizations'. This standard brings together key principles, governance themes and a set of interrelated processes for business transformation through programmes. MSP defines a programme as 'a temporary, flexible organization created to coordinate, direct and oversee the implementation of a set of related projects and activities in order to deliver outcomes and benefits related to the organization's strategic objectives' (TSO, 2011, p. 5). Programme management is 'the action of carrying out the coordinated organization, direction and implementation of a dossier of projects and transformation activities'. It aligns corporate strategy with delivery mechanisms for change and business-as-usual activities. Besides such definitions, MSP delivers insights into programme management principles, such as leading change and focusing on the benefits and threats to them.

In addition, MSP delivers nine governance themes for control and direction of the transformational change programme, as well as for control and sustainability of the wider organization as a corporate entity. The themes are:

- programme organization;
- vision;
- leadership and stakeholder engagement;
- benefits management;
- blueprint design and delivery;
- planning and control;
- the business case;
- risk and issue management;
- quality and assurance management.

A programme management process ('The Transformational Flow') is described in MSP for identifying and defining programmes, managing the tranches, delivering the capability, realizing the benefits and closing the programme. Furthermore, through appendices MSP elaborates on programme information, adopting MSP, the programme office, and health checks.

MSP provides an adaptable route map for programme managers to apply the good practices in their area of responsibilities. An organization and its senior executives may find advice in MSP on how to embed, review or apply the principles, themes and processes proposed. There are various training and certification schemes available for MSP.

'The Standard for Program Management' of PMI

Founded in 1969, the Project Management Institute (PMI) developed into a US-based, internationally spreading not-for-profit professional membership association for the project, programme and portfolio management profession. In the 1980s PMI developed a white paper on project management methodology, which was published in 1996 as the first version of the 'Guide to the Project Management Body of Knowledge' (PMBOK Guide). It identifies that subset of the PMBOK Guide that is generally recognized as a good practice for project management. The PMBOK Guide is process-based, which means it describes work as being accomplished by processes. The processes are described in terms of inputs, tools and techniques as well as outputs.

In 2006, PMI published its first edition of 'The Standard for Program Management'. It presented three key themes – 'Stakeholder Management', 'Program Governance' and 'Benefits Management' – as well as a programme management lifecycle framework based on a 'domain-orientated' approach. The second edition of the standard mirrored the PMBOK Guide approach of processes along the lifecycle of a programme. The third edition of 'The Standard for Program Management', published by PMI in 2013, changed the document to the 'domain-orientated' approach of the first edition. The standard provides information on programme management that is generally recognized as good practice for most programmes, most of the time. It defines a programme as 'a group of related projects, subprograms, and program activities that are managed in a coordinated way to obtain benefits not available from managing them individually' (PMI, 2013a, p. 4).

Programme management is defined as 'the application of knowledge, skills, tools, and techniques to a program to meet the program requirements and to obtain benefits and control not available by managing projects individually'. Through its suite of standards for project, programme, portfolio and organizational project management, PMI shows the interrelations of all these aspects and ways of managing them in an integrated way. All those standards address the business value delivered, the roles involved and competencies required. Like other professional associations, PMI offers training and certification schemes for people involved in programme management.

PMI's Standard for Program Management defines five performance domains for programme management:

- strategy alignment;
- benefits management;
- stakeholder engagement;
- governance;
- lifecycle management.

These run concurrently throughout the duration of a programme and are per-formed by the programme management team. A programme lifecycle comprises the programme definition phase, programme benefits delivery phase and programme closure. Nine processes for communication management, financial management, integration management, procurement management, quality management, resource management, risk management, schedule management, and scope management support this programme lifecycle. They are similar to the processes at project level, but should address considerations of a higher level, depending on the type and/or complexity of a programme.

PMI's standard for programme management defines three categories of pro-grammes as follows:

1. A strategic programme supporting the organization's strategic goals.
2. A compliance programme initiated because of legislation, regulations or con-tractual obligations.
3. An emergent programme, such as improvement or change activities.

Other related standards for programme management

There are many other standards with relevance to programme management. These include:

*   national standards (for example the DIN standards);
*   regional standards (such as the European standards);
*   sector-specific standards (like the V-Model for IT-Systems);
*   standards for assessing and certification of maturity in programme management (for example IPMA Delta).

There are also many books and articles about programmes and programme manage-ment, which could be seen as good practice standards. I shall now focus on standards with a specific approach to programme management.

The AXELOS Standard on 'Portfolio, Programme and Project Offices'

In addition to the aforementioned MSP Standard, Axelos offers a best manage-ment practice standard called 'Portfolio, Programme and Project Offices (P3O)'. First published in 2008, the current edition is dated 2013. P3O provides guidance on portfolio, programme and project offices, aiming primarily at senior managers and managers responsible for the P3O implementation. It defines P3O as follows (TSO, 2013, p. 7):

> The decision-enabling and support business model for all business change within an organization. This will include single or multiple physical or virtual structures, i.e. offices (permanent and/or temporary), providing a mix of central and local-ized functions and services, and integration with governance arrangements and the wider business such as other corporate support functions.

The standard answers the questions of why an organization should have P3Os and how to design, implement or re-energize and operate the office(s). Several appendices of the standard elaborate on roles and responsibilities, and provide a business case example for the development or enhancement of P3Os, examples of tools and techniques through links to a knowledge centre, and case studies on model tailoring.

The Organisational Competence Baseline of IPMA

In 2013, the IPMA released its first version of a new standard, the IPMA Organisational Competence Baseline (IPMA OCB), which introduces the innovative concept of an organizational competence in managing projects. It is a holistic approach for organizations to strengthen their management of projects, programmes and portfolios. The IPMA OCB describes the concept of organizational competence in managing projects, programmes and portfolio-related work and how this should be used to deliver the organization's vision, mission and strategic objectives in a sustainable manner. It also demonstrates how the governance and management of projects, programmes and portfolios (PP&P) should be continuously analysed, assessed, improved and further developed.

The main target audience for this standard is senior executives. They could use the standard to understand the role of PP&P for executing and controlling mission, vision and strategy. It can help them to:

- understand their own role in the concept of organizational competence in managing projects;
- analyse the status of their organization's competence in managing projects;
- identify areas for improvement;
- direct stakeholders, resources and activities for the development of the organization's capabilities in managing projects.

IPMA OCB defines organizational competence in managing projects as the 'ability of organisations to integrate people, resources, processes, structures and cultures in projects, programmes and portfolios within a supporting governance and management system. Organizational competence in managing projects is specifically aligned with the mission, vision and strategy of the organization and is intended to achieve results as well as to ensure continuous organizational development' (IPMA, 2013, p. 19). One chapter elaborates on ways to implement or improve the competence of an organization, and the tools to be used. IPMA's certification bodies use IPMA OCB as the baseline for assessing and certifying the competence of organizations; the approach is called 'IPMA Delta'.

Figure 2.2 shows all the competence elements, including the competencies of programme management.

ISO DIS 21505 'Project, programme and portfolio management – Guidance on governance'

Another standard being developed within the context of ISO/TC258 is a governance standard, the future ISO 21505. Presently, it is available as a Draft International

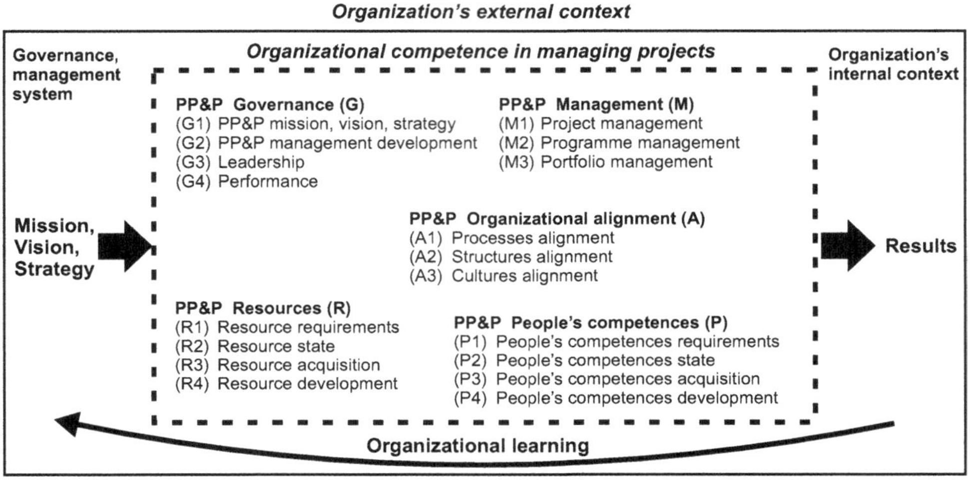

Organization's external context

Figure 2.2 Organizational competence elements

Standard (DIS). The primary target audience for this standard comprises governing bodies and executive managers who influence, impact or make decisions regarding the governance of projects, programmes and portfolios.

The definition for governance is the 'action or manner of governing an organization by using and regulating influence to direct and control the actions and affairs of others' (ISO, 2015b, p. 2). It should be aligned with the overall organizational governance and (if existing) the governance of all projects and portfolios. The governance of programmes in ISO DIS 21505 comprises the principles, governing body responsibilities, guidelines and framework by which an organization directs and controls its programmes. Examples mentioned in ISO DIS 21505 for governing bodies are programme steering committees and a programme board or other management oversight bodies. Important principles are to create the framework, realize value, ensure ethics and sustainability, information security, integrity and disclosure, respect the rights of stakeholders, and establish risk management policies.

The Organizational Project Management Maturity Model (OPM3) of PMI

PMI is also interested in elaborating on frameworks beyond the management of a single project or programme. A standard called 'The Organizational Project Management Maturity Model (OPM3)' was developed, providing guidelines for improving organizational project, programme and portfolio management. The first edition was released in 2003, the second in 2008 and the actual standard in 2013. It is the 'knowledge foundation' and is used for assessing organizations.

OPM3 is based on the strategy execution framework 'Organizational Project Management (OPM)'. It utilizes portfolio, programme and project management as well as organizational-enabling practices. OPM integrates knowledge, processes, people, and supporting tools to achieve business value. The maturity of an organization is 'the level of an organization's ability to deliver the desired strategic outcomes in a predictable, controllable, and reliable manner' (PMI, 2013b, p. 240). OPM3 is a 'framework that defines knowledge, assessment, and improvement processes, based on Best Practices and Capabilities, to help organizations measure and mature their portfolio, program, and project management practices'.

The improvement process is designed to start with acquiring knowledge about organizational project management, based on that performing an assessment to evaluate the current state and managing improvement to gain capabilities identified as needed, and finally, measure the impacts of these changes. OPM3 delivers a 'Self-Assessment Method (SAM)' and an encyclopaedic list of best practices for comparison.

Conclusion

There are many standards available for programme management. The international journey of developing standards started in the 1950s in the USA, especially in the aerospace and defence sector. It continued in this sector, focusing on large projects and programmes with interrelated constituent parts, aiming at synergies through integrative management. Later, the professional associations started to develop their own competence-based or practice-based programme management standards. The type and complexity of a programme are decisive for choosing the right approach. Both the competence of a programme manager and the practice applied are dependent on the programme type. Other programme-related standards touch on organizational settings, roles and responsibilities, including the governance of programmes, and the maturity of its application.

Before reading the standards, the problem should be analysed and defined, the objectives and constraints should be clarified with all stakeholders and an implementation project started. All the aforementioned standards disclose their target readership, the content and the main area for application. That gives guidance on which standard to choose.

International standards are typically very generic, because they are intended to fit all programmes and all organizations. Thus a user needs to understand the standard as guidance for developing an own, situation-specific solution. Implementing or improving programme management is a project (or a programme) on its own. Managing such a project also encompasses change activities, such as stakeholder engagement, communication and conflict resolution. The overall goal is to improve the performance of programme management and deliver value to the organization.

The following chapters of this Handbook will elaborate on several if not all aspects mentioned in this chapter. They may also refer to one or other programme management standard, which shows the significance of the standards in daily application. Because standards are not mandatory, there are many derivates and interpretations at hand, which also help to move the profession forward by exchanging experiences and learning from the application.

References and further reading

APM (2012), *APM Body of Knowledge*, 6th edn., Princes Risborough: Association for Project Management.

GAPPS (2011), *Framework for Performance Based Competency Standards for Program Managers*, Global Alliance for Project Performance Standards.

IPMA (2006), *IPMA Competence Baseline for Project Management*, Version 3.0, International Project Management Association.

IPMA (2013), *IPMA Organisational Competence Baseline*, Version 1.0, International Project Management Association.

ISO (2012), *ISO 21500 Guidance on Project Management*, Geneva: International Organization for Standardization.

ISO (2015a), *ISO CD 21504 Guidance on Programme Management*, Geneva: International Organization for Standardization.

ISO (2015b), *ISO DIS 21505 Project, Programme and Portfolio Management – Guidance on Governance*, Geneva: International Organization for Standardization.

PMI (2013a), *The Standard for Program Management*, 3rd edn., Newtown Square, PA: Project Management Institute.

PMI (2013b), *Organizational Project Management Maturity Model (OPM3)*, 3rd edn., Newtown Square, PA: Project Management Institute.

TSO (2011), *Managing Successful Programmes*, Norwich: The Stationery Office.

TSO (2013), *Portfolio, Programme and Project Offices*, Norwich: The Stationery Office.

Chapter 3

The Nature of Programmes and their Interrelation with Projects, Portfolios and Operations

Rodney Turner

Introduction

Historically, the subject of project management focused on large projects in large organizations. Projects were portrayed as:

- large stand-alone entities;
- separate from other projects and operations;
- with a dedicated team.

Projects were ring-fenced. They had few interfaces with other projects or operations being undertaken by the parent organizations, or with other projects being undertaken by the contractor (if there was one). The project team was confined within the ring-fence and was wholly within the control of the project manager. The project manager might not have had as many resources as he or she would have liked, but those inside the ring-fence were completely within his or her control; they were not answerable to anybody else. That was the view of projects which dominated project management thinking until the late 1980s.

Then people started to talk about 'multiprojects' – projects that were linked to other projects taking place at the same time. In the first edition of my book (Turner, 2014, first edition 1993), I suggested that the large project model described above represented about 1 per cent of projects and a third of all project activity. I suggested further that what represented 99 per cent of all projects and two thirds of project activity was small to medium-sized projects, where:

- the projects are small to medium-sized;
- they have interfaces with other projects and operations;
- they share resources with other projects and operations.

In the late 1980s and early 1990s, we used to refer to a collection of multiprojects as a 'programme', but we quickly began to differentiate between a programme and a portfolio. A programme is a collection of projects contributing to a common objective; a portfolio is a collection of projects sharing resources. We now talk in terms of a constellation of types of multiprojects, including:

- programmes;
- portfolios;

- project networks;
- project-based organizations;
- project-orientated organizations.

In this chapter I shall give a history of thinking on multiprojects and programmes in particular. I shall then define various types of multiprojects, and discuss the particular nature of programmes, their interface with projects, and other types of multiproject and operations.

History of multiprojects

Work at the Technical University of Berlin has shown how the focus of papers published in the *International Journal of Project Management* and *Project Management Journal* has changed over the past 25 years. In the late 1980s, around 70 per cent of the papers published were on single projects, and about 10 per cent were on multiprojects (20 per cent were on other things). By the first decade or this century the number of papers on single projects had fallen to fewer than 50 per cent, and the number on multiprojects had risen to nearly 50 per cent. So, from the focus being almost entirely on single projects there is now equal focus on both single and multiprojects.

Early writings on project management viewed the project as a large stand-alone entity. David Cleland and Bill King (1983, first edition 1966) wrote about the project as a system, and the focus of early textbooks (for example Kerzner, 2013, first edition 1974; Meredith and Mantel, 2012, first edition 1984) was on the single project. Those American books take a systems approach to project management, which in my view produces a very static view of projects, as opposed to the dynamic European, process approach (Turner, 2014; Gareis and Stummer, 2008).

The first time I was aware of someone talking or writing about multiprojects was the IPMA Expert Seminar on multiprojects held in Zurich in 1988 organized by Sebastien Dworatschek (Dworatschek, 1988). I presented a paper on the work I had been doing with H. J. Heinz, which would now be said to trying to establish portfolio management and a portfolio management office. I continued some of that work, and presented a paper at the IPMA World Congress in Florence in 1992, which was published in the *International Journal of Project Management* in November of that year (Turner and Speiser, 1992). Although the title of the paper said it was about programme management, most of what it covered would now be called portfolio management. In the early days people did not differentiate between programme and portfolio management (Reese, 2000; Murray-Webster and Thiry, 2000). The distinction became clear sometime between the publication of the third edition of the *Gower Handbook or Project Management* (Turner and Simister, 2000) and the fourth edition (Turner, 2007).

Geoff Reiss told me once that it was my paper (Turner and Speiser, 1992) that stimulated him to establish APM's special interest group on programme management. (Geoff Reiss has been described as the father of programme management in the UK, which perhaps makes me the grandfather.) From that initiative flowed much of the work on programme and portfolio management in the UK and indeed in the rest of the world. The UK government published its programme management guide in 1997 (Central Computer and Telecommunications Agency, 1997), though somewhat strangely it was 14 years before it published its portfolio management guide (Office of Government Commerce, 2011b). The Project Management Institute (PMI) on the other hand published both its programme and portfolio management guides together in 2004 (Project Management Institute, 2004a, 2004b). So clearly there are several forms of multiproject, which I shall now define.

Definitions

I like to keep my definitions simple, and focus on the key features that distinguish the item being defined. Other people seem to want to cover all the bases and make sure they cover all features of an item, even those which they share with other items.

Project

I define a project as 'a temporary organization to which resources are assigned to do work to deliver beneficial change' (Turner and Müller, 2003; Turner, 2014). By this definition, a project is a temporary organization. We create a temporary organization, to which resources are assigned, and those resources will do a specific task of work. When that task is finished the organization will be disbanded. A project is more than just a temporary endeavour. The making of a cup of tea, the scheduled service of an automobile and the preparation of a company's annual budget are temporary endeavours, but they are not projects. They are routine and so are part of normal operations. The preparation of the annual budget is a temporary task given to the routine organization, whereas the annual audit requires the creation of a temporary organization (which includes auditors from the audit company). However, the audit may also involve some temporary tasks given to the routine organization, the accounting department, and so may be better thought of as a programme, since it involves elements of both projects and operations.

The definition of a project used by other people includes temporary tasks given to the routine organization. For instance the PMI (2013a) says a project is a temporary endeavour. In Example 1.1 of Turner (2014, p. 3), I discuss an engineer from British Telecom who objected to my definition of a project because it did not include his routine, but temporary, maintenance tasks which he labelled projects. At that point, I say the concept of a project is a social construct, and whether you want to view a project them as a temporary organization or as a temporary endeavour depends on what provides you with value. My definition differentiates projects as temporary organizations, and temporary tasks given to the routine organization.

Multiprojects

Many different types of multiprojects have been recognized. Some of these are described below.

Programmes

Keeping it simple, I define a programme as a group of projects which contribute to a higher order strategic objective (Turner, 2014, p. 72). An organization is undertaking a change to achieve a higher order strategic objective, which requires it to undertake more than one project. Reasons for this can include:

1. the change requires the involvement of several different types of resources which it is easier to engage separately;
2. the change requires several cycles, each of which is best organized as a group of projects;
3. the change is poorly defined, and needs to be undertaken as a sequence of well-defined projects, as the definition of the change is refined.

A weakness of my definition is that it says the programme is just a collection of 'projects' whereas the example of the annual audit above suggests that the programme could involve projects and temporary tasks given to the routine organization. Either we need to refine the definition, or take the word 'project' to include temporary tasks give to the routine organization. Other definitions of programme include:

- a temporary flexible organization created to coordinate, direct and oversee the implementation of a set of related projects and activities in order to deliver outcomes and benefits related to the organization's strategic objectives: a programme is likely to have a life that lasts several years. (Office of Government Commerce, 2011a);
- a group of projects, subprogrammes and programme activities that are managed in a coordinated way to obtain benefits not available from managing them individually (PMI, 2013a).

Both of these definitions emphasize that the programme may have other temporary activities which are not projects, and that the objective is to obtain benefits not available from individually managed projects.

Portfolio

Again keeping my definitions simple, I define a portfolio as a group of projects that share common resources (Turner, 2014, p. 72). Projects in a programme contribute to a common output; projects in a portfolio share common inputs. That is the key feature of both.

Other definitions of portfolios include the following:

- An organization's portfolio is the totality of its investment (or segment thereof) in the changes required to achieve its strategic objectives (Office of Government Commerce, 2011b).
- A portfolio is a collection of projects or programmes and other work that are grouped together to facilitate effective management of that work to meet strategic business objectives (PMI, 2013b).

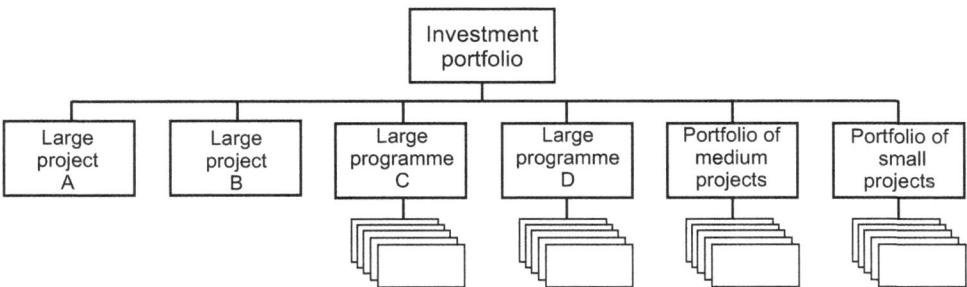

Figure 3.1 An investment portfolio

I believe that the OGC version defines only one type of portfolio. I call this the investment portfolio. Figure 3.1 shows that an investment portfolio can comprise large projects and programmes as well as portfolios of small and medium-sized projects. The PMI definition encompasses the portfolios of small and medium-sized projects and indeed suggests that a programme can include portfolios of smaller projects.

Project-based organization

Anne Keegan and I define a project-based organization as one in which the majority of products made for customers are against a bespoke design (Turner and Keegan, 2000). The concept here is that if the organization is making products against a bespoke design, it will be adopting projects to do that. So most of its work will be projects. This is a bottom-up definition. The work the organization is doing requires it to use projects and so it is project-based.

However, some organizations that ought to be project-based do try to retain functional ways of working because of the dominance of their functional managers. A project-based organization is effectively managing a portfolio of projects, but in a way where it is the totality of the organization.

Project-orientated organization

Martina Huemann (2014) defines a project-orientated organization as one which:

- defines management by projects as its organizational strategy;
- applies projects and programmes as temporary organizations;
- manages a project portfolio of different internal and external project types;
- project management, programme management and portfolio management are specific business processes;
- has specific permanent organizations like a project portfolio group or a project management office to provide integrative functions;
- applies a management paradigm which reflects the ability to deal with uncertainty, contradiction, change and collaboration;
- views itself as being project-orientated.

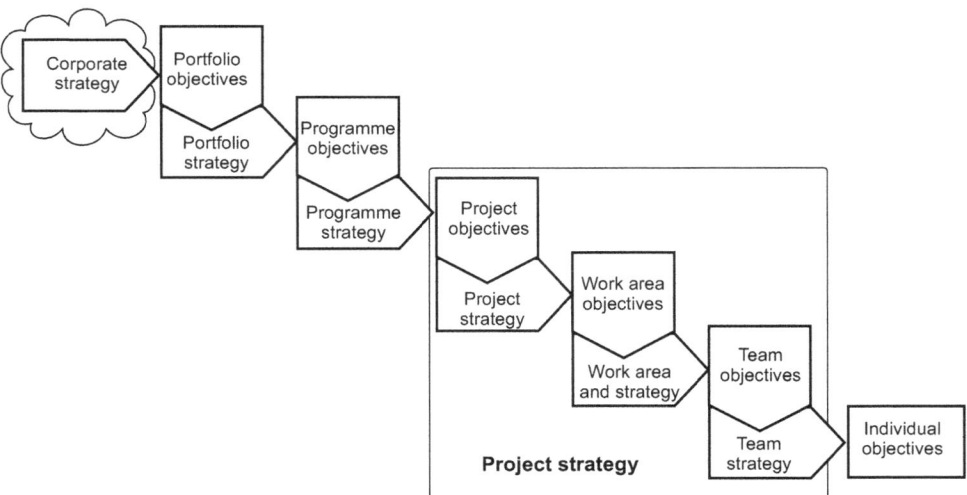

Figure 3.2 The normal (dominant) cascade

This is top-down. The organization perceives itself as project-orientated, and adopts that as its organization strategy. Being project-based and project-orientated should meet in the middle: if the organization is project-based it should perceive itself as project-orientated. Unfortunately, as I said above, in some project-based organizations the functional managers continue to try to manage the organization as a functional organization, and some organizations doing temporary but essentially routine tasks define themselves as being project-orientated.

The cascade

Figure 3.2 illustrates the normal cascade from corporate strategy through portfolios and programmes to projects. This cascade is consistent with the OGC definition of portfolios. The company strategy is translated into a portfolio to fulfil its investment plans. The portfolio comprises programmes of change and links the investment objectives of the corporate strategy into change objectives of the programmes. The programmes are then composed of projects, each delivering individual elements of the programme objectives.

That is the dominant cascade. However, Figure 3.1 showed that the investment portfolio can also comprise portfolios of smaller projects and (as I wrote above) PMI says that a programme can have a portfolio of smaller projects within it.

Three organizations

Figure 3.3 shows three organizations involved in the management of projects.

The organization on the left is a project, or programme. It is a temporary organization, and is being undertaken by the organization at top right to achieve its strategic objectives. The project or programme will be part of the parent organization's

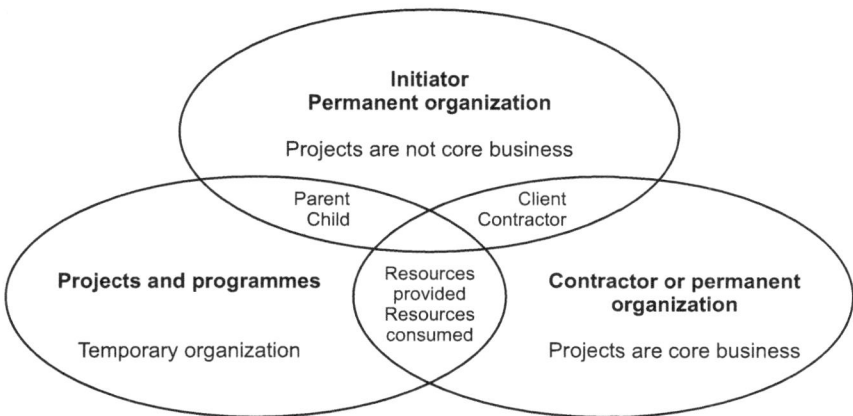

Figure 3.3 Three organizations involved in the management of projects

investment portfolio as shown in Figure 3.1, and will be linked to the organization's corporate strategy through the cascade shown in Figure 3.2.

The organization at the top right is the investor or parent organization. It is a permanent organization. It may or may not be project-based or project-orientated. Its main business might be project-based or routine. It is undertaking the project or programme to achieve its corporate strategy and thereby improve its operations.

The organization at bottom right of Figure 3.3 is a project-based organization. It is a contractor doing some or all of the work of the project for the investor. It too is a permanent organization. Its business is project-based, doing project work for investors.

The nature of programmes

In discussing the nature of programmes, I wish to consider two issues:

1.   Are projects and programmes different?
2.   The relationship of programmes with projects, portfolios and operations.

Are projects and programmes different?

There are people who get quite worked up about this question, and say 'Yes, they are very different.' On the one hand, I think people who take that position sometimes have in their mind a single idea about a project, and are comparing a programme to the projects that make it up. I would say, 'Yes, a programme is very different from the constituents it comprises and is very much larger.' But projects of different sizes are also very different. A €500,000 project is very different from a €50 million project and both are very different from a €5 billion project. I believe that a €50 million project and €50 million programme are more alike than either is to a €500,000 project. However, projects and programmes are different.

Jingting Shao found that the leadership style of programme managers is very different from what Müller and I (2006) found for project managers. Also many people now say that megaprojects are better managed as programmes rather than as projects, and so that would suggest that they can be managed in different ways. There are three significant differences:

1. SMART versus smARt objectives;
2. cyclic delivery;
3. the programme is greater than the sum of its parts.

SMART versus smARt objectives

Projects have smart objectives. These are:

- specific
- measurable;
- achievable;
- realistic;
- timelined.

The objectives of a project are clear, precise and can be well defined quantitatively. They are achievable and realistic and have a clear delivery date. On the other hand, with a programme delivering change, the objectives tend to be smARt. The objectives of the change programme are less clear, and may evolve with time. As early parts of the change programme are achieved and more information is gathered, you might change your ideas about what the final change will look like – and aim for something that is more realistic or achievable. You break the programme into projects with SMART objectives so that you can clearly deliver early parts of the change programme, but as you complete those early parts they might give you new information. That new information might lead you to revise the end objective of the change programme. Because the objectives can change, the time at which they are to be delivered can change and the measurements can also change.

Cyclic delivery

As I have just said, we divide the programme into projects and start delivering early projects to gather more information about the change we wish to introduce. A key part of programme management is that the early projects should be delivered and information gathered from those projects about the change we are trying to achieve, but also the benefits from those early projects should be obtained straight away. If the benefits are obtained straight away it will give us more information about the change we wish to achieve, and the realizability of the benefits. But it also means that the benefits from the early projects can be used to help pay for the later parts of the programme. An issue with projects is that all the money has to be spent before any benefit can be obtained, but with programmes, benefits can be obtained from early projects to pay for later ones.

Often this phased delivery of projects is formalized where the programme is divided into cycles of projects. I use the example of building an out-of-town shopping centre where you might plan to build 50 shops. With the shopping centre, you might plan to do the work in three cycles, building 20, 20 and 10 shops. When you complete the first cycle, the income from the 20 shops will help to pay for the later two cycles. And at the end of the first and second cycle, you can revisit your plans, and decide if you still want to build 20 shops in the second cycle and 10 in the third. You might decide to build more or fewer shops, and you could decide to stop after two cycles or go to a third. There are three types of programme from this perspective:

- cyclic;
- once through;
- mixed.

The cyclic programme is as I have just described. But some programmes must have a specific end date. The construction of Heathrow Terminal 5 consisted of many projects:

- the main building;
- Pier B;
- the railway connecting them;
- road access;
- short-term, business and long-term parking;
- shops.

But the whole thing had to be commissioned together on one day (except that Pier C and the railway connecting Pier B to Pier C was built about 18 months later).

An example of a mixed programme is the new football stadium in Bilbao. I used to teach at the University of the Basque Country, which is next to the Bilbao football stadium. The old stadium was to be demolished and a new one built across the road, then new shops and apartments were to be built on the site of the old stadium and surrounding houses and shops renovated. The new stadium had to be commissioned on one day, but the building and renovation work could be done in cycles.

The programme is greater than the sum of its parts

PMI's definition of a programme emphasizes that the programme will deliver strategic objectives not obtainable from managing the projects individually. So each project in the programme will deliver new capabilities to the parent organization, but the desired change can only be obtained by integrating those new capabilities. There are two related issues here:

1. Several new capabilities are required, and those capabilities cannot be delivered by one project, perhaps because they involve substantially different resources, or they are separate or distinct in some way.
2. But sometimes it is best if the elements of the programme are kept quite distinct. With the computerization of London Ambulance (Dalcher, 2010), at the

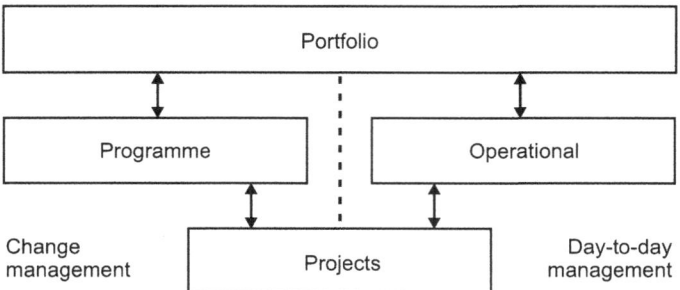

Figure 3.4 Portfolio, programme, operation, projects

first three unsuccessful attempts, the delivery was managed as a single project. At the fourth successful attempt it was managed as a programme. It is easier to coordinate the interfaces between the different elements of the system if they are managed separately. Further, all parts of the system do not need to be delivered simultaneously. Rather than delivering one, large, complicated system at one time, different elements can be commissioned and proved before the whole system goes live.

Megaprojects

Why are megaprojects better thought of as programmes than as projects? It might be primarily related to this last point, but is also related to the smARt objectives. The output from a megaproject usually has to be delivered on a given day, and considering its size, Heathrow Terminal 5 would count as a megaproject. But it is often best if the components are managed separately because the interfaces are then easier to manage. Also many megaprojects tend to be complex and it is the nature of complex projects that small input changes can cause large changes in output. So the end objective might be reasonably unclear in the early stages. Then it makes its management easier if the megaprojects can be divided into subprojects. Many of those will have SMART objectives that can be managed precisely, while the uncertainties introduced by the complexity are refined.

Relationship of programmes with projects, portfolios and operations

Figure 3.4 illustrates the relationship between portfolios, programmes, projects and operations.

Portfolios set the strategic objectives for the organization and are the main vehicle for linking strategic objectives to the programmes and projects being undertaken by the organization. The strategic objectives are primarily about developing new operations, and so in Figure 3.4 portfolios are shown covering operations and programmes.

The investment portfolio will develop a strategy based on the organization's assessment of its context and capabilities, its strengths, weaknesses, opportunities and threats (SWOT) and the needs of its stakeholders. It will develop strategies at the business unit and operational level, and seek agreement between the senior managers and sponsors from the different business units and operations. It will then define objectives for programmes to introduce change to develop new operations.

Programmes will deliver changes to the organization to develop new operations. Programmes will develop clear business cases with defined benefits, and manage across organizational and resource boundaries. As I wrote above, complexity can be reduced if different elements are managed separately but it is the responsibility of the programme to coordinate the interfaces. The programme will set clear objectives for projects to deliver individual elements of change with new capabilities.

Projects will deliver new capabilities. It is the projects that deliver the new operations.

Operations: it is operations that need to manage the transition to the new ways of working. They must ensure business continuity. You do not want your customers to notice any disruption to service. Operations also need to manage the impact on staff, to ensure that they are not adversely affected by the change, and do not become overwhelmed by the changes happening.

Clearly, all four elements (portfolios, programmes, projects and operations) have an involvement in the change process.

References and further reading

Central Computer and Telecommunications Agency (1997), *Managing Successful Programmes*, London: The Stationery Office.

Cleland, D. I. and King, W. R. (1983), *Systems Analysis and Project Management*, international student edn., New York: McGraw-Hill.

Dalcher, D. (2010), 'The LAS Story: Learning from Failure', in J. R. Turner, M. Huam, F. T. Anbari and C. B. Bredillet (eds.), *Perspectives on Projects*, New York: Routledge.

Dworatshek, S. (1988), *Multiprojects: Proceedings of the 12th INTERNET International Expert Seminar, Zurich, March 1988*, Zurich: International Project Management Association.

Gareis, R. and Stummer, M. (2008), *Processes and Projects*. Vienna: Manz.

Huemann, M. (2014), 'Managing the Project-Oriented Organization', in J. R. Turner (ed.), *Gower Handbook of Project Management*, 5th edn., Farnham: Gower.

Jenner, S. and Kilford, C. (2011), *Management of Portfolios*, Norwich: The Stationery Office.

Kerzner, H. R. (2013), *Project Management: A Systems Approach to Planning, Scheduling and Controlling*, 11th edn., New York: John Wiley.

Meredith, J. R. and Mantel, S. J. (2012), *Project Management: A Managerial Approach*, 8th edn., New York: John Wiley.

Murray-Webster, R. and Thiry, M. (2000), 'Managing Programmes of Projects', in J. R. Turner and S. J. Simister (eds.), *Gower Handbook of Project Management*, 3rd edn., Farnham: Gower.

Office of Government Commerce (2011a), *Managing Successful Programmes*, 4th edn., Norwich: The Stationery Office.

Office of Government Commerce (2011b), *Management of Portfolios*, Norwich: The Stationery Office.

PMI (2004a), *The Standard for Programme Management*, Newtown Square, PA: Project Management Institute.

PMI (2004b), *The Standard for Portfolio Management*, Newtown Square, PA: Project Management Institute.

PMI (2013a), *The Standard for Programme Management*, 3rd edn., Newtown Square, PA: Project Management Institute.

PMI (2013b), *The Standard for Portfolio Management*, 3rd edn., Newtown Square, PA: Project Management Institute.

Reiss, G. (2000), 'Information Systems for Programme Management', in J. R. Turner and S. J. Simister (eds.), *Gower Handbook of Project Management*, 3rd edn., Farnham: Gower.

Turner, J. R. (ed.) (2007), *Gower Handbook of Project Management*, 4th edn., Farnham: Gower.

Turner, J. R. (2014), *The Handbook of Project-Based Management: Leading Strategic Change in Organizations*, 4th edn., New York: McGraw-Hill.

Turner, J. R. and Keegan, A. E. (2000), 'The Management of Operations in the Project-Based Organization', *Journal of Change Management*, 1(2): 131–48.

Turner, J. R. and Müller, R. (2003), 'On the Nature of the Project as a Temporary Organization', *International Journal of Project Management*, 21(1): 1–8.

Turner, J. R. and Müller, R. (2006), *Choosing Appropriate Project Managers: Matching their Leadership Style to the Type of Project*, Newtown Square, PA: Project Management Institute.

Turner, J. R. and Simister, S. J. (eds.) (2000), *Gower Handbook of Project Management*, 3rd edn., Farnham: Gower.

Turner, J. R. and Speiser, A. (1992), 'Meeting the Information Systems Needs of Programme Management', *International Journal of Project Management*, 10(4): 196–206.

Part II

Good Practice in Programme Management

Distinguishing Different Types of Programmes

Alan Stretton

This chapter examines the categorization of project programmes. For this purpose I shall review published literature on this subject, some if which is relevant for helping to develop programme categorization further.

Introduction

Only a small amount of material in the literature is directly concerned with *programmes*. In contrast, there are substantial materials on categorizing *projects*, although these are somewhat disjointed and there is no unified view on the subject. Most definitions of 'programme' are fundamentally similar to that set down by Maylor *et al.* (2006), who write:

> The emerging definition of a programme appears to involve the coordinated management of a series of interconnected projects and other non-project work, for the delivery of a specific package of benefits.

I shall follow this definition in this chapter.

The most extensive examination of *project* categorization systems appears to be that done by Crawford, Hobbs and Turner in 2005–2006 (Crawford *et al.*, 2005, 2006). Some of their material is applicable also to *programme* management. Their main concern was with categorization in organizations that manage projects and programmes, which is the first topic discussed in this chapter. They identify three primary purposes for categorization:

1. To help programme (and portfolio) managers to group component projects into programme configurations that facilitate effective management.
2. Aligning programmes with organizational strategy. This could involve categorizing such things as risk management factors and the allocation of resources and budgets.
3. Competency related issues, where categorization could help in choosing such things as types of contracts, working methods, tools and so on. This could particularly benefit effective coordination of interfaces between the component projects of a programme.

Next I shall move on to categorization purposes of 'external entities', such as programme management researchers, professional associations and libraries. Although these have some differing purposes, all three share a common interest in having a standard categorization system for the purposes of accumulating and retrieving knowledge about programmes and programme management. There is some way to go in developing an agreed standard categorization system but some of the following may contribute to this process.

I shall look briefly at some existing categorizations of projects by attributes such as complexity, size and the like. The main purpose of these types of categorizations is to match management styles with different types of projects. These appear also to be relevant to programmes, but with some modifications, particularly with complexity levels.

Next I shall review broader categorizations of programme types. Five different programme type listings from the literature are set down side by side are then cumulated to identify three programme types under the broad heading of strategic programmes (externally focused), and six under the operational programme (internally focused) heading. These should be useful as a check-list for organizations developing their own programme categorizations.

My discussion then progresses to very broad programme categorizations which mainly centre around application sectors, but include other 'technological' programmes, using this terminology for particular types of programmes undertaken in most (if not all) application sectors. Mixtures of these two are common to most general categorizations of programmes and projects. Distinguishing between them is an important prerequisite to developing a more useful and widely acceptable general categorization.

This leads to the development of a matrix model, showing programme application sectors on one axis, and 'technological' programme types which intersect them on the other. In addition to its potential for contributing towards a more widely acceptable general programme application, another purpose of this model is to provide a framework for a more systematic examination of how managing the various 'technological' programmes varies in different application sectors. This should help identify best practices in individual sectors – which could benefit some other sectors as part of a process of building up more comprehensive data on how each 'technological' programme type functions across various programme application sectors.

Categorizations for organizations that manage programmes

At a very general level, Crawford *et al.* (2005) identify two broad thrusts within the project programme and portfolio literature regarding categorization systems:

- The *project* management literature has focused on capability development and on tailoring management styles to suit project type.
- The *programme and portfolio* management literature has concentrated on classifying projects for the purpose of prioritizing them.

Although our primary interest is with programme management, we cannot isolate programmes from their component projects. So there is an inevitable overlap. Additionally, because programmes are typically components of broader portfolios, we are also interested in the latter.

Crawford *et al.* also distinguish between purposes of categorizations for organizations that manage projects on the one hand, and for researchers, libraries and professional associations on the other. But the primary focus of their study was project categorizations as they appear (and are used) in organizational contexts. Many of their findings appear to be applicable to categorizing programmes (as well as projects) within organizations.

Crawford *et al.* (2006) investigate two distinct aspects of project categorization systems:

- the organizational purposes served by such systems;
- the attributes or characteristics used by organizations to divide their projects into groups or categories.

I shall discuss each of these in turn.

Organizational purposes for programme categorization

Crawford *et al.* (2006) give two reasons in their abstract why organizations need to categorize projects:

1. Capability-related: to develop and assign appropriate competencies to undertake projects successfully (do them right).
2. Strategic alignment: to prioritize projects within an investment portfolio to maximize return on investment (do the right projects).

In the specific context of programmes, I shall add a third purpose, quoting from Crawford *et al.* (2006) who include this as one of the focal points of the literature on programme and portfolio categorization:

3. Coordinating interfaces between the component projects of programmes.

I shall now discuss these three purposes, but in reverse order because item 3 is programme-specific and merits priority in discussion. It also happens that there is substantially more programme-specific categorization material regarding items 2 and 3.

Categorization, and coordinating interfaces between component projects

As a general comment there is little helpful material in the literature which is specifically concerned with coordinating interfaces between the component projects of a programme. I find this surprising because this activity is unique to programmes. However, in the context of categorization and coordinating interfaces there are some relevant materials, which I shall now discuss.

Pellegrinelli (1997) and Murray-Webster and Thiry (2000) propose three configurations of programmes – three different ways in which component projects of programmes can be grouped to facilitate more effective programme management:

- portfolio or chunked;
- strategic or goal-orientated;
- incremental or 'heartbeat'.

Reasons for adopting one or more of these particular classifications are reflected in the benefits detailed for each below (quoting mainly from Murray-Webster and Thiry).

Portfolio or 'chunked' configuration

Projects and other associated work are grouped around a common *theme*. This common theme may be a business unit, knowledge area and/or group of resources. Primary advantages of chunked programmes are organizational efficiency. They:

- facilitate project prioritization where necessary;
- provide a mechanism for focusing scare resources;
- enable better resource allocation and utilization;
- identify and manage dependencies;
- exploit existing knowledge and skills;
- highlight weaknesses in capabilities and development needs;
- facilitate control over multiple projects.

Strategic or goal-orientated configuration

Projects and other work are grouped around a common *aim* or *purpose*. This is most often a strategic objective where there can be some uncertainty of the specific final outcomes. Projects and other work will not all be defined at the start of the programme – work can be added or taken away in a coordinated and consolidated way, focused on the primary business aims and benefits. Advantages of this approach are that they:

- translate business needs into tangible actions;
- foster learning and creativity;
- reduce uncertainty and ambiguity through iterative development;
- support integrated review and approval processes;
- allow integration of emergent inputs;
- recognize chaos theories.

Incremental or 'heartbeat' configuration

Projects and other work are grouped around a common *platform*. This platform may be a process, business system or infrastructure. Primary advantages of incremental programmes are related to coordinating and integrating business-wide continuous improvement initiatives effectively. Benefits are that they:

- provide an integrative framework for continuous improvement;
- group initiatives into coherent and efficient actions;

- release changes in controlled 'heartbeats';
- enable continuous reassessment within an holistic perspective;
- support short-term requests with long-term strategy;
- capture bottom-up innovation initiatives.

Murray-Webster and Thiry point out that none of these configurations needs to be used alone. Every situation or organization requires one or more of these programme configurations. The ultimate objective is to find a way to manage the programme that:

- uses limited resources to maximize results;
- achieves business and stakeholder benefits;
- optimizes emergent change and captures bottom-up initiatives;
- avoids delivery of solutions no longer needed by the customer ('white elephants').

Categorization, and strategic alignment of programmes (and projects)

In their Figure 5, 'The organizational purposes mind map', Crawford *et al.* (2006) break down the strategic alignment purpose into three component purposes, the first of which is 'Selecting / prioritizing of projects / programmes'. Here programmes are specifically included, and we can regard their subcomponent purposes as applying equally to programmes:

- aligning commitment with capabilities;
- managing risk/controlling exposure;
- allocating budgets;
- balancing portfolio;
- identifying approval processes.

The second component of their strategic alignment purpose is the planning, tracking and reporting of:

- resource usage;
- performance, results, value;
- investments;
- comparability across projects, [programmes], divisions and organizations.

I added programmes to the last bullet point, because all these subcomponent purposes are evidently applicable in the context of categorizing programmes. The third component is 'Creating strategic visibility', which applies also to programmes.

Categorization, and capability-related purposes

In their Figure 5, Crawford *et al.* (2006, p. 48) break down what they term the 'Capability Specialization' purpose into two component purposes, namely:

1. Capability alignment (which has eight subcomponent purposes).
2. Capability development (which has four subcomponents).

Many of the subcomponent purposes seem to be most relevant to the component projects of programmes rather than to programmes themselves. However some appear to be potential flow-on effects for their programmes.

I shall list my assessment of those subcomponents which appear to be directly relevant to programmes, and those that could have flow-on effects – while acknowledging that others may well assess these differently. My choices include:

- choosing risk mitigation strategy;
- choosing contract type [flow-on];
- choosing methods and tools [flow-on];
- allocating project [programme] to organizational unit;
- setting price;
- adapting to market/customer/client.

Finally, Crawford *et al.* (2006) have a third component in their categorization of projects in organizations: 'Promoting a project approach'. I could comfortably add '/ programme' there.

Concluding these sections on organizational purposes for programme categorization, I have drawn extensively on Crawford *et al.* (2006) whose concern with categorization has mainly been with organizations that undertake projects, particularly in production-based organizations. Although their focus was on projects, a good deal of their categorization materials also applies, to varying extents, to programmes. Those with an interest in pursuing programme categorizations further should refer also to the far more detailed study in Crawford *et al.* (2005) (from which the above is derived). I shall refer to the 2005 publication shortly as I move this discussion from categorization purposes to attributes relevant to categorizing projects/programmes within organizations.

Attributes used by organizations in categorizing projects and programmes

Crawford *et al.* (2005) identified 37 attributes used by organizations to categorize projects. They went on to observe that 'There is a strong similarity, but some slight differences in ordering [ranking] between the ten attributes considered most important to the organizations whose representatives responded to the survey.' The following ten attributes were found to be most commonly used:

- application area;
- nature of work;
- client/customer;
- complexity;
- cost;
- size;
- strategic importance;
- risk level;
- organizational benefit;
- deliverables.

Attributes for building project categorization systems	
Contractual issues	Application area/product of project
Ownership/funding	Stage of life cycle
Customer/supplier relations	Stand-alone or grouped
Complexity	Strategic importance
Risk	Strategic driver
Uncertainty, ambiguity, familiarity	Geography
Project timing	Project scope

Figure 4.1 Map of attributes for building project categorization systems

One of the more interesting differences between the most commonly used attributes and those considered most important for projects was that the two considered most important were (in order) organization benefit and cost. However, the primary interest in this chapter is in what happens actually in practice – so I shall stay with the above listing of the most commonly used attributes.

In the absence of any equivalent analysis of attributes used by organizations to categorize programmes, the question arises: How relevant and/or useful might these project-related attributes be in helping organizations to categorize their programmes? They should surely have some value, even though priorities and/or frequency of usage would probably differ.

Crawford *et al.* (2005) presented a generalized map of attributes for building project categorization systems, which is reproduced in Figure 4.1 simply as a list of attributes. This should be useful as a check-list to help organizations develop their own programme categorization systems. The items are not ranged in any particular sequence of importance or frequency.

Programme categorizations used by external entities

I wrote earlier that Crawford *et al.* (2006) distinguish between purposes of categorizations for organizations that manage projects on the one hand, and for researchers, professional associations and libraries on the other hand (I have labelled the latter three 'external entities' here).

Project/programme categorization by project management researchers

With regard to project management researchers, Crawford *et al.* (2005) say that 'the use of project categories by researchers is based on the belief that different categories of project are (or should be) managed differently'. They also point out that researchers are concerned with the comparability of results from one research endeavour to another, and with the issues of knowledge accumulation, cataloguing and retrieval, concerns which 'create a strong interest in the research community for categorizing projects and project knowledge'. This obviously applies also to programmes and programme management.

Project/programme categorization by professional associations

Crawford *et al.* (2005) also note, 'professional associations share the interest in project categorization systems for purposes of fostering the development, accumulation and retrieval of project management knowledge'. Again, this naturally extends to include programme management.

Categorization used by libraries and document centres

Libraries and documentation centres need standardized project and programme categorization systems for information storage and retrieval. All these external entities share a common interest in having a standard categorization system for the purposes of accumulating and retrieving knowledge about programmes and programme management. This common interest lies behind most of the following discussion. It is to be hoped that this will help to advance the development of a widely accepted programme management categorization system.

Categorization of programmes by attributes such as complexity and size

There is little or nothing in the literature about in the categorization of *programmes* by complexity or size, but there is much pertaining to *projects*. The main purpose of these categorizations appears to be to help to match management styles with different types of projects. Many project aspects appear to be relevant also to programmes, and I shall concentrate on those here.

In the context of projects, Archibald and Prado (2014) discuss (as I and many others have done) the diamond model of Shenhar (2012). This and previous publications written or co-authored by Shenhar essentially describe four categories of projects and their subcategories, as follows:

- technology (low-tech, medium-tech, high-tech, super high-tech);
- complexity (array, system, assembly, component);
- pace (regular, fast/competitive, time-critical, blitz);
- novelty (derivative, platform, new to market, new to world).

These categorizations also appear to be applicable to programmes but with one very significant quantitative difference, which is in the area of complexity.

Additional types of complexities in the programme context

In the context of programmes, complexity assumes a much greater significance than Shenhar's 'array, system, assembly, component' components. This is quite simply because programmes comprise component projects, and the composition of these component projects can often be widely divergent. It hardly needs to be pointed out that the task of managing and integrating divergent (or even several non-divergent) component projects in any particular programme adds a substantial extra dimension of complexity to programme management.

Project/programme size is another typical categorization which is prominent in the project context, but is one of the hardest to get to grips with in the programme context. As a general rule (although there are plenty of exceptions) programmes

Levene, Braganza 1996 (programmes)	Gray and Bamford 1999 (programmes)	Harpham (Davies 2000) (programmes)	Shenhar et al 2002 (projects)	Shenhar and Dvir 2004 (projects)	Cumulative collation
Development (external focus) > bus. strategies	*Delivery* (external focus) > funds inflow	*Strategic* (internal focus)	*Strategic projects*	*Strategic*	Strategic programmes
Delivering new products/services	Product develpmt and introduction			New product development	New product or service developrr ent
	Contracted work for external clients	Assets delivery programmes			Product/service delivery programme
Satisfying legislative requirement					Regulatory compliance
	Platform (internal focus) >*improve infrastructure*	*Key operational* Critical for day-to-day operations		*Operational* Utility and infrastructure	Operational programmes
Creating new facilities	New production facilities		*Problem solving for future projects* New technology, capability, features, equipment, software		New facilities programmes
			Extension of existing products	Product and other improvement	Product improvement programmes
New or improved ways of working		*Support* Business efficiency gains	*Utility projects for organization survival* Re-engineering		Work improvement programmes
			Major maintenance	Maintenance	Maintenance programmes
Change projects New organizational forms Radical transforms	Major organization change activities		Reorganization		Organizational change programmes
		High potential e.g. R&D programmes	*Research projects*		R&D programmes

Figure 4.2 Initial collation of project and programme types from the literature

tend to be larger than projects. Further, it has often been pointed out that what is a large programme for some organizations may be considered to be small by others. An example of this comes from my involvement in consulting with one of the world's largest mining companies, which typically deals with multi-billion dollar programmes (which it describes as 'projects'). The scale of these types of programmes contrasts very sharply indeed with internal IT programmes in most organizations, for example. Greater size does not necessarily involve greater complexity. On the other hand, some types of relatively small programmes can be very complex.

Initial collation of programme types from the literature

Now I shall move to a broader level of programme categorization (which is a first sampling from the literature of types of programmes). Figure 4.2 shows three classifications of programme types plus two project classifications which appear to be directly relevant to programmes. These are grouped side by side, to help identify common types. Vertically, they are divided into strategic programmes (externally focused) in the upper section. Operational programmes (internally focused) are listed in the lower section (with the qualification that these could also be seen as ultimately benefiting strategic programmes).

- The Levene and Braganza (1996) classification is concerned with how to manage different types of projects in project portfolios/programmes. This is in the context of business process re-engineering (BPR), focusing on managing the project interfaces.
- The primary concern of Gray and Bamford (1999) is with managing interactions between the two primary programme categories (delivery and platform) and their subcategories.
- Davies (2000) is quoted by Harpham (undated), and the purpose of his classification is related to their business contribution, which I have interpreted as a programme management related purpose.
- Shenhar *et al.* (2002) and Shenhar and Dvir (2004) are concerned specifically with the best ways of managing different types of projects. These categorizations are included because they appear to be equally relevant for programmes.

The collation of types of programmes in the right hand column of Figure 4.2 could provide a useful check-list for organizations developing their own programme categorizations. As will be seen in the following section, I shall describe these types of programmes as 'technological' programmes, to distinguish them from programme application sectors, as now discussed.

Programme categorization by application sectors (but also including 'technological' programmes)

One of the earlier categorizations of programmes that I came across was Figure 3-1-1 in the Project Management Association of Japan's *P2M – Project and Programme Management for Enterprise Innovation: Guidebook* (PMAJ, 2008), part of which is shown in Figure 4.3. It can be seen that this is a mixture of two categorization groups, which I describe as:

(a) Broad programme management application sectors:
   2. resource business;
   4. plant and factory construction;
   7. commercialization of new business model;
   8. marketing/service;
   9. event;
   12. creative activities.
(b) 'Technological' programmes – particular types of programmes that are undertaken in most (if not all) application sectors:
   1. organization change;
   3. construction;
   5. ICT system;
   6. product development;
   10. large-scale research and development;
   11. capability development (which could also be regarded as part of 1).

A key point for discussion in this section of the chapter is that most broader categorizations of programmes and projects in the literature have varying combinations of the

---

1 **Organizational change**
   Corporate mergers and acquisitions, corporate alliances, restructuring, spinning off a division, shutdown of factories/branches, reorganization/privatization of government ministries;
2 **Resource-related business**
   Resource exploration, oil well drilling, LNG chain, pipeline construction; mine development/operation;
3 **Construction**
   Social infrastructure (airports, railways and so on), large-scale commercial facilities, urban redevelopment;
4 **Plant and factory construction**
   Plant construction (petrochemical, steel, semiconductor manufacture, nuclear/thermal electric power plants);
5 **ICT systems**
   Bank account systems, production control systems, communications/broadcasting;
6 **Product development**
   High-tech industrial products, pharmaceutical drug development, new seed varieties, package software;
7 **Commercialization of a new business model**
   Door-to-door delivery service, online sale of books, Internet search service, online free services;
8 **Marketing/service (including networking)**
   Affiliated dealership for luxury cars, franchise networks, broadband, theme parks;
9 **Events**
   Olympic Games, soccer World Cup, national sports festival, world exposition;
10 **Large scale research and development**
   Space development, nuclear fusion research, human genome research, high-tech military equipment development, global environmental research;
11 **Capability development**
   International partnerships, founding a college, in-house education systems;
12 **Creative activities**
   Film making, television.

Figure 4.3 Types of programmes with case examples

two categorization groupings given above (including my own listing of representative types of programmes in Stretton, 2009, for example). More recently I have recognized that these two categorization groups are very different indeed, as now discussed.

Programme application sectors

These days, programmes and projects are undertaken in practically all sectors of industry, commerce and society. Further, several types of what I have called 'technological' programmes and projects are undertaken within most of these sectors. Therefore, categorizing programmes and projects solely by the sectors in which they are undertaken appears to have limited use for most purposes. But I shall show that differences between such sectors can become very relevant when looking at different ways in which some 'technological' programmes in these sectors are undertaken.

'Technological' programmes

On the other hand, categorizing programmes by what I have called their 'technological' groupings would appear to be useful in several contexts. For example,

	PMAJ 2008 P2M Fig. 3-1-1: Types of programmes	Archibald/Prado 2014 Project categories	Youker 2002 Project types based on project product	Turner 1993 Major grouping of projects by 'technology'	Proposed major 'technological' programme grouping
'Technological' programmes	1 Organization change 11 Capability development 3 Construction 4 Plant and factory construction	2 Business and organization change 5.4 Facility design, procurement, construction	1 Administrative 2 Construction 4 Design of plans	Organizational change Engineering	Organizational change Engineering/ construction
	5 ICT systems	6 Information systems (software)	3 Computer software development	Information technology	ICT development
	6 Product development	9 Product and service development	8 New product development		New product/ service development
	11 Large scale R&D	10 Research and development	9 Research		Research and development
Application sectors	2 Resource related businesses 8 Marketing/ service 9 Event 10 Commerciali- zation of new business model 12 Creative activities	1 Aerospace/ defence 3 Communi- cations systems 4 Event projects 7 International development 8 Media and entertainment 12 Other	5 Equipment or system installation 6 Event or relocation 7 Maintenance of process industries 10 Other		

Figure 4.4 Proposed grouping to provide a skeleton on which to develop further a robust classification of technological projects/programmes

organizational change programmes have already received very wide coverage in the literature (for example, OGC, 2011). These appear to have been undertaken in many different application sectors, and presumably have benefited from cross-sector fertilization. There has also been substantial coverage of some other such groupings, particularly the ICT sector, and engineering/construction.

However, there appears to have been only limited use of categorization by such 'technological' groupings in the literature, even in the project domain. The only one of the latter of which I know is due to Turner (1993), who identified just three categories, all in the 'technological' area. All other categorizations of projects I have seen (for example Archibald and Prado, 2014 and Youker, 2002) have been a mixture of categories (a) and (b) above.

Separating 'technological' projects/programmes from application sectors

Figure 4.4 is a first attempt to separate 'technological' projects/programmes from project/programme application areas. It starts by separating the P2M 'types of

	Major 'technological' programme types					
Example programme application sectors	Organizational change	Engineering/construction	ICT development	New product development	Research and development	Other 'technological' types
Aerospace/defence						
Mining and natural resources						
Telecommunications						
Energy/utilities						
Healthcare						
Other application sectors						

Figure 4.5 Model relating to 'technological' programmes with programme application sectors

programmes' from Figure 4.3 in the left hand column, and does the same for the three project classifications referenced earlier.

The 'technological' projects/ programme types are shown in the upper sector of Figure 4.4 and are organized so that similar types from each source are aligned horizontally. These are aggregated/collated on the right, and comprise five major 'technological' programme/ project types, which should provide a basic skeleton for further development of a robust classification of 'technological' programmes/projects.

The application sectors from these samplings are shown in the lower section of Figure 4.4, with no attempt at horizontal alignment. I acknowledge that the differences between the two major categories are not always absolutely clear-cut, but at least this is a start.

Relating 'technological' programmes with programme application sectors

Because the term 'technological' programmes has been adopted to identify particular groups of programmes undertaken in most (if not all) application sectors in industry, commerce and society at large, it is a natural step to propose the matrix model shown in Figure 4.5. This model has two purposes. Distinguishing between 'technological' programmes and programme application sectors would appear to be an important prerequisite to developing a more useful and widely acceptable general programme categorization. The other purpose of this model is to provide a framework for a more systematic examination of how management of 'technological' programmes varies in different application sectors.

This should help to identify best practices in individual sectors which could benefit some other sectors, as part of a process of building up more comprehensive data on how each 'technological' programme type functions across the whole spectrum of programme application sectors.

I have not attempted to suggest a comprehensive listing of programme application sectors. That would be part of more extensive efforts to develop a widely accepted standard programme categorization system. That is certainly beyond the scope of this chapter. It is to be hoped that others will pick up this challenge.

Summary and conclusions

The first of the two principal sections in this chapter focused on organizational purposes for programme categorization. Although literature on this subject was not plentiful, I was able to list several purposes. These included categorizations of component projects into programme configurations that facilitate effective management. Also, categorizing such entities as risk management, resource and budget allocation in the context of aligning programmes with corporate strategies. Further, categorizations to help in choosing contract types, plus the choice of methods, tools and so on in the context of capability-related purposes. This was followed by check-lists of attributes that can be used by organizations in categorizing programmes, based on relevant project check-lists.

The second main section was concerned with programme categorizations made by 'external entities' such as researchers, professional associations and libraries. Although there were some different purposes, all share a common interest in having a standard categorization system for the purposes of accumulating and retrieving knowledge about programmes and programme management. Much of this section was concerned with taking further steps towards achieving this elusive goal, including particularly recognizing differences between 'technological' programmes and the application sectors in which they are undertaken.

Other categorization purposes that emerged in these discussions included:

* Categorizations of programmes by attributes such as complexity, size and the like, which could be useful in trying to match management styles with programme types.
* A collation of 'technological' programme types from the literature which could be a useful check-list for organizations undertaking programme categorizations.
* The final matrix model could also provide a framework for a more systematic examination of how management of the various 'technological' programmes varies in different application sectors. This should help to identify best practices in individual application sectors. That could benefit some other sectors, as part of a process of building up more comprehensive data on how each 'technological' programme type functions across the whole spectrum of programme application sectors.

In view of the relative paucity of literature on *programme* categorizations, I have used *project* categorization materials as a basis for developing some of the above programme-relevant materials. This seems justifiable to me because I see no real difference between programmes and stand-alone projects, except for the critical need to coordinate interfaces between the component projects of programmes. For that important reason I gave the latter priority earlier in this chapter. This unique attribute of programmes has not received the attention in the literature that its importance deserves. I hope this situation will not prevail for too much longer.

References and further reading

Archibald, R. D. and Darci, P. (2014), 'Maturity in Project Management Series 4: PM Maturity for Project Categories', *PM World Journal*, 3(4).

Crawford, L. H., Hobbs, B. and Turner, J. R. (2005), *Project Categorization Systems: Aligning Capability with Strategy for Better Results*, Newtown Square, PA: Project Management Institute.

Crawford, L. H., Hobbs, B. and Turner, J. R. (2006), 'Aligning Capability with Strategy: Categorizing Projects to do the Right Projects and to do them Right', *Project Management Journal*, 37(2): 38–51.

Gray, R. J. and Bamford, P. J. (1999), 'Issues in Project Integration', *International Journal of Project Management*, 17(6): 361–6.

Harpham, A. (undated), *Bridging the Gap between Corporate Strategy and Project Management. Part 1: Introduction to Programme Management*. Retrieved October 2005 from <www.maxwideman.com/papers/index.htm>.

Levene, R. J. and Braganza, A. (1996), 'Controlling the Work Scope in Organisational Transformation: A Programme Management Approach', *International Journal of Project Management*, 14(6): 331–9.

Maylor, H., Brady, T., Cooke-Davies, T. and Hodgson, D. (2006), 'From Projectisation to Programmification', *International Journal of Project Management*, 24(8): 663–74.

Murray-Webster, R. and Thiry, M. (2000), 'Managing Programmes of Projects', in J. R. Turner and S. J. Simister (eds.), *Gower Handbook of Project Management*, 3rd edn., Farnham: Gower, Chapter 3.

OGC (Office of Government Commerce) (2011), *Managing Successful Programmes*, 4th edn., Norwich: The Stationery Office.

Pellegrinelli, S. (1997), 'Programme Management: Organising Project-Based Change', *International Journal of Project Management*, 15(3): 141–9.

PMAJ (2008), *P2M – Project and Programme Management for Enterprise Innovation: Guidebook*, Tokyo: Project Management Association of Japan.

Shenhar, A. J. (2012), 'What's the Next Generation of Project Management?', PMI Global Congress 2012 North America, Session # RES01, Vancouver, BC, Canada, 20–23 October.

Shenhar, A. J. and Dvir, D. (2004). 'How Projects Differ, and What to do About It', in P. W. G. Morris and J. K. Pinto (eds.), *The Wiley Guide to Managing Projects*, Hoboken, NJ: John Wiley, pp. 1265–86.

Shenhar, A. J., Dvir, D., Lechler, T. and Poli, M. (2002), 'One Size Does Not Fit All – True for Projects, True for Frameworks', in *Proceedings of the PMI Research Conference*, pp. 99–106.

Stretton, A. (2009), 'Programme Management Diversity: Opportunity or Problem?', *PM World Today*, 11(6).

Turner, J. R. (1993), *The Handbook of Project-Based Management*, New York: McGraw-Hill.

Youker, R. (2002), 'The Difference between Different Types of Projects', AEW Services, Vancouver, BC, Canada, February.

Chapter 5

Programme Management in the Space Sector

Séverin Drogoul

Space programmes are often the most visible and complex of a leading nation's strategic investments. A space programme is usually a major undertaking. Stakeholders and key industrial participants engage in tasks of extraordinary risk, complexity and national priority. This chapter develops some key features related to programme management with specific highlights on space launchers.

Main characteristics of the space sector

Space launchers are complex and unforgiving vehicles. They must be as light as possible, yet attain outstanding performance to get into orbit. People, however, are getting better at building them. In the early days, vehicles often exploded on or near the launch pad. This was not so different from early airplanes, which tended to crash often. Aircraft seldom crash these days, but space launchers still fail between 2 and 5 per cent of the time. This is true of just about any launch vehicle (Atlas, Delta, Soyuz, Shuttle, Ariane, Antares) regardless of which nation builds it or the basic configuration that is used. So building and launching is still a very dangerous business. It will continue to be so for the foreseeable future while we gain experience. It is unlikely that launching a space vehicle will ever be as routine an undertaking as commercial air travel – certainly not in our lifetime.

The objective of a space programme is to develop efficient products, which are complex, using many different and advanced technologies. A programme can last for many years, progressing through several stages from conception to disposal or other disposition. These complex products require the collaboration of many participating organizations, often coming from various nations with different languages and cultures. For example, in the Ariane 5 space launcher programme the following countries have been involved (countries are listed alphabetically):

Country	Degree of participation (%)
Austria	0.4
Belgium	6.0
Denmark	0.4
France	46.2
Germany	22.0
Ireland	0.2
Italy	15.0

Netherlands	2.1
Norway	0.6
Spain	3.0
Sweden	2.0
Switzerland	2.0

Thus space programmes can lead to situations in which each participant has a different vision of the product and the limits of responsibilities are not clearly defined. These risk-generating factors can only be solved by setting up a reference system that:

• provides all participants with a common view of the product and the programme;
• guarantees the consistency and compatibility of technical and financial activities.

The key characteristics of a spacecraft and its components are:

• strong economic constraints (changing budgets and hyper-competition);
• complex products with high technical objectives, innovation and high cost;
• strong political and media impact (particularly when failures occur);
• impossibility of complete testing before launch;
• extreme demand on performance (multiple functions, precision, autonomy);
• extreme mission conditions (duration and environment).

These products have long development cycles and few series with strong implications for the customers, complex industrial organizations and numerous speakers; and in addition a higher objective of reliability and safety of the inhabited flights. The space sector is a risky industry (Figure 5.1) for all stakeholders (space agencies and industry).

Mission-driven, with mission success at the cornerstone of the space culture, the stakeholders and actors rigorously manage requirements, schedule, facilities, human resources and budget. The individual people recognize their responsibilities and are

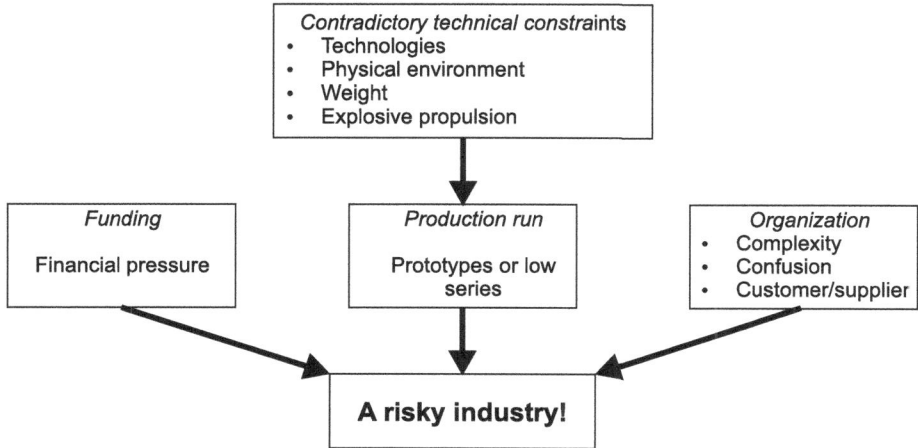

Figure 5.1 Space launcher programmes are high risk

accountable for the important work entrusted to them. Two key factors of the space sector are:

1. Achievement of the highest standards in engineering, research and operations.
2. Constant attention to programme management, which is the cornerstone upon which mission success is built.

Brief history of programmes in the space sector

Defence ballistic missile and space launcher programmes have been interlinked since the 1950s. The application of project management concepts and techniques in space-related projects began with the US Polaris project in the 1950s. In 1958, the National Aeronautics and Space Administration (NASA) was created. During the 1960s, NASA used project management principles and tools to manage large budget, schedule-driven projects, specifically in the Apollo project. Between 1969 and 1972, NASA successfully led six missions to explore the moon. In 1960, NASA set up the Apollo programme office to provide following functions:

*   maintain and schedule Apollo missions using critical path networks;
*   procurement and contract management with suppliers such as GE;
*   develop management systems to measure the performance;
*   provide a focal point for the Apollo programme.

The Polaris and Apollo programmes were huge, complex and with strategic import-ance. They demonstrated the importance of programme management concepts and techniques. They also demonstrated the tiny differences between defence pro-grammes (ballistic missiles) and space programmes (civil launchers).

In Europe, programme management also started early in the 1960s with ballis-tic missiles and civil launcher programmes. In the early days, the Europa launcher started to use programme management concepts and techniques, coming from France and the United Kingdom. But the coordination task singularly failed on this programme, mainly due to people in many European countries not being able to speak a common technical language, and also because of a lack of 'launcher vehicle view'. This is why the 'industrial architect' function was created during the 1970s, and a new era of programme management began using 'management requirements' specifications to align all stakeholders. Those specifications were applied for the first time on the Ariane programme (its development started in 1974 and met success in 1979).

Today building space launchers is still hard even if the year 2014 tallied the highest number of launches compared to the previous two decades. There were more successful space launches in 2014 than in any year since 1992, with Russia, the United States and China responsible for more than 80 per cent of global launch activity. There were 92 space launches worldwide in 2014, and 90 of those missions at least reached orbit. That figure marks the highest number of launch attempts since 1994, when there were 93 launches with spacecraft passengers heading for Earth orbit or beyond. Launch rates have steadily risen since activity bottomed out in the mid-2000s (when NASA's space shuttle fleet was grounded after the Columbia accident, the commercial space industry was reeling from weakness in the communications satellite market, and US military launches were facing delays). Several consecutive accidents raised questions about the safety and reliability of commercial spacecraft, with potential space tourists and companies wanting to place their cargo on these launchers questioning the risk. But three important key successes must be highlighted:

- The most important space achievement of 2014 has to be the Rosetta mission: the European Space Agency's Rosetta, launched by Ariane 5. This successfully entered the orbit of the comet 67P / Churyumov-Gerasimenko after a ten-year journey. This spacecraft first made headlines in 2014 when, after sailing through the inner solar system for nearly a decade, it finally parked itself in a tight orbit with the comet. In November 2014, a tiny oven-sized lander named Philae was released from the mother-ship, and its seven-hour descent to the surface of the comet captivated millions worldwide.
- December 2014: NASA's Orion spacecraft completed its first nearly flawless unmanned test flight. Circling the Earth twice, the Apollo-like capsule designed to carry up to six astronauts tested the heat shield and radiation levels inside the craft as it experienced low-Earth orbit and re-entry. It is hoped this will be the first step to a manned mission to an asteroid in the mid-2020s and to Mars in the 2030s.
- The member governments of the European Space Agency (ESA) agreed to develop a new-generation Ariane 6 launcher to maintain Europe's share of the global commercial launch market, to enhance the power of the current Vega small-satellite launcher and to fund the use of the International Space Station through 2017. The Ariane 6 is designed to carry two telecommunications satellites weighing a combined 9.5 tons into geostationary transfer orbit. This vehicle's cost objective is not far from the current SpaceX price. The business model for this is designed to fit the new joint-venture company created by Airbus Defence and Space and launcher-motor maker Safran.

The challenge for every industrialist anxious to ensure their company's survival in a market against increasing competition is to design, develop and produce faster and more cheaply a product that generally corresponds to the user's expectations.

Development cycles in the launcher industry are very long, largely because of the need to show product maturity and reliability by a demonstration plan and important test. This equates to 'Design the right product first time'. Success demands a culture of excellence (best in class). It requires ongoing commitment by all to organize and enrich for participation in new programmes. Contrary to appearances, this approach is neither obvious nor natural. It requires significant resources to save, organize and classify so that the skills and lessons from past experience are available to the organization and its partners for future programmes.

People in the company must be willing to share their expertise and, conversely, be receptive to solutions other than their own. They must be convinced that the answer to the challenge posed to the company can only be collective and that the best product is often a mixture of a little innovation and industrially validated solutions. All this requires time, conviction and good communication.

Programme management specifications

The attainment of quality, including requirements to meet cost, schedule and technical performance throughout project execution is the overall goal of management. Depending on the nature of the programme or the programme phase, the programme management specifications are issued by the level '0' customer and may include additional requirements or, on the contrary, certain elements which may be deleted with regards to a set of standards requirements.

In order to create the reference for programme management necessary to implement a programme and ensure consistency, a typical launcher programme is supported by management specifications, which play a key role in building the Ariane launchers' culture. Drafting and contractual establishment are important tasks. These specifications are the foundation of the programme and are recognized as essential and indispensable. A big promotional effort was made in the beginning of the programme to all European contractors, with associated videos and presentations in French and English.

Each supplier of a given level acts as a customer of its own suppliers and has to specify the management requirements in the relevant contracts through a specific document or through the statement of work itself.

Everyone recognizes now that these specifications largely contributed to create a real European launcher culture. Written mostly pragmatically, they gave a language and a common approach to all teams across Europe. They have truly been one of the reasons for the success of European launcher programmes. This management requirements structure is illustrated in Figure 5.2.

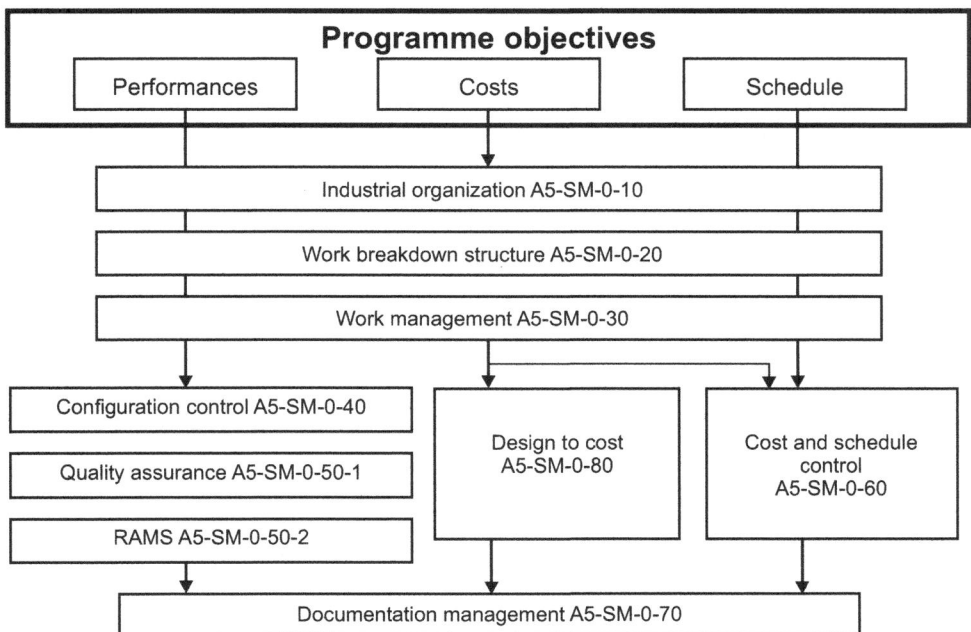

Figure 5.2 Management requirements structure

In response to this programme management specification, each supplier pre-pares a programme management plan. This contains descriptions of main activities, implementation methods and general procedures with respect to its organization. The programme management plan must be submitted to the customer for accept-ance. When accepted by the customer, each plan becomes the basis for determining compliance with the customer programme management requirements. This process applies to all related contractual levels through the customer–supplier chain (tier 1, tier 2, tier 3 and so on).

Programme governance, organization and communication

The space programme organization is the structured assembly of human and material resources used to carry out the programme. This is defined describing the following:

- the roles, responsibilities, authority and reporting lines of the people participat-ing in the programme;
- the situation of, configuration of, and responsibility for the material resources allocated to the programme.

The establishment of a well-structured and coherent organizational structure at all levels in the customer–supplier chain is a key factor for ensuring an effective and effi-cient management approach. This is necessary for consistent programme perform-ance and to control programme execution.

A self-standing programme team can be built at each level in the customer–supplier chain. Each team contains all necessary disciplines within its structure or, more often, it can be built around a core programme team which contains key programme func-tions. Other necessary functions are provided from outside the programme team as external support. Irrespective of the organizational approach, the following elem-ents are relevant at all levels in the customer/supplier chain.

Basic principles

A coherent organization is a prerequisite for the successful execution of a space pro-gramme. The organization must be based on standard requirements which cover all the roles and responsibilities of each actor and their interaction in terms of author-ity and related reporting. These requirements apply to the supplier and customer at all levels when the capability to design and supply conforming product needs to be demonstrated:

- The requirements define the organizational principles (organization at customer and industrial levels for programme/project management) and specify the organization's information circuits (internal and external to the programme/ project).
- The organization to be implemented must take into account the programme phases, the nature of the tasks to be performed and the associated responsibility and authority levels;

- The simplest and most effective management programme as well as contractual relationships must take into account the specific programme aspects (both for national and international programmes).
- The person in charge of defining and implementing the programme organization must be identified.
- The responsibilities and authorities for programme management and contracting have to be specified in readiness for contractual and legal events.
- Each programme organization must be compatible in contractual and technical terms.
- If the programme is associated with other programmes/projects, responsibilities and authorities regarding interface definition and management have to be specified and taken into account when implementing the programme organization.

Organizational structure: responsibilities and authority of the actors

Clear and unambiguous definition and allocation of individual roles is essential, together with their associated responsibilities and authority levels. Roles must be defined with respect to the internal programme set-up as well as to programme interfaces and the external environment (that means both internal and external to the organization).

Phases of the programme phases have to be specified. Programme changes can lead to modifications of the implemented organization during programme execution. Interfaces and relationships with company management should be indicated. Application of the management rules and their effectiveness for the performed or subcontracted programme activities must be verified according to planned and documented audits, analysis of indicators and/or reviews, as contractually defined.

The programme organizational structure must define all functions and disciplines needed, showing clear reporting lines, interrelationships and interfaces. All programme actors below the top level customer and above the lowest level supplier are regarded as both suppliers and customers.

General roles of customers and suppliers

Certain roles are relevant to all actors, some only to customers and some to suppliers (at all levels in both cases). Customers and suppliers have to play their assigned roles for the duration of the programme. In addition:

- When several suppliers jointly play a common role, the responsibilities and authorities of each of them have to be defined. When a supplier plays several roles simultaneously in the same programme, these roles must be clearly defined and carried out separately. But they can be supervised by one authority.
- Each supplier identifies and assigns the main responsibilities and authorities for the programme and implements the internal organization in order to satisfy the contractual requirements.
- When several external organizations and/or internal departments are involved, the responsibilities and authorities of each of them and their interfaces have to be clearly documented and the appropriate measures taken to ensure their

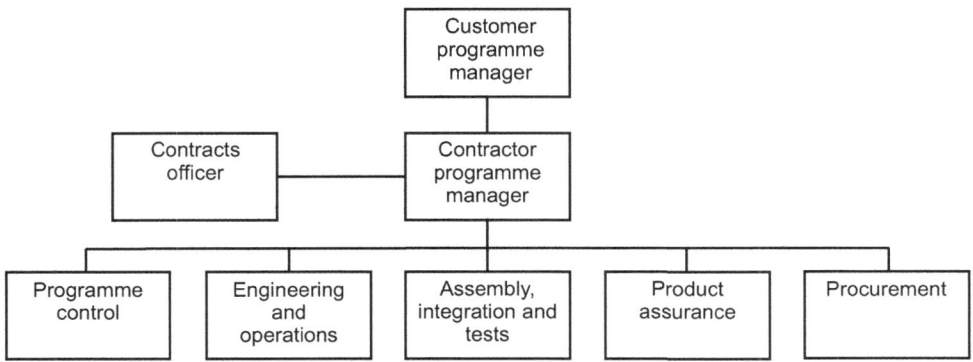

Figure 5.3 Typical programme organization within a dedicated actor (customer or supplier)

coordination. These measures in particular define the nature of the information to be exchanged between customers and suppliers.

The roles of the programme customers/suppliers within each organization have to be defined explicitly and, in particular, the programme organization must indicate who is in charge of each activity from the following list:

- project management;
- contract management;
- cost and schedule control (programme control, including documentation management);
- product assurance (including configuration management, quality assurance and dependability – RAMS);
- procurement;
- engineering;
- manufacturing;
- assembly, integration and verification;
- operations.

See Figure 5.3.

Typical launcher organization

The overall direction of the programme is provided by the ESA, which entrusted the programme management to the French National Space Agency (CNES). CNES is supported by several European industrial prime contractors for the development of major subassemblies (stages), as well as by an industrial architect who is in charge of general design and tests of the launcher vehicle and ensures compatibility of internal technical launcher items and with ground facilities.

The related management specification SM-0-10 defines the precise responsibilities of CNES, the industrial architect, and the following top level industrial contractors:

- Aerospatiale developed the main cryotechnic stage (EPC) and solid booster stage (EAP) and also led the programme industrial architect role.
- SNECMA developed the Vulcain engine and propulsion components of the cryotechnic stage.
- Europropulsion developed the solid booster propulsion (MPS) of the solid booster stage.
- Matra Marconi Space developed the equipment avionics bay.
- Daimler-Benz Aerospace (DASA) developed the upper storage propellant stage (EPS) and the external bearing structure for multiple launch of payloads (SPELTRA or SYLDA 5).
- Oerlikon/Contraves developed the fairing.
- CASA developed Adaptors for payloads.

Since the early 2000s Aerospatiale (France), Matra Marconi Space (France and the United Kingdom), CASA (Spain) and DASA (Germany) merged within Astrium (EADS). These merged since 2014 in Airbus Group Defence and Space (Airbus Group).

The industrial prime contractors generally ensure integration of subsystem tasks and place contracts with various contractors for the development of equipment and components.

The system task is essentially within the industrial architect's role of top level specification and verification which includes:

- conduct of systems design and execution of integrated verification tests (except flight testing);
- development of the specifications: management (SM), technical specification (TS), general design rules (SG), as well as monitoring their technical implementation at all contractors all along the contractual chain;
- definition of electrical systems and their implementation;
- design and production of the outboard calculator flight software.

This task is one that singularly failed on Europa programmes during the 1970s. It requires good cooperation between the Prime Space Agency and Aerospace.

The tasks for development and delivery of stages (upper stage, cryotechnic propellant stage and solid booster stage) do not include the development of propulsion. Propulsion includes the engine, equipment contributing actively to the propellant during flight, and all functional studies concerning packaging and management of propellants during boost phase. This is the concept of 'propulsion' which was the subject of some adjustments during the production phases to simplify the industrial cycle and reduce integration time (and the costs).

All Guiana ground facilities required for the production, testing and launch of Ariane 5 are made according to a similar organizational structure in project management on behalf of CNES. Given the specificity of its commitment in Guiana, CNES kept the development of ground facilities under its direct responsibility as well as the launch team. These facilities are part of the Ariane 5 development programme.

About 150 European companies have participated in the Ariane 5 development programme, each of them in charge of the development responsibilities of their own product items.

Item	Rules to be defined
Information circuits	List and roles of the programme customers and suppliers. Information to be exchanged between customers and suppliers and the schedule of exchanges. Mode of establishment of change and application.
Communi-cation requirements	Information to be exchanged between the actors. Format and tools for communication. Communication timescales. Prerogatives of the customer, including delegation of them to the appropriate organization. *Note: The pre-contractual and contractual relationships should lead to the negotiation of provisions concerning how much visibility is given to the customer.*
Protection of information	Patent rights and intellectual property rights (IPR), levels of confidentiality, external communication and the exploitation of results should be specified by the contract.
Progress reports	For the supplier(s) and the customer, these reports evaluate work in progress regarding technical, performance, commercial and schedule aspects. The content and periodicity of these reports must be contractually defined. The reports and progress meetings must permit communication of information at all necessary levels related to progress of the programme, so that suitable decisions can be made and implementation of decided actions can be followed up. The agenda of progress meetings should be fixed and accepted by all the parties, and each meeting must produce a report that specifies that actions decided.
Customer's prerogatives	The agreement between the customer and each supplier should establish the degree to which the customer will: • monitor the supplier's application of the management requirements; • conduct or participate in audits or reviews of the supplier and be informed of progress made by the supplier in design, manufacturing, inspection and testing. The prerogatives needed by the customer in order to accomplish these tasks should be established by provisions of the agreement. These provisions should cover: • visits by the customer to the supplier's premises; • provisions that should be included in the supplier's direct agreements with lower level suppliers (sub-suppliers) regarding visits by higher-level customers; • the delegation of all or parts of these prerogatives to national surveillance organizations or to other specified organizations.
Action items management	Throughout the programme activities, the actions resulting from relations with the customer (such as meetings, exchange of mail, key events and reviews) and/or those determined by the supplier as part of applying the management rules shall be controlled. Each action is a defined by a form of identification, clear and unambiguous wording, an applicant, a person responsible for its completion and the corresponding deadline (fixed date or programme event. The final status must be formally expressed and accepted by the applicant on presentation of the applicable justifications.
Technical and management indicators	From the start of the programme onwards technical and management indicators (in particular highlighting developments in product quality and the organizational functioning) shall be formally defined, implemented, put to use and updated throughout the programme activities. In case of significant unfavourable developments, measures shall be taken according to the analysis of results. These indicators are defined between the customer and the supplier and shall remain confidential.

Figure 5.4 Key rules for actor interrelationships

Interrelations between actors: information, communication and reporting

The complex nature of space programmes means that effective communication between actors is vital. The activities of organizing a programme consist of setting up the programme internal organization and the external interfaces. This is done by defining the responsibilities and authority of the participants, and their interrelations, taking into account information technologies and subsequently documenting the programme organization. Communication takes the form of direct contact (meetings), actions management, formal periodic reporting (mostly on a monthly basis) and other means. Figure 5.4 identifies key rules.

Effective communication is an essential tool for ensuring clear and efficient interaction between all programme actors, as well as between the programme team and its external interfaces. Information technology is the primary means. Communication serves initially to provide clarity about the programme goals and objectives. Subsequently it supports the day-to-day work of the programme team. Communications have varying levels of formalism associated with them, ranging from informal information exchanges to contractually binding commitments.

The use of formalized action monitoring systems has become established as good practice. Regular reporting is a uniform means of exchanging information concerning the progress of the programme. Monitoring and control activities give the customer the capability to verify the supplied information such as reports. This can be done by subsequent assessments and audits. Clearly, regular reporting is an important tool for exchanging information concerning the progress of the programme. Figure 5.4 tabulates a set of key rules for action monitoring between customer and suppliers.

Work breakdown structure (WBS)

The space sector requires a disciplined approach in establishing programme goals over its lifecycle. It needs streamlined and effective management that is accountable for credible cost, schedule and performance reporting. The WBS is defined as:

- a product-orientated family tree composed of hardware, software, services, data and facilities. The family tree results from systems engineering efforts during the acquisition of a defence materiel item.

The WBS is a critical tool in ensuring that all portions of the programme are covered. The WBS will facilitate the necessary collaboration within the programme team structure for linking performance, cost, schedule and risk information. The WBS also facilitates the required technical rigour and integrated testing and evaluation. It is the backbone for structuring the requirements for integrated master schedules, earned value management (EVM) and other statutory, regulatory and contract reporting information. The WBS is also a critical element in establishing and using milestones.

The systems engineering development essential for all space programmes also needs the WBS. The programme WBS includes the contractual aspects and helps in documenting the work needed to produce and maintain architectural products in a system lifecycle. Creating the WBS ensures that no task has been forgotten.

Related to this is a unique coding system for all the programme tasks, whether these are technical or financial. In particular, the launcher system is broken down into hardware work packages (for example with values up to one million euros). For these work packages each contractor must provide a description of the work, a cost budget estimate, a timetable, the inputs that are required and the outputs provided to the rest of the system.

This WBS design is rigorous, to create the reference system for programme management. To ensure consistency, the programme is broken down in a unique, orderly and exhaustive manner, to allow unambiguous identification of the associated products and models, as well as the tasks and necessary resources.

> [Editorial comment: I strongly endorse this emphasis on the importance of the WBS. Stephen Devaux (1999, p. 59) put this succinctly when he wrote: 'If I could wish but one thing for every project, it would be a comprehensive and detailed WBS. The lack of a good WBS probably results in more inefficiency, schedule slippage, and cost overruns on projects than any other cause.' DL]

Various programme breakdown structures

The purpose of generating and maintaining a set of programme breakdown structures is to provide:

* a framework for ensuring that all requirements, functions and products of the system design are identified and arranged in a logical relationship that can be traced to (and satisfy) the customer's requirements;
* an identification of all tasks and resources needed to generate the system product;
* a cost relationship to the tasks being performed;
* an organizational context for the programme (or project) to perform the tasks needed to generate the system product;
* identification (by name) of the person responsible for performing each task element within the WBS;
* a basis for configuration control (once a particular programme breakdown structure is baselined);
* a framework for identifying risks and subsequent risk management;
* a basis for effective management of changes;
* a basis for financial control and interface responsibilities resulting from business agreements.

Framework and steps for designing a WBS

A WBS displays and defines the product, or products, to be developed and/or produced. It relates the elements of work to be accomplished to each other and to the end product. In other words, the WBS is an organized method to break down a product into subproducts at lower levels of detail. It can be expressed to any level of detail. The top three levels are the minimum required for reporting purposes on any programme or contract, but effective management of complex programmes requires WBS definition at considerably lower levels. This is particularly true of items identified as high-cost, high-risk or high technical interest. Thus it is critical to define the product at a lower level of WBS detail.

Managers must distinguish between WBS definition and WBS reporting. The WBS should be defined at the level necessary to identify work progress and enable effective management, regardless of the higher WBS level reported for programme oversight. This of first importance for understanding:

* the direction for effectively preparing, understanding and presenting a WBS;
* the framework for programme managers to define their programme's WBS and also for contractors in their application and extension of the contract's WBS.

The programme breakdown structures are derived from the level-1 customer's requirements, starting from the functional requirements. These functional requirements can be presented in the form of a function tree. Then the process goes through product tree elaboration, which is the exhaustive definition of the system elements. Delineating the tasks needed to develop and produce an element leads to the WBS. The identification of cost categories facilitates the establishment of the cost breakdown structure (CBS). Allocation of the WBS to the industrial organization results in the business agreement structure and definition of the interfaces.

The primary objective is to achieve a consistent application of the WBS for all programme needs (including performance, cost, schedule, risk, budget and contracts). Based upon the business agreement and the customer's requirements, every level-1 supplier develops a set of specifications (each containing requirements) that satisfies the level-0 (upper-level) customer's requirements. The specifications are organized in a hierarchical specification tree, with lower-level specifications containing requirements that flow down from higher-level specifications.

A function tree is generally generated from the requirements contained in the specification tree. These functions determine what shall be performed by the level-1 supplier's work share of the system (which could be the complete system). The functional requirements in the specification tree specify how well the requirements shall be performed. The specification and functional trees are then used to generate the design elements of the system product, which is arranged as a product tree. This WBS also as a reference for the identification of cost elements arranged into a cost breakdown structure, which is a hierarchical tree of lower cost elements, each of which is related to the next higher cost element.

The WBS and CBS, along with the overall management organization of the level-1 supplier, result in a programme or project organizational breakdown structure (OBS) for the level-1 supplier's work share. This is also arranged as a hierarchical tree of lower organizational elements, with each element reporting or related to the next higher level in the organization.

Business agreement or contract

Each hierarchical element of the WBS is referred to as a work package (WP) and is defined by an associated description. The complete set of WP descriptions defines the entire scope of work in the business agreement or contract between the customer and supplier. Each work package has:

1. a unique identifier, which should denote its position in the WBS;
2. a title (for ease of reference);
3. an assigned WP manager, who is responsible for accomplishing the described WP;

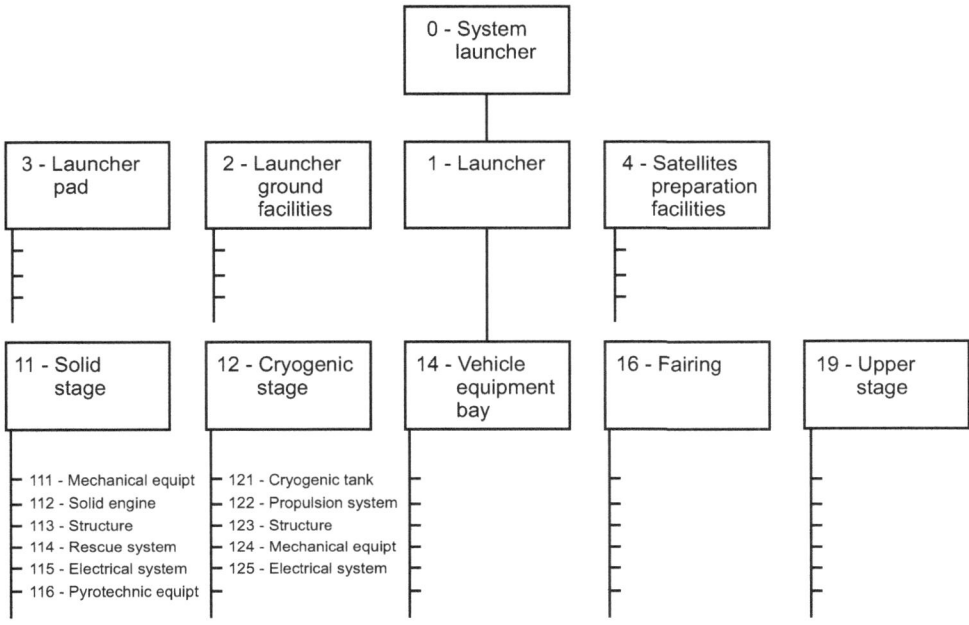

Figure 5.5 Part of a typical work breakdown structure

4. a description with a scope that is manageable and permits progress measurements;
5. planned duration, with specific start and end dates;
6. specific inputs needed to accomplish the WP, along with any WPs or sources from which the inputs originate;
7. resources (such as materials, personnel) identified as necessary to accomplish the WP;
8. specific outputs identified that will result from performing the WP, along with the relationship of these outputs to other WPs and the product tree or other specified breakdown structure;
9. relationships identified to other WPs in the WBS.

The WBS applies to the specific categories of materiel items listed below:

*   space systems;
*   launch vehicle systems;
*   electronic systems;
*   propulsion;
*   ground systems;
*   common elements.

In addition to these common elements, each system has a unique combination of hardware and software which defines the capability or end product of that system. Part of a typical WBS is shown in Figure 5.5.

Development process: phasing and planning management

The objective of programme phasing and planning is to define what shall be done and when it shall be done. Programme phasing and planning should minimize the technical, scheduling and economic risks. The activities required to make the launcher vehicle are defined and grouped into 'phases' (the process is called programme phasing). Each phase has characteristic activities and results in successive baselines of the system or the products. The duration and resources of each activity are estimated and their dependencies are scheduled using this information (programme planning). The customer decides on the authorization of the next phase by formal review and hence controls the progress of the programme.

Key requirements

Management requirements are defined and the specification is provided to all key actors in the industrial chain. Direction of technical task coordination is accomplished by the following means:

- standard process for execution of the work covering the activities of the industrial architect for the launcher vehicle and the activities of the contractors for the component products of the launcher (levels 1, 2 and 3);
- special technical intervention by the prime and/or the industrial architect on the occasion of reviews, or document approval, or acceptance. This technical intervention occurs at intervals depending on the development status of the launcher vehicle and of each individual component product.

Development of the launcher vehicle and its component products is divided into clearly definable phases in such a way that the work accomplished and products manufactured are submitted to reviews at the end of each phase. That can lead either to confidence allowing authorization of the next phase, or reorientation of the current phase.

Finally comes approval or acceptance of all documents prepared during development and on completion of milestones (technical specifications, definition files, production files, justification files, test plans and so on).

The complete technical task coordination process is integrated in the normal cycle of industrial architect and contractor's activities, with special technical intervention by the prime contractor and the industrial architect constituting milestones in the development phase for the launcher system and its component products.

Among other things the specification also sets out the rules related to:

- development and content of the functional specification (FS);
- development and content of the justification file (JF) to establish for each product item:
    - the qualification process;
    - tests management and test review boards;
    - technical task management for software development activities.

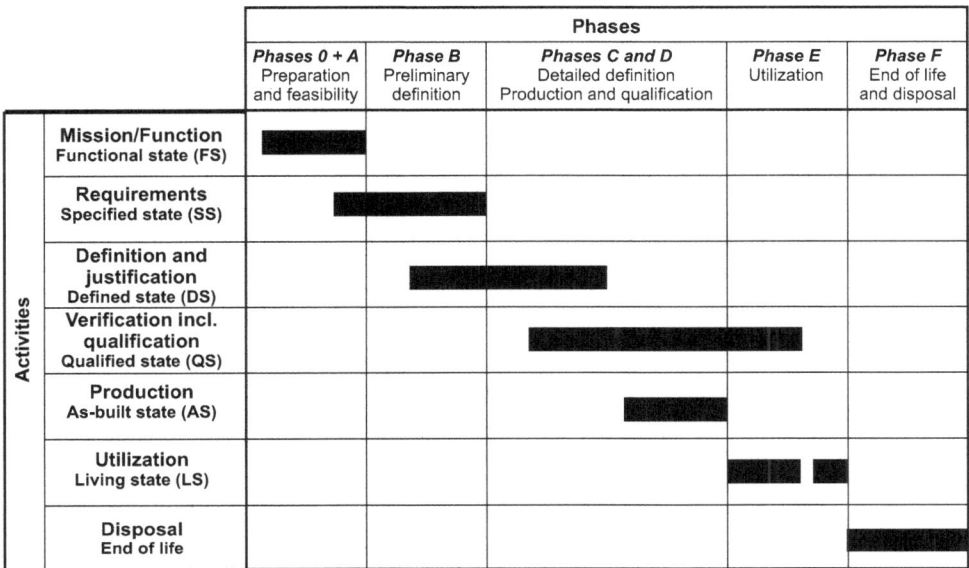

		Phases				
		Phases 0 + A Preparation and feasibility	**Phase B** Preliminary definition	**Phases C and D** Detailed definition Production and qualification	**Phase E** Utilization	**Phase F** End of life and disposal
Activities	**Mission/Function** Functional state (FS)	▬				
	Requirements Specified state (SS)		▬			
	Definition and justification Defined state (DS)			▬		
	Verification incl. qualification Qualified state (QS)			▬		
	Production As-built state (AS)			▬		
	Utilization Living state (LS)				▬	
	Disposal End of life					▬

Figure 5.6 Typical programme lifecycle (simplified)

Basic requirements: development time schedule and logic

In accordance with the requirements and actions to be taken as defined by the customer, each contractor prepares a time schedule and associated development logic, which will serve as a reference document for the activities covered by those requirements. This time schedule must be prepared in accordance with the requirements of A5·SM-0·60: 'Technical Work Control'. For each product, whether classified as a controlled configuration item (CCI) or not, this time schedule must show all essential events such as development testing, reviews, approval and acceptance of documents, and supply of equipment. These are milestones for the technical task coordination function.

Reviews during development programme phases

The programme is structured in phases. These are illustrated in the programme lifecycle in Figure 5.6. The starting of each phase is conditioned by passing a milestone and a review is generally conducted at the end of each phase to verify that:

- the objectives of the phase are met;
- the outputs of the phase have been produced in conformance to the specifications established in previous phases.

The review held at the conclusion of each phase must verify that all information necessary to begin the next phase is available. That information includes the possible best technical definitions, as well as sufficiently detailed planning data for the schedule aspects (and if appropriate, cost) of related activities. This will enable all the actors to commit to the next phase with confidence.

The basic principle applicable to reviews of all space programmes is that a thorough overall examination of the technical status of the programme is performed at crucial steps, involving independent expertise. Reviews assess the work performed by all participants in a programme against the stated requirements, the application of the relevant requirements and standards and good engineering practice. It is essential that the status of all elements of a system under review and its interfaces (such as launcher, spacecraft, ground segment, payloads and operations) are examined during the review process).

Relationships between phases and technical states

It is possible to identify relationships between the planning phases of a space programme and the technical states adopted by the launcher vehicle during development. These relationships equate to the creation of controlled baselines that record the state of the system after each phase. These baselines are verified in formal reviews at the end of each phase; their acceptance allows starting of the following phase(s). Figure 5.7 shows the principle covering the relationships between the phases of a typical space programme and the states of the corresponding launcher vehicle.

Reviews at launcher vehicle level

The development logic at launcher vehicle level includes the following reviews:

- SDSR: system design review, which aims to fix the technical specification (TS) of the launcher vehicle. Previously the need is expressed by a functional specification (FS).
- SDFR: system definition review, which ensures consistency of the technical specifications of the stage contractor and their main constituents.
- SCDR: system critical design review, which freezes the design of the system.
- SGQR: system ground qualification review, which allows qualification approval of the system after all ground tests of the launcher vehicle and related results of stages and components qualifications.
- FRR: flight readiness review. This gives authorization to ship the launcher to the Kourou Space Center in French Guiana.
- LRR: launcher readiness review, which gives the launch permission after reviewing the companion course.
- FDR: flight data review, during which flight result data are examined and validated, which should then make it possible to terminate preparation of the launcher vehicle qualification file.
- UFQR: the unmanned flight qualification review, held after the first Iwo unmanned launcher missions, which confirms the final qualification.

Reviews at constituent products level

The development logic of each product item level (launcher stages and its constituents) expresses needs by means of the FS and then the TS. That design results in

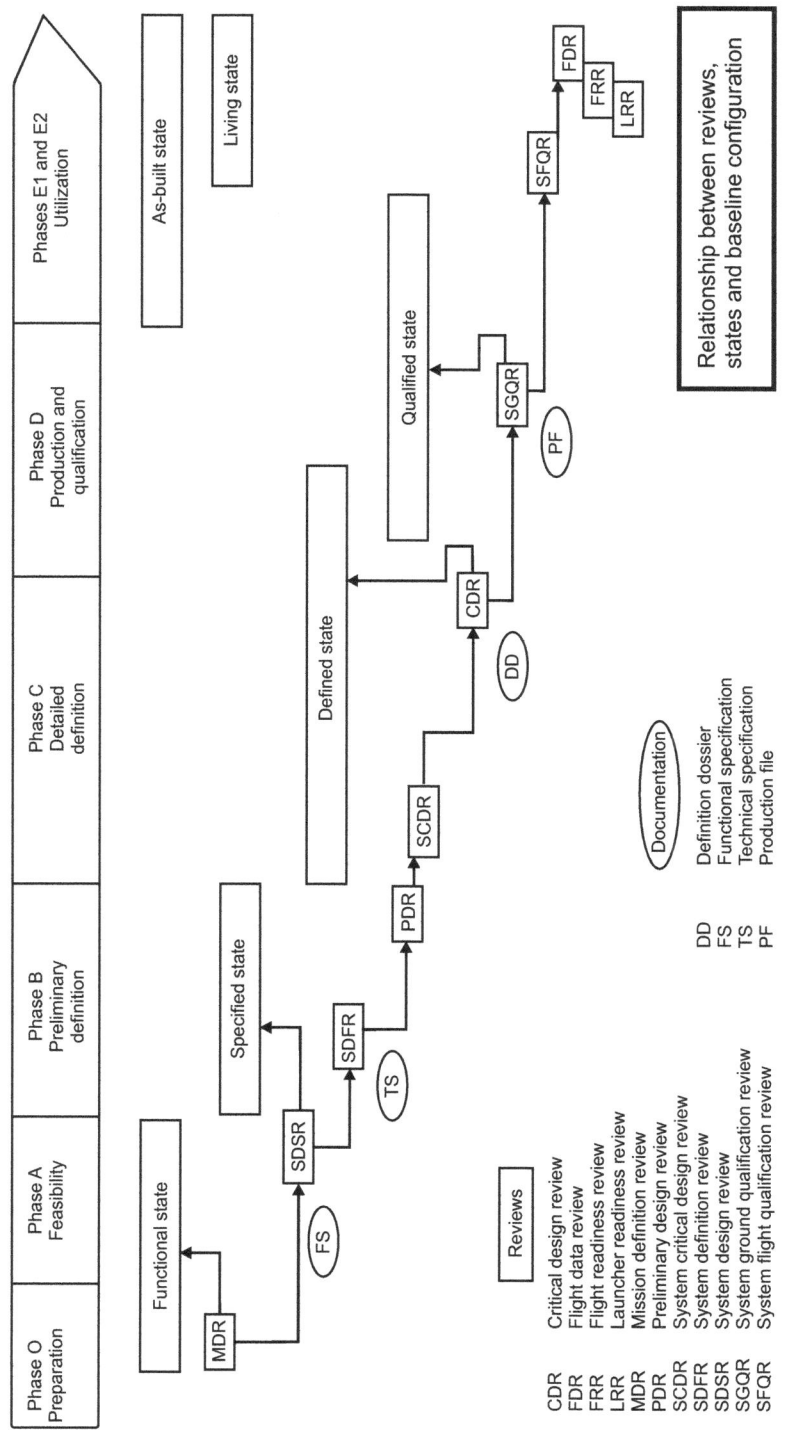

Figure 5.7 Flow chart of programme development showing milestones and phase reviews

| Phase O Preparation | Phase A Feasibility | Phase B Preliminary definition | Phase C Detailed definition | Phase D Production and qualification | Phases E1 and E2 Utilization |

Functional state

Specified state

Defined state

Qualified state

As-built state

Living state

MDR

FS

SDSR

TS

SDFR

PDR

SCDR

DD

CDR

PF

SGQR

SFQR

FDR

FRR

LRR

Relationship between reviews, states and baseline configuration

Reviews

CDR	Critical design review
FDR	Flight data review
FRR	Flight readiness review
LRR	Launcher readiness review
MDR	Mission definition review
PDR	Preliminary design review
SCDR	System critical design review
SDFR	System definition review
SDSR	System design review
SGQR	System ground qualification review
SFQR	System flight qualification review

Documentation

DD	Definition dossier
FS	Functional specification
TS	Technical specification
PF	Production file

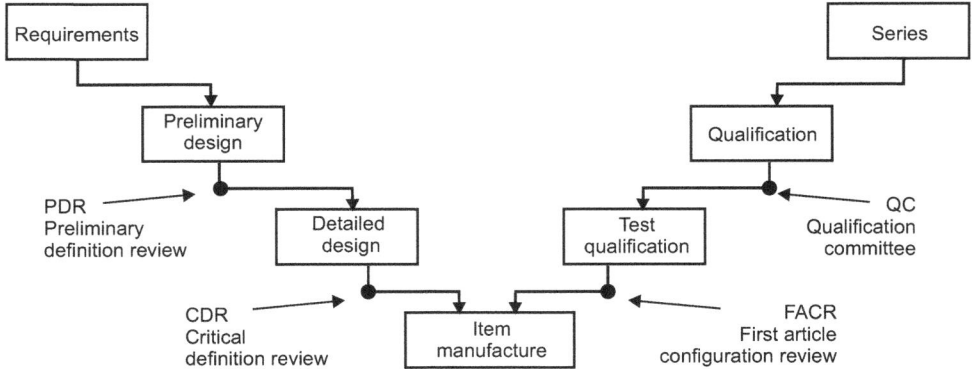

Figure 5.8 Key activities and reviews at constituent product level

the product description and definition file (DF) and the production definition file (PDF), the production of qualification items and qualification of the product design. The steps in this sequence are marked by a series of further reviews, as shown in Figure 5.8.

It is of course possible to identify further relationships in greater detail between the various levels of the launcher vehicle and its subsystems in terms of phases, activities, milestones, documentation and reviews further down in the WBS.

Configuration management

As any programme moves through its lifecycle, various events and changes will inevitably alter the configuration of the system as it is defined in drawings, specifications and other documents. Configuration management covers:

* A limited set of products (hardware or software) for which the prime or industrial architect wants to intervene directly in the formal approval process. These items are known as CCI (configuration controlled items).
* The documentation that exactly describes each CCI. Documents include the TS, interface documents (SI), DF, design industrial file (DID), and so on.
* Documentation rules are designed so that anyone who might be affected by a proposed change shall be informed in order to assess potential impacts and decide on acceptance or refusal of the change.

I have limited space here to go into more detail on this subject and I must now move on to discuss aspects of dependability and risk.

Dependability, risk and quality assurance

From the Ariane 1 Launcher version through to Ariane 4 reliability objectives have been maintained at a figure of 0.90 despite increased performance levels and

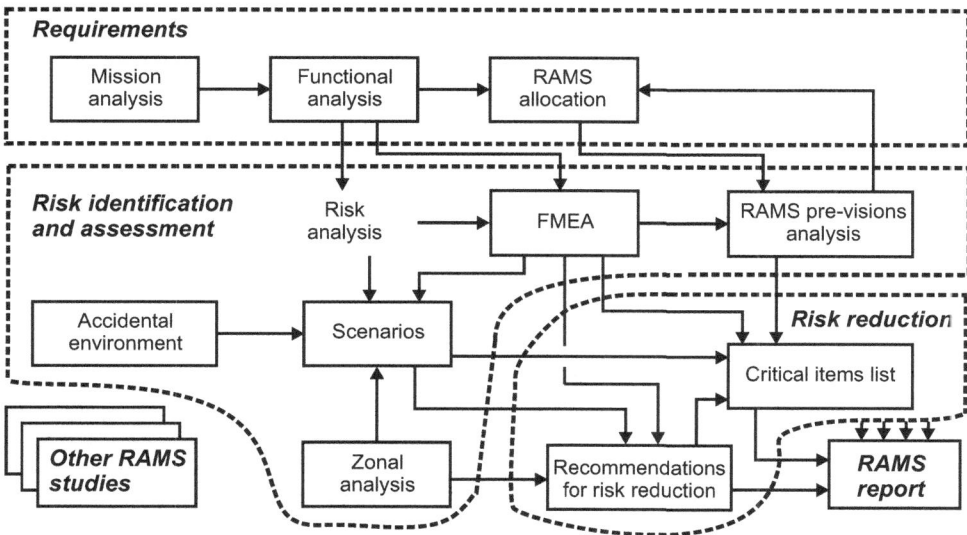

Figure 5.9 Key activities for risk analysis and mitigation

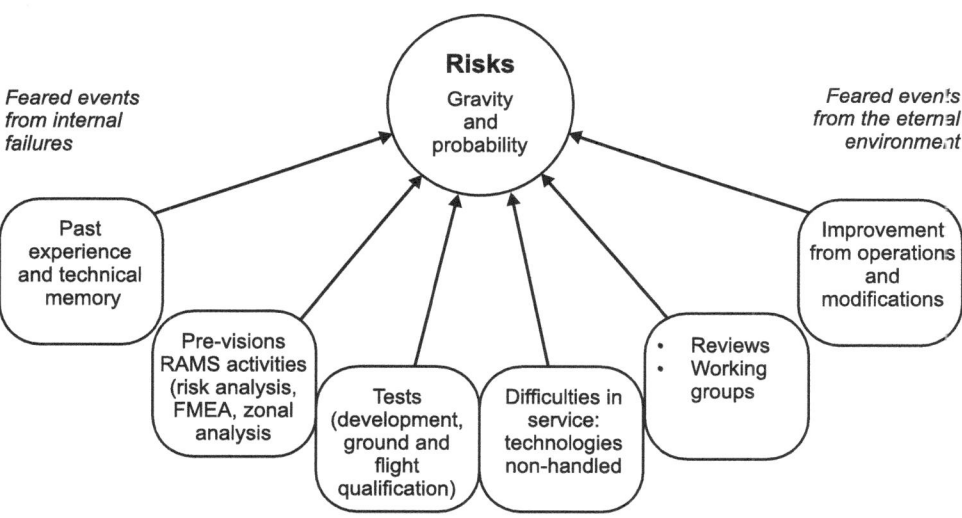

Figure 5.10 Risk identification, assessment and mitigation (RAMS)

technical complexity. The objective for Ariane 5 is 0.98. Dependability embraces the RAMS principle (*R*eliability, *A*vailability, *M*aintainability and *S*afety). The process is outlined in Figures 5.9 and 5.10. The abbreviation FMEA stands for failure mode effect analysis. See, for example, Chapter 7 in Lock (2013) for more on FMEA and risk analysis in projects.

Quality assurance

The following key definitions are essential in the space sector:

- Quality: the quality of a product or service describes its suitability meeting user requirements.
- Quality construction: this covers all actions by which a product or service obtains the required level of quality as defined in the contractual specifications (in technical, cost and time-schedule terms).
- Quality assurance covers the implementation of an appropriate set of predetermined, systematic measures designed to create confidence in achievement of the required quality level (as defined in the contractual specifications).

The programme manager is primarily responsible for product quality. Each contractor is bound by contract as follows:

- to supply products or services throughout the development phase (design, testing, procurement, manufacture, inspection and processing of non-conformances) that are of the requisite level of quality;
- rules apply to ensure that products are identified, stored, handled, supplied and used under conditions which guarantee the preservation of their level of quality;
- rules for processing non-conformances, and preventive and corrective actions resulting from them;
- qualification and training of personnel.

The product assurance manager (or the contract holder's quality assurance manager) must check coherence between quality assurance, RAMS and configuration management plans, and the coherent application of these throughout the programme. The quality assurance plan must take account of product assurance procedures, in particular with respect to coherence of the organization and pre-established rules.

   The industrial architect and the contractors must comply with these requirements, by means of three plans demonstrating the resources applied for this purpose. Meeting quality assurance objectives for the Ariane 5 includes:

- integration development, production and operational experience acquired with the Ariane 1 to Ariane 4 programmes;
- implementation of strict methods throughout the programme in order to control risks;
- integration of all quality assurance activities in the general framework of programme activities, in close liaison with RAMS and configuration management functions.

Quality assurance of each product requires:

- detailed planning for programme activities, and efficient management at all levels;

- definition of tasks concerned with quality assurance, and their integration in the entire process of development, production and utilization;
- assessment of product quality by means of audits, reviews, appraisals and use of technical and management indicators;
- availability of management reports in due time, based on existing documentation in the contractor's premises;
- technical requirements which are compatible between the different research centres, production centres, test centres and operational sites.

Cost and schedule control

A management specification sets out the requirements from the work control process that allows the prime contractor to:

- identify and know precisely the list of programme tasks needed and the associated time and costs;
- monitor progress to ensure that the programme objectives will be met;
- control costs associated with all these jobs;
- collect information in time to take measures for controlling and correcting deviations (variances).

This process allows the industrial architect to exercise authority in planning and monitoring technical progress for the launcher vehicle. Critical path networks are used to plan all the work. This process enables all the provisions that must be met in the following activities.

- Financial evaluation for each work package (annual to completion, monthly for the current year) and timetable including planning significant milestones (key events). Of course, this depends on the nature of the contract (whether or not it is fixed price).
- Monthly reporting, both on cost and time. This information is used in various monthly progress meetings and must highlight even small variances in time and cost to allow effective correction without delay. Milestones are identified and monitored as part of this process.

A common programme calendar is defined for use by all the programme actors.

Design-to-cost management

Management of the Ariane 1 and Ariane 2 programmes was conducted particularly to achieve the following objectives:

- to attain the defined technical performance defined;
- not to exceed the budget allocated for this development.

Since the start of Ariane 3, for Ariane 4 and Ariane 5, the following marketing requirement was added:

- to obtain a competitive product by the end of programme development, in which the optimum balance between technical performance and economic performance is achieved. The purpose being to sell Ariane 5 launchers in a market where the competition will be tough.

To reach this additional target, CNES decided to apply jointly with the industrial firms a method enabling the cost objectives to be given the same importance as the technical, quality and delivery performance targets.

This method is known as 'design-to-cost'. For the first application (the design of liquid boosters and the upper part of Ariane 4) this proceeded as follows:

- from the outset setting the mass production target cost (known as the recurrent cost). The design-to-cost method was intended specifically to control series production and operational costs for products to be developed from the early definition phases;
- with incentives in contracts to encourage the subcontractors to seek out and select technical solutions satisfying both the target costs and the development requirements (quality, performance, delivery);
- to consider the target production cost in the same way as performance, quality and delivery.

This implies:

- that the industrial firm responsible for the contract undertakes to develop a product by design methods that enable the mass production cost and/or launch operations target cost to be met;
- that the work implementation process defined in the management specification is complied with.

Value engineering (VE) was used to help achieve these objectives (for more on value engineering see Mukhopadhayaya, 2009).

Conclusion

Building space launchers is hard. Part of the problem is that space travel is in its infancy. Compare this, for example, with the aviation industry. Since the Russian Sputnik, human beings have launched just over 4,800 launchers towards orbit (not counting suborbital flights and small sounding launchers). But during the first 50 years of aviation over one million aircraft have been built. Unlike aircraft, almost all space launchers can only be used once. There is also the issue of performance. Airplane performance has improved gradually from the early days of the Wright brothers. Aircraft designers and pilots would slightly push the envelope, stop and get comfortable with where they were, and then push on. Orbital launchers, by contrast, must perform perfectly on their first (and usually only) flight. Physics dictates this – to reach orbit, without falling back to Earth, you have to exceed about 17,500 mph. If you cannot vary performance, then the only thing left to change is the amount of payload. The rocket designers began with small payloads and worked their way up.

The space transportation industry is looking for new ways to reduce the cost of access to space. However, this must not come at the expense of losing focus on service quality. The resulting failures and delays would undermine the credibility of the space sector in the eyes of investors and insurers. A significant, but still reasonable cut in launch costs can only be achieved through a thorough, methodical approach to launch vehicle development.

Launch service quality costs money but it also generates value. At the time of writing Arianespace (founded in 1980 and the world leader in commercial space transportation) has fired 285 Ariane launchers. That represents about 330 satellites, contributing directly to the space telecommunications market development worldwide. Thus Europe has played a major role in the development of this sector, which now generates yearly revenues of more than $10 billion. The high quality of launch service has added more than 200 years of orbital life to the satellites launched, which means significant savings for their operators.

The need for effective management of space programmes is still increasing, with fierce competition for space-related programmes. Some of those programmes are the largest cooperative ventures in science and technology ever undertaken. The International Space Station symbolizes cooperation among the world's most industrialized nations to build a permanently orbiting laboratory in space. The pressure is on space programme managers to improve performance – but the application of effective programme management techniques for space-related projects is rarely presented.

There have been some cost overruns and schedule slippages in space programmes. Clearly the success of a programme must be the main objective of the programme manager. The development of a standardized programme management approach is now accepted and recommended for future implementation. Since the mid-1990s the European Cooperation for Space Standardization (ECSS) has developed standards that are internationally recognized and assimilated by the European space industry and agencies. Also the International Standards Organization (ISO) has a technical committee with representatives from about 15 countries involved in the space sector.

References and further reading

Devaux, S. (1999), *Total Project Control*, New York: John Wiley.
Lock, D. (2013), *Project Management*, 10th edn., Farnham: Gower.
Mukhopadhayaya, A. K. (2009), *Value Engineering Mastermind*, New Delhi: Response Books/ Sage.

Chapter 6

Programme Management in the Aircraft Industry

Simon Henley

Programmes for whole new aircraft, engines or re-engineering within the aircraft industry are individually big enough to make or break even the biggest companies or corporations. Thus the management of these programmes has to ensure that they deliver the expected benefits on time and within the expected development cost.

The market

The top tier of the civil aerospace market (complete aircraft, engines and managed services) is driven by two principal considerations:

- performance (especially fuel efficiency);
- time-to-market.

The market is extremely competitive between a few major players. These are primarily Airbus and Boeing for airframes, and Rolls-Royce, Pratt and Whitney, and General Electric for engines. Other prime-level companies are emerging and making some impact (Embraer, Bombardier, Comac and Superjet) but at the moment these have not penetrated the market in large numbers and none is yet in the wide-body market. The market has significant barriers to entry. New development programmes are very capital intensive (typically €15 billion for an airframe and €2 billion for an engine). They are usually internally funded, either by the primes themselves or in collaboration with risk- and revenue-sharing partners. Thus it can be several years before development costs are recouped through product sales and the aftermarket – and that is highly dependent on market share and hours flown once in service.

The defence aerospace market has many of the same players. There are also a few key companies that do not currently have a significant civil aircraft footprint but are primes on combat aircraft or military trainers (notably BAES and Lockheed Martin). The principal drivers in the military market are similar – cutting edge technologies in highly integrated platforms to deliver the competitive edge. But performance is measured in combat effectiveness – not in cost per passenger mile. Almost all defence development programmes are government-funded, as the ultimate size of the market is driven by a number of factors outside the control of the companies concerned (for example, government-to-government relationships, national economic health, export regulations and so on). This has a knock-on effect on the pace of decision-making in defence programmes because government funding comes with a requirement for government oversight and often government agreement to key decisions. Governments often dictate tools and processes to be used in the management of their programmes, so defence programmes are often supported by comprehensive government-mandated tools (such as specified earned value management or risk management).

Quality is a given factor in this market. Quality escapes are highly visible, and can quickly lead to significant impact on market share. Volume is vital, because high competition drives margins on initial sales down to a very low level (and the capital outlay of a development programme is only recovered by volume sales in the aftermarket). Price is held down by competition, with customer airlines driving hard bargains to get discounts. If the product is not fuel efficient or available on time it will not even make it to price discussions.

Success in this market comes from identifying the right time to start a new product development, and then judging what technologies will be sufficiently mature to meet the timeline for availability in the market. The timing will depend on many factors, but will depend on a business case which makes assumptions about forecast delivery of production products, levels of performance (cost per seat mile, range, fuel consumption, dispatch rate) and forecasts of the likely market share/production numbers at the assumed outturn. Key decisions include whether to re-engineer an existing product to re-energize sales and stretch out a product line (for example the Airbus New Engine Option (NEO) on the A320 series, Boeing 737 Max), or to launch a completely new product because the existing offering has run its course (for example, Boeing 787 Dreamliner, Airbus A350).

Reputations can be made or broken with a single product, or even with one technology failure. In the 1970s, Rolls-Royce was driven into bankruptcy and public ownership when the carbon fibre fan blades it had developed for its new engine range were found at a very late stage in the development of the engine to be catastrophically vulnerable to bird ingestion. Boeing was widely considered to have 'cracked the code' for developing new wide-body aircraft when they delivered the 777 programme to time and cost. But they suffered serious time delays and cost overruns on their next major development programme, the 787 Dreamliner, followed by very significant problems after entry into service with the lithium-ion batteries which were a critical part of its more-electric power systems.

The market for whole aircraft is fairly traditional, in that development costs are generally recouped in large part through original equipment sales of new aircraft, with the remainder being recovered through spare parts sales to authorized maintenance, repair and overhaul (MRO) organizations. But an aircraft contains many high-value components with shorter lives than the whole aircraft (most notably engines) and here the market characteristics are quite different.

The original equipment manufacturers (OEMs) sell their components packaged in long-term maintenance contracts. That gives a guaranteed cost per flying hour, or guaranteed engine on-wing availability, or some other way of reducing variability and year-on-year fluctuation in costs for the aircraft operators. In this model, the engine or component is often sold at close to cost price, and the development costs are amortized through the premiums in the servicing contract. This has the interesting effect of incentivizing the component OEM to improve the life and reliability of the product constantly – the less attention it requires in its lifetime the lower the cost incurred in meeting the guaranteed flight hour rate or availability, and the greater the return on the contract. Aircraft operators also benefit from improved on-wing time and lower disruption, so a successfully implemented contract of this type offers a win for both parties.

Governance

Most key players in the aerospace market are not solely dependent on their civil aerospace products to maintain revenue. Many are part of much larger corporations (such as Airbus, Boeing, GE, Pratt and Whitney) in order to give a degree of resilience to the very cyclical nature of the civil aerospace market. Nonetheless the cost and resource implications of a new product in this market are so significant that a high level of governance is a vital part of ensuring that the level of risk is fully understood and contained. It is probably true to say that none of the corporations concerned could sustain a total programme failure of a whole aircraft or engine late in the cycle – the sunk costs would be so great that they would probably bring down the parent corporation.

Thus all the companies in the industry have well-developed governance processes, with escalation of decisions to the appropriate authorization level commensurate with the risk incurred by each decision. Initial launch of a new product is a huge commitment in terms of both cost and reputation, and will always be a group-level decision supported by plenty of independent evidence that the timing and chances of success are worth the risk incurred. Once launched, much use is made of standard 'dashboards' to monitor programme health at the strategic level, with individual decisions on issues such as technology choices, or resource allocation being delegated to appropriate lower levels in the organization.

Organization

Once the decision to launch a major new aerospace product (whole new aircraft, engine, or significantly upgraded aircraft or engine) has been made, a programme director and a chief engineer will be appointed. The programme director will have overall accountability for delivering the business case for the product, which will include delivery to schedule, cost and quality, and ensuring that the product meets its performance parameters. The chief engineer will report to the company's chief engineer/technical director, and be accountable for ensuring the safety and airworthiness of the product; setting the test strategy to deliver the necessary evidence for certification and then continuing airworthiness of the product as it matures from its initial certification standard.

In most cases the staffing below programme director/chief engineer level will be allocated against agreed work packages, with probably only the work package leader (sometimes called IPT leader) being a long-term appointment to the programme. Other resources will be appointed from the various functions as the workload ebbs and flows in a typical matrix organization. Thus the programme director (probably assisted by a programme executive) has to ensure good definition of the work packages and make the case for enough suitably skilled and experienced resources to be allocated to meet the milestones technically and on time. There is usually a small programme management office (PMO) to collate management information and provide reports to the senior executives. Staff in the PMO often have dual roles as work package leaders or IPT leaders.

Programme management impacts

Given the pressures described above, the companies concerned rely on a very synergistic relationship between the engineering and programme management functions. The engineers have to bring the technologies to fruition to deliver performance, while the programme managers have to ensure that the product is delivered affordably and on time. Above all, the senior management need a clear view throughout development of the progress towards meeting forecast production deliveries, and of the maturity of the technologies (which are often vital to delivering the promised performance on which the customer was persuaded to choose that product in a highly competitive market). They must also always have an understanding of the final product cost in terms of development investment and unit production cost – both of which are critical to maintaining a competitive position and to generating enough cash for reinvestment into the next new product.

There are often parallel gated processes; an engineering process to manage the maturation of the technology, and a set of programme management gates to ensure that the programme delivers the business case. Many of the benefits are time sensitive, so the business case reviews will cover the cost, time and risk elements of the programme, and will usually use the output from the relevant engineering review to cover the performance element.

Risk management

Risk management is a critical feature in the way programmes are conceived, activities are prioritized, and outcomes are measured. Almost always a new product will incorporate a cutting edge technology which enables a step change in efficiency or performance, or a significant reduction in running costs, or an enhanced passenger experience which will increase market share for that product. The timing of announcements of new programmes is often predicated on assumptions as to when a new technology will be production-ready. So the major risks to the programme at launch will be the time taken to prove the technology and get a production facility established.

Until a risk has been substantially contained, it is often necessary to run a parallel low-risk fall-back option. Recent examples of slower-than-planned technology maturity impacting programmes include:

- use of lithium-ion batteries in the Boeing 787 Dreamliner, which caused in-flight fires soon after the introduction to service;
- delays to the Bombardier C Series test and certification programme after a failure of the geared turbofan engine (which was crucial to the fuel efficiency promised to customers).

In these cases, the entire programme is constructed to get the critical technologies to test as early as possible, to prove that the technologies deliver the benefits expected, and also to get plenty of test hours to prove the durability and to flush out obscure issues which would otherwise only emerge as the full test envelope is explored. When the technology is proved to be both beneficial and feasible, the fall-back options can be wound down, saving resources and allowing full focus on the primary programme path. The industry's main players have well-founded independent review processes which play a significant role here in judging the point at which a technology is considered mature enough to close down fall-back options.

In parallel to tracking the maturity of critical technologies, the programme risk management system also tracks the key risks to achieving the approved business case for the programme. Key risks here are delays or overruns to the development programme, cost overruns owing to rework, quality issues, or unforeseen extra work required. These must all be managed to contain the programme performance, cost and time envelopes. As an example of the criticality of time overruns, it has in the past proved more beneficial to introduce a new product on time despite failing to meet its guaranteed performance levels (and therefore having to pay performance penalties and the cost of a subsequent retrofit programme once a performance-compliant fix is available) than to suffer the reputational loss and inconvenience to the customer of delaying the product delivery.

It is therefore no exaggeration to say that the ability to manage risk is a real discriminator in the industry, one which can very quickly differentiate between a very successful programme and a very expensive failure.

Engineering development

The pressure on meeting market introduction dates and the competitive nature of the market will always drive concurrency into civil aerospace programmes; the architecture will be committed before the underpinning technologies have proven their maturity; the initial production configuration will be set before certification of that configuration has been achieved; through-life support contracts will be agreed before the true reliability and full lives of components have been demonstrated. All of this concurrency introduces risk – in itself it is not a malpractice but it is vital that the full scale of the accumulated risk due to concurrency is fully understood. Sometimes the risk exposure will exceed the risk appetite for the contractor concerned, and the programme director will have to reconstruct the programme to reduce or remove some of the concurrency, either by adding resources to accelerate development testing, or by delaying the start of the next phase until the outcome of the last phase has been fully understood. The successful contractors in this market are not those who avoid concurrency. They are the ones who can appropriately manage the risk to reap the benefits of a more aggressive technology introduction to beat the competition to market with a technology which stands their product apart from the competition.

The engineering functions in these organizations are very highly developed in terms of recruiting appropriately educated engineers and then imbuing them with the company's engineering culture to develop their judgement and ability to tackle high-risk technology development programmes. That includes understanding of when the risk becomes too high and help is needed from elsewhere in the organization.

Certification

The aerospace industry is very highly regulated for obvious reasons of safety and the potential impact of an airborne failure of design, operation or maintenance. Fundamental to safe operation of air transportation of passengers or cargo is the safety of the design. This is assured through independent certification of the design as being safe to operate within the regime specified in the operational instructions and limitations. Programme development is therefore focused initially on achieving certification of the design and its operating envelope. This requires a highly structured development programme, with rigorous recording, assessment and reporting of results in order to underwrite the performance and safety assessment of every component in the product.

Different levels of safety criticality are defined for systems and subsystems, with appropriate levels of evidence and probabilities of failure assigned by the overseeing bodies (such as the European Aviation Safety Agency (EASA) or the Federal Aviation Administration (FAA), or the national governments in the case of defence programmes). Certification reports are required at every level from component through subsystem, system, and up to whole aircraft. Some large systems (for example engine, propeller, avionics) are subject to separate certification in their own right before their certification reports are integrated into the whole aircraft certification case. The programme manager must therefore establish a certification strategy at the outset of the programme and then have a comprehensive set of metrics that track progress towards certification, with frequent, rigorous management reviews to identify potential risks and issues impacting the ability to achieve certification on time.

Fitness for purpose

One of the biggest tests for a whole aircraft programme occurs just before the initial certification is issued. The aircraft has to prove its fitness for purpose by operating as if it is in service for a period set by the certificating authority. During that time it is only allowed to receive normal scheduled maintenance in accordance with the operating instructions proposed as part of the certification submission. By this time the development aircraft will have performed many hundreds of hours of testing (and individual components many thousands of hours) but this is nonetheless a demanding test, often on the first aircraft built to the production configuration.

Configuration management

The requirements of certification, ability to control the availability of spares for repair or replacement, and the sheer complexity of the systems, subsystems and components of a complete aircraft (and the resultant possibilities for incompatibility between different build standards of items) require the programme to have a configuration management system of very high integrity. Most new product programmes run with a significant degree of concurrency in order to meet the critical entry into service dates. Often this involves committing to a production configuration well in advance of completing all component testing at the standard designated for production.

Should problems subsequently arise, then a modification will be schemed, tested and certified. That modification might need varying degrees of change because of differing modification states across all the components and subsystems in service. With hundreds of subsystems all subject to their own testing and development programmes, the number of moving parts in terms of setting a production configuration is huge. High priority modifications required for safety reasons will be integrated into the configuration as soon as they are available, and pre-modification items already installed will be replaced in similar timescales.

Modifications to ensure that a product meets its original specification may well be introduced by modification 'campaigns' or retrofit programmes, where aircraft fleets are cycled through a modification programme. Lower priority modifications which offer enhanced reliability, lower production cost or improved performance over the original specification may be introduced only when the prior component is replaced at end of life or when it becomes unserviceable.

In all cases the programme documentation must maintain a comprehensive high integrity record of allowable configurations, and ensure that no uncertified configuration occurs (either during production or by introduction of modifications after the product enters service). The top-tier contractor will often set a 'batch strategy' for the introduction of modifications during development and production to impose a degree of control over configuration, so that modifications may only be introduced on the production line at certain build numbers. This is to ensure that batches of aircraft (typically batches of ten aircraft in early production with concurrent development but with much larger numbers per batch once production reaches near steady state) are produced with identical configurations. That will allow standard assembly instructions, simpler spare part management and a simpler aftermarket solution.

This will flow down to sub-tier contractors and may well drive their own modification introduction strategy. Modification development and introduction forms a key part of regular programme reviews between the various tiers of contractors.

An example of the need for (and the use of) an effective configuration control system was the loss of a turbine disc in 2010 from the Rolls-Royce Trent engine of an Airbus A380. That happened on Qantas flight QF32 shortly after it left Singapore. Significant damage was caused to the aircraft in flight. The root cause of the failure was traced to a crack in an oil feed pipe leaking oil into a hot air stream. That caused an oil fire which led to softening of the turbine disc and its eventual failure (Australian Transport Safety Bureau, 2013). Urgent investigation identified a batch of pipes which were susceptible to the crack, and the engines containing these pipes were immediately taken out of service until the pipes could be replaced. The investigation also identified that even after the crack-susceptibility issue was dealt with, a single skin pipe in that area did not constitute best design practice. So a double-skinned pipe was designed, tested and introduced as an urgent modification, campaigned into the fleet by creating spare sets of engines and conducting a rolling programme of removal and replacement to replace all engines fitted with single-skin pipes with modified engines. Additionally the company then reviewed its entire engine portfolio to see if the single-skin pipe had been embodied as a design feature in any other engines. The TP400 engine for the Airbus Military A400M transport aircraft was modified during the design and development phase to incorporate a double-skinned pipe in the equivalent component to ensure that lessons identified from the QF32 were genuinely translated into 'lessons learned'. The ability to identify affected engines fitted with the suspect batch of pipes rapidly, and then further consider the broader implications for other engines, only came about as a result of the comprehensive configuration management system within the engine contractor and Airbus.

[Editorial comment: Some companies refer to configuration records as build schedules or version control. This subject is poorly represented in the literature, which is astonishing considering its relevance to many industries including the automotive industry. However, there is more on the control of changes and recording build schedules in Chapters 23 and 27 of Flouris and Lock, 2009. DL]

Supply chain management

One of the key risks as a new product matures is the ability of the supply chain to ramp up to the required production rates. Top-selling narrow body aircraft typically reach production rates of 35 to 40 aircraft a month. Each aircraft will have tens of thousands of individual parts, many of them very complex subassemblies in their own right. Although the top-level companies will have their own supply chain management function within the procurement part of the company, the programme manager needs to have a good understanding of the supply chain's health and particularly its limitations.

A programme will face many make-or-buy decisions, any one of which might significantly influence the level of risk once the product gets into production. As an example, Boeing (in the 787 Dreamliner programme) decided early in development to outsource the design and build of major assemblies into the global supply chain as a means of increasing the attractiveness of the aircraft to international operators. Several significant introduction-to-service delays were announced quite late during development which were attributed either to poor quality or insufficient maturity in the outsourced supply chain. Some of those problems were overcome only by bringing the design and production of the relevant items back in-house (Tang and Zimmerman, 2009).

There is a limited number of suppliers with the necessary skills and capability to produce some components and subsystems, either because of the specialist materials and processes required or because the complexity of the system requires deep knowledge. When the market is buoyant, these suppliers can become pinch points for production capacity, particularly if (as often happens) they are supplying to more than one top-tier supplier. Hence the programme manager needs to understand the capacity limitations of the existing supply chain and have in place a robust review process and decision process. It is necessary to understand when second-sourcing or more intrusive supplier support is required to reduce risk to on-time delivery.

Aftermarket management

The point of delivery is not the end of the programme in the aviation industry. For many key players it is just one milestone in a 30- or 40-year programme to deliver the business case for a particular product. That is the point at which the product starts to earn revenue and create a return on the investment in development. During the intervening period the competitive market will force the initial sale price for a product down to somewhere near its material and manufacturing cost. This condition applies mainly to those industries where the product has a significant aftermarket cost of regular overhaul and repair. That covers typically engines, undercarriage assemblies and other items which operate at high stress and temperature and are usually maintained by rotating them through servicing cycles (with repair and overhaul performed off-aircraft).

For these industries, a vital part of programme management is a suite of tools and processes for managing the cost of maintaining the performance levels agreed contractually between the industry and the aircraft user (usually at the point of purchase for a significant period of life). This is typically in the form of an agreed cost per flight hour, or a fixed cost per overhaul. The manufacturer can then improve or worsen the business case by managing the time between overhauls and the lives and durability of individual components so that each overhaul requires fewer new components. This type of contract offers opportunities for much greater intimacy with the customer, because the manufacturer often becomes a vital partner in *its* customer's ability to deliver customer satisfaction. That applies particularly where the contract requires an agreed availability or guaranteed dispatch reliability.

The programme manager thus has to be able to manage the short-term requirement to keep customers' assets serviceable to earn revenue while also managing the long-term cost of maintenance, repair and overhaul to maximize return to the programme.

Summary and conclusion

Managing development and production costs is a vital capability within any company in the aircraft industry. Although individual toolsets and processes vary, the outcomes are shaped by a highly regulated industry with extremely detailed certification and assurance requirements. Products have to be delivered into a very competitive market that is populated by knowledgeable customers who demand products of the highest possible quality, combining competitive operating costs with high performance.

Programme management in these organizations has to identify, quantify and manage risk closely through development from the early stages of immature technologies to certification of mature systems. The performance levels demanded by the aviation market have to be delivered at an affordable production and support cost.

The programme management organization must also administer a complex and multilayered supply chain. The risks and limitations inherent in every supplier have to be understood and managed as part of the build-up to successful delivery of the overall programme.

The scope of modern aircraft programmes extends very significantly beyond the point of delivery of a product to the customer. As an aircraft goes through life, its airworthiness must be assured continually. That has to be achieved through replacement of life-expired components, scheduled maintenance to maintain fitness for purpose, unscheduled maintenance and repair of defective items, and modification and overhaul when items, subsystems or systems are updated. Thus the aircraft industry has developed suites of tools for use in programme managing the aftermarket to deliver customer-specified outcomes at prices that are affordable but which deliver appropriate returns for the industry players.

The aircraft market remains buoyant. It is accelerating in the civil market as airlines look to introduce new products ever faster to improve efficiency of utilization, reduce fuel costs and maintain their competitive position. That is unlikely to change for the foreseeable future. Fuel prices will probably continue to dominate operating expenses in the medium to long term. The search for renewable forms of energy to replace current fossil-fuelled systems will ramp up as current reserves are exhausted.

Programme management will become ever more important as upgrade cycles are driven to shorter timescales. The ability to deliver products on time at guaranteed performance levels will become ever more important in this competitive market. That applies to suppliers and also to the operators of aircraft and their related systems.

References and further reading

Australian Transport Safety Bureau (2013), Report *AO-2010–089* released 27 June 2013.

Flouris, T. G. and Lock, D. (2009), *Managing Aviation Projects from Concept to Completion*, Farnham: Ashgate.

Tang, Q. and Zimmerman, J. D. (2009), 'Managing New Product Development and Supply Chain Risks: The Boeing 787 Case', *Supply Chain Forum*, 10(2): 74–86.

Chapter 7

Programme Management in the Automotive Industry

Hans-Henrich Altfeld

Introduction

Project and programme management in the automotive industry is characterized by the following key challenges when developing and launching new products:

- mass production with high quality and safety standards;
- very high variation between delivered products;
- significant number of different products developed and produced in parallel;
- fiercely competitive environment, leading to global design, development and production footprints (all with individual challenges regarding logistics and quality standards as well as multicultural, global and collaborative ways of working;
- very powerful original equipment manufacturers (OEMs), who 'rule' their supply chains and make heavy use of directed suppliers;
- almost never delayed start of production (SOP) deadlines.

Dr Barnes' famous time–cost–quality constraint triangle (Lock, 2013, pp. 23–5) is at the base of the management of all projects and programmes. In the automotive industry there is extreme cost pressure and virtually no compromise on schedule and quality.

Common automotive industry management concepts

For most of its history the automotive industry has tried to generate products that millions of consumers could afford by producing them at the lowest possible cost while assuring high standards of quality. A first major step in this direction was the introduction of conveyor belt-based assembly, which Henry Ford brought to a very high level of sophistication. Ford produced more than 15 million Model T cars and became the first OEM. Ford's key principles, later called 'Fordism', included the decomposition of assembly work into simple one-minute operations ('Taylorism') which could be performed by low-skilled workers thanks to the application of special tools and equipment. Fordism relied on producing cars as (almost) identical copies.

Ford's competitors rapidly copied Fordism, and Ford's competitive advantage started to diminish. Competitors also tried to explore new routes. For example, Alfred P. Sloan, president of General Motors (GM) from 1923 to 1937, introduced fashion and style to automobiles to target new consumer groups. He introduced annual car model changes and different lines, thus creating a portfolio of products for the entire social range of consumers. This 'Sloanist' concept required significant changes from the Ford system, using more flexible machines and equipment capable of producing different car models. However Fordism and Sloanism were process-orientated, focused on mass production at the lowest possible cost.

The European and Japanese automotive industry was heavily hit during the Second World War, and recovery took many years. In Japan, the focus on production processes brought significant improvement. Instead of producing higher and higher volumes, Toyota managers started to analyse the shopfloor value chain and were able to eliminate waste and increase efficiency.

Toyota introduced initiatives such as continuous improvement, and 'pull' instead of 'push' principles. Their 'Andon cord' to stop the assembly line whenever a problem had to be corrected immediately created a sense of urgency for problem solving. Toyota's just-in-time (JIT) processes reduced inventory at the manufacturing facility and reduced work related to sorting parts and matching them to the production schedule. JIT requirements gave suppliers only a few hours to react when systems or parts were ordered for delivery. The innovative Toyota Production System (TPS) reduced production costs, increased productivity and enhanced employee motivation. 'Lean production' was born.

Besides introducing lean production and special customer–supplier relationships, the Japanese also achieved superior quality compared with competitors. They used concepts developed by Deming during the 1940s, later called 'Total Quality Management' (TQM). During the 1980s, when the classical markets in North America and Europe were saturated, Japanese car makers managed to break into the North American market because of their superior proliferation strategies, the TPS, lean production, competitive prices, better quality and greater variety. TPS was so successful that it put the existence of many American and European automotive companies in jeopardy. It became a question of survival for other companies to understand and implement TPS themselves.

Considerable research revealed the main differences between the US and European car makers on the one hand, and Toyota on the other. A study by Clark and Fujimoto in 1991 'became the linchpin for researchers and practitioners alike and set the stage for research on time, cost, and quality performance in [automotive] launch . . . [programmes]' (Witt, 2006, p. 21). It provided evidence that Toyota and other Japanese car makers using TPS principles more efficient in manufacturing and new product development. As it turned out, 'Japanese firms developed new cars with only about 55 percent of the engineering hours required by US and European volume producers' (Cusumano and Nobeoka, 1996, p. 108).

The typical time-to-market required by Toyota to develop a new car was 45 months compared to 60 months for US and European companies (Ellison *et al.*, 1995, p. 11). Clearly these shorter lead times made significant savings. So American and European car makers had to use additional mechanisms to regain their competitive edge. During the next two decades their new ideas included:

* aggressive outsourcing;
* footprint expansion and globalization;
* product variation and modularization.

These innovations moved like powerful waves through the industry. In addition to a process-driven approach as well as leaner product development, these waves affected the way automotive programmes were managed.

Evolution of programme management in the automotive industry

The automotive industry has for a long time concentrated on the mass production of relatively few and undifferentiated, more or less standardized products with relatively long lifecycles. Profits are generated during long, high-volume production periods. When Taylorism and Fordism dominated the culture, programme management was regarded as an unnecessary cost (a view still abundant in the automotive industry).

That started to change during the 1970s when global car markets became saturated and competition increased. Programme management was suddenly seen as a possibility for reducing cost and cycle times. When Japanese auto companies made their inroads into the American and European markets during the 1980s, programme management assumed more importance among major OEMs. However, with management attention in the United States and Europe shifting towards Japanese lean production ideas, programme management still did not achieve the breakthrough it did in the construction and aerospace industries. Instead, the focus on production processes became even more important, given the relevance of volume production to profitability in automotive companies.

During the late 1980s and early 1990s, competition led to developing more vehicles in parallel to bring them to market faster and at lower cost. The management of car development programmes finally had reached 'the heart of corporate strategy' (Midler and Navarre, 2004, p. 1369). As a result, more automotive companies introduced systematic, formalized product development and programme management processes. The use of programme management further improved greatly during the 1990s and then programme management began to be regarded as generating benefits by reducing overall uncertainty during product development and paving the way for lowest possible production costs.

New challenges since the 1990s included mass production of a larger number of *differentiated* products, modularization and platform strategies, customization, globalization, new ways of partnering, leadership of global suppliers and so on. Thus more advanced and customer-focused programme management had to be implemented. As a result, aspects of communications management, human resources management (HRM), supply chain management and multiprogramme management became more developed within the automotive industry as knowledge areas of the overall discipline of programme management.

Programme management applications

Programme management is applied in the automotive industry to a variety of different product developments and programmes.

Programme management with OEMs

Reading Morgan and Liker (2006), Weber (2009, pp. 1–2) and Gusig *et al.* (2010, p. 29) reveals the following programme management applications:

- *New models developed from scratch.* It is the industry standard to develop new models every five to seven years. Designing new models presents the biggest programme management challenges, with a typical programme costing between €750 million and €2 billion.
- *Derivatives: products derived from an existing base vehicle.* Consumers of derivatives should not become aware of commonalities between the base vehicle and its derivative. To achieve this, derivatives usually have new exteriors but up to 50 per cent of the parts are original and unchanged.
- *Variants.* Also derived from product platforms but, in contrast to derivatives, variants visibly build a family of cars around a model line using exterior trim and interior components carried over from the base vehicle in addition to the platform and architecture. Programme management effort depends on whether the variant was already considered as a member of a model line during the design of the base vehicle (for example, a saloon car) or whether it was added later. Each variant adds 10 to 20 per cent to the engineering hours needed to design the base vehicle.
- *Half-term model updates.* These are minor product changes made approximately halfway through the model line's life. Typical programme budgets are around €50 million.
- *Annual model changes.* Product changes required for cost reduction or quality improvement reasons are typically collected over a year and brought into production after the annual summer shutdown. The shutdown period is ideal for changing production equipment because that causes minimal disruption.

Programme management with suppliers

In principle the product and programme differentiations defined above for OEMs also apply to suppliers but the differentiation between half-term model updates ('facelifts') and annual product changes may not be so clear, depending on the degree to which a given supplier is involved in the change. In addition to full product development programmes, programme management at automotive suppliers also needs to deal with other types of programmes, such as:

- pure engineering service programmes (covering, for example, design, development, prototyping, testing or a combination of these) delivering to OEMs or higher tier suppliers with no follow-on serial production contracts;
- build-to-print programmes, where an OEM or other third party hands over a finished design to a supplier who is contracted to bring the design into serial production;
- core (in-house) programmes, which develop new standard products with new technologies towards serial production maturity, which can subsequently be used on many different supplier programmes for different OEMs;
- programmes which involve lower-tier suppliers directed by the OEM.

OEMs and suppliers also need to master the parallel management of many individual programmes. Hundreds of parallel programmes might need to be managed by suppliers, leading to what can be described as 'volume problems' in programme management.

Classical programme management for the automotive industry

It is now common practice to apply any of the following programme management methods:

- a generic, company- and product-specific as well as quality gate based product development process (PDP), which differentiates several phases and subphases;
- a generic, company- and product type-specific WBS, with hierarchical work packages that include predefined work content and expected deliverables;
- for a specific programme, definition of the 'complete vehicle characteristics', from which product specifications for OEM departments or suppliers are derived. These characteristics divide into three levels as follows;
  - level 1, customer domain. Vehicle characteristics which directly influence customers' purchase decisions;
  - level 2, functional domain. Vehicle functions and properties necessary to realize the level 1 characteristics;
  - level 3, physical prerequisites for the functional domain (Weber, 2009, p. 107);
- defining, negotiating and freezing terms and conditions in supplier contracts;
- professional requirements management for product specifications and contractual terms and conditions;
- adaptation of PDPs and WBSs to specific programme needs, including:
  - determination of a vehicle's Start of Production (SOP);
  - determination of each work package's specific work content and expected deliverables;
  - establishment and implementation of a deadlined master schedule which meets the SOP date;
  - detailed, baseline-planned lower level schedules and subschedules, following the WBS hierarchy (detailed schedule plans and the master plan are set up in a consistent manner);
  - resources and budgets allocated to each work package in line with schedule requirements;
- establishment and implementation of a programme organization. Typically, multifunctional development teams are created for product-module related work packages. Clear responsibility is given to one person in charge of each work package to deliver on time, within budget and at the required level of quality and maturity;
- continuous progress checks, including actual versus plan comparisons. Checks cover:
  - product maturity status (quality, safety, parts availability, technology readiness, product performance), for example by careful analysis of testing results;
  - schedule status;
  - cost consumption and adherence to budgets (during development);
  - serial production target cost achievement status;
  - supplier status;

Name	Date first published	Developed by	Based on
QS 9000	1988	Chrysler, Ford and General Motors, who joined forces in a Supplier Quality Requirements Task Force (SQRTF). Now replaced by ISO 16949.	OEM-specific requirements.
VDA 6.1	1991	Verband der Automobilindustrie.	ISO 9001:2008.
Advanced Product Quality Planning (APQP)	1994	Chrysler, Ford and General Motors joining forces in an automotive industry action group (AIAG).	OEM-specific requirements.
ISO/TS 16949	1999	International Automobile Task Force (IATF) and ISO Technical Committee.	QS 9000 VDA 6.1 ISO 9001

Figure 7.1 Examples of quality management tools and standards used in the automotive industry

- – problems and issues;
- – status of the overall programme business case (including impacts resulting from any changed sales volume, price, long-term agreements (LTA) for annual price reduction, exchange rates and so on), including updates of programme financial key performance indicators (KPIs);
- implementation and follow-up of actions to close gaps identified during 'actual versus plan' comparisons;
- forward-looking risk identification, assessment and prioritization, followed by the establishment and implementation of mitigation plans, where deemed necessary;
- application of the company's product and non-product change procedures. For suppliers, this results in the need for professional scope and claims management to deal with customer-induced scope changes.

Quality management standards and tools

To achieve world-class quality, standardization organizations, automotive industry associations and individual automotive companies have developed quality management standards and tools (examples are listed in Figure 7.1). When implemented, these enable an organization to identify, measure, control and improve its business processes. Quality management standards and tools cover the entire product lifecycle from design and development to production as well as product support and after sales.

Standards like QS 9000, VDA 6.1 and ISO/TS 16949 were established primarily to standardize the different OEM requirements applicable at the time for assuring supplier quality, while tools like Advanced Product Quality Planning (APQP – see Automotive Industry Action Group [AIAG], 2008a) were established in order to standardize product quality planning at the OEMs.

There are individual differences between standards and tools. Quality management standards apply a process-orientated approach. Different types of processes are distinguished, among which are *management* processes such as those applicable to product development and programme management. As OEMs have requested their suppliers to be certified according to these standards (most recently ISO/TS 16949), more formalized programme management and product development processes have at last been implemented because these were required to satisfy certification criteria. These processes are therefore usually part of any automotive company's quality management system. By contrast APQP follows a 'Plan, Do, Check, Act' cycle as follows:

- Plan: develop technology and concept;
- Do: develop and verify the product and its associated (production) processes;
- Check: validate the product and process;
- Act: improve continuously.

Many automotive companies have adjusted APQP to their specific quality planning needs. However, the underlying concept is still preserved. In other words: there is 'an industry-wide accepted structure of vehicle development' (Weber, 2009, p. 7). This is why, in the following section, the PDP as described by APQP is presented as an important example.

The APQP-based product development process

As with many other PDPs, an APQP-based PDP incorporates phases, gates, subphases and subgates. It describes which deliverables have to be generated by which department. In addition, it highlights how these deliverables need to be synchronized with the contributions made by other departments, and at which point within the overall product development logic. Gates and subgates are therefore also called 'synchro-points'. At dedicated gate reviews, product development teams have to demonstrate that they are able to converge the different departmental contributions to a consistent product development status.

Before gate reviews, deliverables are often signed-off by higher level management and/or experts of the contributing departments in charge, so that at the gate review itself there is no question about their achieved maturity level. Gates are used to initiate, approve or terminate a programme. In any case, the status of a programme, and the degree to which programme objectives have already been achieved, or are foreseeable to be achieved, are reviewed at gates.

One of the key characteristics of the automotive industry is its capability to deliver sophisticated products in very large quantities while assuring high levels of product quality and safety. This is why the aspect of meeting production process requirements (including for logistics, transportation and so on) appears at a very early stage in an APQP-based PDP: much like for product design activities. Also process-related design activities begin well before programme approval.

In addition, automotive industry PDPs require a series of prototypes for testing and process confirmation. Typically, there are two groups of prototype builds. The first group is used mainly to verify the design. Depending on the design verification test results, design changes may have to be implemented. The second prototype

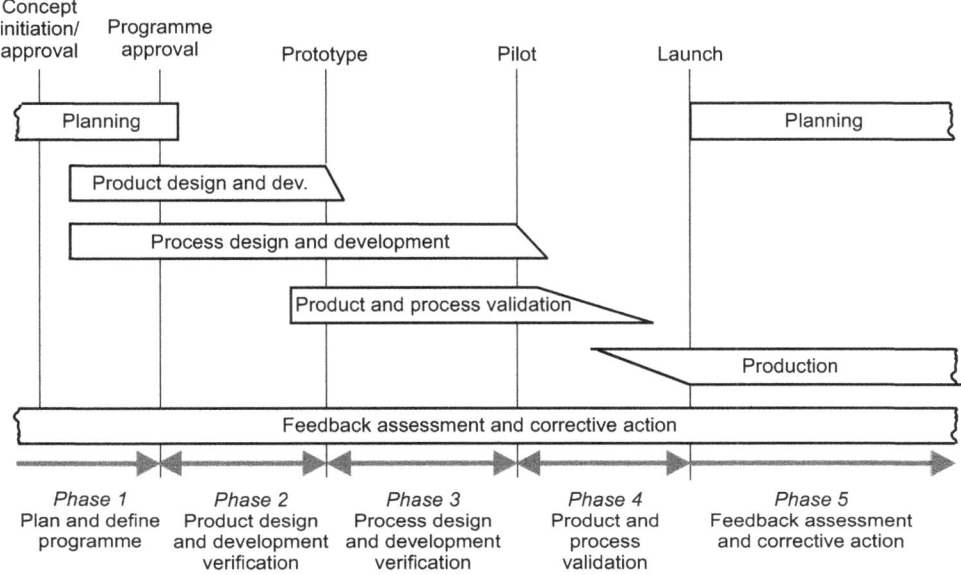

Figure 7.2 The APQP product development process

verifies successful implementation of these design changes. A company's PDP provides guidelines about the timing for building these two groups of prototypes.

APQP's PDP comprises the phases shown in Figure 7.2, four of which are described below in more detail. APQP's PDP also describes a variety of major workstreams which span across one or more phases. As Figure 7.2 shows, these phases overlap, so concurrent working is necessary.

APQP phase 1: plan and define the programme

A programme is usually planned and defined well before it is approved. It is at the point of programme approval that the 'programme clock' starts ticking for all the steps required to develop a new product until product launch (which is when serial production starts to ramp up). Because the clock has started to tick at programme approval, any remaining planning and definition activities need to end within a few weeks thereafter. Thus most planning and definition work for a programme is done before (final) programme approval. This is true not only for the planning and definition activities required by classical programme management, but also for product design and even process design activities.

For each new product development a target framework is generated which captures all the high level requirements derived from company product strategy. This serves as a reference from which it can later be evaluated whether or not a vehicle concept meets the requirements. It 'must be plausible, prioritized and its conflicts resolved' (Weber, 2009, p. 29).

All this information and much more feeds into the business plan for the programme to deliver the new product. The business plan is worked out by the programme's multifunctional development team departments. In particular these include programme management, finance, engineering, manufacturing engineering, production, quality, sales and purchasing. The business plan represents an agreement between all relevant stakeholders within the company, in particular between those stakeholders who want to sell the new product and those who need to execute the programme to make the new product a reality.

A very important element of the business plan is the 'business case' which is compiled to demonstrate the financial viability of the new programme. The programme is financially viable if certain KPIs are better than their corresponding targets (or 'hurdle rates') as defined by the company. Typical KPIs in use by automotive industry companies – either individually or in combination – include: payback period, return on sales (RoS), return on assets (RoA), internal rate of return (IRR) and net present value (NPV). It is also good practice to carry out sensitivity analysis, checking for example how the IRR might be affected by a 5 per cent change in sales price. Chapter 6 in Lock (2013) explains these methods.

At the programme approval gate, a decision is taken to approve or reject the programme, based on:

- a preliminary list of special product and process characteristics;
- the extent to which design, reliability, quality and safety goals will be met;
- a preliminary Bill of Material (BoM), describing the product structure with all its parts;
- a preliminary process flow chart;
- a product assurance plan, which translates design goals into design requirements;
- the presented business plan and business case.

The decision to proceed after programme approval is based not only on a conceptual product design but also on a process design for serial production. In other words, the approval decision also takes into account process feasibility.

In any case, programme approval represents the transition point between the more sales and marketing dominated phase 1 and the subsequent phases which are more programme execution dominated. It also sets the stage for significant cash spending, which now kicks off and ramps up quickly.

APQP phase 2: product design and development verification

At around programme approval, two highly overlapping workstreams, '*product* design and development' as well as '*process* design and development' start (see again Figure 7.2). This is because product and processes are designed and developed more or less concurrently. However a product always needs to be verified first, before verifying the processes. Hence, '*product* design and development' is somewhat in the lead compared to '*process* design and development'.

During the latter, and supported by adequate design reviews, all the classical steps are taken to convert (quality, reliability, weight, safety, cost and so on) requirements and specifications into drawings and computer aided design (CAD) files, and to verify that the design meets these requirements.

Typically, phase 2 is used to demonstrate that a product design is feasible. However, in the automotive industry there is a special emphasis on demonstrating that the design can achieve the very high production volumes. It is crucial to elaborate and prioritize product and process characteristics which require special control. Tools used for this include:

- (design) failure mode and effects analysis (DFMEA) to identify potential failure risks and their severities (described in Lock, 2013, Chapter 7);
- design for manufacturing and assembly (DFMA), a process to optimize the relationship between design function, manufacturability and ease of assembly (see AIAG, 2008b, p. 18);
- prototypes for testing purposes;
- control plan, to determine the special control methods for keeping potential severities of identified failure modes under control.

One important aspect of this phase is the release of drawings to enable the build of critical equipment, tooling, fixtures and gauges for later serial production. Lead times for manufacturing production tools differ widely and some require very early drawing releases. Thus associated drawings need to reach a sufficient level of maturity during phase 2. So design releases and the DFMEA, DFMA and control plan must be programme managed to establish requirements for new equipment, tooling, fixtures and gauges as soon as possible, to help the purchasing department to source them early.

APQP phase 3: process design and development verification

This phase focuses more on developing a manufacturing system for products of the desired quality. Prototype-based testing is again applied, which might need new prototypes. As in phase 2, prototype builds represent significant programme management challenges. Any design change needs identified from phase 2 tests must be implemented and released before building these new prototypes. Should test results from phase 3 still require the implementation of more design changes, there is now much less time available if the SOP date is to be protected. And 'as at this time a lot of the long lead-time serial manufacturing tools already have begun to be manufactured . . . [this may imply] very costly adaption of the series tools' (Weber, 2009, pp. 89–90).

Building these prototypes, rather than their use to yield test results, gives an additional opportunity to verify the serial production methods for each part and assembly step However, thanks to modern CAD systems, the actual build of a prototype can also be simulated on the computer ('virtual build') before ordering parts for the actual prototypes.

Verification activities of this phase use analytical tools which (among others) are widely used in the automotive industry. These tools also need adequate programme management and include:

- process flow chart: a schematic representation of the proposed process flow on the shopfloor;
- (process) failure mode and effects analysis (PFMEA): similar to the DFMEA mentioned above;

- pre-launch control plan, to identify potential non-conformities before future production runs;
- floor plan layout, to check that required control items can be accommodated on the shopfloor;
- process instructions, compiled for all personnel who have direct responsibility for process operations;
- measurement system analysis plan: a document detailing the steps required to analyse whether the proposed measurement system is adequately designed for the desired quality.

The programme management system must provide check-lists to ensure that deliverables are at the right level of maturity.

APQP phase 4: product and process validation

The product and the physical production processes are validated in this phase. The customer for a programme team's ultimate deliverables is the company's production plant(s). While manufacturing engineering and launch managers from these plants might have been involved from the very early programme stages, phase 4 also begins a gradual shift of programme responsibility from the programme team to the plant(s). This is normally completed some time after SOP.

Plant representatives sign off the complete production process following their comprehensive assessment of all production process steps and before kicking off production in their facilities. At the same time plants prepare for production of the first cars (or systems or components).

Phase 4 comprises two validation steps, as detailed below.

First validation step

Activities during the first step are collectively called the 'production part approval process' (PPAP). The objective is to validate that the quality of parts coming out of serial production tools and processes is as designed. For suppliers, parts are submitted to their customers where they are assessed, together with their part submission warrants (PSW) which contain all relevant information regarding specifications, design and tests.

However, before doing so, 'significant production runs' are performed. These are short period production runs at the required rate using serial production facilities, staff, processes, equipment, tools and control systems. The minimum production quantity (typically 300 shipsets for suppliers) can be exceeded at the discretion of the company. Signals from the quality measurement system should reveal whether or not the control items identified in the control plan correctly check product characteristics to the engineering specifications. This includes the validation of gauge repeatability, reproducibility and proper usage.

Before and during significant production runs, the control plan matures further until it is fit to enable serial production. Thereafter it remains a living document because further lessons learned during serial production may be incorporated to maintain product quality and safety.

Significant production runs are key among the elements in the first step for product and process validation. Other involved elements are not detailed here. Any non-conformances to the targeted quality and safety levels are recorded and correction measures taken to close them. More significant production runs may be undertaken to validate these correction measures.

Second validation step

During the second validation step 'Run@Rates' are performed. While the first validation step focuses more on the parts' quality, Run@Rates focus on the production of parts in large quantities. They are production runs to demonstrate that the production line can produce parts without problems for as long as 24 hours at the quoted production rate, and that it can still meet customer demand. The internal or external customer usually joins this validation exercise to witness and assess whether or not all product and process requirements are met.

Some OEMs also require 'capacity verification' where the production line runs more than one part and each part has its own demand. Where it is intended to assemble variants of a vehicle (or a system or subsystem of it) on the same line, these production runs also validate whether the level of variation can indeed be assembled in a robust way. This is a particular challenge because assembly station cycle times might vary from one product variant to another.

The department in charge of product quality and safety ensures that the PFMEA, process flow chart, process instructions and control plan are all consistent and that operators are trained accordingly. It also ensures that the process can make the product at the required volumes and levels of quality and safety.

For suppliers, after successful completion of both validation steps, the customer grants its approval to release the product and process for serial production. The drawing and part releases achieved at this stage now represent a set of legally binding documents.

APQP phase 5: serial production

'Launch' kicks off production of the new cars at the intended plant(s). For many OEMs, the first cars produced (or their bought-in components) might not be sold to customers. Instead, this initial production marks a pre-series subphase during which production is ramping up from low to full daily production volume. Product quality and safety must be monitored continuously. Any deviation caused by manufacturing or design needs immediate correction

For many companies, products are only intended to be sold to customers from the end of this subphase onwards (at SOP). For other companies, cars produced during ramp-up are already sold to customers and so launch and SOP happen at the same time. Whenever SOP takes place, it is around this point in time that sales and marketing activities rapidly intensify.

Some weeks or so after cars have been produced at the planned rate, and it has been demonstrated that serial production runs robustly, the responsibility for the product development programme is finally handed over to the plant(s), and the programme team is dissolved. However, before this happens, a final programme review takes place to assess the degree to which each of the objectives defined in the target framework has been achieved.

Development activities nevertheless continue after this review, as continuous improvement, yearly model changes and facelifts are introduced. Each of these represents new projects and programmes, which follow essentially the same APQP PDP described here, although at a smaller scale and while car production is going on. Product changes may even happen after the end of production, affecting spare parts for service and repair.

Managing programme risks

The automotive industry cannot claim to be the forerunner in risk management. Research and statements made by various authors (see Simister, 1994, pp. 5–8; Burn, 1994, p. 413; Patterson, 2002, p. 14; Weber, 2009, p. 85) give several reasons for this:

- There seems to have been a tendency to ignore risk management, while the industry was focusing on Japanese imported management, operational and production activities and techniques.
- The industry as a whole is not self-regulating and while it relies predominantly on government and environmentally led legislation, there was never a stipulated risk management requirement as is mandatory (for example) with government and defence contracts. It would indeed require customers driving companies to implement risk management methods, processes and tools.
- Most companies in the industry produce components for larger companies. Combined with the fact that there is no stipulated requirement from their customers to use risk management as part of their programme management procedures, risk mitigation, assuring compatibility of components and overall safety of the product or process are left to the end user.
- There is a lack of understanding of how quickly apparently minor problems can become critical if not solved fast enough.
- The risk management adverse, firefighting mentality predominant in the automotive industry leads to managers rewarding and promoting first-class firefighters, and recruiting and training successors with the same abilities.

Only slowly have the industry executives begun to discover that converting company culture from firefighting to proactive anticipation and early removal of potential issues brings about economic benefits and competitive advantage. Implementing this conversion is tricky, because risk management and its associated mitigation activities during the early product development require resources that cannot be released from the firefighting activities of earlier programmes. The fierce competitive environment of the automotive industry does not, of course, allow employing additional resources just to enable this conversion.

However, some risk mitigation concepts are inherent in the PDP. As explained above, the build of prototypes to test the design, analyse potential compatibility issues and validate production processes is common. Prototypes used for different testing purposes represent a stepped (risk mitigating) approach to product development as opposed to a 'first-time-right' concept, thus reducing risk.

Managing parallel programmes

Most automotive firms offer a variety of products. These form a company-level port-folio of products with their associated programmes. The success of an automotive company is therefore not to be judged by an individual programme, but by the returns from its portfolio over time. Similarly, the success of a model line should not be judged by the success of an individual car programme, but rather by 'the coherence and consequent long-lasting attractiveness of the general vehicle concept . . . A commonly accepted measure for the success of a vehicle concept is hence the number of units based on that general concept that could be sold over time' (Weber, 2009, p. 18).

To develop a successful stream of programmes and also to manage the use of common products across many programmes requires a higher degree of coordination than for individual programmes. Automotive companies must therefore manage many (sometimes hundreds) of programmes in parallel to secure optimum financial returns for shareholders.

It is not only the number of programmes that determines the means and ways for how so many programmes should be managed together, but also a company's strategic and financial objectives. In the automotive industry it is common to differentiate three (partially overlapping) types of management approaches to address these challenges:

- programme portfolio management: making choices about which business to acquire and which programmes to execute;
- common parts management: using parts, components, modules and so on that are common to many vehicles on different programmes;
- multiprogramme management: finding ways and means to manage a portfolio of programmes as effectively and efficiently as possible, given that resources are always constrained.

These three approaches are not necessarily applied with the same rigour across the industry. Below, they are explained in more detail.

Programme portfolio management

Programme portfolio management applies a dynamic process, whereby a company continuously makes decisions about:

- which new business opportunities should be addressed in the organizational form and context of a new programme (in which case a programme is added to the portfolio);
- which programmes in the portfolio are accelerated, de-prioritized or even terminated.

Continuous programme assessment results in a dynamic master programme list, which is the company's programme portfolio at any given point in time. Individual programmes have different priorities, but with prioritization done for the company as a whole. Then there is one clear priority setting to be adhered to by all departments. Otherwise, individual departments would tend to prioritize programmes themselves, producing conflicting priorities across the company.

Unfortunately, and despite its proven benefits, programme portfolio management is not well handled in the automotive industry, particularly among those suppliers where professional portfolio management would matter most.

Common parts management

Competition since the early 1990s has resulted in fewer and fewer OEMs offering increasingly larger product portfolios in an attempt to respond to highly different customer needs, tastes, driving conditions and legislation systems in different markets. So vehicle variability started to explode. Fortunately, the automotive industry was innovative enough to invent 'platform' and 'model line' concepts based on common parts and modularization. These allowed for more vehicle differentiation than ever before, while costs could be reduced at the same time. A breakthrough had been achieved.

A key characteristic of a module is that it is interchangeable thanks to its frozen (and hence, robust) interface with its surrounding environment. The term *platform* is used in the automotive industry for a design which defines interchangeable sets of modules connected between each other or individually to their surrounding car area. The intention of a platform design is to share common modules across a wide range of vehicles – even if they belong to different brands or sometimes different OEMs. At the same time, a platform provides a base from which maximum differentiation between brands can be generated very efficiently. For example, the so-called 'Golf platform' is shared by four different brands and 13 different models. It includes most parts of the powertrain, steering and suspension as well as parts of the lower body and interior trim (Weber, 2009, p. 5).

Automakers (notably Toyota and VW) have made tremendous progress with the introduction of modules, achieving significant cost savings. But there are some important downsides and limitations to these strategies. For example, whenever common parts fail in the field owing to quality or safety issues, the cost of recalls may be dramatic compared to a situation where few common parts are in use.

Still, the automotive industry puts forth a lot of effort to achieve the widest possible product variation to satisfy an ever-increasing customer demand for new vehicle designs, while keeping optimum efficiencies of scale and manufacturability. Finding the right product architecture during the early stages of new model development is therefore a vital activity.

Common parts management has indeed gained enormous relevance. It leads to the earlier PDP phases needing more time compared to the times required for the corresponding phases during development of variants and derivatives. It is custom among managers in many automotive companies to put the more inexperienced programme managers and other inexperienced employees on the early phases of product development (because the more experienced ones are needed for fire-fighting during downstream phases of other programmes). In contrast to this, common parts management requires that experienced employees are involved during the early concept phase. Thus implementing platform and model line strategies based on common parts and replaceable modules remains extremely challenging.

Multiprogramme management

Multiprogramme management as described here comprises resource management and product change management. Typically, multiprogramme management is supported by a PMO, but many PMOs have other duties. PMO roles and duties are described later in this chapter.

In principle, programme portfolio management enables companies to allocate their resources (in quantity and quality) to those programmes which matter most to the business. However, as the programme portfolio is dynamic, with continually changing content and prioritization, resource allocation can require significant people movements between programmes. There is a natural limit to the degree to which people can be moved around, because high team member turnover rates will slow progress. Such delays would not be acceptable in view of tight time-to-market limitations. To complicate things further, programme managers and team members commonly work on several programmes.

So, automotive industry companies face a dilemma: programme portfolio management with all its benefits can only be executed up to a certain point. Otherwise programme teams will fall apart too quickly compared to the available time-to-market, or some individuals will be expected to work on too many programmes. To keep this under control, automotive companies take the following (minimum) measures:

* use good resource management processes and tools that provide transparency on:
  - resource availability status and needs;
  - resource turnover rates;
  - succession plans for programme team members;
* determine a company-specific balance between the need for professional programme portfolio management on the one hand and acceptable people turnover rates and dedication levels on the other;
* apply effective methods to manage interchange of people between programme teams.

There are other challenges for multiprogramme management emanating from the management of common parts. Managing a single product change is difficult enough without having to consider the effects of a potential change on other programmes. But if any common part would be affected by a product change, the time, cost and quality repercussions of that change have to be analysed for all other programmes which use that part. With automotive programmes lasting for several years that can be a challenge. It could be difficult even to identify individuals who still have the specific programme knowledge required to perform these analyses and to make appropriate decisions. And what happens if other programme managers disagree with a proposed product change, because it could have detrimental consequences for their programmes (and possibly their personal annual performance objectives)?

Apart from the best IT systems, the following should be in place to manage multi-programme change processes:

- overall governance rules for escalation routes and decision authorities;
- disciplined adherence to the established change procedures;
- a mindset that puts the interest of the company above the interest for a given programme.

It remains to be seen whether the automotive industry will eventually come up with some best practices. At least for today, automotive companies are struggling to find a breakthrough for this problem.

Effects of globalization

Cars have to be available close to consumers ('build-where-you-sell' strategy). A period of liberalization in world trade emerged at the beginning of the 1990s with the collapse of communist countries. Huge investment spaces opened in many new parts of the world. It became possible to offer car products in more and more countries around the globe and to build regional market share. This was achieved by exporting cars into new regions or by assembling them in these markets (which required expansion of a company's footprint).

It was the belief 'that only full-line, global car-makers . . . will survive the transition to the new global economy' (Sturgeon and Florida, 2000, p. 44), which drove OEMs to secure their growth by entering into mergers, acquisitions and partnerships at an unprecedented level. The industry therefore also witnessed a move to further concentration which by 2007 resulted in only a dozen really independent OEMs left compared to 52 in 1964 (see Hab and Wagner, 2012, p. 3).

By the end of the Cold War in 1989, the automotive industry was already very international. But now the new spaces and trade liberalization presented an ideal opportunity to expand internationalization further towards a globalized business. Dealing with a global business introduced many new challenges for the management of programmes, including:

- greater communication distances;
- different time zones;
- working with different cultures and languages;
- different understandings of work hierarchies, leadership and respect;
- different costs of all kinds;
- different laws (intellectual property, for example);
- different quality standards;
- and much more.

Supply chain management

As a response to Japanese competition, automotive companies in the United States and Europe developed new strategies, including more aggressive outsourcing. The main driving factors for that were (and still are) increased price pressures and the strategic desire to eliminate non-core business from the OEMs' portfolios.

Over the decades, the automotive industry's value chains became producer-driven, as OEMs represented larger and larger employers, innovators and traders with enormous buying power. OEMs were able to negotiate lower prices. In addition, they were able to request cost reductions from their suppliers based on long time agreements, forcing suppliers to generate significant increases in productivity.

With more and more outsourcing, the value contribution of the OEMs dropped significantly and is today estimated to be around 25 per cent. As a result, managing and controlling a much larger supply chain became increasingly important. Hence, different programme management methods emerged for assuring procured parts' on-time availability, quality and maturity (see, for example, VDA, 2006). Although these methods provide benefits, their implementation also absorbs a considerable amount of resources for coordination within OEMs as well as suppliers.

In the globalized world, OEMs started to request from their main suppliers 'the same part, for the same price, anywhere in the world'. Only powerful suppliers could satisfy these criteria – and be both close to the OEMs' design centres as well as close to the OEMs' worldwide plants to satisfy JIT requirements. By consequence, Tier 1 suppliers were pushed towards increased consolidation and vertical integration (through mergers, acquisitions and joint-ventures) as well as geographic expansion in order to serve their customers on a global basis.

Programme governance

Since the thorough analysis of Clark *et al.* (1987) and Clark and Fujimoto (1991) (see also Cusumano and Nobeoka, 1990; Ellison *et al.*, 1995) who used a set of 29 criteria to identify the authority of a programme manager, it is common to differentiate between three types of programme managers in the automotive industry (Clarke and Fujimoto called them project managers):

- No programme manager: product development is managed entirely within functional departments and 'coordinated through the functional hierarchy, rules, procedures, and traditions. There is no . . . [programme] manager and no matrix structure' (Clark *et al.*, 1987, p. 752).
- Lightweight programme manager: work is managed within functional departments, with one programme manager in place coordinating all activities across all involved departments. The programme manager typically belongs to one of these departments. His/her authority is limited to engineering questions – that is influence beyond engineering (for example on concept creation, marketing, production aspects) and for topics outside the programme is very limited. As a result, status and level in the company's organization is not very high.
- Heavyweight programme manager: has extensive direct responsibility and authority for all aspects of the programme during the entire product development lifecycle. This includes all product- and process-related development aspects as well as upstream conceptual aspects where market information is analysed in order to develop a vehicle concept which matches demand. Occasionally, the heavyweight programme manager would be supported by

lower level project managers (to run individual work packages) or members of a PMO or both.

According to Clark *et al.* (1987, p. 753), companies primarily utilized a functional structure without a programme manager until the end of the 1950s. In an update of this research, Ellison *et al.* (1995, p. 18) concluded that during the 1990s it became more and more common to use heavier programme management types of organizations in the auto industry.

Thus, over the years, a gradual shift towards heavier programme management systems could be observed. Since then, the role of a heavyweight programme manager in the automotive industry has further evolved (from a coordinator role applying the company's standard processes for product development) to a role in charge of meeting programme objectives and making a vehicle development successful for customers and stakeholders. It has become 'an entrepreneurial job . . . with great autonomy as regards the means for achieving the target' (Midler, 1995, p. 367). The traditional 'time, cost and quality' responsibility of programme managers in the automotive industry nowadays includes a variety of additional aspects, including the following:

- being a team leader for the often globally dispersed development team, facing a degree of team member turnover;
- developing the intended product by applying the established processes for path-to-part, path-to-quality and path-to-safety;
- controlling the programme's development and target production costs as well as recoveries from customers;
- delivering the programme's business case – that is, meeting the defined KPIs;
- improving the integration of programme-related activities in the face of increasing organizational fragmentation (resulting from the need to coordinate many partners as well as hundreds of more or less vertically integrated suppliers);
- identifying an optimized product architecture, satisfying complete vehicle characteristics for an entire family of vehicles (for new model or core programmes);
- managing the product standardization/product differentiation dilemma (that is, the parts commonality between the product under development and other programmes, as well as along the supply chain);
- managing product and non-product change processes;
- achieving optimum systems integration for a given vehicle to be developed;
- increasing the quality and quantity of technical knowledge inputs.

However, an entrepreneurial role for the programme manager does not mean that contributing departments have become relatively weaker with regards to authority and influence, as this would result in other problems. After all, the departments typically own the resources and are the guardians for setting and maintaining product, process and skill-set standards, which are applicable across all programmes of a company. Clearly, future automotive programmes cannot be developed without functional expertise.

It is therefore more and more commonly understood in the automotive industry that only a fair power sharing within the matrix between the programme management authority on the one hand and the functional authority on the other ensures the best possible compromise among all the different alternatives. This is provided that

- both axes of the matrix are sufficiently strong so that the one cannot succeed without the other;
- communication between the two axes of the matrix is well developed;
- individuals working in the matrix are sufficiently competent and empowered, so that the product development team can make most decisions without the need to reaffirm with the respective home functions while possibly committing them.

The last of these is 'incompatible with the Taylorist type of organization, in which delegation is unheard of and competence is strictly divided between high-echelon experts and those who carry out the orders' (Midler, 1995, p. 372).

Required programme manager qualifications

Given the impressive list of roles and responsibilities, experience levels of programme managers in manufacturing (which includes the auto industry) seem to be relatively low compared to other industrial sectors, notably the pharmaceutical, IT and construction industries (see Patterson, 2002, p. 12). With the late arrival of programme management to the automotive industry, it is no surprise that Wirth (1994, pp. CE3.1– CE3.4) states just six years of experience for the average programme manager. It is difficult to gain programme management experience in an environment where firefighting and lean production dominate the corporate culture.

With the increase in importance of programme management for the execution of individual vehicle development programmes as well as for the parallel management of multiple programmes, it is recognized that this does not suffice. However, most midsize companies just cannot financially afford programme managers overseeing a single programme.

Beyond hiring experienced programme managers, most companies in the automotive industry make a dedicated effort to train their employees in the methods, processes and tools of programme management and product development. Thus, there is usually no specific lack of adequate training. But experience in programme management can only be gained through years of managing increasingly difficult and complex programmes. Beyond training courses, career paths for programme managers should therefore be implemented. However, according to the research done by Dworatschek *et al.* (2006), who interviewed 260 German companies from different industrial sectors (including automotive), only around 27 per cent had implemented a career path for programme managers. It can be fairly assumed that this percentage is significantly lower when looking at the automotive industry alone.

Fortunately, there is consensus in the automotive industry that programme managers need to develop skills and competencies in a wide range of areas as tabled in

Management of individual programmes
- Communications management (including stakeholder management, multicultural awareness and pitfalls of globalization.
- Cost, financial and business management.
- Management of issues, risks and opportunities (particularly in view of cultural differences).
- Requirements management.
- Scope management.
- Supplier and supply chain management.
- Team leadership and management (including agile ways of working).
- People and stakeholder management (in particular in the matrix organization).
- Time management.

Management of parallel programmes
- Change management (product and nonproduct).
- Claims management.
- Common parts management.
- Customer and contracts management.
- Resources management.

Product development
- Computer aided design.
- Product architecting.
- Product development process.
- Modularization and platform strategies.
- Quality and product safety management.
- Technical integration.

Operations management
- Operating systems.
- Shopfloor and logistics management.

Other
- Mastering the company's reference language.
- Being able to 'drumbeat' programme teams and contributors while expressing highest levels of social skills.

Figure 7.3 Skills and competencies required for programme managers in the automotive industry

Figure 7.3. In particular, the aspects of supply chain management, financial management, globalization and common parts management call for much more training as well as more opportunities to gain experience.

Today, car companies are investing much more into competence development, particularly for those employees involved in *global* programmes. However, there is the risk that more competent employees seek better job opportunities outside the company that made huge efforts to raise their competency levels. As a result, fluctuation is a constant problem in some countries with a growing gross domestic product, notably China, which makes global programmes even more challenging.

The programme management office

To support the myriad programme and multiprogramme management tasks, as well as tasks related to programme governance and programme manager qualification, many automotive companies have implemented PMOs, of which there are essentially two types:

- central company or business unit PMOs which provide support to individual programmes as members of a programme portfolio;
- individual programme PMOs which provide support to the various work packages of that programme.

German automotive PMO experts recently summarized the roles for PMOs in their industry as listed below (see GPM, 2014b).

Company central PMO

- establishment of programme methods, processes and tools;
- programme portfolio management;
- multiprogramme management;
- competence development for programme managers (including career path development);
- definition of programme management rules and role definitions;
- development of organizational blueprints (such as versions of matrix organizations);
- creation of a programme management community;
- assessment of programme management capabilities within the company, with suppliers and partners;
- to be consulted if and where programme managers are nominated or promoted;
- development of standards for virtual communication.

Business unit central PMO

- programme portfolio management;
- multiprogramme management;
- support to common parts management;
- coaching of programme managers;
- implementation of standard methods, processes and tools.

Programme-specific PMO

- programme planning, monitoring and controlling;
- application of standard methods, processes and tools;
- feedback about their usefulness to company central PMO.

Conclusion

The automotive industry produces high quality products in large volumes, so management focus for many years was on production rather than product development. Management attention went into creating and copying the mass and lean production revolutions introduced by Taylorism, Fordism, Sloanism and the Toyota Production System. The relevance of state-of-the-art programme management systems (such as those in aerospace and construction) was not recognized for a long time.

With dramatic changes in the automotive product development environment (aggressive outsourcing, globalization and modularization):

> it is obvious that a strong product development system is a crucial core competence and fundamental to the success of any consumer-driven company . . . In today's hyper-competitive market, excellence in product development is rapidly becoming more of a strategic differentiator than manufacturing capability.

In fact, it can be argued that product development will become the dominant industry competence within the next decade.

(Morgan and Liker, 2006, p. 8)

It is already apparent that 'companies enjoying exceptional growth differentiate themselves through their product development processes and capabilities' (PTC and RWTH, 2014, p. 13). Also, competitive advantage results from better management of global footprints, supply chains and partners as well as from the use of common parts and modularization principles. All the above lead to shorter times-to-market, lower cost and improved quality, but require much improved coordination across vehicle programmes, departments, companies, countries and cultures.

So the importance of programme management to the industry has increased. With enormous cost pressures resulting from market forces and the need to bring more and more models to market each year, expectations of management capabilities to run all a company's programmes successfully are rising all the time. Significant improvements have already been made with the introduction of more advanced programme management systems.

The complexities involved with automotive product development, in particular the increased level of managing product data across multiple programmes as well as a global supply base, make the application of more effective IT-based information management a top priority. Improved information management must enable concurrent working within a given programme as well as across programmes, and must always ensure accessibility to all relevant product and programme information.

It is also true that programme management in many different industry sectors (and beyond) has benefited lately from the automotive industry's experience. 'Many of today's best practices in [programme] management came out of the auto industry and its suppliers. Twenty years ago, the best practices came from aerospace, defense and construction' (Kerzner, 2005, p. 17). That is because process verification and validation (as well as common parts management) have become part of the programme management systems described and promoted by the various institutions and associations around the world.

Given the traditional industry culture of concentrating on production topics, the introduction of advanced programme management systems represents a massive cultural change for many automotive companies. After all, corporate cultures result from decades of corporate practices. As such, 'the automotive industry is still pretty much characterized by specialization, Taylorism and hierarchical thinking, instead of adjusting to the rapid changes encountered in our times' (Hab and Wagner, 2012, p. 354). It is therefore no surprise that the process of introducing and promoting programme management systems is far from easy or complete.

Much remains to be done. But it seems clear that the automotive industry will eventually be at par with other industries when it comes to programme management capabilities. Not improving those capabilities would inevitably damage competitiveness. No automotive company can afford that to happen.

Acknowledgements and disclaimer

I acknowledge the most appreciated contributions made by the following individuals: Jesse Bedolla, Kurtis Boeve, Heike Bräunlich, Marc De Winter, Jens Erasmus, Lisann Janetzky, Arnulf Kilp, Alexandra Mellin and Thomas Schläger.

Except for quotations from other sources, all observations in this chapter are my personal views and not the views of any other individual person, or of my employer or of any other company or institution mentioned in the text.

References and further reading

AIAG (2008a), *Advanced Product Quality Planning (APQP) and Control Plan: Reference Manual*, 2nd edn., Southfield, MI: Automotive Industry Action Group.

AIAG (2008b), *Potential Failure Mode and Effect Analysis (FMEA)*, 4th edn., Southfield, MI: Automotive Industry Action Group.

Bauer, V. (2013), *Das Schmarotzer-Prinzip: Wie deutsche Automobilhersteller ihre Zulieferer ausbeuten*, 2nd edn., Ebersdorf: 1-2-Buch.

Burn, G. R. (1994), 'Quality Function Deployment', in B. G. Dale (ed.),*Managing Quality*, 2nd edn., New York: Prentice-Hall, pp. 411–37.

Clark, K. B. and Fujimoto, T. (1991), *Product Development Performance: Strategy, Organization and Management in the World Auto Industry*, Boston, MA: Harvard Business School Press.

Clark, K. B., Chew, W. B. and Fujimoto, T. (1987), *Product Development in the World Auto Industry*, Brooking Papers on Economic Activity, No. 3, pp. 729–781.

Cusumano, M. A. and Nobeoka, K. (1990), *Strategy, Structure, and Performance in Product Development: Observations from the Auto Industry*, WP#3150–90, 22 April, Cambridge, MA: MIT Sloan School of Management.

Cusumano, M. A. and Nobeoka, K. (1996), 'Strategy, Structure, and Performance in Product Development, Observations from the Auto Industry', in T. Nishigushi (ed.), *Managing Product Development*, Oxford: Oxford University Press, pp. 75–120.

Dworatschek, S., Kruse, A. and Preuschoff, A. (2006), *Stand und Trend des Projektmanagements in Deutschland*, 2nd edn., Wolfsburg: Volkswagen Coaching GmbH Projekt Management and Institut for Project Management and Innovation (IPMI) of the University of Bremen.

Ellison, D. J., Clark, K. B, Fujimoto, T. and Young-suk Hyun (1995), *Product Development Performance in the Auto Industry: 1990s Update*, Toronto: International Motor Vehicle Programme, Annual Sponsors Meeting.

GPM (2014a), 'Proceedings of Automotive PM Working Group Workshop', Rastatt: GPM, 19 May (unpublished).

GPM (2014b), 'Proceedings of Automotive PM Working Group Workshop, Herzogenaurach: GPM, 15 October.

Gusig, L.-O. and Kruse, A. (2010), *Fahrzeugentwicklung im Automobilbau: Aktuelle Werkzeuge für den Praxiseinsatz*, Munich: Hanser.

Hab, G. and Wagner, R. (2012), *Projektmanagement in der Automobilindustrie: Effizientes Management von Fahrzeugprojekten entlang der Wertschöpfungskette*, Wiesbaden: Springer Gabler.

Kerzner, H. R. (2005), 'Background to Project Management', in E. G. Carayannis, K. Young Hoon and F. T. Anbari (eds.), *The Story of Managing Projects: An Interdisciplinary Approach*, Westport, CT: Praeger, pp. 10–19.

Lock, D. (2013), *Project Management*, 10th edn., Farnham: Gower.

Midler, C. (1995), 'Projectification of the Firm: The Renault Case', *Scandinavian Journal of Management*, 11(4): 363–75.

Midler, C. and Navarre, C. (2004), 'Project Management in the Automotive Industry', in P. Morris and J. K. Pinto (eds.), *The Wiley Guide to Managing Projects*, Hoboken, NJ: John Wiley, pp. 363–75.

Morgan, J. M. and Liker, J. K. (2006), *The Toyota Product Development System*, New York: Productivity Press.

Patterson, F. D. (2002), *'Project Risk Management and its Application into the Automotive Manufacturing Industry'*, PhD thesis, University of Warwick.

PTC and RWTH (2014), 'Product Development Best Practices: Automotive'. Retrieved 18 August 2014 from <http://support.ptc.com/WCMS/files/42954/en/Final_Bench_Auto.pdf>.

Simister, S. J. (1994), 'Usage and Benefits of Project Risk Analysis and Management', *International Journal of Project Management*, 12(1): 5–8.

Sturgeon, T. J. and Florida, R. (2000), *Globalization and Jobs in the Automotive Industry*, Carnegie Mellon University and Massachusetts Institute of Technology, MIT IPC Globalization Working Paper 01-003/MIT IPC Working Paper 00-012.

VDA (2006), 'Reifegrad-Absicherung für Neuteile: Methode', Messkriterien, Dokumentation, Frankfurt, November.

Weber, J. (2009), *Automotive Development Processes: Processes for Successful Customer Oriented Vehicle Development*, Heidelberg: Springer.

Wirth, I. (1994), 'The Generic Project Management Career Path', *Transactions of AACE International*, 38.

Witt, C. (2006), *'Interorganizational New Product Launch Management: An Empirical Investigation of the Automotive Industry'*, PhD thesis, St. Gallen, University of St. Gallen, Graduate School of Business Administration, Economics, Law and Social Sciences.

Chapter 8

Programme Management in the Aviation Industry

Bernhard Dietrich

After a brief introduction this chapter describes the lifecycle of a programme management case in the aviation industry from design to completion.

Characteristics of the aviation industry

The aviation industry is a highly complex service business. It has a fragmented structure of players, all of whom have a high impact on the overall service performance. The industry comprises all the functions needed to operate air transport services for passengers and cargo. These include:

- Airports (with their landside and airside services). These are local business entities that operate in a more or less monopolistic environment.
- Air traffic control. This is usually a government task, sometimes run by government agencies, sometimes incorporated as state-owned companies, or delegated to privately held companies under strict governmental surveillance.
- Airlines and their associated services such as technical aircraft maintenance, catering and so on. Airlines are usually privately held commercial business operations. Under current market conditions they are facing fierce competition which makes change programmes critical for success.

The focus of the present case study is on airlines. This does not mean that there are no programme activities in the fields of air traffic control and airports, but the sheer size of airlines makes programme management in this field a lot more complex and challenging. Airlines represent the biggest part in the air transport service chain but nowadays they generate only a moderate rate of return (see Figure 8.1).

Historically, airlines were state-owned flag carriers. Operating an airline was seen as a national task and airlines were supposed to represent a country in the world. Air traffic is globally organized in terms of governance and traffic rights, but the final decision on traffic rights is made on a national basis and by bilateral agreements. This created an economic niche for flag carriers, with less focus on profitability and a culture dominated by a bureaucratic structure and mentality. A classic flag carrier was an integrated company that handled not just aircraft operation, but also provided all services necessary for operation: technical maintenance, catering, air cargo, IT systems, crew training and so on.

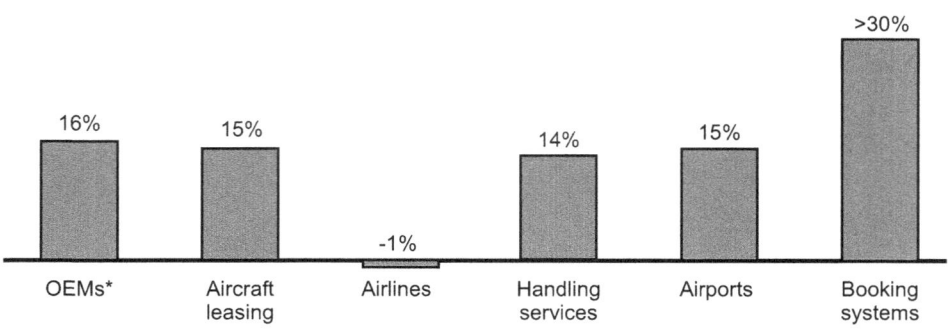

*Original equipment manufacturers

Figure 8.1 Return on capital employed averaged over five years

Recent developments

Two market developments started to change the environment, thus threatening the flag carriers' niche:

1. Market liberalization (the so-called open skies agreements) broke up the 'natural' boundaries of the flag carriers' habitat by permitting more competition from foreign airlines and allowing newcomers to enter the market. Low-cost carriers with a much more simplistic operations system and new tariff structures for pilots, crew and ground staff entered the market offering cheaper tickets based on a cost rate which was more than 20 per cent lower than that of traditional airlines. More recently, Middle East carriers, fuelled by government investments, also entered the market. They are about to create huge hubs, thus threatening European airlines' hub operations.
2. Technological developments in information management led to and supported the break-up of traditional supply chains. The sale of tickets via travel agencies is more or less a niche now. Online booking portals are dominating sales, creating transparency and thus putting air fares and yields under pressure. Standardized information flows broke up internal customer supplier relations, forcing internal suppliers (for example, catering, technical services, accounting and so on) to face external competition.

All these trends led to an overall pressure on airline profitability (see Figure 8.1).

Case study: a holistic business programme in the aviation industry

Typically there are two types of programmes – specific and holistic.

- Specific programmes are designed to address specific tasks. Typical programmes of this kind focus on growth, managing the integration of various services and infrastructure adjustments needed to enable business growth on a substantial scale, or to manage major efforts in the area of improving passenger service solutions (online services, booking, check in, onboard selling and so forth).

* Holistic business programmes target overall profit improvement or aim at business restructuring.

Quite a number of airlines failed to optimize their business in time so they had to go the hard way via insolvency, mainly because the various interest groups were not able to come to a common understanding. There is even a saying in the industry that there can be no turnaround without grounding.

This case study describes a holistic programme for an integrated carrier. The company had been quite successful during recent years; business results (profit, cash flow) were positive and the company was operating on a global scale in all of its service areas. But due to increasing competition, returns on sales were moderate, as were other key financial indicators (such as share price). This company was planning to increase its airline business by investing in new services and aircrafts, which required a higher cash flow. At that time there was a new CEO. This new CEO, along with the CFO, immediately decided to go for a programme to improve business results (especially operating profit). The rationale behind this decision was to create a major momentum to change the business under the regime of the new CEO and to tackle all issues that would lead to better operating results during the following three years.

This vision automatically had some wide-ranging consequences. Driven by the CEO of the group and with the target to improve results for the entire group, all group companies had to participate in the programme. All projects that might be expected to contribute to the improvement of the operating result had to be incorporated into the programme. And a new system to measure the financial success had to be developed and implemented.

Initial programme set-up: pre-phase

As the organization would be alert after an upcoming programme had been announced the pre-phase actions had to be short but effective. This was a decisive phase because key success factors had to be identified and addressed. The key success factors established for this programme were:

* target of the programme;
* team set-up;
* organizational set-up and anchoring;
* board commitment;
* alignment of the management team;
* governance and success measurement;
* communication – internal and external.

The timeline of the pre-phase was determined by a major kick-off event for the programme. The kick-off event is meant to inform and mobilize the management. Therefore it could not be delayed for too long after the first programme announcement and it had to be substantial. The following list describes the pre-phase management tasks.

1. Determine the leader of the programme. That person's job profile had to include experience in project/programme management, excellent leadership skills, good knowledge of the organization, a good reputation within the organization's management team and managerial experience in line functions.
2. The programme targets had to be specified, identifying key areas of improvement and generating first ideas for projects.
3. In parallel with the above, the plan for team set-up and structure had to be developed and a concept for anchoring the programme to the board and within the organization had to be created. Governance on how to run the programme and 'rules of the game' were developed.
4. Internal and external communications had to be organized.
5. A name and slogan for the programme had to be created.

The results of these tasks fed into the kick-off event, for which an appropriate structure was developed. That event had to be prepared.

Specific and concrete steps

According to the steps outlined above, the following concrete measures were implemented.

Target

The prime overall target of the programme was to achieve an improvement of €1.5 billion by 2015. This target was calculated on the basis of the additional cash flow required to finance future expenses for investments and pensions. Baseline was the company's result in 2011, and the target result was calculated for 2015.

In order to further operationalize the target and make it more concrete it was broken down into individual targets for each business unit. The breakdown process was carried out in a transparent and generally applicable way. Best and worst performances in the past, benchmarks from industry peers and reasonable target corridors were all taken into account. The final targets were determined by the management of the respective business units and the board.

Leadership

The board decided on a dual leadership for the programme and thus two leaders were chosen. One of these was a senior manager from the sales and marketing. The other was a younger manager from the finance department. These choices from different departments avoided direct competition between them. Although they differed in age and business experience, both leaders had excellent knowledge of the group's organization and management. Dual leadership meant that both heads were treated equally. Both attended all board meetings and other company events that were important for decisions.

This dual leadership had several advantages for the programme and the team:

- The different business backgrounds and skill sets turned out to be important assets for the management of the programme.
- Leadership presence in committees and steering boards could be established more easily.
- Improved team access to know-how and cross-check discussions ensured a high quality of decision-making and planning.

Team set-up

Apart from the two leaders, three more managers were directly assigned to the programme. Additionally, all of the largest business units were asked to send experienced delegates to the programme team. The team was completed by consultants from the company's in-house consultancy and initially was also supported by several external consultants. The total team comprised up to 16 people.

The rationale behind this heterogeneous team structure was to cover the necessary expertise for all business units and functional skills in communication, controlling, strategy and project management. It also fostered the creation of a platform for exchange of know-how and different viewpoints.

Communication

To promote a programme and to make people inside and outside the company aware of it, a name and a slogan were required. The organization needed an icon to refer to when it came to topics, projects and activities. The name of the programme had to reflect the basic orientation of the areas to be tackled:

- revenue, market and products;
- synergies and shared services;
- material and cost efficiency;
- organization and processes;
- implementation.

The name that was chosen comprised and underlined the programme's holistic approach and vision. Additionally, an escorting slogan was coined to emphasize the need for change and to reflect the change orientation of the programme. It indicated the intention to start a process of change, and it gave a clear orientation with regard to outcome and performance.

Programme management

Organization, roles and processes

The overall organization of the programme is illustrated in Figure 8.2. The group's programme office (programme management group or GPO) was in a direct reporting

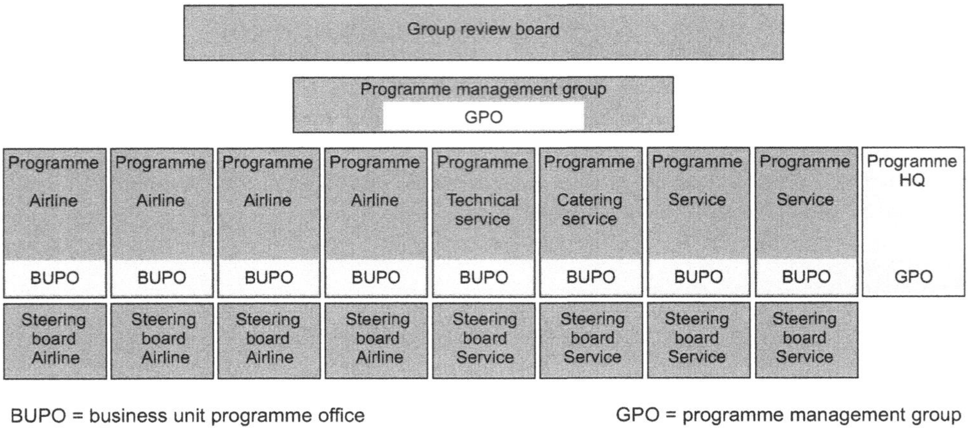

Group review board								
Programme management group								
GPO								

Programme	Programme	Programme	Programme	Programme	Programme	Programme	Programme	Programme HQ
Airline	Airline	Airline	Airline	Technical service	Catering service	Service	Service	
BUPO	BUPO	BUPO	BUPO	BUPO	BUPO	BUPO	BUPO	GPO
Steering board Airline	Steering board Airline	Steering board Airline	Steering board Airline	Steering board Service	Steering board Service	Steering board Service	Steering board Service	

BUPO = business unit programme office   GPO = programme management group

Figure 8.2 Overall programme organization

line to the group s CEO. Additionally, the GPO reported to a group review board for all its programme and project activities.

This structure was mirrored in the business units. All business unit programme offices (BUPOs) were reporting to their respective steering boards. The direct reporting lines of the BUPOs were either the CEO or the CFO of the respective business units. The BUPOs had a dotted reporting line to the GPO, which was also represented in the steering board of the business unit.

The GPO had multiple roles. It served as the overall responsible manager of the programme, but also as the responsible project manager for specific projects. It also initiated new projects. The GPO was responsible for all programme communication and any reporting to the group's board. It set up the targets for improvement for the business units in accordance with corporate controlling. And it supported and coached the BUPOs.

The BUPO's roles were similar with respect to their corresponding business units. They broke down the targets in the business unit areas and departments. They initiated and managed projects, and made sure that ideas and projects were generated and implemented. They gave support to the GPO in communication and controlling. They also made sure that improvement targets were reflected in the business units' budgets.

Regular bi-weekly *jour fixe* meetings of all GPO and BUPO managers served as the platform for joint steering of the programme, for resolving conflicts, monitoring the progress of important projects and exchanging know-how and lessons learned. The GPO shared power with the BUPOs when it came to business unit programme issues, but strictly followed the 'Highlander Principle' ('there can only be one') when it came to rules and governance. This ensured a streamlined programme management throughout the entire group.

The GPO was:

- target-orientated – to achieve the improvement goals;
- pragmatic – to avoid pointless discussions on theoretical issues;

- fair and open – to foster contributions and engagement of all parties;
- trustworthy – to encourage and protect critical voices;
- straight – to address critical issues on all levels.

Rules of governance

The key elements of the governance rules were how to measure the results of the projects and how to handle monitoring and controlling.

Rule 1

The first rule was that, to be relevant for the programme, a measure had to lead to a substantial improvement impact on the operational result compared to the baseline of 2011. This meant that:

- one-time effects and avoided cost increases were not valid and did not count for the programme's target;
- all measures had to lead to an improvement compared to the baseline of 2011; improvements against budget were not valid;
- the impact had to be measurable;
- all other projects were excluded;
- cost reduction had to be real; a reduction of unit costs by increasing the number of units was not accepted;
- revenue increases by an extension of production capacity or driven by exogenous market effects also did not count.

The GPO scrutinized all measures and projects for programme compliance.

Rule 2

The second rule was that all measures had to be registered and monitored using a unique and dedicated programme management tool, as follows:

- The tool had a strict structure for capturing measures and projects and was able to grant individual access and user rights to different user groups.
- All business units' organizational cost centre structures were laid out in the tool, allowing all measures to be assigned to the level where profit was impacted. Additionally, all measures had to be characterized according to project type (sales, cost, procurement, structure and so on).
- A simplified profit and loss structure allowed a distinction between revenue and various cost items (such as material, labour, fees and so forth). Additional key performance indicators for employee capacity and fuel consumption were used for specific reports.
- All measures had to follow the same logic to show the current and planned status. The logic comprised six milestones. These signified boundaries between five project life phases. The milestone were numbered from D10 (project registered)

Degree of implementation

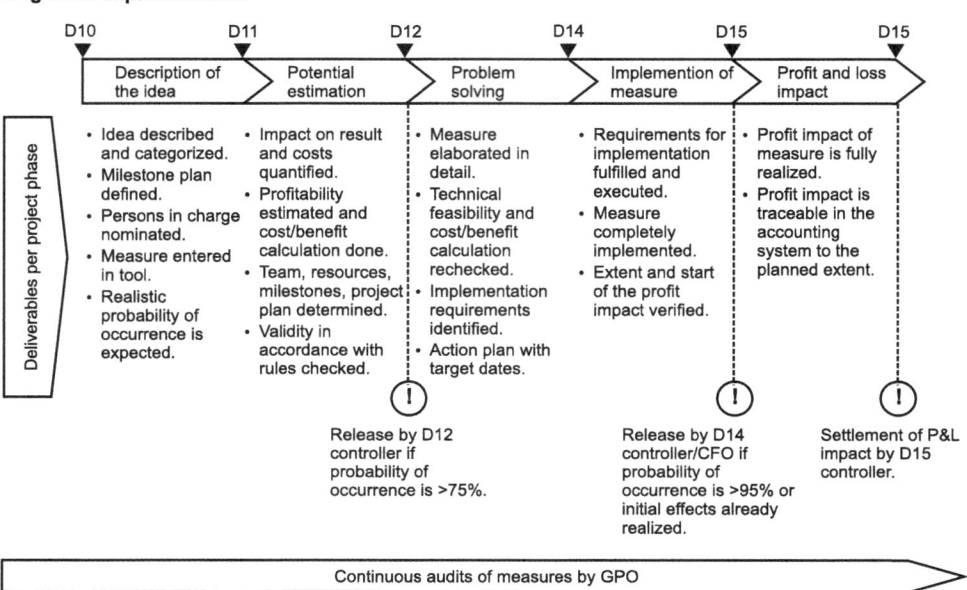

Figure 8.3 Overview of programme phases and status

to D15 (project closed). This is illustrated in Figure 8.3. The phases between these milestones were as listed below:

Phase 1 – description;
Phase 2 – evaluation;
Phase 3 – problem solution;
Phase 4 – implementation;
Phase 5 – the financial impact.

- All measureable parameters (schedule and financial data) had to be planned, forecast and captured as actual data.

The respective project manager was responsible for registering the project and for maintaining and updating the data (description, attachments, schedule and financial impact). He could also set the achievement status for a project phase. Approval for completion of the evaluation, implementation and financial impact phases had to be granted by dedicated controllers of the business unit. This assured high quality of data regarding the financial impact of the projects with respect to planned volume, forecast volume and actual result.

Project types

With the focus on improving operating profit, all kinds of activities could be part of the programme, thus spanning a wide range and a heterogeneous set of projects as follows:

- from strategic projects to incremental projects;
- from total value chain projects to single process step projects;
- from new business projects to market exit projects;
- from single to multifunctional projects;
- from a small to a large volume and impact;
- from easy-to-measure projects to projects with overlapping and/or indirect effects.

All these various types of projects with extreme variations in profit impact value, ranging from just several thousands to several millions of euros, had to be integrated into the programme and managed according to the governance rules. Three factors ensured the successful handling of this task:

1. A central core programme management office (GPO).
2. Decentralized and business unit-specific programme management cells (BUPCs).
3. A standardized programme management tool with a topic-orientated organization structure.

This approach gave a tremendous momentum for the programme. The ability to break down the overall target into business areas and cost centres, and to allocate measures and projects with their impact accordingly, made it possible to assign a relevant value even to small projects. The tool's structure required the allocation of all projects to areas/cost centres and functions (such as sales and procurement) and thus created a double responsibility for success.

Purely internal projects of single business units (such as engine overhaul optimization and waste reduction in catering) were managed and controlled by the business units themselves. Overlapping issues, such as airline-to-services (like aircraft maintenance), airline-to-airline (such as network planning) and group-wide issues (like accounting) were addressed to the GPO (see Figure 8.4). The GPO:

- structured the basic project approach (project manager, team, steering board);
- coordinated the project kick-off;
- participated in controlling the project through attendance on the steering board.

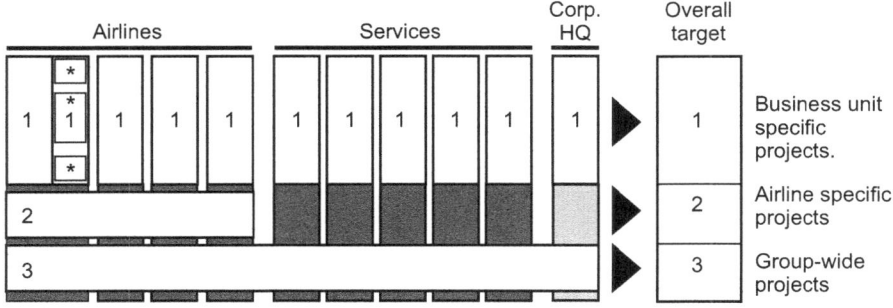

* Including small operational platforms.

Figure 8.4 Overview of project types

Whenever possible, these projects were run by functional and operational managers (such as lean managers and product managers) close to the relevant business to ensure maximum involvement of the responsible stakeholders. In cases where this role was missing or unclear, the GPO itself assumed the project management role to drive the initiative and manage the project. In some cases the result of this process was that new management roles were defined and implemented.

Steering and controlling

The important tasks in controlling the programme's progress and success were to check all measures for compliance, to ensure data quality and to observe project progress (see Figure 8.5). The key reporting task was to create monthly reports and to integrate them into business reporting. The core instrument for controlling was the programme tool, in which all measures were captured and reported. All users were trained regarding the programme's governance and rules, as well as how to use the tool.

Fundamental project data quality could be ensured by integrating all line and functional controllers into the project governance process. Their task was to approve project achievements for:

- business plan and impact evaluation (D12);
- successful implementation and impact forecast (D14);
- financial impact realized (D15).

Additionally, the BUPOs made reports and carried out quality checks within their business units. Final programme approval was granted by the GPO.

The following two types of project audits were conducted by the GPO on a regular basis:

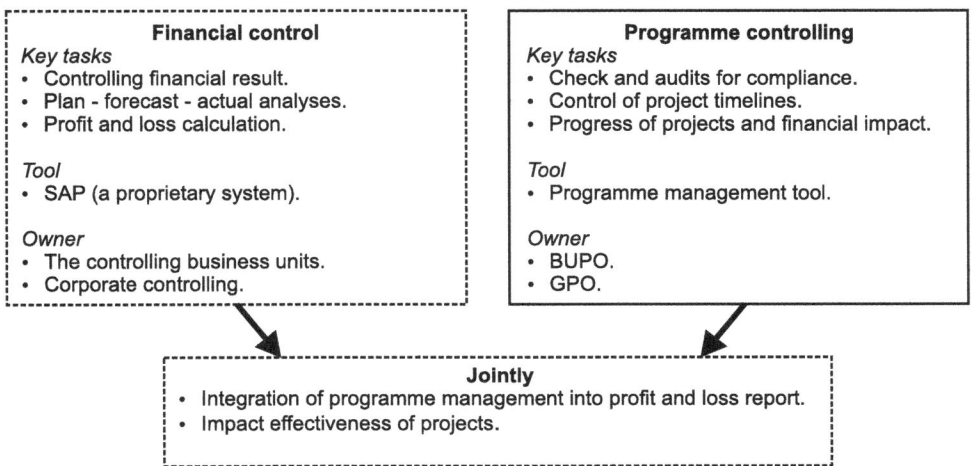

Figure 8.5 Controlling the programme

1. Top ten measures audit. Part of the monthly reporting was a 'traffic light report' on the top ten projects in a selected area. The report showed the project status, its actual and forecast financial impact and (in traffic light colours) the current financial impact and schedule against budget and plan. The topic of these top ten projects was chosen on a monthly basis (sales, structural measures, procurement, processes and costs).
2. General audit. Once a year the measurement data of each business unit were audited. Audits focused on large projects above a certain threshold (depending on the business unit's size) and on projects for which precise measurement was challenging (primarily in the area of sales).

Auditing was carried out in collaboration with the BUPO, the business unit's controlling department and the responsible project manager.

The programme's reporting process was aligned with the general business reporting process. The programme's monthly reports showed:

*   the current status of the overall project pipeline;
*   the current actual improvements achieved;
*   a forecast for the upcoming months until the end of the year and of the next year (see Figure 8.6);

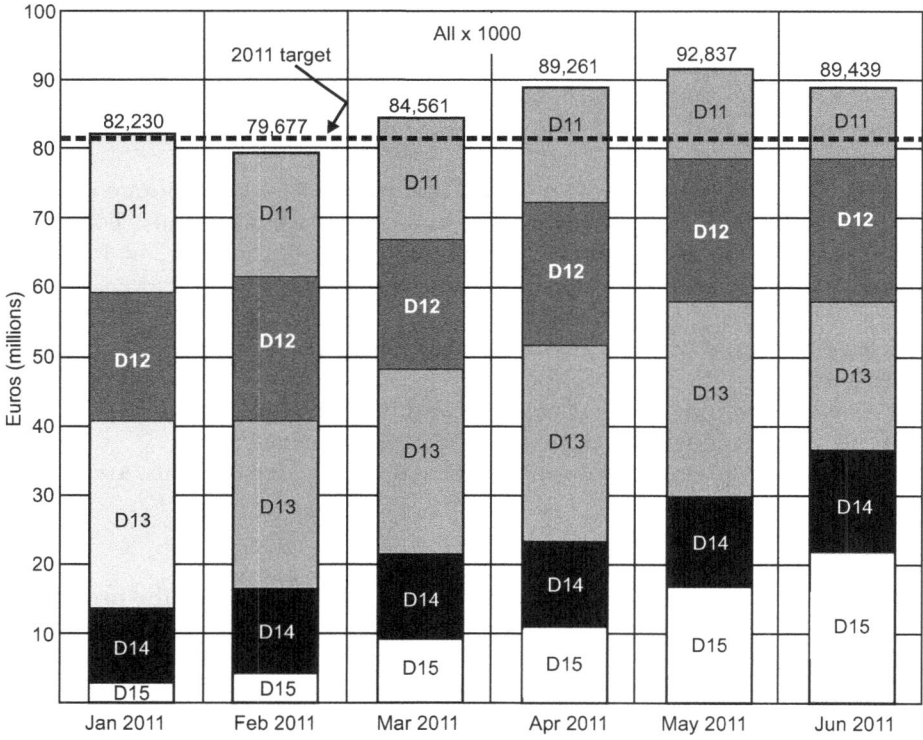

Figure 8.6 Format of monthly development forecasts

- relation to target (degree of fulfilment and/or gap);
- risks (project progress, pipeline meltdown).

Integration of the programme's actual and expected financial impact provided an overview of the current status and an outlook on the group's result. Linking the achieved and planned improvements to the business units increased the quality of forecasting and helped to identify risks. The ability to analyse easily each business unit's project portfolio regarding type of projects and expected date of effectiveness allowed early evaluation of the unit's progress against target achievement.

If the programme portfolio was dominated by revenue-orientated projects, the risk of not achieving the target was high, because market effectiveness and success are highly exogenous and difficult to predict. Units with high overhead costs were expected to present a substantial amount of cost- or process-related types of projects. In this respect the results of portfolio transparency and management provided a valuable input for strategy sessions and budget planning.

Communication

Effective communication is critical for successful programme management from start to finish. One of the essential functions of communication is to keep all employees informed on the progress of the programme and its achievements.

A meeting of all top managers provided the initial impetus, so that the managers were informed and mobilized. The board members collectively presented the rationale for the programme. The designated programme managers presented the structure and the target of the programme. These managers announced the next steps and communicated immediately following tasks for all business units (the first 'to-do' lists).

Communications were driven by the GPO and were linked to corporate communications. According to the programme's overall organization structure, communication managers of all business units were linked to the programme. The following formats were used for internal and external communications:

- articles on selected projects and the overall programme status in the in-house magazine;
- video statements and conferences with board members;
- monthly status and outlook reports for the general management;
- presentations by programme team members for single departments/areas upon request;
- posters of the programme;
- awards for the best-performing projects;
- presentations and question-and-answer sessions with members of the press.

However, communications are determined not only by what is *said*, but also by what is *done*. In this context, the GPO acted as forerunner for all change processes. It demonstrated authenticity of results and fairness to all participants in the processes of change and project management.

Demonstrating respect and appreciation of the project teams is another important aspect of communications. Thus, awards were tendered for the best projects in the key categories of the programme. The award ceremony was turned into a big event, attended by all board members and the managers of the winning teams.

Results of the case study programme

The initiation of the programme, its organization and governance had already triggered a change process. The holistic approach, with programme management cells in each business unit, with the leaders reporting directly to a CEO or CFO, and a governance that assigned responsibility to all line managers, functional managers and controllers created a massive momentum and engaged people on all levels.

One of the most important aspects of the programme was the strict orientation on profit improvement. A new and very efficient attitude towards project management was created by:

- forcing all projects to demonstrate – from the beginning – their impact on improving the operational result;
- defining project completion by the point when the desired financial impact had been realized. Being part of this type of project management as a line manager, functional manager or controller was a challenge because projects became more transparent. Projects became a part of daily business and thus responsibility for projects had to be taken more seriously.

In many cases, line managers and functional managers were forced to leave their departmental 'silo thinking' behind. The question of how a project should be classified had to be answered in a new way. For example, should it be classed as a line project or as a procurement project? In that example it was defined as a procurement project in or for a department. Thinking had to change from 'my project' to 'our project'.

Controllers had to learn that many projects could only provide a best guess regarding the financial outcome. The more complex a project is, the harder it is to calculate the effects. Instead of forcing project managers to produce 100 per cent accurate financial figures right from the start, some vagueness (with a 20 per cent meltdown ratio) had to be accepted.

Managers had to learn that it is the robustness of a project portfolio fed by a constant flow of good ideas and balanced by a wide variety of different measures that guarantees the overall success.

The reporting of the programme's impact in the context of a business result automatically turned the management focus to the effects of economic headwinds – external effects with a negative impact on profit. Putting headwinds into a stronger and more structured focus raised new questions on how to tackle the overall economic situation, which in turn led to new ideas and projects.

Self-mastery

To make a programme successful requires 'self-mastery'. This means the GPO has to have the discipline to change its course and methods if necessary.

Over time, the programme had to undergo several fundamental changes. The first need for change came after a couple of months when the team realized that sticking to the fixed baseline of 2011 as the basis for all improvement effects would create extra work. That made it difficult to calculate effects and feed data directly into reports of business results. Sticking to that kind of baseline would have jeopardized the programme's acceptance in the organization, because reporting would have been tailored to the programme's needs instead of the business's needs.

So the GPO changed the governance to a dynamic baseline. Improvements were subsequently compared directly with the past year on a month-by-month basis. With this modification the programme actually created a new methodology for business controlling. It was then interesting to see that top managers needed more convincing than project managers (who often instinctively filled in their data in the new way because that appeared much more logical to them).

Shortly after this modification the business units requested another change. They asked to open up the tool for other, 'non-programme'-related projects and measures as well. Cost avoidance projects in procurement (such as beating inflation) and also one-time effects could now be managed as proper projects by the business units. Thus contribution to profitability could be monitored.

With a high degree of synergy for the organization in the use of one process and one tool for managing and monitoring projects, the GPO decided to fulfil the change request and provide the additional feature for managing 'non-programme' relevant measures in the same tool and by the same process.

Outlook and conclusion

When a programme comes to the end of its lifespan, the question 'what comes next?' naturally arises. A programme with a focused goal (for example, the design and implementation of a major software solution) will end after going live. Then maintenance will pass to a regular department. For a business-wide holistic programme there are basically two options:

1. The 'ballistic' approach'. This means that the programme will be completed and its office will be closed. The managers and the team will go back to their former or other jobs. In time a new programme with similar or slightly modified goals will be launched, as required by changing internal or external circumstances.
2. The 'orbital' approach. The orbital approach makes use of the momentum achieved by the programme and uses it to reach escape velocity so that a permanent 'vessel' of business change activities will be sent into orbit. It will make use of all the governance and change process achievements reached by the programme. This vessel can be anchored in a formal department and act as a driver for new initiatives for change and keep monitoring business change.

In this case study, the current idea and intention of the group's board is to continue the programme's mission. It is planned to keep the structure of the programme office as a vessel for managing future efficiency initiatives, using the now-existing infrastructure and processes.

Owing to quite a lot of economic headwinds (including massive yield decline, slower than expected market recovery in Europe and Japan) the company is not likely to match its envisaged operational result target for the end of the programme. Nevertheless, the programme was quite a success. It developed and implemented more than 4,000 projects and created a profit improvement impact of more than €2 billion.

Chapter 9

Programme Management in Construction and Engineering

José Reyes

Construction and engineering programmes (C&E programmes) are often large undertakings that can have strategic objectives which give rise to changes in organizations, legal frameworks and people's ways of living. Entire communities can be affected. Some C&E programmes are aligned to government policies or national needs and can be influenced by requirements from international agencies. National and international C&E programmes can even deliver infrastructures or other facilities that strengthen the prestige and sovereign power of the host state.

Introduction

C&E programme outcomes are usually structures, infrastructures or other capital facilities which are expected to have a long life. They often require considerable investment, and so tend to be linked to periods of good economic growth. Every C&E programme should be documented by a business model, followed by a plan setting out the steps needed to attain the expected strategic and economic objectives.

A typical strategic plan will contain a set of main objectives that are delivered by initiatives. These initiatives may involve more than one C&E programme, each of which will have a number of constituent projects. Because a C&E programme can result in a high level of impact on national or organizational strategic objectives it is particularly important to expect a master plan that defines the scheme and its required outcomes.

C&E programmes require a project management approach that provides all managers with proven tools and processes, such as schedule management, cost estimating, document controls, change management, risk management, cash flow management and so on. For these reasons and to facilitate effective interphase management, coordination and partnering, as well as delivering common design, control and construction management, the organization will need a programme/project management office (PMO). There must be logical lines of authority and delegation, under a competent programme director who reports to the chief executive or similar official at the head of the organization

Definitions and characteristics of C&E programmes

It is important to clarify the concepts around infrastructures and C&E programme management. We have to understand the relationships within a framework of linked activities that tend to react increasingly in a synergistic manner. Commonly, an infrastructure is considered as a set of engineering structures or other facilities with the expectancy of a long life, often with high public visibility. In addition to providing productive services, the outcome of a C&E programme can often support political, social and personal needs.

There is an acknowledged relationship between C&E programmes, development and economic growth because C&E initiatives can clearly have a direct impact on the productivity and competiveness of a country or region. Most services cannot be provided without supporting infrastructures and those infrastructures will inevitably have been provided by one or more C&E programmes. We can thus conclude that the provision of services requires adequate development of the supporting infrastructure, and that can only be achieved by effective management of the relevant C&E programmes.

When considering C&E programmes and projects it is important to address the impact to the relevant service or cluster of services. Most programmes are aligned to strategic objectives that will, in many cases, incorporate changes in organizations, legal frameworks and ways of living. This is why C&E programmes are generally classified by the following characteristics:

- purpose;
- economic development;
- social development;
- environmental protection;
- access to information and knowledge.

In many cases, we can also find subgroup classifications that are used arbitrarily for geographic areas (for example: urban, intercity and international).

Different C&E programmes can also be linked in close relationship with each other. For example, a transportation programme and a telecommunications programme can simultaneously support urban, intercity and international traffic. On the other hand, many C&E programmes can by themselves simultaneously achieve economic, political and social objectives.

In relation to economic development, C&E programmes include transport infrastructure, energy and communications networks as well as water supply and sanitation. Among those related to social development may be mentioned hospitals, schools, and again, the networks of water supply and sanitation. Social impacts can be linked to programmes such as:

- protection of the environment through parks and nature reserves;
- ecotourism circuits;
- infrastructures such as cable TV networks, relay stations and networks providing Internet services and so on that enable access to information, knowledge and learning.

Relevance of C&E programmes

The efficient provision of C&E programmes is one of the most important aspects of national development policies, particularly in countries expecting growth.

Inadequate or inefficient infrastructure is a major obstacle to implementing effective development policies and achieving economic growth rates that exceed international averages. Countries need to expand and upgrade their basic infrastructures according to international technology standards, achieve maximum levels of national coverage and effectively meet the needs of infrastructure service operators and people. All these needs can be delivered by C&E programmes.

C&E programmes are central to the integration of economic and territorial systems of a country, enabling transactions within and outside national borders. Thus, such strategic initiatives are the backbone of the economic structure of the countries and their markets as well as the specific mechanisms of articulation of national economies to the global economy. Networks such as electrical power distribution, safe drinking water and sanitation are central to the integration of economic and territorial systems of any country.

The importance of investment in C&E programmes for economic growth has also been the focus of debate among sociologists, planners and researchers. Controversies in the literature and references highlight the complexity of the relationship between C&E programmes and growth.

Role of government in C&E programmes

Government policies regarding C&E programmes often respond to market trends or requirements from international agencies. Efforts intended to solve their problems and needs are frequently influenced by political strategies and interests. The economic sector can be forced to look at the roles of the private sector in public sector investment. That can affect or force revision of the quality of regulation, and legal frameworks of institutions looking for effectiveness of infrastructure programmes and efficiency of the deliverables.

Good practice in C&E programme management allows efficient provision of infrastructure services, which is the vehicle for territorial, economic and social cohesion because these services:

- integrate and articulate all elements of the territory, making it accessible from the outside;
- allow their residents to connect to the environment;
- provide basic services which foster production that should improve the conditions and quality of life of people.

When a government implements a C&E programme to provide infrastructure, that can stimulate private investment and the provision of capital. That facilitates economic and social development.

I have worked for more than 30 years in government agencies as project/programme director (Panama Canal Authority) and have seen how C&E programmes are essential to strengthen the exercise of the sovereign power of the state. No government exercise can execute the legitimate power of public pressure to comply with the law and the development and implementation of public policy in the absence of

C&E programmes. Failure to provide adequate and efficient infrastructure carries the risk of disintegration of the territory and the state.

C&E programmes can be cornerstones of strategic implementation for organizations, regions and countries. Infrastructures delivered by C&E programmes enable internal social integration and substantial improvements in the quality of life of people. Clearly access by people to infrastructure services can satisfy basic needs to a large extent and improve the quality of life for those in the region.

[Editorial comment: In democratic nations, project and programme managers of government-sponsored or publicly funded initiatives are always aware that a change of elected government can cause C&E programmes to be changed or even cancelled for political reasons. That can happen even to work in progress, causing waste of capital and job losses. That can be a powerful demotivator for managers and participating organizations. DL]

Governance and organization of C&E programmes

Most C&E programmes are based in engineering applications which will require all managers to apply the proven tools of good construction and engineering project management, including tools and processes such as:

- clear initial project definition;
- an approved business plan;
- work breakdown structures;
- cost estimates and budgets;
- task and resource scheduling;
- cost and schedule management;
- effective procurement procedures;
- document controls;
- control of modifications and changes;
- quality management;
- health and safety policies and procedures;
- management to prevent unwanted or prohibited effects on the environment;
- contract administration.

Information and communication are critical for C&E programmes. These typically require multiple contracts, many of which have interdependent start and end dates and have to be designed and executed within an all-embracing programme schedule. An effective programme management information system is needed to maintain control and to integrate all the constituent projects and activities. The organization must have a PMO (project/programme management office) with the proper delegation of authority to a competent programme director.

Figure 9.1 outlines a typical C&E programme organization.

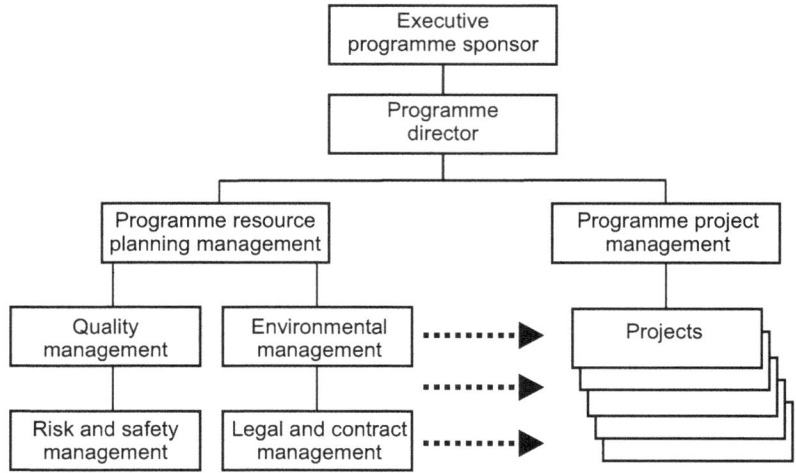

Figure 9.1 Typical organization of a construction and engineering programme

Organization and key roles

The programme director clearly has a key role in any C&E programme and should report to the organization's chief executive. The overall responsibilities could include, for example:

- helping the organization to develop an integrated programme management plan;
- assisting in developing terms of references for contractors;
- providing guidance in programme/project controls for infrastructures;
- reviewing programme estimates and milestone schedules;
- serving as a mentor to the organization in programme management;
- assisting the organization in developing a safety programme for infrastructure programmes;
- providing guidance for quality assurance and quality control;
- advising in communication and stakeholder management and issues;
- following up in environmental plans and programme implementation;
- overseeing the work of project management teams assigned to the projects and activities of the programme;
- reviewing the programme risk register and following up mitigation measures.

The programme director oversees the work of a team of project managers with responsibilities for:

- execution of projects on time and within budget;
- establishing and maintaining relationships with the programme management office;
- recruiting project teams;
- verifying cost and scheduling project performance according to the qualitative and quantitative criteria.

In addition, the programme director should be assisted by a resource planning and programme control team that should manage funding, scheduling, staffing management and control for the programme. This team will supervise risks, safety, legal, environmental monitoring and public relation staffs through designated officials.

An environmental monitoring official should provide technical services to achieve the organizational, country or regional environmental requirements. This official should develop environmental compliance, ecological compensation, monitoring and inspection of documents, reports, reforestation plans and contract sections. It is common that this scope of the work will also include stakeholder management to ensure effective communication and documentation services. One important responsibility for this officer will be developing a communications plan describing public relations, media training and information technology.

The programme safety officer will establish safety plans for the project teams by developing site-specific safety plans and building relationships with the organization and contractors' project managers.

The programme's control officer will develop and integrate technology systems to enable programme and project baseline management and performance status reporting. This officer will also collaborate with the organization financial office for funds management and accounting to establish standard practices and procedures tools.

The legal officer will advise in all infrastructure programme business matters, focusing on contracts and procurements. In addition this officer will coordinate stakeholder communications regarding the programme's legal issues (both within the organization and with third parties). While providing assistance to contracting officers, the legal officer will be responsible for reviewing all contracts and will participate in all changes and claims negotiations, as well as providing support for all programme/project manager-contractors throughout the infrastructure programme.

A risk officer will implement the programme risk management plan and collaborate with programme and project management to identify risks events and evaluate and mitigate such events.

In the event that the infrastructure programme has identified the need to include design/bid/build projects, it might be necessary to incorporate an engineering design group to provide technical solutions. However, the common practice is to outsource this service, unless proprietary and confidentiality issues are part of the works.

Summary of best practices in C&E programmes

So far I have not mentioned the culture that can and should develop in a programme management organization. Indeed, it might be thought that there is no 'culture' related to programme management.

But the fact is that both organization structure and culture are needed, especially in the field of engineering. A C&E programme management culture can develop in an organization if all key players (portfolio, programme and project managers) are clear about the link between the organization business model, the strategic plan and the master plan for implementation.

Tools and processes

A C&E programme management approach should be to provide all parties with proven tools and processes, including cost and schedule management, cost estimating, document controls and change management strategies. All these contribute to facilitating effective management, coordination and completion of the strategic initiatives of an organization to fulfil its mission.

A C&E programme requires multiple projects and contracts. These projects and contracts will be spread over different periods, but they are all interdependent and have to be planned, designed and constructed to fit within the overall timescale. An effective C&E programme management system is needed across all organizations to maintain control at this programme schedule level. All the tasks and project activities have to be integrated within the programme's schedule.

Five principal management elements

I believe that there are five main management elements to consider in order to have a successful outcome for C&E programmes as follows:

1. Have or develop a master plan that will identify those elements of capital investment needed to fulfil the business model.
2. Install one or more high performance teams (in the programme management office) to ensure good programme management.
3. Create a robust method to guarantee the quality of the work.
4. Guarantee completion of the functional elements of the deliverables.
5. Manage contextual requirements related to the environmental and social impacts of the programme.

See Figure 9.2.

Developing and following a master plan

Every C&E programme should be part of a hierarchically arranged structure that starts with the business model, followed by a strategic plan that sets out the way in which to implement that business model. The strategic plan will contain a set of main objectives that are delivered by initiatives. Some of these initiatives will be infrastructure programmes and projects. However, when an infrastructure programme is identified it is necessary to develop a master plan. That master plan will contain the scheme or concept for achieving the particular strategic objective.

A master plan is a flexible, coherent and comprehensive document designed to implement the mission and the vision of an organization over a period of time (called the horizon). The master plan should be read and understood as a living document. It provides a reference for the upper management and programme and portfolio managers. It should set out a comprehensive approach to management and a guideline for operations, rather than being an inflexible thesis. It is packed with options, phases and investment programmes. Particularly for specially infrastructure projects, the plan should be written in conceptual and feasibility form, thus allowing alternatives to be decided in its final design stage according to the most appropriate method or technology at the time.

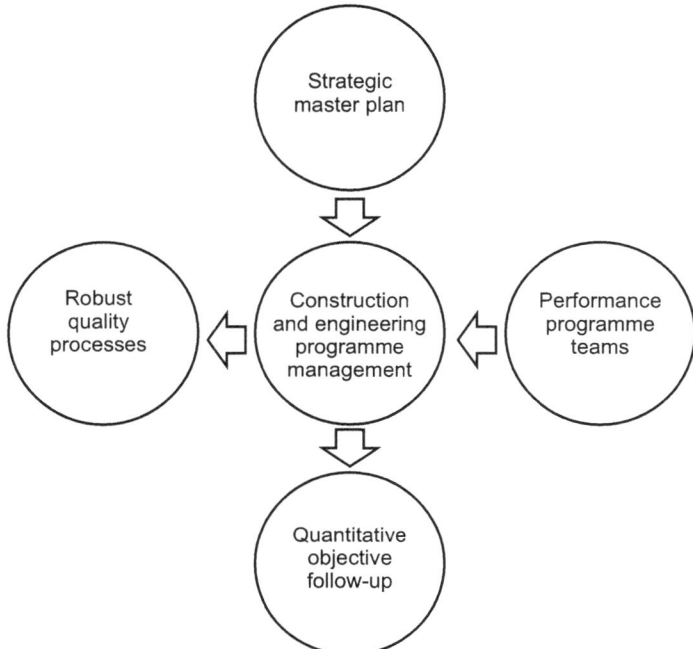

Figure 9.2 Typical construction and engineering programme scheme

A master plan should be flexible so that it can respond swiftly and directly to the requirements of the organization, country or region, subordinate to the behaviour of demand, competition and technological advances. In this sense, for example, the master plan of the Panama Canal is impacted by the behaviour of the demand for transit, identified as the factor that will determine the programming, implementation and proposed speed of the investment programme.

Based on the above example, all master plans are governed by the trends of events in the market, technology and competition, in a defined timeframe. Likewise, since the time horizon should be considered as proposal intent, it must be reviewed and adjusted periodically.

A master plan should contain a summary of the studies and analyses performed and make specific proposals for a programme of infrastructure investments and operating modes. It should also include the elements that embody the strategy of an organization and methods for providing evidence that the intended benefits and goals are achieved. The master plan is a 'living' document – it must be updated continuously by the organization in successive cycles of planning, so that it remains an effective guide and reference document for strategy and decision-making. For a C&E programme should typically include at least:

1.   A memorandum setting out the object of the programme, the programme background and context, and all the factors that must be taken into account.

2. The extent of engineering works required for the works, as well as delineating the occupation of land, return of easements and other property rights (if any) and services affected by implementation.
3. A statement of specific technical or technological requirements, describing the programme and the way it is to be implemented. Also, a description of any necessary organization change.
4. An order of magnitude budget, broken down into parts. This should give unit prices, sources of the estimates and, where applicable, precise details for evaluation.
5. A development programme of work or a work plan guide. Time and cost forecasts should be included where appropriate.
6. All market references on which the estimated level of services will be based.
7. The extent to which documentation standards will come under legal or regulatory nature.
8. A study of the health and safety considerations applicable and at construction sites.

Developing a high performance programme management team

When the programme directors do competency mapping in their PMOs, it ensures that the job profiles are appropriate for the programme objectives. The methodology used in the Panama Canal Expansion Programme followed this competence assessment model which looked at frequency, proficiency and criticality for each of the technical and professional competencies as follows:

*   Frequency: this is a measure of how often the activity will be done in the programme. The scale chosen is: 1 = almost never; 2 = rarely; 3 = occasionally; 4 = frequently; 5 = very frequently; and NA (not applicable or needed in the programme).
*   Criticality rating: a measure of how critical the competency element behaviours are to the programme success and deliverables. The scale used here is: 1 = not critical; 2 = somewhat critical; 3 = fairly critical; 4 = very critical; 5 = extremely critical; and NA (not applicable or needed in the programme).
*   Proficiency; this rates the required proficiency/experience of the team member for the performance of a given element as follows: 0 = no previous experience or awareness; 1 = awareness of this element; 2 = basic proficiency; 3 = intermediate; 4 = advanced; and 5 = expert.

After performing this competency assessment, the programme director will be able to determine the main functions of the PMO and will use the assessment results to adjust human capital strategies as required in terms of education, training and development, targeted recruitment and retention.

As part of the continuous improvement cycle, the competency model should be developed as required to incorporate lessons learned. Finally, a continuous process will define and maintain the competencies required to deliver mission-critical capabilities.

With the PMO organizational function defined, the next step is to develop the elements of responsibilities under each functional area of competency. The process continues with the definition of the different elements of the competency mapping. The aim is to describe the expected deliverables of each role. These will define the performance expectations of the individual and/or the training and coaching requirements necessary to develop the competencies needed to meet the programme goals.

Some programme teams are not really high performers (and perhaps do need to be). However, PMOs should take advantage of the common goal, lasting relationships and the need to work in an integrated environment to contribute to the strategic objectives of the organization in terms of improving core competencies. Perhaps the most valuable legacy that a programme can give an organization is the opportunity of building the competencies of as many people as possible, at all levels, on a day-to-day basis as well as through formal training programmes.

Succession planning

Organizations working with our new generation of professionals should understand the extent of personnel rotation which is associated with modern ways of thinking and competency demands. Programmes can suffer from the sudden exit of key personnel and, because of that risk, steps should be taken to guarantee the sustainability of their jobs. The most effective way to deal with this matter is by the implementation of succession plans.

Succession planning is a process whereby an organization ensures that employees are recruited and developed to fill each key role within the PMO. Through a succession planning process, the PMO retains superior team members because they appreciate the time, attention and development that the organization is investing in them. Individuals are motivated and engaged when they can see a career path for their continued growth and development, especially in projects which in some ways are temporary organizations. To perform succession planning effectively in the PMO, the programme director must identify the organization's long-term goals.

Quality in C&E programmes

Quality in each C&E programme should be defined in the contractual terms and technical conditions of all related projects. It should be divided into two parts: control of processes and unit work execution control. It is good practice that effective implementation of an audit programme should also be performed by independent organizations. These can be official or private as long as they are properly accredited by competent bodies.

A C&E programme quality management system (QMS) should cover both quality assurance (QA) and quality control (QC) policies and standards for the project works. The programme organizational structures responsible for QA/QC are separate and independent from the project functions responsible for performing the works subject to the quality surveillance.

The quality programme director should develop construction and installation quality plans (CIQP) for all work packages that are critical to the project deliverables of a C&E programme (Figure 9.3).

Inspection and test plans (ITP) should be prepared for the implementation and operation of each project CIQP. Each ITP must define the list of successive inspection operations for a particular activity or work package, identifying who carries out the inspections and the follow-up document on which the inspections are reported.

Shipment is one of the final steps of overseas sourcing and likely the most important. Everyone wants to avoid nasty surprises when they receive their goods so it is important to have some way to inspect them before they are shipped. There are different ways for doing this. However, in most situations, a third-party quality inspection is the best course of action.

The quality programme director should never underestimate the importance of proper inspection before a component or equipment is shipped to the project site. The chance for error is always present when making any kind of procurement. With overseas sourcing, the distances as well as shipping times, different legal systems and other factors complicate the process of replacing any defective products. Furthermore, payments are often made in advance and some suppliers may be reluctant to replace goods after they are shipped.

Sometimes improper loading or defective containers can ruin products that were manufactured to specifications. Therefore, inspection during these phases of the works is essential to guarantee the deliverables and achieve the project and programme goals.

A deficiency will be defined in a non-conformance report (NCR), raised by the quality person who identified or has been informed of the deficiency. A non-conforming product may be:

- modified to meet the requirements of the contract;
- repaired to achieve a technically acceptable condition;

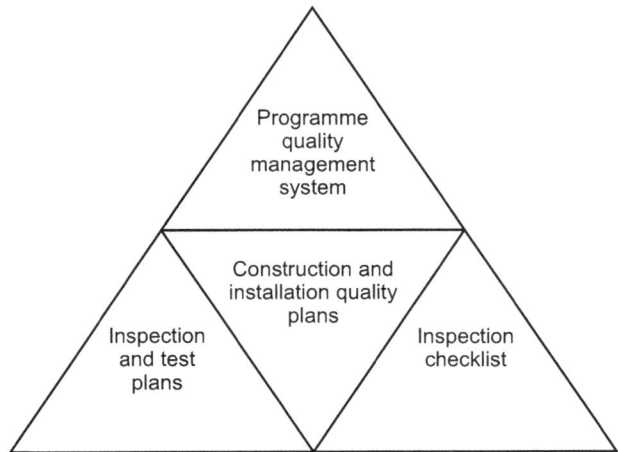

Figure 9.3 Construction and engineering programme quality documentation

- accepted as it stands by concession;
- rejected, scrapped or demolished.

Quality requirements should be clear and verifiable, so that all parties in the project can understand the requirements for conformance. Quality control represents increasingly important concerns for C&E programme directors. Defects or failures in constructed facilities can result in very large costs. Even with minor defects, reconstruction may be required and facility operations impaired. Increased costs and delays are the result.

Completing functional elements of programme deliverables

All C&E programmes should include key progress milestones. These should be included in project contractual terms.

A competent programme director's role includes implementing actions to correct non-conformances or deviations from plan. To complete the projects of a C&E programme successfully in compliance with the objectives and requirements, project milestones produced as part of project deliverables should help to guarantee the achievement of strategic objectives. For this purpose milestones can serve as 'hold points' of the C&E programme projects. As in any auditing process, when recurrent problems are identified the frequency of auditing is increased. Quantified project milestones will give support to these audits of the project works.

The use of quantified methods is the preferable approach in any monitoring process. Specifying programme project milestones in units of measurement (UOM) is the most suitable way to measure progress. Milestones set specific and quantified goals towards achieving a C&E programme. As a minimum the programme project milestone management system should:

1. Have milestones that are specific, attainable and significant to each project of the programme (following established work breakdown practices).
2. Provide a process that will allow a clear and attainable way for the PMO and stakeholders to see and monitor the progress.
3. Increase the focus of all parties by laying out the urgency of achieving each step of the project work packages as required to achieve programme objectives (in other words, highlighting work priorities).
4. Ensure that progress within each project of the programme is followed up using suitable UOM.

I have used the methods described here for projects of the Panama Canal Expansion Programme. The process takes place in three phases, which are:

- Phase 1: defining the milestones and UOM;
- Phase 2: following up, including the use of coordination meetings;
- Phase 3: gaining acceptance for the method.

Phases 1 and 2 are summarized in Figure 9.4. Phase 3 is depicted in Figure 9.5.

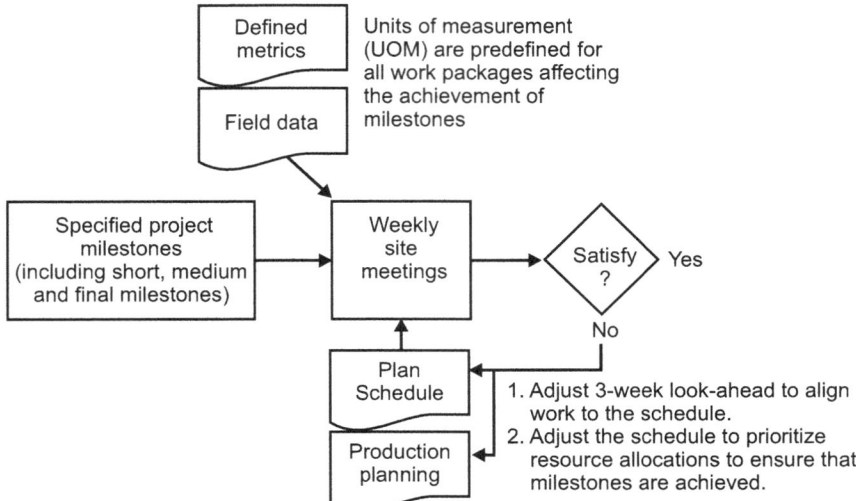

Figure 9.4 Using milestones in construction and engineering programme management

Phase 1: defining milestones with their UOM

Once the work breakdown structure (WBS) of a project is defined and work packages are identified in a way that can supply short-, medium- and long-term milestones, it is important to determine the sources of information that will be used to quantify the level of effort needed to achieve the deliverables.

The UOM which will track the milestones must be defined as metrics of project performance. The sources and method of collection should be assessed in order to guarantee the feasibility and effectiveness of the monitoring effort. All data collected must contribute to clearly show all parties the health of the work package. Monitoring by UOM will allow the project team to track productivity and the effectiveness of corrective actions.

For example, suppose that a project milestone has been set as 'concrete pouring completed' and the foreseen quantity is 10,000 cubic metres. If 8,000 cubic metres have been poured that could imply 80 per cent completion for that milestone. However, the same milestone quantified differently in UOM (for example 'lifts') can give a very different performance result. The delivery might be a pyramid needing 1,000 lifts, with 80 per cent of the concrete in the lower 40 per cent of the lifts. This means that the level of effort necessary to complete the package or milestone is still high compared with the schedule. Then some corrective actions would need to be taken to ensure fulfilment of expectations.

Phase 2: following up as closely as necessary

Follow-up meetings (coordination meetings) are necessary to assess performance against the milestone UOM, and where necessary to decide any necessary corrective

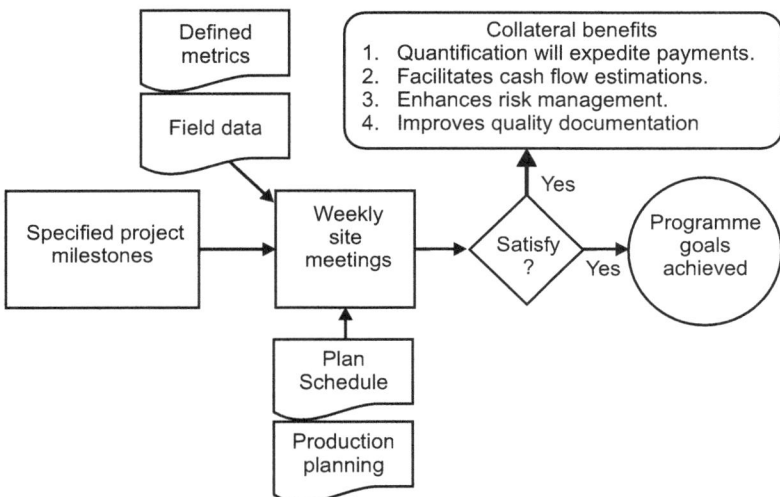

Figure 9.5 Phase 3 of construction and engineering programme controls

action. Meetings should be attended by all interested parties, which certainly means all parties that contribute to the milestone's tasks.

Input from field measurements using defined UOM for each of the monitored milestones should be compared to a three-week look ahead (3WLA) production plan from the field supervisors and each project schedule planned by the estimators or planners. This is needed mainly because the real works planned by the field supervisors take into account the site conditions. Having all parties in the same meeting and allowing them to validate their estimations with real field performance through UOM triggers adjustments to the field supervisors' plans. Estimators and planners can then adjust the project schedule realistically. Both actions are critical to align project efforts and resources to the deliverables (short-, mid- and long-term milestones).

During these meetings, each project team of the C&E programme will gain first-hand information of the project health. That will contribute to achieving the milestone management objectives. This assessment of the project aligned to the C&E programme policies, given an honest approach and the willingness of all parties to meet the project requirements, is the proper way to achieve the overall C&E programme objectives. Using this approach reduces the need for the programme director to deal personally with milestones and works deviations. Applying a collaborative approach to project control tools will improve interpersonal relations – which are important elements in multicultural, multidiscipline and multigenerational work environments.

Phase 3: gaining acceptance for the control methods

Any new control method proposed by the programme management organization will produce reactions from stakeholders. A probable first negative reaction will come from the fact that additional monitoring and reporting resources will be needed from the project sites and these efforts will cost money. Nevertheless, my experience is that this detailed follow-up of work packages through UOM weekly validation meetings will have the following collateral benefits:

1. As the works are being quantified on a weekly basis using UOM, the quantification also serves to validate payment of these units. This will be noticed in the turnaround period of the monthly invoicing by contractors and the time needed for validation.
2. In addition, as the work is quantified, the quality requirements can be identified early in the process. That allows corrective action to take place, reducing the amount of defective products. That can have a positive effect on payment claims.
3. The metrification will serve also to validate or identify risks associated with work packages, so allowing the proper response to any anticipated effects regarding field performance.
4. Knowing in advance the work performed serves to facilitate the compliance of the quality documentation and quality assurance systems. For example, UOM can be the proper way to ensure traceability and scope of non-conformance action plans. That will reduce the cost of quality.

In the long run, achieving each project milestone in terms of UOM aligned to the C&E programme will guarantee that work packages are delivered in a timely manner and minimize interphase problems. This micromanagement of each project milestone will ensure that strategic objectives of the master plan are achieved. That will allow the programme director to be more successful in completing the functional elements of the C&E programme.

Managing contextual environmental requirements

Managing the contextual environmental requirements is one of the most complex parts of a C&E programme. The difficulty lies not so much in the need to establish its content, but with coordination of the various public institutions. This is especially the case when the work of the programme affects more than one community autonomously.

The contextual requirement of a C&E programme includes, in addition to the environmental compliances, elements of stakeholder management and health and safety. Planning and implementation must be documented appropriately because they are subject to audit by international financial institutions, government agencies and non-government organizations. The documentation must describe the procedures, equipment and technical aids to be used to identify foreseeable workplace hazards that can be avoided. The process must involve stakeholders (with citizen participation). Documentation must specify preventive measures designed to control and reduce the risks and assessing the effectiveness of technical safeguards (especially when alternatives are proposed).

Such studies should be part of all C&E programme project contracts and work specifications or, if applicable, the communication plan. Evidence of implementation should be documented at all programme project sites, consistent with the methods required for carrying out and enforcing preventive measures.

Evidence of the budget for environmental, health and safety and risk management must be incorporated in the general C&E programme budget to avoid conflict of interest with projects under execution. A baseline study should be performed whenever the above conditions are not met and this study shall state the environmental, health and safety standards and risk methods applicable to the programme project works.

Outlook and conclusions

Undoubtedly one of the most important tasks in performing a C&E programme is validating the highly significant correlation between the development of the infrastructure through a C&E programme and economic growth, which is based on improvements in factor productivity and systemic competitiveness. The Panama Canal Expansion Programme constitutes an investment of a little more than $5 billion. That has triggered economic growth of the Republic of Panama through collateral C&E programmes in the country's logistic cluster of more than $47 billion. These results indicate that the provision of a strategic plan supported in a master plan of a C&E programme is a key factor in explaining differential growth gaps in the country concerned.

Setting C&E programme projects milestones that are specific, attainable and can be quantified objectively is a process that allows a clear and attainable way to enable C&E programme stakeholders to follow up and manage progress. The implementation of a milestone management system as C&E programme policy will help demonstrate the urgency of achieving each project deliverable in a timely manner. That will allow a smooth workflow with minor interphase problems.

Good programme directors try to ensure that the job is done right the first time with no major non-conformance. The only way to have full control of the process and learn how to manage it effectively is by recognizing the importance of having a high performance quality control inspection organization as part of the PMO.

The use of proven methodology to develop the competencies of a programme team provides the advantage of direct experience and an opportunity to develop a relationship with the programme director and his or her team. The final stage of competency mapping is evaluation of the results as part of the C&E programme's benefit realization assessment. This should consider two aspects:

1. Determine whether the programme competency mapping produced the desired changes in each individual's behaviour.
2. Check if the process implemented contributed to achieving the strategic goals of the organization.

These two aspects will determine if the programme director's implementation techniques were effective competencies that will give the organization a competitive advantage in today's challenging world.

Finally, worldwide, environmental standards and regulations are being strengthened to preserve the planet. Compliance with environmental regulations has become an integral part of the planning and supporting strategic documentation for C&E programmes. Today's organizations recognize the need to deal with issues such as safety, health, management and environmental information disclosure, while complying with international agreements and global regulations.

References and further reading

Carrol, A. and McCrackin, J. (1998), 'The Competent Use of Competency-Based Strategies for Selection and Development', *Performance Improvement Quarterly*, 11(3): 45–63.

Department of Defence (2008), 'Competency-Based Management for the DoD-wide Contracting Community', overview presentation, March.

FERC Engineering Guidelines (1993), Chapter VII: 'Construction Quality Control', prepared under contract with R&H Thomas Inc.

Heathfield, S. M. (2014), 'Succession Planning', Heathfield Consulting Associates, <http://humanresources.about.com/od/glossarys/g/successionplan.htm>.

Mosaic White Paper (2010), 'Corporate Governance', <www.mosaicprojects.com.au/White Papers/WP1033_Governance.pdf>.

Panama Canal Expansion Programme (2011), *Third Set of Locks Training and Coaching Plan*, Panama.

Razzak, A. (2010), *Quality Management in Construction Projects*, Boca Raton, FL: CRC Press.

Reyes, J. and Martinez Almela, J. (2012), 'Procesos de Proyectos y Competencias en Direccion de Proyectos' (extract translated).

Rose, K. (2014), *Project Quality Management*, Plantation, FL: J. Ross Publishing.

Rozas, P. and Sánchez, R. (2004), 'Desarrollo de Infraestructura y crecimiento economico, revision conceptual', CEPAL, October.

Toledo, M. (2004), 'Planes de Sucesion, Metodologia para la efectividad Organizacional', Universidad Diego Portales, ENEFA.

UNIDO (2010), *Good Organization Management and Governance Practice*, United Nations Industrial Development Organization, April.

Vidile II, R. T. (2010), 'Non Conformance Management, Preventive and Corrective Actions', presentation at Strykers Orthopaedic Corporation, February.

Chapter 10

Programme Management in the Mining Industry

Michiel C. Bekker

Mining involves the extraction, processing, rehabilitation and often beneficiation of minerals from earthly as well as offshore geological deposits. The establishment, growth and sustainability of a mining operation provides for a classical application of programme management. The longevity of mining companies is dependent upon on the effective definition, delivery and closure of an extended programme.

Introduction

Even though programme management in the mining industry is often practised, it is hardly recognized as a formal, integrated and synergistic approach towards the management of interrelated projects. As production-orientated businesses, mining companies primarily focus on the effective utilization of assets to extract, process and deliver mineral commodities to favourable and profitable markets. The key performance indicator of a mining operation is the amount of saleable product delivered per month and eventually per financial year. Depending on the type of mine these measurements could be tonnes/month (metals), carats/month (diamonds or other precious stones) or ounces/month (precious metals such as gold and platinum). Programme management provides an additional dimension to the measurement of organizational performance. As opposed to production output measurement, programme performance covers a broader range of measurements and lays emphasis on the effect, and contribution, of interrelated projects on overall benefit realization.

This chapter begins with an overview of the origin of the mining industry and describes what constitutes the development of a mining complex. This is followed by an explanation of the strategic importance of the life-of-mine plan (LOMP) and the derivation of enabling projects. The formulation, or lack thereof, in the mining industry is discussed with some observations from field research.

Definition and main characteristics of the mining sector

Together with agriculture, mining could be considered as one of the oldest industries practised by mankind. Through centuries mining has developed from mere improvement of living conditions to a dominant global industry. The following paragraphs provide an overview of the origin of the mining sector, the stages in the life of a mine and the role of projects and programme management in mining.

Origin of the mining sector

Mining parallels the history of civilization starting with the Stone Age before 4500 BC (Hartman and Mutmansky, 2007). Initially mining activities concentrated on extracting and processing materials to improve living standards and safety such as rock, sand and marble to build shelters and roads. Historically flint was also mined and shaped to be used as weapons and tools. The exploration, mining and processing of metals are so linked to human history that the progression of civilization is often linked to associated metals periods (Campbel and Braidwood, 1970). The first of these was the Chalcolithic or Copper period (*c.*5000 to 3000 BC).

Once it was realized that adding tin to copper hardens the metal, three new periods followed. There were Early Bronze (3000 to 2000 BC), Middle Bronze (2000 to 1550 BC) and Late Bronze (1550 to 1200 BC). During these periods the mining of coal in shallow deposits began, which brought new developments in heating and power generation. With the advent of new processing techniques, iron became the metal of choice, which saw the dawning of the Iron Age from 1200 to 1750 BC. Technological developments in iron processing progressed civilization towards the Steel Age (1750 to 1945). Now society is in the Nuclear Age (1945 to present) with uranium being mined and processed on a large scale.

Mining of metals was not confined to improving living conditions or industrial advancement. Ancient Egypt was the first nation recorded to mine minerals for ornamental value when green malachite stones were produced for decorative purposes. The discovery of gold prompted many ventures in human settlement history. According to Shaw (2000) the gold mining complexes of Nubia (around 3000 BC) were among the first large mining operations, with miners crushing the ore into fine powder before cleaning and rinsing the powder to extract the gold dust. Since the 1700s gold rushes led to large human settlements in South Africa, California, Alaska, Australia and Canada.

The development of a modern mine is hardly done as a stand-alone endeavour and involves multiple business and technical disciplines. Starting with geological investigations and studies, a mineral deposit is found, tested, analysed and confirmed. The feasibility of mining the deposit is confirmed by conducting an economic analysis. Once feasibility is confirmed and capital approved, the design of the mining process will proceed. The procurement of contracting and equipment services will begin and the extraction of the mineral will proceed. Once extracted, the mineral material is cleaned or concentrated. Depending on the type of mineral, the final product will undergo further concentration, smelting, refining or other beneficiation processes. The final product is graded according to customer requirement and, once the minimum specification is met, the product is ready for marketing.

By the turn of the twentieth century mining had become a formidable industry and approached maturity towards the beginning of the twenty-first century. Consolidation of mining companies is taking place to improve economies of scale and improve competitiveness. Most of the world's high quality and easily accessible mineral deposits have been depleted and new techniques are being developed for deep mining and for mining that is less labour-intensive.

Mining stages

Modern mining comprises five main stages. These are illustrated in Figure 10.1 and are summarized as follows:

*   prospecting;
*   exploration;
*   development;
*   exploitation;
*   reclamation.

During prospecting the most favourable mineral deposit is searched and confirmed. Prospecting is the domain of geologists and geophysicists and various methods of direct and indirect prospecting are used to spot, analyse and evaluate geological anomalies. Exploration involves the confirmation of the extent and value of the ore body and is done using drilling and excavation. With the estimated tonnage and grade established, the economic value of the deposit is determined. Based on the economic viability a decision is then made to continue, delay or abandon development. The decision to proceed towards development is dependent on market conditions and is evaluated continuously. Prospecting can take one to two years while exploration can have a duration of between two and five years. Prospecting and exploration are the precursors to mining and they can overlap.

Once the economic viability of an ore body is confirmed and capital approved, development of the mine can begin. A greenfield development can take up to five years and involves critical activities such as:

*   approval of mining rights;
*   environmental impact study and approval;
*   water licensing;

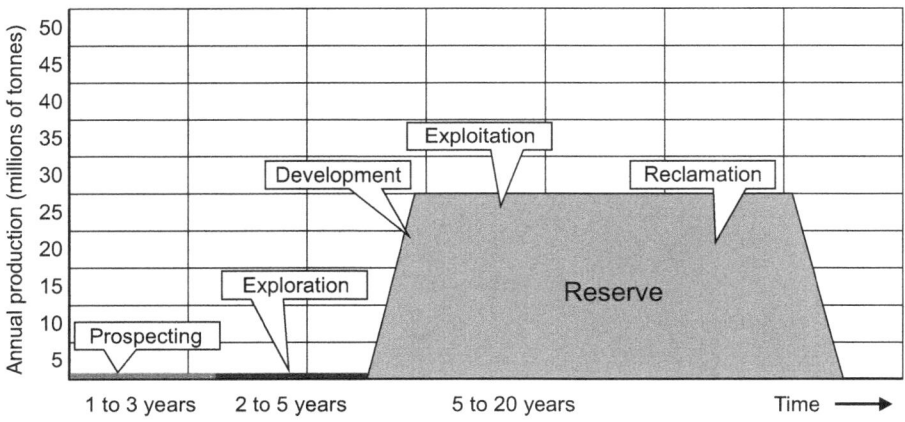

Figure 10.1 Stages of mining

- technology assessment;
- infrastructure development;
- building surface plants and facilities;
- excavation of the deposit by stripping or shaft sinking.

Exploitation of the deposit can start towards the end of the development stage. Ore production gradually increases until full production. During this stage the focus is on optimizing sustainable mining to ensure maximum profitability and honouring customer agreements. As the deposit becomes depleted, reclamation (also known as rehabilitation) is initiated. During reclamation the removal of plants, buildings and equipment takes place as well as the rehabilitation of waste and tailings dumps through the re-establishment of vegetation. In order to establish the current and future capacity requirements to meet the strategic objectives, all stages of mining must be monitored and evaluated for future planning.

Life-of-mine plan (LOMP)

The strategic objectives of a mining operation are usually directed towards production of saleable volumes and cost effectiveness. Mining complexes can typically have one or more reserves. Depending on the quality, accessibility and overall economic viability of the reserve, a greenfield development could potentially start by mining the first reserve (R1). Production will ramp-up to maximum output for this reserve and then start declining. In order to ensure sustainability and growth, the second reserve (R2) will commence development while R1 is still in production. In order to sustain and grow production, the development and operation of more reserves (R3 and R4) will continue in a planned manner until the complex is depleted. The sequencing of reserve mining to ensure a targeted production capacity in the most economical way is planned and confirmed in the LOMP. Figure 10.2 illustrates a LOMP production profile.

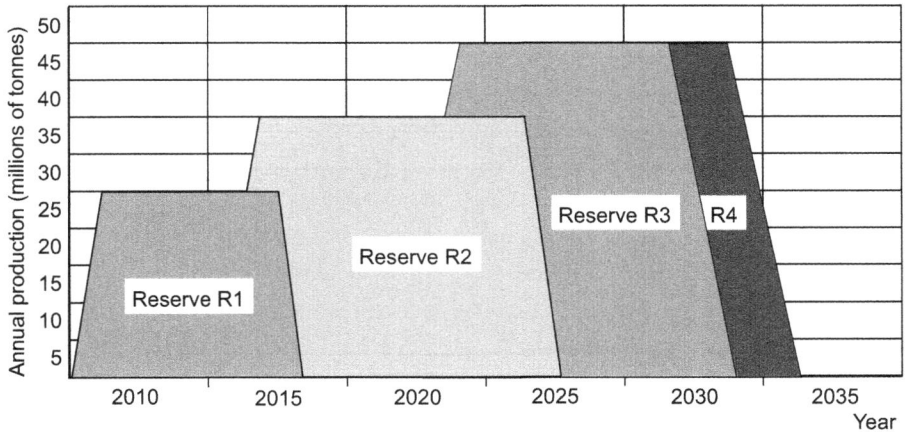

Figure 10.2 Sequenced production profile of a mining complex

Development and implementation of the LOMP, as well as the continuous operation of a mining complex, involves multiple projects over an extended period of time. Even though the development and implementation of a single, greenfield reserve can be considered as a stand-alone project, the continuous development of a mining complex involves numerous projects which are often interdependent. These include projects related to infrastructure, buildings, statutory compliance, socio-economic issues, logistics and common services.

Project management in the mining industry

The management of projects in the mining industry is as old as the industry itself. Apart from the actual mine development, there are numerous other projects that support and enable the intended or current mining operation. Despite the importance of these projects, project management has historically been questionable in this industry. The main reasons for the poor performance of projects in the mining industry are the following:

- Mining is predominately a production-orientated environment. The key performance areas are associated with production rates (such as tonnes per month). Any incident that threatens the ability to meet or exceed the target production rates receives the highest priority. When an incident occurs (for example the breakdown of a transport conveyor system), all effort goes into restoring the conveyor to full operation. Any other activities, such as the management of projects, receive secondary priority. Thus new projects are interrupted on a regular basis by higher priority actions, which evidently result in the loss of project continuity.
- Project management is not the preferred career path for employees who aspire to ascend the corporate ladder. In mining, an established track record in production, legal appointments and hands-on mining experience are the preferred achievements for those aiming to occupy higher corporate offices. Project management does not constitute any legal appointment and by default carries less accountability and authority than operational managers.
- Operational and production requirements often conflict with project requirements. Especially for brownfield projects it is often necessary to shut down sections of operating plants and equipment to allow for tie-ins, construction activities and modifications to existing facilities. These shutdown periods have a negative impact on production which could lead to missed daily production targets.
- Incentives and bonuses in the mining environment are linked to production and sales targets. Anything that could influence meeting these targets is either attended to immediately or completely demoted to secondary priority. The meeting of project targets is hardly addressed or incentivized.

Despite the secondary nature of projects in mining, awareness of the enabling nature of projects and the value of a well-managed project became more evident towards the end of the 1990s. Mine management realized that:

- in order to stay competitive, projects need to be implemented faster and more cost effectively;

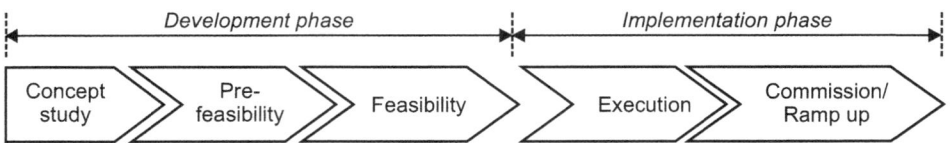

Figure 10.3 Lifecycle of a mine project

- technology in the mining industry is fairly mature, which means that project scope definitions should be more accurate and predictable;
- many projects are scaled repeats of previous projects;
- the mining industry needs a project management methodology to standardize its approach to the development and implementation of project management.

Based on the above, capital and human resources were made available to develop and standardize project management methodologies and systems. By 2010 most large mining companies had developed their own internal methodologies. Even though each company followed its own approach, an informal mining project vocabulary evolved around the definition of a mining project lifecycle (PLC), phase deliverables and decision criteria.

Mine project lifecycle (PLC)

The most commonly used PLC definition by mining practitioners is given in Figure 10.3. The PLC consists of two main phases, namely the development phase and implementation phase. The development phase (also known as the study phase) consists of three subphases:

- concept study;
- pre-feasibility study;
- feasibility study.

Each of these subphases has specific engineering, business and project management objectives and deliverables. They are distinguished by the level of economic evaluation accuracy. The concept study aims for an accuracy of within ±30 per cent. The pre-feasibility study expects to be accurate to ±20 per cent and the feasibility study should be accurate within 15 per cent. Final capital is only approved after acceptance of the feasibility study result and forms the baseline for project implementation. The above PLC is used for all types of projects.

The development of a standardized PLC, methodologies, systems and practices has had a positive impact on project management in mining. Project management is recognized as the discipline required to conduct projects successfully. Still in its infancy, it is believed that the adaptation, adjustment and level of use of project management methodologies will improve overall project performance in the industry.

The mining industry is completely exposed to the cyclic nature of commodity pricing. The continuous search for improvement prevails. As ore bodies become increasingly difficult to access and mine economically, the quest to optimize the project management effort remains.

As with *project* management, the acceptance and application of *programme* management in the mining industry has lagged other industries. The importance and suitability of programme management in mining cannot be questioned; however, the application of the principles and concepts of programme management remains only informal, ad hoc and sometimes intuitive.

Programme management

Although it is not my intention to discuss and explain the principles and practices of programme management in depth here, it is important to provide a short overview of what programme management is, followed by the application of programme management principles in a mining environment. Programme management can be defined as the management and coordination of a group of interrelated projects to realize benefits. Originating from the organizational strategy, the programme is planned, resourced, coordinated and controlled towards the achievement of the programme and organizational benefits.

A programme does not have a finite timespan. As the organizational strategy is reviewed on a continual basis, the programme might be altered and refined to ensure alignment with the strategic objectives. Evidently the programme must deliver defined benefits and it is the realization of these benefits that necessitates a dedicated and focused effort on the management of the programme. Figure 10.4 provides a graphical illustration of a value path towards strategy realization.

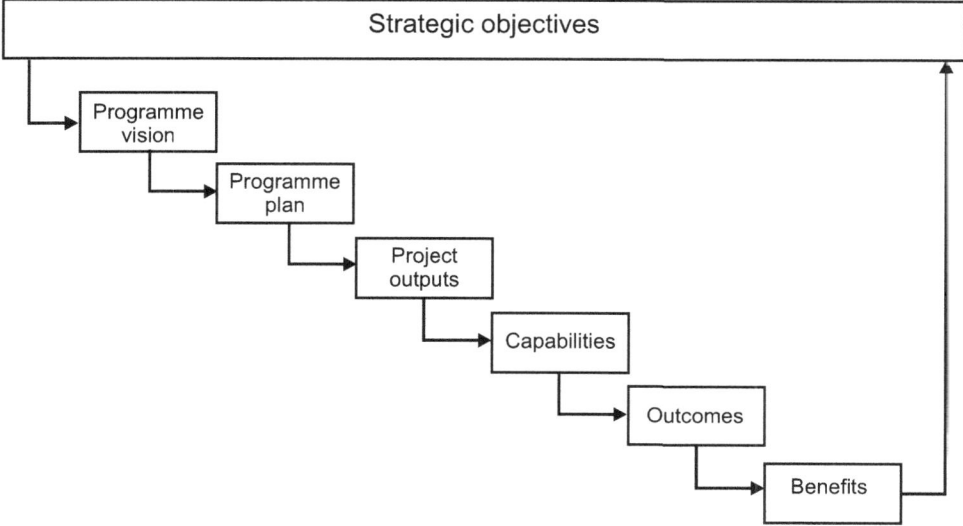

Figure 10.4 Programme value path

Programmes aim to create value and deliver on strategic objectives. This is done through the following process:

- the strategic objectives drive the development of the programme vision;
- the programme vision is decomposed into a programme plan for the future organization;
- the programme plan defines what the various projects need to create;
- the project creates outputs which create capabilities;
- the capabilities are transitioned into outcomes;
- the outcomes enable the realization of benefits;
- the benefits are achieved and contribute to the achievement of the strategic objectives.

Given its importance to the programme, the management of benefits drives many aspects of programme management. Benefits management stretches from inception to beyond the eventual closure of the programme.

Programme management in the mining industry

The adoption of programme management and its formal application in the mining industry is still in its early days. As part of the research for this chapter, an extensive literature search was conducted via academic search engines such as Google Scholar, Refseek, Academicinfo and Deepdyve, with no result. An extensive field study was then conducted, which included interviews with project and mine managers from prominent mining companies such as Anglo American, Lonmin, Exxaro, Glencore and Kumba Iron Ore. During these interviews the following questions were discussed:

- How is programme management defined and applied?
- What drives the programme and how is it aligned with the organizational strategy?
- What constitutes the programme organizational structure and how does it interface with operations?
- How are benefits measured?
- How is the programme designed?
- How is the programme prioritized, planned and controlled?
- How are risks managed?

Consensus from all the interviewees was that programme management is not applied formally in the mining industry. There is evidence of portfolio and project management but programme management is applied informally under another definition such as capital programme management, capital expenditure plan, capital investment plan or capital plan.

The LOMP remains the key driver for meeting the strategic objectives of a mining company and is therefore the basis from which initiatives are formulated, planned and executed, including projects. Given the basic value path of a programme as described above, the application of programme management principles in the mining industry is explained and illustrated through a series of examples based on a case study of a coal mine expansion and information gathered during the various interviews.

Strategic objectives and programme vision

The LOMP encapsulates the strategic objectives of a mining company. Upon formal approval by the most senior executives in the organization, the LOMP is developed into a programme vision and plan.

Example A

Mining company X approves a LOMP that will target to deliver 150 million tonnes of saleable coal product in the next financial year. At $80 per tonne this could create revenue of $12,000 million for the financial year. In order to achieve these objectives, the current reserve will have to be expanded and additional water licences and infrastructure will be required. The infrastructure should also be designed to allow for future expansion beyond the current financial year as well as for the exploitation of the next reserve.

In order to achieve the above objectives, the programme plan (also referred to as the *capital expenditure plan*), is drafted to list all the projects and initiatives that are required and budgeted for under various categories.

Programme plan

Each mining company has its own internal project categorization system. However, the most commonly used categories and subcategories of projects can be broadly defined as:

- capital projects;
  - new developments (greenfield);
  - expansion (brownfield);
- stay-in-business (SIB);
  - replacement;
  - business improvement and optimization;
  - upgrades;
- compliance;
  - socio-economic;
  - safety;
  - health;
  - environmental;
  - legal.

To achieve the strategic objectives as articulated in the LOMP the programme could include numerous projects under these categories. The following example (B) expands on the previous example of Company X and explains the next step of articulating the strategic objectives and programme vision into a programme plan.

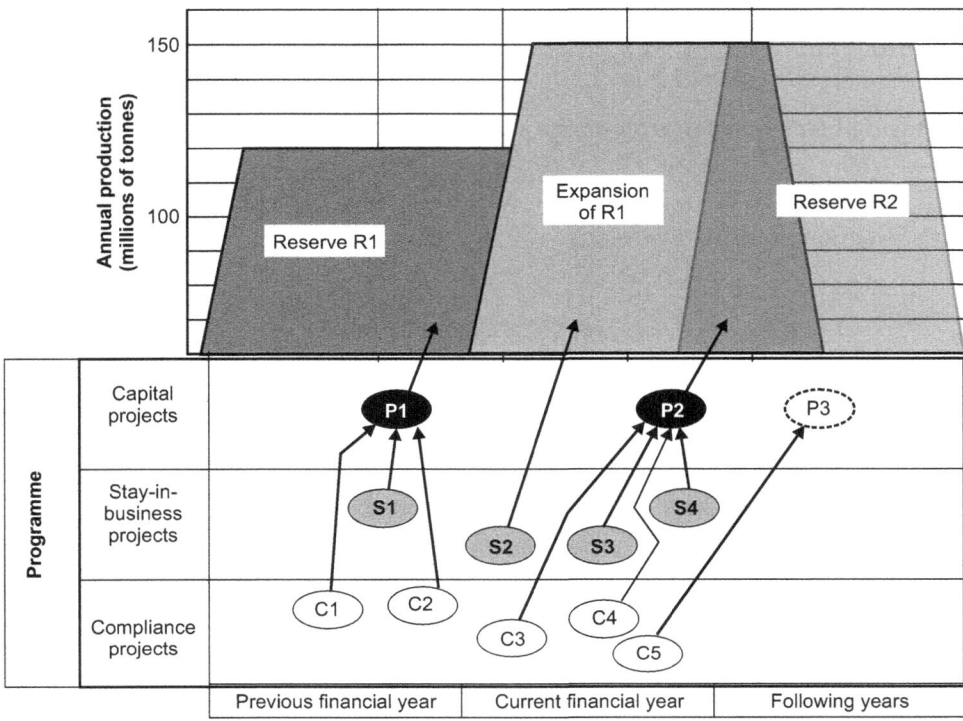

Figure 10.5 Programme plan

A graphical illustration of the project interdependencies is given in Figure 10.5. Please note that this example is for illustrative purposes and does not include all aspects and projects related to a reserve development.

Example B

Upon approval of the LOMP, Company X listed various projects that need to be developed and implemented to achieve the strategic objective. Typical projects included the following under each category:

- Capital projects (total capital approved according to the LOMP $8.60 million);
  P1 – Expansion of R1: $250 million;
  P2 – Mining of R2: $600 million;
  P3 – Exploration of R3: $10 million;
- Stay-in-business projects (total capital approved according to the LOMP $15.5 million);
  S1 – Feed conveyor upgrade to support P1: capital allowed: $10 million;
  S2 – Storm water upgrade: capital allowed: $2 million;
  S3 – Road upgrade for P2: capital allowed: $2 million;
  S4 – Substation upgrade for P2: capital allowed: $1.5 million;

- Compliance (total capital approved according to the LOMP $600,000);
  C1 – Environmental approval for P1: $50,000;
  C2 – Additional water licence for P1: $100,000;
  C3 – Environmental impact study for P2: $300,000;
  C4 – Water licence approval for P2: $100,000 (could be done in parallel with C2);
  C5 – Statutory registrations for P3: $50,000;
- Current total programme value: $876.1 million.

Figure 10.5 provides a visual image of the interrelationships among some of the projects. Although intuitively aware of these relationships, mine management often relies on experience and operational astuteness to manage them, sometimes to the detriment of the programme. For example, the delay in an apparently simple project like C2 (additional water licensing) could have a delay on P1 with a multiplying effect on many of the others. In such a programme there might be few *critical path projects*, let alone critical path activities.

The LOMP includes a list of individual projects. Each project must be justified as a stand-alone project and undergo a formal review and approval process. Often projects could span over different complexes, especially utility and infrastructure projects. Each complex is managed by a legally appointed manager who is responsible for everything within his or her immediate complex boundaries. It is not uncommon for projects crossing complex boundaries to suffer changes and late completion due to insufficient communication and lack of agreement over who takes responsibility at which point. It is often in such cases that the lack of a formal programme management approach impacts negatively on project outputs.

A programme based on the LOMP could span up to 20 years and would be reviewed and updated annually. During each review, the planned-versus-realized benefits of the previous year are reviewed, restated and then the new LOMP targets are added.

Project outputs, capabilities and outcomes

As mentioned, programme management is only starting to emerge as a focus area in the mining industry. With the emphasis on efficient and effective production, the capabilities and outcomes of project outputs are seldom measured. Projects are mostly managed and measured as stand-alone initiatives, with their collective value hardly quantified at an operational or tactical level. At a strategic level, some form of benefit measurement takes place during the LOMP review.

Benefits measurement and strategic objectives

The measurement of benefits and level of strategic objective achievement are usually done during the annual LOMP cycle. Planned versus actual business results are reviewed and based on the results and market developments, the LOMP is rewritten and the forecast for the next financial year confirmed.

In order to illustrate how benefit management is typically measured in the mining industry the example of the LOMP is further expanded. Please note that the example again refers only to a two-year programme window, whereas in reality the LOMP can span over a 20- or even a 30-year period.

Example C

During the previous cycle of LOMP planning a target was set for 115 million tonnes of saleable product to be sold at $90 per tonne for the previous financial year. A total of 120 million tonnes was achieved at $80 per tonne in the year. What also influenced the target benefit was negative cost associated with foreign exchange ($5 million), additional rehabilitation of redundant mines ($15 million), socio-economic projects to allow for additional housing and recreation ($10 million) as well as a new water treatment plant ($12 million). The changes were updated and restated to confirm the realized benefit. Given the approved LOMP and associated projects for the immediate financial year the target benefit is stated. These results are shown in Figure 10.6.

The planning and management of the LOMP is robust and well established in all medium- to large-scale mining companies. The LOMP provides the perfect platform for programme management.

Programme management office (PMO)

Formalization of project management in mining resulted in the emergence of project offices in most companies. However the term *programme office* is hardly used. After further investigation into the functioning of the project offices, it became clear that the programme function is often handled by the engineering management function and not necessarily by project offices. Eventually the project office manages the portfolio of projects and provides support to the respective project managers. The reason for engineering management being unofficially responsible for programme management is that the interrelationships of projects are mostly technical.

The institutionalization of the programme management office in the mining industry remains unclear. In general, major opportunities exist for project, operational, technical, statutory and financial disciplines to synergize their efforts to improve programme planning and implementation in the mining environment.

Summary

Mining remains a prominent global industry. The process of prospecting, exploration, development, exploitation and reclamation of mines is well established and practised by mining companies. The LOMP remains the strategic driver for any mining complex and contains the portfolio of projects required to achieve the strategic objectives. Projects are classified in three categories, namely capital, stay-in-business and compliance projects. The individual and interrelated projects associated with the development of mining operations provide a classical application for programme management. Unfortunately, the formal application of programme management in the mining industry is lagging behind other industries. Evidence of informal programme management is apparent and it is believed that, as with project management, the institutionalization of programme management will continue in future.

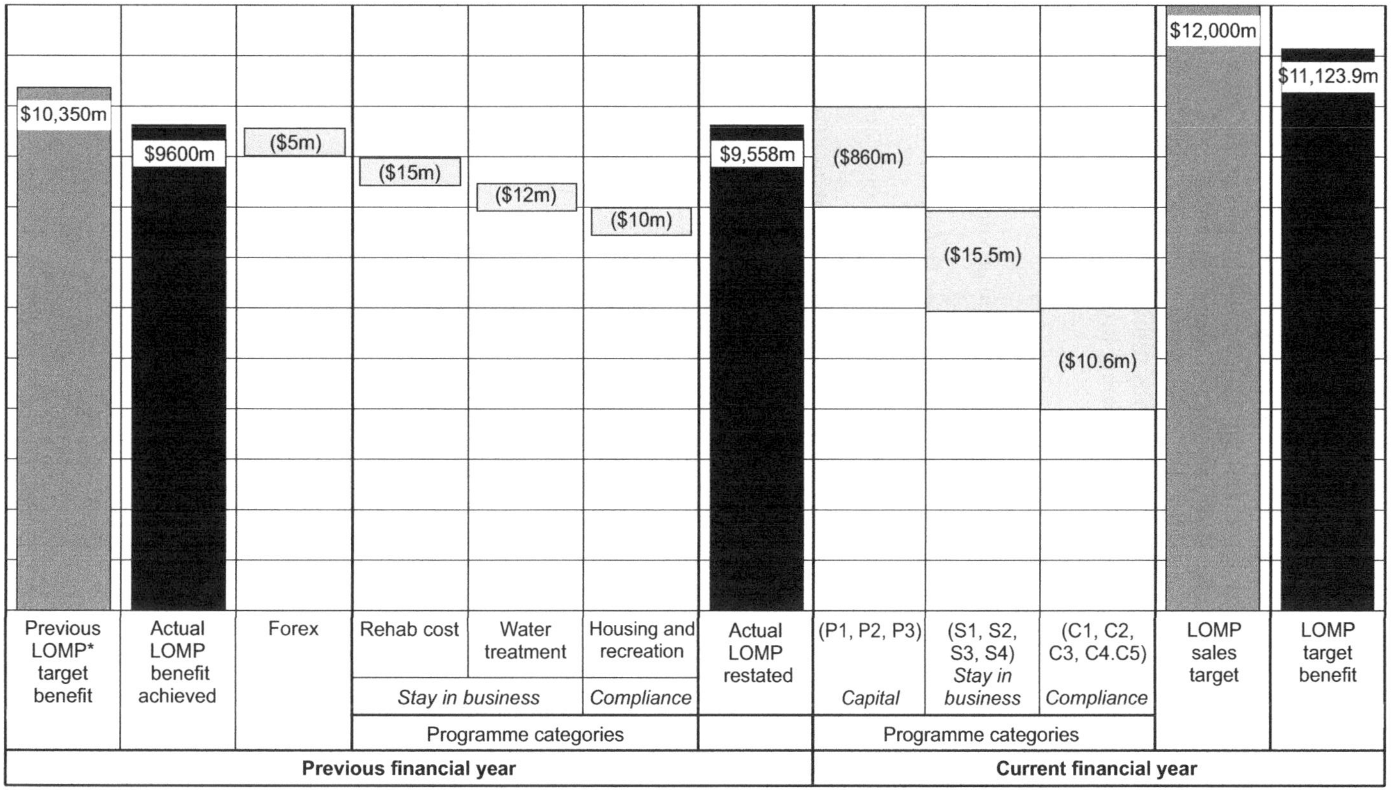

The chart contains the following labeled values and categories:

Previous financial year

Previous LOMP* target benefit	Actual LOMP benefit achieved	Forex	Rehab cost	Water treatment	Housing and recreation	Actual LOMP restated
			Stay in business		Compliance	
				Programme categories		
$10,350m	$9600m	($5m)	($15m)	($12m)	($10m)	$9,558m

Current financial year

	(P1, P2, P3)	(S1, S2, S3, S4)	(C1, C2, C3, C4.C5)	LOMP sales target	LOMP target benefit
	Capital	Stay in business	Compliance		
		Programme categories			
	($860m)	($15.5m)	($10.6m)	$12,000m	$11,123.9m

*LOMP = Life of mine plan.   Financial values are not drawn to scale.   Figures in brackets are negative values.

Figure 10.6 Benefit measurement

Acknowledgements

A word of gratitude is due to the following individuals for their time and valuable input into this chapter: Riaan Blignaut (VP Engineering, Infrastructure and Capital; Lonmin); Pierre Cronje (Portfolio Manager; Kumba Iron Ore); Deon Konig (General Manager; Anglo American); Retief Louw (Manager Projects; Kumba Iron Ore); Johan du Plessis (Project Manager; Lonmin); Johann du Plessis (retired General Manager; Glencore); and Andre Wahl (Project Manager; Exxaro).

I do realize that not everything discussed is covered here but be assured that your inputs, words of wisdom and advice, moulded my thinking and understanding of how programme management is applied in the mining industry.

References and further reading

Campbel, H. and Braidwood, R. J. (1970), 'An Early Farming Village in Turkey', *Scientific American*, 222(3): 51–6.

Hartman, H. L. and Mutmansky, J. M. (2007), *Introductory Mining Engineering*, 2nd edn., Hoboken, NJ: John Wiley.

Kear, P. (2005), *Strategic and Tactical Mine Planning Components*, Sandton: The South African Institute of Mining and Technology.

Lock, D. (2013), Chapter 12 in *Project Management*, 10th edn., Farnham: Gower (contains examples of a work breakdown structure and coding system for a copper mining project).

OGC/Axelos (2011), *Managing Successful Programmes (MSP)*, 4th edn., Best Management Practice series, Norwich: The Stationery Office.

Shaw, I. (2000), *The Oxford History of Ancient Egypt*, New York: Oxford University Press.

Chapter 11

Programme Management in the Pharmaceutical Sector

Lynne Hughes and Susie Boyce

This chapter examines the interlinking complexities of research and development (R&D) programme management within the pharmaceutical industry. It explains approaches for dealing with potential challenges and for delivering robust and auditable data to support product registration.

Introduction

Programme management in the pharmaceutical industry is challenging. It requires meticulous planning, a deep understanding of the medical challenges and standards of care across many countries, and continuous risk mitigation strategies. The aim is to ensure that the global data collected and submitted for review and potential approval are homogeneous and capable of being combined across many different cultures, ethnicities and variations in medical care. It is also essential that robust statistical data can be derived in order to allow a fully informed decision as to whether the tested medicine is safe for launch, with all potential risks and benefits appropriately evaluated.

A structured programme approach is required to bring a new medicine to market. At the phase III pivotal trial stage, there are several factors to consider. If a drug has reached this critical stage, then there is already a wealth of supporting data and launch planning is under way. Smaller, supporting trials are often required to complete the registration dossier. Difficulties and increased complexity arise in the drug development programme if supporting trials are on the critical path which can give rise to delays in final regulatory dossier submissions. Recruiting appropriate subjects who might receive no direct benefit from participation in a trial is an additional factor to be considered. These two factors increase the complexity of the development programme. It is important, therefore, to allow sufficient time for recruitment to a trial in order to achieve planned timelines.

An experienced programme manager is essential in delivering a package of data to inform regulatory decisions on the safety and efficacy of a given medical product.

Background

Medicines are a mainstay of everyday life. People are surviving longer owing to increased knowledge and understanding of the workings of the human body in sickness and in health. Contributing to this increased longevity is the development and use of increasingly sophisticated medicines as our understanding of the pathological nature of disease expands. The early medicines began with a series of chance discoveries of products such as opiates (morphine) and anaesthetics, while the arrival of the penicillins heralded a new era in the fight against infection. Use of vaccination caused diseases that were previously fatal to decrease and in some instances eradicated them. The first randomized clinical trial was conducted in 1948 (Jaillon, 2007), examining the effects of streptomycin on pulmonary tuberculosis. Over the past 20 years, there has been a trend towards more personalized medicines, targeting a specific genotype (BRCA1 for example, in breast cancer) or subtypes of a disease (for example, mild Alzheimer's disease).

Development of these personalized and more general medicines in a rapidly evolving field brings its own challenges to the clinical research team. That applies particularly to the programme/project management team as they try to facilitate the rapid assessment of drugs though a highly regulated and mandated pathway in a controlled, auditable and consistent manner.

The 2014 Ebola crisis might have a significant effect on development timelines. However, traditionally the time from a pharmaceutical company registering a new chemical entity patent to its taking the following essential steps has been 20 years:

- Complete the full package of pre-clinical (animal testing) data.
- Formulate the product so that it can be administered safely and reliably.
- Ensure that large-scale manufacture of the product is achievable.
- Define the clinical indication(s) for the product; ensure that this is an unmet medical need or that the product adds a new benefit to the current range of available products. In other words ensure that there is a market for the product.
- Conduct a full market analysis of the indication, including forward-looking assumptions about the market for the next 10 to 20 years.
- Enter into human tests ('first in human' trials). Most subjects are healthy male volunteers, although there can also be subjects with the target disease (for example cancer patients).
- Liaise with global regulatory agencies to obtain input and advice on the planned development programme.
- Conduct phase Ib and phase II trials in the target patient population
- Conduct the pivotal phase III trials that will ultimately provide the data required to show unequivocally that the product is safe for human usage. Also that it has a defined (and reliable) efficacy plus a characterized risk/benefit assessment. All that is to ensure that physicians and patients are fully informed about both potential risks and benefits.
- Liaise with the relevant payers and regulatory authorities to ensure that there will be an agreed potential level of reimbursement for the marketed product.
- Market and sell the product on the global marketplace, with the goal of recouping development costs and providing continued funding for research and development of future drugs.

Drug development stages

Drug development follows a defined and regulated process with checks and balances at each step of the way. In order to understand the complexities of programme management in the pharmaceutical industry, it is import to have a full understanding of the specific stages of each step of drug development and the outputs required from each step. The lifecycle of a pharmaceutical drug follows the stages detailed below.

Pre-clinical stage

In this stage studies are conducted in the non-clinical setting, involving *in vitro* testing (in the test tube). If the data are positive the trials progress to defined trials on animal populations. As technology has advanced, computer simulations/modelling can also be applied. The objective is to obtain initial pharmacokinetic information and to assist in decision-making regarding further development of the new entity/drug.

Clinical studies

Clinical pharmacology studies are conducted in the clinical setting involving human beings. They follow a strict process from phase I to phase III trials, designed to support registration of the drug for use on global markets. Then further trials take place (phase IV), when a significantly wider population is exposed to the drug.

Phase I

Phase I sees the first introduction of the investigational new drug, using people. Typically phase I studies are performed in healthy male volunteers (approximately 10–40 individuals depending on the drug), although they may be conducted in patients. These studies are usually performed in a phase I unit where the volunteers can be closely observed and monitored by full-time medical staff. The aims of these 'first in human' trials are to assess and determine the metabolism, pharmacological effects (pharmacodynamics and pharmacokinetics), mechanism of action, safety, tolerability, and side-effects of the drug in human beings. The information gained during this phase should enable the design of well-controlled, scientifically valid phase II studies. Phase I trials provide scientific data on the appropriate dosage of the drug, the route of administration, the frequency of dosing and (potentially) what side-effects are to be expected.

Phase II

Studies for phase II are conducted in the clinical setting. They involve approximately 20–300 patients or others with the disease or condition under study. The trials are well controlled, closely monitored, and designed to continue to evaluate safety, tolerability, identification of common short-term side-effects, and to determine efficacy in a larger group. Sometimes phase II studies are divided into phases IIa and IIb. Phase IIa trials are specifically designed to assess the dosing of the drug, while phase IIb assesses efficacy. Development failure in phase II is normally due to toxicity or lack of efficacy.

Phase III

Phase III comprises large-scale randomized controlled trials conducted in larger patient groups (involving 300 to 3,000 or more individuals depending on the disease or condition). These trials capture further and definitive information on efficacy, safety and tolerability and are the most expensive and difficult trials to design. This is the final hurdle to provide the definitive assessment of the new treatment.

Satisfactory results in phase III trials enable the results from the development programme to be compiled into the regulatory dossier for submission to the various regulatory agencies for review and marketing approval. These are often comparative trials, carried out in a blind manner, and against the accepted 'gold standard' therapy for the disease or condition under study. The required statistical outcome is defined prospectively and agreed with the regulatory agencies. No 'data dredging' or 'ad hoc' analyses are permitted to attempt to show efficacy outside the planned statistical plan.

Development failure in phase III is typically due to the investigational product not being better than the existing 'gold standard' treatment. Such failures are extremely expensive, with the developer having invested approximately £1.15 billion by this stage.

Principal regulatory authorities include the US Food and Drug Administration (FDA), European Medicines Agency (EMA), and Japanese Pharmaceuticals and Medical Devices Agency (PMDA). These authorities require at least two successful phase III trials proving the drug's safety and efficacy for approval to be granted.

Phase IV

Phase IV studies are conducted once the new drug is approved and on the market. Post-marketing surveillance is designed to gather further data on safety, efficacy and rare or long-term side-effects from this much larger patient population over a longer timeframe. These studies capture less data per patient than earlier trials. They may be mandated by regulatory authorities (FDA, 2009). It is only when a product is on the market, when many hundreds of thousands of subjects are being exposed to the new drug, and when it is being used outside the controlled environment of phase II and III research, that its benefits and side-effects/risks become more fully known.

The clinical trial stages are generally followed in sequential steps (although they may overlap) with each one designed to minimize risk to subjects while advancing the investigational product and gaining further insights regarding its mode of action, safety and efficacy profile.

This process is fraught with risks at each step and pharmaceutical companies will usually undertake the minimum trials needed to reach the phase III stage. This avoids unnecessary expenditure on smaller trials until companies know that their product has sufficient safety and efficacy to advance into phase III pivotal trials.

The smaller trials which are usually required include the following:

- proof of concept (PoC);
- toxicology;
- pharmacokinetics: to look at how the drug is metabolized and excreted by the body and to determine frequency of dosing;
- dose ranging studies: to determine a minimum effective dose and maximum tolerated dose;
- drug/drug interaction trials involving the most commonly used products in the target population or age group;
- metabolism and pharmacokinetic trials in special populations including the elderly, individuals with renal and hepatic impairment, and children;
- food effect trials to determine whether the product should be administered with or without food for maximum effect.

Thus, the phase III environment is critical for the pharmaceutical company because it tries to manage pivotal and supporting trials in the final dash towards the finishing line of a regulatory dossier. To put all this into perspective, the current metrics for drug development are shown in Figure 11.1.

There has been a general decline in success rate as products move from phase I through phase III and, most recently, a high failure rate at the phase II stage. This reflects stringent testing before companies commit to the lengthy and expensive phase III testing (see Figure 11.2).

An additional complication for drug development had increased the complexity of the clinical trials and dictated the need for a programme director of the highest

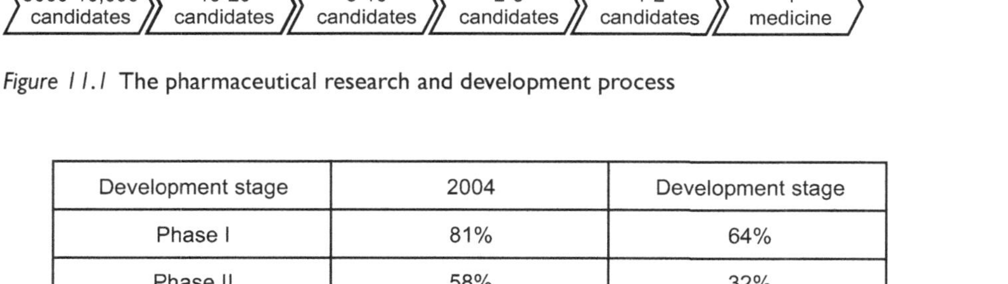

Drug discovery	Pre-clinical testing	Phase I	Phase II	Phase III	Licensing approval	Phase IV
4.5 years	5.5 years	7 years	8.5 years	11 years	12.5 years	
£436 million	£533 million	£710 million	£916 million	£1.1 billion	£1.15 billion	
5000–10,000 candidates	10–20 candidates	5–10 candidates	2–5 candidates	1–2 candidates	1 medicine	

Figure 11.1 The pharmaceutical research and development process

Development stage	2004	Development stage
Phase I	81%	64%
Phase II	58%	32%
Phase III	57%	60%

Figure 11.2 Success rates across drug development phases

calibre. This results from the heterogeneity of the global population. Drug trials are conducted to a strict protocol, which defines the exact population to be studied. The early trials (phases I and II) are very strict and there is no leeway while the basic characteristics of the drug are being defined, including its kinetic profile (how long it stays in the body and at what dose level).

Phase III trials have a little more leeway, in that they attempt to replicate a 'standard' population of subjects with the disease being assessed. However, the requirements are still fairly strict, with the population highly defined. In contrast, when a drug reaches the market, it is used to treat a wide range of 'real-world' patients who vary in age and ethnicity, who have concomitant diseases and who are taking additional medication. It is, of course, impossible to replicate this typical usage in a defined clinical trial but all efforts must be made by the pharmaceutical company to test adequately the most diverse range of patients possible.

During the 1970s drugs were tested and ultimately approved based on clinical trials predominantly conducted in Western Europe and in the United States. It was accepted and acknowledged that trials in Asian subjects required additional early stage testing and separate 'bridging' studies before approval to market was granted. However, such leeway was not afforded to the cultures and nationalities of East and Central Europe and Latin America, and approved drugs were commonly launched on to these markets without robust testing in these specific local populations.

Today, pivotal phase III trials are conducted on a global basis to ensure that people of all races are included in the dataset presented to the regulatory authorities.

Programme management

The 'patent cliff' of the 2000s and the pharmaceutical industry's response to that demonstrates this sector's awareness and strength in portfolio management compared with other sectors. The importance of programme management, and how this differs from project management, remains an area of focus. Recent years have seen increased levels of adoption and maturity of project and programme management in the pharmaceutical and life sciences industries.

The Association for Project Management (APM) defines a programme as: 'A group of related projects and change management activities that together achieve beneficial change for an organisation'. The Project Management Institute (PMI) standard for a programme is 'A group of related projects, subprogrammes and programme activities that are managed in a coordinated way to obtain benefits not available from managing them individually'.

Programme scope in the pharmaceutical industry frequently changes over time with the need to include additional projects or cease projects to adjust to changes in standard of care and emerging needs. The role of programme management in drug development is a critical and integral part of the entire drug development process. In line with other sectors, the process of programme planning, execution variance, monitoring, progress and change control, represents an ongoing, iterative cycle (a feedback loop) and is reliant on people, process, information (data) and technology.

The requirements for a phase III trial programme are usually that a company has to conduct two phase III trials in the target population. These need to deliver the statistical output according to a predefined and agreed level of confidence. By the time a New Chemical Entity (NCE) reaches phase III of clinical testing, there may be less than half the original patent life remaining, and it is therefore imperative that the programme is meticulously planned and implemented in order to maximize the product's earning potential.

A complicating factor in drug development is identifying the most appropriate global investigational sites. A clinical trial is extremely hard work for a principal investigator. The administrative requirements to start up a trial are extremely stringent, and the investigator should be pre-qualified in terms of being trained in 'good clinical practice' (Medicines and Healthcare Products Regulatory Agency, 2014). Each site has to add this trial work into its usual clinical practice and find the appropriately trained and dedicated resources to manage the logistics of the trial and patient visits.

In addition, it is important that the sites chosen have a similar 'standard of care' for the selected indication being tested. The more variable the standard of care, the more the final dataset can vary, thus possibly invalidating the statistical analysis or necessitating the removal of inappropriate subjects from this analysis. As phase III trials are usually very similar – and thus would compete with each other if co-located – then a programme director has to find, identify and qualify a substantial number of investigative sites globally. All sites should have:

- keen and experienced principal investigators;
- a robust and appropriate patient population for trial entry;
- a supportive infrastructure and willingness for timely data entry and sponsor visits and audits.

These sites must be comparable in terms of their disease management and standard of care and the cultures must be appropriate for the selected endpoints. For example, as an endpoint in some trials for dementia therapies, subjects are requested to count backwards in sevens as part of a scale assessment. But if subjects would not be able to undertake this assignment in their 'normal' state, then the measure would not accurately assess the effect of the drug being tested. Thus in addition to applying strict programme management principles, a programme manager in drug development must also take into account the following parameters and variables when planning a global strategy:

- standard of healthcare in the countries selected for the trial;
- availability, experience and qualifications of the principal investigator;
- logistical issues at the site. For example, do they have the human resources to manage trial subjects, facilities to store biological samples at low temperatures, access to appropriate additional medical services such as pharmacy, ECG, radiology, laboratories, and emergency care?
- the need to design a programme which takes into account all global markets so that each subpopulation has some exposure to the product under test;
- managing cultural differences in terms of assessments to ensure a homogeneous and robust dataset;
- ensuring no overlap at sites;
- completing trial recruitment, with quality subjects, within a defined timeframe.

Importance of programme management

Taking into account the numerous variables inherent within a trial programme, it is of critical importance that a very experienced programme manager or programme director is appointed.

Bespoke and meticulous planning is essential. Identification and engagement of all stakeholders is critical to ensure a smooth implementation and execution of the planned trials. For some clinical trials, there may be a number of key and active participants including those providing:

- drug packaging and labelling;
- laboratory analyses;
- imaging modalities;
- translations and back-translations of key documents;
- data management.

Non-participating stakeholders include the sponsor, the regulatory agencies, the payers and patient support groups.

The processes of risk management (including mitigation planning and contingency planning) need to be performed actively at every site involved in a trial. This could involve over 500 sites across 50 or more countries, making such a task and the required follow-up very complex indeed.

Programme management involves, among other documents, a detailed programme plan with various assumptions and slack time (float) incorporated. That ultimately provides a timeline for the overall programme.

Recruitment in clinical trials rarely goes according to plan. Investigators have their patient database, and then have to discuss the benefits and risks of a given trial with each subject and caregiver and/or family members. In addition, specific nuances of a given protocol may exclude particular subjects from the trial. Further, the blood tests and biochemical analysis required to determine a predefined baseline will often exclude potential subjects from a clinical trial. Thus a programme director will often have to track recruitment characteristics per site and have a bespoke mitigation strategy for every site that is not performing according to plan. For some countries this is relatively straightforward, but for others there is a major cultural awareness to take into account because these investigators may ultimately become the end users of the product under assessment.

A strict process must be followed when starting all trials. In the interests of openness and transparency every trial must be registered on a global website, such as www.clinicaltrials.gov (which is managed by the US National Institutes of Health). That website listed details of 179,546 trials across 187 countries in all indications (as at 1 December 2014). This information service allows potential subjects to search for suitable trials within their disease area and location. That increases global awareness of the trials, which is excellent for subjects and offers them potentially more choice of appropriate trials. These factors must be taken into account by the programme manager because recruitment to trials (and managing the expectations of subjects) is key for engagement, motivation and retention of trial participants.

In addition, the ability to search for competing global trials (thus being aware of the entry criteria, knowing the number of participants, the timelines, the global sites and other information within the clinicaltrials.gov website) is invaluable for the programme manager. This allows for a data-driven country and site strategy to be developed which is aimed at minimizing timelines and maximizing the number of sites per country. That, in turn, results in less 'noise' or variability in the final dataset.

The pharmaceutical industry is second only to the airline sector in terms of being the world's most highly regulated industry. In order to start clinical trials in people, there need to be approvals from the regulatory authority in each country in which a trial is planned and also ethics committee approval from each hospital and/or other provider (for example in the United Kingdom the GP surgery, which is taking part in the trial).

Approvals require significant documentation, both from the pharmaceutical company and the principal investigator at each site. Such approval processes are country-specific and can occur sequentially or concurrently. There are published approval timelines, but other factors such as holiday periods, backlog of trials for approval, complexity of the trial or issues regarding the investigational product or device all factor into timelines and are hard to predict. Trials are subject to scrutiny and may sometimes be totally rejected by regulatory and or ethics committees.

Another key factor which has to be actively managed – and one for which it can be equally challenging to make assumptions – is the recruitment rate of subjects into a particular trial at a given site. It is extremely challenging to estimate subject interest in a given trial and recruitment will depend on many factors, many of which the programme manager may not be fully aware of. These include:

- number of ongoing trials at the investigative site (often not disclosed for confidentiality reasons);
- the principal investigator's level of genuine interest and scientific belief in the benefit of the investigational product;
- the number of, and engagement of, nursing study coordinators at the site (managing and coordinating subjects is time-consuming and paperwork is extensive);
- the cohort of subjects at an investigator site (for example, secondary or tertiary referral site);
- the workload of the principal investigator, current hospital duties and other trial commitments;
- the availability of necessary ancillary equipment (such as magnetic resonance imaging (MRI) or Positron Emission Tomography (PET);
- for the trial subjects:
  - stage of disease – are protocol entry criteria being met?
  - concomitant medications;
  - concurrent illnesses such as diabetes or hypertension;
  - insurance status (which can be important in some places);
  - proximity to the investigative site;
  - family support network (if applicable);
  - willingness to be assigned to a placebo arm (although trials are 'masked', subjects may well have a 1:1 or 1:3 chance of receiving a placebo).

Year	NDAs approved	NMEs approved	NDAs received
2010	93	21	103
2011	99	30	105
2012	No data available	39	No data available
2013	No data available	27	No data available
2014	No data available	41	No data available

Figure 11.3 Success rates of NDAs, NMEs approvals since 2010

Outsourcing

Many pharmaceutical companies outsource their phase III trials to a contract research organization (CRO). Leading CROs generally have the country infrastructure to support global phase III programmes across multiple indications, thus assuring that the sponsor is able to assess the efficacy and safety of their product in many ethnicities. Major CROs are able to manage concurrent development programmes, in the same indication, because of their extensive reach and global footprint.

Taking the largest CRO (Quintiles) as an example, this organization currently operates across some 100 countries and employs 32,000 staff. Quintiles is the market leader in programme management for pivotal phase III global trials and can accommodate competing programmes for most indications

Conclusion

Drug development programme management in the pharmaceutical industry presents unique challenges in addition to the usual lifecycle elements of planning, execution, monitoring and close-out. The human factor needs to be taken into account and factored into the planning, design and timelines, and variabilities here are extreme. The other major factor to apply to programme management is the global challenge of utilizing a significant number of countries in a pivotal trial, achieving consistency and harmonization across cultures and ethnicities in order to provide robust and reproducible data.

However, following this robust and defined pathway with meticulous programme management has led to a high success rate of products which pass through to the FDA for ultimate approval (see Figure 11.3).

References and further reading

Abrantes-Metz, R., Adams, C. and Metz, A. (2004), 'Pharmaceutical Development Phases: A Duration Analysis', *SSRN Journal*, 14(4).

APM (2012), *APM Body of Knowledge*, 6th edn., Princes Risborough: Association for Project Management.

Bairu, M. and Weiner, M. (2014), *Global Clinical Trials for Alzheimer's Disease*, Oxford: Elsevier.

FDA (2009), 'Format and Content of Proposed Risk Evaluation and Mitigation Strategies (REMS), REMS Assessments, and Proposed REMS Modifications: Guidance for Industry', *Biotechnology Law Report*, 28(6): 755–73.

FDA (2013), *Summary of NDA Approvals & Receipts, 1938 to the present*. Available at: <www.fda. gov/AboutFDA/WhatWeDo/History/ProductRegulation/SummaryofNDAApprovals Receipts1938tothepresent/default.htm>.

FDA (2015), *Novel New Drugs 2014 Summary*. [ebook] U.S. Food and Drug Administration Center for Drug Evaluation and Research. Available at: <www.fda.gov/downloads/Drugs/DevelopmentApprovalProcess/DrugInnovation/UCM430299.pdf>.

Harpum, P. (2010), *Portfolio, Programme, and Project Management in the Pharmaceutical and Biotechnology Industries*. Hoboken, NJ: John Wiley.

Hay, M., Thomas, D., Craighead, J., Economides, C. and Rosenthal, J. (2014), 'Clinical Development Success Rates for Investigational Drugs', *Nature Biotechnology*, 32(1): 40–51.

Jaillon, P. (2007), 'Controlled Randomized Clinical Trials', *Bulletin de l'Académie Nationale de Médecine*, 191(4–5): 735–56.

Medicines and Healthcare Products Regulatory Agency (2014), *Good Clinical Practice: Guidance and Inspections*. Available at: www.gov.uk/government/good-clinical-practice-guidance-and-inspections>.

Paul, S., Mytelka, D., Dunwiddie, C., Persinger, C., Munos, B., Lindborg, S. and Schacht. A. (2010), 'How to Improve R&D Productivity: The Pharmaceutical Industry's Grand Challenge', *Nature Reviews Drug Discovery*, 9: 203–14.

PhRMA (2007), *Drug Discovery and Development: Understanding the R&D Process*, Washington, DC: PhRMA. Available at: <www.phrma.org/sites/default/files/pdf/rd_brochure_022807.pdf>.

PMI (2013), *A Guide to the Project Management Body of Knowledge (PMBOK Guide)*, 5th edn., Newtown Square, PA: Project Management Institute.

Pullan, P. and Archer, J. (2013), *Business Analysis and Leadership: Influencing Change*, London: Kogan Page.

Pullan, P., Murray-Webster, R. and Randle, V. (2011). *A Short Guide to Facilitating Risk Management*. Farnham: Gower.

Chapter 12

Programme Management for Humanitarian and Development Projects

Ricardo Viana Vargas, Farhad Abdollahyan,
Carlos Alberto Pereira Soares and André
Bittencourt do Valle

[Editorial comment: Programmes of the kind discussed in this chapter are particularly important because of the relief and benefits they can bring to those suffering from natural and other disasters. The writers are well experienced in this field: Ricardo Viana Vargas and Farhad Abdollahyan are both from the United Nations Office for Project Services (UNOPS), and Carlos Soares and André Bittencourt do Valle are at Universidade Federal Fluminense. DL]

Humanitarian and development-driven projects and programmes deal with human-made disasters such as conflicts, terrorism, technological hazards and disasters triggered by natural hazards (such as earthquakes, floods and droughts) or to solve development needs such as lack of health and sanitation, famine and poverty, illiteracy, lack of human resources qualification and lack of livelihood. This chapter covers humanitarian and development projects that are undertaken in a post-disaster environment or in cases of chronic hunger and poverty. The international community contributes to these areas through the provision of funds, experts, food, medicines, farming and other technological tools, and building materials among other items. All these temporary engagements are projects managed with a varying scale of efficiency and effectiveness.

Introduction

Humanitarian projects are 'operations conducted to relieve human suffering, especially where responsible authorities in the area are unable or unwilling to provide adequate service support to civilian populations' (Reliefweb, 2008). That means the environment may be unstable or even hostile to those who provide the aid.

These projects focus mainly on poverty-stricken regions of developing countries in Africa, Latin America and Asia – areas that have been in poverty for a long time and where the living conditions and quality of life are typically below international standards, as measured by the Human Development Index (HDI).

The HDI is a summary measure of average achievement in the key dimensions of human development: a long and healthy life, being knowledgeable and having a decent standard of living. The HDI is the geometric mean of normalized indices for each of the three dimensions (see http://hdr.undp.org/en/content/ human-development-index-hdi). According to the United Nations Development Programme's (UNDP) – *Human Development Report 2014*, 'Overall human develop- ment levels continue to rise, but at a slower pace than before. The 2013 HDI value at the global level was 0.702, while the 2012 HDI was 0.700' (UNDP, 2014a).

Humanitarian and development projects range from complex emergencies (Reliefweb, 2008) to small-scale, stand-alone and output-orientated initiatives with limited scope and importance. The smaller scale projects are outside the scope of this Handbook, unless they are grouped together and managed as an emergent pro- gramme as defined in the UK framework: *Managing Successful Programmes* (OGC, 2011).

Characteristics of humanitarian and development projects

Humanitarian and development programmes aim to provide not only benefits for people and communities, but also longer lasting results and capabilities. It makes sense to either group them together as emerging programmes, or to launch them from the beginning as a vision-led programme (OGC, 2011). Principles (such as transparency, mutual accountability and governance), characteristics (such as complex multi-stake- holder environment) and critical success factors (such as the use of logical frame- works, benefit maps, and results-based planning) are common to all these projects. The programmes are subject to external risks (natural hazards, political and economic instability), and internal factors (such as lack of transparent governance and local cap- acity) that might interfere with, change or even halt their progress. These cases vary in their nature, scale and scope, and most importantly in governance and leadership.

Principles

Some specific principles apply to humanitarian projects. These initiatives follow the global principles of humanity, neutrality and impartiality (UNGA, 1991). Adherence to these principles reflects a measure of accountability of the humanitarian com- munity. Other principles also apply to humanitarian and development programmes (including transparency, national ownership and mutual accountability). There are some cross-cutting concepts (such as sustainability, gender equality and community engagement).

According to the OECD:

> At the Second High Level Forum on Aid Effectiveness (2005) it was recognized that aid could – and should – be producing better impacts. The Paris Declaration [on Aid Effectiveness] was endorsed in order to base development efforts on first-hand experience of what works and does not work with aid. It is formulated around five central pillars: Ownership, Alignment, Harmonisation, Managing for Results and Mutual Accountability. (<http://www.oecd.org/dac/effectiveness/ parisdeclarationandaccraagendaforaction.htm>)

The Accra Agenda for Action (OECD, 2008) reaffirms the objective of strengthen- ing partner countries' ownership of their development strategies and strengthening the ties, making governments accountable for their domestic constituents. It also broadens the concept to include engagement with the parliament, political parties, local authorities, the media, academia, social partners and the broader civil society. The principles of Accra Agenda for Action are:

- Ownership: countries have more to say over their development processes through wider participation in development policy formulation, stronger leadership on aid coordination and more use of country systems for aid delivery.
- Inclusive partnerships: all partners (including donors in the OECD Development Assistance Committee and developing countries, as well as other donors, foundations and civil society) participate fully.
- Delivering results: aid is focused on real and measurable impact on development.
- Capacity development: to build the ability of countries to manage their own future. This lies at the heart of the Accra Agenda for Action.

Risk context

As the latest Human Development Reports (HDRs) have shown, most populations have been doing progressively better in human development (UNDP, 2014b). Progress in technology, education and incomes may eventually lead to longer, healthier and more secure lives. Nevertheless, there is also a widespread sense of instability in the world today – in livelihoods, personal security, environment and global politics. More than 15 per cent of the world's population are exposed to multidimensional poverty. High achievements on critical aspects of human development, such as health and nutrition, can be quickly undermined by a natural disaster or recession periods. Urban violence such as theft and armed robbery can leave people physically and psychologically impoverished. Corruption and impassive state institutions can leave those in need of assistance without alternatives.

There is a convergence among several frameworks that were considered as separate paradigms in the past. In fact, researchers and practitioners in the field

$$\text{Disaster risk} = \frac{\text{Hazard x exposure x vulnerability}}{\text{Resilience}}$$

Hazard	Exposure	Vulnerability	Resilience
A dangerous phenomenon, substance, human activity or condition that might cause loss of life, injury or other health impacts, property damage, loss of livelihoods and services, social and economic disruption, or environmental damage.	People, property, systems or other elements present in hazard zones that are thereby subject to potential losses.	The characteristics and circumstances of a community, system or asset that makes it susceptible to the damaging effects of a hazard.	The ability of a system, community or society exposed to hazards to resist, absorb, accommodate to and recover from the effects of a hazard in a timely and efficient manner, including through the preservation of its essential basic structures and functions. **Higher resilience = lower risk of disaster.**

Figure 12.1 Disaster risk and its relation to resilience

of development regard disaster risk (UNISDR, 2009), building national and local capacity, as well as having resilient infrastructure and communities either as an integral part of humanitarian and development initiatives or as a prerequisite for their success (Figure 12.1). The UNDP considers vulnerability and resilience through a human development lens in its latest *Human Development Report* (UNDP, 2014b).

To treat these uncertainties, UN agencies such as United Nations Office for Project Services (UNOPS) identify and respond to risks in the following risk categories when engaging their partners (governments, donors and implementing organizations) possibly even requiring escalation to the Programme Board level:

- Government and regulatory. Events and conditions that could change the institutional framework governing the programme and affect its business case. For example, a government might change its policies towards international cooperation and hence affect an ongoing programme governance structure.
- Reputation. Any incident should be managed if it might affect the credibility of the implementing organization (as a transparent and politically neutral humanitarian and development agent).
- Human resources. In humanitarian and development programmes, HR risks are related to availability and skills necessary for the programme and its projects. Most of the team members are contracted on a temporary basis and may be difficult to replace.
- Implementation. Risks may be related not only to design and execution, but also to all aspects of procurement and logistics, working environment, security or suppliers/contractors' quality and performance. These risks will affect capability and might delay benefits realization.
- Sustainability. Humanitarian and development initiatives are intended for sustainable outcomes. Thus all events and conditions that could impact environmental, economic, social and national capacity dimensions of the programme should be managed. An example of a sustainability risk would be related to assumptions of future maintenance requirements, such as availability of operational budget for staff to run the capabilities and realize the benefits.

Complexity

In spite of all coordinated efforts (with the participation of rich donor countries, multilateral institutions and their poor country beneficiaries) specialists question the effectiveness of humanitarian and development aid. Fengler and Kharas (2011) observe that in the last two decades, although total aid increased (from US$92 billion in 1992 to US$200 billion in 2008), with more players in the game, aid has declined in *relative* importance in most countries. According to the same authors, a new and much more complex aid environment is emerging, in which direct foreign investment is higher than aid.

The donor landscape has also changed radically. New private players – international non-governmental organizations (NGOs), foundations and vertical funds – are responsible for growing the share of aid volume. Vertical funds are administered by multilateral agencies that focus on a single theme (such as global funds for AIDS,

TB and malaria). Private philanthropy alone now reaches US$60 billion annually. However, most aid still comes from the members of the Development Assistance Committee (DAC), a club of 22 rich countries contributing a total of US$120 billion per year. The 'Third World' is no longer homogeneously poor and some countries (such as Brazil) not only reduce poverty at home but also become donors in Haiti and African countries. This 'South–South' bilateral aid amounts to US$15 billion per year (Fengler and Kharas, 2011).

Although the volumes of aid are growing, the average project size – even of traditional donors – is shrinking. Thus while the number of projects has grown from around 10,000 to nearly 85,000 between 1990 and 2008, the average size of these projects has shrunk, during the same period, from a high point of around US$75 million to below US$15 million. Smaller projects can deliver benefits to isolated communities, but they increase aid fragmentation which increases administrative costs and complicates donor coordination by recipient governments. Clustering small projects into programmes can mitigate this tendency.

One recommendation of Fengler and Kharas supports the idea of emerging programmes in the development aid context:

> The focus should be on the dynamics of development. Individual project success does not always add up to systemic change. Projects that work well are not systematically scaled up. Donors have limited long-term engagement in or accountability for results in a given area. A focus on dynamics can mean changing the institutional setup, with more aggressive monitoring, evaluation, and assessment of development results. Scalable and programmatic approaches commensurate with country needs have to be encouraged. It is important to identify needs, interventions, and gaps at a local and sectorial level, and to monitor progress in these areas systematically over time.
>
> (Fengler and Kharas, 2011)

In other words, a programme management approach will result not only in cost reduction and higher efficiency in use of aid funds, but also more effectiveness through designing the right set of required benefits, planning, monitoring and evaluation of results.

Design, monitoring and evaluation frameworks

Two methods are described here. Both use monitoring and evaluation to ensure that the desired outcomes are reached and that lessons learned are incorporated in the next phases of the programme.

Theory of change (ToC)

Management of most modern humanitarian and development programmes is based on the 'theory of change' (ToC) model developed by Carol Weiss (1995). ToC is a rigorous yet participatory process whereby groups and stakeholders in a planning process articulate their long-term goals and identify the conditions necessary for those goals to be met. These outcomes are arranged graphically in a causal framework. ToC describes the types of interventions (projects) that bring about the outcomes depicted in the outcomes framework map. Each intervention is tied to an outcome in the causal framework, revealing the complex web of activities required to bring about change. It provides a working model against which hypotheses and assumptions can be tested on which actions will best produce the outcomes in the model.

Adherence to the ToC method keeps the processes of implementation transparent so that everyone involved knows what is happening and why. To be clear, every outcome in the theory is explicitly defined. All outcomes should be given one or more indicators of success. As implementation proceeds, organizations collect and analyse data on key indicators as a means of monitoring progress on the theory of change. Indicator data show whether or not changes are taking place as forecast. Using the indicator data, programme staff can adjust and revise their change model as they learn more about what works and what does not.

Rationales in a theory of change explain the connections between the outcomes and why one outcome is needed to achieve another. Assumptions explain the contextual foundations of the theory. Often rationales and assumptions are supported by research, strengthening the likelihood of the theory, accompanied by a written narrative that explains the logic of the framework (the chain of input, output, outcome and impact).

ToC can be a tool for planning and problem-framing as well as for monitoring and evaluation. In formulating long-term outcomes, preconditions and interventions ToC forms the basis of visioning papers, strategic and/or annual plans and goal-setting processes. As an evaluation tool, ToC identifies the specific goals of the programme and ties those goals to particular engagements. Data can then be collected to evaluate progress towards the stated goals, as well as the effectiveness of interventions in producing outcomes. ToC maps out the initiative through the following stages:

- Identifying long-term goals and the assumptions behind them.
- Backward mapping from each long-term goal by working out the preconditions or requirements necessary to achieve that goal and explaining why.
- Voicing assumptions made about what exists in the system without which the theory used would not work, and articulating rationales for why some outcomes are necessary preconditions for other outcomes.
- Weighing and choosing the most strategic interventions to bring about the desired change.
- Developing indicators to measure progress on the desired outcomes and assessing the performance of the initiative.
- Quality review should answer three basic questions: is the theory used plausible, 'doable' (feasible) and testable?
- Writing a narrative to explain the summary logic of the initiative.

LogFrame model

The Logical Framework (known as LogFrame) was originally elaborated by Rosenberg, Posner and Hanley (1970) for the United States Agency for International

Goals	Indicators	Verification sources	Assumptions
Purpose	Indicators	Verification sources	Assumptions
Outputs	Indicators	Verification sources	Assumptions
Activities	Resources	Means	Assumptions

Figure 12.2 LogFrame matrix

Development (USAID). This method has evolved into results-based management (RBM) and managing for development results (MfDR) – used as a standard methodology in multilateral organizations like the UNDP and the World Bank.

The LogFrame is a project management tool to design, implement, monitor and evaluate a project. It presents a wealth of information related to the project in a 4×4 matrix (Figure 12.2).

The LogFrame facilitates reflection on the basic elements of the project, such as its objectives, the activities that should be performed, the resources required, method for monitoring progress and results, and risks that could threaten the project.

The first column of the 4×4 matrix shows the project logic (also called intervention logic) – hence the name logical framework. The project's activities are captured in the bottom row. When these activities are completed, they are expected to lead to tangible outputs. All the different results together will help to achieve the project's purpose (sometimes called 'specific objective' – the main reason why the project was conceived). It is the problem that one wants to solve.

In a broader context, the project's purpose will help achieve one or more goals (or 'general objectives'), which are captured in the top row of the matrix. The term 'project logic' means that one thing leads to another: the activities produce tangible outputs that lead to the project's purpose.

Both ToC and LogFrame use monitoring and evaluation to ensure that the desired outcomes are reached and that lessons learned are incorporated in the next phases of the programme.

Case example: LIFT

The Livelihoods and Food Security Trust Fund (LIFT) is a multidonor consortium fund established in Myanmar in 2009 with the overall aim of reducing by half the number of people living in poverty and hunger. LIFT works in areas that account for about 90 per cent of food poverty in Myanmar. These areas include Ayeyarwady Delta, Dry Zone, Chin, Kachin, Shan, and Rakhine States. The purpose of LIFT is to increase food availability and the incomes of two million target beneficiaries through a network of implementing partners.

In the spirit of the Paris Declaration on Aid Effectiveness and the OECD/DAC guidelines on 'Harmonising Donor Practices for Effective Aid Delivery', the donors agreed on a multidonor trust fund approach. The programme is driven by the conviction that pooling donor resources enables programme coherence and leads to greater impact. UNOPS was engaged to administer the funds and provide monitoring and oversight.

At its start, donors and UNOPS faced the challenge of rapidly mobilizing funds to support livelihood recovery in the cyclone-prone Delta. Operating within the framework of LIFT's overall goal, the $22 million Tat Lan (Way Forward) Sustainable Food Security and Livelihoods Programme began in 2013. Its purpose was to improve the livelihoods of the 214 cyclone-affected communities equitably and sustainably.

The programme management structure and processes have matured since its inception. The LIFT strategy places results at the centre of its funding decisions. There is an overarching logical framework (LogFrame) with headline indicators that summarize LIFT's progress and performance against annual and programme targets. The Implementing Partner LogFrames reflect in aggregate the overall LIFT LogFrame. The LIFT fund staff monitor partner performance through bi-annual reports against an agreed LogFrame and six-monthly field visits. LIFT has an agreed plan for monitoring and evaluation (M&E) against the LogFrame which (given the complexity of the programme) comprises several layers. The LogFrame is reviewed periodically to reflect any changes in the programme approach and targets.

The Department for International Development (DFID) chairs the LIFT Donor Consortium and owns the business case. According to LIFT, results from the 2010–11 cyclone Nargis recovery activities (funded by LIFT) in the Delta have been very positive. As a result of intensive training, demonstrations and on-farm trials of new farming and storage techniques (tillage buffalo, improved seeds, appropriate fertilizer) from the LIFT implementing partners, there was a 20–60 per cent increase in the agricultural area cultivated and a 40–60 per cent increase in crop yields.

In addition to farming activities, LIFT has also supported the creation of 9,579 small village-based businesses such as grocery shops, snack bars, soap house material production, mechanics, and tailoring through training that assists villagers to explore potential opportunities, management skills and book keeping and revolving funds for business start-up. The LIFT programme was originally supposed to close in 2014, but its huge success has led to extension until 2018.

Identifying the programme

According to MSP (OGC, 2011), the idea and the resulting vision that is driving the change generate the programme mandate. That triggers the overall programme management process. In the case of LIFT, discussions began in 2008 among a group of donors on ways to help Myanmar make faster progress towards the achievement of the Millennium Development Goals (MDG).

After extensive consultations with key stakeholders from the Myanmar government, embassies, UN agencies and NGOs, the LIFT Programme Mandate is to assist Myanmar towards the achievement of MDG1. This first goal aims to eradicate poverty and hunger. More precisely, LIFT's purpose was to increase food availability and the incomes of two million target beneficiaries. In March 2009, LIFT was officially launched with the following statement:

> LIFT's vision is to be a collective and influential voice for innovation and learning, and to provide a platform for enhanced policy engagement on sustainable agriculture, food security and rural development. LIFT's goal is to contribute to sustainably reduce the number of people in Myanmar living in poverty and hunger. LIFT's purpose is to increase livelihoods' resilience and nutrition of poor people in Myanmar by focusing on interventions that increase income, food availability, utilization and stability of access to food.
>
> (<http://lift-fund.org/about-lift>)

LIFT's goal and purpose is to be met through the achievement of four outcomes:

1. Increased incomes of rural households.
2. Increased resilience of poor rural households and communities to shocks, stresses and adverse trends.
3. Improved nutrition of women, men and children.
4. Improved policies and effective public expenditure for pro-poor rural development.

According to LIFT's LogFrame, the delivery of eight key outputs will lead to the achievement of its four high-level outcomes. The outputs that drive LIFT's projects are as follows:

*   increased sustainable agricultural production by smallholder farmers;
*   improved market access and market terms for smallholder farmers;
*   increased employment in non-farm activities for smallholders and landless;
*   increased access to affordable financial services by smallholder farmers and landless;
*   improved diets of women, men and children;
*   safeguarded access to and sustainable use of natural resources for smallholders and landless;
*   strengthened local capacity to support and promote food and livelihoods security;
*   generation of policy-relevant evidence regarding smallholder farmers and landless.

The narrative connecting these outcomes can be found in the way LIFT understands the structural dynamics of the rural economy and the implications for its target group (poor smallholder farmers and the landless). The strategy divides its target group into:

1. Households with commercial potential to step up the value ladder and out of poverty. These have the opportunity (as a result of access to land, labour and markets) to invest in achieving higher productivity agriculture and better market terms. LIFT can support them in doing this.
2. Households that can move from agriculture into more productive sectors of the economy over time. This could be a local 'step out', finding better-paid employment in local non-farm activities. It could also be a 'migration step out' to take advantage of opportunities further afield. LIFT can facilitate these processes and minimize any consequential adverse impacts on the household.
3. Households without commercial potential or opportunities to leave agriculture or the rural economy and that have little option but to 'hang in'. For them, own account subsistence agriculture or working as agricultural labour is, in effect, a safety net. For those in this situation, LIFT can take direct steps to improve their food security and nutrition.

A programme requires initial and continuous top-level sponsorship to gain and maintain the necessary commitment to the investment, resources, timescales and delivery of changes.

The sponsoring group in the LIFT programme comprises representatives of contributing donors from Australia, Denmark, the European Union, France, Ireland, Italy, the Netherlands, New Zealand, Sweden, Switzerland, the United Kingdom and the United States. This forms the Donor Consortium, the highest authority in terms of the Fund's governance ultimate decision-making. At the beginning, the Donor Consortium Board met at least twice per year. Since 2014, it meets annually.

The Donor Consortium and the Fund Board are solely responsible for policy dialogue, identification of the Fund's policy and strategy and for approving activities to be implemented by the Fund Manager and implementing partners (Figure 12.3).

Each donor to LIFT will have a bilateral contribution agreement with the Fund Manager. These contribution agreements are the main mechanism through which each donor exerts fiduciary and legal authority over the funds they provide. The overarching objective of the Donor Consortium is to provide a structured forum for donors to LIFT's achievements and current challenges, as well as its finances and main priorities for the coming year (Figure 12.4).

The Senior Consultation Group comprises senior representation from the Government of Myanmar, representatives from implementing partners, civil society and the private sector. It serves as an advisory body and 'sounding board' for the Fund Board. The Senior Consultation Group has no formal decision-making authority within LIFT.

The Fund Board acts with delegated authority from the Donor Consortium, providing strategic leadership and oversight for LIFT implementation. The Fund Board's focus is on strategic decisions, policy decisions, donor coordination, building relations with the Government of Myanmar, and overall performance management of the Fund Manager. The Fund Board also selects the projects that receive LIFT

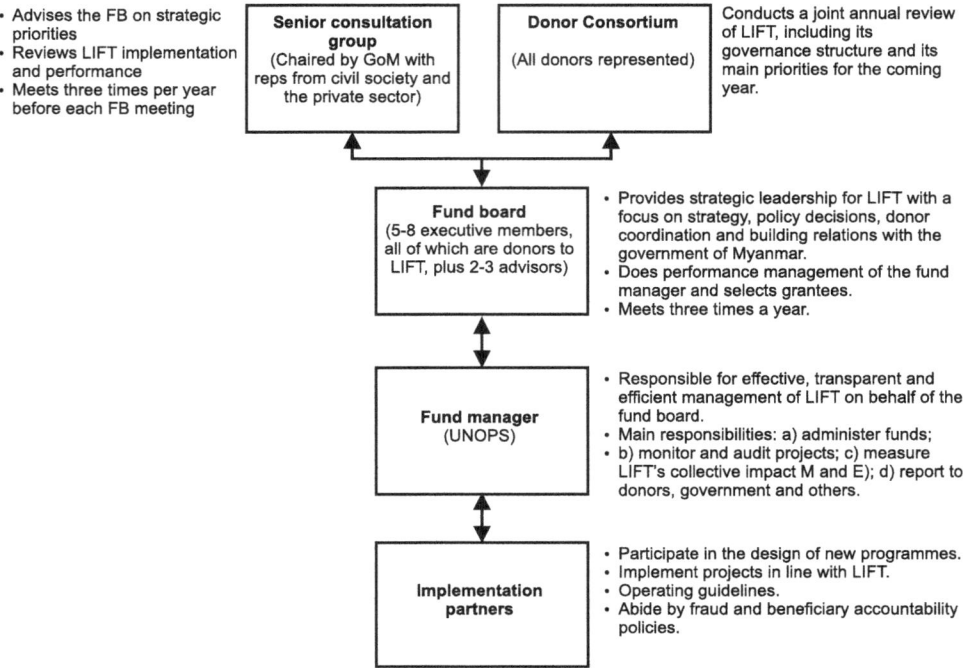

Figure 12.3 LIFT programme governance source

funds with guidance from the Fund Manager. At the time of writing the UK (DFID) chairs the Fund Board as the senior responsible owner (SRO). Australia (AusAID), the European Union, Switzerland, the UK (DFID) and USAID are Fund Board members. There are also three independent members and one donor observer of the Fund Board. The Fund Board meets at least once every four months.

UNOPS acts as LIFT's Fund Manager (the programme manager role defined in MSP). The Fund Manager is responsible for effective, transparent and efficient management of the Fund on behalf of the Fund Board, and has delegated authority for Fund management under the rules and regulations of UNOPS and in accordance with the strategy approved by the Fund Board. The Fund Manager is responsible for the overall management of the fund and for monitoring and overseeing the financial and technical performance of the implementing partners. The Fund Manager is also responsible for implementing monitoring and evaluation, generating knowledge and learning.

For effective application of the funds the Fund Board carefully selects implementing partners using certain criteria. The current implementing partners include local, international and UN organizations.

The LIFT Programme has a series of documents and agreements including a LIFT concept paper. Together these cover items referenced by MSP in the programme brief. There was no formal guide (such as a programme preparation plan) for preliminary mobilization and planning but the approach and schedule were reflected in documents approved by the donor consortium.

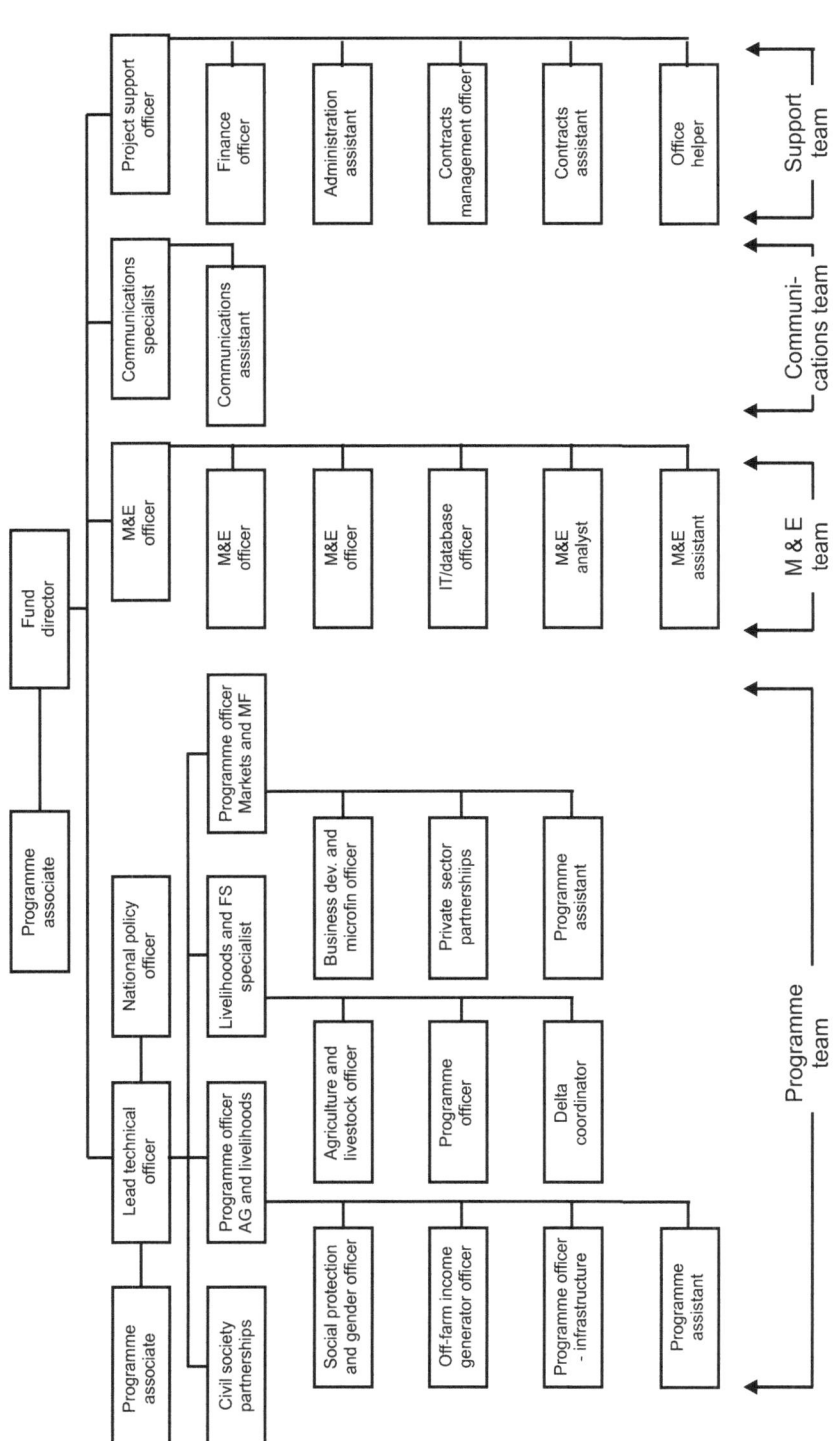

Figure 12.4 Organization of the programme management office

It is highly advisable to conduct an independent formal review of the programme brief to assess the scope, rationale and objectives. But the independent review of LIFT did not follow a structured stage gate review (such as that described in OGC's Gateway Review for UK public sector programmes). LIFT was evaluated using another approach, Value-for-Money assessment.

UNOPS and the LIFT Fund Consortium representatives signed the programme agreement on 2 October 2009. This event triggered the tranches, capability delivery and benefit realization, in accordance with the MSP methodology.

Defining the programme

According to MSP, programme definition provides the basis for deciding whether to proceed with the programme or not based on the detailed definition and plans of the programme. This was therefore used as the starting point for developing the programme definition in more detail.

The programme definition document specifies how the organization will be changed by the successful programme, and how it will be governed in terms of quality, stakeholders, issue resolution, risks, benefits, resources, and planning and control. It must be approved by the sponsoring group and the SRO before the programme can be formally established. Detailed planning is undertaken at this stage to ensure the best – and most realistic – case is put forward.

The programme plan document in this definition stage is vital to provide a structured framework for managing the programme and includes:

- timescales, cost, outputs and the project dependencies;
- risks and issue management;
- a detailed schedule of programme tranches;
- transition plans;
- plans for monitoring and controlling performance and targets.

DFID, as chair of the Donor Consortium, prepared a business case for LIFT. However, that document was elaborated progressively by workstreams based on arising and changing scenarios and events (such as cyclones and other natural hazards). A new LIFT strategy (2014–18) was finalized in September 2014 and approved by the Donor Consortium in October 2014. LIFT attempts to enhance the impact of its projects upon household nutrition, and be alert to possible adverse and often unintended impacts upon household and community resilience. LIFT does that through a rigorous monitoring and evaluation process throughout the programme activities.

Managing the programme tranches

A tranche is a portion of something – in this case a group of projects and activities that deliver a step change in capability. The managing process aims to implement the defined strategies for the programme, ensure that the capability delivery is aligned with the strategic direction of the organization and enables the release of benefits. At the end of each tranche a review can be held to measure the benefits achieved in accordance with the business case and the benefit realization plan (Figure 12.5).

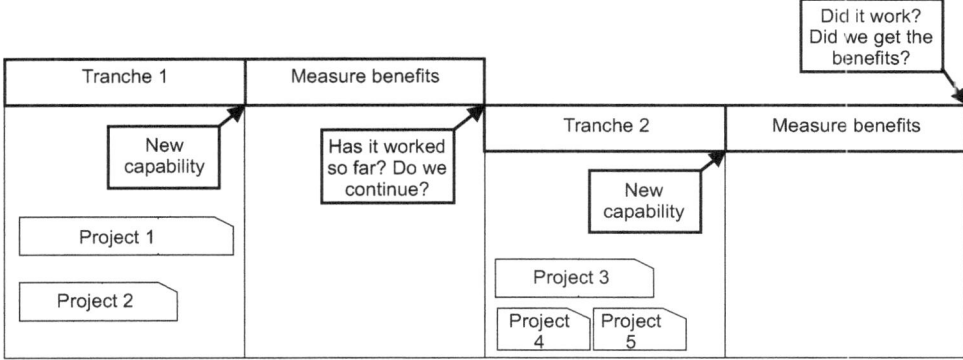

Figure 12.5 Managing the tranches

In October 2014, the programme was halfway through and at the highest level. The end-of-tranche evaluation was carried out and a new tranche was initiated

Of course, the situation in rural areas is fluid and sensitive to exogenous events. New roads and access to markets or new technologies can give households commercial opportunities that did not exist before. Or, natural and human-made disasters and crises can push some people into poverty.

LIFT devotes its resources to positively impacting the rural economy and enhancing the opportunities for all members of its target group through:

- Village-based interventions that are helping households to realize their economic potential as farmers (productivity raising activities); as landless (income-generating activities and jobs in the non-farm economy); or as potential migrants (making migration safe and productive), while protecting and enhancing the resilience of the poorest (through social protection measures).
- Supporting economic activities at regional or national level. That can help to improve the overall environment and offer economic opportunities (for example delivering a range of financial products, strengthening inclusive value chains and making better use of information technology).
- Actively harvesting lessons and generating evidence to achieve systemic change through targeted advocacy that will help to formulate better pro-poor policy and effective public expenditure.

Delivering the capability and realizing the benefits

The results of the LIFT programme are impressive. By the end of 2011, 49 projects had received funds from LIFT, of which 22 were completed in 2011. The 27 remaining projects are being implemented in four distinct agro-climatic regions:

1. Ayeyarwaddy Delta.
2. Dry Zone (the low-lying central part of the country that includes large parts of Mandalay, Magway and southern Sagaing Regions).

	2010	2011	2012	2013
Number of projects	22	27	44	58
Number of townships where LIFT is active (out of 330 townships)	28	94	100	107
Cumulative number of households reached	153,808	223,229	372,528	511,505
Number of studies commissioned	0	2	8	15
Cumulative number of loans disbursed to households (agricultural and non-farming purposes)	1,218	8,103	86,568	151,212
Cumulative number of CBOs strengthened	1,682	3,467	6,391	9,389

Figure 12.6 Activities, reach and impact

3. Hilly Region (upland areas in Kachin, Chin and Shan States).
4. Coastal Region (coastal areas in Rakhine State).

Including the support provided in 2010 and 2011, more than 200,000 households (more than one million people) received assistance from LIFT projects as direct beneficiaries.

In 2013, LIFT disbursed US$31.3 million to its implementing partners, which is 14 per cent more than in 2012. The Fund supported 58 projects in 107 of the 330 townships across Myanmar. Donors increased their funding in 2013 and the Fund welcomed the Republic of Ireland, bringing donor membership to 11. LIFT's mandate was extended for two additional years, until the end of 2018.

Using implementing partner (IP) data, cross-referenced for accuracy with data from LIFT's extensive 2013 household survey, the Fund was able to track steady progress against its output and purpose indicators. By the end of the year, LIFT-funded projects had reached 511,505 beneficiary households, or about 2.5 million people (see Figure 12.6). In addition:

*   More than 290,000 beneficiary households reported that they had increased their food security by more than a month.
*   Nearly 60,000 households reported higher incomes as a result of LIFT support.
*   The number of households accessing affordable credit for agriculture doubled (since 2012) to 130,000 households.
*   The Fund exceeded its progress targets in 17 out of the set of 22 indicators.

The 16/6 Haiti Programme

In 2010 an earthquake killed 220,000 people in Haiti. Low income neighbourhoods in Port-au-Prince had often been established on steep hillsides, with little or no planning, in homes built from poor quality materials. Thus many were severely affected by the earthquake. Some 1.5 million homeless survivors had to be housed in over 1,000 emergency camps. Many people had already been living in poverty and, even though their houses had not completely collapsed, they were living in precarious conditions, exposed to extreme climate conditions and risks of natural disasters. These people had no access to basic services. It was imperative to initiate a reconstruction programme to provide sustainable housing solutions and improve living conditions.

To deal with this emergency, the president of the Republic of Haiti established the '16/6 project' on 30 September 2011. This was to be a two-year pilot programme, supported by the four United Nations agencies:

1.   United Nations Development Programme (UNDP).
2.   International Labour Organization (ILO).
3.   International Organization for Migration (IOM).
4.   United Nations Office for Project Services (UNOPS).

In addition to the rehabilitation of neighbourhoods of the capital and provision of improved housing, this pilot programme, funded by the Haiti Reconstruction Fund and the Canadian Government, sought to improve the living conditions of the inhabitants of affected areas,promoting the development of basic social services prioritized by the community and the creation of income-generating activities. This integrated solution included the closure of six priority camps and the Champs de Mars camp, and the relocation and improvement of the quality of life of the displaced, while meeting the urgent needs of physical infrastructure and social services selected by the communities.

Identifying the Programme

More than half of the houses in the neighbourhoods selected for rehabilitation suffered partial or heavy damage from the earthquake. Many residents in these high-density neighbourhoods had little choice but to resettle in six nearby camps. The pilot programme aimed to facilitate the rehabilitation of 16 neighbourhoods through improved reconstruction of housing, access to basic services prioritized by the community and the creation of income-generating opportunities. Another aim of the programme was to help the return of displaced people living in the six camps. These camps hosted about 5,000 households (mainly from these 16 neighbourhoods). This pilot programme was named the 16/6 Project (although '16/6 Programme' would have been a better name, given its nature and characteristics).

The programme's objectives were to ensure that displaced people in the six camps associated with the 16 districts found a solution to their housing problem. Return to their original neighbourhoods was facilitated by the construction of quality housing. Rehabilitation of the 16 neighbourhoods was undertaken according to people's priorities. Rising incomes and access to employment supported the sustainability of basic social services and access to credit, ensuring the maintenance of adequate housing. The capacity of Haitian stakeholders was strengthened to carry out reconstruction in Haiti by applying the model of the 16 districts.

Rehabilitation of neighbourhoods and access to sustainable housing solutions included subsidies for rents and the repair or reconstruction of housing according to the required standards of quality and safety. The programme also provided support and training for building professionals in micro, small and medium enterprises in the construction sector.

Coordination and a smooth process in the districts were ensured by strengthening neighbourhood committees, which created a platform for dialogue between the different levels of government, the programme and the interests of the community. A communication strategy was designed and implemented to ensure good information and continuous interaction with the programme's beneficiaries.

The protection and equity dimensions played a key role in the programme, particularly in efforts to offer the best possible choice for neighbourhood residents and displaced people regarding housing solutions, priorities for investment in the development infrastructure and access to services. The programme also planned for the investment of an equivalent amount of resources in housing solutions, with interventions to improve living conditions in the area, develop income-generating opportunities and employment, and reduce risks.

There are three levels of programme stakeholders – national, municipal and local. The key stakeholders are the primary councils and CASECS / ASECS (the communal committees), other community leaders and the beneficiary families in targeted neighbourhoods and camps. The programme provided frequent consultations with these stakeholders to ensure the achievement of the programme objectives.

Given the multidimensionality of this programme and the potential overlap with current or planned interventions, the strategy was actively to seek synergies with other projects and initiatives, including the support programme for the reconstruction of housing and neighbourhoods (the Housing Support Project). The Housing Support Project covers many areas of capacity building and data collection which will be useful for:

- this pilot programme;
- the project of shovelling fragments 1 and 2 of UNDP;
- the ILO training programme;
- the income generation for vulnerable women project of UNDP.

Programme planning and controls

The 16/6 Project was structured around four projects or activities, each allocated to one of the UN agencies supporting the Haitian Government in programme implementation according to their mandate and field of expertise. The four projects are listed below.

Project 1: The return process

In February 2011, the International Organization for Migration (IOM), with the support of the Civil Protection Department (DPC), began to register the displaced people. That gave the Haitian government and international agencies reliable data about the needs and the situation of these people.

'Return' in this context meant return to a safe habitat. In other words, returning to the homes and neighbourhoods of origin without risk to the safety of people is linked to the quality of construction, given the natural hazards such as landslides, floods, heavy rains and winds associated with hurricanes and possible aftershocks and posing no consistency problem for urban operation.

It was necessary to focus on the original neighbourhoods and the camps associated with them. The engagement of individuals and communities was a key factor. This workstream of the programme should also promote income-generating activities to meet a priority concern of affected populations. To avoid tensions between communities and to provide equitable support to affected populations, it was also necessary to promote equity in activities in support of return and a broad partnership with the economic and social agents.

Project 2: Housing

The earthquake damaged or destroyed around 200,000 homes, increasing the existing housing deficit. That deficit is estimated at one million homes in Haiti, half of which correspond to Port-au-Prince. This is why the programme through its housing project established four modalities for repair and reconstruction of houses, with the intention to support the affected families in the neighbourhoods of origin, while increasing the capacity of the rental stock. The houses were repaired through two implementing rules (agency-driven and owner-driven). There were two modalities for the reconstruction of houses:

1. Condominiums in situ, with the owner on land allocation.
2. A modality based on available land, where houses were built on higher ground.

Most reconstruction methods had been used by in Haiti since 2010.

Project 3: Rehabilitation of neighbourhoods

When it began in the autumn of 2011 the 16/6 Project helped to reaffirm the local governance structures in each neighbourhood as 'community platforms'. These platforms were composed of different leaders (15–20 members) present in each area, such as leaders of grassroots organizationans, religious leaders, representatives of women's groups, youth groups or other notable people.

Community platforms became single interlocutors, speaking on behalf of the community. Each of these platforms represented the communities of a given neighbourhood and integrated all the different participating groups. A special effort was made to ensure that excluded or marginalized groups in general were properly included. The 'space for dialogue' became an open discussion forum to facilitate dialogue between local and national governments for the expression of the will of the residents. The success of the neighbourhood rehabilitation process depended on the active participation of communities. In this sense, their views were duly taken into account and incorporated.

Participating members of community platforms knew their neighbourhoods, their needs and potential needs. Originally these neighbourhoods lacked urban planning. Leaders were trained to read and understand maps, so as to establish the priorities and to define future interventions. Each of the districts and areas produced an accurate diagnosis and a management plan that would guide future actions and project briefs for each priority identified by the community.

The management plans took into account the zoning maps regulations, which were established through an exercise conducted by the 16/6 Project's technical experts together with the national authorities. These maps determine the level of risk faced by each of the districts in terms of landslides, floods or earthquakes. This micro-zone analysis established which part of the districts could be considered as a red or orange zone. Return to those areas is discouraged because families would be exposed to very high risk and mitigation would not be possible.

Yellow zone areas were classified as considerable risk, but where the risk could be reduced through measures such as pipe drainage, retaining walls and investments, making these areas safer for living. Green zones were those with appropriate living conditions.

These zoning maps are accompanied by a regulation that establishes the conditions of each area and recommends the work and investment to be made and the necessary technical guidance. This regulation could eventually be converted into a standard (law).

Project 4: Monitoring, evaluation and knowledge management

This project represents a balance between humanitarian response and the long-term actions required. For this, a monitoring and evaluation system was set up to monitor the implementation of the programme and its impact on socio-economic indicators, particularly in light of the wide-ranging intentions. The knowledge created in the process is captured by 'lessons learned' documents. This is useful for relevant future interventions. This facilitates progress towards enhanced public proposals and institutionalization of the programme as a urban planning and rehabilitation reference.

Conclusion

Humanitarian and development programmes have changed considerably in the last decades. According to Fengler and Kharas (2011), more funds are being channelled to development aid, as well as emergency humanitarian initiatives; however, the value per projects is decreasing. Therefore, the value-for-money principles – economy, efficiency and effectiveness – are even more required than before. Grouping projects and managing them as a programme appears to be one of the approaches to achieve more value for the investment made by the international donor community. Disciplines such as fund management and monitoring and evaluation techniques ensure that the investment in these kinds of temporary initiative successfully delivers outcomes and, eventually, the impacts expected by the beneficiaries.

The case studies demonstrated that when solid design, planning and governance are in place from the beginning, the chances of success increase considerably.

References and further reading

Fengler, W. and Kharas, H. (2011), *Delivering Aid Differently: Lessons from the Field*, The World Bank Economic Premise (poverty reduction and economic management [PREM], network), No. 49, February. Retrieved 17 November 2014 from <http://siteresources.worldbank.org/INTPREMNET/Resources/EP49.pdf>.

LIFT (2014), *LIFT Strategy October 2014*. Retrieved 22 November 2014 from <http://lift-fund. org/Publications/LIFT-strategy-(2014–18).pdf>.

OECD (2008), *Accra Agenda for Action in Brief*. Retrieved 17 November 2014 from <http:// effectivecooperation.org/files/resources/Accra%20Agenda%20for%20Action%20in%20 Brief%20ENGLISH.pdf>.

OGC (2010), *Gateway Review*. <http://webarchive.nationalarchives.gov.uk/20100503135839/ http:/www.ogc.gov.uk/ppm_documents_ogc_gateway.asp>>

OGC (2011), *Managing Successful Programmes* (MSP®), London: Office of Government Commerce.

Reliefweb (2008), *Relief Web Glossary of Humanitarian Terms*. Retrieved 3 November 2014 from <http://reliefweb.int/report/world/reliefweb-glossary-humanitarian-terms>.

Rosenberg, L. J., Posner, L. D. and Hanley, E. J. (1970), *Project Evaluation and Project Appraisal Reporting System*. Fry Consulting Incorporated. Retrieved 19 November 2014 from <http:// pdf.usaid.gov/pdf_docs/PNADW881.pdf>.

UNDP (2014a), *Human Development Report 2014*, New York: UNDP.

UNDP (2014b). *Summary Human Development Report 2014*, New York: UNDP.

UNGA (1991), United Nations General Assembly Resolution 46/182 (19/12/91). New York: United Nations.

UNISDR (2009), United Nations International Strategy for Disaster Reduction (UNISDR). Geneva: United Nations. Retrieved 30 November 2014 from <www.unisdr.org/files/7817_ UNISDRTerminologyEnglish.pdf>.

Valueformoneyassessment.<www.gov.uk/government/uploads/system/uploads/attachment_ data/file/255126/value-for-money-external.pdf>.

Weiss, C. H. (1995). 'Nothing as Practical as Good Theory: Exploring Theory-Based Evaluation for Comprehensive Community Initiatives for Children and Families', in J. P. Connell, A. C. Kubisch, L. B. Schorr and C. H. Weiss (eds.), *New Approaches to Evaluating Community Initiatives: Concepts, Methods, and Contexts*, Washington, DC: The Aspen Institute.

Chapter 13

Programme Management in the Police

David Stewart

Most of this chapter is about the national police reform programme in Scotland. That saw the merger of eight police forces and two other policing organizations to become the Police Service of Scotland. Merging those separate organizations into one entity was the largest public sector reform programme in Scotland (and arguably in the United Kingdom). Although extremely complex, this programme had to be delivered before 1 April 2013 because legislation introduced by the Scottish government meant that the pre-existing organizations would no longer hold the powers necessary for policing after that date.

Definition and main characteristics of the sector

Policing in the United Kingdom is a public sector service solely funded by the government. Before the police reform programme in Scotland, there were 52 police forces in the United Kingdom, 43 in England and Wales, one in Northern Ireland and eight in Scotland.

Each police force in the United Kingdom is led by a chief constable (chief of police). These are not elected, but are instead appointed through competitive interview processes held by a governing 'board' or 'authority'. These police boards were historically made up of councillors from the relevant local authorities. However, in 2012/13 that changed. In England and Wales the government decided that, instead of a board, the oversight for chief constables should come from a single elected individual known as a 'police and crime commissioner' (PCC). 'The role of the PCCs is to be the voice of the people and hold the police to account' (<http://apccs.police.uk/role-of-the-pcc>).

The Scottish government determined that, instead of the pre-existing eight boards, the new police service should be governed by a single Scottish Police Authority (SPA), members of which would not be elected to the posts but instead would be appointed after application and interview. The SPA eventually comprised 12 members. The defined role of the SPA was 'to maintain policing, promote policing principles and continuous improvement of policing, and to hold the chief constable to account' (<www.spa.police.uk/about-us/>).

Creation of the new SPA body at the same time as the new police service was very relevant to the programme in terms of stakeholder engagement. That will be covered later in this chapter.

Relevance of programme management to policing

Policing in the United Kingdom, like policing elsewhere in the world, has undergone considerable change over the past 30 years. Significant focus in recent times has been upon technology-driven change, with a variety of programmes and projects to develop and implement new information communications technology (ICT) policing solutions. Most (if not all) police forces either employed project and programme managers as dedicated resources, or provided relevant training in addition to other day-to-day activities. The Association of Chief Police Officers (ACPO) and their Scottish equivalent had dedicated programme teams, as did the College of Policing for England and Wales and the Scottish Police College. As with most other public sector organizations, however, media focus on programme management in policing tends to focus on things that have not gone to plan.

The issue of poor overall project management standards owing to inadequate training, or occasions when project management is seen as being a 'side skill' to the normal job is highlighted by Butler and Reid (2010) in relation to Warwickshire Police as follows: 'This leads to multiple standards of Project Management from a qualified Prince2 Practitioner following globally recognized Project Management Standards, to a member of staff becoming the "Accidental Project Manager" with little or no formal training. This diverse range of skills meant that Warwickshire Police managed projects in many different ways however simple or complex.'

A 2012 review of an ICT programme in Surrey Police also highlighted concerns about project management capability: 'The Surrey Integrated Reporting Enterprise Network (Siren) was commissioned by Surrey Police in 2009 but was abandoned last year. The report, by auditors Grant Thornton, said it was an "ambitious project that was beyond the in-house capabilities and experience" of the police force and police authority' (<www.bbc.co.uk/news/uk-27911416>).

These issues were not restricted to England, as the following extract, relating to the ACPO(S) platform programme highlights:

> a state-of-the-art police computer system, overseen by the Association of Chief Police Officers in Scotland (ACPOS) has been abandoned before being put into service. The £7.7m Common Performance Management Platform aimed to put the crime figures for the forces on an equal footing for detailed analysis. It should by now have saved the country's eight police forces more than £30m, but it cost at least five years of officers' time and failed to deliver.
>
> (<www.heraldscotland.com/news/home-news/8m-it-failure-beyond-probe.18618724>)

Notwithstanding these high-profile 'failures', many other projects and programmes were concluded successfully following well-established programme management methodologies. However, none of these was as large, complex or as time-constrained as the national police reform programme in Scotland.

The national police reform programme in Scotland

The context of police reform in Scotland was unusual. Recorded crime was at a (then) 35-year low, violent crime detection rates at a 35-year high and there were record numbers of police officers (17,000 officers and 7,000 staff). The annual investment budget was £1.4 billion.

Policing in Scotland is devolved to the Scottish government at Holyrood and decisions made by the UK government at Westminster regarding policing generally only affect England and Wales. However, as the overall funding for the Scottish government was provided by Westminster, any reduction in funding had the potential to impact on spending. As such, the pressure of the global economic crisis on the UK government meant a reduction in finance from Westminster to Holyrood and this presented the Scottish government with the challenge to reduce costs.

Historical context

The previous significant police reform in Scotland took place in 1975 when 20 police forces were reduced to eight. That structure had remained in place ever since with the only addition being the creation of the Scottish Police Services Agency (SPSA), which provided ICT and forensic services to the Scottish forces and also governed the Scottish Crime and Drug Enforcement Agency (SCDEA).

There was significant disparity between the eight forces. The largest (Strathclyde Police) had over 8,000 officers and 2,000 staff while the smallest (Dumfries and Galloway Constabulary) had only 500 officers and 300 staff. In fact Dumfries and Galloway was smaller in numerical terms than the smallest Strathclyde Police Divisions, but it had a chief constable and deputy chief, as well as various senior staff members. Clearly that was not conducive to economies of scale.

This meant that, across Scotland, there was significant expenditure on senior ranks with eight chief constables, nine deputy chief constables, 14 assistant chief constables, associated director posts, and 24 territorial divisions, all governed by nine separate police authorities (eight forces plus SPSA).

As a result of the new financial challenges, the Scottish government asked ACPOS to establish a taskforce to consider how to reduce police expenditure in 2009. This taskforce subsequently reported that significant change to structure was the only option and, in September 2010, the Scottish government created the 'sustainable policing project'. That comprised senior police officers and staff as well as civil servants. In March 2011 it was decided to consider three options:

- a single national police force;
- three regional police forces (North, East and West);
- an enhanced eight-force model with the SPSA taking on responsibility for greater functions.

It quickly became obvious that the third option had little professional support and so the debate concentrated on the other two options.

Despite the fact that there were only eight chief constables in Scotland, it was soon clear that there was no unanimity on this matter. The chief constable of the largest force, Strathclyde, suggested that as his force already encompassed half of all police officers and half of the population base, expansion to a single police force was the obvious choice. Not surprisingly perhaps, those from smaller forces were less enthused by the single force option, with the chief constable of Grampian

Police warning of the imposition of culture and practices that would fail to take account of the unique nature of policing in the North East (<www.bbc.co.uk/news/uk-scotland-north-east-orkney-shetland-14733641>). Other chiefs espoused a similar position and, for some time, it seemed that the vocal objectors would sway the argument towards the three-force model.

However, in September 2011 the Scottish government, following the report of the Sustainable Policing Project, decided that the only way to make the necessary savings and take advantage of economies of scale was to create a national police force. In November 2011 the National Police Reform Team (NPRT) was established to deliver this and the Scottish government determined that the effective date of implementation would be 1 April 2013, which allowed less than 18 months for the task.

Aims of the reform

Forces elsewhere in the United Kingdom had faced similar financial and restructuring challenges before and had, in the main, employed three main techniques to reduce costs:

- reduce the number of police officers;
- make police staff redundant;
- outsource significant areas of business to the private sector (such as contact centres and custody).

The Scottish government set out three main strategic aims for the police reform programme:

- protect and improve local services despite financial cuts;
- create more equal access to specialist support and national capacity;
- strengthen the connection between services and communities.

However, at the same time, they insisted on three constraints, namely:

- maintain police officer numbers at no less than existing levels (17,234);
- no compulsory staff redundancies;
- no significant outsourcing of services.

A target was also set to reduce costs by £186 million over three years with an overall target of delivering a £1.4 billion saving over 15 years. However, over 80 per cent of annual budget was staff (salary) costs and of that figure over 70 per cent was for police pay. This meant that the amount of budget from which savings had to be found was relatively small and therefore this savings target was extremely challenging, to say the least.

Programme methodology

The NPRT was set up in November 2011, overseen by one of the eight existing chief constables (the then President of ACPOS) and run, on a day-to-day basis, by the deputy chief constable of Strathclyde Police. A programme management structure was initiated, which saw the creation of three programmes:

1. Core policing (uniformed policing).
2. Policing support (CID and specialist operations).
3. Organizational support (corporate departments such as human resource management (HRM) and finance).

Each of these programmes was led by a senior individual (deputy chief constable, assistant chief constable and director respectively). From a stakeholder management perspective this structure was important for a number of reasons. Not only were those people 'in charge' senior with significant experience but, with the 'command and control' culture of the police as an organization, ensuring appropriate rank of those in the key decision-making roles was designed to ensure a clear path in terms of driving 'top-down' change.

However, while the structure should have worked on paper, the reality was initially different. The process of appointing the first chief constable of the new Police Service of Scotland did not take place until 1 October 2012, only six months before the impending legal merger date of the legacy forces. Between November 2011 and October 2012, the proposals for change put forward by the NPRT had to be approved by the ACPOS Council (which comprised eight legacy chief constables).

Personalities and policing styles differed from individual to individual in the ACPOS council, so there was reluctance to make any significant decision. The general opinion was that whoever became the new chief constable would undoubtedly want the service designed around their own policing philosophy. Thus while the project teams undertook the necessary work, their proposals were in effect left only as 'options' until the appointment of the chief constable. Firm decisions about the number of territorial divisions, structure of specialist departments or location of back-office departments could not be made at an early stage.

The impact of this on the staff who would be affected by any kind of change was to introduce significant questions and uncertainty. Although attempts were made to communicate with staff, the lack of certainty meant that many of these communications could only lead to more questions being asked – questions that simply could not be answered. This was not the fault of the NPRT. It was a consequence of the circumstances in which they found themselves operating.

The programme underwent a gateway review. That highlighted areas for improvement around the overall management of the programme. A firm of consultants was subsequently appointed to review the programme. This revealed that although the existing programme manager's focus on the technical aspects of the program was understandable, the programme itself was drifting and was in danger of not delivering the required outputs in time. The consultants recommended that a senior police officer with programme management experience should be appointed as programme manager. That was done only six months before the 'go live' date of 1 April 2013. That date became known as 'Day 1'. The remainder of this chapter will describe those final six months of the programme.

Programme analysis and review

The newly appointed programme manager instigated a programme review. There was lack of clarity about the programme structure, including how many projects and associated workstreams actually existed. Finding the answers was not easy and it took almost six weeks to find that there were in fact 14 projects and 85 separate workstreams. Nomenclature had to be standardized. Some projects had individuals identified as project managers, while others had 'project leads' or 'project advisers'. The review also examined project risks and issues.

The 'Day 1' plan

The programme review outlined that the 14 projects had required over 1,800 actions to be completed by 31 March 2013. It was immediately clear that there was a significant risk of this not being achievable.

Workshops were then held with each project to go through the project plans in detail. The project management office (PMO) team was tasked with reviewing and challenging what the projects were calling 'essentials'. This 'bottom-up' review was complemented by a top-down review of the essentials necessary for the new organizational set-up.

The identified Day 1 changes were captured within a plan for each project/workstream and placed in categories as follows:

- Category 1: essential (for example, a legal requirement);
- Category 2: expected to provide savings in the first year of the new service;
- Category 3: producing wider benefit;
- Category 4: other.

It was then agreed that the focus for Day 1 would be restricted initially to Category 1 and 2 items. This highlighted that, of the 1,800 actions, only 180 were critical and 'must do' within the allowed timescales. The remaining 1,620 were considered as 'nice to do' activities. The programme manager immediately instructed that the programme had to focus on the 180 'must do' activities and give those priority.

Following the functional workshops to establish the critical Day 1 activities, an analysis was undertaken of the outputs and a dependency matrix was created. This was followed up with a series of workshops with the 'enabling' areas of the business (HR, ICT, Finance, Estates, Procurement) to ensure that dependencies were known across all functions and that owners were clearly identified. This same process also provided the opportunity to identify any gaps within the programme in order to ensure that the programme was focused on proactive and not reactive activities.

What became clear during this process was the importance of the enablers for success, both to ensure delivery of the Day 1 essentials and also to achieve the ongoing savings. That caused the programme manager to reconsider the timing of some changes because with both Finance and HR essential to help enable the changes, reforming those functions would have been extremely detrimental at that critical point.

Programme control

A structure had been put in place to provide support to the project teams from a variety of sources from across the legacy forces. However, while the overall programme had been based on the principles of MSP (Managing Successful Programmes), and used Prince2 methodology, the provision of support from different sources had caused complications. Each of the legacy forces had slightly different practices. Some project support staff were fully trained in Prince2 but for those in different forces, the lesser known PRIDE was the preferred methodology (<http://it.toolbox.com/wiki/index.php/PRIDE>). Although most used Microsoft (MS) Project software, different versions were in use and they were not always compatible with each other.

It was clear that consistent reporting and control had to be applied. The programme review included a review of the individual project plans and associated documentation (such as risk and benefit plans). These were tweaked as necessary by the PMO team to ensure consistency of approach across the entire programme. The decision was taken to simplify the reporting process for the individual projects. The central PMO was tasked with developing and pre-populating highlight reports in Excel, which ensured that all used the same format. Similarly, while the PMO retained MS Project internally, further external reporting was completed using simplified Excel and PowerPoint documents. As the timeline to Day 1 shortened, the spans of programme reporting schedules shortened, from monthly to fortnightly and then finally, weekly. Internal report formats also had to change. The delivery to senior management of a 33-page A3 Gantt chart had proven 'unpopular' and senior management needed something more palatable and easy to understand at a glance. A series of reporting documents were produced that were designed to do just that – a 'plan-on-a-page' timeline in simple PowerPoint, accompanied by an Excel action plan, colour coded with red, amber and green status against each of the projects. This improved senior management team confidence as the pressure to deliver Day 1 increased.

Approvals

One of the biggest changes to the programme had been the appointment of the first chief constable in early October 2012. Before that, although a programme structure had been in place, there was reluctance to approve formally any of the business cases produced by the projects because it was felt that the new chief constable should make the final decisions. While this was undoubtedly correct, the reality was that this lack of decision-making made the challenge facing the newly appointed chief constable massively more severe. This meant that the reform programme leading up to the official merger had to be transformational but undertaken with significant haste.

The newly appointed chief constable immediately instigated a weekly 'design authority' meeting at which he considered the previously prepared options papers. Some were very quickly approved, while instructions were given for others to be rewritten as the proposals did not support his policing ethos. It was initially anticipated that the chief constable would perhaps only chair one or two design authority meetings and then delegate the remainder. However, he chaired all design authority meetings up to Day 1 and this ultimate grip on leadership made a significant difference to the programme's momentum.

Implementation

A firm programme management grip was also placed on this process to ensure that the new senior management team was aware of progress against the fast-approaching Day 1 target of 1 April. The programme was rearranged into one comprising 14 projects with a total of 85 workstreams. The deputy and assistant chief constables were appointed in January 2013 and they took on the roles previously occupied by the NPRT leads. Also a senior role of 'executive lead for transformation' was created to provide further oversight of the change programme.

A number of 'quick wins' were identified and these were implemented successfully well before the 1 April deadline. These included the following:

- launch of a new national non-emergency contact public telephone number;
- the launch of the Specialist Crime Division;
- the new 'divisional' structure for operational policing.

Internal testing

Programme testing and project plans became crucial as much of the focus swung to Day 1 and the ability of the new organization to maintain a smooth transition while still delivering a service to the public. A two-pronged approach was taken as follows:

1. Internal project and programme dependency workshops were held, which became known as 'speed dating' events. In these workshops, representatives of the central PMO and the 'enabling' workstreams joined all 14 projects. The 'enabler' and PMO functions (planning, risk, benefits) each sat and remained at the same table for the entire session. Each project was allocated a table to start at and then, after 20 minutes, they moved on to the next table, much like speed dating. This meant that, by the end of the workshop, the representatives from each project had spoken to each enabler as well as the key functions within the PMO. Such was the success of the initial session that these workshops were held every four weeks until Day 1. After Day 1 they became the basis of the new dependency management format for the continuing change programme within Police Scotland.
2. The second form of testing was to hold a 'day in the life of' workshop. At this, each of the 14 commanders of the new territorial policing divisions worked through a number of routine scenarios, supported by colleagues from specialist departments and the support functions of HR, finance, ICT and so on. This allowed them to test their readiness for day-to-day business in the 'new world' that would exist after 1 April.

Both of these internal testing methodologies were ultimately crucial in delivering the programme of change.

Stakeholder engagement

Stakeholder engagement was enhanced by the appointment of the new senior team, with weekly updates being published. Each of these contained a personal message from the chief constable. Use was made of intranet sites, FAQ pages, and online question and answer sessions with members of the senior team. This communication could not realistically keep up with the pace of change owing to the restricted timescales, but the effort put into engaging with those affected by the change was genuine. Internal stakeholders included staff affected across the legacy organizations (each with its own unique culture), trade unions, the Police Federation and other police staff associations. Significant effort was put into internal stakeholder communications using

- intranet site daily updates (including minutes and decisions of 'change' meetings);
- regular change newsletters with a personal message from the chief constable;
- weekly line manager briefing slides;
- weekly project manager meetings;
- weekly meetings with legacy force transition teams;
- weekly senior management team and design authority;
- monthly dependency workshops;
- briefing sessions by senior managers around the country;
- web chat sessions with executive officers.

Stakeholder engagement was not limited to internal staff. There were also some challenging moments from a governance perspective. The Scottish government was a key stakeholder with ultimate responsibility for the decision to introduce a single force – a fact to which political opponents were paying close attention. There was much debate (in parliament and the media) in the run up to the legal merger. A new single Police Authority had also been established and was also finding its feet and trying to establish the extent of governance it should deploy. This led to some lengthy and intense debates (which unfortunately played out in the media and did nothing to settle the fears of those impacted upon by this change).

Beyond that, other stakeholders such as local authorities also had to be engaged with. However, the most fundamental stakeholder was the recipient of the service – the Scottish public.

Benefits management

A dedicated benefits management team had been an integral part of the PMO from the outset; however, their comprehensive approach had been difficult for members of the Scottish Government Programme Board to understand and, at an early meeting after the appointment of the new programme manager, members of this board expressed concerns that they were not clear as to what tangible benefits would look like for the new service.

The programme manager then worked with the business benefits team to develop a number of 'benefit scenarios' using policing incidents of vandalism, domestic abuse, murder and a terrorist incident to then explain (in simple terms) what the benefits of the new service would look like in reality in these scenarios. This simplified version was presented to the next programme board and met with universal approval. At a subsequent OGC Gateway Review of the programme the reviewers

Senior management structure before the reform programme

	Dumfries and Galloway	Central Scotland	Lothian and Borders	Fife	Strathclyde	Tayside	Grampian	Northern	SCDEA	Totals
Chief constables	1	1	1	1	1	1	1	1	0	8
Deputy chief constables	1	1	1	1	1	1	1	1	1	9
Assistant chief constables	4	1	2	1	4	1	2	1	1	14

Senior management structure after the reform programme

Police Service of Scotland	
Chief constables	1 (total)
Deputy chief constables	4 (total)
Assistant chief constables	6 (total)

Figure 13.1 Comparison of senior management numbers before and after the reforms

described the benefits plan and approach as 'The best that the Review Team has seen' (OGC Gateway Review, February 2013, not externally published).

Result

Figure 13.1 compares the senior management structure in the Scottish police before and after the programme. The most telling result of the programme was that, on 1 April 2013 (Day 1), the vast majority of the Scottish public noticed no difference to the service they received from the police. This belied the fact that the programme had delivered the following:

- a new divisional structure of 14 divisions;
- 32 area commands aligned to each of the 32 local authorities;
- 32 local policing plans agreed with each local authority;
- 353 community policing teams;
- 353 'ward plans' set in consultation with local communities;
- national major investigation teams;
- a national rape task force;
- a national human trafficking unit;
- a national tactical support group;
- national air support;
- a national trunk roads patrol group;
- a national alcohol and violence reduction unit;
- a separate suite of ICT projects including new website, intranet site, email systems and so on.

The perception of success was not shared by all concerned though. The restrictions on the sources of savings imposed by the Scottish government (which you will remember from earlier in this chapter included maintaining police numbers, with no compulsory redundancies and no significant outsourcing) meant that most savings had to be delivered by a longer-term restructuring programme that would result in thousands of posts becoming surplus to requirement and staff leaving through a voluntary redundancy/retirement process. Other planned savings will be achieved by relocation of dispersed staff to centralized locations and even the closure of some local police offices. All of these effects will receive much negative publicity and it therefore remains to be seen if the perceived success of the actual merger within a hugely challenging timescale will be reflected in the longer-term view of the resultant change programme in the coming years.

Lessons

It is clear that this time-bound and challenging merger could not have been achieved successfully without strong leadership and a single vision for the future of the police service. The fact that this only came with the appointment of the chief constable six months from the effective date is testament to the endeavours of all concerned in the planning and delivery of this change programme.

Stakeholder relations are crucial and, unlike private business, change in policing encompasses multiple stakeholder groups, internally and externally, and the earlier this process commences the better.

This programme would also not have been delivered on time without an extremely firm grip on the process through project and programme management and the earlier that is put in place, the more control can be applied as timescales collapse. This also ensures early identification of risk and allows mitigations to be put in place. It also allows for comprehensive reporting to those stakeholders with ultimate responsibility to give them a sense of assurance.

Change on this scale cannot be undertaken without an impact on morale – for those driving the change process and those on the receiving end. Managers need to be aware of this and do all they can to support staff throughout the process.

Finally it is fair to say that, certainly in the UK public sector, change never truly stops. The first day of April 2013 was not only the effective merger date for the police service of Scotland but it was also the first day of a change programme that is likely to last for five years or more. This has to be undertaken in such a way that the ethos of what police do is unaffected – the provision of service to the public. Whenever and whatever change is introduced, that fact must remain at the forefront.

References and further reading

Butler, M. and Reid, M. (2010), *The Transformation Project: A Case Study of Project Partner Collaboration with Warwickshire Police.* Warwickshire Police.

OGC (2009), *Prince2*, Norfolk: The Stationery Office.

OGC (2011), *Managing Successful Programmes (MSP)*, 4th edn., Norwich: The Stationery Office.

Chapter 14

Programme Management in the Transport Sector

Ben Ganney and Arnab Banerjee

This chapter describes the application of key elements of programme management in a transport environment, using Transport for London (TfL) as the case example.

Introduction and a profile of Transport for London

A short description of the business will show the appropriateness of TfL as the choice for our case study. The statistics have been taken from TfL's annual report and statement of accounts for 2013/14.

Transport for London is the overarching body for public transport in London. TfL is responsible for the day-to-day operation of the capital's public transport network, managing London's main roads and planning and building new infrastructure. No other city is as defined by its transport system as London, with its red buses, black cabs and Tube trains instantly recognized the world over. TfL manages London's buses, the Tube network, Docklands Light Railway, Overground and Tramlink. TfL also runs Barclays Cycle Hire, London River Services, Victoria Coach Station, the Emirates Air Line and London Transport Museum. As well as controlling a 580 km network of main roads and the city's 6,000 traffic lights, TfL regulates London's taxis and private hire vehicles and the Congestion Charge Scheme. Every journey matters to TfL and it does everything it can to keep the city moving, making sure the transport system is safe, reliable and fit for the future.

To illustrate the volumes, in 2013/14, London Underground (the Tube) served 1.3 billion passenger journeys, buses carried 6.5 million passengers a day, 8 million people used river transport in the year and cycling increased by 176 per cent compared to 2000 values. Overall, there are about 30 million journeys every day across TfL's network.

The need to keep pace with the needs of the city drives a significant level of capital investment. Capital expenditure – spending on projects and programmes – is about £3 billion a year. TfL's funding comes from income from fares, central government, business rates, borrowing and central government. The challenge to deliver 'value for money' drives close scrutiny of the business and efficient delivery of programmes and projects is at the core of TfL (see Figure 14.1).

The Transport for London story

Our goal

To keep London working and make life in London better. We will deliver a transport system that secures London's position as a world-leading city and the engine of the UK economy. Our services will ensure that those who live and work in London can access all the Capital has to offer in terms of jobs, leisure, health and education.

Our strategy

This has four pillars:

• **Our customers and users** – we will demonstrate that every journey matters, putting customers and users at the centre of everything we do.

• **Our people** – we will be accountable, actively seek solutions to problems, and work with other people directly, fairly and consistently.

• **Our delivery** – every day we will deliver safe, reliable, clean, sustainable and accessible transport. We will introduce new assets without any disruption to services, and we well deliver our major investment programmes efficiently, getting them right first time, every time.

• **Value for money** – we will continually ask 'can we do this better, simpler or cheaper?' and we will deliver clear value for fare and taxpayers; money, helping us to secure funding for major improvements to our transport infrastructure.

Our priorities

• Deliver high and consistently improving standards of operational performance and service to customers and users across the full range of our responsibilities, building on the success of our delivery during the 2012 Games.

• Deliver our investment programme on time and to budget, with the upgrade of our Tube, rail and road networks, plus Crossrail, at its core.

• Continually strive to be collaborative, innovative, lean and integrated.

Our organization

We are a single, fully integrated authority which exists to serve London, and which our people are proud to represent. We work together as a team to ensure that we deliver for, and listen to, our customers, businesses, users and stakeholders and that they find us easy to do business with. We will work together with high levels of personnel accountability, proactivity and collaboration and continually strive to be more innovative, lean and integrated.

Figure 14.1 The Transport for London story, showing the importance of infrastructure delivery

TfL's programme delivery in context

We shall now describe briefly the TfL delivery methodology (TfL Pathway) in the context of the wider organizational activities. The broad range of programme delivery requires a flexible and scalable approach to the method used.

TfL is primarily an operating and asset management company. Capital investment and programme and project delivery is clearly necessary for an ever-improving city infrastructure. The vast majority of the organization's direct employees are targeted at operations and planning; the projects are mostly delivered by a supply chain of third-party suppliers under the direction of in-house programme and project managers and other relevant functions such as engineering, health and safety, controls and so on.

The place of 'delivery' (under the TfL Pathway) is shown in Figure 14.2 in the context of the overall organization. Mayoral and strategic priorities, 'opportunities' – effectively programmes and projects – are generated from long-term business plans that reflect government. These are delivered by teams and handed over to operations, where the ultimate benefits are realized. These then feed further opportunities.

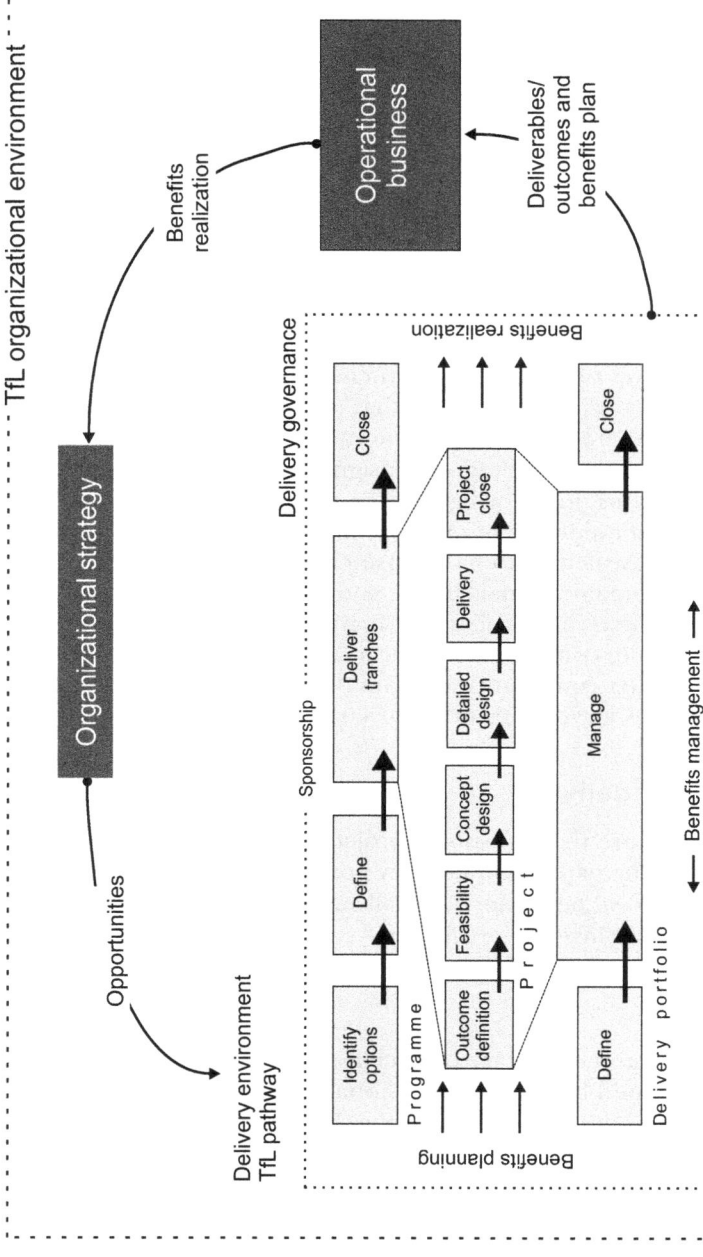

Figure 14.2 The delivery environment in the context of the TfL organizational environment

The fundamental importance of effective sponsorship for effective delivery is now recognized industry-wide. Sponsors play a critical role (and contribute to all aspects of the cycle) by making sure that investment is focused on the right priorities and delivers the benefits required to facilitate London's growth and meet the needs of customers.

What TfL delivers

TfL delivers a huge range of programmes that fall into two broad families, infrastructure and business change programmes. Programme management adds value in any environment but needs to be a delivery model able to cater for the full spectrum.

The significant level of planned investment in TfL's network involves upgrades to infrastructure and changes to the way that transport across London is managed. This is the traditional arena of programme management and is the bulk of spend in the business. TfL delivers rolling stock, signalling, bridges, tunnels, roads, track renewal, control systems, monitoring systems, complex IT systems and many other programmes covering every type of professional function to technologies.

Alongside the infrastructure arena lie business change programmes. These may be internally focused – organizational change and new ways of operations for example. They are also often externally focused – driving behaviour change to encourage modal shift or reducing congestion at critical stations through better travel demand management and better communication with the travelling public. Programme costs across the two families may vary from £100,000 to several billion.

The structure of delivery

TfL works in a structure that consists of projects, programmes and delivery portfolios. In this context the expression delivery portfolio must not be confused with an organizational *investment* portfolio. The delivery portfolio is a convenient structure for delivery and not for investment choices.

Project lifecycles

Projects follow the familiar six-stage project lifecycle shown in Figure 14.3, although stages can be combined based on professional judgement. For example, a simple project may combine outcome definition with feasibility, and then combine concept design with detailed design before going on to delivery and project close.

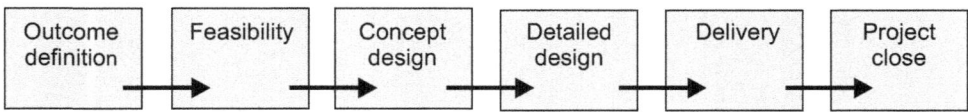

Figure 14.3 The project lifecycle

Figure 14.4 The delivery portfolio lifecycle

Delivery portfolio stages

A delivery portfolio is defined as a grouping of an organization's activities, schemes or projects, likely to be agreed annually, taking into account resource constraints. Examples are surface roads resurfacing, surface traffic signal replacement, track replacement and ICT server replacement. In this environment, there are significant numbers of similar projects that are not interrelated and may be run under annual budgets. All delivery portfolios should follow the three-stage lifecycle shown in Figure 14.4.

Delivery portfolios are subjected to a formal review at least every 12 months to ensure that the requirements and business case remain valid and achievable. The delivery portfolio is likely to contain several projects, each of which would be delivered using the project lifecycle.

The programme stages

A programme is defined as a temporary structure which has been created to coordinate, direct and oversee the implementation of a set of projects and activities in order to deliver outcomes and benefits related to the organization's strategic objectives. Examples within TfL are Barclays Cycle Hire, Northern Line Extension and the Oyster card service. All programmes follow the four-stage programme lifecycle shown in Figure 14.5.

Following Stage B, a family of projects would be set up in classical fashion to deliver the tranches of the programme. These projects would each be delivered using the project lifecycle.

The product matrix: underpinning the lifecycles

The TfL Pathway delivery framework is 'product based'. Each of the lifecycles described above is supported by a series of 'products' forming the key documentation that a programme would be expected to produce. Each product follows a common format, an example of which is shown in Figure 14.6. This illustration has been rescaled to fit on to the page, but contains all the relevant information. The document is almost self-explanatory and covers the following topics:

- Contents: used when a template is not available – otherwise the template would cover contents.
- Quality criteria: what makes a good product?
- Document management: the product's place in the programme document structure.

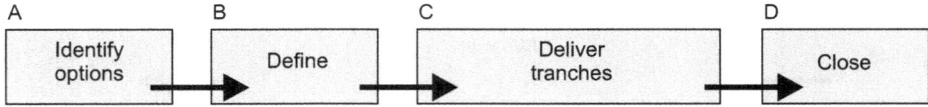

A   *Identify options*

Look at the programme from a high level. Consider strategic fit, vision, costs, duration, risks and prepare for the future.

B   *Define*

Explore the options for delivering the required outcomes and benefits together with robust and detailed planning for delivery.

C   *Deliver tranches*

Implement the governance strategies to ensure that capability is delivered and aligned to organizational objectives - manage the projects. Every programme will have one or more delivery tranches.

D   *Close*

Confirm that ongoing support is in place. Disband resources and infrastructure so that the programme does not drift into normal operations.

Figure 14.5 The programme lifecycle

- Roles and responsibilities: the responsible, accountable, consulted and informed chart with the following definitions:
  - Responsible (R): responsible for producing all or part of quality product;
  - Accountable (A): accountable for ensuring timely delivery of quality product;
  - Consulted (C): must be consulted when product is being produced;
  - Informed (I): a copy of the signed-off product must be sent to (the person named).

The example shown in Figure 14.6 is a core (or mandatory) product. It must be produced for all programmes. In other cases (for example an infrastructure programme) there will be the need to produce significant technical products, while that will not be needed for a business change programme. This provides the applicability and scalability.

Figure 14.7 is a substantial extract from the associated product matrix. While most of the products in this product matrix are dependent on the complexity and particular circumstances of the programme, some are required for every programme. These are:

- programme requirements;
- programme execution plan;
- schedule;
- risk register;
- progress reporting (the regular reports);
- integrated assurance and approvals plan (summarizing agreed governance);
- project close report and stage gate certificates.

Programme Requirements (Stages A and B)

Purpose

To deliver the scope and objectives of the programme; the business and user requirements the programme must deliver and the criteria against which deliver will be accepted.

Programme Requirements is the central document used to manage all requirements on the Programme during Stages A and B. As such it forms a 'contract' between the sponsor and the Programme manager and the basis against which the Programme is change controlled. It will also form the basis of any requirements documents for sub-programmes or projects.

It is the foundation against which all other Programme deliverables must be written - including the Programme Authority Submission, Business Case, Estimate, Schedule, Benefits Managements Plan and Programme Execution Plan (PEP).

Applicability

This product is mandatory and must be produced for all programmes.

Templates

- Programme Requirements template.
- A template is also available for the Requirements Management Plan.

Contents

- Contents is defined by the template.

Quality criteria

- The supplied template must be used.
- The objectives set out in the Programme Requirements must be consistent with, and linked to, the TfL Business Plan.
- The document must be fully signed off at both Stage A and Stage B. Any changes after Stage B can only be made through the change control process.
- It must demonstrate consideration for multi-modal interchange as per TfL's Interchange Best Practice Guidelines.
- It must demonstrate consideration for all stakeholders.
- The TfL Corporate Requirements Management Process details an approach to assist the attainment of quality in developing requirements and also provides further guidance.

London Underground Specific Requirements

If the programme is being managed within London Underground the following points also apply.

- This product is used to discharge part of the requirements for a Change Assurance Plan under LUL Category 1 Standard 1-538. As a consequence it is mandatory that the supplied template must be used.
- Consideration for all stakeholders should be as per LU's Stakeholder Engagement Framework.
- This document should take account of the Network Asset Work Schedule.
- Must follow the guidance in the second term of the Capital Programmes Directorate Weekly Bulletin May 2013.

Documents management

Programme Requirements must be filed in accordance with the document filing structure.

Roles and responsibilities

For information on the roles and responsibilities in the table below, refer to the Pathway Glossary.

The comprehensive RACI table used with IM can be found here.

Responsible (Responsible for producing all or part of quality product.)	Accountable (Accountable for ensuring timely delivery of quality product.)	Consult (Must be consulted when product is being produced).	Inform (A copy of the signed-off product must be sent to).
During Stage A	Sponsor	Operations representative.	Programme Director
Sponsor			Business planning
During Stage B		Maintenance Representative	
Programme Manager			HSE Adviser Programme Engineer Subject Matter Expert Commercial Lead Systems Engineer Stakeholders

Feedback

If you have any queries, feedback or improvement suggestions about this Product Description then please contact tflpathway@tfl.gov.uk.

Document History

Revision	Date	Reason for change	Author
A1	30/11/2012	Issued for consultation	IPPM
A2	08/04/2013	Issue for use	IPPM
A3	11/12/2013	Amended Quality Criteria	TfL PMO

Figure 14.6 A typical TfL Pathway product

Pathway	Programme lifecycle				Core roles							
	A Identify options	B Define	C Deliver tranches	D Close	Sponsor	Programme manager	Programme engineer	Subject matter expert	HSE advisor	Commercial lead	People change manager	User representatives
Governance												
Pathway project management plan (PPMP)	Created	Updated	Updated	Updated	A	R	C	C	C	C	C	C
Stage gate certificate	Created	Undertaken	Undertaken	Undertaken	A	R	C	C	C	C	C	C
Authority submission	Created	Created	Created		AR	R			C	C		
Business case	Created	Updated	Updated	Updated	AR	C		C	C	C		C
Programme close report				Created	A	R						
|— Financial close report				Created	C	C				R		
Lessons learned	Created	Updated	Updated	Updated	ARC	R	C	C	C	C	C	C
Integrated assurance and approvals plan (AAP)	Created	Updated	Updated	Updated	A	RC						
Sponsor and requirements												
Programme requirements	Created	Updated			ARC	R	C	C	C	C	C	C
Feasibility report	Created	Created			A	R						
Operational concept	Created	Updated			A	I	C	C	C	C	C	R
Maintenance concept	Created	Updated			A	I	C	C	C	C	C	R
SDR - scope/design review (Buildability)	Undertaken	Undertaken	Undertaken		A	R		C	C	C		C
Manage the programme												
Programme execution plan (PEP)	Created	Updated	Updated		C	AR	RC	C	C	C	C	C
|— Benefits and value management strategy	Created	Updated	Updated	Updated	A	R					C	C
|— Estimate	Created	Updated	Updated	Updated	AR	A		C	I	R		C
|— Risk management strategy	Created	Updated	Updated			A				C		
|— Stakeholder engagement plan	Created	Updated	Updated		A	R					C	
|— External consultation strategy	Created	Updated	Updated			R					C	
|— Communication plan	Created	Updated	Updated		A	R					C	
Schedule	Created	Updated	Updated		A	R			I	C		
Risk register	Created	Updated	Updated	Updated	C	AR	C	C	C		C	C
|— Issue register	Updated	Updated	Updated	Updated		AR						
Resource management	Created	Updated	Updated	Updated		AR						
Change control register	Created	Updated	Updated	Updated	C	A				R		
Integrate assurance review (IAR)	Undertaken	Undertaken	Undertaken	Undertaken	A	R						
Progress report	Created	Updated	Updated	Updated		AR						
People change												
People change plan	Created	Updated	Updated	Updated	C	A					R	C

Figure 14.7 Product matrix

[Editorial comment: The 'product matrix' shown in Figure 14.7 is very similar to a valuable tool that would be known in other organizations as a linear responsibility matrix but I suspect it is not used as widely as I believe it should be. This TfL case is an excellent example. The concept is described in Lock (2013). DL]

The products are supplemented with a series of handbooks, the applicability of which will depend on the content of the programme. The handbooks cover the following subjects:

1. Governance – instructions and guidance on programme, project and delivery portfolio gates, governance and reviews, including funding.
2. Sponsorship – instructions and guidance on the role and activities of sponsorship.
3. Manage the project, programme or delivery portfolio – instructions and guidance on planning and control.
4. People change – instructions and guidance on people change management – how to manage people through transition.
5. Construction – instruction and guidance on managing construction works.
6. Commission and handover – instructions and guidance on managing assets during the design and construction of the works and their handover into operational use and maintenance.
7. Consents – instructions and guidance on consents.
8. Health, safety and environment – guide on TfL's health, safety and environmental (HSE) arrangements.
9. Commercial (procurement and contract management) – instructions and guidance on how to procure goods, services and works.
10. Risk management – instructions and guidance on successful risk management in TfL.
11. Benefits and value – instructions and guidance on tools for benefits and value management in TfL.
12. Engineering – instructions and guidance for the delivery of engineering products and services.

The objective of these handbooks is to provide the programme team with the context for the products and ensure specific organizational and statutory requirements are satisfied. The handbooks are written for competent practitioners and assume that readers understand the generic principles of the subject. They are not intended to provide training on the subject covered in each handbook.

Roles, responsibilities and core functions

The following paragraphs contain high-level descriptions for a number of key roles and activities in TfL Pathway. Those that are 'standard' across many organizations are mentioned but not detailed. Those which have particular nuances in TfL are shown in more depth.

Core roles are typical roles that exist within a project team to assist in the delivery of the project. Depending on the business unit, size and type of project, not all these roles will be required. Each area will adjust to suit its needs and this is part of professional judgement within the TfL Pathway. In other words, it is not suggested that every programme has all these roles – rather that such roles are typical in this environment and each area will adjust to suit its needs.

Core functions provide business support to the project delivery team.

Core roles

Sponsor

The sponsor acts as an 'internal client' and as such is accountable for identifying the business need in order to deliver against corporate and Mayoral Transport Strategy objectives. There must only be one sponsor of a project at any one time. For programmes there may be a leading sponsor, supported by a team of project sponsors or representatives.

The sponsor may change during the life of the project; for example it may transition from TfL Planning and Strategy to Surface Transport or Rail & Underground as it moves from a strategic to a delivery focus.

Figure 14.8 positions the role of the sponsor within TfL's organizational structure. It is intended to illustrate how the sponsor function translates high-level business strategy into a set of specific projects and programmes in order to achieve a defined set of outcomes:

- Organizational direction is set at the strategy level, defining the strategic priorities in alignment with the Mayor's strategy.
- Those priorities are then translated into *strategic requirements* for TfL's services, operations and assets; identifying the optimal investment portfolios to align resources to strategic priorities.
- From these strategic requirements, specific deliverables are identified, including concepts for major programmes, renewal of existing assets, maintenance, and

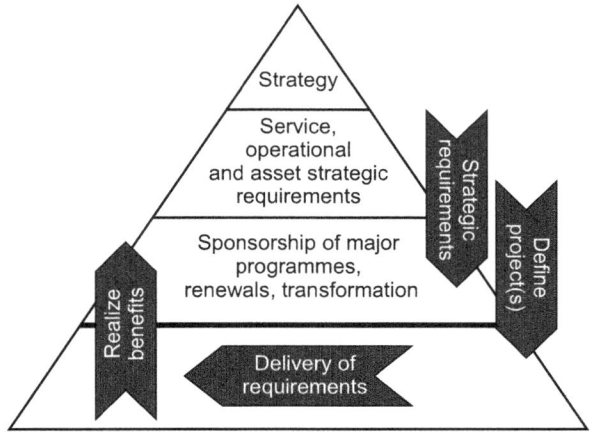

Figure 14.8 The sponsor in context

change programmes. The sponsor role defines projects, while the delivery organization is responsible for delivery of requirements. During the delivery the sponsor maintains oversight of the project and retains accountability for the business case ensuring that the business case remains valid and achievable and that the benefits are realized.

Figure 14.9 illustrates the relative involvements of the sponsor, the deliverer and the operator and maintainer in relation to the lifecycle of a project. The same principles hold good for the programme. This is for guidance only and the relative involvement of the sponsor may need to be different; for example soft, business change projects may require an enhanced level of involvement from the sponsor at different stages of the lifecycle.

Figure 14.9 reflects the fact that the sponsor is involved before and after the 'delivery' period as defined in the TfL Pathway (see also Figure 14.2). In particular, sponsors are involved in the development of strategic requirements and participate in business planning processes before projects are initiated. This assists the sponsor in understanding how the project fits with TfL's strategic objectives and to identify dependencies with other proposed activities. Providing this context to the project team and stakeholders will help to ensure that activities and decisions are aligned with the strategic direction.

The sponsor should, at the outset of the programme, project or delivery portfolio, agree with the deliverer, the operator and maintainer and other stakeholders about their relative involvement so that all parties are clear on what can be expected from the sponsor. The sponsor retains accountability for the business case and benefits realization.

Although there is no definitive list of sponsor functions, the following are typical sponsor activities:

- makes the project visible within the organization;
- provides direction and guidance on strategic objectives and initiatives;

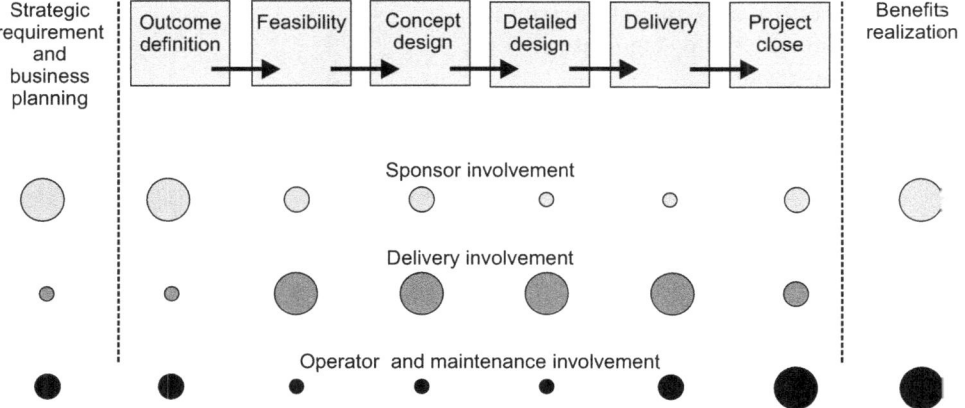

Figure 14.9 Sponsor involvement (characteristic)

- identifies and quantifies benefits to be achieved by the project;
- makes decisions that affect the business case;
- secures the necessary authorities to fund the project;
- actively participates in project initiation and planning;
- reviews and approves changes to plans, priorities, deliverables, schedule and cost;
- identifies project stakeholders and encourages their involvement through effective communication;
- resolves differences in opinion between stakeholders when they occur;
- assists the project team as and when required by exerting authority and the ability to influence;
- helps resolve inter-project boundary issues;
- supports the project manager in conflict resolution;
- advises the project team of governance, political issues and potential sensitivities;
- evaluates project success upon completion.

It is clear that a good sponsor will perform different functions throughout the lifecycle, serving as leader, mentor, catalyst, motivator and mediator. While the application of sponsorship functions varies according to operating businesses and to the context of specific activities, there are fundamental, key skills and competencies which are consistent across TfL.

TfL has developed the 'Sponsorship Role Family' that sets out the technical skills and experience which sponsors need to fulfil their functions. It also assists sponsors by identifying development and training opportunities required to fulfil a career in sponsorship.

The role family framework comprises the following technical skills and general TfL competencies:

Technical skills:

- apply whole life cost principles and appraise investment options;
- project success and benefits management;
- business case;
- change control and impact assessment;
- project lifecycles and stage gate reviews;
- project governance;
- strategic risk management;
- requirements and scope management;
- value management.

TfL competencies:

- building capability;
- commercial thinking;
- communication and influence;
- customer service orientation;
- planning and organizing;
- problem solving and decision-making;

- responsiveness;
- results focus;
- stakeholder management;
- strategic thinking;
- team leadership.

These common principles of the roles of sponsor and delivery team apply across TfL. The sponsor can also be known as an SRO or sponsor's agent.

Programme or project boards

All programmes and projects in TfL must be governed by a combination of boards and reviews. The project board is accountable for the success of the project and reports to the programme or delivery portfolio board. It is the decision-making body for the project, but can delegate responsibility (not accountability) to the project manager for certain decisions subject to the tolerances and change control approach. It must be chaired by a sponsor.

Programme manager

The programme manager is accountable for leading and managing a programme or delivery portfolio from strategy to successful delivery, through effective coordination of the programme or projects, their interdependencies and risks.

Project manager

The project manager is given authority to run the project on a day-to-day basis, within agreed constraints and authorizations.

Construction manager

Construction managers are responsible for managing the construction works process.

Project engineer

The project engineer is the doer, who is principally responsible for doing the work required to deliver technical products. The engineer can draw on support from the project manager, subject matter expert (SME) and other project resources to help deliver his/her obligations under the project.

Subject matter expert

The SME is a person who is an expert on a particular domain, area or topic. The SME will bring expert knowledge to a project or programme to help steer and direct products influenced by that area of expertise. Their input to the project is to steer, direct, review and provide technical validation of products to ensure that they meet and integrate with existing or future business requirements as appropriate.

In a transport context, within individual business units this could translate into roles including, but not limited to:

- real time operations;
- traffic maintenance and control systems;
- traffic technology;
- network performance;
- traffic infrastructure;
- discipline engineer;
- asset engineer;
- systems integration.

User representative

The user representative is responsible for the specification of the needs of all those who will use the final product(s), for user liaison with the project team and for monitoring that the solution will meet these needs within the constraints of the business case in terms of quality, functionality and ease of use.

People change manager

This manager leads key activities that need to take place to implement successfully the people change management within projects – in particular, working with the programme manager to ensure that 'people change' considerations are factored into the project as a whole.

HSE adviser

The HSE adviser's role in the programme, project or delivery portfolio team is to ensure that TfL and its suppliers comply with relevant health, safety and environmental (HS&E) legislation and TfL standards in the delivery of the programme, project or delivery portfolio.

Core functions

Strategy and planning

This function is responsible for defining the transport strategies and associated package of projects, programmes and delivery portfolios required to meet the business plan objectives for the coming business cycle. It also involves utilizing transport planning analysis to ensure that future investment is aligned to delivery of the key outcomes in the Mayor's transport strategy. The function is custodian of the Strategic Assessment Framework (SAF) which is used as the consistent means of appraising and comparing future investment options and essential components of any business case. Another responsibility is leading in the initiation of major infrastructure projects in partnership with relevant parts of the business, including business case preparation, stakeholder engagement and securing consents.

Performance and project controls

This function is responsible for periodic and quarterly reporting on the delivery of the investment programme to approval boards within each business unit, the projects and planning panel and the TfL board. It also involves management of change control processes for project authority, project baselines and milestone target dates

Commercial

The commercial function is responsible for implementing and managing contractual requirements with suppliers.

Risk management

The risk management function provides permanent TfL risk experts to champion and lead risk development and training. That includes risk awareness courses and workshops. Management of Risk (MoR), as delivered by AXELOS, has been adopted as a reference standard. These, together with the accredited training modules are offered as part of PYRAMID training courses. This function leads the Risk Management Special Interest Group (SIG) with membership across TfL.

Benefits and value management

This function provides value and benefits leadership across TfL. Management of Value (MoV), as delivered by AXELOS, has been adopted as a reference standard, together with the accredited training modules and are offered as part of a PYRAMID training course. The benefits function leads the Value and Benefits Special Interest Group (SIG), with membership across TfL.

Each of the different types of programmes delivered within TfL will have very different objectives which will influence how the risks and benefits should be approached. The choice and application of Pathway products should be scalable, applicable and relevant to the particular subject in question. For example in terms of the approach to value, a typical new programme could create a value management strategy which would aim to prioritize drivers and balance the consensus of opinion among diverse stakeholders. In comparison the upgrade of an existing asset might look at creating a value engineering product to ensure that the design is optimized and any unnecessary cost or design is reduced.

In support of these different approaches to value, benefits management may differ in that some investments are measured through qualitative indicators which might take several years or even decades for the public to appreciate the benefit fully. Conversely, the benefits measurement might be far more quantitative, with the benefits demonstrated much closer to the delivery timescales.

Business case

In TfL, the business case has to subscribe to thresholds and criteria set not only by the organization but also United Kingdom government requirements set by the Department for Transport and the Treasury.

Conclusions

This chapter has described TfL in brief, shown 'delivery' in the context of the wider organization and explained the building blocks of programme management. The key role of the sponsor has been shown in some detail.

A critical point to make is that the range of programmes requires customization of the TfL Pathway framework (assurance levels, which products to produce and application of core principles such as risk management and benefits and value). The recently approved 'Garden Bridge', a pedestrian and ornamental Thames River crossing, would have very different risk, benefits and stakeholder profiles than, for example, the Hammersmith Flyover, which is still a bridge but designed to carry road traffic. The differences are even starker when comparing an infrastructure programme like the Northern Line Extension to Battersea to a business change programme that radically alters the working practices in London Underground's stations. To use a final example, a programme of office moves will use far fewer products and have a far simpler structure than a programme of road improvements.

The TfL Pathway – like any method – provides contextual tools and criteria but it is the skill of the delivery professionals to use them effectively and appropriately that mattters.

References and further reading

Lock, D. (2013), *Project Management*, 10th edn., Farnham: Gower.

Chapter 15

Programme Management in the ICT Sector

Burkhard Görtz and Silke Schönert

This chapter uses the case of a large programme in the German armed forces as an example of programme management in the information and communication technology (ICT) sector.

Introduction

The objective of the HERKULES programme in 2006 was to equip the German armed forces with modern, reliable, secure and economical ICT. The BWI service alliance was founded in the same year. This alliance combined the expertise of the German armed forces and industry to master the programme, which was scheduled to last for ten years.

The new nationwide IT infrastructure includes 140,000 end user systems, 300,000 landline and 15,000 mobile phones, as well as a 12,000 km high-performance wide area network. In addition there are central services, such as the intranet, internet and operation of the Lotus Notes integrated communication system. The range of services is completed by data and telephone networks, as well as service organizations such as the User Help Desk (UHD), Directory and Exchange Services, and the Operational Competence Centres (OCC) or on-site services which BWI has set up for the German armed forces. Almost 45,000 users work with a centralized and fully integrated software solution called SASPF.

BWI rolls out the software, trains the users and operates the solution in fail-safe, state of the art data centres. Central operation of the consolidated and virtualized systems on a few powerful servers saves energy and makes it easier to roll out new functionalities at short notice. BWI also runs the existing application systems used by the German armed forces and keeps those up to date. Crucially, BWI not only runs the ICT but the service alliance is also responsible for keeping it up to date in accordance with clearly defined specifications.

The initial situation

The HERKULES project was initiated by the federal government through a number of pilot projects for the privatization of public tasks. Until now it is the biggest public private partnership in Europe.

The main objective was to relieve armed forces personnel of non-core activities, such as the IT operation. Another objective was to resolve a year-long investment backlog and modernize all the non-military information and communication technology.

Negotiations of the comprehensive agreement were formulated in a contract with a total of 17,000 pages. That took six years. In the end a consortium consisting of Siemens AG and IBM Germany won the ten-year contract. The contract goal was primarily to modernize the IT of the German army. For that purpose, the wide area network had to be expanded and encrypted with the security requirements of the appropriate hardware.

Owing to the long-running contract negotiations, an additional modernization issue arose because the system could not be changed during the contract negotiations. The investment in new hardware has thus been reduced because of the tight household budgets.

In most locations of the German army local area networks (LAN) had to be built from the ground up. Furthermore central services like a single-user help desk, software distribution, file service and so forth were designed and implemented. In addition, 140,000 desktop computers and 300,000 telephones were issued.

The IT of the German army was spread over several responsibilities. So there was no standardized process, no single asset management and no complete documentation. It was not possible to describe the specific technical structures and achievements during contract negotiations. Owing to lack of time (and the high costs which could be expected) the IT of the German army had to be estimated without due diligence.

Three companies were responsible for the modernization and operation of the IT contracted services. Each of them had their own rules and regulations, but they worked towards the same goals. The client also had two roles:

- as a contractor;
- operational involvement in the implementation of projects as supplier and decision-maker.

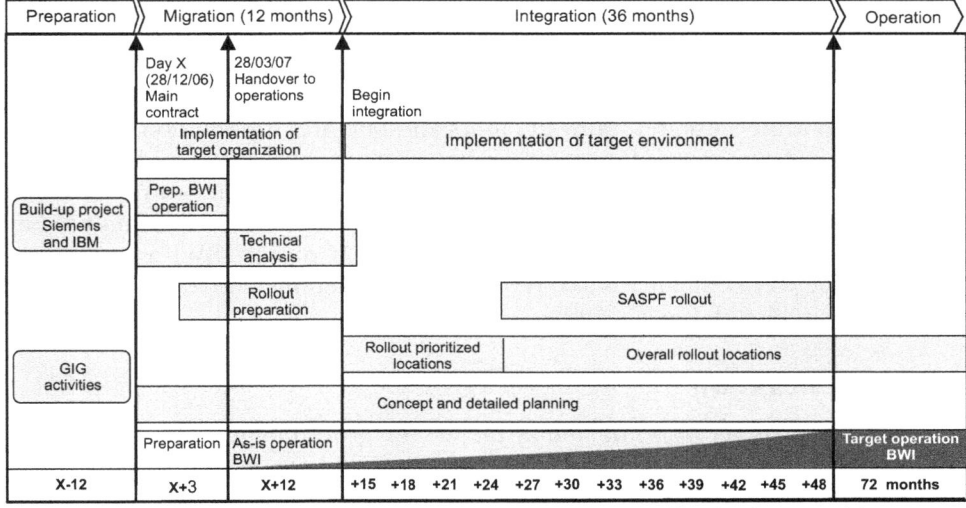

Figure 15.1 First implementation plan

Upon conclusion of the contract negotiations the companies were established. Then the structures and processes had to be built within organizations and two different headquarters were behind the companies.

The first comprehensive plan (shown greatly reduced in size in Figure 15.1) included extensive preparations necessary at own risk by the contractor. In addition, a migration phase was planned for 12 months in the contract, during which the existing IT operation should be incorporated gradually. Then, over the following three years, the entire IT would be modernized in an integration phase.

A programme was established within composite responsibilities to coordinate and control the entire project. Programme management had the objective of coordinating and reporting upon all contractually required project deliverables. In addition, uniform project governance was set up for all the constituent projects.

Challenges

Unclear base

The investment backlog caused by the household budgeting (which was sufficient just to keep the existing IT operational) grew worse because of the very long negotiations for HERKULES. A very ambitious master plan for the migration and integration of many individual projects was set up. In essence, that plan contained the takeover of operations, modernization and innovation. The starting point was to conclude a contract which contained many unknowns.

Programme governance and tools

The companies were established at time zero (referred to on the plans as x + 0). This meant that the migration phase was also defined and established at the same time. There was no common project management methodology, and no common planning tool. There was not even a common project language and understanding of the project.

Staff had to be integrated from two different corporate structures and armed forces personnel. The German army had to take on a new role; in addition to the role of the customer from the contract negotiations they now had to assume the role of customer management.

Complex overall planning

From a technical point of view the contract itself was not highly complex. But complexity was created by the large number of projects which had to be planned in detail and provided at different locations (Figure 15.2). These projects were almost suppliers for other subsequent projects. At the same time they depended on services from other projects. Because of these interdependencies between projects, the schedule made high demands on overall planning.

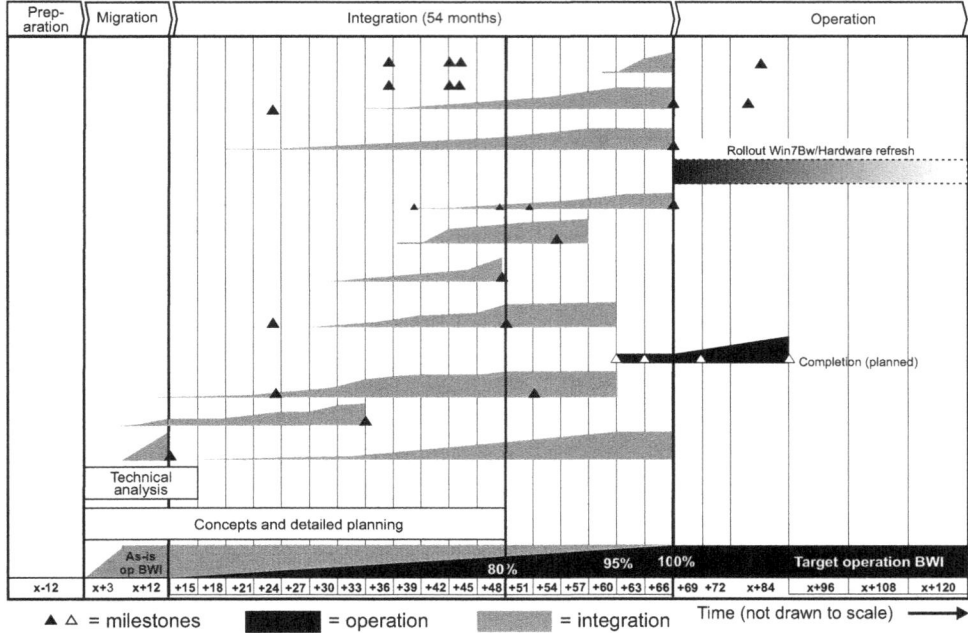

Figure 15.2 HERKULES meets reality

The solution and factors for success

The unclear starting position for IT operation made due diligence necessary during the contract negotiations. Assumptions had to be made to compensate for unclear positions regarding the existing operating and IT equipment. In order to verify these assumptions a one-year migration phase took place before takeover. However, there were many demands, such as a project methodology, appropriate tools and a comprehensive plan. The organization had to be capable of running large complex projects.

The programme manager of the HERKULES programme was defined as a key role. Each of the contracted companies had its own management, its own human resource management (HRM) department and so on. Thus a programme management link had to be established, with all projects linked across all the companies. There was only one overall plan which included the contracted project deliverables. The projects had multiple interdependencies, creating all kinds of links between the projects. That led to a demand for standardized planning, coordination and reporting. That was an important mission of programme management and the essential content of the HERKULES programme.

Project methodology

Methods had to be devised to make the projects more manageable and reduce complexity. Programme management objectives also included creating transparency, support of corporate objectives, cost efficiency, optimization of resources and controllability. Management has been characterized particularly by:

- standardized governance;
- focused project planning;
- risk assessment and control at the programme level.

Existing methods from project management alone were not sufficient for this purpose and had to be supplemented by programme-specific methods. So the tasks of programme management were (for example) coordination of resources, coordination of schedules, comprehensive risk management and common change management.

To ensure all this, a project and programme management methodology was developed. This was based on existing methods of Siemens and IBM as well as on the current German army project methodology. It was most suitable for the programme elements, so that each could be selected and matched. Here processes, templates, concepts and so forth have been harmonized and laid down in a guideline for project and programme management.

Project governance

A large number of projects in a programme with different requirements usually require clear and effective project governance. Each project was given very clear guidelines through the project methodology. Project organization (with roles, responsibilities, planning and reporting) was controlled. Defined links to the master plan at all levels were clearly defined for the links into the master plan over several levels. Each project phase and each complete project had to be completed by passing a quality gate (Q gate). Larger individual projects had a nominated member from the programme management for support.

Programme risk management

In addition to the complexity, one main difference between a project and a programme is that a programme combines all individual project goals into a common programme objective. A programme is established to achieve the strategic objectives of the company. In the case of HERKULES this was the migration and integration of the agreed deliverables.

However, there are always changes in a programme. These can occur due to technical constraints, by changing demands from the client or by changes in the company's management. Programme management must be able to consider and implement those changes. For this reason, corporate risk management was also established in the context of HERKULES programme management with the aim of identifying and evaluating critical business risks and taking action. Linking programme management and risk management makes it possible to identify the influence of programme risks on the strategic risks – and vice versa.

Overall planning problems

With a planning system containing up to three million transactions, information can only be managed and retrieved with a strict hierarchy and aggregation of data. For this BWI Informationstechnik GmbH created a solution based on the Microsoft Office Project Server, which has been adapted to the specific needs of HERKULES. In this the milestones at the top of the pyramid are formed from the overall plan.

Common tools supported the planning on that basis. There were general parameters for project planning, which were not covered by standard products on the market. The pressure of time (and the fact that the first projects had to be planned and carried out in the migration phase) did not leave time for complex development. So standard tools had to be used and adapted. The dates and dependencies among the projects had to be represented transparently. It was not possible to create a meaningful and, above all, manageable plan on one level owing due the high number of milestones. A hierarchical plan was needed.

Overall planning with reduced complexity

The objective of the overall planning was to decompose the total order of the programme in measurable and connected results. In this way, individual results are used to support the planning and control of the programme. A result may not be identical to the milestone of a project or subproject. In this respect the project results differ from programme results. The objective is also to regard the programme from the result. In other words, the result is anticipated and then operationalized and broken

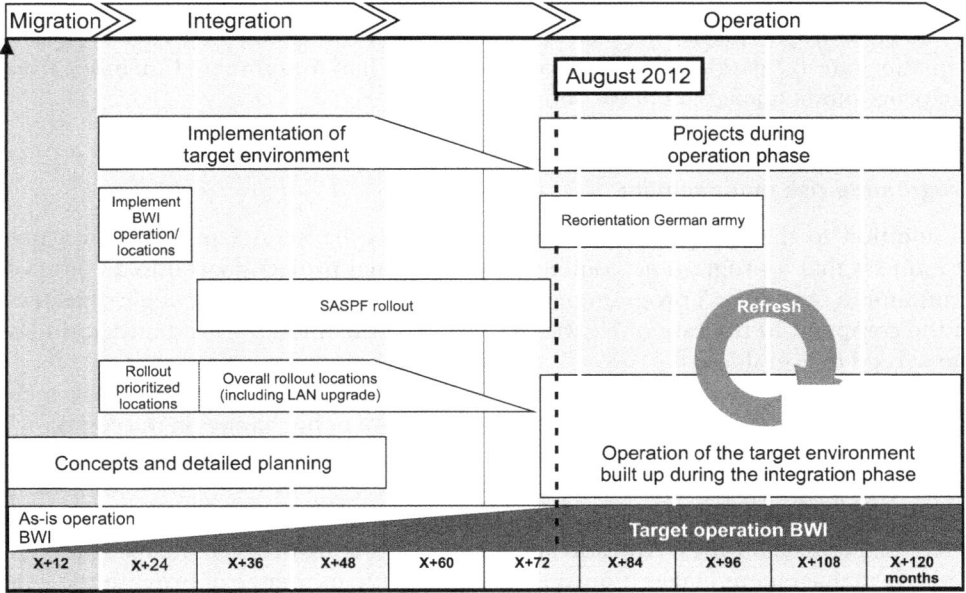

Figure 15.3 Overall implementation plan

down into partial results. Such results help to make the complexity of the programme manageable. Results are meaningful measurable points. Results are not the same as milestones, because milestones represent only measurement points where there might be no finished or semi-finished product.

Overall, planning for results provides the ability to recognize different levels of aggregation and the progress of the programme. Because it is an integrative planning approach, results and partial results are synchronized and harmonized by planning in two ways:

- by the aggregation of project-based detailed planning;
- on the other hand by the overall planning objectives and milestones.

Result plans depict these results and present them with a view of the programme in a relationship.

In summary, result plans are geared primarily to the management of a programme and any associated reporting lines such as management or client. The overall integration plan is shown in Figure 15.3.

Interrelationship management

The task of interrelationship management is to integrate (partial) results to reflect the overall structure. The overall structure cannot be represented by a linear plan or a list of dates. Interrelationships are influences between projects that have an impact on the progress more than one project. These interrelationships may be technical or informational. Identifying these interrelationships between projects is a particular challenge in a complex programme.

A matrix chart can be used to show interrelationships between demanding and supplying projects. Colour coding can be used on the chart to show whether the interrelationship is known and whether or not the situation can be solved between projects or must be dealt with by escalation. In addition, a project status will also be shown before and after the interrelationships, using colours. The interrelationship matrix shows at a glance which projects are interrelated. But it does not show how many interrelations between two projects exist – only whether interrelations are available. A project's degree of cross-linking can be represented here by a characteristic number.

Concluding summary

As part of Europe's largest public private partnership, cooperation between industry and the German armed forces has achieved its major goals. As part of this, the German armed forces had their previously separate networks combined and operation of the ICT infrastructure was handed over to a joint IT company, the BWI service alliance. This has created the following advantages for the German armed forces:

- The German armed forces now possess a modern ICT system which specifically supports the personnel in fulfilling their missions in Germany and abroad.
- In BWI, the German armed forces have a reliable IT service provider to provide services at all times.

- Systems have been standardized and harmonized. Information can now be consistently exchanged.
- The ICT infrastructure is operated on the basis of high service levels and industry standards, which can be clearly understood.
- The German armed forces personnel have been relieved of IT responsibilities and can focus fully on their core duties.

Chapter 16

Managing Change Programmes

Oliver Mack

Today companies are faced with a high rate of change in their competitive environments, with an increasing dynamic in global business. To stay competitive or be one step ahead of competitors, changing the company efficiently and effectively becomes more and more important. Instead of optimizing the operations, optimization of the transformation itself becomes a key top management task. Programmes can be the tool of choice when significant organizational transformations are necessary.

Organizational change management: continuously needed and still challenging

VUCA environments

Organizations all round the world are confronted with an environment that is getting more and more global, dynamic and driven by technological progress. The world becomes more and more VUCA. VUCA is an increasingly used acronym standing for (V)olatility, (U)ncertainty, (C)omplexity and (A)mbiguity. It expresses certain challenges that lie in the increasing dynamics and interconnectedness of the global economy (Mack and Khare, 2015). This increasing speed of change and complexity in the environment forces organizations of all types either to adapt continuously to keep up with the changes, or proactively initiate changes to get or stay ahead of the competition. Adaptation of the organization is a main success factor for competitiveness (Greenwood and Hinnings, 1996). Especially in larger companies, more and more huge and complex change activities are started but often fail to deliver the expected results (Towers Watson, 2013). Today, most of those change endeavours are realized through programmes, a formalized approach to implement complex changes in cross-functional teams which are also used in other, more technical project-orientated environments.

This chapter gives an overview about the specifics of change programmes and their management, including some innovative ideas using a systemic background that might help to improve the results of such programmes.

Organizational change

There is no common definition of organizational change. Various facets exist in literature and practice. I follow a definition that defines organizational change as the simultaneous transformation of several organizational elements (like strategy, processes) that affects different levels of an organization (Pescher, 2010 with further references). Organizational change appears in many facets. As a first step I shall look at different types of change, different change purposes and the objects of change.

A model from osb international (Figure 16.1) differentiates between five types of change, depending on the frequency of change (episodic or one-time) and the severity of change (three levels). Organizations are always changing and never stand still. This is reflected on level one, covering the evolutionary development of an organization. Second-level changes can be understood as actively controlled changes within the current structure of the organization. Third-level changes are more fundamental changes of strategy, structure and culture.

The four consciously controlled types of change all have different characteristics and different underlying approaches. While permanent change is reflected in the permanent management structures and systems of an organization (for example Six Sigma for Type 1, or innovation management for Type 3), the episodic change is normally handled by specific projects or programmes. Type 2 changes are more reactive, for example solving a current organizational crisis with a restructuring project. A Type 4 change 'Radical Transformation' is normally driven by a larger and more complex strategic programme. This is the area which I shall focus on in this chapter.

Looking a bit more into practice, we can differentiate between various change triggers and objectives (see Figure 16.2). Often several of those aspects are touched upon in a radical transformation. Each of the different change triggers and objectives has implications on the set-up, approach and management of the change and needs specific intervention designs to be successful but I shall develop some general ideas in the following sections.

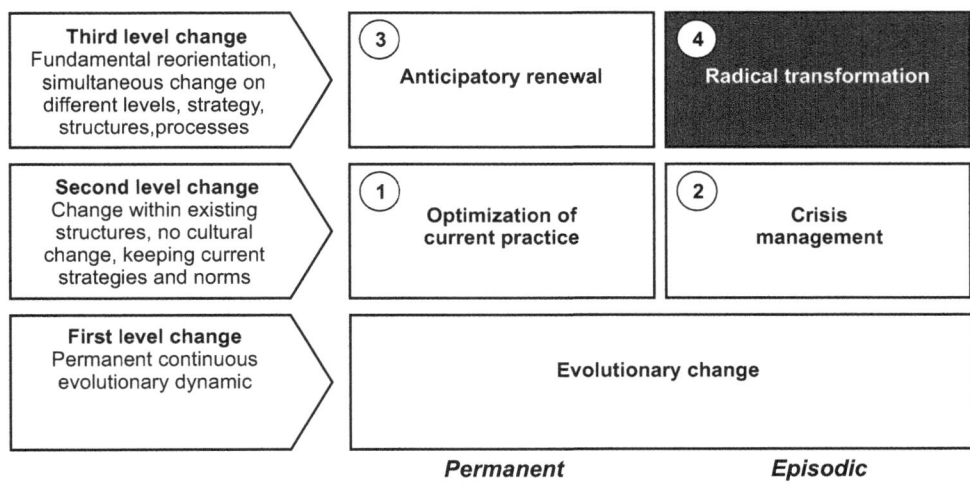

Figure 16.1 Change types

Purpose and culture of the organization	Develop or change organizational culture or values	
	Develop/sharpen or implement vision/mission	
	Implement strategic repositioning of new/adapted business model	
Value chain/business activities	Concept development	Develop ideas/concepts on: • Organizational structures; • Processes; • Systems
	Rollout of (centrally) developed concepts	Adapt organizational structures: • Integration of new entities into existing structures (for example a new groupwide staff function or department) • Addition of a new entity into an existing structure (for example a new country organization) • Removal of an entity from the existing structure (for example, carve-out and sale of a business unit; closing a department) • Merger of entities into one new structure (for example, company post-merger of two sales regions into one)
		Adapt processes: • Core processes • Support processes • Management processes
		Adapt systems: • IT systems • Management systems
Improvements	Improvements within existing structures	Improve: • Efficiency • Innovativeness • Changeability

Figure 16.2 Different objectives of change projects

Change management

Change management is the systematic set-up, conception and implementation of measures to change an organization in a planned direction. It focuses on specific interventions on three different levels that are interwoven and have to be considered and addressed simultaneously, as follows:

• Individual level: change requires dealing with behavioural change by learning and unlearning of a single person during the organizational change effort as well as dealing with psychological aspects such as fear, power and anger.

- Group/team level: change at this level means dealing with changing patterns of social groups and the underlying organizational (as well as pycho-social processes) of changing teams and interaction/communication patterns.
- Organization level: change requires dealing with the overall aspects of new governance structures, rules or purpose of the part of the organization to be changed (which could be the whole organization).

Various change management approaches exist in literature and practice. Most of the traditional process-orientated approaches consist of the following areas of interventions (Stolzenberg and Heberle, 2006; Pescher, 2010):

- Change vision: these interventions focus on developing a clear picture of the desired future state that should be reached when the change programme has ended. All actions needed to attain the vision have to be listed. The current status also has to be recorded, allowing before and after comparison.
- Change communication: this area contains all activities dealing with the planning and execution of communication measures to inform the organization of the desired state and the progress of the change endeavour. These interventions adress several groups like participants, affected employees and stakeholders.
- Employee participation: these interventions focus on the involvement of the affected employees in the transformation process. On the one hand participation helps to integrate the expertise of a broader audience into the process. On the other hand the idea is also to reduce resistance due to participation and increase active support of change measures.
- Employee qualification: this area contains all activities needed to support the learning processes during a transformation. It includes the identification of competence gaps based on new requirements and the identification of specific training needs for all affected employees. It also includes the development and execution of training and other qualification measures related to the transformation.

Change programmes: a special type of programme

A programme can be understood as a group of projects executed and managed together to reach a specific benefit, which would not be possible by managing the projects individually (PMI, 2013a). By comparison with a project portfolio, a programme follows specific common goals, reflected in the benefits. While a portfolio is a collection of projects of a specific type, a programme can contain a set of different projects of various types.

The management of a programme contains two separate but interlinked levels, the programme level and the project level. Both levels have specific characteristics that have to be dealt with simultaneously by specific roles and structures, processes and tools (Mack and Jungen, 2015). While the project level focuses on the results of the individual projects, the programme deals with the overall programme benefits and objectives by coordination and control of the programme's set of projects.

To understand the specifics of change programmes better, I shall differentiate between three types with different characteristics. These can appear as programme types or as project types within a programme (see Figure 16.3). These types are as follows:

- Type 1 – physical result. Starting with an idea, this project/programme type ends with a specific product or service. Engineering or construction projects are typical members of this type. Normally these kinds of projects can be clearly split into a concept and an implementation phase. The traditional project management methodology with its well-established tools and concepts was developed with this type in mind.
- Type 2 – research and development. Again starting with an idea, this project/programme type explores a certain area and narrows down the expected result over time and the result becomes more and more clear. By comparison with Type 1 the result is a much more 'moving target' and can differ significantly from the initial idea. Typical examples of this type are all kinds of research projects or software development projects. Normally these projects need a different approach which is much more iterative and dynamic in planning and execution. Solutions for handling this project type are agile methods like SCRUM (Schwaber, 2004; Stellman and Greene, 2014). Compared with Type 1, these projects deal with increasing complexity working simultaneously on two levels – on the delivery of the result and on the result itself (which might change as a whole or in terms of its concreteness). In these projects the project team's view of the project result will develop over time.
- Type 3 – change. Change projects and programmes focus not on a particular product or service, but on the structural change of social systems like organizations. The results involve behavioural change from people. Typical examples are restructuring, reorganization, post-merger integration, process redesign or

1. Technical projects

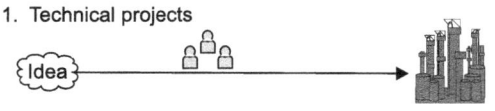

- Clearly defined result
- Concept > implementation
- Breakdown of clearly defined tasks
- Best practice, or good practice

2. Research/development projects

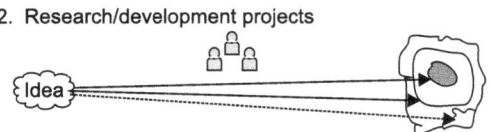

- Unclear result - moving target
- Iterative approach - search for result
- Time boxing (phase-gate, milestones and step-by-step dealing
- Trial and error

3. Change projects

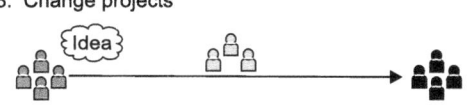

- Different behaviours/system change as project result
- Project team is part of change/result
- Transformation of a complex adaptive system (actors and system change simultaneously
- Context control.

Figure 16.3 Project types

cultural change projects. These kinds of projects have a self-reflexive character, as the people to be changed are not just a group outside the project or programme. The project or programme team will have to change during the project/programme lifecycle to achieve success. This is the most complex of the three types, because behavioural and social aspects are not just enablers (as in Types 1 and 2), but are part of the core objectives. Ideas on how exactly to deal with this kind of project type and its described differences are just at the beginning in the literature and practice of project management.

The following discussion will focus on specific aspects of Type 3 programmes (change programmes).

Change programmes

A change programme can have several objectives but at its core the objective is always the implementation of measures to change an organization in a specified direction. This usually requires significant behavioural change of a large number of people in an organization. To reach the objective, several projects can be defined under the programme umbrella covering various aspects, like changes in the organizational structures and processes, activities towards the market, the implementation of new systems and tools, and so on. The programme might include projects from all the types described above.

As an example, consider a restructuring programme undertaken during a financial crisis that has as its objective to reach a 'black zero' result, needing more than 100 million euros in financial improvements. For that purpose, ten projects might be needed to deal with various issues, such as increasing sales in existing markets, entering two new markets, reducing debtors, reducing fixed costs and so on. Many employees will have seen the company surviving economic downturns in the past, and most will see no need to change their behaviour, which would require additional change aspects to be included in the programme.

As this example shows, a change programme is normally not always focused on change as such but on a more specific purpose. But programmes can be called change programmes if change is a major success factor for the whole programme and its primary objectives.

Managing change programmes: some aspects from a systemic perspective

In this section I shall look at the management of change programmes from a more integrated and systemic perspective, combining some aspects of change management and programme management for greater effectiveness.

Establishing the change role in a programme

If the change aspect in a programme is a critical success factor, that should be clearly established in the structure and processes from the beginning. Change management can be established either as a separate function or as an integrated part of the core work (either at project or program level). Four kinds of approach can be identified, as shown in Figure 16.4 and outlined below.

Option 1: separate change project

A common approach (especially in large IT projects such as enterprise resource planning (ERP) implementations) is to define a separate project for change management on the same level as all other projects in the programme. This change project bundles together all the activities that have to be done from a change perspective. It is a service entity for the other projects, helping them to deliver the implementation of concepts under the clear responsibility of a project manager. On the programme level the change project is controlled like all other projects, with status reporting, an activity/milestone plan, resource and cost planning, progress control and so on. The benefit of this approach is that it fits well into traditional programme thinking and separates change activities from the 'content' work.

There is also a negative side, because running the change as a separate project puts the focus only on operational tasks like communication, information and training. The distance from the other projects in the programme, as well as to the senior level decision-makers on the programme level is too high.

Option 2: function/responsibility in all projects

Another approach is to make each project in a programme individually responsible for all the change activities within the scope of the project, either fully

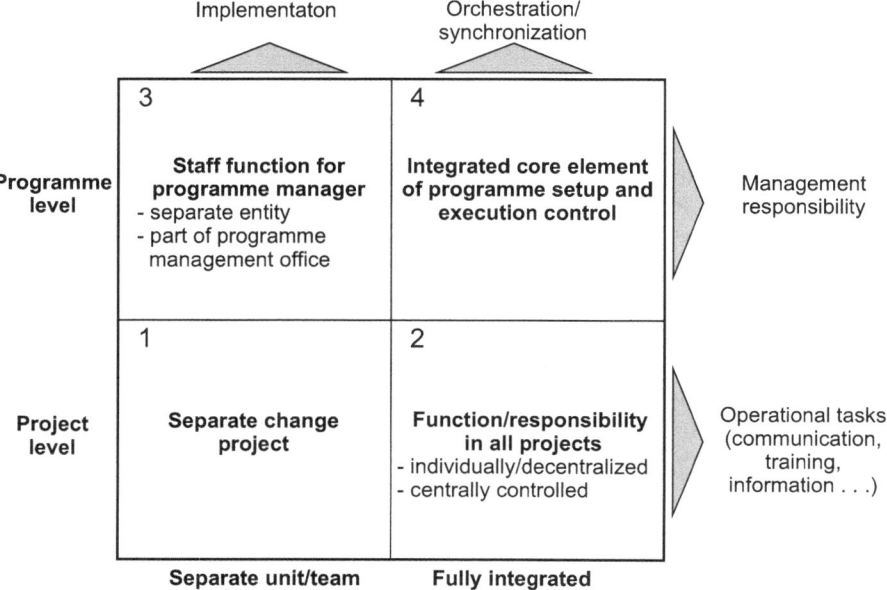

Figure 16.4 Change role set-up in a transformation programme

independently for each individual project or centrally coordinated. The change management is fully integrated on an individual project level. Project management and change management are not seen as separate activities but as an integrated approach on the project level. The benefit of this approach is that change is understood as an integrated part of each individual project and can support its concrete needs with high effectiveness.

The disadvantage of this approach lies in the decentralized set-up, which leads to lower efficiency of the measures and a high risk of uncoordinated activities that might address the same stakeholders several times. This could lead either to confusion or to an increased coordination effort.

Option 3: staff function for the programme manager

In this approach, a specific support function for change is formally installed on the programme level. This can be a change manager or a change office reporting directly to the programme manager. Or it could be a separate entity within the programme management office, where the change manager is reporting to the programme office manager. The change function takes over all change management activities on the programme and individual project level.

The advantage of this arrangement is prominent positioning close to the programme manager and the programme decision-makers as well as centrally coordinated change activities. On the negative side is the risk that the change management is too distant from the operational projects, possibly not understanding or willing to pick up their needs.

Option 4: change management as an integrated core element of the programme set-up and control

In this approach the change management is fully integrated on the programme level. This means that change management aspects are not regarded as separate planning and control actions of the individual projects, but are an integrated part of the programme management. By comparison with the other approaches, change management is not understood as a separate activity in addition to the programme and project management but as an integrated part on both levels. Change aspects are considered in all areas and phases of the programme set-up and execution as well as on the individual project level. The benefit of this very new approach is the high efficiency and effectiveness of the change efforts within the programme. Programme and project participants can share an integrated approach.

The challenge of this approach is the high level of leadership required from the people involved. An advanced attitude towards a holistic perspective as well as experience in systemic thinking is necessary, both at the senior management level (acting as programme owners) and at project manager level.

Integrating change aspects into programme management

As mentioned, project and programme management and change management complement each other very well from a traditional perspective. A more integrated approach goes one step further so that these areas are no longer separated but combined, seen as two sides of the same coin. When setting up and running a programme, the ideas of change management are used in programme management. Also, when developing and executing interventions in change management, the programme and projects (with their structures, processes and objectives) are explicitly used to facilitate change.

Programme visibility, roles and committee structures

A first important and often underestimated aspect to discuss from a change perspective is the clear and well-considered definition and set-up of all roles and committees of a programme.

To ensure the full impact of a change programme, the programme itself has first to be established as a specific structure or subsystem of the organization in addition to the well-established organizational subsystems of hierarchical structure and organizational processes. Only a clear visibility of the new subsystem makes the programme a recognizable place where the change can happen and start to spread across the whole organization. To draw a clear distinction between the running business and the change programme, the definition of a clear border and the naming of the subsystem as a programme are important aspects. For more details on distinction and form see the groundbreaking work of Spencer-Brown (1969).

Sometimes line management does not understand (or underestimates the importance) of these issues. They ask if the effort of establishing projects or programmes is necessary. That weakens a new change programme from the beginning. Even if the project level is well established, the programme level needs to be established as another layer of control (the programme layer) in order to generate sufficient impact on the line organization. Visibility on both programme and project levels can be supported by nominating clear project and programme roles or by giving the programme and project recognizable names and branding.

Establishing a change programme in such a clear way can also help to manage the change stability paradox (Feldman and Pentland, 2003), dealing with the issue that organizations need both stability and change to develop and prosper. In times of change, where the main organization undergoes significant transformation with all uncertainty, the change programme can temporarily give the necessary stability for the people involved and the rest of the organization.

The second aspect requiring attention is, as already mentioned, the clear set-up of all roles on project and programme level from the beginning. These should include at least project managers, project team members, project owners, programme manager, programme owner and programme steering committee (PMI, 2013a, 2013b). In practice there are often discussions about the need for all these roles and the unnecessary complexity generated by establishing separate roles on programme and project level. Especially in change programmes we see both layers as important as they focus on different aspects.

On the project layer the roles focus on implementing the content of the individual projects. On the programme layer the focus is on more general aspects like the overall transformation, setting up of new projects or correcting/closing existing projects as well as on keeping an eye on the overall change progress. Mixing up those layers in practice often leads to unclear situations and sometimes conflicting priorities.

The importance of the right 'interpersonal links' between the roles and the two layers is often underestimated as a parameter of programme design. One person can take over several roles on programme and project level. Intelligent configurations can help to improve the necessary information flow between the teams and can control politics.

The programme layer should be linked to the operational project level via a 'top-down steering link'. This could mean steering committee members from the programme level also being nominated as steering committee members or project owners in the individual projects. Also a 'bottom-up link' should be set up to ensure that the individual project is also linked to the overall programme on the operational level. This can be done for example by forming a programme core team that brings all project managers together.

The set-up is mainly driven by the individual situation, company culture and programme goals. As an example, in a large change programme, the executive board members acted as a programme steering committee (with the CEO as the programme owner). They made it very clear that they did not act in the executive board role when dealing with the programme manager and the project managers. Each programme steering board member took over the sponsorship of one or more projects within the programme. Each led as a project owner on the relevant project steering committees, together with other senior leaders from the affected divisions. All project managers together formed the programme core team, led by the programme manager, to discuss operational programme-wide topics as well as change aspects of the programme.

The programme structure should be simple to understand and transparent for the whole organization. Complicated matrix structures and multilevel responsibilities beyond the traditional project and programme roles should be avoided. In one programme the programme manager role was split into an 'operational programme manager' (OPM) and a 'strategic programme manager' (SPM). The first of these was held by an experienced project manager and the second by a senior manager from the company. During the programme lifecycle, the organization got totally confused about this set-up as it was unclear who was really managing the programme because the OPM needed to get approval for all major decisions from the SPM. That caused several delays. Also the SPM used the programme role to position himself as a potential new candidate for the executive board, which influenced the programme significantly.

Programme goals, change goals and activity

A second area of programme management that can be discussed from a change management perspective is the definition of the programme goals and project goals. As it is well known how to define clear goals for projects and programmes in general (PMI, 2013a, 2013b) and how to break down programme goals on individual projects, additional aspects are important for change programmes. In comparison to other programme types, where programme goals are mainly important for the communication and understanding within the programme structures themselves, the goals of change programmes fulfil an additional role: they should be also suitable for communication to the whole organization.

In practice, this fact is often underestimated and the solution is often a split between programme/project goal setting and change communication, which could lead to coordination and consistency issues and confusion across the whole organization. To gain a better insight on this topic we need to discuss goal setting and executed behaviour in organizations on a more differentiated level. Setting up good change programme objectives is itself a challenge.

On the one hand the objectives should be as clear and concrete as possible to make the whole organization understand what the major aspects of the change are and why the change is necessary – clarity is especially expected from inside the organization on lower levels. The goals should give a clear indication of the future expected state of the organization or at least of the expected impact of the programme. A good change vision should be imaginable, desirable, feasible, focused, flexible and communicable (Kotter, 1996, p. 72).

On the other hand the goals should be open enough to allow flexible interpretation while the programme is progressing, helping to adapt the programme to the changing context. This view is also supported by the understanding of organizations as loosely coupled systems (Orton and Weick, 1990), working in practice very well with various vaguely and badly defined goals (Caluwé and Vermaak, 2003, p. 10; Orton and Weick, 1990). Brunsson (2009) sees this aspect as a useful mechanism, because top management vagueness in objectives is useful in communication to important external stakeholders (like owners or shareholders) as the risk of a change programme failure is high. Unclear objectives help to reinterpret the results of a change initiative in the desired way.

However, developing clear goals and intentions does not mean we should act in that way. Often individual behaviour is strongly decoupled from intention and opinion (Orton and Weick, 1990). This means that although a change programme was initiated and run with a good intent to change, and although the change topics were communicated and discussed with a supportive attitude, people on all levels might act differently.

This has significant consequences for the management of change programmes:

- Definition of the programme's goals should be a good balance between clarity and vagueness. It should not be too short, as the process as such is important for the programme and project teams to form a subsystem within the organization beside the hierarchical structure. It also helps to be able to communicate with one voice to the organization. But it also shouldn't be too long as the real impact on behaviour is limited. The process should be used to work on implicit and explicit opinions to get a better common understanding across management levels. It is not only the goals themselves which are important, but also the process of developing them (Caluwé and Vermaak, 2003).
- Besides the focus on change programme goals, a strong parallel focus should be set on behaviour and action. Beer *et al.* (1990) emphasize that the starting point should not be the idea of changing individual attitudes and know-how as a basis for organizational change. Instead, the focus on individual behaviour is key where change can be understood to adapt recurring behaviour patterns.
- Goal-setting in change programmes is very context-dependent. Programme managers should get a clear picture of how much operational change is expected and

possible, based on all stakeholder interests. The definition and measurement of success criteria should be defined. Effects always occur on two dimensions with context-specific importance – on the operational level and on the attitude/cultural level. Even if a programme doesn't change much on the operational level ('real changes'), it might still have significant impact on the cultural level, which is much more difficult to measure (Brunsson, 2009).

Balanced change project portfolio

Another important but often underestimated lever of control in change programmes is the project portfolio. From my practical experience some portfolio set-ups work better than others. This is not surprising as on an organizational level the change programme as a whole, as well as the individual projects, are recognized by the entire staff of the organization as the broader audience of the change programme. Also programme and projects are linked to each other (as already discussed) in a complex way which could lead, if not consciously designed, to unexpected impacts. The following parameters should be kept in mind when setting up a change programme.

1. Minimization of project interdependencies. A first portfolio requirement is to make sure to cut the programme objectives into projects with few or no conflicting goals, overlaps or dependencies. This simplifies the coordination between projects on the programme level, as complex interdependencies with unexpected effects can be reduced. Therefore this should be considered as a design parameter from the beginning.
2. Balance of project types. A more change-orientated aspect is the portfolio balance related to the project impact. Using the so-called Triangle of Belief Polarities (TBP) as an underlying pattern (for further details see also Mack and Jungen, 2015), we can split change aspects of projects into three different types concerning their organizational impact. A first type focuses on structural changes of the organization, adapting organizational governance like roles, responsibilities and structures. A second type focuses more on the processes and interaction patterns between people in the organization, targeting adapted communication and interaction. Finally, a third type focuses on the changing competencies and know-how needed by the individuals in their specific roles and responsibilities. All three types are interdependent and one or more aspects can be found in one individual project, but often one dominant aspect per project can be identified. We have the practical experience that if the overall project portfolio is in good balance on these three types on the programme level, this causes a positive impact on the overall success of the change programme. This seems to be the case, as always all three aspects have to be considered in parallel for good progress in change, either being addressed within the programme or outside (Mack and Jungen, 2015). The dynamics and effects between the different projects can also be used to initiate specific interventions moving the organization into the desired direction. As an example, imagine an initial programme set-up for an ERP roll-out with two projects (beside the IT project itself) focusing on setting up new processes and training people on the new system. Automatically discussions start about responsibilities and the need

to realign organizational structures. Depending on the situation, this can be ignored on the programme level and will be then covered in the line organization, or it can be picked up as a new project focusing on the structural redesign. Different constellations of projects might lead to totally different dynamics of a change programme.

3. Alignment of project effects. Each project in a change programme follows a certain timeline in regard to the impact of the planned change measures on the organization. Some projects target shorter-term changes, such as the formal adaptation of structure, publishing a new standard or procedure, or behavioural/attitude changes in a very small team. Other projects take effect only on a longer timescale, like those focusing on some behavioural change or changes in attitudes of a larger group of people or the whole staff of an organization. The project portfolio of a change programme should have a good balance of short- and long-term projects. An imbalance in favour of short-term projects would create a risk that the programme might lack sustainability in the organization. Conversely, an imbalance in favour of long-term projects would risk the programme lacking acceptance because of missed 'quick wins' (on quick wins for leaders see Van Buren and Stafferstone, 2009).

These three aspects should give an idea of how the project portfolio can be used to control the dynamics of a change programme actively. These aspects are often underrated and programme managers should bear them in mind when setting up and running change-related programmes.

Programme lifecycle and timelines

A final aspect to be considered is the lifecycle of a change programme. By comparison with Type 1 and 2 projects (technical and R&D), change projects and programmes follow their own logic related to time and speed. While theoretically Type 1 project timelines are mainly determined by technological restrictions and Type 2 projects by the intellectual capacity of the researcher, Type 3 change projects are additionally determined by the complex social system dynamics.

- Change programme roadmap. A programme roadmap can be defined as the chronological representation of a programme's intended direction. While details are planned on a project level in the projects' schedules, the programme roadmap helps to organize the programme in major stages or blocks (PMI, 2013a; Thiry, 2012). A change programme can be split into major phases to reduce its complexity. Programme milestones are defined as gates at the end of each phase (mandatory for all projects). Depending on the overall set-up (see below), this helps to synchronize the progress of the individual projects on programme level by time-boxing, while keeping their individual flexibility and freedom of action. The milestones on programme level can also be used as review points for the programme owner/programme steering committee to discuss the projects' change impact and realization of planned benefits (Thiry, 2012, p. 140). The OGC recommends an approach in tranches, delivering the new capabilities as a set of step changes (OGC, 2011, p. 98).

- Waterfall versus agile iterative set-up. A traditional form of structuring the program lifecycle comes from Type 1 (technical projects as described earlier). This is mainly based on the idea of a desired future state at the end of the programme and an assessment of the current state of the organization, identifying the gaps and deducing a top-down approach of how to close them. This leads to the traditional approach of phases and gates (Cooper, 1990). Either specific tranches are defined (OGC, 2011), or traditional phases are identified (such as concept, implementation and final review). The projects interact with each other in this framework and work in synchronization. Alternative approaches becoming more and more popular in software development are iterative approaches, like agile development or SCRUM methodology (Schwaber, 2004; Rubin, 2012). Taking seriously the idea of Type 2 and 3 projects (where the final result cannot be defined at the beginning), these approaches focus on time-boxing and decentralized responsibility rather than on upfront top-down planning. This gives more flexibility for the individual projects as well as for the whole programme, but it also needs other leadership skills and cultural context. Agile approaches place people over processes and responsiveness to changing context over following a plan (Stellman and Greene, 2014). On the individual project level, the agile approach is broadly used and first applications on change projects are discussed (Little, 2014). Although not applied to change programmes so far, some ideas can be used from the application of agile methods in multiproject environments (Heusser, 2015).
- Rhythm of change. Another almost always forgotten dimension is the 'rhythm of change' in programmes and projects (Huy and Mintzberg, 2003). Although the research in this area is still in a very early stage, we know that oscillation and specific rhythmical approaches lead to better results than non-rhythmical design of the time dimension of change programmes and projects (Klarner and Raisch, 2013). Considering the importance of rhythm and oscillation in nature (like the heartbeat or the tides) this should not be surprising and is often done intuitively by experienced change programme and project managers. Defining the right rhythm needs to be considered on all levels in programmes, starting from the right reporting and meeting structure on the individual project level, up to the definition of regular programme steering committee meetings.
- Multilevel intervention design. A final aspect of time, specifically important in change programmes, is what can be called 'multilevel intervention design'. This means the systematic alignment of all change activities across all projects in a programme – not just with regards to content, but also in terms of timing. By comparison with other programme types, change programmes need an integrated view of interventions on all social levels across projects simultaneously owing to their self-referentiality (the projects and programme change the organization and therefore the project and programme participants themselves). Interventions on individual level (behavioural change), team level (change in configuration, roles, communication processes) and organizational level (cultural change) need to go hand-in-hand, but also need to be aligned with the programme's technical progress. Interventions on people and teams need to be congruent with changes on the other subsystems of the organization, like the formal organization or the value-generating activities (Nadler, 1993). As an

example, if one project in a change programme works on the implementation of a new software tool (including the training activities to enable the affected employees) and another project works on the integration of two business units affected by the software tool at the same time, it is obvious that conflicting or complementing dependencies can appear. Systematic design and control of the change interventions on programme level may help to keep the congruence and give the overall change process the uncertainty and stability needed at the same time (Leana and Barry, 2000).

Conclusion and outlook

The starting point of this chapter was the idea that change programmes are significantly different from other programme types. These differences need to be reflected in tools and concepts, which are just beginning to evolve. There is the need for a clear awareness of these differences when setting up a change programme, as well as a clear idea of how change will be managed during programme execution. Beside establishing a specific role on the programme level, various parameters can be tuned to integrate the change aspect in a programme systematically from the beginning. Staffing and interaction of the programme roles are underestimated key success factors. Traditional elements like the project portfolio, the scope of the individual projects as well as the definition of project goals can be viewed and designed differently from a change perspective. Another important aspect is the timing in change programmes, which needs a much broader perspective than in other programme types.

Many aspects mentioned in this chapter are at an early stage of understanding in theory and practice. Although there is much literature on change management, change through implementation of change programme management is just at the beginning. More research is needed. From practical experience it seems that agile project management methods are the right way to conduct change projects and programmes, but it seems that most change endeavours (at least in larger companies) are still designed and managed with a traditional, mechanistically driven, centralized, top-down approach. The future will show whether we can benefit more from unexplored generic principles from biology, sociology and other natural and social sciences that can be incorporated into management science for a different understanding and management of large change endeavours.

References and further reading

Beer, M., Eisenstat, R. A. and Spector, B. (1989), 'Why Change Programs Don't Produce Change', *Harvard Business Review*, 68(6): 158–66.

Brunsson, N. (2009), 'Mythos Change Management', *Harvard Business Manager*, 30 July. Retrieved 29 May 2015 from <www.harvardbusinessmanager.de/heft/artikel/a-621442.html>.

Caluwé, L. de and Vermaak, H. (2003), *Learning to Change: A Guide for Organization Change Agents*. London: Sage.

Cameron, E. and Greene, M. (2012), *Making Sense of Change Management*, 3rd edn., London: Kogan Page.

Cooper, R. G. (1990), 'Stage-Gate Systems: A New Tool for Managing New Products', *Business Horizons*, 33(3): 44–54.

Feldman, M. S. and Pentland, B. T. (2003), 'Reconceptualizing Organizational Routines as a Source of Flexibility and Change', *Administrative Science Quarterly*, 48(1): 94–118.

Greenwood, R. and Hinings, C. R. (1996), 'Understanding Radical Organizational Change: Bringing Together the Old and the New Institutionalism', *Academy of Management Review*, 21(4): 1022–54.

Heusser, M. (2015), 'Introducing the Scaled Agile Framework', *CIO online*, 17 June. Retrieved 2 July 2015 from <www.cio.com/article/2936942/enterprise-software/introducing-the-scaled-agile-framework.html>.

Huy, Q. N. and Mintzberg, H. (2003), 'The Rhythm of Change', *MIT Sloan Management Review*, 44(4): 79–84.

Klarner, P. and Raisch, S. (2013), 'Move to the Beat: Rythms of Change and Firm Performance', *Academy of Management Journal*, 56(1): 160–84.

Kotter, J. P. (1996), *Leading Change*, Cambridge, MA: Harvard Business Press.

Leana, C. R. and Barry, B. (2000), 'Stability and Change as Simultaneous Experiences in Organizational Life', *Academy of Management Review*, 25(4): 753–9.

Little, J. (2014). *Lean Change Management*, Happy Melly Express.

Mack, O. and Jungen, M. (2015), 'Program Management in VUCA Environments: Theoretical and Pragmatical Thoughts on a Systemic Management of Projects and Programs', in O. Mack, A. Khare, A. Krämer and T. Burgartz (eds.), *Managing in a VUCA World*, Berlin: Springer.

Mack, O. and Khare, A. (2015), 'Perspectives on a VUCA World', in O. Mack, A. Khare, A. Krämer and T. Burgartz (eds), *Managing in a VUCA World*, Berlin: Springer.

Nadler, D. A. (1993), 'Concepts for the Management of Organizational Change', in C. Mabey and B. Mayon-White (eds), *Managing Change*, 2nd edn., London: Sage.

OGC (2011), *MSP – Managing Successful Programmes*, Norwich: The Stationery Office.

Orton, J. D. and Weick, K. E. (1990). 'Loosely Coupled Systems: A Reconceptualization. *Academy of Management Review*, 15(2): 203–23.

Pescher, J. (2010), *Change Management*, Berlin: Springer.

PMI (2013a), *The Standard for Program Management*, 3rd edn., Newtown Square, PA: Project Management Institute.

PMI (2013b), *The Standard for Project Management*, 5th edn., Newtown Square, PA: Project Management Institute.

Rubin, K. S. (2012), *Essential Scrum: A Practical Guide to the Most Popular Agile Process*, Harlow: Addison-Wesley.

Schwaber, K. (2004), *Agile Project Management with Scrum,* Redmond, WA: Microsoft Press.

Spencer-Brown, G. (1969), *Laws of Form*, London: Allen & Unwin.

Stellman, A. and Greene, J. (2014), *Learning Agile*, Sebastopol: O'Reilly Media.

Stolzenberg, K. and Heberle, K. (2013), *Change Management*, Berlin: Springer.

Thiry, M. (2012), *Programme Management*, Farnham: Gower.

Towers Watson (2013), 'Only One-Quarter of Employers are Sustaining Gains from Change Management Initiatives, Towers Watson Survey Finds'. Retrived 25 June 2015 from <www.towerswatson.com/en/Press/2013/08/Only-One-Quarter-of-Employers-Are-Sustaining-Gains-From-Change-Management>.

Van Buren, M. E. and Safferstone, T. (2009), 'The Quick Wins Paradox', *Harvard Business Review*, 87(1): 55–61.

Chapter 17

Programmes and Collaborative Working

David E. Hawkins

The complexity and stakeholder profile of programmes has changed significantly in recent years owing to economic challenges and the increase in multiparty solutions. As organizations strive for enhanced performance, traditional hierarchical contracting models have given way to more integrated configurations that foster a more interdependent collaborative programme management profile.

Introduction

Involving a contractor early in a programme can bring the potential to optimize design, reduce costs and accelerate execution. Constraints to engagement are mostly like to come from reliance on relationships, both from the contractor selection process (where optimum designs and solutions cannot be traditionally evaluated) and where downstream execution performance is planned through integrated teams. In these models the focus is on combining the best individual skills irrespective of their organizations and where risk and reward are built around joint responsibilities and performance.

The dynamics of these integrated configurations raises the prospect of clients, contractors and their competitors removing the more traditional boundaries between their organizations and, while most will acknowledge that relationships are important, few have the structures in place to replace personal relationships with organizational relationships. Reports dating from Latham (1994) to the more recent McNulty Report (2011) highlight the potential benefits of integrated collaborative working. In 2005, Partnership Sourcing Ltd (now the Institute for Collaborative Working) reinforced this concept by predicting that by 2020 these alternative collaborative business models would be the norm – not just in programme delivery but across a spectrum of business activities and delivery solutions.

The impact of these developments must inevitably lead to changes in the more traditional aspects of programme management and the need to enhance skills and operating models. In response British Standards (BSI) in association with ICW published BS 11000 in 2010, the world's first standard for collaborative business relationships (at the time of writing this was due to become ISO 11000). It provides a robust framework for developing and embedding collaborative working best practice to facilitate the transition from reliance on personal relationships to more sustainable business-to-business relationships. The underlying theme for effective collaborative working embedded in this framework standard is the behaviours that organizations and individuals adopt within operational programme management across a variety of contracting models.

It can be challenging to predict concrete benefits before programme teams are given the authority to venture into what many might consider uncharted waters. There are no absolutes, although most would agree that collaboration within any programme will deliver benefits (whether these are direct cost and time savings or greater confidence and risk mitigation). Some examples are:

- Network Rail reduced a two-year 'de-bottlenecking' project to 20 months using a collaborative alliance approach.
- The @one Alliance achieved significant savings and (at the time of writing) is on track to deliver 20–30 per cent savings, while providing innovative and sustainable solutions including a 30 per cent carbon reduction programme.
- Collaborative planning significantly stabilized a water treatment works programme, saving four weeks and $600,000.
- Collaborative planning achieved £2 million savings on a motorway viaduct project valued at £100 million.
- BAA T2 working in partnership with an incentivized programme reduced design time and accelerated construction start, delivering savings of 8–10 per cent.
- Traffic management enhanced through the integration of four prime contractors generated £1 million savings in supplies and plant and a 20 per cent reduction of the commissioning programme.
- A city council increased its front-line performance, saving £1 million per annum. The council's savings are used to limit local tax increases.

Recognizing the potential value that collaboration can deliver is only the first step. The challenge for programme managers is to embed a robust and sustainable approach, particularly when looking at long-duration projects where inevitable changes in personnel can alter the balance of behaviours. It was to address this focus on sustainable relationships that the Institute for Collaborative Working introduced the CRAFT methodology which ultimately became the foundation of BS 11000. It establishes an eight-stage lifecycle model (Figure 17.1) that enables organizations:

- to evaluate their internal strategies and capabilities for collaboration;
- to develop appropriate engagement plans for partner selection;
- to develop a platform for building effective governance and a structure to support behaviours (and thus performance).

The unique feature of this standard is that while it outlines in a process the key principles of managing evolving relationships, each of the best practice requirements is included because of the impact these have on behaviours. In the following text I shall outline the principles of the framework, together with case studies of major organizations that have already embraced the standard, demonstrating key aspects that should be considered in future programme management.

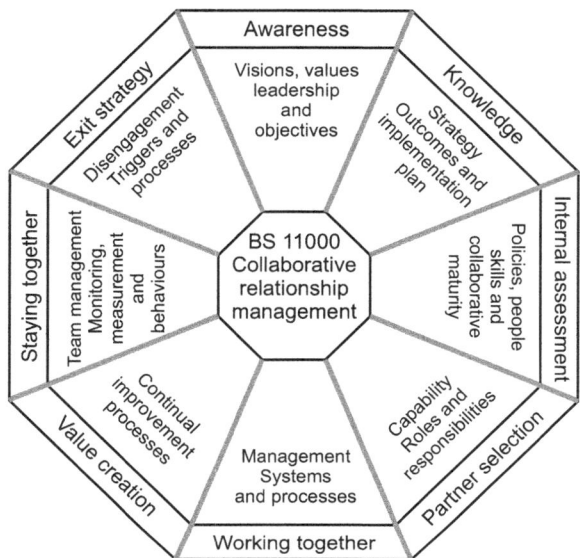

Figure 17.1 CRAFT/BS 11000 eight-step model

The underlying theme for effective collaborative working is the behaviours that organizations and individuals adopt and display within operational business relationships. It is generally recognized that for most people collaboration is the preferred way of working. However, evidence suggests that in practice this is frequently diluted either through individual corporate policy or more often by the nature of the leadership. It is relatively easy to define how we expect others to behave but it is frequently less common to find those same expectations reflected in the way in which organizations present themselves. The list in Figure 17.2 identifies some general examples of attributes and abilities that should be considered if collaboration is to be successful.

Collaborative programmes where multiple organizations share a common focus can create a complex arena for programme managers. When considering both the behaviours and competencies together it should be recognized that programme managers not only need to consider collaborative skills but also to ensure that the basic competencies and organizational enablers are in place.

While every effort can be made to bring organizations together through compliance with formal procedures and processes, it will be the informal issues that will define success, because knowledge sharing and joint responsibility can be impacted by the individual interpretations of those involved. Therefore how each individual views the challenges will be reflected in their effort and commitment. More importantly, these background pressures will significantly influence the ways in which they respond to others. Understanding these issues and being aware of how critical behaviours are reflected in the operation is the crucial step towards fully optimizing performance. There are many aspects of behaviour, but

Context	Core competency skills	Organizational enablers
Business skills required in the management of collaborative programmes	Key competencies specific to the role of developing and managing collaborative programmes	Key cultural aspects that enable collaborative working and underpin operational practices
• Leadership • Business planning • Communication skills • Team management • Negotiation skills • Conflict resolution • Commercial management • Change management • Project management • Contract management • Risk management • Knowledge management • Business process development	• Leadership through influence • Coaching and mentoring • Stakeholder management • Cultural awareness • Creating strategic alignment • Value proposition development • Collaborative negotiation • Partner selection • Governance development • Measurements and matrix • Collaborative working • Joint business planning • Organizational alignment • Relationship management • Transition management • Problem solving	• Leadership development • Joint governance structures • Shared goals/objectives • Cultural alignment • Joint business planning • Appropriate measurement • Strategic alignment • Collaborative ethos • Defined roles and responsibilities • Processes and infrastructure • Issue resolution mechanisms • Risk and reward sharing • Clear accountability • Adequate resources • Stakeholder management • Competency skills development • Delegation of authority • Aligned incentive programmes

Figure 17.2 Skills and organizational enablers

in endeavouring to distil these to a functional platform the key element comes down to 'RESPECT' as follows:

* Responsive;
* Ethics and integrity;
* Service to customers;
* Professionalism;
* Enthusiasm;
* Creativity;
* Teamwork (RESPECT model © 2014 Midas Projects Limited).

It is often said that *authority* can be bestowed but *respect* can only be earned.

Using this simple profile as a measure to test a course of action provides a valuable measure for assessing the potential impact. It is not possible to change the basic nature of an individual, but managing how it is reflected to others is a factor of self-discipline. Internally there are many interfaces that impact the performance of an organization. It is important to recognize that while many of these individuals might not be directly involved in the delivery process, they will significantly affect the performance of others.

It is equally important to recognize that external organizations tend to view the whole operation and that effective performance comes from an integrated approach that might affect numerous internal boundaries. In the context of high performing operations the key traits that blend across its leadership, management and staff are factors of managing behaviours and that lead to success (Figure 17.3).

Sound communications are at the heart of any relationship. The essence of that is in understanding how behavioural traits affect the way in which messages are given and received (Figure 17.4). The broad range of attitudes and approaches

Context	Managers	Staff
• Commitment to goals and values • Meeting stakeholders' needs • Ethical and transparent decisions • Encourage innovation • Harness diversity • Non-discriminatory • Recognize and reward performance	• Clear goal setting • Performance feedback • Model organizations values • Foster risk and reward • Ensure work-life balance • Develop skills • Equal opportunity • People management • Transparent	• Contribute fully • Take responsibility • Demonstrate commitment • Show initiative • Develop skills and knowledge • Support corporate values • Communicate openly • Be innovative • Commit to goals • Responsive to change

Figure 17.3 High performing organizations

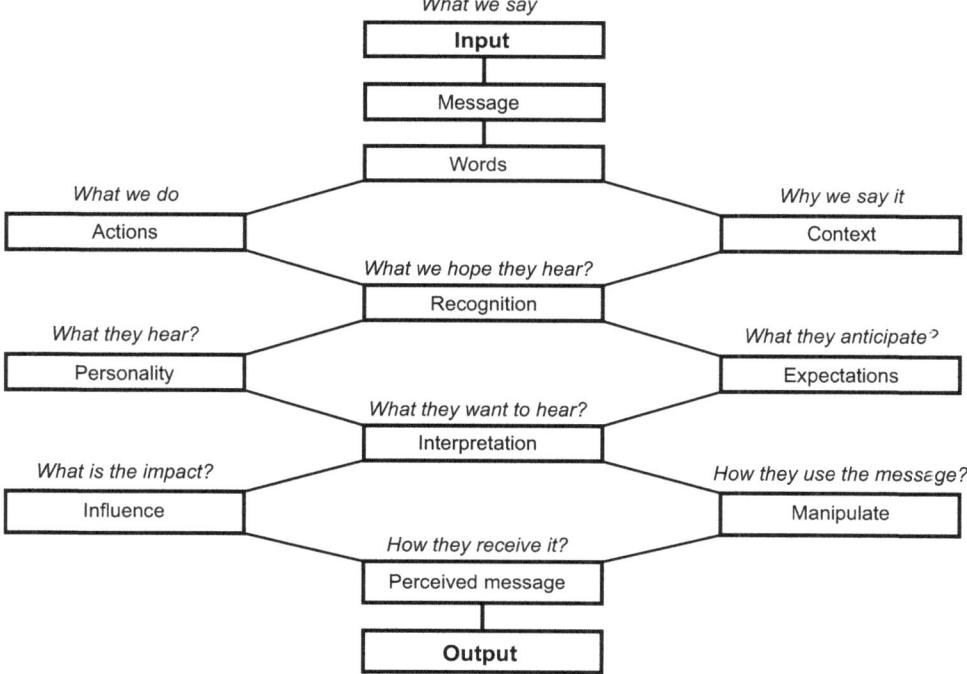

Figure 17.4 Interpreting communications

Figure 17.5 Understanding Maslow's hierarchy of motivational needs

that individuals present to others is critical in creating empathy and trust between individuals and organizations. It is important to understand and recognize the key influences, through communications and otherwise, that affect people and motivate them. Individuals will adapt their general attitudes to respond to organizational change and to other influences such as performance monitoring and incentives. Maslow (1970) recognized that personal motivation is a complex subject that affects different people in different ways (Figure 17.5).

Despite individual enthusiasm for collaborative approaches, the reality is that the organizational structure has a major influence. How individuals are led, managed and incentivized will significantly affect the way in which they consider they need to behave. Dynamic leadership is a key facet of every successful programme in a collaborative model. Developing an effective team focus is a challenge in most environments. But where the traditional command and control structure is replaced by cross-functional operations, coordination and direction of the team are even more complex and motivation and influence are critical for success.

The best practice principles of BS 11000

For programme managers seeking to implement integrated collaborative approaches, the BS 11000 standard framework provides a structured model that draws on a wealth of experience to identify factors that could undermine performance if they were not dealt with appropriately. The backbone of this standard is the relationship management plan. That initially defines internal rules and guidance and is developed into a joint plan with partners that evolves through the life of the relationship.

Stage 1: awareness

Relationships of any kind have a lifecycle. To maximize the benefits of a collaborative approach, an organization needs to consider the longer-term implications of its actions for value-creating relationships. Such approaches will affect every internal function and a clear executive mandate is necessary. Collaborative working in any form is not easy; it requires investment, resources and often policy or process changes. It needs strong support from the executive level and clearly defined policies, providing a backbone to any prospective programme that is understood across all involved organizations, thus empowering staff to challenge internal friction if and when it arises.

At the same time it is crucial that the adoption can be clearly aligned with the business goals and objectives. In this way the whole organization can appreciate the potential for a collaborative approach rooted in a robust business case. Collaboration offers greater tangible benefits than more traditional models. Focus must be on a sound cost-effective solution which in turn will give individuals the necessary confidence and motivation.

Historically terms such as partnering or collaboration have been used too liberally, often neither necessary nor appropriate. That has led to confusion, misalignment of goals, failure based on expectations and lack of effective management. It is important to focus only on things that can add real value.

Collaborative approaches can introduce alternative ways of managing risk, but they can also introduce new risk elements which need to be recognized throughout any development from the start. Collaborative working might not suit everyone and, while individuals could be excellent in one domain, the concept and skills for operating in a mutually beneficial environment might challenge some. It is a crucial aspect of leadership to ensure that the programmes are driven with the right people in the front line.

> EMCOR UK was the first facilities management provider to achieve the BS 11000 certification, recognizing EMCOR's track record in developing long-term client relationships. EMCOR's clients have always benefited from its collaborative approach, but since April 2010 an independently assessed framework has been in place that effectively ensures the knowledge, skills, processes and resources to meet mutually defined objectives are in place. BS 11000 sets out a framework that will enable companies like EMCOR to apply good practice principles to its own way of working, and has wide applications on how to manage valuable business relationships within the supply chain.
>
> (Christopher Kehoe, Director, EMCOR UK)

Stage 2: knowledge

Having identified the potential for collaboration, the next stage is to develop specific strategies and risk management that will deliver the required outcomes. What do you want or need to achieve, and what skills are needed or exist to support the complexities of these integrated models? Pushing collaboration forward without considering the available skills and the resources needed will probably affect the behaviours of those charged with delivery. Every relationship is different whether vertical or horizontal. However, the key issues will be common to most, while each relationship will probably have varying drivers which will shape the approach.

A major benefit from collaboration is the ability to share knowledge. That can create a challenge for many organizations in identifying and managing what can and cannot be shared to avoid clashes later. More importantly, if individuals are not informed that will impact their behaviours in trying to protect what they are empowered to share externally.

One frequently ignored concept in the development of collaborative programmes is the exit strategy. While this may seem negative, it is in fact crucial to effective development. On the one hand it allows organizations to consider the end game but equally it has a strong influence on those involved in the programme (because understanding the rules of disengagement will provide clarity for individuals and thus enhance engagement and reduce concerns).

> Lockheed Martin has long recognised that in order to deliver a successful programme the parties involved have to work together. Programme objectives are more likely to be successfully achieved if all parties involved are focused on those end goals, encouraging positive behaviours and remove road blocks to the ability to work together. The type of long term, large scale, complex programmes that form the core of Lockheed Martin's business often demand a different type of working relationship to the traditional 'arm's length' contracting models of the past. The parties involved need to work collaboratively over the long term to successfully deliver challenging programme objectives. The BS 11000 standard has provided LM with a framework for implementing and objectively measuring the benefits of collaborative working. Using the standard to evaluate past activities, LM has been able to identify repeatable collaborative working good practice, as well as areas that could benefit from increased focus.
>
> (Mark Cooper, MD Lockheed Martin UK IS&GS Civil)

Stage 3: internal assessment

Most organizations are very good at defining what they want from others. But they may be less willing to assess their own capability to meet the challenges of collaboration (which by definition has to be through two-way relationships to achieve the desired goals, requiring commitment on all sides). This is not just about processes, procedures, systems and contracts (the 'hard' process issues) but also the people drivers (the so-called 'soft' issues such as leadership, skills and motivation) that will govern behaviours. Programme managers need to understand the internal enablers that build trust between the parties, based on mutual benefit and equitable reward.

Building robust collaborative programmes needs the appropriate rules of engagement clearly embedded in operational approaches where current operating practice might constrain effective collaboration. These can vary widely but include programme ownership, cross-functional barriers, incentive and performance measure policies, together with management systems and procedures.

In attracting the right partners, organizations should consider their collaborative profile to evaluate if they would make a suitable partner (so that potential partners see an organization with which they can work openly).

At the same time, as part of this internal assessment it is useful to establish in each case what the ideal partner should look like. It is perhaps wise at this stage to let the delivery team develop these perspectives, because it is they who will have to work with the partner(s). Imposing a partner without joint agreement could build up reservations that surface later.

It is unlikely that every organization will have an abundance of skilled professionals ready to take on a collaborative role. Recognizing the gaps and building capability development into the process is important particularly for those individuals who might find the approach at odds with previous roles within the organization.

> In Skanska we a have a long history of collaborative working with our clients, our joint venture partners and our supply chain. Collaboration in business is not an easy option as it always involves additional effort to ensure that the terms and the direction remain clear to everyone, and to ensure that trust remains at all times – even when time and money are tight. However, we are convinced it is absolutely the right way to deliver best value to our customers and to our stakeholders – the benefits far outweigh the disadvantages. BS 11000 provides a framework and a language to improve the way we create and sustain our collaborative business relationships. It reflects our existing best practice, but some of this is not formally captured and in other areas we know we can yet collaborate more effectively. We view BS 11000 implementation as an opportunity to record, rationalise and improve our approach to collaboration so that everyone in Skanska understands how we should manage our collaborative relationships.
>
> (Jonathan Morris, Business Improvement Director,
> Skanska Civil Engineering)

Stage 4: partner selection

Collaborative relationships can be used in many different circumstances. Finding the right partner should not be left to chance. Too often the choice is by default or based on long-term experience in a traditional relationship, where individuals may bring 'baggage' based on previous engagements which will inevitably influence their level of commitment. It is important to understand the differing dynamics of a collaborative approach and assess the partner's strengths and weaknesses.

Programme managers must ensure that any selection maintains the appropriate competitive edge. To build confidence in the selection process, a competitive starting point should be used, while focusing on the end game to avoid confusion later. Collaboration goals need to be defined together with the relative value that will be placed on their collaborative capability. The selection process should also consider the potential partner's objectives as well as building a dialogue around common objectives and outcomes. These may not always be the same but should be evaluated for alignment and compatibility.

Negotiating style can have far-reaching implications and is one of the high risk areas because the nature of negotiations will set the tone for future relationship. While a win/win approach may be the aim, the reality is often that most exchanges if not managed effectively will revert to traditional 'arm wrestling' and 'poker playing'. This is not to suggest that negotiations should not be robust and commercially focused, but to ensure that the ultimate relationship is kept in mind. Establishing a negotiation strategy should be embedded in the process and supported to ensure individuals are supported when taking a more engaging approach.

> NATS made a conscious and deliberate decision to invest in the concept of a Collaborative Working standard because of the value it believes it will add to its business. It was Supply Chain Management that initially recognised its potential in managing our Strategic Supplier relationships, determining supply chain/supplier strategies through working closely with internal stakeholders. NATS decided to adopt the standard to manage its supplier partner relationships, building on existing collaborative processes. Based on successful application of BS 11000 when working with Partner Suppliers, we are introducing it into relationships with major customers. Through adopting a collaborative framework with individual customers, a strong message is established of a committed relationship that can generate mutual benefit.
>
> (Adrian Miller, Supply Chain Manager, NATS)

Stage 5: working together

It is crucial to establish the governance model on which to create a collaborative relationship. In most cases there will need to be an agreed contract or agreement. However, this should be developed jointly, setting out the appropriate terms that will support collaborative working and behaviours that will ultimately deliver value. There needs to be joint executive sponsorship to provide overall support for a clear and transparent agreement, focused on the desired outcomes and objectives of the relationship. The agreement should reflect joint ownership of the principles and behaviours. This is often captured in a collaborative charter. That is not a document to just 'hang on the wall'. It is important that the collaborative principles are kept alive.

Establishing a joint management team with a clearly defined profile of roles and responsibilities ensures that all participants fully understand their contribution. The team should be supported by a joint assessment of the competencies and skills and where appropriate an agreed joint development plan. Effective management of knowledge and information is important to ensure that individuals are clear on what and how to share information. Key to maintaining a successful relationship is ensuring effective joint management of risks, including those of the partners which may impact the relationship.

When initiating a relationship it is valuable to undertake a joint review of the delivery processes to clarify potential internal and cross-border conflicts which could affect performance. All parties must understand how the relationship and delivery performance will be measured, ensuring that incentives support the behaviours.

> For Costain the main drivers for collaborative working were already there – it is fundamentally the way we work, and is key to our Choosing Costain strategy. So adopting BS 11000 was a 'no-brainer' and doing so will demonstrate to our customers that we do what we say, and our collaborative capability has been independently verified. Another key driver is that BS 11000 provides a standard

approach with a common language that (as more organisations adopt the stand-ard) can be adopted and readily understood by all parties. It has helped bring structure and process to a subject that had in the past been a little 'intangible' and is particularly important as we form many joint ventures, alliances and rela-tionships. One of the first challenges was to map our existing collaborative pro-cesses to the standard, and not to reinvent the wheel or cause duplication, and then looking to see where any gaps were, for example, planning for 'disengage-ment' before selecting a partner was something that was not formally done at this early stage of a relationship.

(Tony Blanch, Business Improvement Director,
Costain Group)

Stage 6: value creation

Most collaborative relationships will tend to plateau over time if not driven to main-tain continual improvement. Those which are particularly focused on long-term benefit must maintain a relevance to markets and customer needs. Even with a clear vision on agreed objectives the major value from collaborative approaches comes from the ability to share ideas and harness alternative perspectives. Those who look for additional benefit often exceed their original objectives and perform much bet-ter overall. A parallel benefit can come from adopting a structured approach to joint continual improvement. Working jointly to achieve business and product value cre-ation improvement beyond the initial aims helps to engender improved engagement across collaborative teams. The key to optimizing this co-creation is to ensure that identified issues are regularly reviewed. If necessary, efforts that are not delivering the intended results have to be culled. This ensures that resources are not wasted or distracted from the primary objectives.

One of the major challenges in any relationship is to define what value means for those involved. This is the responsibility of the joint management team and execu-tive sponsors, who must recognize that these longer-term values might be common or complementary.

As organizations begin to work together more closely it is equally important to capture the lessons learned. This is a key aspect of creating value and setting the agenda for innovation. Few business activities will stay constant for very long and (particularly in a technology focused environment) innovation is crucial to maintain competitive edge for the partners. While there might be many common opportun-ities, it is important to recognize that some aspects might on occasion benefit only one party – but support for these is equally important.

SELEX–ES expected the standard would strengthen our business benefits by building and maintaining relationships throughout our supply-chain, and we were not disappointed. The economic challenges of the current market place even greater emphasis on the value of collaborative relationships. This standard offered an innovative, structured approach to Relationship Management which, in addition to dedicated Board commitment, had the potential to yield trans-formational long term benefits.

(Tim Mowat, Business Development, Selex-ES)

Stage 7: staying together

Business relationships will probably change over time as a result of either internal or external factors. Even where partners have invested in creating a firm foundation and governance, the people involved will develop or move on. That will change the dynamics of an integrated team and is a strong reason for embedding the collaborative behaviours in the operating model to maintain a sustainable relationship.

The joint management team must focus to maintain performance and monitor, measure and review behaviours. Additionally they should consistently monitor innovation and continual improvement to ensure the teams are exploiting their joint knowledge and enhancing their skills. Inevitably issues will arise and too often these are left to fester until they can in some cases irreparably damage the relationship. A crucial factor for any collaborative approach is to ensure that there is a robust approach to identifying and managing disputes. If handled well, these issues can significantly strengthen a relationship. The final aspect of maintaining the relationship is to ensure the exit strategy is jointly developed and regularly reviewed and updated if necessary.

> At Network Rail we identified the adoption of BS 11000 as a means of enabling greater collaboration with our supply chain. In addition to supporting the goals of greater efficiency and enabling the cultural and behavioural change associated with more collaborative working and delivering a more consistent means of engaging with our supply base. Perhaps the single biggest benefit of working to BS 11000 that we have found is the requirement for greater structure and process in the management of the relationship; something that can be described as 'having different conversations' from those that would normally be the case for traditional contract management. The requirement to focus on continual improvement and demonstrating value through the collaboration rather than only meeting the project outputs has helped to create a focus on the effectiveness of the relationship for our project teams and its overall contribution to success. One of the major benefits to date has been the sharing of information and knowledge with key partner organisations who have responded positively to our policy to adopt BS 11000 as they embark upon their own journeys to certification. This knowledge sharing process has already facilitated the sharing of best practice collaborative working from other industry sectors. Such learning represents a key driver in our own continual improvement drive as we respond to the ongoing Value for Money challenge in the rail industry.
>
> (Mike Pollard, Head of Collaborative Working,
> Network Rail Investment Projects)

Stage 8: exit strategy

Although exit strategy is the final stage in the lifecycle, it is key aspect that should be addressed as part of the initial thinking and carried through the whole lifecycle, recognizing its impact on individuals and their behaviours. Exit strategy should not be confused with contract termination which, while important, is relevant to another aspect of contracts. Exit strategy should focus on how the parties plan to disengage when necessary and ensure effective business continuity and customer support.

Jointly developing and maintaining a focus on disengagement ensures that the partners have a clear focus on the value of the collaboration. This may seem to many to be a negative approach, but experience suggests that organizations which maintain a realistic perspective will enjoy greater engagement, enhanced behaviours and increased value from collaboration.

It is important to define clearly the boundaries of the relationship, though it is accepted that these may change over time by mutual agreement. This should include the business risks and regular joint reviews of both the market and the relationship to ensure it is still relevant and delivering value. If the relationship has been well managed and delivered its objectives, then the way should be open to consider future possibilities for collaboration.

> Raytheon Systems recognises the importance and significance of achieving success both for customers, suppliers and the company. This understanding is reflected in the company's core values. BS 11000 complements these; it underpins and sustains Raytheon's approach to relationship management, both internally and externally. BS 11000 provides an independent and reliable benchmark against which each participating entity can rely on a common set of measurable relationship principles, outlined against a balanced and equitable process of relationship management. While Raytheon has always had a strong collaborative working culture, adoption of this standard has provided 'structure to our culture'. Adoption of the standard has supported the necessity for significant self-realisation in the form of mandating internal due diligence as well as the obvious external due diligence before entering a collaborative arrangements. From experience, we know that application of the standard has added significant value to existing and new relationships.
>
> (Mike Woodstock, Commercial Executive
> Raytheon Systems Limited)

Conclusion

Developing trust in the relationships and ensuring the appropriate behaviours is vital. As trust increases, the relationship should increase the value it delivers. Wrong behaviours will quickly undermine the levels of trust and the investment with obvious impacts on output.

There can be little doubt that the essence of building effective collaborations is seen where organizations and their personnel not only present the right behaviours but embrace them. Too often organizations may profess to be collaborative ('it's in our DNA') yet in reality there is little internal focus on assessing, evaluating and developing individual capability or in establishing the appropriate environment where the required behaviours can be encouraged. While there may be corporate values, principles and policies in place, it is often the performance measures and incentives that dictate behaviours.

Traditional command and control business models still have their place but, if programme managers wish to exploit the potential of collaborative approaches, then greater emphasis must be focused on ensuring that the right behaviours are fostered and supported. Relationships are a crucial factor in the success of any programme. They should not be left to chance but must be effectively developed and managed through a structured approach such as the BS 11000 framework.

References and further reading

BSI (2010), *BS 11000–1: Framework Specification for Collaborative Business Relationships*, Milton Keynes: British Standards Institution.

BSI (2011), *BS 11000–2: Collaborative Business Relationships. Guide to Implementing BS 11000*, Milton Keynes: British Standards Institution.

BSI (2013), *Raising the Standard for Collaboration*, Milton Keynes: British Standards Institution.

Latham, M. (1994), *Constructing the Team*, London: HMSO.

Lock, D. and Scott, L. (eds.) (2013), *Gower Handbook of People in Project Management*, Farnham: Gower.

McNulty, R. (2011), *Realising the Potential of UK Rail*. Independent report of a study chaired by Sir Roy McNulty and commissioned by the Secretary of State for Transport <www.gov.uk/government/policies/rail-network>.

Maslow, A. H. (1970), *Motivation and Personality*, 2nd edn., New York: Harper & Row.

Chapter 18

Managing Strategic Initiatives

Terry Cooke-Davies

It is commonplace to hear the word 'strategy' used in conversations between executives, managers and staff when the topic of an organization's intentions, aims and objectives are being discussed. Similarly, organizations' leaders are prone to launch 'initiatives' that are designed to change something about the business, to help implement its 'strategy'. Such 'strategic initiatives', therefore, are highly likely to consist of work that can best be viewed as projects, programmes or collections of projects and programmes.

Introduction

An important study sponsored by the Project Management Institute (PMI) as a part of its 2013 *Thought Leadership* series (Economist Intelligence Unit, 2013) reported that during the three years before publication an average of only 56 per cent of strategic initiatives had been successful. The report defined a strategic initiative as 'a project, portfolio of projects, other discrete programme or series of actions undertaken to implement or continue the execution of a strategy, or that is otherwise essential for the successful implementation or execution of a strategy. This includes some (usually high priority) projects, but does not entail the entire project portfolio.'

Given the prominent role that projects and programmes play in such strategic initiatives, and the newspaper headlines that so frequently report on the failure of this or that major programme (especially if paid for out of taxpayers' funds), then this should come as a surprise to no one. There is considerable evidence from the field of projects and programmes to suggest that a low success rate is not particularly abnormal. Whether the data come from the field of IT projects (El Emam, 2008), from major infrastructure projects (see, for example, Flyvjberg, 2014) or from major organizational initiatives (Lovallo and Kahneman, 2003) all the results point to a higher rate of failure than might be expected, given the importance of projects and programmes.

It is not as if the critical success factors for projects and programmes are not well documented. They have been extensively researched since the 1970s and are not controversial. Summaries can be found in many papers such as Fortune and White (2006) and Cooke-Davies (2004). The trouble is that, like losing weight or giving up smoking, the principles are easy to grasp but the behaviour (in this case organizational behaviour) is very hard to change, particularly because transformational change involves large numbers of people needing to do things differently.

Since the 1960s management research and management gurus have wrestled with the problem of bringing about transformational change and, in the course of this journey, they and we have learned a lot about why it is so challenging. One could categorize the most important of these lessons into four key areas or 'strands of thinking' as follows:

1. The first strand concerns what we might call the 'nuts and bolts' of good programme and project management. That means being clear about what we need to accomplish, knowing how well we are progressing towards those goals, and having the right means to make course corrections along the way.
2. The second strand concerns the people who are impacted in some way by the change. The past 20 or 30 years have seen tremendous advances in our understanding of what makes human beings 'tick', as fields such as cognitive neuroscience and psychology have started to gain insights from each other, and new fields such as behavioural economics have been developed.
3. It is being recognized just how important it is to design programmes in different ways from projects (but incorporating projects and project management) while at the same time avoiding all forms of dysfunctional complexity. CEOs increasingly see complexity as a major challenge facing their organizations, yet they doubt that their organizations have the necessary capabilities to respond to it effectively.
4. Finally, there is a shift in dialogue away from 'managing' transformational programmes towards 'leading' them. An increasing emphasis is being placed on leadership and on talent management.

Each of these four strands of thinking has contributed important lessons that must be learned if strategic initiatives are to be delivered successfully. So I shall expand on each of these in the following sections and describe just what those lessons are.

Outcome, process and control

This first strand itself pulls together several different sets of insights and the research that underpins them. Fundamental to all strategic initiatives is the question, 'What is it that you are trying to accomplish?' Indeed, during the 1980s the emphasis was all on this aspect of transformation.

Business Process Reengineering, for example, seemed to be very much the order of the day, particularly when the then newly developed practice of 'benchmarking' (Codling, 1995) allowed Xerox to thrive in the face of intense competition from Japanese photocopying manufacturers (Camp, 1989; Codling, 1995), or pointed to massive efficiency gains that could be made such as in Ford Motor Company's accounts receivable department, which employed 500 people, while Mazda's (admittedly dealing with only half the Ford volume) had only five (Hammer, 1990).

However, in many cases, process re-engineering alone failed to deliver the promised results, and so we learned how important it was to start from the required outcomes, rather than on the activities needing to be changed or those needed to bring about the change (Schaffer and Thomson, 1992). The concept of key performance indicators (KPIs) began to appear as measures of outcome, rather than as measures of improved activity and you will find considerable emphasis on these throughout this Handbook.

Interestingly, the logical conclusion of this in the world of projects and programmes has still failed to be universally recognized, let alone widely practised. Many organizations have not yet recognized how important it is to adopt a benefits realization perspective (Crawford and Cooke-Davies, 2012), although there is increasing evidence of the influence of benefits realization management on project and programme success (Serra and Kunc, 2015).

Poorly implemented project management can become a bureaucratic burden on an organization. Too easily, programme management can be seen as a way of imposing top-down control on project management (Maylor et al., 2006). Smart processes are needed that can be understood by all and minimize misunderstandings between leadership, management and the people doing the work (Sirkin et al., 2005). Techniques such as Boston Consulting Group's 'DICE' and 'Rigor Testing' provide management with ways of testing that all is well and that all remains on track. But, to be effective, the underpinning methods used to manage projects and programmes must also be simplified. Crucial checkpoints (such as milestones) must be related to outcome measures that are of strategic value to the organization. The success or otherwise of changes must be assessed not simply in terms of the traditional triangle of cost, time and performance, but more significantly in terms of the value or benefit to the organization.

Transparent control is the goal of such smart processes and value-related progress checkpoints, which is why different control tools are important for strategic initiatives. Programmes cannot be adequately controlled using only the tools of project management: there needs to be a programme structure that knits the projects together, copes with an increased level of uncertainty, and allows project managers to focus their efforts on the specific outputs and deliverables that their projects need to produce (Pellegrinelli et al., 2015).

Strategic initiatives often affect many different divisions, functions or regions within an organization, and thus the controls and processes used to manage and implement them need to be common to all the different units involved. That in turn calls for a framework of project and programme management which is consistent and coherent throughout the organization, and aligned to the demands of its strategy (Cooke-Davies et al., 2009). If these practices are not the norm in an organization, then it is now understood that the process of introducing them is itself a significant programme of management innovation which must be approached as carefully as any other strategic initiative. There are many ways of doing that, not all of which are likely to be successful (Thomas et al., 2012).

Engaging people in changes

The second strand of thinking concerns the 'people' side of transformational change. That is perhaps the area which has seen the greatest strides (at least in our understanding if not our practice) during the past ten years or so.

The first thing to be said in this very broad field is that the leadership of strategic initiatives is not simply the responsibility of the programme managers who are tasked with responsibility for implementing the initiative. All too frequently the cause of difficulties lies with the lack of intelligent involvement of senior executives. That was highlighted earlier in this chapter in the Economist Intelligence Unit report (2013).

This problem is not restricted to strategic initiatives. Even from the simpler viewpoint of project management there has been a growing recognition of the important role played by the executive sponsor (Crawford *et al.*, 2008). Leadership of all these initiatives requires a partnership between senior executives and programme managers, a partnership that allows their two very different perspectives to lead to balanced decisions on the basis of shared understanding. That is easier to say than it is to achieve.

Coherent leadership, however, is only the first of the people-related challenges facing strategic initiatives. As a result of the failure of so many process re-engineering programmes in the 1980s, the 1990s saw an emphasis on the importance of 'engagement programmes' to win the 'hearts and minds' of those who need to change. That insight is backed up by current evidence, as shown in a report from the Project Management Institute (PMI, 2014). This is particularly important, given what we now know to be our human biases (Kahneman and Tversky, 2000) and the need for leaders of change to demonstrate high emotional intelligence (Earle, 2013).

Because the benefits of a strategic initiative are experienced not in the programme itself but in the operations that use the programme's outputs, there is growing recognition of the need to involve operational units in the benefits realization process (Serra and Kunc, 2015). However, at the same time we have to avoid placing too great a burden on those units (for example in the form of unpaid overtime) in their efforts to help the programme to deliver change to them (Sirkin *et al.*, 2005).

An area in which there have been great strides during the twenty-first century has been the confluence of psychology, neuroscience and behavioural economics. The person who strides this field like a giant is Daniel Kahneman, a psychologist who in 2002 won the Nobel Prize for Economics. He proved beyond doubt that people do not make economic choices rationally. The theory for which he was awarded the Nobel Prize is known as 'Prospect Theory' (Kahneman and Tversky, 1979). It shows that human beings are *loss averse*: we go to great lengths to avoid losing what we already have.

Building on that foundational work, our understanding of human biases has been widely investigated for the impact they have on our judgement, decision-making and behaviour. Our apparent lack of rationality (Sutherland, 2009) underpins many of the behavioural challenges encountered in the management of strategic initiatives. Anyone wishing to explore this topic in greater depth could do no better than to read Daniel Kahneman's masterful and beautifully-written book, *Thinking Fast and Slow* (Kahneman, 2011).

In his keynote address to the 2006 PMI research conference in Montreal, Professor Bent Flyvbjerg traced the link from Kahneman's work to his own work on 'Megaprojects and Risk' (Flyvbjerg *et al.*, 2003), which has become a classic. Professor Flyvbjerg also made the point that (left to their own devices) both project promoters and the contractors who bid for the work conspire in a series of lies: because the promoters want to believe that their projects will be affordable, and the contractors want to win the work. Specific examination of the costs of Olympic Games held since 1960 appears to provide compelling evidence to support this (Flyvbjerg and Stewart, 2012). The impact of these human behaviours on complexity has been explored elsewhere (Cooke-Davies, 2011). I shall discuss complexity in the following section.

Complexity

There are many different definitions of complexity, but none really does it justice. Almost by definition, complexity is beyond logical definition, which is why Terry Williams' description seems to me to be so apt, 'If you don't know what will happen when you kick it, then it is complex' (Williams, 2002).

It's worth distinguishing between 'complex' and 'complicated'. Something can be said to be complicated if it is composed of many interconnected and interrelated parts. Complexity, on the other hand, is related not only to the number of moving parts and how they relate to each other, but also to the predictability of each part (and thus of the ability of the pieces to be melded together in ways that are foreseeable). Traditional project management tools such as the work breakdown structure (WBS) are excellent for complicated projects but, on their own, are inadequate for complexity.

Complexity is also relative to what we know. At the boundary our most ambitious efforts will always seem complex. Ancient building projects such as the pyramids or Stonehenge must have seemed highly complex at the time, particularly with respect to the surrounding logistics, but they would be considered simple today in comparison with modern strategic initiatives such as the massively international programme to develop the Lockheed Martin F35 Lightning fighter aircraft.

Generally, it is not technology that provides the greatest challenge in such complex programmes. A team at Cranfield University demonstrated the preponderance of problems caused either by what they called 'socio-political complexity' or by 'emergent complexity' (Maylor et al., 2013).

Socio-political complexity refers not only to the behavioural challenges described in the previous section, but also to the cultural and political dynamics within the programme team and in the wider stakeholder communities. *Emergent complexity* refers to the inherent uncertainty that arises from the intermixing of novel technological, human and social arrangements which give rise to unforeseen and unforeseeable consequences – what you might call the unknown and unknowable unknowns. These phenomena have been explored within the collection of scientific disciplines loosely known as 'complexity science' and in works such as Mitchell (2009).

A particular aspect of the socio-political complexity involved in many strategic initiatives is that they themselves are embedded within an organization, like cuckoos' eggs in a nest. The systems established to run the business often clash horribly with the systems in place to run the organization.

Writing in the *McKinsey Quarterly*, Suzanne Heywood and her colleagues distinguish between two types of complexity – dubbed by them as 'institutional complexity' and 'individual complexity' (Heywood et al., 2007).

Institutional complexity arises out of the strategic choices made by the organization, the external context within which the organization operates and the management and operating systems that it employs to supply its products or services.

Individual complexity, on the other hand, refers to the ways by which individuals operating within the organization experience and deal with complexity: 'how hard it is for them to get things done' (Heywood *et al.*, 2007). As individual complexity rises, so employees find it harder to work efficiently and effectively, and both the individuals' and the organization's performances suffer accordingly. When hard-pressed individuals are then expected to contribute to strategic initiatives on top of their already challenging 'day jobs', it is easy to see why this particular form of complexity provides so many challenges for strategic initiatives (Sirkin *et al.*, 2005).

All this means that complexity has to be *navigated* (as the early navigators such as Vasco da Gama or Christopher Columbus did) rather than *managed*. And this calls for highly developed qualities of leadership at the head of strategic management – the fourth of our strands of thinking.

Leadership

The classic work on leading organizational change is from John Kotter of Harvard University (Kotter, 1995). Maintaining that transformation is a process rather than an event, he argues that transformation efforts advance through a number of stages which build on each other. When managers are pressured for results too early, they skip stages and fail as a consequence. Having been around for more than 20 years, these stages are fairly familiar and have given rise to many imitators. Nevertheless, stages such as the following still make sense in many strategic initiatives that involve transformational change:

- establish a sense of urgency;
- form a powerful guiding coalition;
- create a vision;
- communicate that vision;
- empower others to act on the vision;
- plan for and create short-term wins;
- consolidate improvements;
- produce more change and institutionalize new approaches.

However, not all strategic initiatives are only (or even mainly) about transformational change, although many will include such elements. Under these circumstances, general advice on leadership that is more broadly applicable is useful. Just such good advice (grounded in extensive experience) is provided by Ronald Heifetz (Heifetz and Laurie, 1997). He talks in terms of the *adaptive challenges* faced by people in organizations when they are confronted by the execution of new strategies (that is, by strategic initiatives or their consequences) and the role of leaders in mobilizing them to make the necessary behavioural changes.

Bringing this back more closely to the topic of programme management, in 2013 PMI introduced what it called 'The new triple constraint of project management skills' comprising:

- technical project management;
- leadership;
- strategic and business management.

PMI has subsequently renamed these the 'Talent Triangle'. Surveys such as PMI (2013) place the weighting heavily on the leadership end. The general recognition is that technical skills are the easiest to train, whereas leadership skills are the most important and the hardest to train.

Pulling it all together: managing strategic initiatives for success

Each of the four strands of thinking that I have identified points to a different imperative if strategic initiatives are to be successful:

* smart processes focused on the delivery of value that enable senior executives to provide strategic direction to empowered management;
* engaged people throughout the organization, working to implement the initiative in their own units and aligned behind the initiative's purpose and concept;
* flexible navigation of inevitable complexity and avoidance of unnecessary dysfunctional complexity;
* capable and knowledgeable leadership that delivers the first three imperatives.

Books, papers and articles abound about each of the above. There is no shortage of good advice, or of evidence showing the high cost of deficiencies.

Because this is a chapter in the context of programme management, I have to emphasize once more that each of these four imperatives is necessary to manage strategic initiatives successfully, but even collectively they are not sufficient to guarantee success. They will deliver success only if the organizations involved in the strategic initiative have taken the time to develop those organizational capabilities that are essential prerequisites to good project, programme and portfolio management (Cooke-Davies, 2015).

Strategic initiatives play an extremely important role in the world's economy. A recent article in the *Harvard Business Review* described the problem: 'Since Michael Porter's seminal work in the 1980s we have had a clear and widely accepted definition of what strategy is – but we know a lot less about translating a strategy into results. Books and articles on strategy outnumber those on execution by an order of magnitude' (Sull and Spinosa, 2015).

Put that together with the alarming data from the Economist Intelligence Unit (to which I referred at the beginning of the chapter), from the Boston Consulting Group (Keenan *et al.*, 2013) and from the PMI (PMI, 2014) and the need to improve the management of strategic initiatives comes into sharp focus.

References and further reading

Camp, R. C. (1989), *Benchmarking*, Milwaukee: ASQC Quality Press.

Codling, S. (1995), *Best Practice Benchmarking*, Aldershot: Gower.

Cooke-Davies, T. J. (2004), 'Project Success', in P. W. G. Morris and J. K. Pinto (eds.), *The Wiley Guide to Managing Projects*, Hoboken, NJ: John Wiley.

Cooke-Davies, T. J. (2011), 'Human Behaviour and Complexity', in T. J. Cooke-Davies, L. H. Crawford, J. R. Patton, C. Stevens and T. Williams (eds.), *Aspects of Complexity: Managing Projects in a Complex World*, Newtown Square, PA: Project Management Institute.

Cooke-Davies, T. J. (2015), '*Delivering Strategy. What Matters Most, Capability or Maturity?*' Paper presented at the PMI Global Congress EMEA, London.

Cooke-Davies, T. J., Crawford, L. H. and Lechler, T. G. (2009), 'Project Management Systems: Moving Project Management from an Operational to a Strategic Discipline', *Project Management Journal*, 40(1): 110–23.

Crawford, L. and Cooke-Davies, T. J. (2012), *Best Industry Outcomes*, Newtown Square, PA: Project Management Institute.

Crawford, L., Cooke-Davies, T., Hobbs, B., Labuschagne, L., Remington, K. and Chen, P. (2008), *Situational Sponsorship: A Guide to Sponsorship of Project and Programs*, Newtown Square, PA: Project Management Institute.

Earle, D. (2013), 'Emotional Intelligence in Project Management', in D. Lock and L. Scott (eds.), *Handbook of People in Project Management*, Farnham: Gower.

Economist Intelligence Unit (2013), *Why Good Strategies Fail: Lessons for the C-Suite*, London: EIU.

El Emam, K. (2008), 'A Replicated Survey of IT Software Project Failures', *Software, IEEE*, 25(5): 84–90.

Flyvbjerg, B. (2014), 'What You Should Know about Megaprojects and Why: An Overview', *Project Management Journal*, 45(2): 6–19.

Flyvbjerg, B., Brunelius, N. and Rothengatter, W. (2003), *Megaprojects and Risk: An Anatomy of Ambition*, Cambridge: Cambridge University Press.

Flyvbjerg, B. and Stewart, A. (2012), *Olympic Proportions: Cost and Cost Overrun at the Olympics 1960–2012*, Said Business School, Oxford University.

Fortune, J. and White, D. (2006), 'Framing of Project Critical Success Factors by a Systems Model', *International Journal of Project Management*, 24(1): 53–65.

Hammer, M. (1990), 'Reengineering Work: Don't Automate, Obliterate', *Harvard Business Review*, 68(4): 104–12.

Heifetz, R. A. and Laurie, D. L. (1997), 'The Work of Leadership', *Harvard Business Review*, 75: 124–34.

Heywood, S., Spungin, J. and Turnbull, D. (2007)' 'Cracking the Complexity Code', *The McKinsey Quarterly*, 2: 11.

Kahneman, D. (2011), *Thinking, Fast and Slow*, New York: Farrar, Strauss & Giroux.

Kahneman, D. and Tversky, A. (1979), 'Prospect Theory: An Analysis of Decision under Risk', *Econometrica*, 47(2): 263–92.

Kahneman, D. and Tversky, A. (2000), *Choices, Values, and Frames*, Cambridge: Cambridge University Press.

Keenan, P., Bickford, J., Doust, A., Tankersley, J., Johnson, C., McCaffrey, J., Dolfey, J. and Shah, G. (2013), *Strategic Initiative Management: The PMO Imperative*, Newtown Square, PA: Project Management Institute.

Kotter, J. P. (1995), 'Leading Change: Why Transformation Efforts Fail', *Harvard Business Review*, 73(2): 59–67.

Lovallo, D. and Kahneman, D. (2003), 'Delusions of Success', *Harvard Business Review*, 81(7), 56–63.

Maylor, H., Brady, T., Cooke-Davies, T. J. and Hodgson, D. (2006), 'From Projectification to Programmification', *International Journal of Project Management*, 24(8): 663–74.

Maylor, H., Turner, N. and Murray-Webster, R. (2013), *How Hard Can It Be? Actively Managing the Complexity of Technology Projects*, Cranfield, UK: Cranfield University.

Mitchell, M. (2009), *Complexity: A Guided Tour*, New York: Oxford University Press.

Pellegrinelli, S., Murray-Webster, R. and Turner, N. (2015), 'Facilitating Organizational Ambidexterity through the Complementary Use of Projects and Programs', *International Journal of Project Management*, 33(1): 153–64.

PMI (2013), *PMI's Pulse of the Profession ® In-Depth Report: The Competitive Advantage of Effective Talent Management*, Newtown Square, PA: Project Management Institute.

PMI (2014), *PMI's Pulse of the Profession ® In-Depth Report: Enabling Organizational Change through Strategic Initiatives*, Newtown Square, PA: Project Management Institute.

Schaffer, R. H. and Thomson, H. A. (1992), 'Successful change programmes begin with results', *Harvard Business Review*, 70(1): 80–9.

Serra, C. E. M. and Kunc, M. (2015), 'Benefits Realisation Management and its Influence on Project Success and on the Execution of Business Strategies', *International Journal of Project Management*, 33(1): 53–66.

Sirkin, H. L., Keenan, P. and Jackson, A. (2005), 'The Hard Side of Change Management', *Harvard Business Review*, 83(10): 109–18.

Sull, D. and Spinosa, C. (2015), 'Why Strategy Execution Unravels: And What To Do About It', *Harvard Business Review*, 93(3): 58–66.

Sutherland, S. (2009), *Irrationality*, London: Pinter and Martin.

Thomas, J. L., Cicmil, S. and George, S. (2012), 'Learning from Project Management Implementation by Applying a Management Innovation Lens', *Project Management Journal*, 43(6): 70–87.

Williams, T. (2002), *Modelling Complex Projects*, Chichester: John Wiley.

Part III

Programme Governance, Organization and Culture

Chapter 19

Programme Governance

Martin Samphire

There is a strong correlation between good governance and successful projects. Good governance is taking on a more prominent role in senior executives' minds as greater scrutiny is exercised and accountability for performance is expected. So what is good project and programme governance and how can it be achieved? This chapter sets out some core principles, identifies the key players and provides ten golden rules of good governance.

Introduction

Project failure rates and reasons for failure are little different now from 30 years ago. The UK Cabinet Office and National Audit Office (NAO) list common causes of failure that have been well publicized over the last ten years (similar to a list published by the Harvard Business School 30 years previously):

- Lack of clear link between the project and the organization's key strategic priorities, including agreed measures of success.
- Lack of clear senior management and ministerial ownership and leadership.
- Lack of effective engagement with stakeholders.
- Lack of skills and proven approach to project management and risk management.
- Too little attention to breaking development and implementation into manageable steps.
- Evaluation of proposals driven by initial price rather than long-term value for money (especially securing delivery of business benefits).
- Lack of understanding of and contact with the supply industry at senior levels in the organization.

All these are mainly poor governance issues.

One cause of governance failure is that organizations become 'comatose' and do not always enforce learning from past mistakes and successes. Also the project environment is becoming more dynamic so organizations need to be more agile and flexible in their governance response. 'I've started so I'll finish' is no longer an appropriate strategy.

Importance of project and programme governance

Organizations invest at least 30 per cent of their turnover on projects (many much more). There is now greater recognition that good governance of projects and corporate portfolios is core to success, and this is borne out by research. For example 'Fit-for-purpose governance strongly influences project and programme success' (PwC, 2014).

At times some members of senior teams neglect good governance until things go wrong. Boards (whether in the private or public sector) have a duty of care to shareholders and other stakeholders when investing in projects that will impact their bottom line and reputation.

Governance needs to be a strategic focus for all organizations. The UK NAO report (2013) on the Universal Credit Programme revealed a number of governance failures, including:

- overambitious timescale;
- unclear implementation strategy;
- lack of appropriate controls;
- use of a novel (for the department) methodology;
- lack of sponsor continuity.

Similarly, reviews of the failed franchise competition for the West Coast Mainline in 2012 found a number of governance failings:

- unclear objectives;
- poor sponsorship and continuity;
- poor oversight;
- lack of transparency;
- poor planning;
- roles and responsibilities for approvals were unclear;
- too much reliance on quality assurance reviews;
- 'the Department's governance lacked efficacy'.

The governance landscape

The overriding aim of project and programme management governance is to ensure that an organization achieves the objectives successfully with confidence, transparency and control. It should ensure that the organization is aware of risks, minimizes failures and maximizes the beneficial outcomes (value) from its overall portfolio of projects in a sustainable and transparent manner.

The link between corporate governance and the governance of projects, programmes and portfolios (sometimes abbreviated to 3P) and project, programme and portfolio *management* (which abbreviates to 3PM) is paramount. Most organizations have a governance hierarchy and landscape that can be simplified as shown in Figure 19.1. It is critical to differentiate projects (new or change) from 'not-projects' (business as usual) in any organization because the required governance and management approaches are different (PwC 2012 global survey).

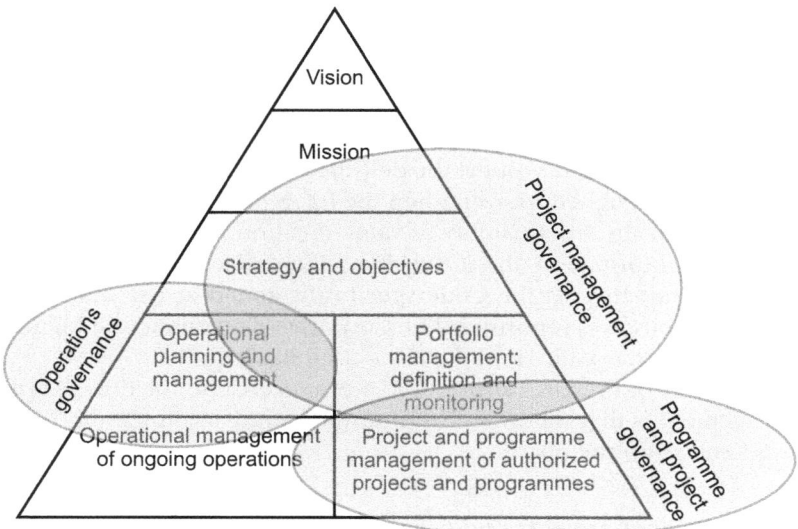

Figure 19.1 Generic organizational governance linkages

Equally it is important to differentiate the 'governance of project management' from the governance of individual projects or programmes and also to understand how these relate to the overall operations or 'business as usual' (BAU) governance. Publications like Prince2, MSP and PMI's PMBoK describe methods covering aspects of the governance of individual projects and programmes. The governance of project management is described in publications such as the APM BoK and particularly APM's *Directing Change*.

OECD framework

The Organisation for Economic Co-operation and Development (OECD) lists three main elements of a corporate governance framework:

1. A set of relationships between a company's management, its board, its shareholders and other stakeholders.
2. A structure through which the objectives of the company are set and the means of attaining those objectives and monitoring performance are determined.
3. Proper incentives for the board and management to pursue objectives that are in the interests of the company and its shareholders.

This governance framework is also relevant to project and programme management.

UK Corporate Governance Code

The UK Corporate Governance Code states that 'Governance is about what the board of a company does and how it sets the values of the company.' Good governance is about: accountability, transparency, probity and focus on the sustainable success of an entity over the longer term.

One of the key roles for the board includes establishing the culture, values and ethics of the company. It is important that the board sets the correct 'tone from the top'. The directors should lead by example and ensure that good standards of behaviour permeate throughout all levels of the organization. This will help prevent misconduct and unethical practices and support the delivery of long-term success. The 2014 update of the Code was designed to strengthen the focus of companies and investors on the longer term and the sustainability of value creation and requires the provision by companies of information about the risks which affect longer-term viability. There is addendum guidance to the Code specifically aimed at risk management, internal financial and business reporting. The Corporate Governance Guidance and Principles for Unlisted Companies in the UK has a similar focus.

The crucial element of the UK Corporate Governance Code for the governance of project management is that the overall responsibility and accountability for good governance sits firmly with the board.

Governance of individual projects and programmes

Governance arrangements for individual projects and programmes are linked to the overall governance of project management primarily through the role of the project/programme sponsor, the corporate project management method, portfolio management and review and assurance bodies. Key success measures include:

1. Delivery of the project to time, cost and quality/performance criteria (the project manager measure).
2. Realization of desired benefits (the sponsor measure).

Governance of project management

The governance of project management concerns those areas of corporate governance that are specifically related to project/change activities – across the whole enterprise. I would define it as:

> the set of policies, regulations, functions, culture, processes, procedures, relationships and responsibilities that define the establishment, management, control and reporting of projects, programmes and portfolios. Good project management governance sets the environment, boundaries, culture and regulatory framework for individual projects, programmes and the overall portfolio to succeed.

Governance of the portfolio includes choosing and prioritizing projects to best meet strategic objectives. Stopping a project in the portfolio may be seen as a failure for the project sponsor and project manager, but a success for the overall business and portfolio manager – but that must be done at the earliest opportunity. Failing early is the new success!

Established guidelines

We should all support the purpose of good governance, but what does 'good' look like and what do you need to put in place? Often boards of directors want an instant 'already engineered' solution. However, as David Shannon (chairman of the APM Governance Specific Interest Group from 2003 to 2012) said 'Governance is like nailing jelly to a wall.' Good governance in one organization looks different from that in another.

Governance of project management principles

Good practice guidelines for governance have been developed over many years to deal with common causes of failure. The best published guidelines for project management governance are contained in the APM publication *Directing Change* which states that:

- The board has overall responsibility for the governance of project management.
- The organization differentiates between projects and non-project based activities.
- Roles and responsibilities for the governance of project management are defined clearly.
- Disciplined governance arrangements, supported by appropriate cultures, methods, resources and controls are applied throughout the project lifecycle. Every project has a sponsor.
- There is a demonstrable coherent and supporting relationship between the project portfolio and the business strategy and policies, for example ethics and sustainability.
- All projects have an approved plan containing authorization points at which the business case, inclusive of cost, benefits and risk is reviewed. Decisions made at authorization points are recorded and communicated.
- Members of delegated authorization bodies have sufficient representation, competence, authority and resources to enable them to make appropriate decisions.
- Project business cases are supported by relevant and realistic information that provides a reliable basis for making authorization decisions.
- The board or its delegated agents decide when independent scrutiny of projects or project management systems is required and implement such assurance accordingly.
- There are clearly defined criteria for reporting project status and for the escalation of risks and issues to the levels required by the organization.
- The organization fosters a culture of improvement and of frank internal disclosure of project management information.
- Project stakeholders are engaged at a level that is commensurate with their importance to the organization and in a manner that fosters trust.
- Projects are closed when they are no longer justified as part of the organization's portfolio.

Key enablers

Before moving on to the ten golden rules for good governance, we need to look at the key underpinning enablers that allow an organization to get started on the journey to better project management governance. Implementing good governance principles is not easy. There are two essential enablers:

- acceptance of a framework for project management in the organization;
- the crucial role of the board.

Framework

Organizations need to recognize that routine business operations need a different governance and management approach from projects. Failure to understand this differentiation results in waste of resources and staff confusion. Organizations must ensure that people who perform both business-as-usual and project activities have clearly defined performance criteria to ensure that their motivations are aligned to the right outcomes for each. Organizations need to commit to project working and be able to overlay project roles on to 'business-as-usual' job titles – and translate between the two. In the project world someone's business-as-usual job title is interesting but not as useful as their 3PM role title.

With maturity, most organizations quickly recognize the need for a formal framework for 3PM across the business and also move to ensure that there is a 'line-of-sight' between every project and specific corporate objectives, in some cases via programmes. The same needs to be true for the line of sight accountability through governance roles from project team member, project/programme manager, sponsor and thence to the main board.

Crucial role of the board of directors

A board of directors is typically responsible, among many other things, for risk over-sight and maintaining sound systems of internal control. The board is accountable for the overall governance of project management. It must be convinced of the need for, and support of, a robust framework for 3PM. The board must define the port-folio direction for the business (set the 'strategic roadmap') and ensure good organizational capability.

In large organizations, many of the day-to-day accountabilities of the board for 3PM governance can be delegated to a subcommittee of the board (such as an invest-ment or change board or committee). However, the link back to the main board is crucial and the board members must recognize their role and accountability at the apex of governance.

The board is responsible for 'picking' the right projects, ensuring they go through robust business case assessments and clear priorities are set and articulated. Once the corporate portfolio is established the board should regularly challenge the port-folio and individual projects, assure progress, create the 'environmental' support (and culture) and put in place the organizational capability. This is how the board controls the strategic roadmap and entry/exit of projects to ensure maximum value from the corporate portfolio.

Ten golden rules

Now it is time for me to outline the ten golden rules necessary for good governance.

Rule 1: alignment and relationships

The board must recognize and ensure a strong link between each project and its intended impact on strategic objectives. In turn each board member and project or programme sponsor should be able to articulate clearly how each project or programme is aligned with strategic objectives and how they will affect key performance indicators (KPIs). The board should define and own the entry, exit and prioritization criteria for the portfolio. That requires regular challenges and reviews with a clear methodology to ensure maximum alignment. Those reviews should take place at least quarterly. The board should be aware of the constraints on the major projects and how they are being addressed.

Rule 2: vision and strategic roadmap

A key board role is to set the strategic direction of the business and the roadmap to achieve the goals. The board should have hands-on engagement with the corporate portfolio of projects, or at least with the *vital few* highly strategic or high risk programmes. Further other oversight can be delegated to a board subcommittee.

At all three levels of portfolio, programme and project (3P) there should be a clear vision or 'end state' that defines clearly the destination for each (for example: market positioning, target operating model and so forth). The overall method for the journey towards the vision must be clearly articulated and understood by the team and stakeholders. At portfolio level the board owns and articulates the vision. The relevant sponsor has this role at the programme and project level.

Another key decision at the project start is choosing the most appropriate delivery method. For example choosing a traditional 'waterfall' approach to deliver into a rapidly changing environment where the objective and method of getting to the result is uncertain is likely to lead to project failure because the rate of change might outpace the rate of project progress. In this circumstance the board ought to consider the merits of an incremental delivery approach like MSP, DSDM or Agile. References for MSP and DSDM are given at the end of this chapter and guidelines on the governance of Agile projects are available from the APM. The important issue is matching the method to the circumstances and challenges – and ensuring that the governance regime matches the delivery method and remains flexible.

Rule 3: golden thread of delegation

A key part of governance is to delegate an appropriate level of executive power to the key managers. Delegate too little and the managers' freedom will be excessively constrained. Delegating too much risks that managers and the board will lose touch with each other.

It is vital that each key governance role aligns with another for accountability. Organizations should have a systematic and documented corporate governance policy defining where (body or role in the organization) each type of change (3PM) decisions can be most effectively made, by whom and to what authority level (often defined by financial limits). Often organizations do have financial approval limits set by job description or seniority in the organization – but for the 3PM governance world this needs to be also by project role, for example sponsor, project manager, stage review panel.

There should be a hierarchy of accountability in the way each level in the organizational hierarchy is granted defined responsibilities and powers. It is important that each level and person understands the expectations regarding their responsibilities in order that accountability leads to the most appropriate behaviours. That, of course, applies to any business organization.

A basic principle of good governance is that no individual should have unfettered power over decision-making. Checks or audits should exist that oversee the actions of individuals. Big decisions should be made on a collective basis. The corollary to this is that the board maintains effective oversight of delegated decisions – receiving information, challenging, assuring and supporting to evaluate the effectiveness of performance and behaviour.

Rule 4: framework, process and decision gates

We already know that organizations need to distinguish between projects and business-as-usual. But organizations which aspire to good governance go much further than this. They develop a comprehensive framework of lifecycles, defined role descriptions, 3PM governance roles, rules and detailed processes to ensure consistency of application and language across an organization.

A crucial element of this framework is to have review and decision gates (also known in some organizations as stage gates) so that all projects are reviewed objectively at key points in their lifecycles. Good governance will specify when these critical decisions need to be made and name those involved in making them. Decision gates operate at three levels:

1.   Portfolio level, to enable controlled entry and exit of projects to realize maximum value and monitoring and forecasting of strategic outcomes.
2.   At programme level, to enable a clear business blueprint or target operating model, strategy, appropriate funding and benefits delivery at specified gates.
3.   At project level, to enable appropriate definition, development of information, business case and delivery of 'product' at each gate. A particular focus for projects is to ensure that the appropriate level of focus is given to the 'front end'. Rushing into implementation without ensuring solid definition up front is always a false economy on projects. If a project is doomed to failure, then 'failing early' and cancelling the project is best in the long-term interests of the organization. If an Agile approach is adopted, 'time boxing' is crucial (for example, delay to a planned gate review is unacceptable).

There should also be consistent processes at all three levels in (for example) funding, reporting, quality, stakeholders, risk, value, benefits, cost, time and issues management.

The gate approval process should be carried out by competent senior managers to ensure that continuation of projects is in the best interests of the business. A benchmarking study of governance by the APM's specific interest group for governance found that 70 per cent of organizations had five or more gate reviews during a typical project.

Any framework should include targets for data collection, making key governance decisions and enacting them. Quick key decision-making is particularly important in Agile projects (within 24 hours, for example).

Rule 5: have clearly allocated roles

Organizations need line-of-sight accountability from project team member, via a project manager, sponsor and thence to the main board. 3PM roles and responsibilities should be made clear and accountabilities allocated – aside from 'business-as-usual' job titles. Having clarity and avoiding overlap or gaps between role responsibilities is vital for good governance and getting true accountability. I have seen many examples where, when things go wrong, key players are heard to say 'I didn't realize that was my responsibility'. In other cases an individual (often the project manager) is blamed for failure when it was, for example, the sponsor's responsibility.

Even if someone has a big job title in an organization, the question should still be asked: 'What is their 3PM role and responsibility in this specific situation?' Only then can we be clear on who is accountable for making the key decisions.

So at both the project and programme levels we need to understand who the named individuals in the following roles are:

- sponsor or project executive (who might be supported by a sponsor team, steering committee or project board). This is not to be confused with a stakeholder group;
- project manager;
- senior user;
- senior supplier.

Sponsor continuity is also important. A change of sponsor during the lifecycle of a project is often cited as a key reason for failure. An APM benchmarking study found that fewer than 25 per cent of projects have the same sponsor throughout. The NAO highlighted that the 'challenged' Universal Credit Programme had no fewer than five different sponsors in 18 months. Change of sponsor should be treated as a reason to relaunch the project – going through the requirements, strategy and key success factors to ensure that the new sponsor is supportive.

We also need clear role definitions at the portfolio level, where the politics become ever more complicated. These roles need a clear linkage to individual programme and project governance – no matter where in the organization they sit or are driven from. So we need to name the body and its membership that is responsible for selecting and prioritizing the corporate portfolio of projects (for which the main board is accountable).

In this regard, in the benchmarking study by the APM's governance special interest group found that one of the key determinants of good governance was seen as having a project management representative on the board (a 'chief projects officer' or equivalent, for example). Over half of the organizations represented in the study had such a role.

Rule 6: requirements – keeping the end destination in sight

Project management is about achieving a desired result or change. So requirements definition and planning is crucial. But how many times do teams lose sight of the end objective or business case?

We carry out the task of planning by representing activities from today and then into the future (in the Western world from left to right). But we need to keep checking that the forecast result is still appropriate and that the 'left to right' activities, once completed, will result in the desired outcome. Hence we also need 'right to left' planning. This is essential in programmes, because the end result cannot always be defined precisely at the outset. The programme can keep changing in shape as the team learns and the programme environment develops. Then the need for 'right to left' planning and re-forecasting the outcome is even more important.

Traditionally project practitioners like to 'lock things down' and are trained to define things in a progressive level of detail from concept through to testing and completion. 'Locking on to delivery' too early can mean that a subtle change to the environment into which you are delivering can result in the end product being perceived as a failure – failure to meet what is necessary. Good governance needs to overcome this propensity and keep a focus on the end outcome and needs, especially if the environment is dynamic. In short, the higher level governance bodies need to 'stay conscious' and compensate for the lower levels sometimes becoming 'comatose'.

At the portfolio level the board's governance activity would be to re-forecast constantly and check to see if the desired business performance (the strategic objectives) can still be delivered within the dynamic business environment with the selected portfolio of projects. If not, the portfolio must be modified.

Rule 7: transparent reporting

There must be transparency of change decisions or actions and communication of their outcome using one version of the truth. Good governance should ensure that reporting is open and honest and that there are clearly defined criteria for reporting 3P status and for the escalation of risks and issues to the levels required by the organization.

The board has a key responsibility to set the appropriate reporting 'tone'. This should include ensuring that information published is suitable for easy absorption by the reader or audience. It should match the main measure of progress to the priority objectives – for example time, cost, quality, benefits. In addition the board should be explicit about 'whistle blowing' and reporting of bad news.

Reporting needs to be hierarchical. Each report should be addressed specifically to the audience it is intended to serve. Reports should be available (in the most appropriate format) to all the key stakeholders in order to ensure transparency.

Rule 8: capacity and competence

A core area of governance is ensuring that appropriate numbers (capacity) and skilled and experienced resources (competence) are in place for delivering projects. People deliver projects! There must be enough of them – with competence in their roles and with the right tools.

We would not expect to win a soccer championship without competent players. Why then do we assume we will have project success by fielding incompetent people on the 'project field'? In this respect the competence of all 'players' (including sponsors, senior managers and board members) is vital. We can assume that these people must be competent in their domain to have risen to their senior roles. But they all need to be fully competent in their 'project role' and collaborate effectively. This involves not just knowing the rules and language of the 'project game' but also having and practising the skill to achieve project success.

Good governance is not just about appointing a competent project manager. That manager is only one of the players on the 'project pitch'. Good governance is also about ensuring that the other key players are competent in their roles and that they perform as a coherent and collaborative team.

A poll conducted by the APM revealed that the key principle from directing change which gave organizations most difficulty was the competence, authority and resources of decision-makers. Both private and public sectors have invested heavily in increasing the competence of project managers in recent years, but less so in other roles. The most important of these other roles are the sponsor and the board members at portfolio level. A series of studies have shown that, on average, 50 per cent of sponsors do not know what is expected of them or do not feel competent to carry out their role. An APM benchmarking study found that only 8 per cent of the organizations used a competency assessment model for selecting sponsors. Further, only 40 per cent of the respondents had project benefits measures in their sponsors' personal performance measures.

I have already written that sponsor competence improvement is a key requirement for good governance (and project success) and an area for general improvement. Some organizations recognize this issue and are helping to build sponsor competence by having 'sponsor agents' (programme or business professionals to provide vital support to busy strategic sponsors) or sponsor coaches to help fill competency shortfalls.

The PMI (2014) Pulse Survey demonstrated a direct correlation between effective talent management and better project performance. Organizations with the foresight to recognize that organizational capability improvement is a strategic objective appoint a 'chief projects officer' (or similar). They develop a community of project professionals and establish a 'centre of excellence' – opening project management academies to develop talent. They encourage and expect staff to join reputable institutes and gain formal qualifications as part of professionalizing project management.

Rule 9: assurance

Corroboration of project status through rigorous independent review is the penultimate golden rule. Again the board (or its delegated subcommittee) needs to decide when independent scrutiny of projects, programmes or project management systems is required and implement such assurance accordingly. Independent scrutiny is a vital tool for the board to get a second opinion on the health of projects and project management in general. An independent view on a specific project does not necessarily mean using a body external to the organization – a peer review might satisfy that need and increase cross-business learning or sharing.

Assurance is the final safety gate for ensuring that a board or project/programme team has not become 'comatose' and lost sight of the desired outcome. A key assurance role is to ensure that the board is fully conscious of what is happening and is making decisions accordingly.

But beware! Boards need also to ensure that they don't 'just' rely (or over-rely) on assurance reviews, because these are often only a 'snapshot' in time. The board must remain conscious and ensure that other normal governance structures and reporting are also in place.

Rule 10: leadership, collaboration and supportive culture

I have left this rule to last because it is the most important and has the greatest impact on effective governance. Put simply, good governance is about how people behave. These behaviours need to be set from the top.

The right culture has to be driven from the top as the board members sit at the top of governance. Only the senior people can set, reward and enforce a culture of transparency, openness, collaboration, performance focus, empowerment, single point accountability, role adherence, ethical working and so on. The board members need to demonstrate individually and collectively good behaviours of governance. The board has to ensure that the policies, ethics, culture and 'tone' are set appropriately and that adherence to good governance principles is not compromised. Board members need to foster a culture of improvement and of frank internal disclosure of information. Board members influence this (directly or indirectly) by what they say and do.

Improving and delivering good governance comes mainly through a change of culture, behaviours and relationships. Organizations need a coherent structure and processes for project management transcend the business, but they primarily need a culture and behaviour of people that actually believe in the culture and want to do things in the right way. An organization might have the best structure in the world with all the right review/authorization bodies, but if the behaviour is wrong (with someone wanting to 'play a game' or circumvent lessons learned and good practice) good governance is destroyed.

End users are running today's business and often feel they are too busy to spend time thinking about a project that will not deliver for months or even years. But we all know that early user involvement is crucial to avoiding late user changes when they don't like the deliverable. Again this message to emphasize the need for early user involvement needs to come from the top.

I have written much about the role of sponsor on individual projects and their leadership role as being critical to directing the project team, via the project manager. That role includes protecting the delivery team from organizational interference. The sponsor needs to lead from the front and champion their project at every opportunity, not only within the organization but also with key external stakeholders.

The key players in governance

The key players are shown as a simple governance structure in Figure 19.2. This is not an exhaustive list because each organization needs a governance framework that is proportionate to its needs. For example, the structure will be far larger for complex and multi-owned projects. The important requirement is that roles, authority and accountability lines are clear.

How much governance is enough?

One problem for organizations is answering the question 'How much governance is necessary?' The answer will vary from one organization to another. Many factors have

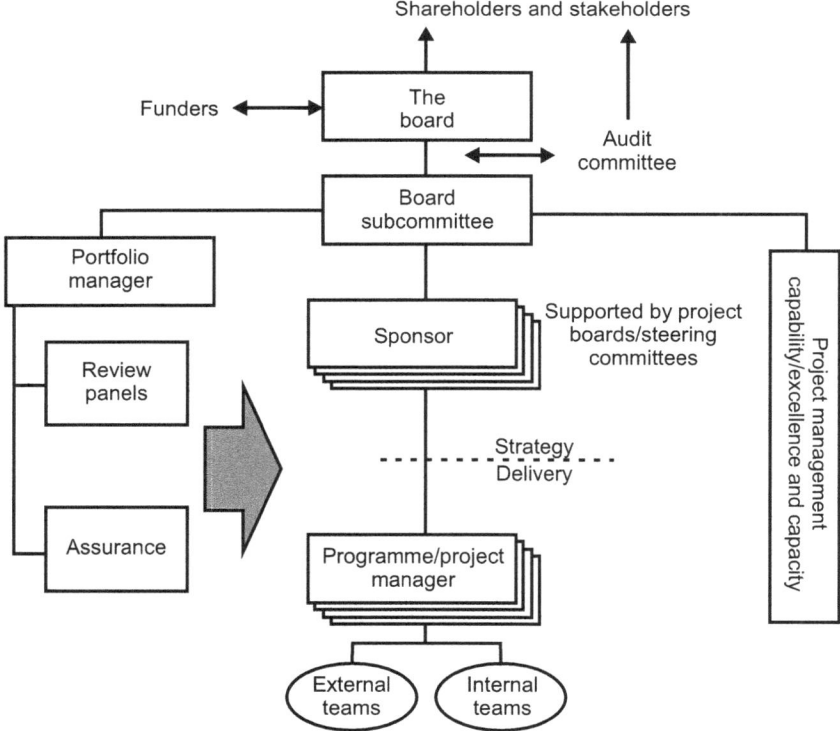

Figure 19.2 Key governance players and accountability lines

to be considered, among which are maturity, appetite for risk, management style, history, personalities and competence. There is no one right way of delivering good governance, but the basics and suggested ten golden rules must be observed.

In smaller organizations the board would probably be intimately concerned with all their projects. In larger organizations with bigger portfolios I would expect responsibility for governance to be delegated. However, that delegation must be in a hierarchy where the board still has visibility of the most significant strategic projects and is assured that all other projects have appropriate delegated levels of governance with links back to the top.

The key requirement is that the governance framework should be proportionate and realistic. It should be structured and applied in a flexible and pragmatic manner. It is not an end in itself but a means of adding value to an organization, providing continuity, increasing transparency and controlling risk.

Case study 1: transformation programme in a global services company

After a period of rapid growth due to acquisitions and market pressure a business decided to develop and implement a more global approach. Growth over the company's previous ten years had meant that numerous and varied platforms, processes, systems and data standards had evolved to meet specific local customer needs. Much of that had operated effectively in local countries.

The business had tried unsuccessfully to roll out an IT cloud-based tool to support global and consistent working. After much hard work from the IT-driven team, user adoption was poor. It was clear that there were some fundamental problems. The business took a 'time out' and assembled the business leaders from the countries at a workshop to assess the problem.

The problems – and their relationship to the ten golden rules

This project had been driven by IT as a 'new IT platform' as part of an IT portfolio. No one had sufficiently defined the vision in business terms or aligned the project to the business strategic objective to transform the way that the business worked for the benefit of strategic global customers. Not every golden rule was followed, as explained below.

- *Rule 1 (alignment and relationships).* The fundamental driver of the business strategy was to put in place a new operating model for the business, supported by a new tool and aligned to the needs of strategic customers. But the project had not addressed the business model, the country managers or the ultimate vision for the project. So there was no consistent approach globally. Unfortunately the board had not seen the project as anything more than part of the IT portfolio. Instead the project needed to change people's working relationships, performance measurement and reward mechanism. Just delivering the technology didn't get to the 'destination' and many stakeholders were not engaged.
- *Rule 2 (vision and strategic roadmap).* The team had tried to implement the platform as a 'big bang' project. However, it was necessary to allow the new ways of

working to evolve alongside the capability of the technology. Part of the reason for the business users not adopting the technology solution was that the initial versions did not satisfy their ultimate requirements. There was no roadmap to show how the initial releases would satisfy only partial requirements. The roadmap should have shown how the full system capability would be achieved through a series of releases, learning from each one alongside development of the operating model, processes and reward mechanisms.

- *Rule 5 (clearly allocated roles).* Being driven from the IT department had resulted in the project manager being IT-based. Also his boss, the chief information officer (CIO), had ended up being the sponsor. That was inappropriate for the project, which had become a business transformation programme.
- *Rule 7 (transparent reporting).* Top managers in the various countries were blind to reporting progress and problems of the project. This did not seem important to them.
- *Rule 8 (capacity and competence).* Insufficient business user resource had been involved. Those who were involved felt the platform was being 'imposed'. Also they didn't see a natural business focus in the project team with which associate. The IT project manager was not sufficiently competent to deal with business users in their own 'language', or to handle the transformational change approach needed.
- *Rule 9 (assurance).* An assurance exercise had been started (by someone from the IT department) and they were about to carry out a post-project review.
- *Rule 10 (leadership and collaboration).* As stated above, the sponsor was effectively the CIO, not the business unit head. There was poor cross-business collaboration, with little support given to user staff from their managers (and in some case complete resistance).

So some significant governance problems had to be dealt with. However, the 'time out' was effective and a new approach was agreed and adopted.

The governance response

The IT-led 'post-project review' was cancelled and a business-led 'transformation programme' was established. The business unit head took over as sponsor and developed a clear vision and appointed a professional programme director. A new IT project manager was put in place. A senior business unit manager was appointed 'business architect' to drive development of the global operating model and processes and be the main link with country key users (speaking their 'business language'). A *programme*, rather than *project*, model was adopted so that incremental delivery of operating model, processes and technology could be achieved across multiple countries.

A video was created to explain the new model. This focused on strategic customers and a programme approach. This emphasized the priority and importance of the transformation, with key staff being interviewed.

A steering group was established with the country managers and other key stakeholders so that they were kept informed. The project and its priorities were thus emphasized.

The core team carried out an intensive 'engagement and adoption' campaign, with each country being treated as a unique entity and their specific issues being addressed (but within the global operating model). The team emphasized the new behaviours (collaborative working) at the core of the transformation and a standard 'change toolkit' was offered to each country, tailored to their requirements.

Success for the new operating model, processes, technology and resulting performance was achieved through a series of tranches and incremental steps.

Case study 2: project management capability improvement

The subject of this study is a global systems contracting organization. They identified the need to improve radically the creation and delivery of bids and projects across the business. Bid success rate was dropping, so that resources were being wasted on failed bids. Project delivery was highly variable across all divisions of the business, with reduced customer satisfaction. A high proportion of their business comprised projects – both for external customers and for internal new product development. Individual divisions competed for their share of development funds, mainly based upon the size and revenue of the division.

Each division had evolved its own framework and processes for project management. Project managers did not feel valued in the organization, where technical excellence was highly regarded. Senior management reviews of key customer projects and internal investment projects were either not carried out at all, or they were infrequent and haphazard. Resource planning was poor. There was little cooperation across the business regarding resources or reviews.

Remedial action

The board decided to deal with the problems. Again I have set out the remedial actions with respect to the ten golden rules.

- *Rule 1 (alignment and relationships)*. The board decided that all requests for development funds would be reviewed by the board across all divisions of the organization. Requests would be prioritized using new criteria that balanced future strategic value against operational necessity. This allowed some of the smaller growing divisions that were important to the future business to gain a greater share of investment and also the entire portfolio of internal projects to be formally aligned to strategic and business unit objectives.
- *Rule 2 (vision and strategic roadmap)*. The board instigated the creation of a new department to focus on building increased organization competence in bids and project management. This new unit gained 'buy-in' from the board and the whole business to a vision for improved project management, and a roadmap of the steps needed to get there. This included addressing the key elements of status in their industry, role in the business, project governance, individual competence and qualifications, processes, tools, technology and performance measurement.

- *Rule 3 (the golden thread of delegation).* The company's rules on delegated powers were reviewed. New rules were put in place specifying the levels at which particular decisions could be made. It was made clear who should/must attend formal reviews of bids and projects, what questions they should be asking and the decisions they should be making. Visual aids were produced to help reviewers to carry out their role better. The reporting and accountability lines between project managers and their business directors were made clear.
- *Rule 4 (framework, process and decision gates).* A new framework was designed with well-defined decision gates at key stages in bids and projects. It was made mandatory for board members and senior managers to attend the relevant reviews. Weekly board reviews of key bids were also instigated to ensure that effort was being focused on 'winnable' bids and that low probability bids were declined at the outset. Core processes for bidding and project management were developed and implemented, supported by an intranet based tool.
- *Rule 5 (clearly defined roles).* Core roles on bids and projects were defined better, with role descriptions to help consistency of allocation and accountability lines. The internal sponsor role for development projects was enforced.
- *Rule 6 (keeping the end destination in sight).* Monthly reviews were instigated to review the progress of each improvement initiative against a dashboard and also an annual assessment was made of performance and the resource and budget requirements. Significant changes in direction were made owing to the impact that was being made in the business.
- *Rule 7 (transparent reporting).* Monthly progress reports were made to the business leaders. Also a monthly bulletin was distributed to them plus everyone in the project management community to keep them informed and to continue to develop the 'community' focus.
- *Rule 8 (capacity and competence).* The board initiated actions to improve capacity management, most notably putting in place a formal competence for bids and projects and appointing a director responsible to the board for the bids and projects department and for driving through the initiative on their behalf. Also the board put in place a formal resource forecasting process to ensure that project and bid resources were properly forecast and managed.

The new director for projects developed the vision, articulated the case for change and put in place a software-based competency assessment tool for all project staff. He arranged training courses with external providers to allow project staff to gain formal accreditations and qualifications. He also developed and implemented a new HR strategy to improve recruitment and development, set up a series of lunchtime knowledge share (lunch and learn) workshops and presentations, arranged annual conferences for the community and gained corporate accreditation for the business. He was personally involved in project reviews and trained and coached his board colleagues in the way to run reviews competently.

- *Rule 9 (assurance).* Assurance reviews of all projects were planned and carried out using peers from across the business. Annual surveys were carried out to measure the state of project management and quantify the improvement.

- *Rule 10 (leadership, collaboration and supportive culture).* The director of bids and projects worked tirelessly to emphasize to his board colleagues and senior managers the importance of demonstrating support for the new arrangements and encouraging collaboration across the business. The result was that the project managers finally started to feel valued.

Summary

Project delivery has not improved markedly over the last few decades. The reasons for failed projects are the same now as then. Most causes are the responsibility of the governance of project management – and specifically the sponsors of projects and board members. Good governance of project management is not a dream. By following the principles and golden rules outlined in this chapter, organizations can move towards better governance, and thence to more successful projects.

Structure, process and tools are essential enablers to improve governance. However, the crucial enabler is the behaviour and leadership of the board or top team and project sponsors. Organizations need to make good governance a strategic objective. Directors and executives of organizations must stay conscious, avoid becoming 'comatose' and become more professional in their roles associated with projects and change. Above all the key success factor in projects is having an engaged sponsor.

Two suggestions

There is no silver bullet for project success. However, to counter governance (project) failures I suggest two simple interventions to make a difference.

1. I have focused this chapter on the role of the board or executive team. However, project managers also need to take some responsibility for governance and project failure. They often spot issues of poor governance but do nothing about them because they feel impotent. My message to project managers is to be more challenging and demanding of their organization. Use the rules and principles of good governance, spread the word, hold them up to those responsible for governance, and ask them to challenge themselves as to how they are doing. Attaining good governance is a journey to which all must contribute.
2. At each project start senior teams need to be a little more circumspect and *imagine failure*. Instead of thinking that everything is going to go right, imagine the worst case scenario. Challenge the sponsor, reflect on the usual reasons for failure, revisit lessons learned from previous projects and ask what special steps are being taken to deal with those usual reasons for failure upfront.

During projects ensure that they and their colleagues remain conscious – things will change but keep asking the same questions. This simple good governance approach can be taken by any board or senior leadership team. Also, in this small way they can demonstrate their overall responsibility and pro-activeness.

Ultimately the board is accountable for good governance and has to ensure the right process, competencies, culture and behaviours are in place.

References and further reading

APM (2011), *Directing Change*, Princes Risborough: Association for Project Management.

APM (2012), *APM Body of Knowledge*, 6th edn., Princes Risborough: Association for Project Management.

APM (2015), *Factors in Project Success*, Princes Risborough: Association for Project Management.

DSDM Consortium (2014), *Agile Project Framework*. <www.dsdm.org>.

Financial Reporting Council (2014), *The UK Corporate Governance Code*, London: Financial Reporting Council.

IoD (2010), *Corporate Governance Guidance and Principles and Guidance for Unlisted Companies in the UK*, London: Institute of Directors.

National Audit Office (2013), *Lessons from Cancelling the Intercity West Coast Franchise Competition*, London: National Audit Office.

OECD (2004), *Principles of Corporate Governance*, Paris: OECD.

OGC (2007), *Managing Successful Programmes (MSP)*, London: Cabinet Office/AXELOS.

OGC (2009), *Prince2*. London: Cabinet Office / AXELOS.

PMI (2014), *Pulse of the Profession: The High Cost of Low Performance*, Newtown Square, PA: Project Management Institute.

PMI (2015), *A Guide to the Project Management Body of Knowledge (PMBoK)*, 5th edn., Newtown Square, PA: Project Management Institute.

PwC (2014), *4th Global Portfolio and Programme Management Survey*, London: PwC.

Chapter 20

Mastering Integration in Programme Management

Martin Sedlmayer

This chapter is about integration of a programme into its context, described at the example of the Virtual Centre programme at 'skyguide', the Swiss air navigation service provider that manages air traffic to ensure safe and efficient flights in Switzerland.

Introduction and background

The Virtual Centre programme described in this chapter changes completely the way in which skyguide produces and provides its services, in a unique way: Because a physical consolidation is not conceivable, a single unit with methods of operations, information, procedures, technical means and equipment fully harmonized shall be implemented, albeit operating in multiple locations. The complex geographical and topographical area, the densest traffic in Europe, the state dominance and strong unions make the initiative even more demanding.

The strategy is straightforward, with the following main objectives:

- Run a single unit, operating from two different physical locations, including sharing of business between both sides.
- Base on a fully harmonized common data centre, supporting both operation centres with standardized services.
- Influence the development of services in Europe and convince the industry to adhere to the idea.
- Integrate external services as soon as they appear on the market and are of economic advantage.
- Provide service continuity to avoid building a contingency centre.
- Influence the development of services in Europe and convince the industry to adhere to the idea and integrate external services as soon as they appear on the market and are of economic advantage.

This chapter describes the Virtual Centre programme in its context. Strategy, cultures and values, demands and ambitions, structures and processes led to the programme approach chosen by the Virtual Centre management team. I shall describe aspects of the programme, discuss its rationale and conclude with a couple of learnings from this programme, which was initiated in 2011 and will go beyond 2022.

An air navigation service provider (ANSP) manages air traffic to ensure safe and efficient flights from aerodrome to aerodrome. It also provides services for pilots and other airspace users (including weather and airport information, rescue assistance and more). Typical characteristics of the ANSP industry include:

- As a High Reliability Organization (HRO), the industry is totally committed to avoiding incidents, accidents and catastrophes in an environment subject to heavy risk factors and to the complexity of the business. The five characteristics of HROs (Weick and Sutcliffe, 2007) include preoccupation with failure, reluctance to simplify the interpretations, sensitivity to operations, commitment to resilience, and deference to expertise. This preoccupancy drives significant efforts to human factors especially related to safety and makes projects longer and more expensive compared to other industries.
- Because no single private organization could bear the consequences of a potential catastrophe, the world agreed in the middle of the Second World War that the states themselves shall be responsible for the safe and free operations of the air traffic. The ICAO, a UN specialized agency, was created in 1944 upon the signing of the Convention on International Civil Aviation (ICAO, 2006). This characteristic yields a lot of regulations and heavy state controls into projects.
- In addition to the regulations based dominance of the states on air traffic management, the military air operations strengthen isolation tendencies, because every nation claims its own sovereignty, also in term of flight operations even in times of peace (for example, air policing). This aspect makes it demanding to cooperate with ANSP in other countries, especially when it comes to exchange of data.
- The labour force in the ANSP industry is very well organized. Many strong unions exist, and their influence on corporate decisions is very high. This drives the need to involve the unions' representatives directly in all phases of a project, but especially in the requirement engineering and test phases.
- The Air Traffic Controller (ATCO) is personally accountable for the work he or she is doing. This direct personal liability together with the HRO mindset has at least two main impacts on projects: First, a solution is directly influenced by the individual end users which causes a very high complexity to be defined from many individual solutions. Second, the ATCO is very reluctant to change: If a solution has been accepted, a new one has to be at least as good as the previous one, with all functionality the former solution offered, just from the start of the implementation.
- The industry requires very high investments, especially for technology infrastructures like radars, communications and networks. Most single element require being at least available twice, in several cases the infrastructure is tripled (with both hot and cold standby). These high investments slow down the technology evolutions significantly.
- The technology in place must be very reliable. The availability of the communication chain for example has to be 99.999999%. This aspect makes it hard to invest in modern technology; the old fashioned technology in place is often more reliable than an emerging new one (for example VoIP).

- Technology has always to be downwards compatible. Because for any technology improvement, the airline industry has to adapt all aircrafts, from the antique 'Wright Flyer' to the most modern 'Airbus A350' or the fifth generation fighter jet 'F-22 Raptor', across all users of the airspace, often worldwide. This aspect drives towards very complex technology solutions. Too often different solutions for the very same purpose have to be operated and maintained in parallel for a long-lasting period of the evolution.

Begun in the late 1990s, the Single European Sky initiative (Eurocontrol, 2014) dictates how the design, management and regulation of airspace shall be coordinated throughout the European Union in a more efficient way to cope with increasing demand. Europe experienced during this period a dramatically increasing amount of delays in the airline business, with enormous cost, safety and environmental issues.

In recent years (after the 2000 crisis), the European Sky faces a completely different challenge. Now traffic volume only increases marginally in central Europe (the growth happens in Eastern countries). This stable traffic situation (together with some implemented Single European Sky Advance Research (SESAR) results, many individual ANSP initiatives and a better cooperation in Europe) means that manageable delays have fallen to an extremely low level.

This change in the business environment has turned the focus of the industry from increasing capacity to using available resources more efficiently, thus reducing operating costs. However, the industry still expects an increase of traffic very soon. It also believes that the measures taken to increase capacity remain the same, namely to use existing resources more efficiently (reducing costs). These assumptions are highly questionable and lead to too many misconceptions.

Although many billions of euros have been spent in research in Europe, there is still no common understanding of a cooperative business model, with no innovative rules of cross-border sharing of revenues and costs in place. The states with their national ANSPs are still the dominant players, and cross-border collaboration is still without a common understanding of a business model or strong guidance when it comes to executing initiatives of any kind.

The Air Navigation Service industry (ANSP) in Switzerland

In Switzerland, skyguide (skyguide, 2014) manages and monitors the Swiss and delegated airspace on behalf of the Swiss Confederation with specific characteristics such as:

- Airspace with the highest density in Europe.
- High density of airfields (64 in the very small geographical area).
- Challenging geographical issues (for example, Alps) and weather conditions.
- Military operations fully integrated into the civil air navigation services.
- Two major airports (Zurich and Geneva) geographically situated very close to the national borders; to manage these airports efficiently, skyguide controls a large area over neighbouring countries too. Skyguide ensures safe and efficient

operations not only of all Swiss airspace, but also of adjoining airspace areas in France, Germany and Austria that have been delegated to its control.

- Switzerland operates its two area control centres (ACC) of approximately equal size and importance in two culturally disperse regions; the Geneva centre belongs to the French speaking region of Switzerland with a strong relation to France, and Zurich to the German speaking part with close relation to Germany – at least in terms of business relations.
- Switzerland is a basic democratic country with high local influence; therefore the local government of the Cantons of Geneva and Zurich have a high influence on key decisions of skyguide, not just the Swiss Confederation.
- Skyguide is the most expensive ANSP in Europe, partly explainable by the complex airspace, partly by the unfavourable foreign exchange rate (costs are spent in CHF, revenues generated in euros).
- A mid-air collision occurred in 2002 which was partially caused by shortcomings in the Swiss air traffic control system supervising the flights at the time of the accident.

The technology used is quite remarkable. The detection, allocation and prediction of the flights in the three-dimensional space is technology-wise quite challenging, especially because of physical barriers like the Alps. Its combination with flight information and environment data like weather makes it even more demanding. The ground-air communication with limited capacity and reachability like all technology outbid the physical possibilities in a constantly changing environment and a dynamic traffic, changing radically by time, season, weather conditions and so on. This makes the engineers highly knowledgeable experts in their specific area of technology.

In contrast to the basic technology, the applications (for example planning, controlling and managing the traffic) are at least partially outdated and have grown in an uncontrolled manner. Although there was an investment strategy in place, several applications today serve the same purpose. The decision on how they were implemented was based too often on personal preferences and resource availability and not on a commonly agreed architecture.

The two different centres in Switzerland, comparable to two different national ANSPs, have each worked well. But from a pure management standpoint one ANSP would also work perfectly well. Over the last 80 years continuous investments and improvements have been made, but they were site specific. Only during the last decade has network technology enabled closer collaboration and joint development. But changing the complete infrastructure is costly and very time consuming, and that influences significantly the way ATCOs are managing air traffic.

The challenge

After a series of studies, skyguide decided in 2010 to go for a virtual consolidation strategy. This includes flexible operations, sharing traffic across the two centres (East in Zurich and West in Geneva) based on a harmonized infrastructure. In addition, the flexible centres are to be supported by a shared data centre providing the services required for the operations (see Figure 20.1). Additional external services are to be implemented if available and economically reasonable. This approach was chosen mainly because:

- a cross-border solution together with France and Germany (at a new site near Basel) was politically not possible;
- physical consolidation was too expensive (owing to very high transition cost) and was not supported socially or politically.

The strategy for the Virtual Centre is straightforward and described in the Virtual Centre Business Model (skyguide – the Virtual Centre Model, 2014) as follows:

- Run a single unit, operating from two different physical locations, including sharing of business between both sides.
- Base on a fully harmonized common data centre, supporting both operation centres with standardized services.
- Influence the development of services in Europe and convince the industry to adhere to the idea.
- Integrate external services as soon as they appear on the market and are of economic advantage.
- Provide service continuity to avoid building a contingency centre.

For the approach chosen by the Virtual Centre programme management team, it is important to recognize that neither this kind of operation (sharing traffic across centres), nor the data centre approach, nor the integration and use of external services, has ever been implemented in the ANSP industry in Europe. Parts of the technology objectives are in place in the US for shared services, but with a completely

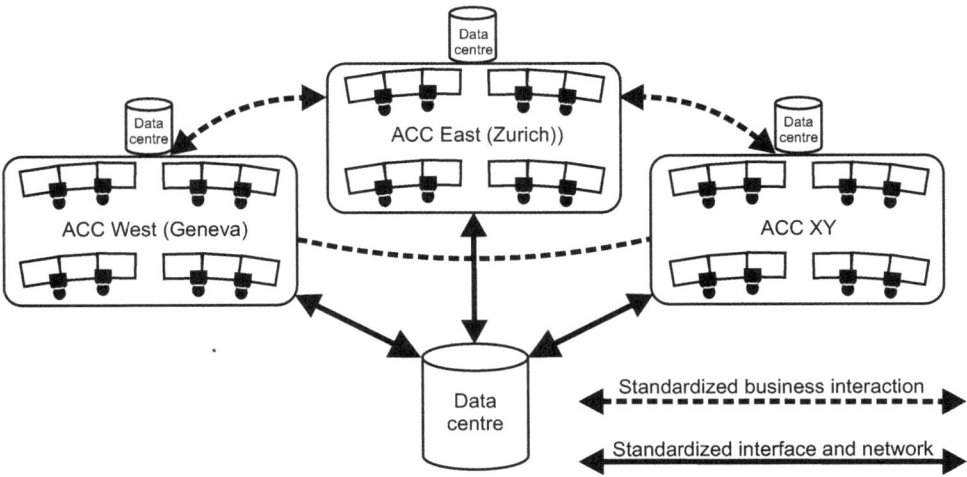

Figure 20.1 The business architecture

different institutional set-up. Even the general objective of a virtual consolidation (virtual merger) is not a very often practised approach to gain benefits.

Contextual dimensions

The contextual dimensions are described in Version 4 of the ICB International Competence Baseline (IPMA, 2015, which was not published at the time of writing).

Strategy

The corporate strategy defines the Virtual Centre as the 'strategic initiative No. 1', part of the set of four 'beacon statements', which are:

1. zero serious incidents;
2. a successful virtual centre for Switzerland;
3. being the preferred ANSP for customers and partners;
4. being a company where outstanding people enjoy doing an outstanding job.

However, when digging deeper into the meaning of the Virtual Centre, the strategy does not provide enough answers. The questions 'What exactly is a Virtual Centre?' and, more important, 'For what future challenge is the Virtual Centre an answer?' were not considered sufficiently at the beginning.

With the exception of the management, individuals at working level often do not even recognize the need for any change. Partially this is due to the perception that skyguide cannot have a financial problem. Although the Swiss ANSP is the most expensive provider in Europe, the charging mechanism in place guarantees a small benefit every year (route charges are simply calculated on a budget basis). The only option for an airspace user to avoid these high charges would be to fly round the Swiss geographic area, incurring longer cruising time and higher fuel costs (fuel adds up to one third the cost of a commercial flight, so the shortest route is important).

Hence, the European Commission implemented rules forcing the ANSP to optimize the cost structure, but that pressure is not widely recognized as being very threatening. That is partly due to the ANSP's position as a public service provider, where the financial performance of the company plays a minor role in comparison with the financial and operational performance of its customers. If an ANSP reduces cost and therefore the level of service (or the level of reserves the ANSP keeps for managing peaks or unexpected situations) the impact on the airline industry would be much higher than the cost reductions achieved within the ANSP.

Partially the issue lies in the relatively small amount an average passenger has to pay for air navigation services. Which passenger would not be willing to pay approximately eight euros for safety per flight? Consequently, safety and service will always be the first priority, provided that the associated costs are perceived as reasonable.

As a consequence, management and the Virtual Centre (VC) programme team had first to develop a common understanding of what exactly VC is all about and, especially, why skyguide should undertake the programme. In addition to the employees, the addressees for this message included the board members and the owner, because these stakeholders had to agree to the significant investment required.

Compliance, standards and regulations

An almost unmanageable amount of regulations exist in the ANSP industry. The programme Compliance Management Plan lists 46 different sources of references that have to be taken under consideration. The most important sources include:

- European Parliament and its Council (although Switzerland does not belong to the EU);
- European Commission (EC);
- International Civil Aviation Organization (ICAO), Eurocontrol (the European organization for aviation safety) and the Civil Air Navigation Services Organization (CANSO);
- European Aviation Safety Agency (EASA);
- Safety oversight of ANS procedures of the national supervisory authority (FOCA);
- Swiss Federal Department of the Environment, Transport, Energy and Communications (DETEC);
- Swiss Federal Department of Defence, Civil Protection and Sport (DDPS, military law);
- an enormous amount of internal processes and work instructions.

In terms of rules it is important to recognize, that Switzerland – in the specific field of air traffic management – adapts directly the given regulation in Europe. Although this general rule is in place, there remain many controversial issues, like military operations and state sovereignty.

Governance, structures and processes

To ensure safe operations, a very distinct and clear governance regime is in place. Transparent structures and a large number of precisely described processes support the decision-making at usually quite a high level. As a consequence, but also typical for these kinds of business, the company is clearly managed through line management. A project team member usually performs the part of the job that his/her department is supposed to do, but not more.

As part of the corporate governance, a framework for project management planning and execution is well-established within the company. Because the company is almost purely state owned, skyguide focuses almost exclusively on financial aspects. Well-established budgeting processes cover the whole company, but they do not fit the specific needs of projects well because annual budgeting is stronger than project budgeting. For the VC programme this leads sometimes to quite confusing situations on what is the true basis, because several different budgets exist, as follows:

- budget for the programme over time, per tranche;
- budgets for the various projects, per phase;
- budget for the year.

The strong line management has a negative consequence because team spirit is quite fragile. Team members usually understand themselves as delegates from the line, and pursue the distinct objectives of their departments. Clear barriers exist between the team members. A joint project team spirit is usually not well established: skyguide is still far away from being a project orientated organization. With the exception of technical replacement or upgrade projects, projects are still seen as being disruptive to the daily business. Projects are not regarded as interesting challenges for coping with the future and usually are not welcomed.

In addition, before the start of the VC programme, the term 'programme' was used for big projects, or for multiple (sometimes loosely linked) projects. But real programme management focused on change and benefits was almost unknown to the company. Therefore a suitable programme approach and organizational set-up had to be established first.

Culture and values

Skyguide employs approximately 1,400 people from more than 35 nations. This rich diversity is a big advantage. It increases productivity because it brings different talents together using different skill sets, especially in the context of an HRO. Also it increases creativity and problem-solving by combining different and diverse minds. For individuals it can help to enhance language and communication skills. However, the challenges are also manifold. Integration can be handled but communication is always an issue. Formal communications are in English, which for almost everybody is a second or third language. That makes it difficult to communicate precisely. But the true meaning of words and a common understanding are particularly important for the ANSP business and its projects.

Analysing the culture of both the Swiss context and the skyguide/ANSP specific culture using the Hofstede framework (Hofstede, 2014) reveals the following picture:

- *Power distance* (defined as the extent to which the less powerful members of institutions and organizations within a country expect and accept that power is distributed unequally) is at the lower end of the scale in Switzerland (34). But this value seems to be even lower within skyguide because of the distinct expert culture. As a consequence, experts have to be integrated more intensively in solution selection and design.
- *Individualism* (the degree of interdependence that a society maintains among its members) is quite high for both French and German speaking parts of Switzerland (68). It is expected to be similar for skyguide.
- The high score in *masculinity* (70) indicates that Switzerland is driven by competition, achievement and success. In skyguide, a significant difference is recognizable between the French speaking region (with significant lower masculinity) and the German speaking part, with a direct impact on project execution. While German speaking Swiss love to have very detailed project plans and controlling mechanisms in place, the French speaking Swiss usually focus on cooperation within team members, and get results through joint achievements rather than through sophisticated plans. As a consequence, the Virtual Centre programme teams are mixed wherever possible to reflect both worlds.

- In *uncertainty avoidance* (the way that a society deals with the fact that the future can never be known) Switzerland is average (58). Interestingly, the French speaking people have significantly higher uncertainty avoidance. In skyguide this dimension seems to be significantly higher owing to the high reliability organization (HRO) paradigm and the strong safety focus (with a negative impact on project duration and cost). This is dealt with in the Virtual Centre programme by binding or linking projects together where human factor and safety activities can be shared.
- *Pragmatism* describes how every society has to maintain links with its own past while dealing with the challenges of the present and future. Switzerland, scoring 74, is definitively pragmatic. This might be true for the whole ANSP industry, but is definitively true for skyguide's corporate culture. The HRO paradigm challenges this pragmatism in terms of reluctance to simplify interpretations.
- *Indulgence* is defined as the extent to which people try to control their desires and impulses, based on the way they were raised. Switzerland with a high score (66) exhibits a willingness to realize desires with regard to enjoying life and having fun. This aspect might be similar in skyguide.

Power and interests

As a relatively small ANSP, skyguide cannot play a major role in Europe like its large neighbours France and Germany. Also, Switzerland is not part of the European Union, although its strong economy makes Switzerland an important EU partner.

Switzerland's geographical position in the heart of Europe and the challenges given by the Alps make skyguide an interesting partner for challenges in air traffic control. Further, the long history of Switzerland, its openness for cross-border collaboration, its democratic basis and its long-lasting independence drive a strong ambition of skyguide to contribute to the global development.

Therefore, skyguide defines its ambition not as a follower, but as a creative cooperator in the future of air navigation services (skyguide – 'What we stand for', 2014). Skyguide intends to take its due position in Europe. This implies (because of the lack of directive power) intensive negotiations, firm conviction and long-lasting, smooth non-disruptive changes.

The programme approach

Based on the corporate strategy, in 2011 skyguide launched a bundle of large projects to modernize until 2016 the toolset that the ATCOs use for managing their day-to-day work. Until 2013, the ATCOs in ACC East (Zurich) and lower sectors in ACC West (Geneva) used paper-based procedures. These are being replaced by IT tools. These tools are partially available already in the higher sectors in Geneva. They will support new ways of managing air traffic control. Manual interfaces within a centre between different airspace sectors, and between the two centres will disappear.

In addition, the mandate included harmonization of the procedures between the different airspace sectors and the two centres. This was the first step towards the Virtual Centre. The intention included the sharing of workload across centres, and the use of external services (if available and of economic advantage). The whole technical harmonization, based on a service orientated architecture, had not yet been addressed.

In 2013 skyguide management recognized that without a holistic approach and an integrated view they would never reach the Virtual Centre objectives, at least not in the foreseen timeframe and at affordable cost. The management decided to apply a programme management approach and hired an experienced programme manager.

At the end of 2013, in parallel with developing the overall programme mission, structure, CBA, roadmap, processes and so on, the programme delivered successfully the biggest change in recent history: the implementation of a stripless world in Zurich ACC, bringing the operations of the two sites closer together. But the procedures and tools at the two sites are still not fully harmonized, the underlying technology has not been harmonized and the services have not been designed and implemented.

On 1 October 2014, skyguide reorganized its operations, which dealt with the lack of a top-level manager accountable for the organization cross centres. Since then, an operations manager is no longer responsible for operating either Zurich or Geneva, but one manager is responsible for the transit traffic for the whole managed airspace East and West, one manager for the two international airports, including tower, approach and departure, and one manager for the regional airports and the military operations.

This fundamental organizational change gave the programme new drive. A clear owner of the Virtual Centre was inaugurated. A line manager was in charge of the harmonized and modernized processes and systems.

Understanding values, power and interests

A very early task in setting up the programme structure included a holistic analysis of the relevant stakeholders. It was imperative to understand the values and interests of the key players, including regulators, board members and unions. These stakeholders are shown in Figure 20.2.

The main interest of the stakeholder groups include the following:

- The owner (state) is primarily interested in a seamless service, without safety issues, without negative publicity. In addition, the state is interested in a high performance of the Swiss economy for a reasonable price.
- The oversight body wants to make sure that air traffic control, despite the changes, is acceptably safe and complies with regulations.
- The board of directors and the executive management team want to ensure the future of skyguide and the provision of an above average performance.
- The air traffic controllers are interested in providing a non-disruptive service. They simply want to avoid any kind of harm.
- The technical engineers are interested in the most modern technology to support the airspace users and ATCOs in the best possible way.

One of the core insights of this analysis was that the different stakeholder groups understood the idea of the Virtual Centre very differently. Operations people often did not understand why at all something had to change, or the change was about technology only. Many groups just understood that the change would be minor and

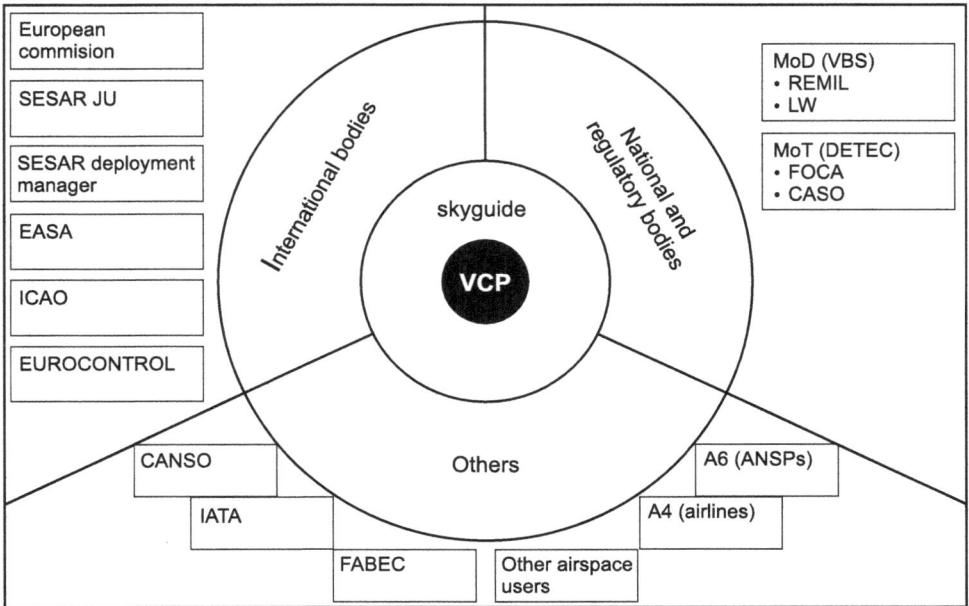

Figure 20.2 The relevant stakeholders

influence mainly others. This divergent understanding of the programme content drove both further development work as well as the intensifying of communication with increasing success.

Developing the mission

The mission of the Virtual Centre programme was developed based on corporate targets and the identified value and interests – the 'picture of a better future' (OGC, 2011). It contains all relevant interests from the major stakeholders both in terms of outcomes and in terms of process. An animated sketch was also developed to make the mission understandable. This sketch was often used to demonstrate the vision to the wider audience. The mission statement is shown in Figure 20.3 and the animated sketch in Figure 20.4.

Decomposition of the work

After defining the programme's target situation, the work necessary to achieve that desired outcome had to be defined and decomposed. The approach chosen was to conduct a series of workshops under the label of 'how to operate in 10 years' time' where many participants from different internal organizational units were involved.

It was imperative to define the programme scope properly by amalgamation of all the tasks to be performed. Because the Virtual Centre as a whole reflects the future of skyguide, the boundaries of the programme itself had to be set clearly – not everything of the future has to be part of the Virtual Centre programme. It

> Within the context of skyguide's vision and mission, the Virtual Centre Programme transforms skyguide by the way it provides ATM/AIM services, into a service-based organization to take its due position in the European network in order to deliver the best possible future for skyguide by:
> - Creating a single unit (albeit in multiple locations) with fully harmonized methods and operations, information, procedures, technical means and equipment
> - Standardizing and focusing on the most appropriate systems and technology
> - Improve _safety_
> - Implement _service continuity_
> - _Improve_ efficiency
> - _Reduce_ complexity of legacy systems
> - Proceeding in a _socially and politically acceptable manner._
> Skyguide's approach of the Virtual Centre is anchored on FABEC and European level to ensure that the European Air Traffic Management develops into a modularized network of competitive service advisers.

Figure 20.3 Programme mission

was in fact more important to define what was not part of the programme than the other way round. Finally, a draft was developed and visualized in seven building blocks (see Figure 20.5).

After this analysis, the management decided that the Virtual Centre programme would concentrate on the following five core building blocks:

1. Harmonized operations based on a stripless Human Machine Interface (HMI).
2. Common infrastructure, based on a service orientated architecture.
3. Combined air traffic control out of the Zurich and Geneva locations.
4. Flexible and optimized sectorization for the managed airspace.
5. Support development of and migrate to external services.

Cost-benefit analysis

Preparation of a cost-benefit analysis was a core programme activity. The result was too late for decision-making because the main decision was made years ago by defining the corporate strategy. It was quite hard to identify benefits. This difficulty could have been avoided if the cost-benefit analysis had been done when the strategic options were analysed (Sedlmayer, 2008). The financial expert asked to perform the analysis made a comment to the effect that 'How does one ask frogs how they shall dry their pond?'

To overcome this challenge, a separately developed, integrative target situation of the future of skyguide (including costs) was created, where the Virtual Centre was the core of the consideration, but also included side initiatives in the next 10 years to come. This work was executed on top management level, with the executive board members as the key contributors. This frame will provide sustainable benefits – and ensure their realization by the line organization at the right time.

A traditional cost-benefit analysis focuses on the influence of the investment on profit and loss account of the company and cash flows seen from the company's balance sheet. Other (external) effects are usually not taken into consideration. But,

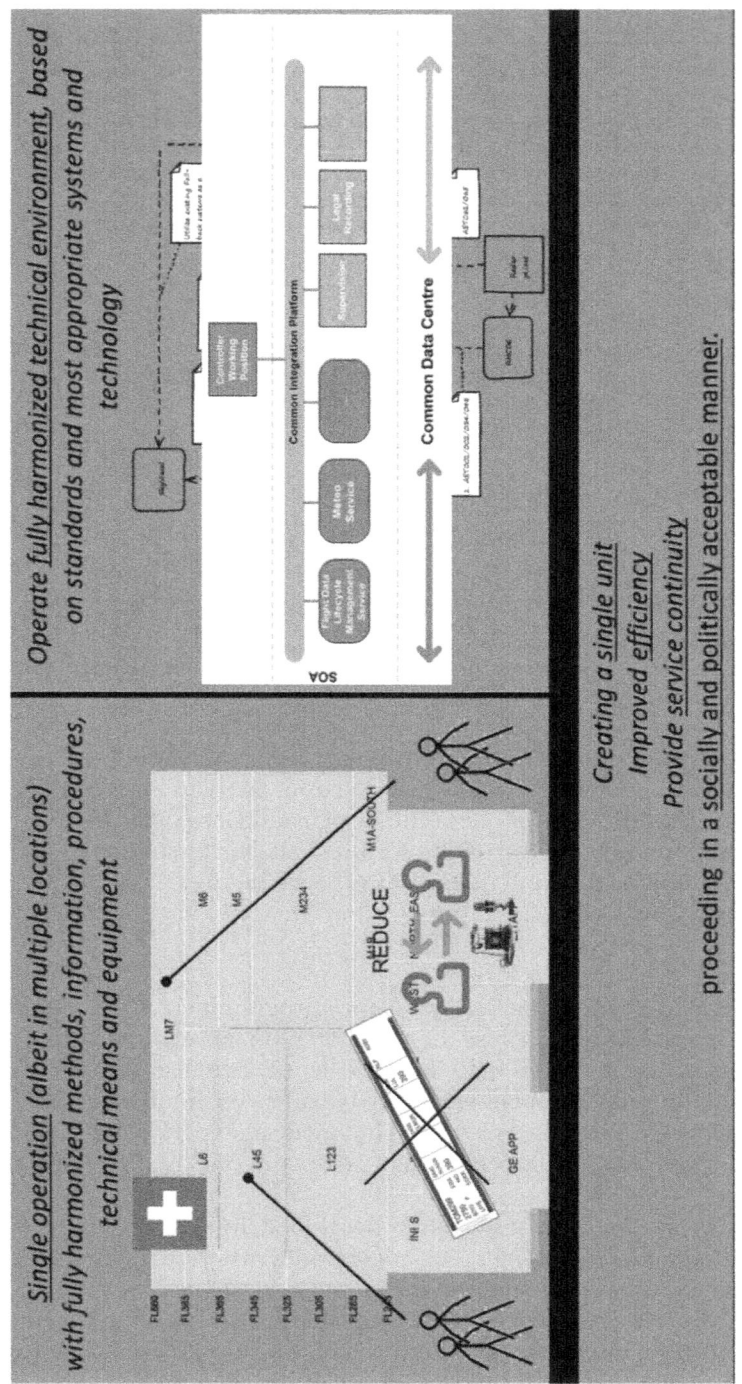

Figure 20.4 The Virtual Centre programme as a sketch

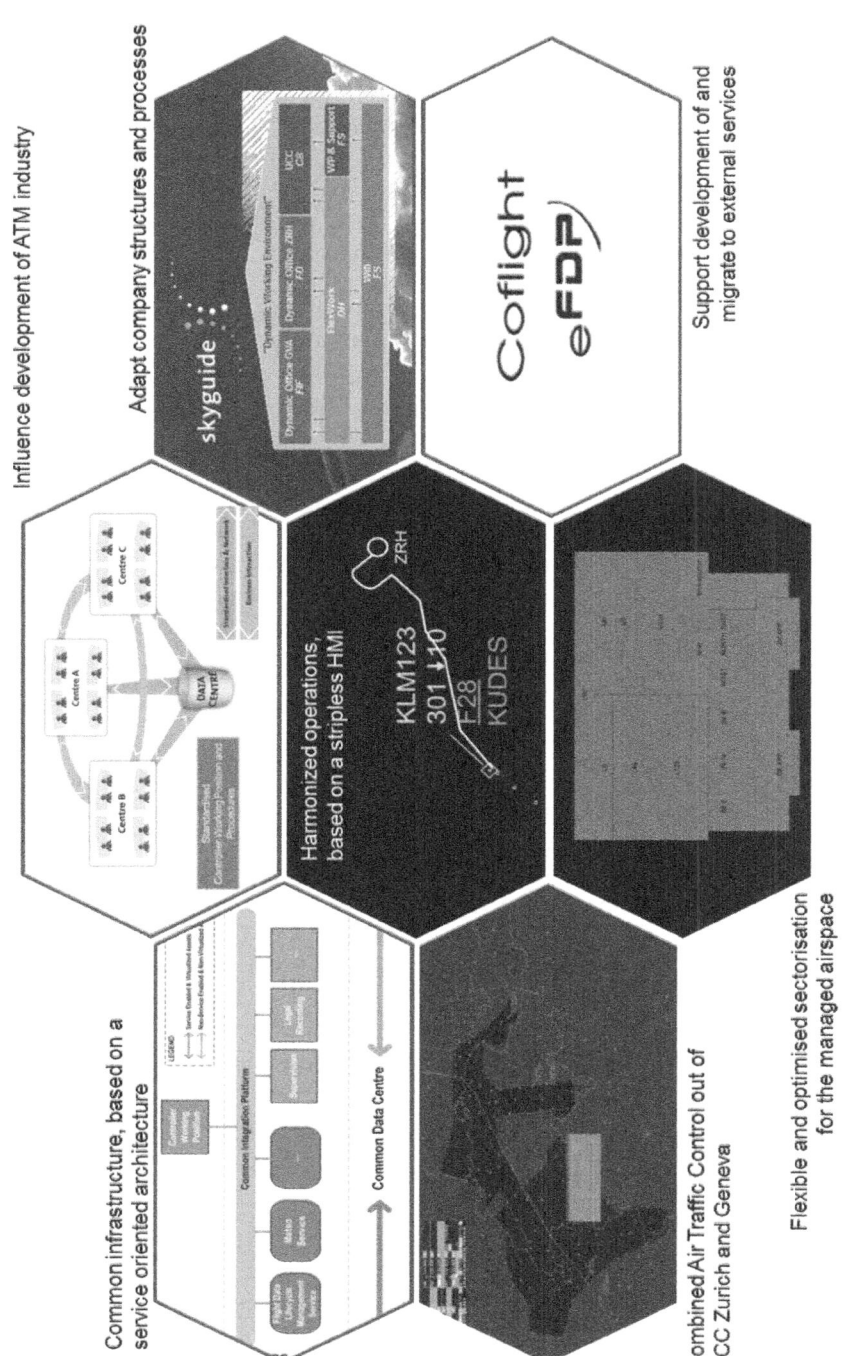

Figure 20.5 The seven building blocks

perhaps typical for an ANSP, the performance with our customers is much more important than profit. An ANSP can easily reduce its cost basis, but that would have a negative impact on the customer. For example, reducing the headcount will produce delays with the carriers (a really unwanted effect). This situation also forces the ANSPs to focus on four different targets – not just financial performance but also: safety, capacity for our customers and the environment.

To overcome this issue, the cost-benefit analysis was calculated and presented threefold. The costs of the programme were compared to:

- pure (internal) cost reductions and impact on future revenue streams;
- additional benefits for the customers (shorter routes, low delay rates), environment (noise and emissions) and the wider economy (ensure service continuity);
- additional, non-financially measurable benefits like safety and perception/positioning of skyguide in the European context.

Net present value calculations were made. While the costs of delays were quite easy to calculate, the programme failed to evaluate environmental cost (mainly noise), and safety (mainly because of ethical reasons). In addition, a kind of cost comparison was conducted. The team evaluated the costs of alternative ways for reaching the same safety, capacity and environmental objectives and put these (avoided costs or investments) into the benefits part of the cost-benefit analysis.

Managing the change

The structural set-up of the company is dominated by accountability to a single person. As a consequence, the line organization is very powerful. Projects and programme with their cross-functional, integrative role have almost no direct power.

Therefore, it was imperative for the management of the programme to have the whole top management team integrated in the steering of the programme. But this was not sufficient. Because skyguide is an organization of highly qualified experts, many operationally driven decisions are not taken by the board, but by the experts on the lower hierarchical levels. Thus it was important for the programme to have the directly involved line managers at the table, too. The portfolio steering body of the programme (called UMB+) was used to do this integration work, although it was set up primarily to steer the project portfolio within the programme. The governance structure is illustrated in Figure 20.6.

Virtual Centre programme organization

As could be expected, the CEO is owner of the Virtual Centre programme. Consequently, the programme reports directly to the steering committee, headed by the CEO, comprising all executive board members, a member of the unions, a representative of the military and the head of corporate development. Because of the impact of the programme on the company, it reports regularly also to the board of directors.

The VC project portfolio (projects related to the programme) is also managed within the programme itself, but is also integrated in the normal project portfolio

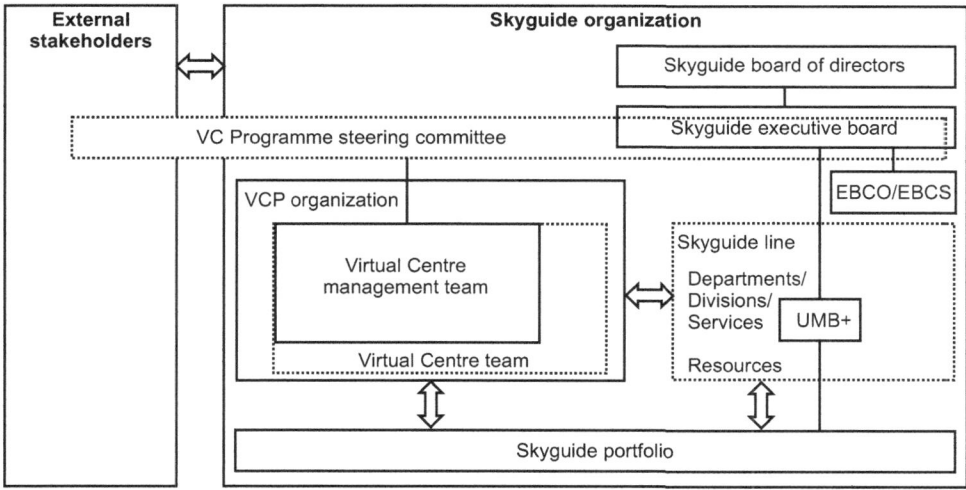

Figure 20.6 The governance structure

processes within the company. This provides the programme management with the opportunity to discuss things such as prioritization within and across projects directly with the organizational unit heads.

In addition to a programme management office (PMO), the programme management incorporates five core functions, which are shared across the programme:

1. safety, security and human factors;
2. compliance and regulations;
3. communications;
4. business architecture;
5. IT architecture.

The organization is shown in Figure 20.7.

The execution is managed twofold: The projects with clear sets of deliverables are implemented under sponsorship of the most affected line manager and executed by a dedicated project manager. The programme is accountable for the integration, and ensuring that all projects are launched according to the programme plan and that the benefits can be realized. The link between the VC programme and projects is implemented on various levels:

- on programme steering committee level where all top (line) managers are involved;
- on portfolio level, where all project sponsors are involved;
- on project steering level through direct participation of the programme director;
- on project management level through involvement of all project managers;
- on architecture level where detailed solutions are discussed.

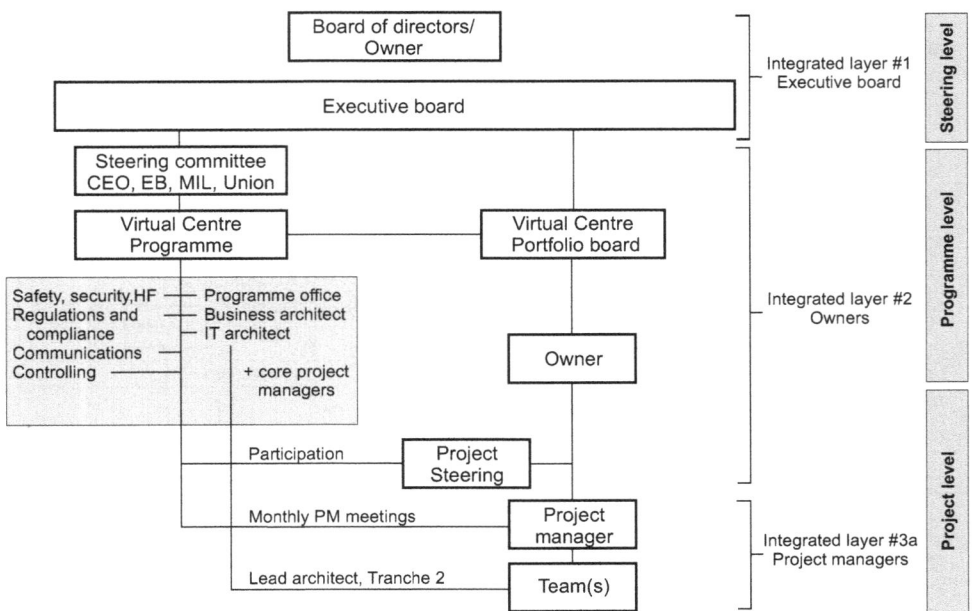

Figure 20.7 Programme organization

Organizing the execution

To manage the execution properly, a stepwise approach was selected. The agile programme management approach (DSDM Consortium, 2014) was selected for the underlying theoretical framework. Four main tranches were defined, to keep the development under control, as follows:

- Tranche 1 shall provide fully technical means for the ATCO, including electronic coordination between the sectors. The paper strip shall be completely eliminated.
- Tranche 2 shall demonstrate the feasibility of sharing traffic across centres. The top levels of the managed airspace (FL375 and above) shall be managed from either site, in an identical way, throughout all traffic situations 24/365.
- Tranche 3 shall provide the roll-out of the concept of sharing traffic to all sectors of the upper airspace into more challenging geographical sectors.
- Tranche 4 shall bring the implementation of remotely produced services (for example centralized services available cross countries, and new ways of providing ATM services in a supranational harmonized operational concept).

It is imperative that tranches are prepared well in advance. For example, the implementation of external, remotely produced services for Tranche 4 must be prepared well in advance, because these kinds of services do not exist today. Therefore, even though Tranche 4 will not come until 2021, preparatory studies and projects are already in execution. The 'roadmap' of this programme is shown in Figure 20.8.

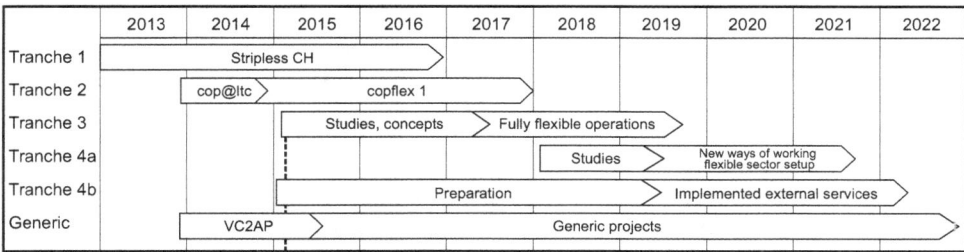

Figure 20.8 Roadmap of the Virtual Centre programme

Funding

The Virtual Centre programme is financed mainly through CAPEX (capital expenditure) and the amortization is refinanced by the customers through unit rates. Every year the funding is allocated to initiatives in a well-organized project portfolio process. This process overlaps the project budgeting process and often leads to significant changes in projects and programmes.

To minimize the financial burden to the customer, the programme management team regularly seeks additional funding. Funding could come from European or national research programmes like SESAR or NRPs (National Research Programmes are the Swiss government's research funding tool).

Because realization of the Virtual Centre is demonstrating the practical feasibility of 'shared infrastructure between centres', enabling new ways of cooperation of European ANSP (which in turn is an element of study in SESAR), skyguide is seeking membership in SESAR. But because the external funding bodies require sticking to specific rules (for example, SESAR projects have a chance for 50 per cent EU funding if there are at least three European partners involved), projects often have to be adjusted time wise or content wise.

A second important external funding provision is envisaged to come from national governmental agencies. From an economic standpoint, the availability of seamless services (especially of service continuity even in case of a complete disaster at one centre) is crucial for the Swiss economy. For instance, a study in the Netherlands about the consequences to the Dutch society of a potential total failure of Schiphol Airport predicted disastrous results within just a couple of days!

Service continuity – without building a contingency centre – is one of the core objectives of the Virtual Centre programme, and therefore the programme should be at least cofinanced by public funding.

Risk management

The risk management process follows long-standing common practice (PMI, 2006). A series of workshops were held with the Virtual Centre management team members with the objective of identifying the important risks related to the programme itself (not the risks of the core projects). Based on this list, an evaluation in terms of likelihood and impact was done by every team member individually. The generated synopsis was very interesting. These individual assessments produced varied results. Consequently, another workshop followed where all ratings were intensively discussed.

This discussion about the differing perceptions of the risks and their possible impact was more straightforward than the evaluation itself. It offered very interesting insights into risk scenarios and possible measures for keeping the risks under control on programme level. Finally, the risk process was incorporated into the risk process of the whole company. Today, the risks of the Virtual Centre programme are fully integrated, managed and reported regularly to top management and the board of directors.

Processes, tools and technologies

All projects in the Virtual Centre programme follow a predefined stage process, similar to all other projects within skyguide. A stage-gating process (implemented in 2013) is used as follows:

- The first stage is a 'Change Proposal' where the sponsor or the programme manager requests a change (usually a project). An accepted change proposal puts the change into the portfolio.
- Gate 1 represents the start of the concept phase.
- Gate 2 represents the start of solution development.
- Gate 3 represents the going life and includes the important ODD (operational deployment date) with many requested approvals.
- Gate 4 represents the close-out of the project.

Gates (and change modification requests needed to adjust significant deviations from the original plans) are controlled and managed on Virtual Centre programme level in a separate body called 'unit management board' (UMB+). The programme itself controls the projects belonging to it although decisions made on UMB+ level have to be confirmed by the executive board.

A simplified earned value management process was implemented. Every project has planned deliverables, with budgets allocated to the deliverables. Progress measures during each project's lifespan use simple indicators as follows:

- 0 per cent, not yet started;
- 20 per cent started;
- 80 per cent completed;
- 100 per cent, finished and approved.

This method is easier to implement than the fully-fledged earned value measurement approach but is adequate for steering the projects on programme level.

Programme charter

All important aspects of the Virtual Centre programme are documented in the programme charter, which is signed by the executive board members and the Virtual

Centre programme director. It forms the mandate given by the executive board to the Virtual Centre programme management team and contains the following elements:

- background;
- rationale (business requirements, corporate strategy, corporate mission, expected benefits);
- the blueprint;
- mission;
- main objective;
- scope;
- outcomes;
- expected end-state;
- expected benefits;
- necessary conditions, assumptions and constraints (political, economic, social/human, technological, environmental, legal);
- impacts on skyguide (operations, technics, safety, quality, security, finances, culture and personnel, national and international business relations, governance and line organization);
- success factors and show stoppers;
- environment and structure;
- external stakeholders (European institutions and organizations, other international entities of interest, national regulatory bodies);
- programme governance (skyguide organization and key roles);
- programme organization (structure, organization and key roles);
- stakeholder engagement;
- programme management;
- benefits management;
- change management;
- communication management;
- compliance management;
- financial management;
- human factors and human performance management;
- issue management;
- material management;
- outcomes management;
- portfolio management;
- quality management;
- requirements management;
- risk management;
- safety management;
- security management;
- annexes.

Maintaining focus

In such a long-lasting programme it is very important to keep focus on the programme's outcome, although there are changes within and around the company that influence the programme, and have to be selectively taken on board. To keep the focus, the following tasks have been implemented:

- Deliver results. It is imperative that results can be delivered on a very regular basis. Delivery also helps people to start believing in the idea.
- Celebrate success. Success is celebrated and made visible at every meaningful moment. Success helps people to start believing in the outcome and the Virtual Centre gets reality.
- Involve people, not just communicate. It is much more important to involve people than simply to provide communications. Various channels have to be established to allow regular discussions with the people involved throughout the whole programme.
- Avoid brand erosion. The brand of the Virtual Centre – after the idea became known on a European basis – is more and more used by others with a complete different meaning. Also within Switzerland, little jokes were invented. This has to be prevented and the original intention of the programme has to be communicated continually.

Major difficulties with the delivery of a big project part in 2014 (three months' delay and a 6 per cent cost overrun) also showed an important insight. Clearly such problems are commonly recognized as being negative events. But they can also present a positive aspect. If a problem can be overcome through an orchestrated common effort, it can weld together all the people involved.

Lessons learned

The following lessons have been learned after four years of this (at least) 12-year programme:

- A fundamental change through a programme can hardly be successful through the programme alone: changing the organizational set-up of the company was essential to unlock endless discussions.
- A very high involvement of the top management alone is not enough, especially in an expert company. The subordinated managers and the staff had to be involved much more intensively and directly.
- In a merger of equals, none of the existing solutions can be chosen successfully. In the context of the Virtual Centre programme, only by creating new ways of working could the change from both former worlds be successful. Neither the Geneva nor the Zurich way of using strips could be implemented Swiss-wide. Only removing the strips and working with technology unlocked the situation.
- A change takes its due time. The very complex Virtual Centre programme needs at least 12 years.
- Commonly agreed barriers against change have to be overcome: In the ANSP industry, safety is always the first key to block possible changes. After overcoming that hurdle, pride was next ('it is impossible to make something better or more efficient than the way it has been done so far'). Only after overcoming these hurdles was it possible to discuss options.

- Identify milestones and stage gates. A long-lasting change programme needs clear decision points with distinct, meaningful outcomes where management can make decisions and adjust the programme as necessary.
- A big-bang approach will most probably fail. It is impossible to plan a programme completely and precisely for such a long period. Thus a more agile approach is needed, followed tranche by tranche with decreasing errors in prediction of results and tasks.
- Fundamental change requires strong belief in the idea from real leaders, from both management and those involved in executing the programme.

References and further reading

DSDM Consortium (2014), *Agile Programme Management Handbook*. Dover: Buckland Media Group.

Eurocontrol (2014), <www.eurocontrol.int/dossiers/single-european-sky>. Brussels, Belgium.

Hofstede, G. (2014), <http://geert-hofstede.com/switzerland.html>.

ICAO (2006), *Convention on International Civil Aviation*. Montreal, Canada: International Civil Aviation Organization.

IPMA (2006), *ICB – IPMA Competence Baseline for Project Management*. Nijkerk, The Netherlands: International Project Management Association.

IPMA (2015), *Competence Baseline for Individuals*. Nijkerk, The Netherlands: International Project Management Association.

OGC (2011), *Managing Successful Programmes*. Norwich: The Stationery Office.

PMI (2006), *The Standard for Program Management*, Newton Square PA: Project Management Institute.

Sedlmayer, M. R. (2008), 'The Architecture for Effective Strategy Implementation: Value Creation through Integration of the PMO into the Strategy Process'. In IPMA, *Values and Ethics in Project Management*, Zurich: International Project Management Association.

skyguide – 'The Virtual Centre Model'. <www.skyguide.ch/en/company/innovation/virtual-centre-model/>. Geneva, Switzerland.

skyguide – 'What we stand for'. <www.skyguide.ch/en/company/vision-mission/>. Geneva, Switzerland.

skyguide.<www.skyguide.ch/fileadmin/user_upload/publications/brochures/E_sky_chiffres_et_faits_13_new.pdf>. Geneva, Switzerland.

Weick, K. E. and Sutcliffe, K. M. (2007), *Managing the Unexpected*, San Francisco, CA: Jossey-Boss.

Chapter 21

Programme Management Offices

Eileen Roden, Lindsay Scott and Dennis Lock

The term programme management office (PMO) has acquired several meanings as programme management has become more common. For the purposes of this chapter, we understand a programme management office to be 'a temporary collection of functions that provide decision-enabling and delivery support services to a programme'.

Introduction

Many of the PMO characteristics described in this chapter can apply also to PMOs that provide services to multiple projects and/or programmes. That kind of PMO is often a permanent office (called a departmental or enterprise programme management office). However, our focus is on a temporary programme management office that provides services to a single programme.

A programme might also have separate *project* management offices (confusingly also called PMOs) established for some or all of the projects within the programme. These project management offices may undertake some (though not all) of the services discussed here, alongside local duties specific to their projects. Please note that we have used the abbreviation PMO in this chapter only for programme management offices and have not abbreviated portfolio or project management offices – hopefully that will avoid confusion.

It is not always necessary for all the functions of a PMO to be located in the same place. Those locations are most likely to be influenced by the geographic and organizational scope of the programme.

Reporting lines

Ideally and commonly the PMO will have a manager to oversee its various functions and services. The PMO manager will typically report to the programme manager. However, in an organization with a permanent departmental or enterprise PMO, the manager of a temporary PMO could have two reporting lines – one to the permanent PMO and the other to the programme manager.

Figure 21.1 shows how a temporary PMO might fit within a large organization's full complement of programme and project management offices (designed to support the various change initiatives). Each organization will need to design and implement a structure aligned to the blend of programme and project management activity that exists within it.

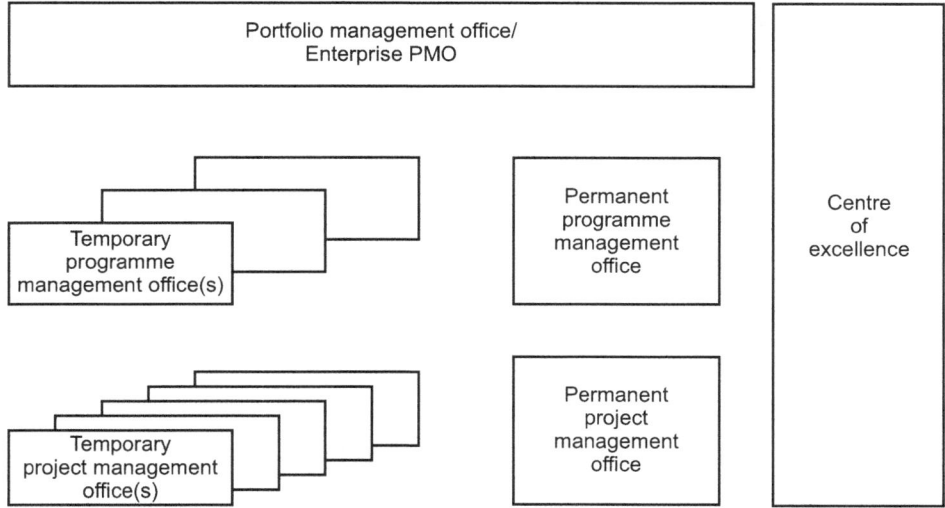

Figure 21.1 The full range of PMO types within organizations

PMO functions and services

Using the nine-quadrant [sic] model (Pinto *et al.*, 2010), a PMO can be classified as strategic, tactical and/or operational (Figure 21.2).

Strategic PMOs provide functions and services that link programme activity to the strategy of the organization. That might include, for example, providing programme information to the enterprise PMO to support the organization's capacity planning at portfolio or organization level.

Tactical PMOs provide functions and services that focus on the delivery of specific programmes. Examples could be maintaining a consolidated programme schedule, or the development of reporting standards.

Operational PMOs provide functions and services that support individuals involved in the delivery of programmes and their associated projects. That could include anything from coaching and mentoring to the production of project team meeting minutes.

There is no defined list of functions and services that must be provided by every PMO. The range of functions and services provided will be defined and agreed for the specific PMO in question, with the associated costs and benefits of each validated within the programme's business case. Similarly, where projects within a programme require a dedicated project management office, the range of functions and services which that provides should be allowed for in the project business case.

Where a permanent or enterprise PMO exists, specific requirements or constraints should be imposed on it so that it aligns with existing corporate or departmental functions and services (for example relating to reporting requirements).

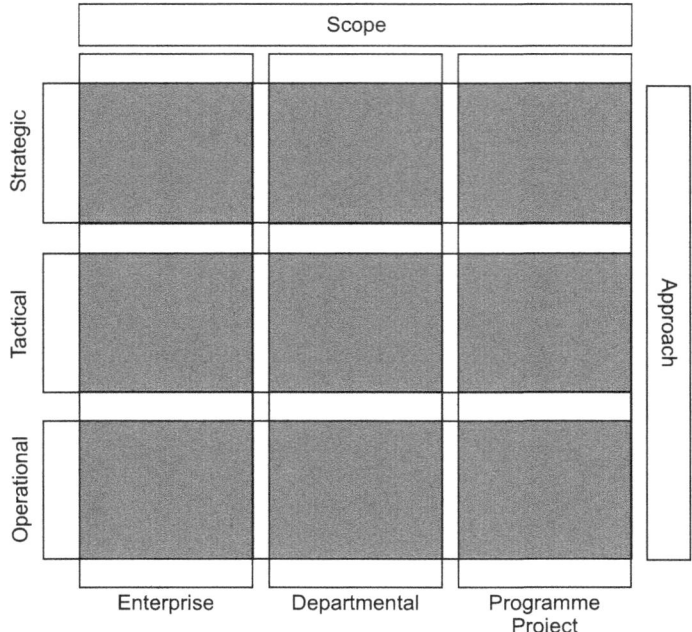

Figure 21.2 The three segments resulting from the relationship between the scope and the approach relationship

Specific PMO functions and services

A PMO can provide services to many stakeholders, both within and outside the programme (Figure 21.3). Some of those services are summarized here. These functions and services will enhance programme delivery and Figure 21.4 shows some aspects of the added value which a well-managed PMO can bring to a programme.

Compatibility of systems and methodologies

One fundamentally important job of the enterprise PMO is to ensure that all programme management and project management systems are compatible with each other across all projects and programmes throughout the organization. That compatibility includes the scheduling methodologies, project management software, reporting methods, terminology and (although often difficult) things such as numbering and coding systems. In this sense the PMO oversees project management offices within the programme. Figure 21.5 illustrates this overarching aspect and also summarizes typical PMO functions.

Task scheduling

One of the principal reasons why project management offices were formed in the first place was to carry out task scheduling, usually using some form of critical path

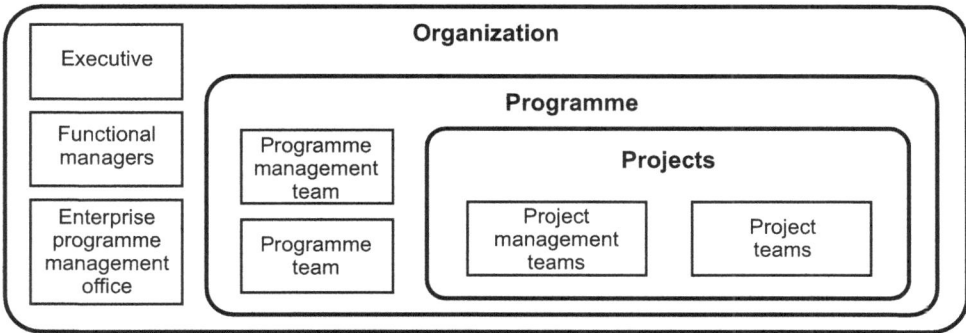

Figure 21.3 Programme management office stakeholders

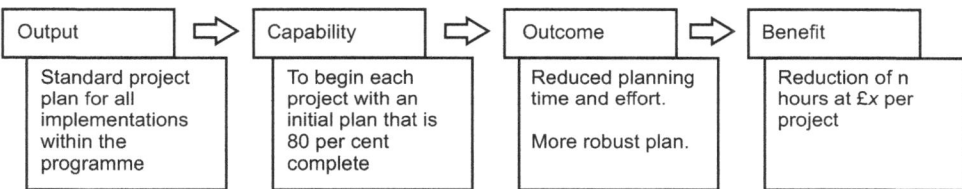

Figure 21.4 Value of the programme management office

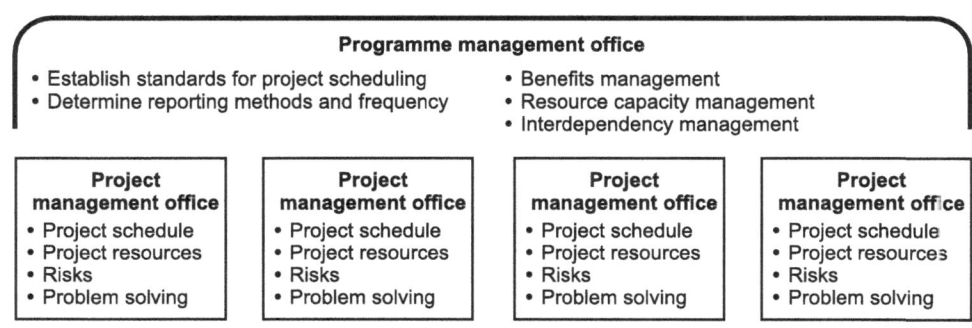

Figure 21.5 The programme management office as an overarching entity

network analysis. That function is also carried out in today's PMOs. Scheduling sets all task priorities, is the basis for progress control and reporting, and is an important factor in resource scheduling. We assume that all those involved in programme management will be familiar with project scheduling methods and there is no need to elaborate further on those here.

Resource management

The objective of resource management is to ensure that the programme has the right resources available at the right time to deliver the programme successfully. Resource management includes establishing the relative priorities and resource requirements of all the individual tasks and ideally all those data should come from one or more critical path networks. Typical PMO resource management services include the following:

- resource requirements capture across all projects;
- providing or helping to provide a consolidated programme resource plan;
- scheduling and deployment of staff across the projects and programme;
- forecasting and providing what-if analyses;
- demand and capacity management;
- management reporting;
- recruitment support and forecasting (in-house and where required for contractors);
- training support.

Resource management deals mainly with human resources, but anything that can be quantified in numbers can also be scheduled by the same methods (and that includes cash flows, given the right level of expertise). Resource management at its very basic level means being able to provide the programme manager with:

- an overall view of the resources needed (people and otherwise);
- whether or not those resources are available;
- making sure they are allocated to the right projects and suitably prioritized.

Low level resource management services in a PMO tend to concentrate on human resources. A competent PMO can forecast future needs, which is invaluable either for recruiting staff or for making arrangements with temporary staff agencies. This function can be a challenge, requiring mature processes and robust tools. It can also sometimes demand ingenuity. The PMO should be able to provide a consolidated view of resource requirements across all projects within the programme. It should also hold a database of the available resource pool, aligned with individual staff capabilities.

An advanced service from the PMO would be to carry out 'what-if' simulations and scenario analyses, with the ability to manipulate resource data and schedules to provide differing outcomes that could help the programme manager or superior management to make decisions.

Resource management is seriously neglected in the literature but there are detailed descriptions with illustrated examples in Lock (2013), where those who need to can also read about task scheduling and other basic project management methods.

Budgets, timesheets and cost control

One important function of a PMO is the monitoring and reporting of costs against budgets. That usually requires close collaboration with the organization's accounts department (more specifically the cost and management accountants). PMOs are often responsible for administering timesheets, which can in some circumstances include certifying that the times entered are correct. Absolute timesheet accuracy is usually an unrealistic goal, but reasonable accuracy in timesheet entries is important for several reasons which include:

- comparison of actual times against estimated times for tasks:
- establishing records that might prove useful in comparative cost estimating for future similar work;
- supporting invoices, where programme or project management services are being charged out to an external client.

Benefits management

The PMO objective in benefits management is to ensure that benefits identified are realized throughout delivery and completion of the programme. That function includes, but is not limited to the following services:

- creation of templates for benefit management strategy, benefits profiles, and so forth;
- facilitation of benefits management workshops;
- setting up a benefits realization management system;
- tracking and reporting on benefits realization.

The programme office is initially concerned with ensuring that the standards and methods for benefits management are agreed and that the guidelines with supporting documentation and templates are created. Guidance stemming from an organization (enterprise) PMO might already exist. If they do not, the PMO works with the programme manager to establish the process and the role that the programme office will play in supporting benefits management.

Generally, programme offices provide the following two core services for benefits realization management:

1. Establishing the benefits management system, which captures the initial benefits identification and analysis and then tracks benefit realization throughout programme lifecycle.
2. The PMO then establishes a reporting cycle around the benefits data.

In advanced PMOs (where the programme is particularly large or complex) there could be a need to establish a role dedicated to benefits realization. That work broadens the focus on benefits across the programme by using more advanced methods to embed value management, opportunity exploitation and benefits realization. This dedicated role is also often that of a mentor, developing the relevant programme and project managers' personal skills.

Managing interdependencies

The objective in managing interdependencies is to consolidate and integrate project level plans and activities into a programme level view to enable better planning and control. Contributing tasks include the following:

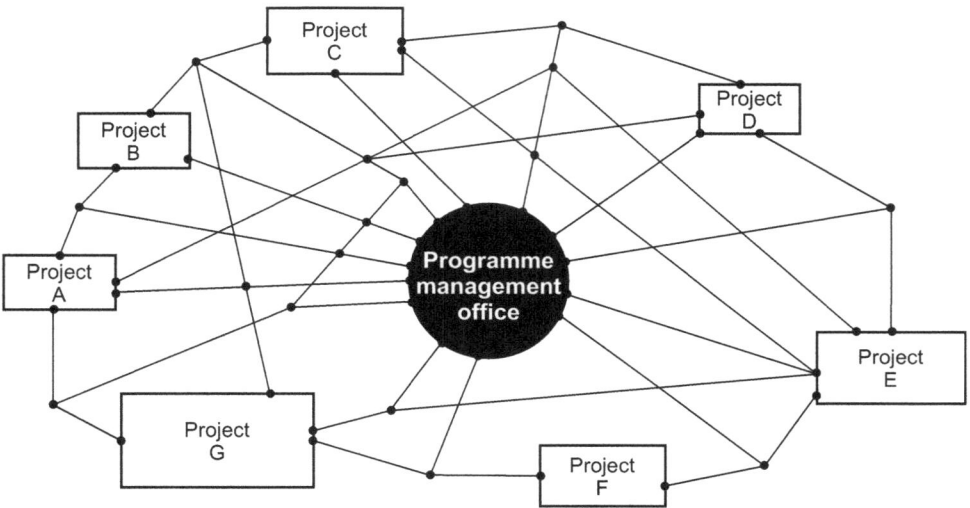

Figure 21.6 The programme management office hub

- setting up the 'programme management dashboard' (infrastructure) to enable reporting;
- creating standardized reporting schedules;
- providing consolidated programme plans and schedules;
- creating registers for risks and problems at programme level;
- programme systems support.

At its very basic level, a PMO should be able to provide the most current project schedules from Projects A, B and so on. The programme office should also be able to provide a programme-level plan which includes all the major milestones from each of the projects – to produce a consolidated plan. As a PMO matures and gains credibility it may provide a level of assurance, provide constructive challenge and scrutiny to the various elements and make recommendations for corrective actions.

The PMO is often referred to the hub or central point of a programme. The more projects that exist within the programme, the greater the amount of information and communication required to make sure everyone is working towards the same goal. If all information can be made to flow through a central hub like a PMO there is a greater chance that the PMO will become the 'single source of truth' (Figure 21.6).

Skills within the PMO

Clearly a PMO needs appropriate skills and experience to deliver the required functions and services. Within each programme office it is likely that there will be people with different levels of skills, ability and experience. Job titles will obviously vary from one organization to another, but the roles of PMO members can be grouped into three levels, as follows.

1. Aside from the PMO manager, a programme office needs someone to provide the basics of programme support (who might be called a PMO coordinator). That person or group will provide the core services of reporting, planning and risk/problem tracking.
2. More advanced services include consolidation and analysis (in areas such as what-if? analyses and scenario planning) tend to be delivered by a more experienced PMO analyst. Planning specialists are typically employed when the programme is vast and the intricacies of planning require a particularly focused and experienced capability.
3. Other specialist roles include people who are expert in particular tools and methods, resource managements and quality assurance. One or more financial specialists are often needed (sometimes known as cost engineers or PMO accountants).

Clearly the number and skill levels of the PMO team will be driven by the size and complexity of the programme and the range of functions and services provided. Here are three examples:

- PMO coordinator; duties include reporting, planning, risk/problem management and secretariat jobs;
- PMO analyst; carries out analysis and forecasting, scenario predictions and assists in decision-making;
- PMO specialist, who is a person with expert and specific skills as required.

Strategic and operational PMO functions and services

So far the emphasis has been on tactical functions and services. Because the typical PMO is very much intended for supporting programme delivery activities it might not have a great strategic role.

One area where the PMO contribution has a link to the strategic elements of the business is in relation to reporting on actual progress. Programmes and projects are the actualization of strategic direction for an organization and the programme office might be required to report on how that actualization is progressing. That will take the form of reports, statements and (possibly) balance sheets.

The PMO can also perform more operational roles. For example it could provide consultancy and support to individuals within the programme and projects. With more experienced PMO managers this could, for instance, take the form of mentoring and guiding junior or new programme managers.

PMO staff can also provide direct support to the projects and project management offices, especially in areas such as training, mentoring, and facilitation.

Tools

PMOs rely heavily on technology to enable them to provide the functions and services they offer. In recent years there has been an explosion in the different types of project management software on offer. Gartner's annual series of research-based reports called Magic Quadrant aims to provide unbiased insight into the popular tools on offer and is a respected source.

Regardless of the advance in project management software, the most popular tools in programme offices today are still Microsoft Excel for reporting and analysis; Microsoft Project for individual project plans; and Microsoft SharePoint for the storage of project and programme documentation. While these tools are popular, the most common complaints are that they are labour intensive because rolling up plans, looking at dependencies and trying to provide good analysis requires a lot of complex formulae to make it work. Also (personal comment from DL) the most popular project management software is by no means the best. The best software might not be the cheapest or easiest to use and some will require special training. Choosing and using an appropriate project management tool relies heavily on upfront and ongoing investment and, rightly or wrongly, in the early days of setting up a programme office that is often way down the list in order of priorities. There are guidelines (with a questionnaire) on choosing project management software in Lock (2013).

A programme office working as part of a departmental or organization portfolio office might already have access to enterprise-level project management tools and can use that functionality for the programme. Yet there are smaller and less expensive tools that can do specific jobs for the programme office. One danger in that approach is that it could lead to a proliferation of software that is incompatible with company standard and will not interface with other systems in the organization. In large programmes that affect more than one company it might be essential that the software used in all the companies is compatible, at least for the exchange of data and access to a common database.

PMO structures

In many cases a PMO is established as a temporary structure, in place only for the duration of the programme. Of course, for large programmes lasting for several years 'temporary' is a relative term and a PMO could last for several years before finally being closed.

The PMO structure will be influenced by the location, programme scope and size, staff available, the services required by the programme manager and the authorized budget.

Temporary PMO structures

The following temporary PMO examples highlight a few of the possible variations.

Variations dependent upon PMO size

The smallest PMO known to exist is the 'Programme office of one' (POO) which denotes one person providing a subset of services. The POO (or should we say perhaps the POO person) will report directly to the programme manager and be responsible for the main services of reporting, interdependencies, planning and resource management – a busy person indeed.

The next size up from a POO is a POT (the 'Program office of two'). The extra person will allow extended services or could provide 'granular' levels of support in key areas.

Interestingly (largely anecdotally), most PMOs are either POOs or POTs. This is mainly due either to the existence of a larger permanent PMO elsewhere in the organization (on which the programme can call for services) or the programme is not sufficiently large or complex to require anything more.

PMOs based on location

The larger and more complex a programme is, the larger the PMO becomes, both in the range of services it offers and the number of people needed to deliver those services. As a general rule, the programme office function should cost between 3 and 5 per cent of the programme's life costs (Roden, 2013). Unsurprisingly, these costs arise mostly from providing the PMO staff.

The numbers and types of resources required to staff the programme office will depend on several factors including:

- the overall maturity of programme delivery in the organization;
- the state of existing processes and tools;
- the nature of the programme itself (complex, locations, third party involvement and so on);
- the peaks and troughs of the programme lifecycle.

Typically a large, complex programme with many projects and interdependencies will require resources that are specialized in certain service areas. Within the PMO there will be resources that purely provide reporting information, planners who maintain the programme plan, cost controllers overseeing the budget requirements, and communications coordinators managing (and where necessary recording) information flows.

A large PMO of this nature will typically be found in one location, reporting to the programme manager and within easy physical reach of the programme (and possibly) project teams (co-location).

For national or international programmes, the PMO will become a virtual entity for many people working on the programme. The PMO staff might be placed in one location, typically where the programme manager spends most of his or her time. Alternatively, the PMO staff might be dispersed, working at different office or home locations.

A dispersed PMO relies heavily on advanced systems and tools in order to carry out most of its work. In programmes which 'follow-the-sun' during their lifecycles the PMO must be able to hand over effectively to its remote colleagues, so that they can pick up the work.

PMOs based on resourcing options

The typical structures described so far are internal PMOs that support an organization's own change initiatives. For organizations such as consulting and professional services firms, the programme is a commercial venture for a client. In these cases there might be two PMOs, one within and serving the external consultancy and the other within the client organization. Each PMO will provide services to its own organization. Both PMOs will be required to work together to provide information and support for the overall programme.

Outsourced PMOs

Outsourced PMO services are becoming increasingly common as an option for reducing costs or gaining the required PMO skills. Outsourcing works well when the role carried out is very process and data driven (principally reporting) and the objectives are clear. Then there can also be an internal PMO that outsources the data collation and reporting aspects, while retaining other duties themselves.

The arrangement will obviously be arranged to suit both the hirer and the external provider because two PMOs are never quite the same.

The PMO lifecycle

Where the PMO is a temporary structure (unlike a permanent enterprise PMO) its lifecycle will clearly be influenced by the programme lifecycle. Here are typical lifecycle stages:

- decide the PMO functions, structure and staffing;
- establish the PMO;
- start up the PMO functions;
- check on the PMO performance as the programme proceeds and, if necessary, make adjustments (such as providing instructions, additional training and, where necessary, making staff changes);
- close the PMO and, if possible, redeploy the staff;
- keep notes of lessons learned that could be useful for setting up a PMO in the future.

The timing and duration of each stage will clearly depend on the needs of the programme and on any existing PMO services that might be available within the organization.

Realizing the value that a PMO might bring could result in setting one up sooner than strictly necessary for the programme. However, a PMO set up before creation of a programme business case (which itself would need to include the costs and potential benefits associated with the PMO) would be unlikely to give due consideration to the functions and services required and valued by the stakeholders. The resultant early PMO might then contain a set of 'expected' functions and services rather than those that are essential for adding value to the programme.

Designing and setting up a PMO

The PMO design (structure, reporting line, functions and services) needs to be tailored for the specific programme and will evolve as the scope and definition of the programme is developed. It is important to maintain a clear definition of the PMO scope throughout, along with an understanding of when each function and service will be required by the programme. Rad and Levin (2002) remind us that 'attention should be paid to the project objectives in terms of administrative placement, schedule, cost and metrics by which the project is measured'. Tjahjana *et al.* (2009) recommend the use of a Charter to document and maintain a shared understanding of the programme office's vision and mission, objectives, responsibilities, critical success factors, stakeholders and structure.

If there is an enterprise PMO, its manager and the programme manager (with input from key stakeholders) should design and set up the new PMO. Hatfield (2008) suggests that three specific skills are required, namely:

- leadership conceptualization (for design);
- articulation (for gaining understanding and buy-in from resources and other stakeholders);
- execution (for the delivery of functions and services).

Where a PMO manager has limited conceptualization and articulation skills and experience, the design and set-up may be assisted by resources from the organization's portfolio office, centre of excellence or from external consultants.

Hallows (2002) suggests that PMOs take a year or longer to establish. Hobbs and Aubry's study (2010) also found that setting up a PMO will usually take between one and two years, depending on the type of PMO. Roden (2013) suggests that it is 'reasonable to allocate up to 10 per cent of the programme or project lifecycle timescale for the establishment of the temporary programme office', and provides the following sample timescales:

- where the programme lifecycle is 12 weeks, allow one week to set up its PMO;
- for a programme lasting six months, allow two and a half weeks to set up the PMO;
- for a 12-month programme, expect PMO establishment to take five weeks;
- allow 10 weeks for a 24-month programme.

As with the PMO design, set-up can 'evolve in small incremental steps' (Hallows, 2002), but it is recommended that a project/change management approach is taken to setting up the PMO. This further supports the assertion from Block and Frame (1998), who suggest that the establishment of a programme office is 'a visible sign of an organization's commitment to pursue project management in the best way possible'.

Using a project approach to setting up the PMO has many benefits including piloting, finessing and demonstrating the value of a number of the processes, procedures, tools and templates that will be used on the projects within the programme. If the PMO is to be set up in stages, more careful consideration will be required to ensure that the resources are kept balanced and able to provide the required programme support at all times. That could mean employing temporary staff for specialist tasks that will not be needed throughout all stages of the programme.

It is important to establish good working relationships between the PMO and all other departments and stakeholders in the programme. Those will stretch beyond the programme and project delivery teams to include (for example) the organization portfolio office, other delivery teams and operational business units. Building those relationships and explaining the role that the PMO will assume should be part of the programme's agreed stakeholder engagement strategy.

Managing the PMO

Axelos (2011) describes the PMO as 'the nerve centre and information hub of a programme'. It should be the centre for coordination of information, communication, monitoring and control at programme level.

The PMO office sets the heartbeat for the programme in terms of reporting. Clearly defined metrics and milestones require measuring and consistent, regular reporting throughout the life of the programme. A significant challenge for any PMO is the accuracy, integrity and timeliness of the information provided. From the outset, the PMO needs to establish its multiple roles, as described earlier in this chapter.

The services offered to the programme manager and the team(s) for programme governance and control are designed to support effective decision-making and assurance of due process. That should increase the speed, efficiency and effectiveness of programme and project delivery. For large projects within the programme, and where there is justification within the project's business case, one or more separate project management offices may need to be established, preferably by or in consultation with the PMO. The PMO manager will need to work closely with the project management office manager(s) to define clearly the demarcation of accountabilities between the PMO and the project management office(s). If a programme charter exists, that should clarify how the processes, procedures, tools and templates will be tailored for each project within the programme.

The PMO has a key role in the close-down of all projects within the programme, focusing on three clear areas for each project:

1. Information: if not already done, all project information must be integrated within the programme information repository. Then formal ownership has to be transferred from the project to the programme (access rights must also be updated accordingly). This will include any residual content of the project registers, such as risk/problem/actions and so on, which must be transferred to the relevant programme registers.
2. Benefits: benefits profiles will need to be updated to reflect the deliverables/ outputs from the project and, if it has not already done so, the PMO can begin measuring and reporting the associated benefits.
3. Lessons learned: the PMO is central to knowledge management across the programme and all its projects. That includes ensuring continuous improvement for the organization, benefiting from lessons learned from the programme and its constituent projects. Lessons from each project should be reviewed for application across the current programme and, through the enterprise

PMO, to other projects and programmes (current and future) throughout the organization.

Often, at the close of the project, incomplete documentation might be identified. A pragmatic approach should be taken to the effort needed to complete documentation retrospectively. That should only be undertaken for specific governance and legislative requirements or where there is likely to be specific need for reference to the documentation at a later stage.

The PMO might also be involved in the review and reallocation of the resources from the various programme projects.

Although the primary focus of a PMO is on supporting the delivery of the programme it is also necessary to review the performance of the PMO itself, to ensure that it continues to meet the needs of the programme.

Aubrey *et al.* (2011) did not find any general pattern that drives changes in PMOs but they did identify four reliable factors, which they name as:

- portfolio management and methods;
- collaboration and accountability;
- project management maturity and performance;
- work climate.

Throughout the life of the programme it is likely that one or more of these factors will change, so the PMO will need to reflect those changes in its functions and services. The PMO might also have a direct impact on the performance of the programme as a strategic driver for organizational excellence by enhancing the practices of execution management, governance and strategic change leadership (Donselaar *et al.*, 2011).

Closing down a PMO

It is important to distinguish between closing down the programme and closing its PMO. As we have already written, the PMO has a key role to play in the close of all projects. The PMO has a similar key role in closing down the programme.

Closing the programme has similar elements to those involved in closing each project (information, benefits and strategy delivery and, finally, lessons learned). Where there is an enterprise PMO, that might take the lead in determining the activities to be undertaken.

Where there is no enterprise PMO, programme ownership output (information, benefits and lessons learned) will have to be established. The worst case scenario is that the output is to be just archived or 'mothballed' without any defined ownership. Additional effort will then be needed to ensure that the various elements of the output are easily accessible at a future date.

The PMO has been the hub and nerve centre for the duration of the programme. During this time relationships have developed with key stakeholders outside the programme, within the wider delivery team, the enterprise PMO (if that exists) and operational business units. Some PMO processes, procedures and systems will have been integrated into the company operations and their sudden 'switch off' could have operational consequences. In that case a project/change management approach is recommended for the close-down and reallocation of programme office resources.

In some organizations, where the benefits of the programme office have been recognized, the organization might decide to create a divisional or enterprise PMO, building on the processes, procedures, systems and methods developed and used within the closing PMO. That can be done in parallel with closing down the PMO. However, the efforts and costs in doing that should not be allocated to the outgoing programme, but must be authorized through a separate business case.

Challenges and trends for the PMO of the future

Challenges

A PMO within an organization with a mature approach to programmes and projects, with well-developed and skilled staff and the right tools to support delivery in a flexible and adaptive way should face few challenges. But a PMO operating without these optimum conditions can expect to face challenges from the very people it supports and serves. Some of these challenges are as follows:

- *Bureaucracy.* A charge often levelled at the PMO is that it is 'overly bureaucratic' which relates to the problems that can occur when trying to find the balance between supporting the delivery side (the programme manager, project managers and teams) and providing the oversight required by stakeholders like senior managers. Too much process and control or rigidly enforced standards tend to be seen in immature delivery organizations and are often a consequence of repeatedly failing programmes or projects. Also, an under-skilled PMO team can find it difficult to bring pragmatism into their work; they stick doggedly to check-lists and processes without understanding the nuances of project and programme delivery.
- *Funding.* If the programme manager sets the business case for the PMO resources and services needed, the funding will come directly from the programme. In organizations where a departmental or enterprise portfolio office already exists there will also be additional requirements needed from the PMO (which the programme manager might not want and might therefore not see the value or justification for those extra costs). That could include, for example, providing additional reporting requirements needed at the department or enterprise level.
- *Services.* Programme office functions and services have to be current and in line with customer expectations. New services require time to embed and become standard. Some service areas are considered to be too difficult to implement at all. A frequently highlighted service area causing a challenge for PMOs is resource management (ESI International, 2015). Within many knowledge economy based organizations there is still a lack of organizational processes, standards or tools for allocating the workforce. That has a knock-on effect for resource capacity planning, allocation and demand management at programme and project levels. The basics of understanding current resource capacity and capability levels in an organization are simply not available, offering nothing to the PMO to benefit from. Further, resource management at programme/project level also

suffers from a lack of investment – not only in creating a robust system but also in the supporting technology.

*   *Technology.* Investment in technology to support the work of the programme office is still lacking, regardless of the fact that there has been an explosion of project management tools available. The ability to use increasingly sophisticated project management tools relies heavily on resolution of the bigger problem of organizations being able to 'unify communications' across their business. While we wait for organizations to invest in technology that supports the collaborative nature of programmes and projects, the PMO will continue to rely on common desktop products from Microsoft which are still considered as PMO staples. The difficulty facing PMOs is that as programmes become increasingly more complex they will continue to battle with customized spreadsheets to drive complex data collation and reporting. Where that is the case, PMOs are opting for 'consumer grade solutions' for tools, starting a new trend for programme offices.

Trends

Consumer grade PMO tools

The explosion of social media and 'apps' development has brought a wide range of project management tools that are inexpensive, easy to implement and access and do not need to be part of the organization's existing architecture and infrastructure. Such tools are classed as 'consumer grade' because by and large they do not meet the corporation's standards for performance, reliability and security. In other words, programmes need data management and improved collaboration – and programme managers and PMO managers are not prepared to wait until an 'enterprise grade' solution comes along.

Innovative and progressive PMOs are quick to find solutions that enable them to get the job done.

The consumer grade solutions range from document storage (using Dropbox instead of its enterprise grade alternative, Sharepoint) to internal messenger services (such as Skype rather than enterprise grade alternatives such as Saleforce's Chatter and Microsoft's Yammer).

To meet the PMO challenges of data collation, reporting and tracking there are literally hundreds of alternatives to the 'big four' project management enterprise tools such as Oracle's Primavera, CA Technologies' Clarity, Microsoft's Project and Hewlett Packard's PPM.

The PMO role in collaboration

'Working collaboratively' is one of the latest trends to emerge as programmes become more complicated and complex, with team sizes becoming increasingly larger, more diverse in terms of the types of people who work on projects and more virtual in nature.

The PMO response to supporting true team collaboration varies, depending on the locations of team members. The PMO role can, for example, include providing a physical space for the programme manager and teams to hold workshops (possibly organizing video conferences for programme meetings with the wider virtual teams).

Within only one physical location the team can collaborate much easier just because of their proximity to each other. However, team collaboration doesn't just happen because colleagues happen to work next to each other. It is here that the PMO can help and support team collaboration, as follows:

- The PMO can create 'programme/project rooms' which are available for team members wanting to work on a problem together away from the hubbub of daily work. Such rooms (sometimes called 'war rooms') contain everything a team needs to collaborate well such as whiteboard, pens, sticky notes, flipcharts, projector and so on.
- Organizing daily 'stand up' meetings for everyone on the team. The PMO can facilitate these meetings, freeing up the programme manager to concentrate on getting the team working in the right direction, spotting where smaller groups may need to work together on a particular problem or knowing when to bring in a new resource to add new knowledge and experiences.
- Providing visual overviews of the programme and its progress. The PMO office can create 'programme walls', which display information that everyone on the team needs to know about. The visual representation of where the programme is in terms of milestones, work package completion, potential risks and known problems is a great way of sharing the status, keeping the common goal visible and building a sense of co-ownership and trust.
- Using specific project collaboration software and tools also enables the PMO to build virtual programme walls and provide a channel for informal communications. One of the biggest problems with dispersed teams is the amount of information they miss out on when it is being informally communicated. Teams that work closely together often take for granted the amount of information they are picking up through informal channels, which helps them perform their role as well as feeling like part of a well-functioning team.
- The PMO can play a central role in making sure that informal conversations are available to the wider dispersed team by adopting the role of reporter and commentator. The messaging and discussion areas of project management software are the obvious places to do this and have been used by innovative PMOs.
- More advanced PMOs have thought about the advantages of mentoring programmes, where individual team members can be paired with more senior and experienced colleagues for more effective learning and knowledge transfer.

References and further reading

Aubrey, M., Hobbs, B., Muller, R. and Blomquist, T. (2011), *Identifying the Forces Driving Frequent Change in PMOs,* Newtown Square, PA: Project Management Institute.

Axelos (formerly the Office of Government Commerce) (2011), *Managing Successful Programmes,* 4th edn., Norwich: The Stationery Office.

Block, T. J. and Frame, J. D. (1998), *The Project Office.* Menlo Park, CA: Crisp Publications.

Donselaar, J. W., Hedeman, B. and Portman, H. (2011), *Competence Profiles, Certification Levels and Function in the Project Management and Project Support Field*, Zaltbommel: Van Haren Publishing.

ESI International (2015), *The Global State of the PMO*, London: ESI International.

Hallows, J. (2002), *The Project Management Office Toolkit*, New York: American Management Association.

Hatfield, M. (2008), *Things Your PMO is Doing Wrong*, Newtown Square, PA: Project Management Institute.

Hobbs, B. and Aubry, M. (2010), *The Project Management Office (PMO): A Quest for Understanding*, Newtown Square, PA: Project Management Institute.

Lock, D. (2013), *Project Management*, 10th edn., Farnham: Gower.

Pinto, A., Cota, M. and Levin, G. (2010), 'The PMO Maturity Cube, a Project Management Office Maturity Model'. Presented at the PMI Research and Education Congress. Washington, DC. <www.pmotools.org/arquivos/PMOMaturityCubeEng.pdf>.

Rad, P. F. and Levin, G. (2002), *The Advanced Project Management Office: A Comprehensive Look at Function and Implementation*. Boca Raton, FL: St Lucie Press.

Roden, E. J. (2013), *Portfolio, Programme and Project Offices*, Norwich: The Stationery Office.

Sowden, R. (2011), *Managing Successful Programmes*, Norwich: Axelos.

Tjahjana, L., Dwyer, P. and Habib, M. (2009), *The Programme Management Office Advantage*, New York: American Management Association.

Chapter 22

Programme Culture

Steven Raue and Louis Klein

A systemic knowledge of culture, of the nature of real possibilities and the power of context, lies at the very heart of any understanding of managerial responsibility. Only if we understand culture can we manage responsibly.

Programme culture: winning or losing the benefits

There is only one reason to engage in programme management – benefits or (better still) cross-benefits. Programmes provide the frame (and hence the immediate context) for projects. And as we know from systems sciences, the logic of the context is always stronger than the logic of the system (or in our case the logic of the project). Or to argue more philosophically with Theodor W. Adorno (2010 [1951]), 'There is no right life in the wrong one.' Knowing and managing the context of projects is the number one critical success factor for excellent programme management.

However, this assumes an understanding beyond recognizing the context. Following Scott's principles of observation, successful programme management implies the understanding that there is always a bigger picture, there is always more detail and there is always an alternative perspective (Scott, 2009). And the ability to acknowledge and master these different perspectives resides beyond technical skills and political aspects in the culture as the sense-making frame of the organization. This is why our chapter on programme management looks at programme culture from two perspectives:

- What is the culture of programmes?
- What is a corresponding organizational culture?

Dealing successfully with these two perspectives is crucial to winning or losing the benefits.

In the first part of this chapter we identify culture as the paradigmatic reference for certain communities of practice. Culture defines the realms of organizational possibilities and limits. It allows programme culture to be seen in three different ways:

1. Only a reflective and learning organization gains maximum benefits from programmes by understanding the systemic conditions for the possibilities of a desirable practice.

2. Programmes create what is known as path dependency and left shifts. They rule.
3. Meeting the challenges of programmes requires a management that cascades along the hierarchy of structural, procedural and personal implications.

Later in this chapter we transfer these aspects into the organizational perspectives on programme culture, asking what does the programme do for the organization and with the organization. Programmes follow a strategic ambition. They focus projects and the organization on a desirable goal. They integrate. However, looking at the culture of programmes implies a generic perspective on emerging properties. Each project inherently carries the quality to change the world (or at least a part of it) and hence the organization.

On the one hand, a project dynamically increases complexity. And multiproject programmes significantly increase complexity, both for projects themselves and for the organization. Complexity challenges the ability to act and the capability of management. So what are the cultural conditions that facilitate the ability to act and to reclaim management? It will be a lesson on how we relate to the world.

On the other hand, beyond managing complexity, projects can be regarded as change themselves. Some projects change the organization, and that change must be managed. And again (beyond technical and political aspects) the key for successful change management lies in the cultural context of the organization and to what extent the organization is ready for change. We shall discuss practical approaches to deal with this topic and note ways of exploring and mapping the world of change.

In our final paragraphs we refocus these approaches in making sense of programme management and its context in the world. In this chapter sense-making is used both as a tool for reflection and guiding the understanding of programme culture to manage it successfully. We shall explore four cardinal skills and their interdependence:

- self-observation;
- self-description;
- self-realization;
- self-creation.

This is not all you need to know about culture, but it is what you need to manage programmes responsibly.

Understanding programme culture

There are many ways to refer to culture. The most common and the most misleading way is to distinguish so-called national cultures from each other. We use the term culture to refer to religious or ethnic differences and particularities. An entire industry of trainings and seminars revolves around statistical research into the various clusters which we refer to as nations (Klein, 2006). We are taught what to expect from the typical American or the typical Chinese. We are guided to adapt to this statistical avatar which regularly renders us helpless when meeting real people.

Real cultural competence does not lie in the first order of observation and adaptation but in the second order of understanding people in a given context. Based on this systemic notion, understanding culture means understanding how people attribute meaning to their behaviour. Culture serves as a reference system. It provides a reference for choosing a specific behaviour out of a range of possible behaviour in a specific context. In that respect culture explains a world, its possibilities and limitations.

These possibilities and limitations do not need to be factual. A specific world view is functionally sufficient if it provides a guideline for appropriate and successful behaviour. In this sense a religion, a world view, or a profession provide a set of beliefs which allow navigating the world. In systemic terms culture is a paradigmatic reference of a community of practice (Klein, 2013a). This combines the world view and belief system on the one hand and a group of people doing something together. Although this sounds abstract, it has a very concrete and practical implication for programme management. Its culture provides a reservoir of answers to those questions that arise when you run any kind of programme management. It ranges from *why*, to *what*, to *how*. It provides possibilities and describes limitations. And certainly it is not black and white and there is rarely a right or wrong.

If we want to explore culture in an organizational context, the 'TPC' matrix comes in as a very helpful tool (Tichy, 1983). This concept, illustrated in Figure 22.1, distinguishes three perspectives: technical, political and cultural:

- The *technical perspective* entails all the models, methodologies and instruments which rule a specific discipline (which in our case is programme management).
- The *political perspective* refers to micropolitics. This is to acknowledge that different stakeholders pursue different interests and that this creates a heterogeneous ecology ranging from the one extreme (clash of interests) to the other extreme (a symbiotic co-evolution of intentions).

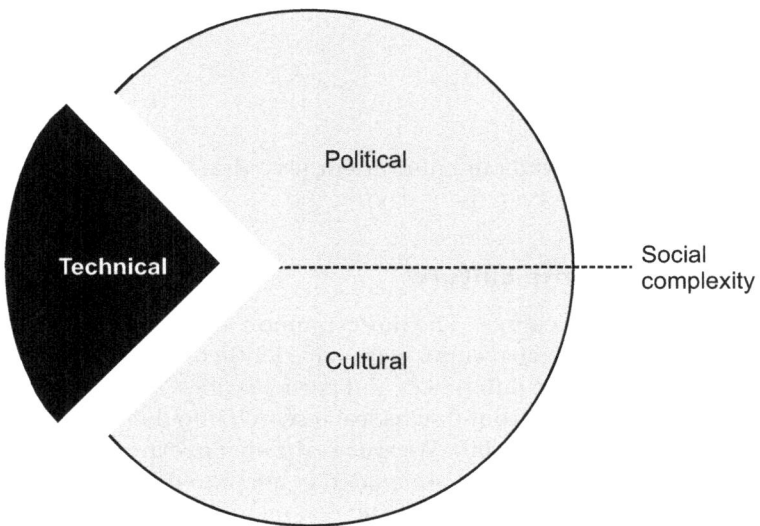

Figure 22.1 In Tichy's TPC matrix social complexity evolves in the political and cultural dimensions

- The *cultural perspective* is an embedding perspective: it informs, makes sense. and creates meaning within a given context. We can say that it creates the context for a person, a group or a community. In that sense, programme management culture informs programme management what programme management is. why it is and how it works. It does not provide scientific proof, it is not chiselled in stone; it just works.

All that we could say about programme management can only be formulated within the cultural paradigm of programme management. In this respect a programme management culture provides the conditions for the possibility of any activity that can be described as programme management. In a very systemic sense 'culture' is the 'context of the context'. We know that programmes provide the context of projects. In a deductive or generic approach, programmes provide a frame and a corridor for possible projects and their development. Systemically we are looking at the figure of path dependency (Gleick, 1998). The initial conditions, the regulations and settings of a programme become overly important for the further progress of the programme and its projects. The criticality of setting the programme right from the start creates what is referred to as the necessity for a 'shift left strategy' (Boehm, 1981). Or more simply, if we get it wrong in the beginning it will not come out nicely.

The reason for programme management is to gain cross-benefits. A programme is set up in a way to realize commonalties and synergies so as to:

- lower the cost;
- reduce the timescale;
- improve quality of projects.

The various projects in a programme provide experience which can be used in a learning loop to prove the programme and its abilities to improve projects. This refers to the ideal type of learning organization (Klein, 2013b). Closing the loop, as in a plan–do–check–act cycle (PDCA) is the prerequisite for further improvement. Culture provides for this learning loop the legendary 'box' – we need to get out of that box with our thinking if we really want to innovate. We do not only want to improve what we are already doing, but we also want to do something new which hasn't been there before (Klein and Wong, 2012). The informed system thinker knows that we only 'get out of the box' at the price of finding ourselves in the next larger box which is providing a frame and containment for the initial box (Glanville, 2009, 2013).

If we refer to programme management culture as the framework or the box for programme management, we might want to acknowledge that this culture is only one of several very different paradigmatic references for a multitude of different communities of practice. This points at a phenomenon which has been described as the 'ecology of paradigms'. Paradigmatic references for specific behaviour offer a reference which *can* be choosen, but not necessarily *has* to be chosen. There are always different offers, different explanations and different guidelines from which we might want to choose.

Looking at this complexity of cultures is confusing. However, it comes with very practical and pragmatic implications. Culture may appear very determining and rigidly ruling the context at any given time. Over time, however, it is changeable. It changes and *can* be changed for more desirable outcomes. This is still challenging, but it provides some comfort.

Before we engage in a notion of change, we want to close this first part of the chapter with a short exercise in cascading programme management culture along the hierarchy of structural, procedural and personal implications of a specific practice. If programme management wants to improve a certain project's management practice it needs to provide a guideline for a desirable operating and governance model. A programme provides a corridor to focus a desirable practice and rules out a lot of possible practices and activities. Any organizational practice is stabilized by contextual rules and regulations.

The first level of stability is provided by working out the procedural implications of a desirable practice. We can refer to those as business processes, describing the course of action for operations and management.

The second layer providing further stability is the structural implication, attributing roles and responsibilities and providing clarity about who does what.

Third and finally, personal or individual implications of a desirable practice focus on the person over time. This relates to career paths, learning and qualification.

Although working out these procedural and structural implications of a desirable practice seems to be a managerial commonplace, it can only be successful if it is coherent with the overall culture. And even if it seems to be logical in a micro context, if it does not fit the overall context it will not be viable let alone successful.

The organizational perspective

If we engage with the organizational perspective of programme management we have to answer two questions. First, what does programme management do *for* the organization? Second, what does programme management do *with* the organization? Certainly (as we wrote earlier) the reason for programme management is to realize cross-benefits. We engage in programme management to improve projects and their results across the entire portfolio. This refers to the management of commonalities and synergies. However, that is mainly a business perspective. Organizationally it should be of equal interest to look at the effect wich programmes have on the organization. Two very specific aspects come into play, namely *complexity* and *change*.

Complexity is rooted in interdependence and qualified by the 'property of emergence' (Klein, 2013c). The relationships are not linear and the various aspects are mutually influencing. Programmes provide a corridor for projects. The corridor may be wide or narrow and compliance might be managed rigorously or laissez-faire. In any case it can predict that programmes will be challenged by the different project developments.

We mentioned the chance for learning earlier but with all this come a lot of challenges for programme management. Leaving the managerial details aside it can be said that any venture, be it a simple hike or a large battle, will be managed more easily if we have a better knowledge of the landscape. So before engaging in action, there comes the art of exploration and map making. What can we know about our possibilities to act and our chances to manage? We have already seen one tool, the

TPC matrix, which allows us to approach the various organizational aspects from technical, political or cultural aspects.

Another tool to introduce here is Scott's principles of observation (Scott, 2009). These are illustrated in Figure 22.2.

Scott's first principle is that for any given observation there is always a bigger picture. This relates to our understanding of culture – there will always be a larger context for organizational possibilities.

Scott's second principle states that for any given observation there are always more details to be observed. This points back to our habits and routines for observing the world. A lot has been written about attention to detail under the headline of mindfulness. That relates to early warning systems and the idea of weak signals. In a functional sense this provides the ground for the improvement of risk management – beyond that it addresses a broader competence of attention and awareness in management. We should be alert if details are not in tune. We know that many reporting checks and balances are in place in good project management; but we also know that there are often details which are out of tune (variances), which are not captured by controlling, measurement and milestones.

We have a tendency to refer to experience (or gut feeling). Nevertheless profound insight in programme culture provides us with a superior source for checking those 'out of tune' details. In most of the cases we find a reflection or follow a story, an anecdote, or a narrative in the cultural domain. It's a trace worth pursuing.

Scott's third principle states that for any given observation there is an alternative perspective. The essence of this third principle became popular with Edward de Bono's *Six Thinking Hats* (2008). De Bono described an exercise where six thinking 'hats' represent six different perspectives from which to think about a given problem. The same applies to any observation we undertake to explore the landscape in which we are operating. This third principle addresses a point that accounts for many situations both culturally and in terms of project as well as programme management. It is not only critical to measure right, it is also always worth asking if the

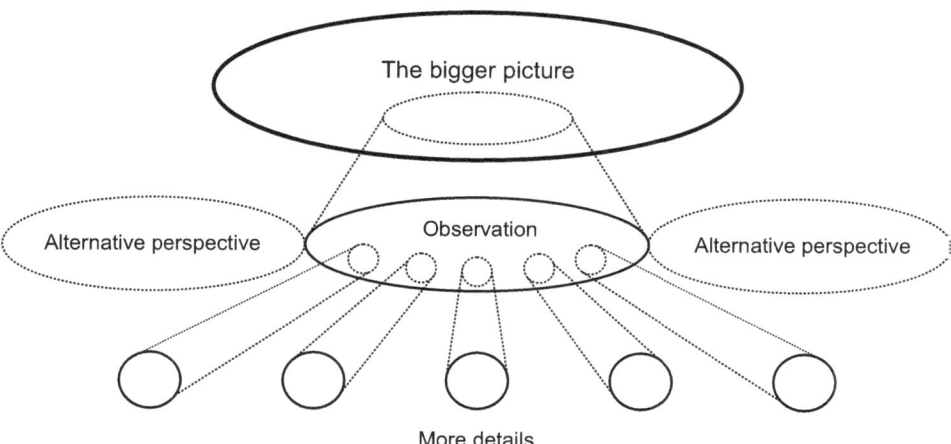

Figure 22.2 Scott's three principles of observation

measures taken are the right ones. In other words, it is not only important to be careful about the details, it is also worth reflecting if the perspectives taken need to be changed or complemented. Different perspectives may capture the main aspects of an organization, different stakeholder interests, or other relevant or critical aspects worth exploring. Exploring and mapping are the major managerial skills required to understand and meet the complexity of any situation where we want to maintain our ability to act and react.

Change management is one of the most underrated disciplines in the area of management. The main stream of change management runs in two not-so-favourable directions. Either change management is conceptualized in a mechanistic fashion or it tries to operate on the ground of burning platforms, leaning on the idea of heroic management – the idea of the change manager as the heroic mechanic fixing what is broken. That is not a very helpful image. At the other extreme, the philosophical notion that everything is changing constantly and that the only constant is change, is not very practical. If we dare to say that we are actually able to manage change, the analogy of the lazy gardener seems to be the most appropriate (Vetter, 2008). You can be a successful gardener, but not by micromanaging every single plant in your garden. And your garden will always be exposed to nature's raw forces; sunshine and cold, rain and wind. Yet successful gardening is possible. You can care for the ecology, you can care for your garden, you can care for people. And based on your knowledge and experience you can intervene. The outcome will be likely but not certain. It is always a question of balance. When we look at change it is always the balance between integration and transformation (Klein and Wong, 2012).

The idea of programme management is to integrate, to manage commonalities and synergies, to focus and integrate, to learn and improve. On the other hand every project carries the potential to challenge the limits, to jump out of the box, to fuel transformation. It is the balance between central governance and distributed action. If we are looking at good change management, we need integration and transformation plus improvement and innovation. We need to learn from experience and we need to dare to try new things. As we know from the ancient Tai Chi philosophy, we do not only need a balance – we need sufficient improvement and innovation (Klein and Wong, 2012). Programme culture needs to take account of this necessary balance. It needs to carry the notion of good change.

Mastering culture

The first two parts of this chapter on programme culture were very much concerned with the dynamics and complexity of culture and the corresponding organizational perspectives. Now we focus on a more systemic perspective on the cultural side of social systems and mastering those cultural aspects. Following Niklas Luhmann's theory of social systems (Luhmann, 1984) we acknowledge that communication lies at the heart of social systems, be they groups, societies or organizations. Every social system is qualified by its communication.

To qualify itself as a system, a system (and hence an organization) needs to realize itself as a system distinct from its environment. Its members need to observe themselves, and they need to describe themselves. Observation and description are activities and as such they constitute a practice. As we have seen earlier, a practice as such is stabilized by its paradigmatic reference. Hence, the ways in which organizations observe and describe themselves constitute specific cultures of specific organizations. In this sense culture is inevitable. It is a given context for any organization.

Once we acknowledge this relationship we may as well change the self-observation and self-description of the organization and by doing so change the organization as such. This sounds rather abstract yet it implies that you cannot change the organization without changing the culture and that you cannot change the culture without changing the organization. Or, to put it positively, you can change the organization by changing the culture and you can change the culture by changing the organization.

Organizational mastery can systemically be described as an oscillating process which changes from self-realization to self-creation and back to self-realization feeding into self-creation (Klein, 2009). It's a little bit like a PDCA or learning cycle. Self-realization can be understood as an act of self-awareness. In this it relates to what was said about self-observation and self-description.

The interesting thing about social systems is that they possess not only the ability to observe and describe what they are, but also what they could be. In this sense they describe both actuality and possibility. The interesting part is that with this opening of actualities and possibilities, limits come into sight. Possibilities can turn into actualities. But only those things (activities or changes) are possible for an organization which are observed and described as such. Those things which an organization does not observe and describe as possible are simply not possible for that organization. The implications of this cannot be overestimated. It explains why so many attempts to realize best practices fail – because what is identified or provided externally as a best practice cannot be realized if it is not also observed and described within the organization as possible.

Self-realization comes first. Self-creation is the flip side of the coin. Organizations need to create themselves based on decisions. Once possibilities are identified they can be turned into actualities based on the decision to do so. Choosing a possibility brings something into the world which has not been there before. It changes the world. It changes the actualities and, since choosing an option usually comes at the price of not choosing other options, changes the realm of possibilities as well. Changing the actualities changes the possibilities. And these changes require a next turn of self-realization. The cycle starts again.

Summary

In summary, this chapter on programme culture discussed conditions with regard to the possibility of stability and change in organizations. The way in which we conceptualize programmes determines not only each programme as such. It also affects the following projects and their outcomes. It makes a substantial contribution to the organization's development. More than all that, it determines the possibilities of an organization to learn, to improve and to change.

References and futher reading

Adorno, T. (2010 [1951]), *Minima Moralia*, London: Verso.
Boehm, B.W. (1981), *Software Engineering Economics*, Englewood Cliffs, NJ: Prentice-Hall.

Bono, E. de (2008), *Six Thinking Hats*, revised and updated edn., Boston, MA: Back Bay Books.

Glanville, R. (2009), *The Black Boox Vol. III: 39 Steps*, Vienna: Echoraum.

Glanville, R. (2013), *The Black Boox Vol. I: Cybernetic Circles*, Vienna: Echoraum.

Gleick, J. (1998), *CHAOS: Making a New Science*, London: Random House.

Klein, L. (2006), 'Führung, Kultur und Kontingenz: Social Design im Kulturdreieck von Werte, Institutionen und Praxis', in R. Bouncken (ed.), *Interkulturelle Kooperation*, Berlin: Duncker & Humblot.

Klein, L. (2009), 'Organizational Excellence: Die Kompetenz zur Selbst-Innovation', in K. Henning and C. Michulitz (eds.), *Unternehmenskybernetik 2020*, Berlin: Duncker & Humblot.

Klein, L. (2013a), 'Notes on an Ecology of Paradigms', *Systems Research and Behavioral Science*, 30(6): 773–9.

Klein, L. (2013b), 'Soziale Komplexität in Projektmanagement', in R. Wagner, A. Wald, T. L. Mayer and C. Schneider (eds.), *Advanced Project Management (Vol. 3): Komplexität. Dynamik. Unsicherheit.* Nuremberg: GPM Deutsche Gesellschaft für Projektmanagement.

Klein, L. (2013c), *Die Organization der Personalentwicklung: Entwicklung und Anwendung eines systemisch-kybernetischen Modells*, Auflage 1, Heidelberg: Carl Auer Verlag.

Klein, L. and Wong, T. S. L. (2012), 'The Yin and Yang of Change: Systemic Efficacy in Change Management', in G. P. Prastacos, F. Wang and K. E. Soderquist (eds.), *Leadership through the Classics*, Berlin: Springer.

Luhmann, N. (1984), *Soziale Systeme: Grundriß einer allgemeinen Theorie*, 15th edn., Berlin: Suhrkamp Verlag.

Scott, B. (2009). 'The Role of Sociocybernetics in Understanding World Futures', *Kybernetes*, 38: 863–78.

Tichy, N. M. (1983), *Managing Strategic Change: Technical, Political, and Cultural Dynamics*, New York: John Wiley.

Vetter, R. (2008), *The Lazy Gardener: Wie man sein Glück im Garten findet*, vol. 1, Appenzell: Appenzeller Volksfreund.

Part IV

Programme Lifecycles, Processes, Methods and Tools

Chapter 23

Programme Lifecycles

Andrea Demaria and Joseph Sopko

Introduction

Programmes have been described as 'a vision with no clear path to get there'. At the inception, the vision may be great, but the technology and architecture of the future state may not even exist or be mature enough to execute predictably. Requirements for projects must not only be collected and managed – they must be created. Even before valuable and scarce resources are committed to defining the detail, the programme must be evaluated to understand if the programme vision is achievable and the business case is feasible. In many cases, only the first stages of the programme can be determined and the programme must adopt a certain amount of management agility to iteratively make its way to the final solution for the future state.

Although much of the terminology used in programme management appears similar to projects or even portfolios, the context is very different. A different lifecycle must be engaged which not only delivers a multitude of related capabilities, but delivers them in an effective and coherent manner, orchestrates the transition of these capabilities into common practice by the organization and works together with the 'business-as-usual' element of the organization to deliver the expected value. Owing to their complexity, uncertainty and extended duration, programmes must explore new technologies and approaches during their lifecycles to evaluate the best way forward in the light of ever changing market and organizational environments, while sustaining stability for the component projects that ensures their success. Finally, because a key principle of programmes is to add value, the evolution, management and realization of benefits play an important role in shaping the programme lifecycle.

Benefit lifecycle: from opportunity to full benefit delivery

The principal objective of programmes is to realize benefits effectively. Therefore, the lifecycle of programmes is closely interrelated with the lifecycle of benefits. By having a clear understanding of how benefits are identified, defined, systematically realized and delivered it is possible to better distinguish between project and programme activities and clearly determine the boundaries of different programme phases.

According to the *Oxford English Dictionary* a benefit is 'an advantage or profit gained from something'. But that definition is too general in the context of projects and programmes. According to that definition both programmes and projects deliver benefits. For example if a hospital runs a project for a new building one could say that the project delivers an immediate benefit, since the owner of the building can legitimately claim to have an advantage from the additional space available in the new building. But programmes do not limit the focus to creating the enabling capability. So in the hospital case we would consider not only the new building with trained staff and equipment, but also the realization and sustainment of benefits. The full benefit is realized once the potential capability to create a benefit is actually put in use (that is, the new building is being used to care for additional patients or increased healthcare enhancement). This distinction might seem trivial but plays an essential role in the business.

There is a fundamental difference between having the capability and actually getting the full benefits of this capability. For example, installing new production machinery and training workers might establish the capability to produce 1,000 pieces per hour. However, only once the production is started, those 1,000 pieces per hour are sold, and the profit is collected can we declare that the business has realized the benefits and the objectives defined in the business case have been achieved. Before that we only have realized costs and 'potential' benefits. While potential benefits can be considered an advantage, they are not the aim of a programme. Accordingly a benefit in programme management can be defined as the result of the performance of an organization that is considered to be a strategic advantage to the organization.

The reason for a programme benefit to be strategic is twofold. On the one hand, programmes focus on advantages that are important enough to justify the costs of the programme. On the other hand, the advantage must be aligned with the strategy of the organization. As an example, if an organization has chosen to reduce production costs as a strategic objective, an increase in production speed (for example by acquiring new production machines) is not considered a benefit. A higher production speed is generally an advantage, but in this case it has been achieved at the expense of additional costs and therefore does not support the strategic objective of the organization. Figure 23.1 shows the path from the deliverables building a new capability to the resulting benefits, contributing to strategic objectives.

The process of benefit creation can be structured in several steps and is described in the *benefit lifecycle*. The benefit lifecycle begins when the opportunity to realize a benefit is first identified and ends when the benefit has been fully delivered. It can be divided into seven phases. Some of the phases described below may overlap and may be more or less explicitly implemented. It is possible to realize and deliver benefits without knowingly implementing these specific phases. Nevertheless whenever benefits are created it is generally possible, at least a posteriori, to recognize the seven phases of the benefit lifecycle outlined below.

Phase I: opportunity identification

When an opportunity to realize a benefit is discovered, the strategic relevance of the opportunity is assessed and the first traits of the potential benefit agreed between the key stakeholders. In the hospital example, let's say that a new expansion strategy is adopted and additional space is needed. Opportunities for creating a new building near the current hospital will be identified and discussed.

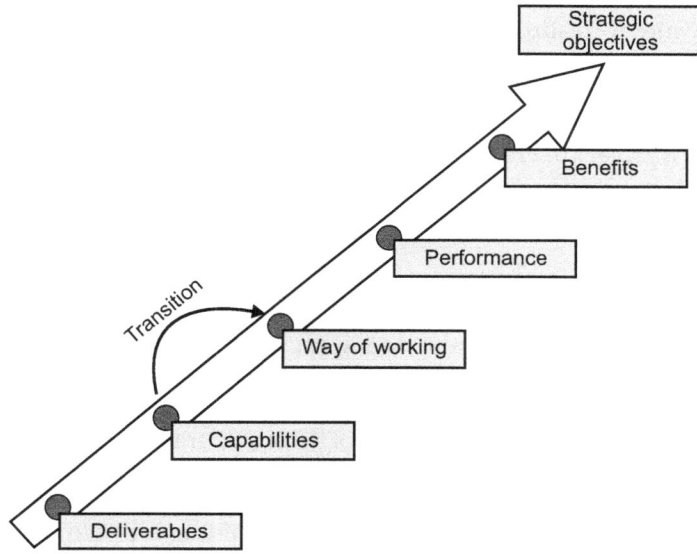

Figure 23.1 Realization of benefits from deliverables

Phase 2: benefit definition

Once it has been determined and agreed that the opportunity should be pur-sued, the key characteristics and frame conditions for the delivery of the benefit are defined. Examples of benefit characteristics are the benefit owner, associated costs and risks, expected timeframe, measurement of the benefit, current bene-fit level, and expected magnitude to be achieved. In the hospital example, the benefit owner(s) can be the department(s) to be moved into the building or the healthcare management that will be responsible for providing care. The business case will also be defined. It is important to baseline the current state of the benefit measurement in an effort to quantifiably determine the trends and to confirm the achievement of the benefit as the programme progresses. The difference between the current state of the benefit and the future state of the benefit is a component of the business case that will be compared against the costs to determine the value delivered.

Phase 3: capabilities definition

Once it has been determined that the defined benefits should be realized, the new and improved capabilities necessary to realize the benefits are defined and docu-mented in a blueprint of the future states of the organization. Definition of the cap-abilities should consider what processes, organization, technology and information must be established to deliver each new capability fully. In the hospital example, the definition will include the high-level layout of the building as well as the way in which hospital departments will operate and make use of the processes, technical infra-structure, personnel, data reports and so on.

Phase 4: capabilities delivery

In this phase the activities to realize and roll out the new capabilities are chartered, started and completed. After this phase, transition activities may begin to adopt, perfect and institutionalize the new capability. This step usually overlaps in time with the next because benefit realization can be started once the new capability is proven. In the hospital example, a project to create the new building is chartered, the new processes for training staff, care delivery and administration are defined, the technical infrastructure is acquired and installed and the required personnel are recruited.

Phase 5: benefit realization

The first real benefits are delivered and reported when the organization adopts and starts using the new capabilities Benefit realization can be a step change or a gradual improvement. What is most important is that the benefit, once realized, remains stable at the desired level. This is the confirmation of successful transformation. After this phase the organization will have achieved the desired transformed state. In the hospital example, as soon as parts of the building are usable, the departments will methodically begin to use the new space until the whole building is put 'in production'. The increased revenues and potential healthcare improvements are measured to ensure that the planned benefits are achieved.

Phase 6: stable benefit delivery

This phase depends on the type of benefit being delivered. It will be skipped if the benefit was a one-time delivery. In other cases this phase can take several decades. The delivered benefits become the new normal 'baseline' of the transformed organization's performance.

Phase 7: end of benefit delivery

At some point the old capability (such as legacy systems), previously 'business as usual' in the organization, will be either stopped or replaced by new capabilities and a new level of performance achieved. In the hospital example, the original building can be sold, repurposed or torn down, legacy systems are shut down and old processes are terminated.

The programme business case

Two distinctive characteristics of programme business cases play a key role in the nature of the programme lifecycle. These are the investment-dependent nature of a programme and the fundamental characteristics of a programme to add value and lead change.

To understand the difference in context between projects and programmes, one simply has to look at the business cases for both. The business case for a project is often focused on the ability of the project team to deliver a defined scope at a planned cost and schedule. The performance metrics are typically efficiency based (such as earned value, which evaluates the cost and schedule performances related to the planned baselines). For most projects, completing the delivery of the defined scope at a schedule and cost performance index greater than or equal to 1.00 is often considered as a success.

Programmes on the other hand use the new capability or future state to deliver benefits, and those benefits are typically some multiple of the cost invested. Therefore, programme success is often measured using value models such as net present value (NPV). For more on methods of financial appraisal, see Chapter 6 in Lock (2013). The programme must not only break even – it typically must deliver value or benefits that are significantly greater than the investment costs. The success of an IT infrastructure programme is not only indicated by 'going live' within the set time and on cost parameters. It is also about improving company performance (perhaps even aiming to produce the best run company).

Another contrast between projects and programmes is the value of time. In projects, assuming that adequate risk management is performed, cost often bears a direct relationship with the project duration. The longer the project takes, the more money is spent and the more it costs. The impact on the business case is typically one of either overspending or of cost savings. For the programme, time or the quality of new capabilities will often have a far greater impact on the value it is defined to deliver.

For example, delays in a new product launch might not only cost more to the development project, but could mean the total loss of the funds invested if the market window is missed or a competitor advances before it. Conversely, a higher cost to accelerate a project or add a new product feature might bring market or organizational benefits far beyond the cost of accomplishing it. This large impact might be detected and measured only at the programme level where the benefits are managed.

It is therefore important that the sensitivity of programme benefits to changes in schedule, cost and scope are known, so sensitivity analysis should be part of the business case programme components. This not only provides a business case for evaluating the proposed changes but also encourages innovative approaches with a sound investment foundation.

A successful programme adds value and leads change. Any change is easier to conduct if the organization performing and undergoing the transformation realizes that the resulting future state will deliver some advantage for each of the stakeholders. Tools such as benefit maps can be developed which depict and trace the value delivery stream from the project outputs and capabilities through to the planned benefits to be realized. This traceability allows for a type of value stream analysis to show the relationship between the project component work and its effect on the programme's benefit goals. Since programmes are generally of long duration and the programme environment can change over time, the benefit map is useful for programme gate reviews in validating the contribution of programme components and identifying a lean approach to programme execution.

Programme lifecycle boundaries and phases

It is not always easy or even possible to determine when a programme actually begins. The time at which some budget is explicitly assigned to the execution of the programme is usually recorded and clear, but this formal act is only done once the programme has been clearly identified and it is recognized that the potential benefits provided would outweigh the cost of that initiative. In order to evaluate benefits and costs of a programme a number of activities are necessary, sometimes including benchmarking activities and feasibility studies.

It is a chicken and egg problem: in order to start the programme the benefits and costs must be clear but in order to determine benefits and costs preliminary programme activities must be started. Sometimes these activities are performed driven by other functional departments of the organization such as a programme portfolio or by line management.

To complicate things further, many strategic initiatives are often started as projects or run for some time with a hybrid structure before they eventually are recognized as programmes and formally organized as such. These are typically referred to as emergent programmes.

At the other end, when a programme is no longer needed, there is usually a clear decision point determining its closure. Because formal decisions were made to launch the programme, a similar level of formality is necessary to end it.

The start-to-finish lifecycle of a programme can typically be divided into six distinct phases (see Figure 23.2). These phases are as follows:

- initiation;
- definition;
- preparation;
- capability delivery;
- benefit realization;
- closure.

Each phase has a different purpose and should be started only once defined preconditions have been fulfilled, according to clear decision points. Programmes can also be implemented in steps and can include recursions or waves in their lifecycles, during which the phases from definition to benefit realization are repeated.

Initiation phase

The initiation phase starts when one or more sponsoring stakeholders intend to support the achievement of one or more strategic objectives through a programme. For example, a benchmarking activity might have exposed areas that need improvement, or a new regulation could create the need for change. Or the application of a new technology might offer the opportunity to improve a product. Perhaps,

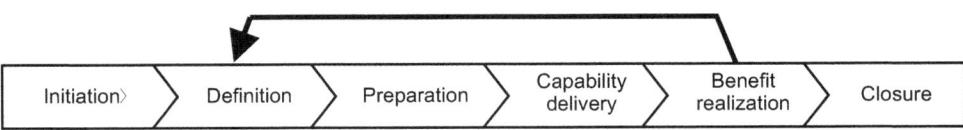

Figure 23.2 Programme lifecycle phases

more generally, the current performance level of the organization requires improvement to remain competitive. Whatever the origin of the expectation, it is important that the opportunity be sufficiently relevant to justify at least the execution of this initial phase.

The main purpose of the initiation phase is to provide all key stakeholders with a common understanding of what is needed against what the programme could be expected to achieve. Then they have to come to a well-founded decision on whether or not the programme should proceed to the next phase.

The sponsoring stakeholders can express their initial expectations in a document that is sometimes called the 'programme mandate'. A programme manager can be appointed to examine the feasibility, explore possible implementation and provide one or more options for realizing the programme. That investigation will consider the expected benefits, need for change, time constraints, available resources, external influences and other important factors pertinent to the programme environment.

A plan and cost estimate of the next phase (definition) can also be conducted. This, together with a first outline business case and programme vision statement, contributes to the 'programme profile'. If the key stakeholders come to an agreement that everything described in the programme profile should be executed, then the programme can proceed to the next phase.

Programme definition phase

The fundamental elements of the programme must now be defined (definition phase). This will detail the programme profile further and ensure that the most viable approach is going to be implemented. In this phase it is essential to involve all stakeholders responsible for the programme implementation (those responsible for creating new capabilities as well as those who will be responsible for ensuring a successful change and sustainable transitions).

The objective of this phase is to define clearly the key points of the future way of working in order to maximize the benefits listed in the programme profile. The new way of working will usually be achieved in several steps or waves, so the intended benefits will generally not all be realized at once.

The capabilities to be created at each wave will be defined and documented in a document which might be called the 'future states blueprint', focusing on what is expected to change. A 'benefit profile' will be developed for each intended benefit, specifying how, when and under which responsibility the benefit will be realized. The activities needed to create the new capabilities and organization transitions are then identified and organized, usually in single projects.

The sequence and timing of waves with the relative projects and other programme activities is documented in the 'programme roadmap'. The logical connection between project activities and benefits to be achieved is explored and documented in 'benefit maps'. Now the programme organization, including 'sounding boards' and a steering committee, can be defined based on the amount and quality of work to be executed by the programme. The overall governance of the programme is also defined, together with the methodology to be applied (tailored to fit best the requirements of the programme).

At the end of this definition phase the business case is finalized. Now the programme sponsor and steering committee have all elements to decide whether or not the programme should be implemented and the funds needed for the first wave should be committed.

Programme preparation phase

The programme preparation phase begins after approval for programme implementation. All prerequisites for executing of the first (or next) wave of the programme smoothly will either be made available or updated/finalized. The complete programme organization must now be defined in detail and role owners empowered, including the (candidate) project managers for the delivery of capabilities. Now a programme management office (PMO) will usually be established, freeing the programme manager from the burden of administrative and repetitive tasks. If not already present, the programme support infrastructure must be established. Accounting structures, document management systems, communication infrastructure and facilities are set up and made available to the programme team.

It is a good practice to define the programme handbook in this phase. That will document the processes to be used in the programme (for example risk management, quality management, escalation paths, responsibilities, reporting rules and templates). All these elements are necessary because after this phase projects will be started to develop the new capabilities. Projects expected to start in the next wave now have to be chartered or otherwise authorized properly to ensure the agreement of project managers and project sponsors.

At the end of this preparation phase all resources should be in place and ready to start with the delivery of the capabilities. The programme sponsor, supported by the steering committee, will take the decision to proceed into the next phase.

Capability delivery phase

In this phase, which will be repeated for each programme wave, the capabilities defined in the future states blueprint will be created and made available by components of the programme which are called 'enabling projects'.

Newly created or enhanced capabilities will be used later to improve the current status of the organization and these are aligned with the organization's strategic goals defined in the benefit maps. Many projects, with their own phases, milestones and quality gates, are interrelated. They must be managed in a coordinated way under the programme. Although the beginning of the capability delivery phase is marked by a clear decision point, the projects in this phase are not necessarily started all at once. Rather they are timed with the intention that they should finish at the same time, at the end of a wave. A late start is usually preferable to finishing too early (pull principle) because of the risk that the results of the projects become outdated before the start of transition. Projects can be stretched over more than one wave as long as their completion is aligned with the end of their last wave.

Programme work during this capability delivery phase will be carried out both at project and at programme level.

Project level

The objective of the enabling projects is to deliver one or more capabilities, or at least elements of them. A 'capability' consists of all elements needed by an organization to be able to apply a new way of working. What belongs to a new capability is described on a high level in the future states blueprint defined during the definition phase. That can include resources, methods and processes, tools and systems, information, organizational structures and value flows.

The projects will first define and plan in detail the deliverables necessary to implement the new capabilities, based on the requirements provided by change and transition managers as well as by the business managers responsible for the benefit realization. Once the capability elements needed to realize the programme benefits are defined and the project plans developed, the projects will proceed with the development of the deliverables and with their roll-out. If necessary, pilots will be performed to verify that the developed deliverables can enable the organization to apply the required capabilities effectively.

Programme level

Once started, the component projects are expected to deliver according to their charters and 'get their scope done' without major changes. At the programme level, the programme sponsor will work closely with the programme manager and the business managers responsible for the benefits to ensure that the programme remains aligned with the organizational strategy and objectives and takes advantage of upcoming opportunities. This involves continuously verifying that the original strategic objectives of the programmes remain valid and that new opportunities to improve the benefits further are identified early and the projects directed accordingly.

When changes are beneficial, the scope of the affected projects is adapted. In some cases, projects already in execution may be stopped using a well-defined change order management process (see Chapter 23 in Lock, 2013). In all cases, the future state blueprint as well as the benefit profiles and benefit maps will be updated. The steering committee and the expert boards provide essential input to guide the programme in this phase.

At the end of the capability delivery phase of a given wave, the capabilities needed to implement that wave have been created and made available (Figure 23.3). A handover between the project managers and the transition managers takes place after the business managers responsible for the benefits give acceptance for the deliverables produced.

Benefit realization

In the benefit realization phase the rolled out capabilities (usually those achieved in the previous wave) are activated for operational use in the day-to-day business. These transitions from the existing way of working to a new one are usually organized in projects and directly report into the programme. Alternatively they can be handed over to the operational units to organize. In most cases, current operations cannot be stopped and must continue in order for the organization to sustain its current

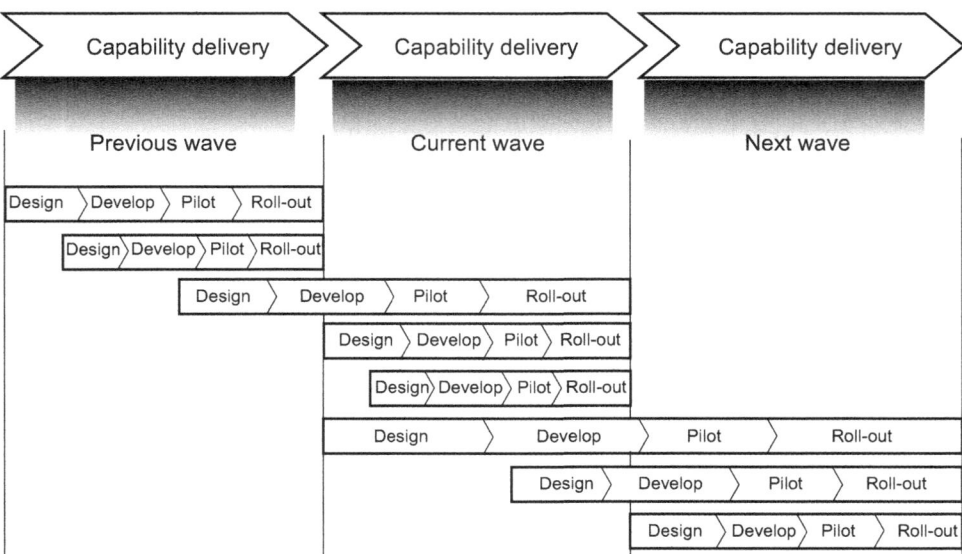

Figure 23.3 Relationships between enabling projects and programme waves

state. Temporary facilities might be needed in parallel with the programme improvement work. The transitions of the capabilities into operation of the current wave are aligned in time in order to ensure that disruptions to normal operations are kept to a minimum. The focus of this phase is on ensuring the realization of the intended benefits besides implementing the new or enhanced processes and capabilities. The work in this benefit realization phase is also carried out both at project and at programme level (Figure 23.4).

Project level

The change to a new way of working includes ensuring that all elements rolled out in the capability delivery phase are put in operation. From a process point of view new roles, tools, materials and information will start at a defined point in time to interact and produce new outputs from the currently available inputs. This change happens during the transition phase. Before the actual transition, in a mobilize phase, the individuals involved must be trained, organized and motivated to support the new operational mode. Moreover the elements to be used for the first time must be prepared and made ready. After the transition phase, in a stabilize phase, any necessary activity to ensure the effective application of the new capabilities is undertaken in order maximize the benefits and minimize negative consequences (for example verifying that the old capabilities are actually not used any more, ensuring that the new ones are applied in the best way, correcting existing flaws in the tools). Once the new capabilities are working in a stable way and the desired benefits are realized the outdated systems and infrastructure of the old ones are removed.

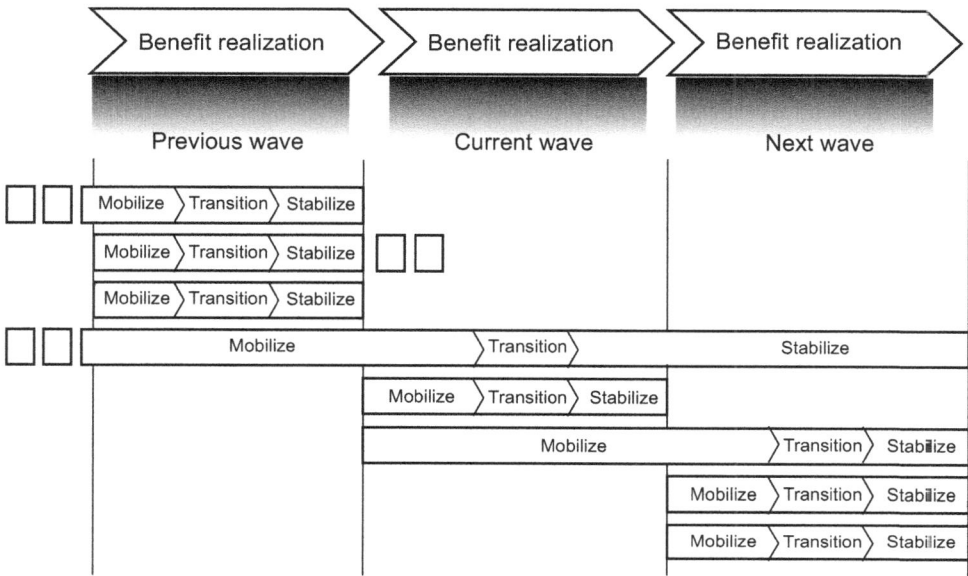

Figure 23.4 Relationship between transition projects and programme waves

Programme level

The realization of benefits is the main objective of a programme and is achieved during this phase. All transitions are chartered and steered at the programme level to ensure the most effective sequencing and minimize disruption of ongoing operations. Only when the new capabilities are operative can the benefit realization begin. In order to measure the level of benefit achieved, it is necessary to begin with the measurement of the aimed benefits before any transformation activity starts (earlier referred to as establishing the baseline). After the transformation, the benefit level will be closely monitored and corrections necessary to maximize it will be executed, usually by the transition projects in the stabilize phase.

The end of this phase is determined when, ideally, all capabilities that were decided for transition have realized their intended benefits or when the next set of transformations starts being implemented, that is, the next wave is started.

Closure

Handover and closure take place in the closure phase. There are three kinds of reasons for terminating a programme, as follows:

1. The programme has realized the expected benefits.
2. The programme cannot realize any or all of intended aimed benefits (for example the costs would be higher or the environment has significantly changed).
3. Realization of the programme benefits is no longer relevant.

The capabilities successfully implemented and the benefits realized are formally reviewed for completeness and the realization of benefits not yet achieved can be planned during programme closure to ensure that they can be confidently realized and sustained without programme support.

Handover to the business managers is performed by the programme sponsor and the programme manager with the aim of ensuring proper coordination of any remaining projects and activities. After handover, the final documentation of the programme is produced and archived. The programme team is released from the programme responsibilities and disbanded.

Interaction between programme components

At the onset, programmes typically have a degree of complexity and uncertainty with multiple alternative solutions. For example, a new product might be needed to fulfil an emerging market demand, but multiple technologies and design solutions have to be considered and evaluated. These technologies could themselves be emerging in their development maturity and must be evaluated and tested, not only for their capabilities but also to ensure that their stability will allow for predictable project delivery. Additionally, is the market demand understood well enough to establish clear and stable requirements? As the sponsor of the component projects, the programme manager may call for market research projects to understand more thoroughly the customer need and to develop product and project requirements.

Often, analysis alone cannot solve these issues. One has to build something and observe it in the expected field of use. Techniques such as rapid prototyping or technology 'run-offs' might be conducted to determine which solutions will enable success and which will not. The elimination of outputs from some projects is as much a success as it is to select the ones that provide the best solution. Lessons learned from preceding work are often used in improving the final outcomes of the next projects. To deal with this constant refinement of the programme on the way forward while maintaining the stability needed for project delivery success, programmes often take on an iterative nature which resembles an aspect of agility in resolving the best approach by conducting smaller scale, but stable, projects while continuing to make forward progress. A discussion of the various types of programme component work follows.

Explorative projects

Explorative projects are those work components initiated to analyse unclear or uncertain objectives and deliver the information necessary for programme requirements development, risk reduction, and to support later decisions. Explorative projects establish the foundation for the programme objectives and scope and reduce programme risk exposure for later work. Explorative projects are usually started during the programme definition phase and completed before the start of capability delivery phase. Examples of explorative projects are:

- new technology development, maturity evaluation and selection;
- market studies for better understanding of a new or changing market;

- business case refinement – costs versus benefits; programme viability;
- modelling and prototyping of new technologies, tools or capabilities;
- requirements development and refinement of the capabilities needed as part of the future state (for example, the 'blueprint').

Enabling projects

Enabling projects are programme components that are intended to deliver the building blocks of new or improved organizational capabilities. These are the capabilities that constitute and define the future state 'blueprint' such as the new processes, technology, organizational structure (for example, staff competency, roles, responsibilities and the flow of information) that enables the organization to achieve the expected outcomes leading to benefit realization. Enabling projects are the principal work elements in the capability delivery phase of the programme.

Transition projects

Transition projects are work components directed at implementing a new or improved capability in an organization and establishing new ways of working. This work is normally conducted and led by the 'business-as-usual' or operations area of the organization that will actually utilize the new capabilities and is responsible for benefit delivery. Transition projects are performed during the benefits realization phase of the programme. Examples of transitional projects are:

- controlled introduction of new capabilities (for example, low rate initial production, operational evaluation);
- operational analysis to ensure that desired outcomes are achieved;
- capability refinement and improvement (for example, lean, six sigma projects);
- all of the above in one project.

Operational functions

Operational functions are critical components of programmes because they will be responsible not only for accepting the new capabilities and transitioning them to stable use but also for ensuring sustained delivery of benefits as programme support is removed. Expertise from the operational functions is key in several areas of the programme, especially in the definition, benefits realization and closure stages, as follows:

- defining capability requirements and acceptance criteria;
- defining and developing staff competency requirements;
- transition activity planning and execution;
- defining, measuring and confirming benefits;
- establishing realistic benefit expectations.

Support functions

Support functions provide guidance, assurance and technical expertise to the programme. These functions could range from senior technical experts, quality and safety consultants to organizational programme and project methodology processes, templates and tools. Strategic suppliers could also be considered in this group. A PMO is an example of a support function within the programme that can provide administrative, financial accounting and information support.

As owners of the new capability infrastructure as well as having responsibility for the realization and sustainment of benefits long-term in the organization, both operational and support functions are instrumental throughout the programme lifecycle (especially in the benefits realization and closure stages).

Interactions between project and programme portfolios

Portfolios provide the alignment of the organization's programmes and projects to achieve the strategic vision. Where organizational transformation is required, programmes are established to deliver that change and to deliver and sustain the benefits envisaged by the portfolio. Programme sponsors are typically selected from the portfolio leadership to ensure linkage between the portfolio objectives and the programme.

As programme managers are often the sponsors of component projects to ensure the alignment with programme objectives, programme sponsors are the vital link between the programme and the strategic goals of the portfolio. In that capacity, programme sponsors are typically accountable for delivering the programme outcomes to the portfolio leadership and are best suited to guide the programme in delivering strategic value to the organization. This would include:

- assurance of adequate resource allocation for the programme;
- management of strategic stakeholders;
- orchestrating cooperation across the organization to facilitate the acceptance of change.

Additionally, adjacent programmes might exist which provide enabling capabilities across multiple programmes. One example might be a research and development programme that is responsible for developing new technologies across the entire organization's product lines. Although supporting programmes may not be under the immediate direction of the lead programme, the lead programme is considered a customer. These complex relationships must be clearly understood and managed at the portfolio level as the benefit objectives of one programme could adversely affect the benefit objectives of the adjacent programmes.

References and further reading

Lock, D. (2013), *Project Management*, 10th edn., Farnham: Gower.

Chapter 24

An Overview of the Programme Management Process

Robert Buttrick

This chapter outlines programme management processes and procedures and discusses their significance and the relationships between them.

Programme management: process or method?

Programme management processes define how a programme is directed, managed and undertaken. This usually means that these processes are:

* Directed by the programme sponsor. The sponsor is accountable to a higher level or authority in the organization, owns the business case and is the primary risk taker, decision-maker and change agent (known as the 'senior responsible owner' in the MSP [Managing Successful Programmes] method).
* Managed by the programme manager, who is accountable to the programme sponsor for the day-to-day management of the programme and for ensuring that the stated objectives are achieved.
* Undertaken by the programme team, which is accountable to the programme manager and may be working at 'programme' level or on any of its constituent projects or work.

These terms are used in this chapter. But beware: they may be used differently in your own organization or even be mixed up with job titles. For example, on one major programme, costing £1 billion over ten years, the job title 'CEO' was used for the programme sponsor and 'COO' for the programme manager, as these fitted the prestige and level associated with the roles.

The programme management processes comprise the practices which should be followed by the programme sponsor, manager and team to ensure that the programme's business objectives are achieved. As such, they are a vital part of the governance of a programme. But they are only a part; following a process rarely achieves anything on its own. For programme success, a number of bases need to be covered, as shown in Figure 24.1 (Buttrick, 2009).

* *Accountability and structure* define what the roles are and who each role holder is accountable to. If a person is not accountable to anyone, they are not accountable.

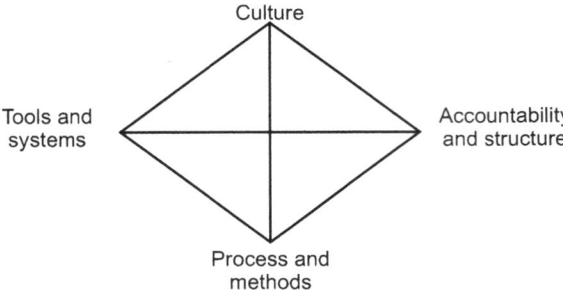

Culture

Tools and
systems

Accountability
and structure

Process and
methods

Figure 24.1 Efficient programme management requires more than process or methods, culture (values and mindsets)

- *Processes (or methods)* should be used whenever value is added by undertaking an activity in a consistent way. If consistency is not important, then no process or method is needed; the person accountable undertakes the activity in whatever way they want. Do not define processes just for the sake of it.
- *Systems and tools* should make the undertaking of repeated activities more efficient and effective, especially facilitating information flow.
- *Culture and behaviours* determine people's mindset when using the processes and systems. With the wrong mindset, even the best processes and systems will fail to deliver the required results. We are all familiar with 'tick-box' management, where the completion of forms takes precedence over real management thought and action.

Note in Figure 24.1 that each of the four bases is connected, meaning that a change in one is highly likely to affect any or all of the others. Looking at culture in this way can explain why processes which work well in one organization might fail in another. Similarly, even a stable process may stop working within an organization with a change of senior leadership, where the new incumbents have different values from the previous regime.

Another cultural factor affecting the successful management of a programme is trust. The less trust there is in an organization, the more checks and controls management tend to put in place. Numerous checks and review loops add to the number of roles needed and, in turn, increase the complexity of the processes. If these extra processes are supported by systems, this will be reflected in the system design and workflow options. On the other hand, with a greater level of trust and personal responsibility, processes and systems can be simplified, allowing people maximum freedom in their work. This concept of trust is at the heart of agile practices. It does not mean there should be no 'must do' processes, but these should be restricted to those that add value, enhance customer experience and ensure compliance with higher level governance and risk management needs. Getting the balance right is not easy, because this can change over the life of a programme. So do not think that once you have defined your method or processes they can be fixed. They must be managed, enhanced, simplified and developed to respond to the changing context, needs and people associated with the programme.

Programme management processes and methods: context is key

Programme management processes should help a team to achieve the programme's objectives. The design of these processes is dependent on the context within which the programme is undertaken. Key considerations are:

- Is the programme a stand-alone business entity?
- Is it under the direction of a formal portfolio managed environment?
- Does it cross institutional boundaries?
- What else is happening which might affect it?
- What is the level of maturity of the organization managing the programme and how does this compare to any suppliers?
- What specialist work is needed and where?
- Does the organization have an enterprise method or processes for programme management?

Different viewpoints of contractors and suppliers

A programme seen from the viewpoint of a contractor or supplier may look very different from a programme as seen by the promoter, even though they appear to be the same programme:

- The promoter will be interested in the business outcomes and benefits they seek to achieve, which will be related to their strategic objectives. They may have more than one supplier for their programme and may also be undertaking work themselves. They are primarily taking the risk (regardless of any contractual indemnity clauses with suppliers). Their business case is based on increased revenues, reductions in working capital, efficiency and improved service levels set against the costs incurred in their organization, plus those of any contracted parties.
- A contractor will be interested in the revenue gained from a major contract. Their interest is limited by the scope of the contract and is likely to exclude many of the activities critical to their customer's success. Their business case relies on the revenue they can gain against the costs they incur.

These differences are not always clear-cut and can become more ambiguous if a contractor's scope goes beyond the development of outputs (say software) and includes change management, operational and service aspects. Many 'build–operate–transfer' contracts are best managed as programmes.

Formal, informal, light or tight?

Processes define the activities to be undertaken, who is involved, and usually include templates for important and frequently used documents (such as the business case and programme management plan). They may also include product descriptions with quality criteria, guidance in the form of booklets (online and/or physical) and videos, which act as educational vehicles for the programme team.

The degree of formality in programme direction management is a matter of context, culture and choice. It ranges from very prescriptive (process-driven) to a looser approach, giving the programme manager a large degree of freedom on the detail (this is often called method-driven). Some organizations are clear on the difference between 'process' and 'method' and find the distinction useful, while for others this is irrelevant. It is very much a matter of how the words are perceived and used in those organizations.

Recent focus has been on improving programme and project management success rates by using reliable, repeatable processes. CMMI's approach (SEI, 2010) is based on the assumption that the quality of the output is highly influenced by the quality of the process used. Many (but not all) organizations have gained significant improvements as a result. Consequently, there is growing concern that an overemphasis on 'process' or being 'process obsessed' might have the opposite effect to that intended in terms of improving business performance. For this reason, 'methods' are gaining more attention.

A method defines the broad approach, leaving much of the detail for the user to define. Methods are less prescriptive than processes, which can be seen as a straitjacket. For this reason, many believe that 'management', being more of an art, is better defined in terms of methods rather than process. Again the context and words used in your organization may paint a different picture; the terms 'process', 'activity' and 'practice' are used differently and often interchangeably in different organizations, published methods and standards. Do not, however, confuse the freedom 'methods' give over a pure process approach with how 'tight or light' your management is. Programme management needs to be tight in terms of ensuring that every part of the programme is aligned to:

- strategy;
- meeting business objectives;
- managing interdependencies;
- acceptable overall risk;
- work being started (such as for project gating) or stopped when it should be and information flows to the programme management team, ensuring that progress and status are being accurately reflected.

Programmes, by their nature, are usually too large to be predictable enough to let an unmanaged plan drive them.

With both a 'method' or 'process' approach, the practices and activities comprising the management of a programme can be looked at as falling into three main groups:

1. *Management processes or methods* which ensure the programme as a whole, including its component parts, is adequately governed, integrated, under enough control and likely to meet the defined objectives. This is the core of the process set.
2. *Supporting processes or methods*, which determine how a particular facet of management is undertaken (for example risk management). Such processes include the detail and may be used within the components of a programme or even outside

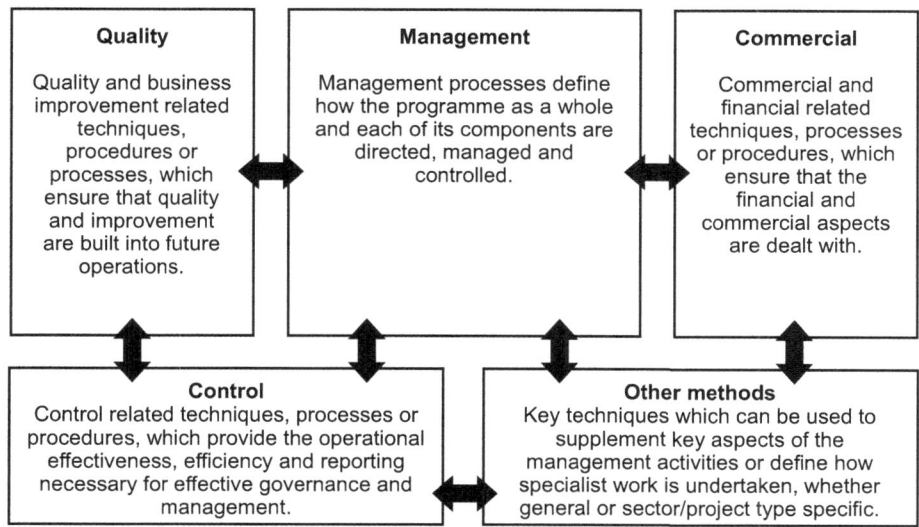

Figure 24.2 Management support and specialist programmes: high-level architecture

the programme. Typically, they comprise processes for the control, quality and commercial work on the programme.

3. *Specialist processes or methods* are dependent on the type of outputs and outcomes expected from the programme (for example a software development process or method). These are outside the scope of programme management but as they form part of the context, they can have a significant effect on programme management. For example, programme management information flow and management practices for agile delivery would be different from those for more tangible deliveries, as in civil engineering projects.

An outline for an architecture is depicted in Figure 24.2. For simplicity, the term 'process' is used in the rest of this chapter to cover both 'method' and 'process'.

Ensuring an architecture for programme management processes

None of the processes can exist in isolation and the key to developing them for a particular programme, or as part of an enterprise-wide programme management approach, is to ensure they fit into the host organization's management operating model, culture and level of maturity. As a general rule, the less mature an organization, the greater the need for documented guidance and processes. Unfortunately, the heavier the document load, the less likely people are to use it. Programme processes must be suited to the competencies of your people. So the processes need to be designed for use at varying levels of detail. The levels start with summary descriptions and end with detailed templates and guides, supported by step-by-step instructions. Designing the process architecture makes the processes simpler to use, less ambiguous and easier to maintain and develop, as the organization matures.

Architecture design may be based on international or national standards, proprietary methods, such as MSP (OGC, 2011), or particular bodies of knowledge from various professional organizations, like the Association for Project Management (APM, 2012). Design may also draw on practices defined in maturity models, such as CMMI for Development or CMMI for Services (SEI, 2010). Do not restrict yourself: take what you need from wherever. Each published standard or method takes a slightly different approach and uses different terminology; you must decide which standard or method to base your approach on and select your own glossary of terms. Having done this, you can then include any features from any of the other approaches. None of them on their own is likely to cover your full needs, nor (if you are a contractor) the requirements of every one of your customers, so you will need to build a process architecture which suits your context and needs.

An important first action is to define what work components your programme comprises, as this forms the basis of the management structures. For example, a programme is likely to have projects and so a project management process would be required. Figure 24.3 shows a typical breakdown of a programme into its management components, showing a programme divided into project and other work and then decomposed into work packages.

You will also need to ensure that your programme management processes fit with the other management processes in your organization by aligning your programme process (and systems) to your organization's systems and process for activities, where they exist, such as:

- performance reporting;
- enterprise resource management;

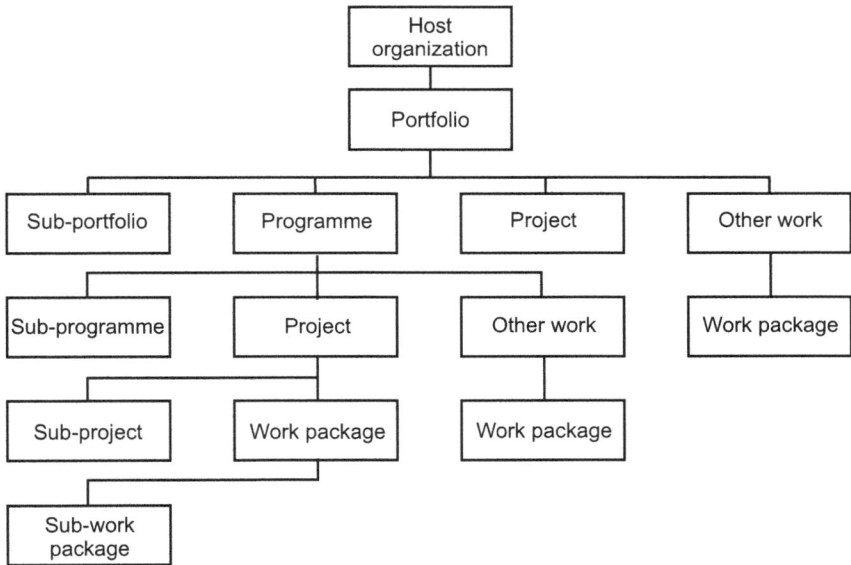

Figure 24.3 Decomposition of a programme into components

- enterprise risk management;
- financial management;
- procurement and supplier management;
- portfolio and project management;
- management of change;
- quality management.

Despite what some standards say, few, if any, processes (and their supporting systems) are unique to programme or even project management and would need to be shared with other management functions and roles. Risk management, for example, is an activity which should be undertaken as part of:

- enterprise risk management;
- portfolio management;
- programme management;
- project management;
- service and operations management;
- work package management.

It therefore makes sense to use the same fundamental approach to risk management for all these, rather than have different methods, processes and systems for each. This is even more critical because programme management, being a higher order activity, includes the management of its component parts (including projects and other work, such as operations and service management). You certainly would not want your project managers using a different approach from your programme management team. This argument applies to all the 'supporting processes' which are discussed later in this chapter.

By taking such an approach, you are unlikely to be able to replicate any of the architectures from the published standards and methods exactly. Yet, this does not mean that your approach does not comply with them. For example, companies have developed programme management methods and processes which can be demonstrated as complying with *all* of the following (and often others):

- MSP;
- APM and PMI bodies of knowledge for portfolio, programme and project management;
- Prince2;
- DSDM Atern;
- CMMI for Development and Services;
- ISO 21500, Guidance on project management;
- ISO 9000, Quality management;
- ISO 31000, Risk management.

It is a matter of demonstrating where, in your method or process, the particular aspect of the standard or method is covered. An example of this is in the UK's Cabinet Office White Paper which shows how Prince2 aligns with both ISO 21500 and BS 6079 Part 1 (Buttrick, 2012).

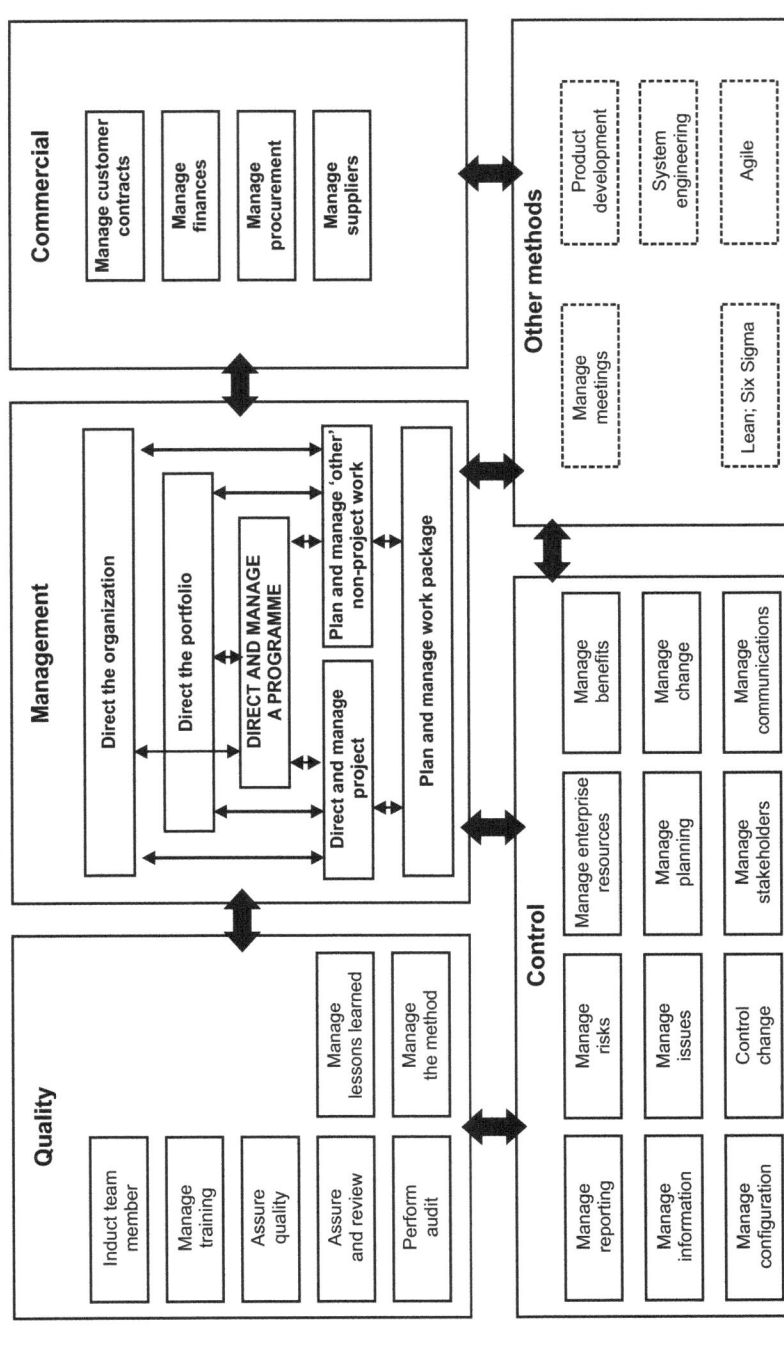

Quality

- Induct team member
- Manage training
- Assure quality
- Assure and review
- Perform audit
- Manage lessons learned
- Manage the method

Management

- Direct the organization
- Direct the portfolio
- **DIRECT AND MANAGE A PROGRAMME**
- Direct and manage project
- Plan and manage 'other' non-project work
- Plan and manage work package

Commercial

- Manage customer contracts
- Manage finances
- Manage procurement
- Manage suppliers

Control

- Manage reporting
- Manage information
- Manage configuration
- Manage risks
- Manage issues
- Control change
- Manage enterprise resources
- Manage planning
- Manage stakeholders
- Manage benefits
- Manage change
- Manage communications

Other methods

- Manage meetings
- Product development
- System engineering
- Agile
- Lean; Six Sigma

Figure 24.4 Starting to build detail into the architecture: choosing the activities which are key for the programme

You need not decide to use the same terminology as a particular method or standard, nor even exactly match the detail in each. That is your choice. It is your organization and your programme. You need to decide what is important for you, tailoring the standards to fit your needs and context. Remember, standards and proprietary methods are simply the consensus of what represents good practice, and none was designed specifically for you. Tailoring is a feature of any good method and is discussed later in this chapter.

Figure 24.4 is an example of a high level architecture, which will be developed in the rest of this chapter.

Management processes

Management processes pull together various strands from the supporting and specialist processes to ensure the programme as a whole is adequately governed, defined, planned, under control and likely to meet its objectives. As 'integrating' processes, a programme and its components parts (such as projects) are often interrelated. A programme management method should be designed as a 'complete architecture' to ensure that the different aspects fit together and that terms are used consistently (which is why pure standards, MSP or Prince2 terminology cannot always be used). The management procedures are summarized in Figure 24.5, with the arrows depicting information flows. For example, the 'Direct and manage a programme' procedure controls the 'Direct and manage a project' and the 'Plan and manage other work' management processes.

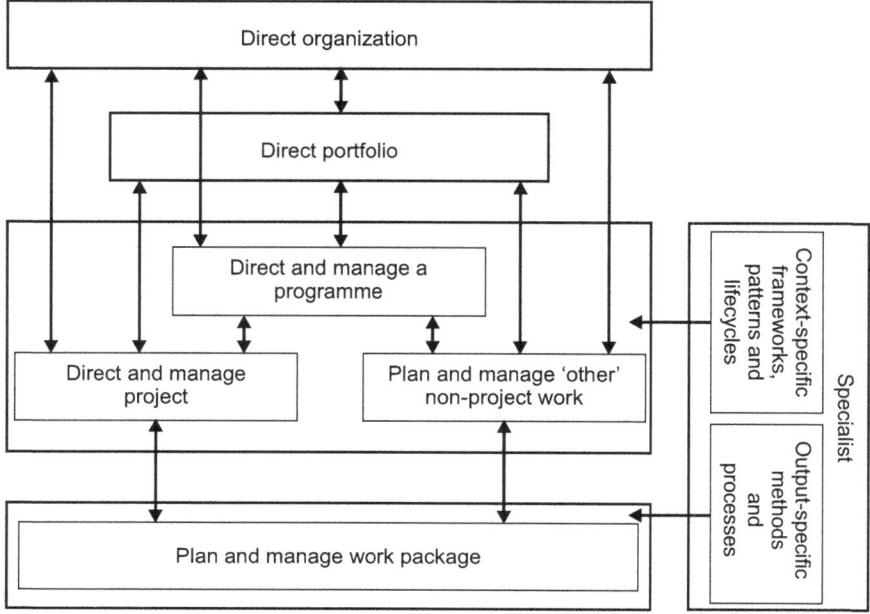

Figure 24.5 Programme management architecture in the context of organization, portfolio, programme, project and portfolio management

Managing a programme

A programme comprises two types of component work:

- project-related work;
- other work (not managed as a project).

'Project-related work' usually involves the building, development or creation of outputs for new capabilities or services, or the withdrawal of existing capabilities or services. A project may, however, include the work involved in transforming an organization to ensure outcomes are achieved (change management). This is what many standards term 'an extended project lifecycle'. Then the scope of the project (and hence its lifecycle) is extended beyond the creation of outputs. It ensures that the outputs are actually used and the organization is transformed. Business adoption, and hence benefits realization, are then more likely to be achievable. It is an approach advocated in Isochron's D4 method, using 'Recognition events™' and 'Value flashpoints™' (Fowler and Lock, 2006).

As a programme is likely to comprise more than one project, project portfolio management is key in undertaking this work, together with a gating process to ensure that each stage of a project starts when it is meant to (if the risks are acceptable). Project gating should be more about decisions to start the next stage, rather than backward facing quality checking on the previous stage. Retrospective 'quality gates' are a feature of some waterfall IT development methods which are often ignored or block progress. Good project gating ensures that a project stage proceeds even if the previous stage is incomplete, providing the risks are acceptable.

'Other work' relates to work which is not run as a staged and gated project, but is essential as part of the programme. A key example relates to operating the capabilities and services, including the measurement of performance and benefits. 'Other work' also applies to the management-related aspects of the programme (for example, running the programme management office).

By taking this approach, a programme may include both project and non-project work and might not even include any projects at all. Examples are where a Six Sigma approach is used to enhance operations on a continuous basis or where agile delivery techniques are applied as part of 'business-as-usual' platform enhancements.

The typical activities, roles and information flow relating to managing a programme are summarized in Figure 24.6 and described below.

Identify a programme

Identifying a programme is the first step in launching a programme. If the programme is internal to an organization it should be identified within a business area as a need or opportunity, derived from the business strategy and plan. The people within the business area who require the programme to be undertaken (for the benefits it will realize) are the sponsoring group. In a contracting context, if the programme is related to a bid for a customer, the identification happens as part of putting the bid response together.

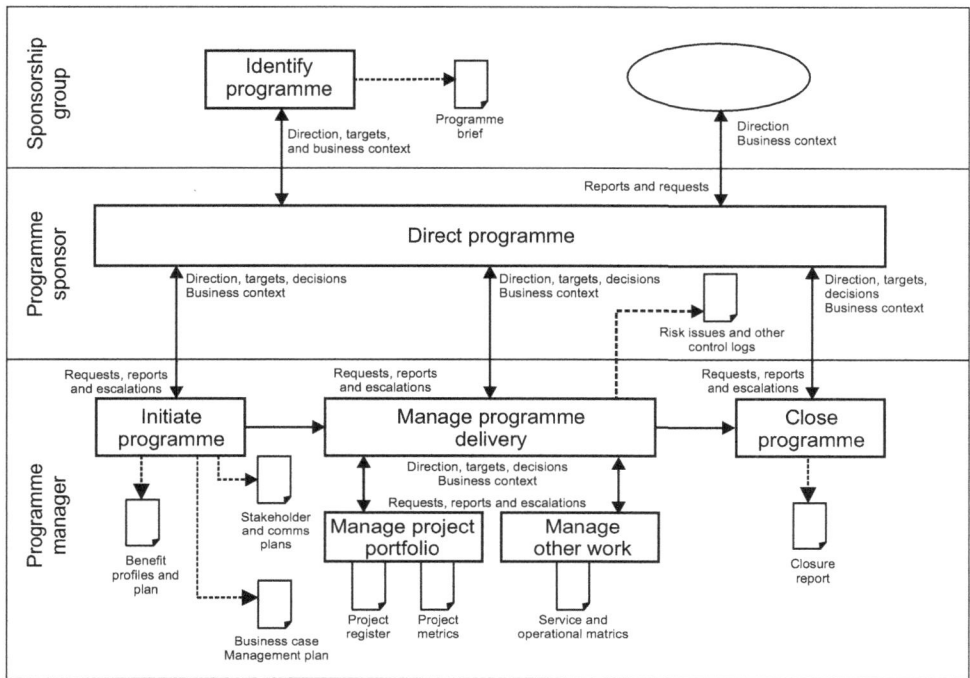

Figure 24.6 Information flow and activities for directing and managing a programme

The primary output from this activity is a programme brief or charter, summarizing why an organization's senior management wants to undertake the programme and outlining their expectations. Note that the programme is not started through the immediate creation of a programme management plan and full programme plan. In programmes the complexity and amount of work undertaken is so great that development of the programme plan and programme management plan can themselves be an expensive undertaking. For this reason, a shorter programme brief is created, to ensure alignment within the sponsoring group, explaining what the programme is for. Then, this is used as the basis for selecting the appropriate programme sponsor, manager and team.

Direct a programme

The role of the programme sponsor is to ensure the programme is always viable in business terms. If the programme becomes unviable, it must either be changed or terminated. Ensuring continued viability is the focus of this activity and is the responsibility of the programme sponsor. Tasks include ensuring the programme manager and team are aware of the changing business context and risks, requesting and receiving direction from the sponsoring group, dealing with requests and direction from the programme manager and reporting on the programme status to the sponsoring group and key stakeholders. The programme sponsor is also accountable for engaging senior stakeholders. The scope, complexity and size of a programme may be such that the programme sponsor might delegate certain aspects of the role to others (which would be defined in the programme management plan). Such delegation does not, however, absolve the programme sponsor from overall accountability for the success of the programme.

Initiate a programme

As soon as the programme brief is approved the 'initiate a programme' activity is triggered. This means setting up the programme correctly from the start. The programme brief forms the basis for this and the programme manager is accountable for ensuring that it happens. The programme's internal processes are defined here. The key tasks to be undertaken include: mobilizing the cross-functional team, reviewing lessons from previous programmes, identifying and engaging stakeholders, determining how quality will be managed and outline planning of the programme. Large programmes often need establishment of a number of capabilities to ensure effective management and will probably include a programme management office and programme infrastructure:

- procedures;
- house style;
- intranet;
- document and information management facilities;
- specialist tools such as for planning, risk and issue management, change control, configuration management, requirements management, testing and so on.

In addition the governance arrangements for the programme should be defined, taking into account the needs of the key stakeholders and (if relevant) the customer. Each governing body should have clearly defined terms of reference and responsibilities. All this is documented in the programme management plan. With an enterprise programme management approach, each programme team need only cross-refer or define any tailoring, dramatically simplifying and reducing the extent of any documentation.

The above deals with setting up programme operation (how it will be undertaken). Work also needs to be undertaken to develop a future state to be created by the programme (MSP calls this a blueprint), to develop an initial, outline programme plan for achieving this and justification through a business case. Often, programme delivery will be phased (undertaken in 'tranches'). Phases or tranches are convenient ways of segmenting a large, complex programme to gain early benefits, facilitate understanding and simplify the planning aspects. You can think of them as 'subprogrammes'. Those phases/tranches which are well into the future need not be planned until necessary. For many programmes, even if the business need remains stable, plans for achieving the desired outcomes are likely to alter during the course of the programme. Programme management is ideally suited to this ambiguous form of business activity. The 'initiate a programme' activity includes work that will itself be undertaken as a project or simply as a 'work package'.

Manage programme delivery

The programme manager is accountable for controlling the programme on a day-to-day basis, ensuring that delivery and benefits realization remain on track. Throughout the programme the programme manager will receive reports and confirmation of completed deliverables, outputs, outcomes and benefits from the project and other managers and will be reporting progress to the programme sponsor and key stakeholders. Advice, decisions, business context and risk are covered by the programme sponsor from the 'Direct a programme' activity.

The issue of an instruction by the programme manager to start work on a project triggers the 'Direct and manage a project' procedure. If the programme is for a customer, the programme manager will need to ensure that not only is the programme's baseline controlled (in terms of benefits, costs, schedule and scope), but also that it is still consistent with the contract and any variations. In many programmes suppliers are engaged to create the outputs or operate services. It is the programme manager's accountability, through the programme team, to ensure that these are run effectively, supported by specialist supplier managers, where appropriate.

Manage project portfolio

The key activities required to manage the project portfolio include maintaining the project register, managing interdependencies, dealing with escalated risks and issues, receiving and responding to project reports and giving direction to change the project's status (proposed, in progress, on hold, terminated, completed). Finally, this activity oversees any post-project review to assess project effectiveness in terms of enabling benefits realization and the performance of any operational capabilities produced.

Plan and manage 'other work'

I wrote earlier that 'other work' often relates to managing operations and services and can be very diverse. For this reason, the approach has to be determined on a programme-by-programme basis, depending on the type of work undertaken. Nevertheless, the key activities include planning, monitoring continuing operations and services (using metrics), dealing with escalated risks and problems and providing direction to the teams.

Close a programme

Programme closure can happen in three circumstances:

- the programme is completed;
- the programme is terminated because the risks have become unacceptable or a problem has arisen which cannot be resolved;
- the context has changed (for example a business takeover, reorganization or competitor activity).

The programme manager should decommission the programme and prepare a programme closure report to confirm the state of the programme at the point of time when it closed and should include a summary of the key lessons learned. This document forms the basis for formal approval of programme closure by the programme sponsor. On receipt of formal approval, the programme manager should manage the final closure actions, communicating to all stakeholders, ensuring that all facilities are decommissioned and people are reassigned.

Supporting processes

The management procedures described above outline 'integrating activities' that the programme sponsor, programme manager and core programme team need to undertake. They do not necessarily describe how some of those activities are undertaken. The detail for many of these, such as managing risks and issues, controlling change (as in baselined plans), managing information and so on may be defined in a set of supporting processes (which might not be unique to programme management). Documenting the supporting processes separately ensures that the management procedures are as concise as possible, common supporting procedures can be used across all programmes and projects, and variants of the procedures can be slotted into place for use on specific types of programme or project. It also enables a common tools strategy to be deployed. The support procedures can be divided into three groups:

- control (planning, risks, problems and variances, change control and reporting);
- quality (reviews, audits, lessons learned, document management, induction);
- commercial aspects (contract and supplier management, procurement, financial management).

To make these procedures mutually consistent they need to be designed as part of the overall architecture, showing how each relates to the other. Figures 24.7, 24.8 and 24.9 give an example of the procedures or processes for each group.

Remember, these groups are simply a way of categorizing processes to make them easier to understand; you may choose, as part of your architecture, to have different groups.

Specialist or 'other' processes

Specialist processes are dependent on the type of outputs and outcomes expected from the programme. To be successful, not only does the programme have to be directed and managed effectively, but the specialist work relating to the programme's outputs and outcomes has to be undertaken well. Although the specialist processes are outside the scope of this chapter, the way they are undertaken is relevant to how the programme is managed and achievement or progress measured. The programme manager needs to be confident in the progress metrics and operational or benefit metrics used. For example, some of the software work in the programme may be undertaken using agile delivery techniques, while others might use other traditional or proprietary approaches (frequently supplier-led). The challenge for

Process	Description
Planning	Planning ensures that outputs and outcomes from a programme are likely to be delivered in sufficient time, within cost, and at a required quality so that the expected benefits will be realized. The different aspects have to be planned as a whole. For example, changes in the schedule might affect costs and benefits. Planning should be holistic, covering scope, schedule, resources, costs and benefits, because each impacts the others. For example, an increase in scope could trigger a schedule slip, increased costs and reduced benefits. The objective is to ensure that the plan takes risk into account and ensure the programme is always viable.
Reporting	Reporting ensures that all programme team members and key stakeholders are aware of the current programme status and the outlook for the future; particularly achievement of the objectives and benefits. Reporting generally relates to information flow within the programme and immediate set of interested parties. Note that communications management is used for stakeholders outside the core team (see below). Some organizations combine these in a single process, even though the tools and approaches are different.
Risk management	Risk management ensures that programme objective are likely to be achieved and that the risks are acceptable to the organization. It covers the identification, treatment and monitoring of risk, including threats and opportunities.
Issues management	Issues management ensures that events do not impact negatively on achieving the business objectives. Issues may result from a known risk 'happening' or could be totally unforeseen.
Change control	Change control ensures that only approved and fully assessed changes are adopted into a programme, so that the objectives, benefits, scope, schedule and cost baselines for the programme or project are defined, mutually consistent and reflect the current status at any point in time. The main danger is of progress being slowed by non-value-added bureaucracy. Making sure that change control decisions can be made as low in the management chain as possible is key.
Configuration management	Configuration management ensures that each project deliverable is identified in terms of status and version. Also that the composition of all higher level outputs is known of the constituent deliverables/components. Some organizations treat this as a specialist process, relating to IT development or service management.
Information management	Information management ensures that the programme team understand where all information and documentation is held and how it is management and distributed. It usually defines how all documents are created, reviewed, approved, version-controlled and ultimately withdrawn.
Resource management	Resource management ensures that the programme manager has the resources to undertake everything in the plan. If resources are not fully allocated to a programme, this needs to interface to any enterprise approaches used. Even if resources are fully allocated they may still be shared across the programme's different work components.
Stakeholder management	Stakeholder management identifies and manages all stakeholders to ensure programme objectives are achieved. People are at the heart of any change and we need to understand the impact they might have on the programme. Ignoring stakeholders is a quick route to failure.
Communications management	Communications management ensures that communications to all programme stakeholders are effective and coordinated - so that the programme objectives can be achieved. This relates to wider communications outside formal reporting and might include press releases, advertisements and exhibitions. The 2012 London Olympics made great use of this to build momentum and support to ensure a successful Games and legacy.
Change management	Often called the 'management of change' or transformational change to distinguish it from change control (see above). This is about winning hearts and minds to lead to acceptance of changes the programme is designed to implement. If people are not supportive the changes and benefits will not happen. 'People create change, people constrain change' (Obeng, 1997). Some organizations treat this as a specialist process.
Benefits management	Benefits management ensures that the programme or project benefits are identified, managed and realized. Because the only reason for undertaking a programme is for the required benefits, this process is fundamental. Its outputs, like a business case, drive many of the critical business decisions on a programme (Jenner, 2013).

Figure 24.7 Typical processes and control methods

Process	Description
Quality assurance	Quality assurance ensures that the outputs from the project are fit for purpose so that the project objectives are achievable. Typically this covers the standards to be applied, how quality is built into the outputs and how outcomes will be assured from a business perspective. Audit is often planned as part of this.
Audit	This is usually found only in large programmes. It covers the activities carried out by an independent team to give a programme sponsor, higher management and (where appropriate) the customer with objective, timely and effective insight into the performance of the programme. Traditionally, audits tend to focus on compliance with defined processes and procedures. They identify non-compliance issues tracked to a viable resolution. However, blind compliance with processes can deflect the team from the programme's primary objectives. Good audits look primarily at whether the management approach, culture and documentation are best for the programme, whilst ensuring that corporate governance is adequate and whether the programme team is likely to achieve the required objectives.
Review and assurance	The purpose of reviewing a programme or project is to ensure that it is still likely to meet the stated business objectives and to provide recommendations for any improvements. Reviews tend to be less formal and quicker to undertake than audits. They can be planned in advance on known, complex parts of the programme or before major decisions. Or this could be a reaction to a major issue that requires resolution.
Induction	To be effective, new joiners to a programme need to be briefed on the background and context of the programme and its operational procedures. Induction is needed either where the programme has created its own management approach or is tailored from an enterprise method. It includes routine aspects such as security, access and working methods, as well as values and behaviours.
Training	This procedure ensures that programme-specific training is delivered to team members to make them more effective in the operations, procedures and methods of the programme. This is a key aspect of CMMI, which takes the view that people are unlikely to perform well if they do not have the necessary training, development and experience. Training can also be used as part of change management, when training and development is needed to use new systems or equipment.
Lessons learned	Managing lessons learned ensures that any positive or developmental lessons are passed to the respective managers (for example, procedure owners or trainers) to avoid repeating past similar mistakes and to reuse good practice.
Method/ process management	Managing the programme processes or method and its components (procedures and so forth) ensures that these remain fit for purpose and that lessons learned are incorporated. This process also applies to any locally-managed tailored variants of enterprise processes. Without management, any process or method will degrade over time and become irrelevant. Too often organizations invest heavily in processes and methods and then mistakenly believe that these can be left to look after themselves.

Figure 24.8 Typical quality related processes

the programme manager is to understand how progress reporting and delivery are undertaken to ensure an overall view of the programme as a whole can be collated and harnessed to manage the entire programme.

A list of specialist processes would be as long and as varied as the different deliverables created.

The importance of change management

Key among the specialist processes is that related to the management of change, which determines transition from a current state to a future state, turning any 'outputs' into 'outcomes' or changes to the business. Change activity may be managed in different ways (for example, as part of a project or simply as part of managing

Process	Description
Financial management	Managing finances ensures that revenue and costs are controlled effectively, whilst overruns are contained and savings are made where possible. This usually includes budgeting, setting up accounts codes, time recording, time costing and forecasting. Cost forecasting should be related to cost and resource planning. Financial management usually includes processes to make sure that legal and regulatory requirements for good governance are covered (such as in Sarbanes Oxley).
Customer contract management	This is only needed if the programme is managed from a contractor or supplier. It covers the activities required for management and delivery of the contractual obligations to the customer This includes contract finances, contract risk, contract changes and variations. A contrac: generally limits an organization's degree of freedom of action.
Procurement	Procurement ensures that products or services bought to further a programme's objectives are of the appropriate quality and represent value for money for the buyer.
Supplier management	Managing suppliers ensures that their products or services are fit for purpose and that value for money is achieved. Procurement and supplier management are sometimes documented as a single process.

Figure 24.9 Typical commercial processes or methods

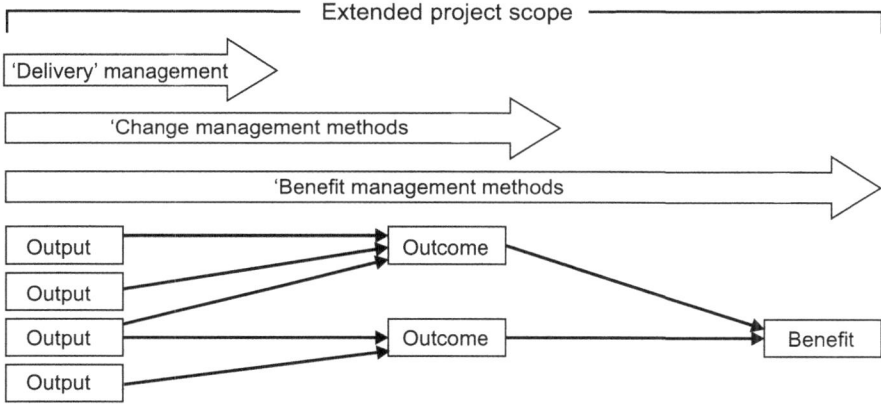

Figure 24.10 Project scope encompassing both outcomes and benefits, as used in an extended project lifecycle

business operations). A number of proprietary and 'home grown' approaches are available to use and professional standards are starting to be developed (such as in the Change Management Institute).

Do not constrain yourself by thinking that a project only creates outputs and then that the 'business' implements these to deliver 'outcomes'. Projects may be scoped based on outputs, outcomes or benefits. Figure 24.10 shows an extended project scope or lifecycle, encompassing outcomes and benefits (APM, 2012; BSI, 2010). Note, however, that even if a project scope is restricted to outputs (such as in an enabling project), work relating to benefits and change management still needs to be done within the overall programme.

The amount of change an organization can handle is not fixed. Organizations reach their limit of change tolerance because no one has a high-level view of the entirety of change under way and the collective impact of those changes on employees when added to 'business as usual'. When the cumulative and collective impact of change is not monitored and managed, people-related consequences arise, preventing realization of the programme's objectives. The consequences can be seen at the individual, programme and organizational levels.

At the individual level in a change saturated environment, employees can become disengaged, frustrated, fatigued, resistant, confused and more cynical and sceptical because they are already dealing with so much change.

At the programme level in a change saturated environment, projects do not realize benefits. There is a lack of resources to devote to each project, changes are not sustained, and projects fail to gain momentum because priorities are ignored and resources scarce. The same can apply to 'other work' (by which I mean change which is not managed as a project).

At an organizational level, operating at or past the point of change saturation can result in higher staff turnover, reduced productivity, increased absenteeism, loss of focus on business basics and negative morale.

You need to ensure that you have change management methods which are appropriate to your needs (Blake and Bush, 2009). Change management originated with psychologists and academics and is seen as a 'touchy-feely' discipline (usually controlled by HR or organizational development departments and specialists); it had an emphasis on how humans react to change. To make it more usable, engineering and project management approaches were integrated (for example in Kotter's eight-step model, Beer's six-step model and business process re-engineering). Unfortunately, with such approaches the human side of change can be undervalued and underfunded and is responsible for many so-called 'IT project failures'. Whatever techniques are applied the most important contribution a leader can make is passion, conviction and confidence in others. Too many senior managers announce a plan, then simply expect the team to find the solution.

Tailoring

Not every programme will need all the available processes and the extent to which they are used can vary from programme to programme or even within a programme. In addition, any commercial obligations in contracts associated with the programme should not conflict with the programme's processes. Allowing tailoring is, therefore, essential; this gives the programme manager the freedom to define the detail and rigour for the application of each aspect of programme management. If working within an enterprise-defined method, tailoring should only be done when it adds value, not as a matter of personal preference. Tailoring should be undertaken on a cascade basis, for example as shown in Figure 24.11. The higher level sets the contracts and degrees of freedom within which all lower levels operate. Those working at the lower levels have to tailor and choose their working methods accordingly.

Documenting processes

Whether you are creating a set of processes for a specific programme or as an enterprise method, you need to ensure that your documentation is easy to obtain and use.

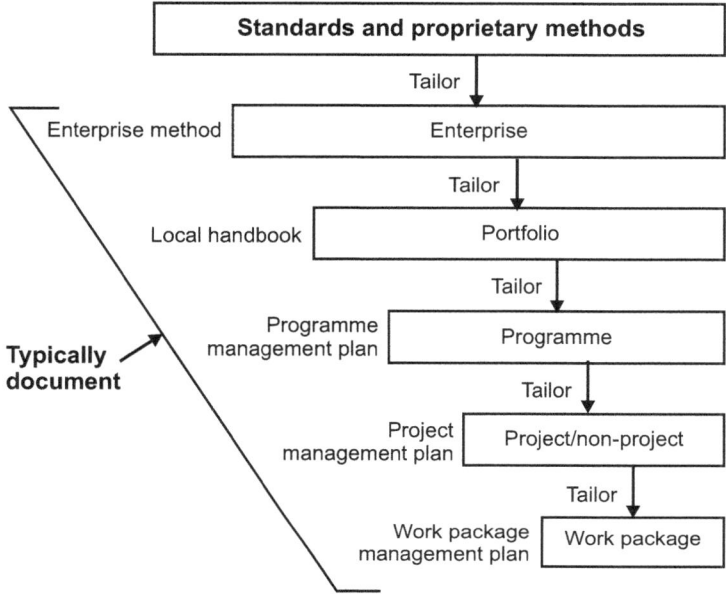

Figure 24.11 Cascade for tailoring

This usually takes the form of a website which users can view and from which they can download those parts they need to use. Modern systems can make the creaticn and maintenance of processes and methods easier, providing online and 'offline' versions (say, as a pdf), allowing people to share the methods and find what they need. Such systems can integrate a programme management process set with other enterprise methods and information, providing the user with what they need in as few pages or 'clicks' as possible.

Programme management should not be considered separate from overall management of the enterprise because it shares so many common techniques and processes. Web-based systems allow tracking how much the method is used overall and which parts are most used.

To conclude, here are some points of advice on how to document and manage your processes:

- *Have an architect who knows what they are talking about.* You must have someone who knows the overall content for your management approach before you start. This person should understand the context (otherwise you risk creating an inconsistent set of processes, with overlaps and gaps). Usually such a person would work in an enterprise or programme management office (OGC, 2008).
- *Create a house style.* Before you write or web-publish even ONE word, you must define the house style for documents and web pages and use this from then onwards. You have to ensure that your websites and documents are easy to navigate and read. This will prevent hours or days of rework. Many organizatiors have standards for this, in which case adopt them.

- *Have a defined glossary.* To be precise in your communications, choose your words carefully and always use them in the same way. Keep the glossary up to date and redefine terms if necessary.
- *Use plain, precise language.* Plain language is easier for everyone to understand. Use short words wherever possible (for example 'use' rather than 'utilize'). Avoid contentious or ambiguous words, jargon and acronyms. Ensure that activities are defined unambiguously, using verbs. For example, 'Business case' as an activity name is less informative than 'Develop and obtain approval for the business case'.
- *Have trusted knowledgeable advisers to keep you on the right path.* Even if your architect is a world-class expert, they should always seek advice from other knowledgeable people who might see things differently. The most important people are those who use the processes, and everything should be written with them in mind.
- *Use rigorous documentation management.* Use version control methods. If you have many processes, templates and guides you need to ensure that people have and use the latest version. So, use a document management system and categorize and use its version control features.
- *Encourage people to provide targeted feedback.* If it is easy to give feedback, then people might do it. Always respond to feedback; never ignore people (even if you do not take up their suggestion). Be prepared to react to feedback and change things, remembering that an elegant process set is not the end objective. The processes should enable the programme team in delivering a successful programme. Provide a feedback form on every page of your website to make it easy. Accept feedback in any form (for example, verbal or email). Do not insist that people use only the formal system.
- *Keep your processes up to date.* Keep your site up to date. A site which is out of date reduces user confidence. Do not just update quarterly. Update in real time whenever you get relevant feedback. People must be encouraged to realize that their feedback is really valued and used.

References and further reading

APM (2012), *APM Body of Knowledge*, 6th edn., Princes Risborough: Association for Project Management.

Blake, I. and Bush, C. (2009), *Project Managing Change*, London: FT/Prentice-Hall.

BSI (2010), *Project Management – Part 1: Principles and Guidelines for the Management of Projects*, 3rd edn., Norwich: British Standards Institution.

Buttrick, R. (2009), *The Project Workout*, 4th edn., London: FT/Prentice-Hall.

Buttrick, R. (2012), White Paper: *PRINCE2® and the National and International Standards*, Norwich: The Stationery Office.

Change Management Institute. <https://www.change-management-institute.com>. Accessed 19 December 2014.

Fowler, A. and Lock, D. (2006), *Accelerating Business and IT Change*, Farnham: Gower.

Jenner, S. (2012), *Managing Benefits*, Norwich: The Stationery Office.

Obeng, E. (1994), *The Project Leader's Secret Handbook*, London: Pitman Publishing.

OGC (2008), *Portfolio, Programme and Project Offices*, Norwich: The Stationery Office.

OGC (2011), *Managing Successful Programmes*, 4th edn., Norwich: The Stationery Office.

SEI (2010), *CMMI®(R) for Development*, Version 1.3, Pittsburgh, PA: SEI.

Chapter 25

Programme Identification and Initiation

Colin Bailey

A programme's success or failure can be heavily influenced by what happens in its identification and initiation.

Introduction

This chapter is in three main parts. The first of these begins by answering three questions:

1. What does it take to start a programme successfully?
2. What do we mean by identification and initiation?
3. What are the processes really trying to achieve and how do we know when we've got there?

After discussing the pitfalls that can often occur in early days of a programme start-up, I shall describe a completed identification and initiation, the end state of the processes and outline the goals of a successful start-up. I shall then explore other important things to achieve at the end of initiation, including:

- initial alignment of the projects towards the common goal;
- understanding of the programme from a project perspective (its key attributes of milestones, dependencies, resources and, ultimately, risks).

The second part of this chapter explores an approach for programme initiation (a plan for a plan). Initiation can be tricky, and in some cases recursive. There are several aspects of initiation that are heavily dependent on each other and which must be refined iteratively until the optimum mix of risk and reward has been discovered from a stakeholder perspective. I shall discuss the emergence of a business case and some of the trade-offs than can be made during the process.

My last main section is concerned with establishing the supporting infrastructure of a programme, and the advantages of getting things in place and working early. This concept of 'instant governance' is discussed in terms of avoiding some of the pitfalls mentioned in the first part of the chapter.

Part 1: where are we going?

It all starts with someone's good idea. Whether a minor change in the office layout or a large-scale corporate change, all changes begin the same way. How that idea is developed, shaped and crafted into a set of actions and activities that will deliver that idea are proportionally different, but the processes are similar. Programme management is ultimately a set of processes designed to deliver change on a large scale, dealing with many associated complexities and ambiguities, and managing the risks associated with an underpinning business case that supports a good idea. Programme identification and initiation are the foundation processes that establish and then protect the business case, ensuring that clear direction and focus can be maintained throughout programme delivery.

Identification

Identification is really a formal statement of intent. It allows an organization to consider a potentially good idea and determine just how much effort and resources are required to develop a detailed description (programme definition) of how to deliver the benefits associated with the good idea. Creating a programme definition can take significant time and effort, and consume valuable corporate resources. Making these investments cannot be taken lightly. Identification allows a governance structure to be established, empowering and controlling a team targeted with developing a plan for subsequent programme initiation.

Identification can be done relatively quickly and allows some fundamental checks to be put in place to protect an organization from bad investments. It formalizes basic questions such as:

- Just how good is this good idea?
- Does the business case make sense?
- Is it aligned with our corporate strategy?
- Is it aligned with other in-flight programmes?
- Will this make best use of our resources?
- How likely are the benefits?
- What are the risks?
- How quickly will the investment pay back?

Identification must ultimately confirm that the business case is good enough to invest some potentially scarce organizational resources into compiling a detailed programme definition. When programme identification concludes, there should be a clear outline programme description, including a vision of the good idea, the benefits it will bring, the business case supporting it, a strategy for creating the vision, and the risks and issues associated with it. There should also be a plan for developing the detailed programme definition, including required resources and timings as well as a supporting governance structure, committed to providing the required resources and delivering the benefits.

Ambiguity regarding any of the identification outputs at this early stage should be considered a major risk and a reason not to proceed. Lack of clarity regarding the

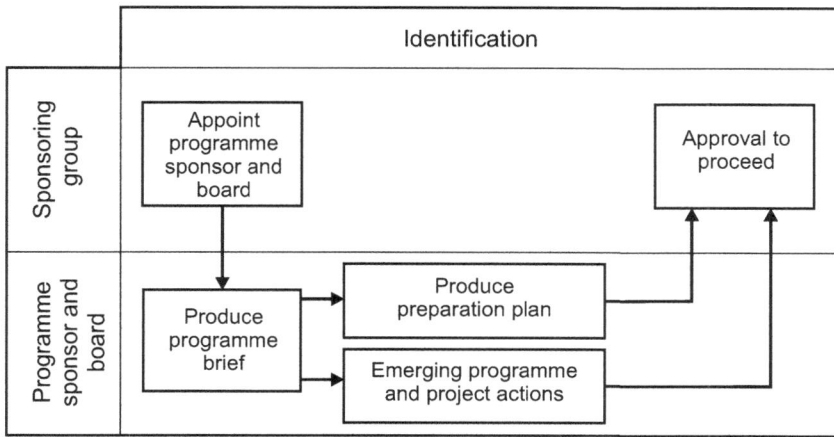

Figure 25.1 The process of programme identification

business case, benefits or organizational commitment is an early sign that the 'good' idea is not good enough. Care should be taken to ensure that the organization really does have the ability to deliver this change. Failure to spot an over-ambitious plan at this stage could lead to significant future waste.

Programme identification is an easy step to overlook. Good ideas generate enthusiasm and usually a demand for pace. This desire for early progress can lead to some of the basics demanded by good programme management discipline being overlooked. Programme identification gives the organization the opportunity to commit formally to the good idea and assign the right resources to nurture it. Failure to have these basics in place and failing to invest properly in the preparation for a plan can have catastrophic results – certainly not worthy of a good idea.

Figure 25.1 briefly outlines the identification process. The formality with which the process is started varies by organization. Invariably there is a very brief paper trail asking for some work to start. MSP refers to this as the Programme Mandate (OGC, 2007).

Initiation

Programme initiation is the consolidation of a number of detailed planning activities that define precisely what the programme will deliver, how the programme will operate and the business case behind the good idea. On completion there must be a fully formed definition of where the programme wants to go. In Chapter 8 of MSP (OGC, 2007) this is referred to as the *programme blueprint*. This is the detailed description of exactly what the good idea will look like after it is implemented. It contains a Current Mode of Operation (CMO) and a Future Mode of Operation (FMO) for the area of change. Both must be clearly defined in terms of people, organization structures, processes, systems and supporting infrastructure. The transformation strategy (how the change will be implemented) must also be described. This is the journey from CMO to FMO. The result of this strategy will be a set of projects and associated benefits delivered, with timings, and of course, the resource costs that correspond with them. This really defines the scope of the programme.

There will be implementation risks and issues that could impact the business case with any given transformational strategy. As well as a blueprint, the programme definition will need to describe fully the programme stakeholders, the business case, benefits of the programme, the programme organization and its approach to governance. I shall explore the links between blueprint, business case, benefits and project portfolio in more detail in the section 'Are we there yet?' The development of the remaining elements of the programme definition (stakeholders, organization, and governance) is discussed in the section 'Putting the support in place'.

All the programme definition components must be aligned at the conclusion of programme initiation. This should be ratified by the sponsoring group, and also possibly by independent review.

Programme initiation is a complex process of clarification, removing ambiguity, adopting organizational learning points and refining propositions until the costs, benefits, requirements, timings and risks all reach alignment. Ultimately, finding this balance can be tricky and care should be taken to ensure 'buy in' from all relevant stakeholders. It may not be possible to meet all requirements, but failure to consider the needs of influential stakeholders could introduce a significant risk of programme failure.

To help manage organizational risk, care should be taken to ensure that the programme business case has as much ambiguity removed as rapidly as possible. Only when all the detail is fully documented should the programme gain full authority to proceed. The principle of 'plan to the level of detail you understand' is recommended in this circumstance consistent with the MSP and Prince2 planning principles (OGC, 2009).

However, depending on the nature of the projects that make up the programme and the transformational strategy, it might not be possible to have a detailed understanding of the entire programme benefits and costs at this stage. If this is the case, the programme should not be implemented in full, but in specifically defined tranches, allowing the programme to proceed at each stage with a level of understood investment. Large-scale programmes typically have such stage gates or review milestones for funding to be released as progress in business case development is made. (The OGC Government Gateway review process makes excellent use of this approach.) Major changes in the outline business case could result in programme closure at any of these review points. Clearly these should be put in place at carefully chosen intervals to manage and limit the risk faced by the organization as it invests in the programme.

What else to consider?

Programme initiation can be a lengthy and intense process and, at its end, projects will start to be executed under the umbrella of the programme. Detailed plans might have been created for these Tranche 1 projects during programme initiation process, or possibly they might remain at a high level. In either case, while benefit profiles must be understood for conclusion of initiation, internal project dependencies can very often be overlooked when bringing together many complex disparate elements. This can lead to large areas of discrepancy in an overall programme plan at a very early stage.

Care should be taken to ensure project alignment within the project portfolio, before going firm on the individual project plans within the overall programme plan. This is also true for published milestones and benefit profiles. When communicating dates for dependencies, milestones and building benefit profiles, risk-adjusted dates should be considered. Allowing for the impact of known risks when concluding programme initiation permits a level of expectation-setting with stakeholders. Early confidence can be eroded quickly if a programme starts off badly due to the impact of early issues.

What if we have already started?

Creating programmes around existing projects presents special difficulties during programme identification and initiation. In this situation there are projects already running that will now be potentially grouped into a programme, possibly with new projects to complement them. This introduces the added complexity of assessing in-flight strategic fit.

During initiation, each active project must be assessed for strategic fit with the new programme. The fundamental question is really – how does this active project impact the original good idea? If it works well with it then you have a head start! The project should be well understood, and be relatively easy to incorporate into the new programme definition. However, an active project might not fit. So it should be left alone, to be executed independently. If an existing project conflicts with the programme vision it should be stopped.

Whatever the outcome, the clear requirement is for initial assessment criteria. These should be agreed during the programme identification and result in recommendations for each project. Stakeholder analysis must be undertaken with care during these situations, especially when closing potentially competing projects.

Part 2: are we there yet?

At the end of identification the 'good idea' has been accepted as good, and an outline business case exists. But now the problem of creating a fully detailed programme definition presents itself. At this point it is very easy to get lost in the detail. There are many parts that need to be consolidated and these are linked together with heavy dependencies. It is not easy to understand where to start and know when or if you have really finished. In trying to answer the question 'Are we there yet?' some of these dependent parts are now considered as the business case develops.

As already discussed, the definition must include a blueprint or statement of the current and future states (CMO and FMO), together with the programme vision (derived from the good idea). The FMO definition will form a major part of the benefits profile for the good idea. So before anything else, a good understanding of the FMO state is vital. Associated benefits and their profiles can be articulated once an FMO design is available. Similarly, the CMO state must be described to ensure that the starting point of any change is understood.

The CMO and FMO definitions between them also implicitly define the change that the programme needs to implement – the transformational journey. This change is delivered by a series of interrelated projects, possibly in tranches of change. Each of these projects needs to be designed with the objective of creating the FMO state from the CMO state. There will be many choices regarding this project portfolio design, such as:

- Are the projects grouped by discipline?
- Are the projects developed to avoid certain risks?
- Perhaps some quick benefit wins are possible if a certain set of deliverables are grouped together?

Some projects may have to be executed first as enablers for other later project benefits. This may be too big a change to achieve in one step and several tranches of change are required. The choices are very wide. No matter how the project portfolio is constructed, certain attributes for each project will be required for the programme definition to conclude.

Each project will need to have a clear contribution to overall requirements mapping, to ensure that all programme requirements are met when the portfolio delivers and FMO is attained. At the conclusion of each project there will be a set of project outputs – leading to outcomes and ultimately benefits enabled, with an associated profile which will need to be understood. Delivering each project will take organizational resources, time and money. Risks associated with each project will need to be understood and managed.

Once the transformation strategy is articulated and the project portfolio is designed, each of the previously mentioned project attributes can be consolidated into a programme plan and a benefits realization plan. Bringing these two plans together (with their associated timings, costs and risks) produces a refined business case.

This business case then needs to be considered against the organizational criteria for a good business investment. Various techniques are possible: profitability, investment appraisal against internal rate of return, risk and reward, payback period, discounted cash flow and so on. Ultimately a decision must be taken as to whether the programme is good enough to be accepted in its current form at the closure of programme definition. If not there are two options to consider.

One option would be to refine the FMO state, and therefore change the benefit profiles and as a result the project portfolio to reach FMO. It is important to remember that this new FMO state must remain in line with the programme vision.

An alternative option would be to create a different project portfolio to deliver the existing FMO state with a different cost or risk profile. This could potentially impact the timing of benefits realization plans, as well as directly influencing costs and/or risk.

Once an option has been selected, and changes implemented, the creation of the business case should be revisited. This is then the beginning of an iterative process that continues to repeat until an acceptable business case has been produced or it is concluded that there is no acceptable business case and the programme is cancelled.

A typical trade-off that may occur during this iterative approach to business case development would include increasing implementation risk with speed (to implement faster with higher risk, with the potential reward of earlier benefits). Each organization will have its own appetite for risk when it comes to decisions such as this. When reviewing the business case it is very important to test just how achievable the benefits are. Unrealistic benefits could significantly damage a programme business case and should be guarded against. Some projects might introduce negative effects with the move to FMO and these negative benefits should be profiled along with the positive ones to ensure that the programme is reviewed holistically.

Business case assessment is at the centre of this process and a stakeholder viewpoint is essential to the evaluation. But just what is an acceptable business case? The business case should be considered from various perspectives to ensure that the many stakeholders of the programme have all been considered carefully when comparing various iterations of a business case. What could be a perfect solution for one stakeholder group could be seen as a total disaster for another! Only by reviewing the programme from the many and varied stakeholder perspectives will a truly well-rounded viewpoint be possible.

The programme initiation process is depicted in Figure 25.2. Most of the responsibility for this process is shown as falling upon the programme manager, who typically will delegate this to various members of the newly formed programme team. Creating the supporting infrastructure and strategies that will enable the programme to be successfully managed is the subject of the following section.

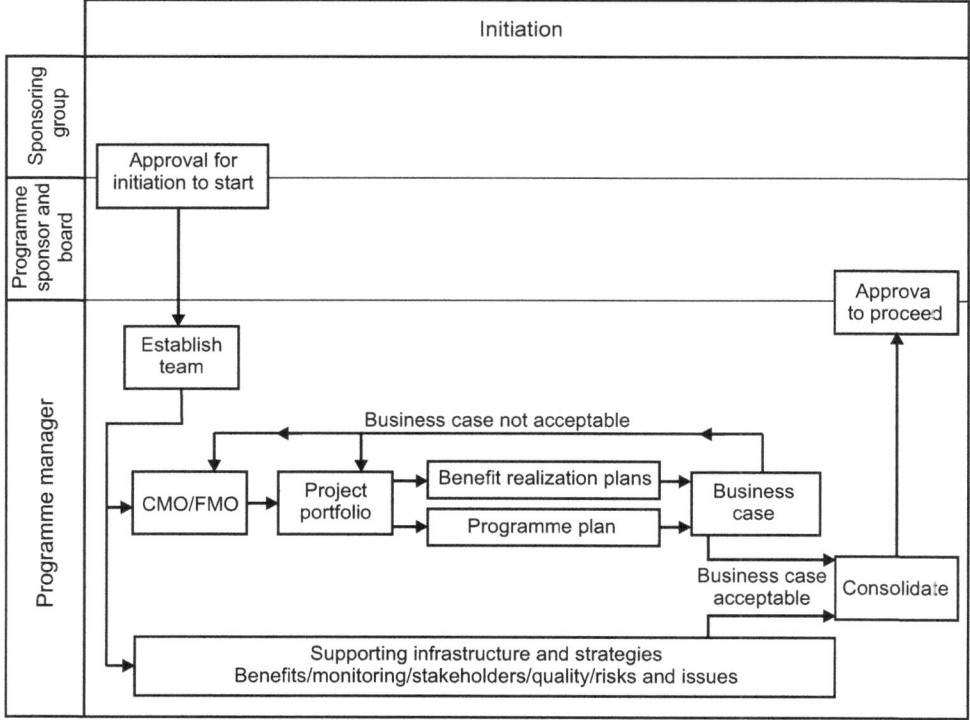

Figure 25.2 The process of programme initiation

Part 3: putting the support in place

Before launching a major programme successfully the basics must first be in place. The fundamental programme support needed includes such things as an early programme initiation team, office space, supporting IT and software and so on. It also includes processes that must be established early. Programme identification and initiation can go seriously wrong in the early stages where this programme support is lacking.

Identification and initiation team selection is a key early step in the programme lifecycle that will enable the programme to start with the early pace that a stakeholder will be keen to see. Without the right team in place, too many things become serial activities and generally impact on early progress. A good programme brief from the identification process will enable clear selection criteria to be developed for team creation. Once in place the initiation team needs to plan to expand as the programme initiation stage is reached, typically growing in size with individuals who will be capable of planning and executing the main programme from initiation through into execution.

The end to end nature (where design activities lead to delivery activities) encourages the right behaviours in a team who must show a clear sense of ownership and accountability for the programme, its integrity, and the benefits that it promises to deliver. The transformation strategy and the design of the project portfolio are key deliverables that enable this to happen. Some areas, however, are fairly consistent at a programme level, enabling parts of the programme organization design to be completed early. A programme management office (PMO) is a typical example of this.

Many of the other more process-driven elements of the support infrastructure can be put in place while the programme's business case is being constructed. These include strategies for benefits management, information management, risk and issue management, project monitoring and control, quality management, resource management and stakeholder engagement. Each of these strategies is equally important and an absence of any of them will introduce unnecessary risk. Many organizations will have strategies for each of these elements and where possible, unless the programme has very specific and unique needs, these should be utilized as soon as possible. This will help to facilitate rapid programme initiation and, at the very least, establish a more stable programme support environment while the alignment of blueprint, project portfolio, benefits and business case proceeds.

Having the process structure in place during business case finalization has a number of benefits. Typically as the project portfolio design emerges, workstreams establish themselves by project, for the creation of the required artefacts to demonstrate an aligned business case. These include profiles of benefits, costs and risks as well as project scope statements, project plans and the more detailed resource plans and requests. When this split of the work happens and teams start to work in parallel, having standards for the production of artefacts is invaluable to ensure speed of development, consistency and ease of consolidation. Also, if team members move around project workstreams, they will be familiar with the templates and therefore more efficient during change in assignment.

An additional benefit of early availability of process is the possibility of instant governance, where immediate project reviews can begin, following the structure of the programme from the moment the workstreams split out. This enables the programme management disciplines to be deployed at a project level extremely early in the project lifecycle, establishing good habits and identifying the areas where projects are not making the progress required as soon as practically possible.

Clearly not all the project disciplines will be possible until each project definition is recorded and baselined. However, the sooner the project teams are behaving in line with the future programme governance arrangements, the less likely it is that projects will fall out of line in the early days of programme delivery. This is effectively preparation for Tranche 1 and makes the move to managing the programme easier for all the programme management team and their stakeholders.

Instant governance allows programme management to take control of the programme initiation workstreams at a point where it is quite common for the complex dependencies of blueprint, benefits, projects, risks and business case to enter into a recursive discussion about who should change first. It is not difficult to imagine how these relationships could become confused and misaligned when worked on by parallel (sometimes competing) workstreams. This concept of continual alignment is crucial when considering the timing of risk-adjusted dates for specific programme events. Maintaining the integrity and alignment of the programme plan, and benefits realization plan, where the risk profile is being updated in parallel by multiple workstreams, needs a carefully managed integrated approach such as that offered by instant governance.

Conclusion

There are many good ideas that never deliver what they promise. For a good idea to be successful it needs to be assessed and confirmed, and the required change to be planned fully and rapidly. The good idea needs the support of bought-in stakeholders (with their enthusiasm, desire for benefits and resources) to make it happen. These things need clarity – clarity of the destination, the journey and the risks involved. Establishing these attributes lies at the core of programme identification and initiation.

The programme identification and initiation processes can be used to ensure that a programme of change uses organization resources wisely, with the appropriate level of risk, and delivers change that maximizes the possibility of business case success. To achieve this, the processes establish a number of artefacts including a programme future state, a benefits realization plan, project portfolio, programme management plan and a business case.

While executing the initiation process, care must be taken to ensure that each artefact aligns with the others through iterative refinement, so that the business case finds its optimum configuration. This enables the balance of risk, and benefits from scarce organizational resources. Establishing programme support mechanisms during the early stages of initiation provides a level of consistency across the programme. That enables various workstreams for the project portfolio to work at pace, in parallel. This early oversight of the initiation processes, using an instant governance approach, can establish good programme behaviours at the start of the delivery, simplifying the route to a clearly defined programme and building a solid foundation to launch the programme.

References and further reading

Government Gateway Process. Accessed 7 January 2015 at <http://webarchive.nationalarchives. gov.uk/20110822131357> and <http://www.ogc.gov.uk/what_is_ogc_gateway_review.asp>.

OGC (2007), *Managing Successful Programmes*, 3rd edn., Norwich: The Stationery Office.

OGC (2009), *Managing Successful Projects with Prince2*, Norwich: The Stationery Office.

Chapter 26

Programme Planning

Joel Crook

Clearly programmes that are not properly planned are likely to fail. Carefully integrated planning is essential for reducing risk and costs, improving quality and finishing on time.

Introduction

The following should be considered as part of the planning process:

- how the programme will integrate its subordinate projects, programmes and resources while maintaining strategic alignment with the larger organization;
- the scope of the programme and how it will be defined and controlled, including the delivery of anticipated benefits;
- the scheduling approach and how it will allow actual achievements to be measured against the intended plan;
- stakeholder engagement;
- communications, including stakeholders' information needs, periodic reviews and reports, and their formats;
- risk management for both threats and opportunities;
- the quality of products, processes and services;
- supply chain management for products and services;
- the financial management plan including financial framework, cost estimating and budgeting;
- programme closeout and transfer of benefits to the organization.

I have excluded the programme governance plan from the above list because that subject is dealt with exhaustively in Chapter 19.

Programme planning processes are iterative, because they depend upon information generated by subprogrammes and projects which have not yet been initiated. The requirements in the programme management plan should be allocated to all subordinate documents, and those subordinate documents should be traceable to this plan. Iterations cease when all the process inputs, outputs, tools and techniques required for programme success have been defined. For greater efficiency and quality, these processes should if possible use existing policies, processes, procedures and lessons learned from similar work.

Case study

Here is a true story from the world of medicine that illustrates the importance of programme planning (Crook, 2014b). A young lady (in the United States) was diagnosed with breast cancer. Tests found the tumour to be grade 3, BRCA-2 positive. Grade 3 meant that the tumour was fast growing and BRCA-2 is a genetic mutation that indicates a raised potential for breast, pancreatic and ovarian cancer.

The standard treatment for this diagnosis requires a mastectomy and removal of the ovaries. It was also determined that both chemotherapy and radiation therapy would be administered, given the aggressive nature of the cancer. Because of the positive BRCA-2 finding a team of doctors, with different roles, was assigned to the case as follows:

- an oncologist (in charge of administering chemotherapy);
- a radiation oncologist in charge of post-operative radiation of the cancer site;
- a gynaecological oncologist to remove the ovaries, to prevent the possibility of future ovarian cancer;
- a general surgeon for the mastectomy;
- a plastic surgeon for reconstructive surgery.

This team was assembled within one week to discuss the case. The team's response was impressive. The time from the initial medical examination to the start of treatment was only six weeks. The patient emerged free from cancer and full of life. She was thankful for the prompt response of the healthcare providers.

However, there is far more to this story. The patient's prognosis was initially threatened due to the lack of adequate programme planning. Five different medical specialists were treating the patient. This team of doctors met during 'tumour board' to discuss the appropriate course of treatment. The board discussed the treatment plan before having the results of the BRCA test. This was considered to be a low-risk decision, because this diagnosis is relatively rare. It was assumed that the first order of business would be to remove the cancer. An appointment was made with the general surgeon.

During the patient's initial visit, the surgeon suggested immediate surgery to remove the tumour (lumpectomy) and all the lymph nodes from the adjacent arm. This is considered to be the standard treatment, but removal of the lymph nodes can result in unpleasant and lifelong side-effects.

Then the BRCA test came back positive, which meant that a full mastectomy was the standard of care, whereas a lumpectomy would leave the patient with a high probability of cancer recurrence. Thus, had the lumpectomy been performed immediately, subsequent mastectomy would have been required.

The oncologist had decided on an approach where chemotherapy would be used before surgery in an attempt to shrink the tumour. This treatment has the advantage of allowing the efficacy of the chemotherapy to be measured directly and using alternative drugs if it is not working. If the surgeon had removed the tumour as originally intended there would have been no way to determine the efficacy of the chemotherapy. If the chemotherapy drugs were ineffective in this scenario, it would have been possible for the cancer to survive microscopically, only to reappear later without warning.

The surgeon was approaching his patient's care like a project – he was driving to an *output*, rather than an *outcome*. In his eyes, his job was to open up the patient, remove the tumour and close without incident. 'Who could criticize a surgeon for doing that?' he might ask.

After witnessing this lack of coordination I asked the surgeon a key question: 'Who is responsible for integrating care between all the attending physicians?' The surgeon replied that the physicians had achieved a consensus on treatment. But that was the wrong answer. The consensus to which he was referring was the tumour board meeting mentioned earlier. That was a one-time event, conducted with incomplete information (no BRCA test results). Each doctor was doing what was right in his own mind. All were approaching the care of the patient as an individual project. Each was striving to achieve an *output* but none was responsible for the overall *outcome*. That is one of several distinguishing characteristics between projects and programmes. A few days later the patient fired the surgeon and replaced him with a new surgeon who answered the question correctly.

The oncologist began to integrate care towards the desired outcome. Discussions between the specialists increased. Chemotherapy was started. After the chemotherapy was completed, an MRI scan confirmed that the tumour had gone. Now the efficacy of chemotherapy in this case was proven. So only a few lymph nodes were removed, which greatly reduced the likelihood of the patient from suffering the life-long side-effects mentioned above.

Initially, each doctor had treated their work as an isolated project – driving to an expected output. When the patient's care was managed as a programme the focus shifted to the patient's outcome. Lateral communication between the specialists improved. In the end, the coordinated plan prevented one surgery and eliminated the ancillary node dissection, the patient side-effects, and the cost of long-term medical care for lymphedema. Most importantly the patient now had a better outcome and prognosis.

It is undeniable that good programme management in this case improved the outcome (benefits), improved the schedule, reduced risk, improved quality and reduced the cost. The same can be true for your programme – but not without good programme planning.

Programme management plan

The programme management plan is the output of the planning process. It details the integration of component projects and programmes, people and other resources needed to deliver the programme's anticipated benefits. The requirements in the plan should be allocated to all subordinate documents, and all those subordinate documents should be traceable to this plan. All programme plans should be subjected to a 'parent/child' requirement analysis. The programme planning processes are iterative and are dependent upon information generated by subordinate programmes and projects.

The programme management plan should cover the following:

- programme overview;
- applicable documents;

- integration;
- scope;
- schedule;
- stakeholder engagement;
- communication;
- risk;
- quality;
- supply chain management;
- financial framework;
- governance;
- programme closeout and transition.

Infrastructure

Programme infrastructure includes an organization's command media, policies, procedures, lessons learned, document templates and others. Programme infrastructure normally represents organizational learning, so whenever possible it should be used to support programme planning.

Figure 26.1 illustrates a typical set of programme planning documents. New programme managers can be discouraged by the number of documents needed. However, if an organization has a good programme infrastructure the task is not as difficult as it might first seem.

Programme infrastructure should be consistent with nationally and internationally recognized standards, which are generally developed through collaboration by industry practitioners around the globe (based on the current practices that make their organizations successful). To achieve a consensus, the programmatic processes are generally defined at a high level, so that considerable scaling and tailoring is possible and necessary when they are applied to specific organizations. That approach is important for keeping the processes from becoming excessively onerous and bureaucratic.

Most recognized programme standards organizations offer their members useful research papers, books and other complementary resources that can expand an organization's infrastructure for little or no cost. This includes professional development opportunities, which eliminate the need and expense for companies to develop their own training. Additionally, an industry of consultants has based its practices on many of these standards, and they offer relatively inexpensive consultation, consistent with their use of the standards.

The organizational infrastructure should be evaluated as part of the programme closedown process. Recommendations for changing the programme infrastructure should be considered as part of the organization's continuous improvement efforts.

Some organizations have very few formal processes, which appears to work for them. However, their programme managers will still be required to manage cost, schedule, scope, risk, communications and so on, even if that is done informally. That results in an inconsistent and unpredictable programme outcome, which is entirely dependent on the skill of the programme manager. When processes are

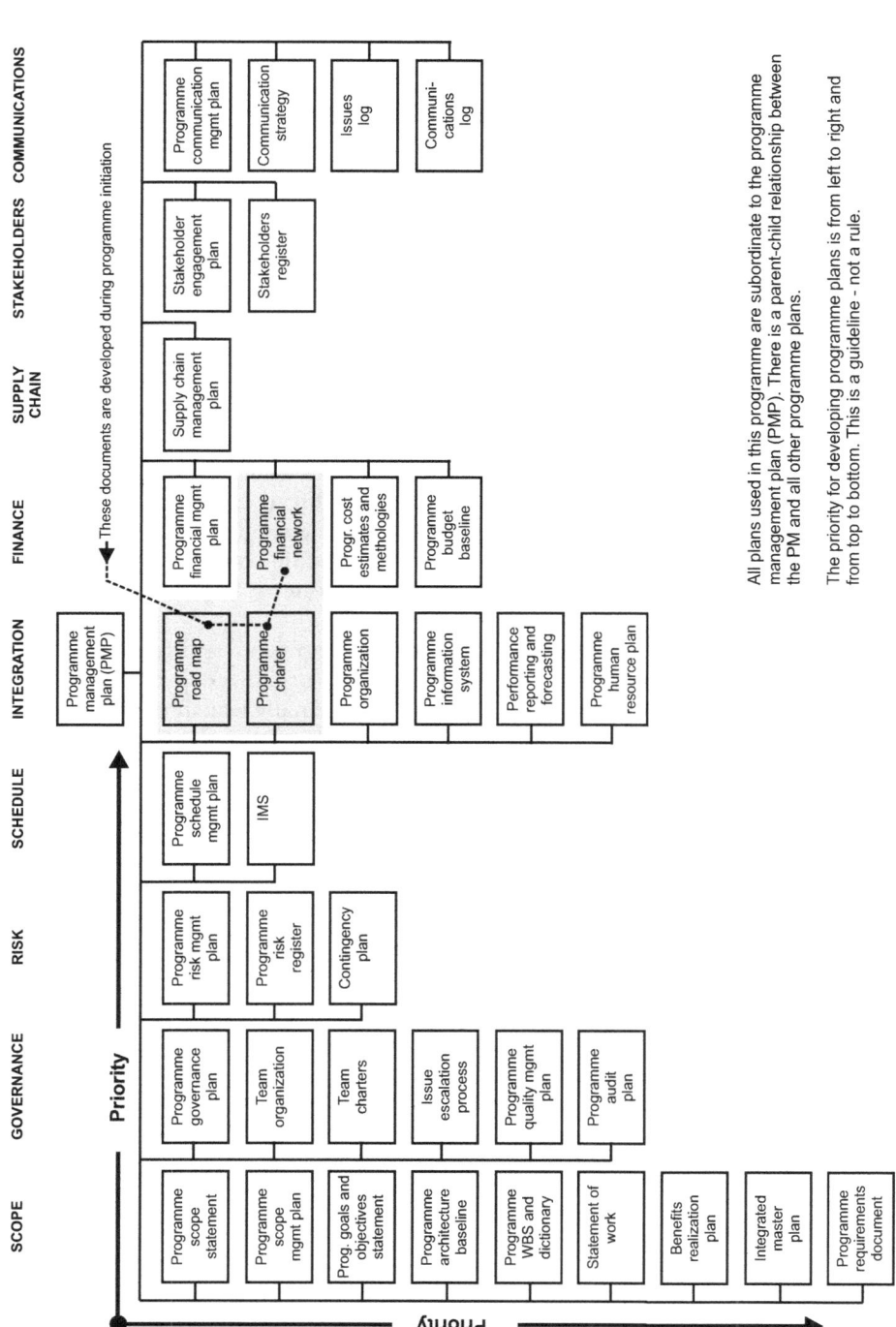

SCOPE | GOVERNANCE | RISK | SCHEDULE | INTEGRATION | FINANCE | SUPPLY CHAIN | STAKEHOLDERS | COMMUNICATIONS

Priority

These documents are developed during programme initiation

Programme management plan (PMP)

SCOPE
- Programme scope statement
- Programme scope mgmt plan
- Prog. goals and objectives statement
- Programme architecture baseline
- Programme WBS and dictionary
- Statement of work
- Benefits realization plan
- Integrated master plan
- Programme requirements document

GOVERNANCE
- Programme governance plan
- Team organization
- Team charters
- Issue escalation process
- Programme quality mgmt plan
- Programme audit plan

RISK
- Programme risk mgmt plan
- Programme risk register
- Contingency plan

SCHEDULE
- Programme schedule mgmt plan
- IMS

INTEGRATION
- Programme road map
- Programme charter
- Programme organization
- Programme information system
- Performance reporting and forecasting
- Programme human resource plan

FINANCE
- Programme financial mgmt plan
- Programme financial network
- Progr. cost estimates and methologies
- Programme budget baseline

SUPPLY CHAIN
- Supply chain management plan

STAKEHOLDERS
- Stakeholder engagement plan
- Stakeholders register

COMMUNICATIONS
- Programme communication mgmt plan
- Communication strategy
- Issues log
- Communi-cations log

Priority

All plans used in this programme are subordinate to the programme management plan (PMP). There is a parent-child relationship between the PM and all other programme plans.

The priority for developing programme plans is from left to right and from top to bottom. This is a guideline - not a rule.

Figure 26.1 Programme documents arranged by subject matter and priority

standardized and used consistently across an organization, the effects of process variation on the output are eliminated. This makes it easier to troubleshoot and improve the process. Standardizing programmatic processes is always the first step to improving their output.

Integration

Integrating the programme's components should be a primary concern for the programme manager. As shown in the medical case above, issues occur at the boundaries between the programme components. Component interfaces must be controlled and managed. Knowledge must move both vertically and horizontally through the organization. Information concerning test results, programme changes, design requirements, constraints, dependencies, assumptions and others must be available to the entire organization. Otherwise there will be problems.

Physical and functional integration may also be required. An example of physical integration is the mating of two components produced by different projects. Physical integration is concerned with verifying that the mated components fit. An example of functional integration is verifying that electronic controls are capable of operating the system as intended, once all of the components have been physically integrated.

The efficiency and effectiveness of programme integration is directly dependent on the way the programme is organized. A poorly organized programme will struggle to integrate its components. Work may be informally transferred from one component to another, giving the contributing component the appearance of efficiency, but at the expense of the overall programme. Processes will be only locally optimized.

Programme organization

An organization's structure has a direct effect on its ability to perform its function and deliver its anticipated benefits. Figure 26.2 uses the medical case above to illustrate the programme organization before and after intervention. After intervention the communication paths became clear. The oncologist acted as the programme manager responsible for the medical outcome. Initially each doctor behaved as a stove-piped project, locally optimizing to do what was right in his own mind.

Cost, quality and availability are not mutually exclusive. It is possible to concurrently improve all of these metrics using internationally recognized programme management techniques.

Programme information and reporting

It is important to establish a programme information system. This is the central, electronic repository for all programme-related information. It is the place where programme stakeholders go to retrieve information or to post information.

Once the programmes key performance indicators have been defined, performance reporting and forecasting should be considered as part of programme planning.

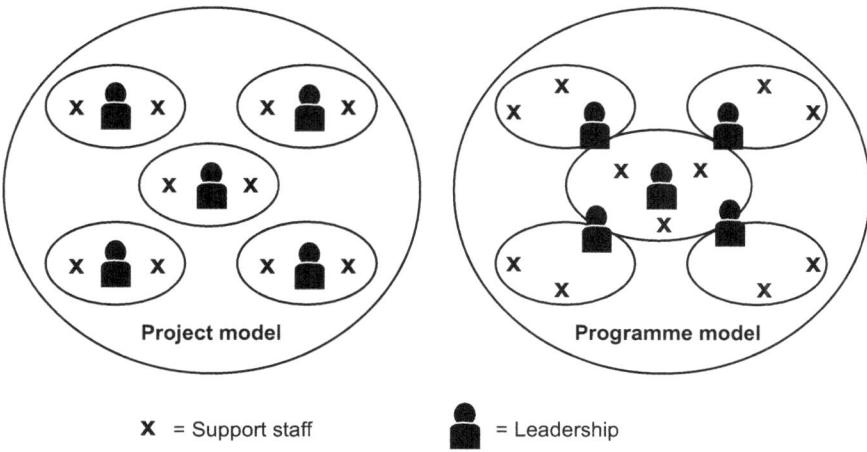

X = Support staff   = Leadership

Figure 26.2 Project 'stove-pipe' organization compared with an integrated programme organization

Performance reporting and forecasting against key performance indicators must be predictive, to allow timely corrective actions.

Human resource plan

The human resource plan forecasts the resources and skill types needed to complete the programme. It is an input to the business case and the supply chain management plan in cases where staffing is augmented by subcontracted services. The human resource plan should contain:

- identification of required skill sets;
- staff forecasting;
- hiring plan;
- employment development plan;
- the outsourcing plan.

This plan should be updated with data from the fully resourced integrated master schedule (when that becomes available).

Scope management

The approach to scope management should be documented in a formal plan. Scope changes should be controlled using standard and formalized change control procedures. The scope plan must not allow 'gold plating' or 'scope creep' (which would add benefits not specified in the requirements documents and are thus not authorized). Gold plating gives the customer more than they expect but can become a 'poison pill' because it creates requirements for which no authorized budgets exist and which were not part of the business case. Such additions would escape risk analysis and more problems can arise when the programme manager attempts to deliver unplanned benefits to an organization that has not prepared to receive them. The programme scope management plan should contain the following:

- scope definition;
- scope management process;
- roles and responsibilities.

Scope definition identifies the baseline scope at programme initiation. Any subsequent change to the baseline should be documented here, together with the relevant change authorization details (including forecast impacts to cost, schedule, risk and so on).

The scope management process must clearly define the process for allowing and making scope changes. The process must tightly control the scope because any change might damage performance. It is important to announce the points of contact for scope change requests and name those allowed to authorize changes. All personnel must clearly understand that any change initiated outside the defined procedure is not valid.

The programme scope statement should describe the objectives that must be achieved for the programme to deliver its anticipated benefits. The delivery of these benefits must be timed in line with available budgets and the business case analysis that was used to justify the programme. The scope statement should also include known assumptions, dependencies and constraints upon which the programme is based.

Work breakdown structure

The work breakdown structure (WBS) is a hierarchical breakdown of the work necessary to complete the programme. It is the important task framework from which the programme is supported. The objective of the WBS is to break down the work into smaller, more manageable packages. Then a parent–child relationship forms. The 'parent', or upper level work, is decomposed into smaller, lower level 'children'. There are a few simple rules that should be followed when constructing the WBS:

- the sum of the work at the child level must equal all the work at the parent level;
- branches should be consistent with how the WBS elements will be integrated;
- the WBS should describe products and services, not functions.

Once the WBS is complete, its elements need to be defined. This becomes the WBS dictionary.

A statement of work (SOW) must specify in clear terms the work to be done. The SOW is constructed using the WBS dictionary as the primary input and should have the following key attributes:

- requirements are specified with adequate detail to allow estimates of the resources needed;

- describes only what is required and not how it will be done;
- invokes only the minimum applicable standards and specifications needed.

Another relevant document is the work authorization. Different organizations use a variety of names for this but I use the term work authorization package (WAP). This authorizes the scope of work and identifies the functional organization(s) responsible and accountable for its completion. It divides each element of the SOW into assignable work packages.

Benefits realization plan

Clearly the intended benefits must be realized and delivered on time within the estimated budget. The benefits realization plan should contain:

- a quantified description of each benefit;
- cost–benefit analysis;
- benefit owner;
- key performance indicators;
- person responsible and accountable for delivering the benefit;
- performance reporting requirements.

Programme benefits are of course identified before programme initiation as part of the business analysis but it is not unusual for those benefits to be refined during the programme planning activities.

Any change to the benefits realization plan should be included under the scope management and change control process.

Integrated master plan

The integrated master plan contains major programme events (MPEs), significant accomplishments and accomplishment criteria (AC).

MPEs are chronologically organized gate reviews designed to assess the maturity of the system. Examples include the system requirements review and the critical design review. To complete an MPE list successfully all its exit requirements must be satisfied. These exit criteria are known by some as significant accomplishments (SAs). An example of such a significant accomplishment event might be the completion of the design trade studies, or the completion of the system requirements allocation. Accomplishment criteria describe the content of the SA. An example of an accomplishment criterion (AC) is requirement allocations to a specific component.

The MPE, SA and AC are the top three levels of the schedule, but they do not contain any specific tasking. Criteria can be either quantitative or qualitative, but they must be measurable. Until an MPE is complete, the programme should not be allowed to progress further.

The integrated master plan (IMP) should contain:

- introduction;
- major programme events, accomplishments and criteria;

- IMP narratives;
- glossary.

The introduction should include: a description of the programme and its associated assumptions, dependencies and constraints; and an MPE dictionary. The MPE dictionary should provide sufficient detail to explain the purpose of the event. This will provide context for the SAs and ACs described in following paragraphs.

The associated SAs and ACs for each major programme event should be described in this section. This is a very important part of the document. Organizations that fail to provide this information as part of their programme planning will typically identify the SAs and ACs within days or weeks of conducting the MPE. These discussions tend to become negotiations over content. When the content of MPEs is diluted they lose their ability to indicate the maturity of the programme.

The narrative section is a good place to capture standard processes that will be used to mature the programme. This includes design analysis cycles, risk management and others. This section may also be used to describe other information necessary to execute this plan, such as technology and manufacturing readiness levels.

The glossary should include all of the terms and acronyms used in the IMP.

[Editorial comment: Anyone who has read this far in this chapter will certainly agree with the need for that. All acronyms are listed in the general index at the end of this Handbook. DL]

Programme requirements document

A rigorous list of programme requirements should be developed and maintained and recorded in a programme requirements document. The most common requirement types are:

- customer requirements;
- company requirements (business plan, programme schedule);
- functional requirements (what must be accomplished);
- performance requirements (how well the functions must be executed, including margin, reliability, availability, safety);
- performance constraints;
- physical constraints;
- design constraints – environments, interfaces;
- design requirements – codes, processes, manuals;
- derived requirements – implied or transformed from higher-level;
- allocated requirements – established by dividing or allocating higher-level requirements.

All these requirements should be:

- achievable – the potential solution is technically feasible and affordable;
- verifiable – allowing objective verification by test, analysis, inspection, similarity or demonstration;
- unambiguous – should have only one meaning;

- complete – all information regarding the customer's need is stated;
- expressed as a need, not a solution;
- consistent with other requirements;
- appropriate for the level of hierarchy.

System engineering management plan (SEMP)

The SEMP is the foundation document for requirements development and technical activities required to support the programme scope. The SEMP is a type of contract between the programme office and the functional engineering organization. The SEMP is subordinate to the programme management plan. The SEMP should contain the following:

- purpose and scope;
- applicable documents;
- technical summary;
- common technical processes;
- technology insertion;
- requirements compliance matrix.

Programme schedule

In the late 1980s the US Air Force recognized the need for a new approach to developing programme schedules. They found (as others had before them) that conventional programme schedules only measured the passage of time and did nothing to indicate programme maturity. So they adopted an approach that is promoted here, namely start with the programme's desired end state and then measure the current state as a percentage of that end state. The key elements of this approach are the integrated master plan (mentioned above) and the integrated master schedule (which is described below).

Schedule management plan

The schedule management plan provides an overall description of the tools, processes and procedures used to develop and manage the integrated master schedule (the IMS is described later). The schedule management plan should identify the schedule management tools that will be used for the integrated master schedule as well as the following:

- activity definition;
- activity sequencing;
- activity duration estimating;
- schedule integration;
- schedule management;
- schedule status;
- baseline control process;
- performance metrics and reporting.

Critical path network

The critical path network (or networks) should include all activities that must be performed and the milestones to be achieved. Activities should cover all tasks down to the lowest level of the WBS. The sum of all these activities should equal the total scope of work as defined in the programme SOW. Activity sequencing identifies the predecessor and successor relationships of the activities. There are several options for estimating the durations of individual tasks. These include parametric models, analogical models and engineering estimates.

The integrated schedule is a logical network that identifies the interdependencies of the activities. Several statistical models are available to improve the quality of the integrated schedule, such as Monte Carlo simulations, three point estimates (PERT) and others. These should be used to establish the schedule baseline.

A discussion of schedule float (also known as slack) should be included in this section, as well as the schedule methodologies to be employed (such as critical path method, critical chain, pull system, Agile and others).

[Editorial comment: Estimated task durations are best made, wherever possible, by the managers who will later be expected to achieve the result. Of particular interest in scheduling is the overall float after time analysis. This must be driven by the required programme completion date. It often happens that the first results of critical path analysis predict a finish date well beyond what is wanted. Imposition of a target date on the final activity will then create negative float for some or all activities. When the total float is negative, steps must be taken to accelerate the schedule using fast-tracking or by employing more resources. The critical path results will not be practicable without subsequent scheduling of resources, to make certain that the appropriate skills are available when they are needed. Lock (2013) gives detailed and illustrated descriptions of the critical path method, resource scheduling and fast tracking. DL]

Schedule management

The schedule management section of the plan should detail the process that will be used for plan management, such as rolling wave techniques.

[Editorial comment: The rolling wave method is used for projects and programmes of very long duration when there is insufficient knowledge to plan work in detail for the distant future. The solution is to plan in detail for as far ahead as possible and then to bridge the gap between the end of detailed knowledge and the required completion date with summary activities. As the work proceeds and more becomes known, the detailed part of the network can be extended, replacing summary activities and moving forward like a rolling wave. DL]

A discussion should also be included on how the schedule will be used to prevent the over-allocation of resources (using a suitable resource levelling method).

This discussion should also consider schedule crashing and fast-tracking if the timescale is critical or tight.

Schedule status and baseline

A properly constructed IMS will allow filtering so that personalized schedule updates can be distributed to those responsible for schedule performance. The master planner will typically update the schedule according to feedback of progress.

Progress has to be measured and reported against the original schedule information (the baseline). Control of changes is important because unauthorized changes can wreck progress, cause wasted work and delay completion. Many companies set up a change board or change committee to question every change request. Formal procedures are also needed to ensure that any authorized deviation from the original programme specification results in updated records, so that eventually the documentation will record the programme in its 'as-built' state.

Performance metrics and reporting

It is necessary to decide at what level of the WBS the schedule will be managed. Then consistent cost accounts must be created. The cost account manager should be assigned the responsibility, authority and accountability for accumulating cost records and the associated schedule performance.

If earned value measurement is to be used, the cost account manager can administer this, although in many cases this work will be centred in a programme management office. The following four earned value metrics can be considered:

- schedule variance (SV);
- cost variance (CV);
- schedule performance index (SPI);
- cost performance index (CPI).

If the SPI has a variance outside predetermined values, the cost account manager should report the exception, identify its cause and develop a recovery plan. The programme manager should be responsible for providing an aggregated report for the entire programme.

[Editorial comment: Earned value methods are described with examples in Lock (2013). But beware. Earned value measurement takes considerable effort from many people, adds cost without adding any value, and produces results that are not always reliable. DL]

Integrated master schedule (IMS)

The integrated master schedule is a logic network that identifies activities and milestones to a level of detail sufficient to document the interdependencies among work elements. A work element is a scope of work that has a specific budget, schedule and a responsible person assigned to its completion. This schedule incorporates the IMP, WBS and the SOW. This allows for filters to be used that enable reports from the IMS database to be presented in a number of different ways, based on need. The IMS should be viewable by WBS element, by major programme event and so on.

Stakeholders

Programmes that create organization change tend to divide people into supporters and adversaries. The reasons are complex, but people often feel threatened by change and feel discomfort when their familiar world is replaced by something new. Additionally, people once recognized as subject matter experts might view change as a demotion in status. Some others will welcome change because it shifts power in their favour.

Stakeholder engagement plan

Internal and external programme stakeholders must be identified and distinguished between those who will gain or lose when the programme is completed. A strategy for engaging stakeholders should be developed. The primary objective of the stakeholder engagement plan is to sustain and improve support for the programme. This plan should contain:

- stakeholder register;
- stakeholder analysis;
- stakeholder strategy.

The stakeholder engagement plan will probably contain sensitive information that should be carefully protected.

Major programme stakeholders should be recorded in the register. The stakeholder register is a repository of information including:

- the stakeholder's name and organizational position;
- programme advocacy – friend or foe;
- the stakeholder's needs and expectations;
- stakeholder classification (customer, sponsor, suppliers, programme team and so forth).

Stakeholder analysis should focus on the attitudes of stakeholders and their causes. It is important to understand the type of each stakeholder (key decision-maker, influencer, approver and others). Identify those that can influence the programme's outcome, and define the relationships between stakeholders. Stakeholder issues should also be identified here.

It is extremely challenging to manage the large numbers of stakeholders touched by some programmes. Stakeholders should be prioritized, keeping in mind that the amount of time spent engaging each stakeholder will increase according to their priority ranking. A strategy should be developed for each stakeholder issue and concern. Potential responses to their issues include: monitor, provide them with push communications, educate, collaborate and others. An effective strategy will help the programme team to anticipate reactions to reports and engage stakeholders proactively in advance (to exploit positive reactions and avoid negative reactions).

Communications management plan

The communications management plan considers the specific communication needs of key stakeholders and defines the periodicity and format of reports to meet their needs. The calendar for standing meetings and their agendas are also found in this plan. The stakeholder engagement plan described in the previous section is an input to this plan. The communications management plan should contain:

- communication strategy;
- stakeholder communication needs;
- communication methods;
- standing meeting agendas and attendance;
- email rules:
- issues log;
- communication log.

Communications strategy

Visual communication systems and multimedia need to be considered as part of communications strategy. Visual management can provide key stakeholders with a clear and common understanding of goals and measures. It allows all the teams to align their actions and decisions with the overall strategic direction of the programme. It is also provides an open window to performance, providing the same unbiased information to everyone. A visual system allows for rapid assessment of where problems exist.

Multimedia can be very effective at communicating change to larger audiences of stakeholders, both internal and external to the organization.

When problems or issues are encountered they need to be entered into an issue log which documents the issues and monitors their resolution. It can also be used to facilitate communications and promote a common understanding of issues.

The communication plan should also establish a programme communication log. The purpose of this log is to record all significant communications, including (but not limited to) requests for information, submittals required by contract, status reports and others.

Risk management plan

Risk should be considered during the planning of each work activity at all programme levels. Risks can be positive (opportunities) or negative (threats). Both must be managed. The risk management plan should describe the risk management process and how each risk can be avoided or mitigated. These decisions should be entered in a risk log, which must also show the name of the person who 'owns' the risk (the person responsible for taking action). Risk management policies and procedures should allow for appropriate scaling or tailoring of the risk management plan. This is necessary given the variation in project and programme size, duration and scope.

We need to distinguish between risks and issues. When a risk event occurs it no longer has uncertainty associated with it and ceases to be a risk. For example, when driving a car there is a risk of a flat tyre. Once a tyre is flat, it is no longer a risk. It's no longer probabilistic but is now an issue that must be dealt with. When issues are encountered they need to be entered into an issue log, as part of programme communications management (already discussed).

Risk identification and analysis

Risks should be identified using one or more of the following methods:

- reviews of programme assumptions, dependencies and constraints;
- brainstorming;
- interviewing;
- using check-lists built from lessons learned reviews;
- SWOT analysis (strengths, weaknesses, opportunities, threats);
- scenario analysis.

Risk analysis can be qualitative or quantitative. Qualitative analysis is valuable for prioritizing risk for further analysis using quantitative techniques. During the qualitative analysis, the probability of occurrence of a risk event and the potential impact are estimated. The event can then be plotted on a probability versus impact matrix (see Figure 26.3). Threats and opportunities that fall within the matrix 'area of interest' should be prioritized for additional, more rigorous quantitative analysis. Examples of quantitative analysis include Monte Carlo simulations, failure modes and effects analysis (FMEA), and effects criticality analysis (FMECA), all of which are described in Lock (2013).

Risk response planning

A response plan must be developed for each threat and opportunity. Risk response plans should maximize opportunities and minimize threats. This will enhance the organization's ability to predict its performance, with reduced likelihood of operational loss. The chosen strategies must be translated into actions and integrated into the programme plan for execution. Actions available at the programme level for executing specific strategies include:

- redefining the programme scope;
- changing priorities of constituent components.

Generally speaking, managers are accountable for owning the risks that affect their work scope responsibilities, and for systematically working to reduce or eliminate risks and realize opportunities.

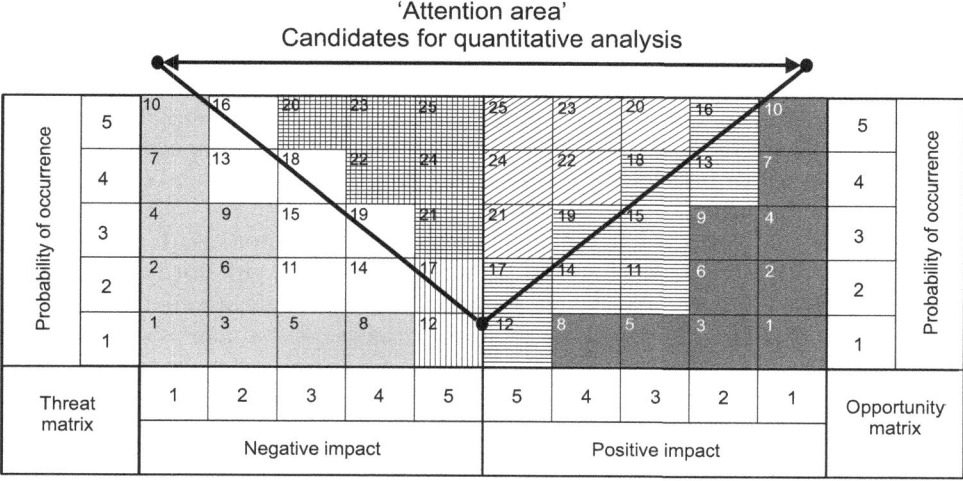

Figure 26.3 Probability-impact matrix showing the 'area of interest'

Risk category	Definitions
Cost	The costs incurred in delivering the programme benefits.
Schedule	Meeting established internal and external milestones.
Quality	A measure of an organization's ability to meet the requirements, objectives and expectations of its customers.
Technical	The use of engineering or applied science to accomplish an objective.
Safety	The state of proactively ensuring the health and well-being of employees and the community by identifying, responding to and controlling workplace hazards.
Environmental/ sustainability	A measure of protection offered to employees and the public by preventing pollution, complying with applicable requirements and continually taking actions towards improvement and sustainment of the environment.

Figure 26.4 Risk category examples

Risk categories will vary depending on business sector and other factors. Some of the most recognized risk categories are defined in Figure 26.4. Each threat or opportunity can be mapped to a WBS element, so that a risk breakdown structure (RBS) will emerge. The RBS facilitates identification of relationships between risks.

The probability and impact of each risk should be evaluated. It is not uncommon for a project to have risk in multiple categories. Some of these risks will be financially tangible while others are not.

Risk normalization and aggregation

There is a logical process used to aggregate risk which begins with risk normalization. To normalize risk one must first view each risk in terms of its cost impact. This allows for financially tangible risks, financially intangible risks, and other seemingly disparate risks to be summed. For example, an environmental impact risk could cause a cessation of operations for a period of time, which would equate to a specific monetary impact on sales. Once risks have been normalized in this way they can be summed to indicate an overall risk position.

Figure 26.5 is a tornado diagram that shows the aggregated risk for a notional project, expressed in dollars. This illustration also shows that risk normally has both a downside (threat) and an upside (opportunity). For example, a well-managed risk response might cost less than anticipated in the project cost estimate, so it is then an opportunity.

Scenario analysis

The ability to aggregate and disaggregate risk enables scenario analysis, which focuses on the interrelationship and interdependency of many risks as opposed to single, isolated risks. This more realistic view of risk improves the probability of meeting business objectives and preparing the organization to manage future risks.

Programme risk register

The risk register (or risk log) is a database for all risks. It typically includes the following information:

- a description of the risk;
- the impact of this risk should it occur;
- the probability of its occurrence;
- the difficulty or otherwise of recognizing the risk event, should it occur;
- risk score and how it is calculated;

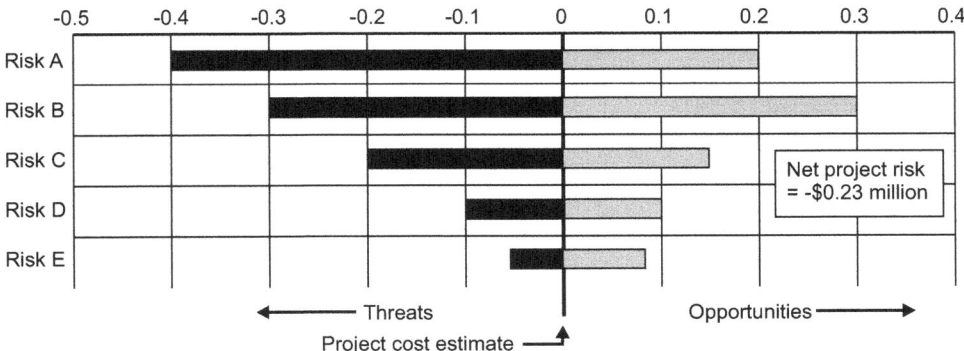

Figure 26.5 Example using a tornado diagram to show the risk position for a project

- the risk response;
- the risk response plan, which is designed to reduce the probability of occurrence or the consequences of the event should it occur;
- the name of the person who must take appropriate action against the risk.

Risk registers are standard features in most leading risk management software tools.

Contingency plan

Low probability, high impact threats (for example, risks ranking 12 on the probability/impact matrix in Figure 26.4) should not be dismissed as requiring no further action just because they are unlikely to happen. It is precisely because of the severity of the impact that these risks should have a planned contingency response.

There should be a contingency reserve budget. This needs a burn-down plan which tracks the consumption of reserves over time to a predetermined curve. If the consumption of contingency reserves is too great, a recovery plan should be developed.

Supply chain management plan

Although not strictly part of programme planning, bought goods and services can account for well over half the cost of a typical programme, so I cannot ignore supply chain management strategy.

Some organizations decide it is cheaper for them to support only core activities, and subcontract work out. Other organizations choose to do all work in-house because they believe that to give total control of their customer's experience with their product and services. These are relatively easy decisions when the product or service is considered to be a core capability of the company. The decisions become more difficult when the product or service can be subcontracted through multiple sources. A make or buy decision process should be included as part of the supply chain management plan, to provide consistency and alignment to the organizational strategy.

Companies establish a list of qualified or preferred suppliers to save time and money during the source selection process. The list should be routinely revised with up-to-date information.

The programme supply chain management plan should contain:

- contract strategy and type;
- make or buy plans;
- qualified supplier list;
- terms and conditions of contracts.

There are many different contract strategies and types. Each has a specific purpose. Some of the major categories of contracts that should be considered are: firm fixed price, cost reimbursable, and time and material.

Financial management plan

A financial management plan should be established which contains:

- financial framework – funding sources and type;
- cost estimates and methodologies;
- performance metrics and reporting;
- forecast schedule of net cash flows;
- budget baseline.

Owing to the large amount of money normally involved in programmes, the time-phasing and amounts of costs could constrain the programme. The business case depends not only on keeping costs within budgets, but also managing the timing of payments as part of cash flow management. Ignoring this could violate the business case or even cause the company to run short of cash.

Performance metrics and reporting

The programme manager needs to specify at which level of the WBS the costs for the programme will be managed. Control accounts must be created at this level to accumulate incurred costs. A cost account manager needs to be assigned the responsibility, authority and accountability for each account. Earned value management can be used in this context, as described earlier. Any gap between the programme investment and delivery of the programme benefits must be closed to the greatest extent possible to provide the best cash flow possible.

Quality management plan

The approach to quality should emphasize that quality cannot be 'inspected into' products, processes or services – it must be planned and designed into them. Everyone in the organization should be made 'quality aware' so that a 'quality culture' results. Metrics should be established and used to measure the effect of the quality plan throughout the programme's lifecycle.

The quality management plan should be flowed to all assemblies, subassemblies, components, materials and procured items. This plan should contain:

- quality requirements and standards;
- quality assurance;
- quality control.

The applicable quality requirements and standards should be identified. There should also be a discussion of how compliance with these requirements and standards will be verified. Both product and process quality should be addressed.

The quality assurance section of the plan should stipulate the process for monitoring adherence to quality standards and requirements and the metrics that will be used.

The quality control section is used to document quality control for parts and processes. Details should be included for statistical process control methods for processes and statistical quality control methods for materials, parts, assemblies and others. Also included should be the process for monitoring and recording the results of these activities, assessing performance and recommending necessary changes. Alternative quality control methodologies should be considered where statistical methods are impracticable.

Other plans

Audit plan

A programme audit plan should provide a schedule for periodical audits that will assess the adherence of the programme and its components to programme plans, policies and procedures. Recovery plans should be made for identified deficiencies.

Closeout and transition plan

This plan should detail how the programme will be closed, how programme resources are to be released and how benefits will be transferred from the programme to the organization. The contents of this plan will vary greatly depending on the programme. For process-related programmes, the transition plan might require an operational readiness inspection that includes (but is not limited to) the following:

- demonstration that a preventive maintenance plan for the new process is in place;
- compliance with applicable codes and standards has been demonstrated;
- agreement by the process owners that all necessary operator training has been completed and the process is ready for production.

It is very important that all stakeholders have been engaged and their concerns have been addressed before transitioning benefits to the organization.

References and further reading

Crook, J. (2014a), White Paper: Developing the Programme Management Plan, unpublished.
Crook, J. (2014b), White Paper: Programme Management in Health Care, unpublished.
Lock, D. (2013), *Project Management*, 10th edn., Farnham: Gower.

Chapter 27

Controlling Programmes for IT and Business Change

Gerrit Koch and Dennis Lock

Clearly the object of control is to obtain success. A programme is controlled successfully if all its constituent projects have been finished as specified, the key performance indicators are achieved (or are on track for success) and all the shareholders and other major stakeholders are satisfied. The process begins with the business case and does not end until the organization and its people have adapted to implement all the required changes.

A few golden rules

As other contributors to this Handbook have written, programme authorization and primary responsibility for control must be led from the top of the organization, which in most cases means the board of directors.

Suggestions or requests for a new business change project or programme can arise anywhere in a large group or company. Such suggestions should never be discouraged, even if they originate from a relatively junior person. However, there are some important rules that should apply before a programme is authorized.

Programmes for systems or organization change are disruptive and can cause distress to people within the organization because they have to learn new methods, fit in with a changed command structure, face apparent demotion or even lose their jobs. A very bad condition will be created if a new change programme is allowed to begin while another, earlier programme is still in the process of being completed or is 'bedding down'. Then people will become confused, demotivated and even aggressive. So one golden rule is to allow only one programme to be in active progress at a time. Never cause disruption and confusion in an organization by expecting it to accommodate new changes while it is still in the process of trying to make an earlier change succeed.

Every new project and programme will cost money in a number of ways (some of which might not be anticipated before the programme starts). That money has to come as an indirect cost to the business, unlike normal operations that are funded by revenue from clients and customers. The aim of every organization must be to keep its indirect costs as low as possible. Otherwise it cannot sell its services and products at economic prices.

Change usually comes associated with risk – risk that the proposed change will not produce the beneficial results expected or that other targets are not met. The normal business operations could even be seriously disrupted, with consequent damage to the key performance indicators (KPIs) that the change programme was expected to improve.

The authorizing body has to take all this into account, and a key ingredient to help their decision must be a sound business case. The initiation process has to be done very carefully to set the scene for success. All involved stakeholders have to agree on what is expected from them and what their responsibilities will be.

The business case for a change programme

The person or group that sees a need for a programme must be asked to prepare a business case for the board to consider. A business case sets out details of the proposed programme and attempts to justify the reason for authorization. Sometimes that reason is compelling (for instance to comply with changing legislation). Most programmes, however, promise benefits, defined as a contribution to the various KPIs set by senior management. A few examples of KPIs are:

- increased revenue;
- improved cash flow;
- reduced indirect costs;
- improved inventory turnover;
- better employee satisfaction and lower staff turnover;
- improved service to customers (which can be measured in several ways).

A business case that omits one or more cost items would clearly lead to work and cost estimates that are too low, with all the consequent risks which that would entail. Some companies that conduct programmes and change projects habitually develop check-lists. The example in Figure 27.1 is also arranged in the hierarchy of a work breakdown structure.

Consideration of the business case

The task of approving or rejecting a business case must be loaded on to an executive at board level, but preliminary filtering and recommendations can be done by a strategic portfolio board (SPB), always provided of course that one exists in the organization.

Now suppose that you are responsible for reviewing several business cases, each coming from some part of your organization, and each claiming to the best thing since the advent of sliced bread.

Your task of sorting out the good, the bad and the ugly from the pile of documents on your desk will be easier if they all conform to a common layout. So you should encourage everyone who wants to submit a business case for a new project or programme to adhere to a predefined common format. Then your comparison task as a portfolio manager will be somewhat easier.

If it would compete with other programmes, a proposed new programme must be challenged by top management or, if there is one, the SPB or its equivalent. That authority will compare the contribution to the organization's KPIs, the positive cash

Code	Category/sub-category/cost element
010000	**Business analysis**
010100	Business redesign
010101	Major process procedures design
010102	IS procedures design
010103	Data model design (logical)
010104	Report and management information design
010105	Develop procedures documentation
010200	Current state assessment
010201	Information systems review
010202	Use organization assessment
010203	Process assessment
010204	Reporting and MI assessment
020000	**Business change**
020100	Business user training
020101	Identify communities to be trained
020102	Conduct training needs analysis
020103	Develop training plan
020104	Develop training course material
020105	Schedule training events
020106	Administer training events
020107	Deliver training courses
020108	Monitor training feedback
020200	Communications
020201	Identify communication audiences
020202	Develop communication strategy
020203	Select communication media
020204	Develop communication plan
020205	Implement communication plan
020206	Assess audience understanding of key message
020207	Update communication plan
020300	Project contract development
020301	Identify objectives
020302	Identify event milestones
020303	Identify business values
020304	Match flashpoints to value drivers
020305	Quantify values
020306	Determine project cost
020307	Balance value against cost
020308	Develop project contract
020309	Obtain approval

Figure 27.1 Initial task check-list for a management change project
By kind permission of Isochron Ltd.

flow generation forecast, the probability for success, the portfolio's risk appetite and the available resources. Even a new programme showing extremely good promise could jeopardize the success of the whole portfolio (for example if it would place too much demand on scarce resources).

Code	Category/sub-category/cost element
020400	Stakeholder management
020401	Develop stakeholder management plan
020402	Implement stakeholder management plan
020403	Stakeholder analysis
020404	Develop stakeholder role transformation plan
020405	Implement stakeholder role transformation plan
020406	Manage stakeholder issues
020407	Integrate stakeholder management and communication plans
030000	**Project running costs**
030100	Facilities
030101	Accommodation charges
030102	IT charges
030103	Room hire
030104	Food and refreshments
030105	Printing and stationery
030200	Overhead allocations
030201	Other contributions to central funds
030300	Project administration
030301	Project accounting
030302	Resource management
030303	Project facilities management
030304	General administration
030400	Project management
030401	Project structuring
030402	Project planning
030403	Project control
030404	Project monitoring
030405	Issue management
030406	Change management
030407	Project reporting
030408	Travel
030409	Hotel
030410	Subsistence
040000	**Technology solution**
040100	Applications support
040101	Design support model
040102	User environment design
040103	IS environment design
040104	Procedures design
040105	Training design
040106	Implement support model
040107	Monitor support services

Figure 27.1 Continued

The forecast net present value (NPV) and internal rate of return on investment (IRR) are the principal financial factors usually taken into account when authorizing any programme. So these must be calculated as part of the business plan. For a crash programme with a very short duration (say 12 months) simple arithmetic will

Code	Category/sub-category/cost element
040200	Custom development
040201	Application infrastructure development
040202	Business system design
040203	Testing design
040204	Data conversion application development
040205	Application software development
040206	System testing
040207	Implementation planning
040300	Hardware
040301	Servers
040302	Clients
040303	Connectivity
040304	Peripherals
040400	Implementation
040401	Data conversion
040402	Acceptance testing
040203	Installation of production system
040204	Refine production system
040205	Evolution planning
040300	Package integration and testing
040301	Installation and environment set-up
040302	Package integration design and pilot
040303	Package business system design
040304	Package application development
040304	Package integration testing design
040305	Data conversion application development
040306	System testing
040307	Implementation planning
040400	Package selection
040401	Package requirements analysis
040402	Vendor and package screening
040403	Package shortlist evaluation
040404	Final evaluation and selection
040405	Contracts and technology acquisition
040406	Development planning
040407	Licences

Figure 27.1 Continued

suffice. The full benefits from programmes typically take several years before they are fully realized and then it is necessary to discount all the cash flows to take into consideration the changing values of money over time. Examples of discounted cash flow methods and time-spaced cash flow spreadsheets for projects can be found in Lock (2013).

A negative NPV forecast would clearly be a first indication that a programme should not go ahead. The question arises of where to set the discounting rate, and a common answer is to choose a rate at least equivalent to the percentage rate that the company could earn by investing the money elsewhere instead of pursuing the proposal.

However, another approach is to reiterate the NPV calculations several times using different discounting rates until a result is found that gives an NPV of zero. The discounting rate which gives that zero NPV result indicates the expected IRR.

A higher IRR clearly makes a programme more desirable and increases its priority in the portfolio. As such, IRR forecasts can be used to rank several prospective programmes and projects being considered for approval. Assuming all other factors are equal among the various programmes and projects, the project with the highest IRR would technically be considered the most attractive to be undertaken first (as long as it fits in the portfolio's risk appetite).

The business case must answer questions such as:

- the required total budget;
- the required budget per year and/or per programme tranche;
- the time needed to execute the programme;
- the time needed to harvest the business benefits;
- the expected KPIs;
- the development of cash flow relating budgets, spending and business benefits;
- the forecast IRR, to adjust priorities in the portfolio;
- risk mitigation related to the business case;
- in addition, anything requested by the portfolio office (PFO) and/or the SPB.

When reviewing any business case the data must be subjected to critical questioning. People enthusiastic to promote a programme as their personal cause are apt to emphasize the positive aspects, give optimistic estimates of time and costs and play down the risks. It is clearly in the organization's best interests to ensure that all the data are calculated as fairly and accurately as possible. Also, any risks and potentially disruptive aspects must not be ignored or understated. Predictions of the KPIs have to be fair and honest.

Programmes in an organization

From initiation until closure the focus must be to direct the programme towards 'right first time'. Coordination with other programmes has to be focused on avoiding contradicting changes or competing benefits.

When a business case is considered, all possible double counting of benefits with other programmes and other initiatives in the permanent organization need to be detected and eliminated. The organization that will own the intended benefits must be the driving force in their realization. That drive must come from senior management, but success will depend largely on keeping all staff who would be affected or involved by the proposed programme positively motivated. No matter how good the programme expectations are, and with the best possible business case, the outcome can be wrecked if all the participating staff in the permanent organization are not fully supportive. There is more on this subject in Fowler and Lock (2006).

Overall programme control helps to make the ambitions SMART (SMART is an acronym pertaining to business objectives and is generally accepted to mean specific, measurable, achievable, relevant and time-bound). Methods for measuring results (time, cost and work done) have to be set up. Then any deviations from budgets and plans (known differently as exceptions, non-conformances or variances) have to be reported up the line of command so that appropriate actions can be taken.

People in the organization have to know what their responsibilities are and what will be expected of them. The London Transport example in Figure 14.7, although titled there as a 'product matrix', is really an illustration of a universal tool for assigning organizational and task responsibilities which is more widely known as a linear responsibility matrix. That kind of document can record and inform all programme participants and stakeholders about the control responsibilities of all the key people in the organization.

Stage-gating

Programmes tend to last for several years. Breaking the programme into stages (or tranches or phases) makes it easier to envisage the work and improves programme control. A critical review at the end of each stage allows the board or the sponsor to call a halt ('pull the plug') and stop the damage if it becomes clear that the programme is headed for failure. This process is called stage-gating. Stage-gating is particularly important when a programme is allowed to start when the business plan is incomplete or some of its contents are not fully defined.

Assumptions and general rules

The most important stakeholders (those who are most concerned about the programme's outcomes) should be represented on a programme steering committee. The programme manager is usually responsible for the projects that run in the programme. Here, accepted and well-known project management rules apply. The programme manager should report to the programme steering committee about all projects in or related to the programme.

The permanent organization will have to implement the required organizational changes and be committed to delivering their part of the business benefits. Effective programme control facilitates the business change managers in their benefits management. It will encourage managers of individual projects to report and exchange experiences. Programme control consolidates all this information to programme level.

As the closure draws nearer, the programme delivers the last output, completes the final activities in the permanent organization and benefits are measured to ensure that the KPIs have been achieved. Commitment of the permanent organization to take over the responsibility for the programme's continuing commitments is a prerequisite for closing the programme. A programme is usually closed as soon as the organization feels itself capable of taking over responsibility for tracking results to achieve the KPIs. Sometimes the benefits realization is well on its way when the programme closes but in other cases it can take a year or more after closing the programme before all the benefits become apparent.

Controlling and closing a programme requires a control-based management style related to the projects, plus a consulting style to enable and support change. It should not be assumed that every *project* manager or change manager will be a competent *programme* manager.

Project, programme and portfolio management controls

The definition of a programme according to the International Project Management Association (IPMA) is an endeavour set up to achieve a strategic goal. A programme consists of a set of related projects and required organizational change to reach a strategic goal and to achieve the defined 'business' benefits.

Programmes contain a number of related projects that are executed to deliver the programme's benefits. Multiple programmes and their projects can be managed in a portfolio. The absence of programmes is sometimes referred to as the missing link between high-level strategic goals and getting the work done (Figure 27.2).

Competence of the organization

An early step is to examine the organizational environment in which a programme will be performed. Several different viewing angles will help to analyse this including:

- the organizations involved;
- the intended programme;
- the principal stakeholders;
- the critical resources.

Opening new programmes should be aligned with the competence of an organization to select and initiate them, to execute all the individual projects well, and to improve work methods as a programme proceeds.

Sessions with relevant stakeholders should be held at the end of each tranche and at final closure to discover and list all the lessons learned. That experience can be used to advantage in a following tranche or future programme. An organization that builds up and maintains competence will clearly show a higher success rate in

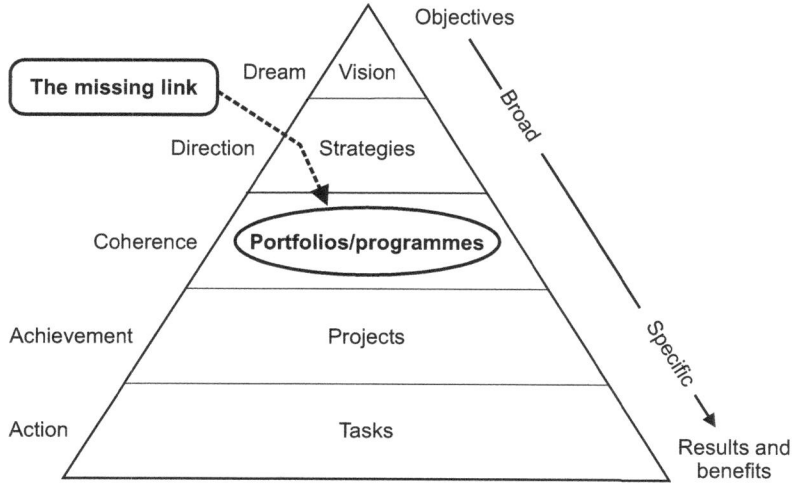

Figure 27.2 The missing link

performing future programmes. The current competence of an organization can be tested by asking questions such as:

- Does the organization have a vision related to projects, programmes and portfolios (PP&P)?
- Does the organization align programmes to its strategy, to the PP&P vision and its medium- and long-term plans?
- Does the organization have experience in using programmes to achieve strategic goals?
- Does the organization have enough mass in its critical functions to keep control over the programme?
- Does the organization align projects and programmes in a portfolio to optimize the outcomes?
- Does the organization apply benefits management and change management?
- Does the organization facilitate good preparation involving the main stakeholders?
- Does the organization have a mature and independent control function with project and programme control experience?

Every organization needs a clear and binding methodology to perform programmes. It also needs adequate standards and procedures that tailor programme management methodology to the organization and to the programme's specific needs. The organization's relevant departments and functions have to be well aligned and competent to support and control the programme. To examine the setting in and around a programme one should ask questions like:

- Does the programme involve the relevant stakeholders well?
- Are the steering priorities for the programme (time, money, outputs) set, understood and agreed by the stakeholders?
- Are the programme's goal, benefits, outcome and output clear and accepted by all stakeholders?
- Do the contextual parties (such as facilities management, HRM, HSSE [health, safety, security and environment], finance and legal) know what the programme needs from them and does the programme management know what these contextual parties expect from the programme?
- Will the programme's organization evolve into a new part of the permanent organization?
- Is the permanent organization well involved and participating to keep control over intended output, outcomes and benefits?

A programme that is set up to achieve a strategic goal will of course be of great concern to senior management, So the programme management team needs to be competent to act or report at board level. Reporting has to be two-way, with the board taking ultimate responsibility.

When considering the individual people involved in a programme, views of their competence and suitability can be built up using questions like:

- Do participants in the programme understand their roles and responsibilities?
- Is everyone competent to perform their expected tasks and responsibilities?

- Are there fallback options for critical resources and are these secured?
- Is there a good balance between leadership roles, management and execution capacity?
- Are there clear feedback loops with the stakeholders and do the contextual parties know what their representing participants in the programme need?
- Is everyone aware of what/who the critical resources are?
- Is every participant given enough challenge for their own development?
- Is the benefits management accepted in the programme as well as in the part of the organization represented by the business change manager(s)?
- Is the role of programme control well-defined and is the programme controller competent in this role?

This assessment should be done at the beginning, involving the programme executive, programme manager and the programme controller. That should indicate how to set up a control function that will suit the organization, the programme and the resources in and around the programme. This should lead to a finalized and validated control plan.

Control cycles

All individual projects in a programme should be controlled and coordinated by a programme management office (PMO). Unfortunately those initials can also stand for a project management office, and large constituent projects in a programme might each need one of those too. In the remainder of this chapter we shall use PMO to describe the programme management office, which consolidates all projects and activities in the programme.

Figure 27.3 describes the following control cycle. All the programmes and the independent projects should report to the organization through the portfolio office (PFO). The PFO will receive regular instructions from the portfolio board to pass on to the projects and programmes. In addition the PFO provides regulations and

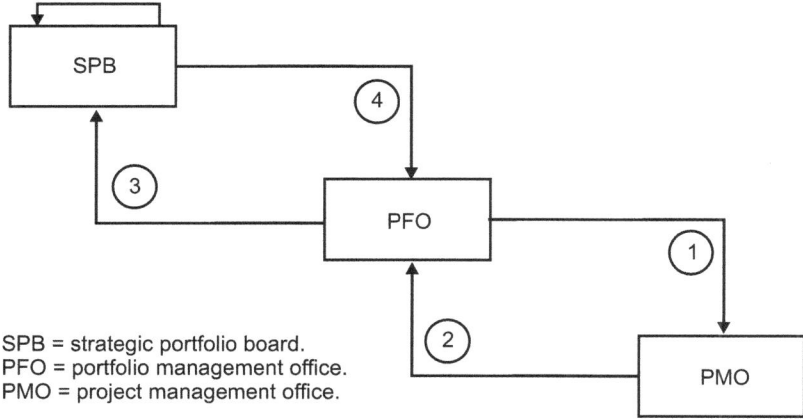

SPB = strategic portfolio board.
PFO = portfolio management office.
PMO = project management office.

Figure 27.3 Programme control loops

guidelines for reporting. It also checks whether the reports are compliant with regulations and guidelines and whether they are true, complete and timely. This kind of cycle is known as the Deming continuous improvement cycle or the PDCA (**p**lan, **d**o, check, **a**ct; see Deming, 2000).

Conflicts can occur during consolidation (for example between individual projects). The PFO should make proposals or recommendations to resolve any conflict. The consolidation results should be reported to the SPB for decision-making or any other necessary action.

The SPB is usually at director or executive level. Large project-orientated organizations tend to have a portfolio for each division or geographic area, plus one portfolio for all organization-wide projects or programmes. Significant management information from each portfolio would be reported to the board of directors. This arrangement is obviously closely aligned with the structure on board level.

Double loop control cycle

The following describes the control cycles for one portfolio. The SPB is chaired by the end responsible manager or executive responsible for PP&P. This person is responsible for the final decisions and for resolving conflicts between different participants in the SPB. The SPB consists of senior management, responsible for their annual plans and the profit or loss for the part of the organization that they represent.

The senior management of the (internal) suppliers are typically also members of the SPB. Often in larger organizations the chief financial officer and the chief information, communication and technology officer represent the staff in the SPB. Portfolio management by the SPB generally involves those corporate projects and programmes that exceed the responsibility of individual SPB members.

Historically in most organizations projects and even programmes have emerged from the bottom. The vast amounts of money often involved and the need to do these endeavours right first time demanded good coordination. Pre-project or programme steering committees were formed. Directing and management were still per project or programme. The next step was to involve the board on an escalation basis to avoid problems between projects and programmes. For early and impartial information a PFO was initiated. The next step from that moment on was to support projects and programmes with templates, formats, procedures and so on. The second step was to check the reports. The PFO acted primarily as timekeeper and not so much on the content or the comparison of various reports.

The third step was to deliver the reports to the SPB. The board required more information on progress, issues and risks and the PFO started to define additional requirements and information needs related to the reports on the projects and programmes. The projects, being part of a programme, reported through the programme. This limited the work per project and helped the programme to maintain focus on the goals.

To consolidate the reports the PFO requested the SPB to define SMART goals and subsequent relevant KPIs. This way the PFO enabled the SPB to prioritize between projects and programmes aligning with the organization's goals. The SPB was also able to improve its own alignment in the decision-making-processes. Now the two Deming cycles are fully interrelated (Figure 27.4). One could even argue that there

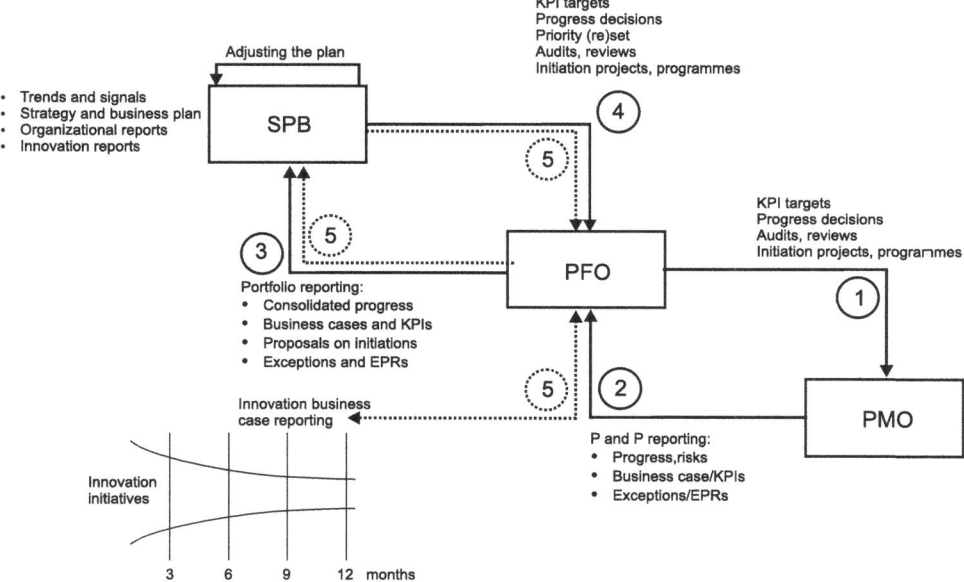

Figure 27.4 Elaborated control model

are three loops if you add the project/programme internal goal setting and reporting interrelating with the PMO.

Competing objectives of money, time and scope

Money, time and scope are the control steering variables. Some might think that
quality should be included, but quality is not a variable. A mature definition of quality is that any product should be 'fit for purpose'. Clearly the programme must be fit
for purpose.

Sometimes there is competition between money, time and scope if one takes priority over another. Dr Martin Barnes originally expressed this as a triangle of objectives,
and those who are interested can see examples in Lock (2013). Especially during
initiation, planning and start-up the programme management must be clear about
the priority of the steering variables because that will to some extent guide the management processes.

If the top priority is cost and budget control there is no room to exceed the budget.
Time can exceed planned dates, perhaps by up to some 10 per cent of the intended
duration and the scope is a little flexible.

Product development often puts the priorities in descending order of time, scope
and money. With that sequence it is crucial the make the development cycle as short
as possible to be the first on the market and repay the investments.

Luxury goods can be an example where scope and functionality become the
important variables, taking all the budget that is needed.

Control has to be adapted in relation to the chosen prioritization. The impact of this distinction can be severe if the different parties do not have the same view (or no view at all) on the priorities set. The control arrangements and organization can differ tremendously depending on these priorities.

The programme plan and the underlying plans for each tranche have to make clear which priority setting is chosen for the sake of clear and unambiguous decision-making.

Managers can now more easily detect whether or not programmes will run out of control. A clear priority sequence helps to see early if criteria will not be met with an unchanged plan. Control flags this situation if one of the steering variables' settings cannot be met; it does not have to wait until this is visible in the financial statements of the progress reports.

Communications and reporting

An important control factor is the need to ensure that all people involved in the programme are given appropriate information through regular and dedicated communication. Communications are extremely important horizontally across the organization and vertically through the command and reporting structures. Communications can be either formal or informal.

A good example of formal communications are the work-to-do lists which have their roots in the schedules from the constituent projects. Time analysis from critical path scheduling will establish the priorities of all tasks and the task list should be personalized for each manager, so that each manager gets only that part of the total work schedule pertaining to his/her responsibility. That personalization is achieved by developing an organization breakdown structure, with each element of the organization (or better, each functional or department manager) given a unique code. Then all instructions and work-to-do lists can be filtered using these codes. All this demands the use of good software, remembering that the most commonly used software is by no means always the best.

Another important breakdown structure is the cost breakdown structure, which overlays and interacts with the work breakdown structure.

These three breakdown structures, with their codes, provide formal channels of communication for command and instruction. These same channels, in reverse direction, are important for collecting and analysing results and performance data.

Breakdown structures for single projects are described thoroughly in Harrison and Lock (2004) and the methodology is easily adaptable for programmes.

Defining roles

Disagreements are probable between people from different functions. Some say that discussions can be more productive and carry less risk of hurting personal relationships if we think of and address our colleagues by their role names instead of their personal names. Whether or not we agree with that, clear role descriptions are essential for all who are involved, at least at senior level.

The PFO can take the lead in ensuring that roles are adequately defined and also in taking care that training and support are provided where needed to bring competence to the roles. Often the roles are not known or understood, especially by senior management and by some staff functions.

Different names are given to corresponding roles by different companies and professional organizations. George Jucan provides a comprehensive discussion of role titles in Chapters 15 and 16 in Lock and Scott (2013).

Cost control

Clearly people must be informed about who is mandated to allow expenditures, especially those that would exceed the authorized budget. The procurement and control people need to know who can decide on the money. That of course also requires that all in the management structure know what the budgets are and also what portion of the overall budget is allocated to their control personally.

Programme cost budgeting and reporting can be different from specific project cost reporting because most change programmes are charged against overhead (indirect) costs – they cannot be charged out and recovered from clients or customers but have to be borne by the business itself. However, programme budgets, costing and cost reports have to be kept separate from general overheads if good control is to be exercised, so a cost collection and reporting structure has to be established in a similar way to the cost and reporting structures for direct work. Colin Drury (2012) has long been a leading authority on cost and management accounting, for those needing to learn more about this subject.

Change control

The business case will have set out the scope of the programme, together with cost estimates from which working budgets have been derived. Any proposed change to scope or any part of the programme that would cause significant deviation from the original business case must be considered at senior level before it can be allowed. The operative word here is 'significant' and some discretion can usually be allowed to senior managers.

It can make sense to allow the programme manager a budgetary discretion of perhaps 5 or even 10 per cent of programme costs. Budgets should be calculated in the first place to set aside reserve amounts for such contingencies. More significant changes need formal consideration before they are allowed and for that purpose it is customary to have a change board or change committee, comprising senior managers. The change board will not only prevent unnecessary changes and 'scope creep' but will ensure that the programme records are updated to accommodate the changes.

Particular attention must be paid to the costs of bought equipment and services, because these can amount to a very significant proportion of the total costs. So a competent contracts or purchasing manager must be part of the programme operation.

The projects specified in the programme have to be managed within the programme with the programme manager as the project owner. All these projects should report to the PMO, which should consolidate progress reports to present the programme overview (typically on a bi-weekly basis). The PMO will typically report costs, progress, conflicts and risks for the whole programme to the PFO on a four-weekly basis. The PFO consolidates reports from the various programmes for the SPB. Then the SPB will decide on any possible priority and resource conflicts for decision, usually also on a four-weekly basis.

In recent implementations R&D initiatives have also been brought under this regime, typically on a three-monthly basis. Each R&D manager reports progress, a reassessed or confirmed business case and a plan for the flowing three months. At these stage gates, half the initiatives might be stopped for various reasons. Those which 'get through the funnel' are usually awarded project or programme status for further development. This reduces the risk of wasting money. The most important advantage is to give the SPB (operation at board level) an overview of work in progress and an outlook for three to five years ahead on expected benefits from the programme and R&D portfolios.

Exercising control at portfolio level

Several organizations target their individual projects for their realization not to differ more than 20 per cent from the last accepted budget, while their programmes have to stay within 10–15 per cent of the budget. The portfolio has to be able to stay within 5 per cent of the total budget of the underlying projects and programmes. The idea is that the more projects that are in joint control, the better the PFO should be able to manage the total deviation within very limited margins because good and poorer individual project or programme results compensate each other.

Benefits realization and measurement

One or more business change managers (BCMs) should be appointed by senior management to oversee the changes needed to realize the intended benefits. BCMs are represented on the programme's steering board and should report to the SPB. A BCM is responsible among other things for:

- contribution of the specified benefit to the business case requirements;
- delivering specifications for the benefits to be realized;
- delivering specifications for benefits measurement tools;
- implementation of changes and capabilities to realize the benefits;
- informing and aligning senior management;
- getting and keeping those who need to know involved and informed about the programme.

Each BCM prepares, supports, implements the measures, reports, advises and assumes the responsibility for realizing the business benefits.

BCMs are at most times accompanied by the programme controller and/or by the programme manager. Their task is to keep the business case aligned with the benefits realization and with the programme's goals and outcome. A BCM's first job is to create a cross-reference table relating the programme's benefits to the organization's KPIs. The BCM makes a benefits card for each organization as an element for its benefits management. An accounting principle is applicable here, namely be clear about disbenefits and book those realistically. Also, be conservative about the expected benefits realization. Benefits tend to come later and not to their full extent in the first one or two years.

There could also be some additional benefits, more indirect, less quantifiable and related to issues where the organization does not have much experience. It can be worthwhile to define those measurements in any case. Measuring should begin early, with everything kept under close control. After six or twelve months it should become clear whether some things really contribute, to what extent, and to actualize the business case for this programme.

The programme manager and the controller assist the BCM to build the 'goal tree', the benefits cards, the benefits realization plan and the measurement instruments needed. The BCM involves the relevant senior management, helping them to recognize the benefits. Other senior managers will involve their business controllers as counterparts for the programme controller.

Measurement of the benefits can be developed in various ways:

- If the contribution of a business department is relevant to a particular KPI, then probably this KPI will be measured already and the BCM needs to connect to this measurement. This can define, for example, the need to develop additional questions in a client satisfaction inquiry to measure the department's contribution to this KPI.
- If contribution to the KPI is an absolute requirement, then adequate measurement methods must be developed. Often these methods can be made available for other programme contributors as well.
- If the goal is to reduce costs and to achieve this through personnel reduction, there needs to be clarity where this reduction will take place and under whose authority. The programme cannot enforce this. In addition, it is wise and important to involve the labour committee or the relevant trade union early and before committing to any target.
- The management of the organization has to realize that improvements from the programme will not be fully successful if the personnel affected are not informed, involved and motivated.
- Closing a programme team organization can clearly be related to the real end, when all outputs and benefits have been delivered and are accepted by the receiving management. The alternative is to close the programme team early, when the BCM's organization is capable of taking over responsibility for finalizing implementation and managing benefits.

Closing a programme

It is important to involve all major stakeholders in closing a programme and to look for findings and lessons learned. Calling a programme 'successful' requires that the permanent organization is satisfied with the delivered benefits. This does not necessarily mean that the programme organization has to be maintained until this very end because the permanent organization can sometimes be capable of resolving any remaining open issues and integrating benefits management in the regular management process.

It is easier to close a programme that was successful because all who could have an opinion like to identify themselves with this success. From a programme that was not or only partly successful there is still much more to learn however (such as defining better procedures for future use).

Questions to evaluate the programme should be asked of the major stakeholders. Here is a check-list:

- Did the programme ensure independent reviews from various functions like the business management, facilities management, quality management, legal, HRM, HSSE and financial management?
- Are the organization's departments that were involved satisfied? Did they get what they expected? Are the outputs, outcomes and benefits satisfactory?
- Have the business change managers succeeded in implementing the outputs, outcomes and benefits measuring systems and getting acceptance from their senior management?
- Did the programme achieve qualitative goals such as the professional development of staff and an organization fit for the future?
- How does the programme team and the permanent organization ensure that output, outcomes and benefits will continue and develop further after ending the programme?
- If a programme is ended because of changing priorities or because the permanent organization takes over the remaining output, outcomes or benefits, how will the programme and permanent organizations ensure a successful handover?
- Were products, process, benefits and programme documentation accepted in the handover to the permanent organization?
- Have responsibilities, tasks and qualifications for maintenance and development after the programme been defined and implemented?
- Have programme personnel been handed back to the permanent organization in a way that satisfies all parties?
- Is the core business organization satisfied and can they achieve their targets and harvest the benefits as promised?
- Are the newly implemented systems performing as intended?

In many organizations the programme manager is held responsible for the closing process. Independent reviews deliver more and better information for further development. Even programmes that were not successful provide sources for learning, provided that relevant stakeholders are open and honest.

Fast systems development

Many programmes have new or renewed IT systems as one of the outputs and these are crucial for the success of the programme. Fast-track developments like Scrum and Agile require specific set-ups allowing the development teams to develop small packages of functionality in sprints, every few weeks. In this case time and subsequent budgets are difficult to predict. The teams benefit and improve from learning and get more productive along the way. This requires the business representatives to be closely aligned with or be part of the development teams. Programme management and control have to align their way of working to this situation as well.

The bigger picture

Many organizations may have a mission, vision and strategy related to their core activities and their organization. In general, however, there is no vision or strategy yet related to projects, programmes and portfolios. The emerging portfolio management in organizations can contribute to clear selection criteria about which projects and/or programmes to do and what, given the organization's KPIs, the priorities should be. This way projects and programmes are easier to control, while resource optimization is solved in the best interest of the organization at large.

It is no longer necessary for the individual managers to fight for the best resources. That has become part of the managerial decision-making. The PFO signals to the SPB for the organization to decide about changes overseeing the whole portfolio and its impact on the organization. The vision, strategy and annual plans create clear expectations and clarity for the projects and programmes to plan, realize and prove their added value and contribution to the organization. Development of a clear vision on PP&P, implementing that and making it work with professional staff is the highest priority in many organizations.

References and further reading

Breese, R. (2012), 'Benefits Realisation Management: Panacea or False Dawn?', *International Journal of Project Management*, 30(3): 341–51.

Deming, W. E. (2000), *Out of the Crisis*, Cambridge, MA: MIT Press.

Drury, C. (2012), *Management and Cost Accounting*, Andover: Cengage Learning.

Fowler, A. and Lock, D. (2006), *Accelerating Business and IT Change: Accelerating Project Delivery*, Farnham: Gower.

Harrison, F. and Lock, D. (2004), *Advanced Project Management*, 4th edn., Aldershot: Gower.

Lock, D. (2013), *Project Management*, 10th edn., Farnham: Gower.

Lock, D. and Scott, L. (2013), *Handbook of People in Project Management*, Farnham: Gower.

Chapter 28

Using Modern Technologies for Programme Management

Mark Phillips

The message in this chapter is that we should not be driven by unrealistic ideals of what software tools can do for programme success. Instead we have to be realistic and pragmatic about their choice, relevance and application. As stressed in many other chapters, people are the most important tool.

Introduction

Picking a programme management software tool is probably one of the least important decisions you will make when implementing successful programme management. This comes from several decades of experience. For the better part of the last two decades I've been the co-founder, CEO, CFO, product manager or lead spokesperson for a project management software company. I've been involved with the boards of industry organizations, closely working with senior executives and salespeople from leading programme and project management software providers. I've attended numerous industry events and spoken to countless programme managers. I've led several very successful innovative programmes. The message I hear is always the same. The tool doesn't make a difference. I shall present some cases that prove this point.

Case 1

Take, for example, an extremely large, global smartphone and computer manufacturer. Let's call it the XYZ company. Over the course of a year or so they were looking for a new programme management software tool to support one of their global lines of business. This line of business crossed into nearly every one of their products and touched their major profit drivers. The business owners and programme managers spent over a year researching tools. They read websites and White Papers, had demonstrations, talked to salespeople and narrowed the choice down from the myriad tools out there to a handful of potential competitors.

The XYZ company then spent six months whittling that list down. Programme managers from different groups engaged in telephone calls and web demos with potential vendors to express their needs. The various vendors described how they could meet those needs. The vendors shared their product roadmaps. Many changed their roadmaps to incorporate this customer's specific long-term needs.

The company shared their current workflows, programme management methodology, project portfolios and business goals. They explained why they needed a new tool now and why there was urgency to implement change before the next product launch. The company described discussions they'd had on their ideal approach – their dream future state for how programmes would be managed.

Together the tool makers and the XYZ company uncovered valuable intersections of the tool makers' technology and XYZ's ideal programme management approach. Finally, XYZ chose a single tool maker with whom they had the best relationship and who they believed could help power the next generation of successful programme management for this global enterprise. To help bring this deal to a close, the programme managers brought in the business owners for final conversations, questions and relationship building.

XYZ team members planned site visits to the software company's headquarters, development office and customer support centre. Everything seemed to be lining up. The programme managers envisaged a bright new future with the new ideal tool in place. The tool maker dreamed of adding another prominent customer to its portfolio.

While the final conversation and visits were being scheduled, XYZ brought its purchasing department into the process to begin negotiating a final deal and making sure that the supplier could meet the strict vendor policies and guarantees that XYZ required. Given the potential impact this software decision could have and how integral it was going to be to the overall operations of this line of business, and therefore to the entire enterprise, it was critical that the purchasing department should craft the most advantageous structure for a long-term deal.

Each party liaised with legal counsel. The tool vendor circulated potential deal structures with its board of advisers. This was going to be a major decision for both sides. Over the course of months of negotiation it seemed that a deal was close at hand. Only a few signatures from the XYZ company were needed and the formal relationship could begin in earnest. Each side looked forward to the incredible impact expected from the use of this perfect programme management software tool. And they waited . . . and waited. No signatures. Messages left, but unreturned. Emails sent but not answered.

Two months after the target start date for the deal, the tool vendor got a call from one of XYZ's programme managers explaining that they had decided not to do anything. They had chosen instead to keep going with their current practices and the current tool. XYZ might revisit the topic later but they were sticking with the status quo for now. Disappointed, the tool vendor expressed understanding and continued with its own business.

As for the XYZ company that so desperately needed a new tool, the right tool to support their next phase of global growth, can you guess what happened to them? They executed all their programmes successfully. They delivered business value. Their revenues skyrocketed, they introduced market-dominating new products, they kept customers happy and their net worth grew astronomically. They innovated, achieved good speed-to-market and maintained a high standard of quality. Their brand equity went up. Their ability to do all this had nothing to do with picking the right programme management software tool.

There are programme managers who swear by one software tool or another. I have found that this is usually based on past experience rather than objective evaluation of the importance of a tool. They feel comfortable with one tool. It helps them do their job so they make the case for sticking with that one tool.

There are also executives or IT folks who become enamoured with one technology or another, believing that the tool can help drive change, or force a different way of thinking or different behaviour. Like the saying 'the truth shall set you free' they believe that implementing one tool or another will free the organization from its previous habits. They believe a particular tool will drive accountability and rational decision-making. They believe the software will empower team members in new ways and cause team members to act in completely different ways from the past. Of course, that doesn't happen. People remain the same. Behaviours don't change simply because of a new tool.

Case 2

I knew an experienced programme manager at a well-funded, late-stage start-up. The company was probably making around $50 to $100 million annual revenue. Senior executives at the company decided it wanted to get serious about disciplined programme management and implement a software tool to help drive the change. My colleague was brought on board to help choose and implement a tool that would meet the executive's needs and deliver the desired change. Jill (not her real name) had an extensive background in implementing and using tools at Fortune 100 companies. She knew her stuff.

Jill's first step was gathering all the executives' requirements. She wanted to create a picture of the executives' ideal state for how the company should operate when programme management was taken seriously. She held numerous requirements fact-gathering workshops and one-on-one meetings. She mapped out processes and end-state diagrams. She put together Visio drawings and PowerPoint presentations describing the current state, the future state and a detailed plan on how to get from the current state to the future state.

The plan was heavy on the kind of changes people would need to make to their weekly workflows. These included items such as recording times into an online time tracking system to gain a better understanding of how productive specific processes work. There was a need to update project and task status on a timely basis. The plan also contained ways people would log change requests into a system and the way they could centralize communication using specific online communication tools.

The plan described keeping programme performance metrics current and regularly evaluating performance against updated business priorities and defined goals. It was a thorough plan on the necessary human-generated inputs that any system would need to help automate programme management processes and facilitate business decision-making.

The executives loved it. They were thrilled they'd hired the right person, someone who understood what they were looking for and could describe it thoroughly and accurately. They gave Jill the green light to 'go find' and implement a programme management software tool that would get them their desired future state.

Jill found a tool set that would do the job. She got authorization to license it, completed the deal and implemented it. She spent a large amount of time at the beginning creating and entering every programme and project schedule into the tool. She designed permission groups, set up users and specific roles for each person on a programme, mirroring the parts they played in the programme or project.

Working with the tool vendor, Jill held role-specific trainings, admin trainings, executive trainings and workshops to empower everyone in the organization to maximize the capabilities of the tool. It was a textbook roll-out and implementation.

Everything worked great for the first month or so. Timelines were up to date. The new reports looked good and were accurate. People did not have to put a whole lot of effort into the tool because of the work the programme manager had put into the tool during the setting up. But after a while, there seemed to be a disconnection between the data in the reports and what appeared to be going on with the programmes. When executives talked to programme managers they heard a different story from that which the tool was telling them. When they listened to the on-the-ground chatter around the offices from the people doing work on the programmes it sounded different from the messages that the tool was giving. It was clear that the data were out of synch. The tool was gradually becoming less useful. In fact, it was becoming downright wrong.

The executives held a meeting with Jill and asked her why the tool had stopped working. She had come prepared. She showed that people never updated the tool. The tool was working just fine but people's behaviour hadn't changed. The executives understood, but asked if that was because the tool was not user-friendly enough. Jill understood where they were coming from. She showed the executives that being user-friendly was one of the key selection criteria for the tool. In fact, she had made sure to run a pilot with the tool before they went all in. Almost everyone in the organization interacted with the tool during the pilot. To a person, they all agreed that the chosen tool was the most user-friendly software they had seen or used. It was intuitive and friendly.

'So,' the executives asked, 'what can we do to make this tool more accurate and generate the kind of reports we're looking for?' Jill replied that they would have to incentivize people to change behaviour – they would need to build a culture around the type of behaviour they were looking for. The executives thanked Jill for all her work and ended the meeting. As you can guess, nothing changed at the company. Jill, seeing this lack of change, became dispirited and moved on to a different organization. The company ended up sticking with the tool. But the executives were never able to get the exact reports, visibility and accountability that they originally wanted.

Where did the executives go wrong? They were looking at software as a magic bullet, the tool that could drive unwanted behaviours out of their company, leaving behind only the behaviours they wanted. They knew that the company and its culture had to change to provide the required visibility. They hired people and built a culture that behaved one way. They wanted information generated by people who behaved in a different way. They were totally aware of this. They believed a tool could take the folks they had and turn them into the folks they wanted – all without losing what they liked about the people they had. I don't have to tell you that things never work that way.

It is worth pointing out the trade-off the executives made in this case. They settled for substandard reports and less automated programme management. But, they maintained the people and organizational strengths responsible for their revenue growth and profitability. There is always a balance between reporting and performance.

It is an easily observed truth that asking people to report on what they do will change their behaviour. While it is true that people can only improve what they measure, it is equally true that people will focus on making what is measured improve. This means that metrics can easily be 'gamed' or worse, that people feel incentivized to hide information that might make the metrics look bad. And, of course, there are always managers willing to encourage this type of behaviour. They will do anything to make the numbers look good because that is what their performance is based on. Metrics take the place of actual programme results. There are many programmes which have been green throughout their lifecycle but which ended up delivering zero value to the enterprise. In the drive for automating programme management it is important not to kill the goose that lays the golden egg.

Choosing the right programme management software tools seems important since tools promise so much, including the right metrics. But without getting the big decisions right, the small decisions (like a programme management software tool) will not matter. And if you get the big decisions right, the specific tool you use will not be that big a deal for successful programme management. Sure, some will be more time saving and others will take you more time. But as long as it fits with your two big decisions you'll be fine.

So, what does matter for successful programme management? There are two big decisions for successful programmes. These are *leadership commitment* and *having the right people*. Make sure that whatever tool you use fits in with your leadership, getting them the information they need. When it comes to developing the right people, make sure a tool helps your people to be themselves. A tool should amplify people's talents. It should be a multiplier of the factors you hired them for, making them better at being the people you hired. When you've got the right people, going in the right direction and doing the things you want them to do, get them a tool that enhances the existing good things.

Concluding case

To conclude, here's an experience I had on one of my programmes. I had two team leaders who desperately needed a programme management tool. They were doing a great job but the sheer volume of projects and tasks they were managing became too much to handle. Staying organized was overwhelming them and, frankly, whittling away at leadership's confidence in them. The team leaders were spending more time keeping track of people and tasks than they were spending time actually leading. This had to change. These leaders were two highly skilled professionals, brought on to help envisage and execute leading edge workstreams. But they were being reduced to being jugglers.

The need made itself felt in other ways. The amount of energy needed to stay organized had other effects. It smothered the team leaders' productivity and dampened overall team morale. These were exciting programmes that were carving new territory into undefined areas of the enterprise. However, instead of excitement at the range of possibilities, the sheer enormity of the possibilities and efforts needed created a sense of chaos. This, in turn, jeopardized the team's ability to innovate. Because instead of feeling as if they were safely exploring new terrain, they felt they were continually dodging falling rocks while trying to scale an unwieldy cliff face.

This is a case where a modern programme management tool really came in handy. It helped the two team leaders put everything that was going on in one place. But, note that it did not automate anything. It helped the team leaders to create a taxonomy of programme-related information. It created a bucket or category to put activity into. Everything now had a place it could go. The programme was run using Agile so each programme had its Epics. Each Epic had its user stories. Each user story had its tasks, and so forth. The tool promoted a hierarchy which provided places to keep track of the mountain of activity the programme required.

It was a game changer. Once it was put in place the team leaders had room to breathe. They could focus on leading and moving the programme forward. They could encourage risk-taking and innovation. They could feel excited about the wide range of solutions the programme could provide and the wealth of business value they could generate for the enterprise. And the excitement became contagious. Needless to say, morale improved and the overall mood of the team was happier. Furthermore, the tool made it easy for other people (namely senior leadership) to see what was going on. The tool was continually being used. Because it was continually used it meant that the artefacts produced from the tool were up to date and always appeared to be reflective of what was going on with the programme. Leadership rarely actually delved into the details of the tool's artefacts. But the perception that the artefacts were current gave leadership confidence in the programme managers. It also gave credibility to the programme managers' status reports. It created a bond of trust that carried through change requests, scope changes, budget pressures and schedule modifications. Leadership saw the tool being continually updated and therefore believed the programme managers were genuinely on top of things.

One of the secrets of the tool being used was that it didn't require much overhead from team members. It was primarily a manager's tool. The little daily updates required from team members were worked into the daily rituals that the programme managers had set up. The updates were part of daily stand-ups and check-ins which the manager would do with the team members.

Mind you, rolling out the software did not happen overnight. The team leaders inherited a tool which the enterprise was already using and had to find ways to put it in place effectively. This was helped by leadership support for their efforts and IT's willingness to help out. But with sufficient patience, creativity and gentle nudging for change, the tool did the job it needed to do and made a big difference in allowing the team leaders to deliver a successful programme.

It is worth mentioning that, until the formal tool was in place, I allowed them to use free, online tools 'unofficially' to help them do their job. When the need is there, focus on what can get the job done without getting lost in the promise of perfectly automated programme management. Remember, leadership and people deliver programme results. Get those things right and the rest will follow.

Chapter 29

Managing Programme Benefits

Andrew Hudson

> To begin with the end in mind means to start with a clear understanding of your destination. It means to know where you're going so that you better understand where you are now and so that the steps you take are always in the right direction.
>
> Stephen Covey

Introduction

There is no other purpose in doing a programme than to deliver value and realize benefits. That is the true measure of a programme's success. To illustrate this, consider which of the following is better:

- a programme that was delivered on time, on budget and created some value;
- a programme that was late and over budget but created significant value.

Some might dispute that the second of these examples is better, but it delivered more value despite being late and over budget.

> [Editorial comment: Many programmes and large projects could have been considered as failures on their completion, yet were successes because their benefits, although delayed, proved to be substantial. Eurotunnel is just one of many examples. DL]

This chapter explains how being more effective at managing programme benefits can accelerate performance improvement and enable organizations to achieve their strategic objectives better. It explains common benefit management practices and explores reasons for programme benefit success and failure. I shall also give practical guidance on the most effective management strategies for achieving programme benefits, including guidance on how to tackle some of the barriers to successful adoption.

Benefits management is at the heart of an organization's strategy. It is a central discipline that connects strategy with change and operations, enabling strategy to be executed and performance targets to be achieved. Figure 29.1 illustrates how benefits management sits at the heart of the strategic process.

Figure 29.1 Connecting strategy with change and operations

The need for programme benefits management

The beneficiaries of a programme, who could be internal or external consumers or operators, need to know that the programme's outputs will enable them to realize their objectives.

Programmes start with high expectations and levels of motivation. That motivation ebbs over the lifecycle of a typical programme as issues relating to quality, cost and time crop up. Programmes may be 'de-scoped' to ensure that they deliver on time, with insufficient awareness and consideration given to the impact on delivered value. This is an example of why programmes fail to deliver their expected benefits.

A study conducted in 2013 by the International Centre for Programme Management (ICPM) found that of the 21 programmes researched over a two-year period (valued from £10 million to over £100 million), six achieved their stated objectives, nine were partially successful and six failed to achieve any objectives or were abandoned. Findings from this study and other research show that for programmes to be more successful they need to have a clear purpose, be strategically aligned with a recognized need and be supported by a strong financial case.

Programme benefits management is the practice that brings this together. While organizations lack people with the skills and experience to do this effectively, consultants and contractors are often appointed to facilitate programme benefit management on behalf of the organization. There is, therefore, a big opportunity for leaders to emerge within organizations who can lead benefits management practices and their adoption.

Executives' attitudes to investment in programmes

Programmes require a significant investment in terms of financial and human resources. Executives know that programmes are complex and challenging, so they do not invest in them lightly. Executives might:

- have their personal performance objectives and remuneration tied to the success of a programme;
- want programmes to become a focus for the organization and its teams to improve performance while not distracting from current operational issues;
- have high expectations that programmes will deliver the expected outcomes and performance improvement;
- rely on a turnaround or transformation programme to sustain the organization and reduce the risk of takeover or failure.

The nature of programme benefits management

Programme benefits are the positive outcomes of change enabled by programme investment and capability delivery. Programme benefits management involves organizing and facilitating the identification, evaluation, commitment and realization of benefits throughout the programme lifecycle. Some points to be considered in this context include the following.

- Programme benefits are generally aligned to one or more organizational strategic themes and objectives (for example to transform the customer experience, to develop new products and services or improve productivity) or to a major change activity (such as a big system upgrade or a compliance project).
- Programme benefits might be identified before the programme has been initiated. For example, a strategic review or transformation blueprint could have identified performance improvement targets that are subsequently assigned to a programme.
- Programme benefits don't just happen as a result of new IT systems or process capabilities. They need business or behavioural change activities to realize the potential value.
- Programme benefits can be dependent on complex cause and effect relationships with changes and intermediate benefits that are difficult to articulate. Benefit dependency maps are a valuable and engaging technique to model these interrelationships.
- Programme benefits must be owned and ideally managed by the operational and functional leaders and teams who derive value from the capabilities being delivered by the programme. It is incumbent on those leaders and teams to ensure that their programme delivers the right capabilities to maximize the value. Programme and benefits managers need to facilitate benefit adoption.
- Programme delivery should be aligned to the critical programme benefits with opportunities for quick wins deployed at the earliest opportunity. For example, the process design for an IT project may identify operational changes that can be deployed before the system deployment.

- Programme benefits are measurable and contribute to one or more financial or non-financial measures (such as revenue growth, cost reduction, defect reduction and customer satisfaction). Measures are metrics or measurements that define achievement of an outcome or benefit. An outcome or benefit that cannot be measured is likely to be a deliverable or an activity.
- Programme changes and benefits can lead to additional risks and disbenefits that must be identified and understood. Minimizing the negative effects of disbenefits can make a significant difference to the programme's return on investment.
- Programme value (or worth) is the general term used to describe the net effect of benefits *minus* investment and ongoing costs.
- Programme financial value is the return on investment (typically measured using discounted cash flow [DCF] techniques including net present value [NPV] and internal rate of return [IRR]; see Chapter 6 in Lock, 2013 for more on financial appraisal tools).
- Benefits will continue to be realized after the programme has completed delivery. There should be no need for a handover of benefits because the operational leaders and teams should already be handling their realization.

Programme benefits lifecycle

While there is no global standard for benefits management, the diagram in Figure 29 2 is reasonably aligned with leading practices. The steps involved in each stage will vary by organization and will be aligned to internal budgeting and investment procedures and governance rules. I shall now outline the five stages.

Stage 1: identify

This stage involves identifying programme benefits and outcomes from the following perspectives:

1. The primary strategic objectives to which the programme will contribute and the programme's contribution relative to other initiatives.

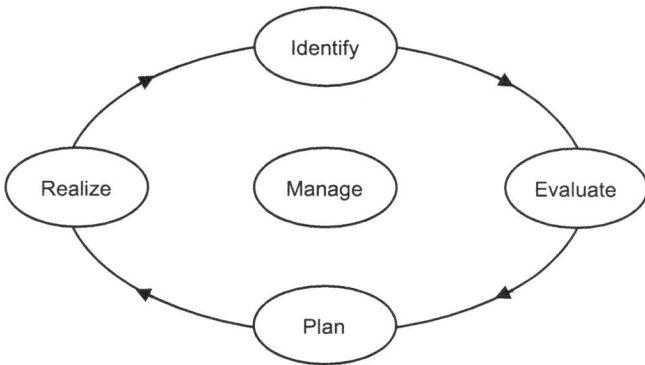

Figure 29.2 Programme benefits lifecycle

2. Intermediate and end benefits that can be mapped out in a cause and effect diagram (called a benefit dependency map).
3. Assessment of stakeholder and operational issues to identify improvements and benefits that is relevant to end customers of the programme deliverables.
4. Understanding the impact and benefits of the key programme deliverables, capabilities and enablers.
5. Alignment and identification with strategic, operational and financial measures.

Benefit mapping workshops enable engagement, a shared understanding and strategic context for the programme for a range of stakeholder groups. If programme delivery teams are also involved, they will be more motivated if they know what the value and contribution of their efforts are to the organization and its strategy.

Benefits need to be SMART – specific, measurable, agreed upon, realistic and time-bound. Benefit profiles (templates) are used to articulate benefits and include details such as description, ownership, measurement, risks and the dependent benefits, enablers and capabilities. Measures may also include an initial profile of expected performance.

Stage 2: evaluate

The evaluation stage involves a more detailed value assessment before funding and budget approval. The value assessment is prepared using a business case that includes both financial justifications and forecasts of non-financial benefits. Key sections of the business case should include the following:

1. Financial justifications. These are evaluated by subtracting the initial investment and ongoing costs from the financial benefits. Discounted cash flow projections are used to determine the return on investment (ROI). Financial forecasts are reviewed with the finance department and the relevant beneficiaries. These reviews will decide whether the benefits are cashable or non-cashable.
2. Non-financial benefits, with measures that are specific to the programme (or multiple projects and programmes). Where there are multiple project and programme contributions to a measure, the use of high, medium or low contribution ratings will be sufficient (because quantified contributions are often arbitrary).
3. Evaluation of the relative contributions of programme and project deliverables to benefits and strategic objectives. This will enable better discussions with the programme delivery teams on the relative priorities and contributions of each deliverable.
4. Changes and 'quick win actions' that can be performed by the beneficiary with minimal up-front effort (for example, actions that do not require a major system change).
5. Benefit risks with a financial impact can also be assessed to identify the level of risk management reserve required for the programme.

The programme or project level business case (or cases) will then be submitted for approval by the appropriate investment committee. This is likely to coincide with the annual budgeting and strategic planning cycle, with either departmental or organization-wide investment decisions being made. On approval the benefits and costs are baselined and budgeted in the overall financial plan and strategy. Each approved project may also have a tolerance threshold (above which the project would be subject to review or cancellation). Agreeing to stop a programme or project before it starts is a less emotive decision than cancelling later, and leads to more positive conversations on how the resources and funds can be better utilized.

Stage 3: plan

This stage involves forecasting and reconfirming the expected benefits, taking into account available resources and more detailed delivery plans. Benefits need to be translated into specific measures that the operational teams can use to drive performance improvement. Specific 'business' changes will also be planned to ensure that the value of capabilities delivered can be realized by the operational teams. Other planning activities include:

1. Reconfirmation of the financial cost benefit and cash flow analysis from more detailed programme delivery planning and scoping.
2. Plans for stakeholder engagement, communications and capability deployment identifying the changes required to ensure adoption, minimize risks and realize benefits. The work required to realize the benefits of change is often underestimated by those involved in delivering the capability.
3. Timing of benefit realization aligned with the availability of resources needed to deliver the required capabilities.
4. Consolidation and prioritization of benefits and benefit measures to ensure delivery and operational team focus.
5. Confirmation of measurement data sources, measure forecasts and any measurements that need to be set up for tracking and reporting.

Stage 4: realize

Benefits realization is the responsibility of the programme's benefit owners – not the programme. Owing to the lack of personnel and capability to identify, track and report on operational measures, it is often incumbent on programme benefit teams to coordinate this task in support of the benefit owners. In the case of financial benefit measures (such as increased revenue or reduced costs), these may be reported centrally by the finance department, with value contributions assigned to each programme in consultation with measure owners.

During the programme delivery phase the programme's benefits are reviewed and forecast again to confirm the programme's viability with recorded quick win benefits. Programme deliverables (capabilities) must also be checked for benefit contribution, with additional benefits highlighted or operational issues tackled through programme changes. Disbenefits are also tracked to minimize 'value leakage'.

As the programme progresses, reviews will be needed to validate that the expected benefits are achievable and that there will be a return on the remaining programme investment. Quality reviews should also establish that the benefits have been

Challenge	Explanation	Mitigating actions
Maturity	Low organizational maturity with poor governance frameworks, practices and know-how.	Appoint advisers who can shape benefits management strategies and practices.
Long lead times	Long lead times to benefits realization with changes in accountability, organizational strategy and external events lead to disenfranchisement of beneficiaries.	Quarterly or bi-annual reviews of programme outcomes, alignment with strategy and financial justification. Identify quick wins to show programme contributions to beneficiaries.
Complexity	Programmes are complex by nature, with multiple internal and external dependencies. Programme benefits are complex to articulate and difficult to measure.	Take time to understand the complexity and use techniques such as benefit dependency maps, risk assessments and scorecards to simplify the logic.
Practice understanding	A diverse range of stakeholders who do not understand the practice and find it too complicated.	Build the education of practices into programme communications.
Poor forecasting	Benefit measures are forecast in isolation from the actual operational measures used by the organization, with over-optimistic expectations.	Aggregate common benefit measures (such as savings) to operational measures where operational measure owners forecast benefits across multiple programmes.
Information quality	Inadequate and inaccurate information and insights to manage benefit performance to enable effective decision making.	Establish a benefits reporting framework and tools that is run and managed by a central programme office or strategy team.
Delivery pressures	Programme pressures to focus on delivering to time cost and quality - even though the programme success is ultimately measured by outcomes (not capability).	Programme leadership needs to use benefit or outcome criticality and consequence to inform decisions on programme delivery.
Stakeholder engagement and support	Programmes involve diverse stakeholders, many of whom are beneficiaries or blockers to successful outcome delivery.	Understand stakeholder needs, motivations and concerns related to programme outcomes and ensure that these are addressed with an agreed engagement plan.
Benefit accountability	Programmes are not accountable for the benefits. They are responsible for ensuring that the right capabilities are being delivered to achieve them.	Ensure programme beneficiaries are assigned to and reported by operational managers.

Figure 29.3 Programme benefits management challenges and mitigations

defined to the right standard and that the beneficiaries remain committed to them. Disbenefits will also need to be considered to ensure that any negative impacts are minimized.

After programme delivery, benefits realization should have switched into standard measurement reporting by operational areas. There might also be a central performance reporting unit that would handle team reporting.

Stage 5: manage

This stage involves ensuring the effective management and governance of benefits from the programme. Ideally there should be a central function to oversee benefits (improvements) planning and reporting as a continuous process across all depart-ments and programmes. If no central function or organizational standards exist, the process, templates and reporting formats for benefits management will need to be established by the programme benefits manager.

At relevant stages in the programme benefits lifecycle the overall benefits man-ager will need to ensure that programme benefits have been identified, assigned, evaluated and confirmed by the respective benefit owners. They must also ensure that the programme's deliverables have been assessed and aligned with the needs of the operational areas.

Some of the challenges involved in managing programme benefits are tabled in Figure 29.3, which also suggests possible actions that can be undertaken to mitigate or handle them.

Programme benefits management roles

This section describes roles commonly involved in programme benefits management and provides guidance to individuals on their responsibilities and the behaviours required.

Benefit owner

Benefit owners are the senior beneficiaries (such as line managers, directors or exec-utives) within an organization accountable for committing to and realizing a bene-fit or improvement target. Benefit owners can consider benefits as the outcomes required to deliver their team's part of the organization's strategy or to deal with specific operational performance issues.

Before committing to a benefit, benefit owners need to be confident that their team can achieve the targeted performance and that there is a coherent plan in place to deliver it. Risks can be used to qualify commitment and highlight uncer-tainties and concerns in benefit achievement. Benefit owners need to be proactive at resolving issues and concerns. Focusing on a few critical benefits and measures also increases their chances of success.

While benefits may relate to a single programme, benefits typically depend on the contributions from multiple initiatives, internal actions and change programmes. Owing to the complexity of benefits analysis and assurance, benefit owners rely on analysts and consultants to facilitate, assess and report benefits from multiple stake-holder perspectives. As well as providing the overall management responsibility for benefits realization, benefit owners will also need to report or escalate issues to the executive committee or board levels for consideration.

Benefit manager

Benefit managers are responsible for facilitating and managing benefits within a pro-gramme or across one or more organizational areas. They will be aligned with (or report to) one or more organizational areas but may also report to the programme manager, central strategy or change office.

Benefit managers need the knowledge and skills to apply benefits management practices. While experience of the sector or process is invaluable, they need to be adept at interpreting operating procedures, process models, performance reports and benchmark data.

Responsibilities include facilitating the development of benefit dependency maps and producing benefit profiles for review and agreement with the relevant benefit owners and stakeholders. They may be required to prepare business cases, working with the benefit owners and programme sponsors, but more commonly to focus on validating the financial benefits, ongoing costs and scope of programme deliverables. Benefit managers are responsible for ensuring that the relevant change transition activities are in place to realize the planned benefits. They are also responsible for reporting benefit measure performance, with exceptions (variances) reported for review by senior management.

Benefit managers need to be expert facilitators who can translate and articulate benefits and benefit measures in a way that stakeholders can understand and own. They need to be competent at interpersonal skills and understand behavioural drivers. Senior benefit managers will lead and inspire change working within operational or cross-functional teams.

A benefit manager's role may also involve the planning and coordination of business change activities or a specific 'business change manager' role might be required in its own right.

Programme sponsor

A programme sponsor is the senior manager or executive who is the primary beneficiary of the programme's outputs (that is, the area benefits most affected by the delivered programme capabilities).

Programme sponsors are accountable for the successful delivery of the programme (time, cost and quality) and benefits realization in their organizational area. They are also accountable for ensuring commitment from other benefits owners to the delivery of the programme-specific benefits in other organizational areas.

Programme sponsors need to ensure that the aims of the planned change continue to be aligned with the organization's strategy, and overseeing and directing the transition from change delivery to business-as-usual.

Benefits management practice leader

The benefits management practice leader is responsible for defining, agreeing, deploying and overseeing benefits management practices and governance within a programme or across the organization. While they would be likely to have a role as a benefit manager they would be granted the remit to lead benefits management practice adoption across the organization (as part of a central or specific strategy, or programme or a project management office). In some organizations the benefits practice leader may be appointed to run a benefits (or value) management office with its own terms of reference.

This position involves supervising the team that provides benefits management support services and escalating process compliance issues relating to quality, ownership and reporting timeliness. The role may also be responsible for maintaining measures on practice adoption, quality, achievement, skills, satisfaction and communication. Benefits management maturity may also be judged in terms of an organization's ability to measure the process and improve it continuously.

Programme benefits management practices

This section describes common practices and techniques required to manage programme benefits including advice and guidance on strategic alignment, benefit mapping, cash flow modelling, benefit measures and realization planning.

Strategic alignment

Strategic alignment involves understanding the relative contributions of projects and programmes to the organization's strategic objectives. If the organization's strategy has not been articulated as a set of strategic objectives then the programme or benefits manager might need to define strategic objectives using available reports, presentations, scorecards and measures. During an initial qualification of projects and programmes this technique helps to evaluate whether the programme is worth doing. It also highlights objectives where the contribution from programmes and projects is too light. Beyond the initial qualification, the objective contributions can be used as a starting point for benefit mapping, business case development and contribution status reporting.

The simplest way to visualize strategic alignment as a technique is through a grid or matrix. In Figure 29.4 the relative contributions of projects and programmes are assessed against the strategic objectives. Contribution values of 1, 3 or 7 are used to represent a low, medium and high contribution respectively. Strategic alignment scores are calculated by summing the contributions multiplied by the objective weightings.

	Objective 1	Objective 2	Objective 3	Objective 4	Objective 5	
Weighting	2	1	2	1	1	**Score**
Programme A	7	3		1		18
Programme B		1	3	1		8
Programme C		7		3	1	11
Programme D	7		7	1	3	32
Programme E		3		1	1	5
Programme F			3	1		7
Programme G	3				3	9
Contribution	34	14	26	8	8	

Figure 29.4 A strategic alignment matrix

Benefit mapping

Benefit dependency maps (BDMs) are a visual representation of the value chain from project and programme work products to the end objectives. This mapping technique is a valuable way of engaging programme teams and other stakeholders to understand and articulate the benefits of a project or programme (and the required deliverables and changes). This technique will be found invaluable for programmes that are difficult to articulate in terms of value and benefits. One of the key techniques is identifying the organizational and behavioural changes required to ensure that programme and project deliverables and capabilities translate into benefits. For example, a new system provided to users may not deliver the expected benefits until these users have been trained, know how to use it effectively and have adopted new behaviours.

BDMs have evolved into a range of formats and conventions that are broadly similar. The example in Figure 29.5 shows the programme or project enablers and capabilities, the business changes, benefits and strategic objectives. Disbenefits can also be shown, since minimizing their impact might affect whether the programme is considered worthwhile or not. Balanced scorecard strategy maps are related, because they show the overall strategic themes and objectives mapped out in a value chain by a general scorecard perspective.

Maps are ideally formulated in workshops that are set up and run by experienced 'independent' facilitators. Facilitators need to ensure that there are contributions from all participants. Well-run workshops create a shared understanding and vision on how to achieve the objectives. One of the challenges for the facilitator is to consolidate scores of ideas and thoughts into very specific and relevant items. A map with more than 30 items becomes unwieldy, difficult to interpret and communicate.

A simplified version of the map with key items might be required for general communications. Benefits and outcomes should be measurable and describe what the outcome has achieved (for example, reduced expenditure leakage with a measure,

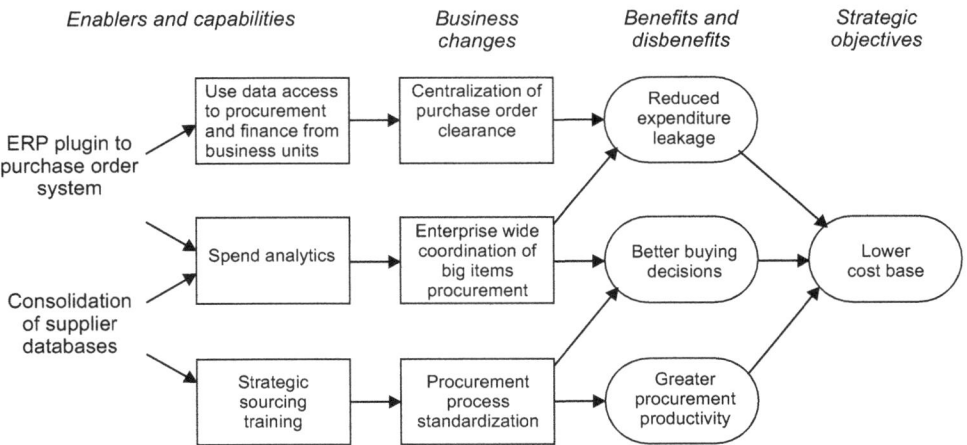

Figure 29.5 Example of a benefit dependency map

		Year 0 2015	Year 1 2016	Year 2 2017	Year 3 2018	Totals
Financial benefits	Procurement saving	200	800	425	425	1,850
	Gross financial benefits	**200**	**800**	**425**	**425**	**1,850**
Investment costs	Procurement optimization	650				650
	Gross investment costs	**650**	**0**	**0**	**0**	**650**
Ongoing costs	Procurement savings maintenance	50	80	80	80	290
	Gross ongoing costs	**50**	**80**	**80**	**80**	**290**
Totals	**Net cash flow**	**-500**	**720**	**345**	**345**	**910**
	Cumulative cash flow	**-500**	**220**	**565**	**910**	**96.9% IRR**
	Net present value (NPV)	**-471.7**	**169.1**	**458.8**	**732**	

IRR = internal rate of return   All figures are $'000s.

Figure 29.6 Example of a cash flow profile

baseline and target for leakage). Enablers, capabilities and business changes often turn into detailed dependent tasks and actions. These need to be consolidated into specific items with detailed task plans for each item. Benefit measures and risks may also be shown on the maps or included on a benefit profile.

Cash flow modelling

Determining the value of a programme is difficult because the value of money in the future is not worth as much as earnings today and there are different ways to measure the value of future cash flows. Cash flow models are used to calculate the annual and cumulative return (that is, the financial benefits net of the investment and ongoing costs). Net present value (NPV) is a factor used to evaluate the financial returns of an initiative, taking into account a discount rate for the cost of capital. The precise rules and choice of discount rates vary by organization and type of programme but some organizations use a discount rate equivalent to depositing the money in a bank. The example in Figure 29.6 shows four years of cash flow with an initial investment in Year 0.

For budgeting purposes the budget holders and finance departments need to know whether financial benefits are cashable or non-cashable and whether they are tangible or intangible (see Bradley, 2006, for more specific categorizations of benefit types). Benefit owners also need to review financial benefits and ongoing costs across all initiatives by the type of financial measure (for example, revenue or cost) to ensure that the sum of financial benefits is valid and not double-counted, as is often the case. A useful test is to review all the approved business case financial benefit forecasts and compare those with the business plans and budgets.

Benefit measures

Measures are something you can put an amount, quantity, size, ratio or a percentage against (such as the number of claims). Measures are fundamental to benefits management since they tell you whether you have achieved a benefit or not. Imagine trying to do high jump without a bar. Bar height is the measure and the target is how high you set the bar. Measures by themselves can inspire better performance if they are meaningful, motivating and rewarding. Benefit measures also tend to be the leading measures that drive performance improvement, which is why they are so valuable.

Every benefit needs to have at least one associated measure. Measures can only be assigned to one benefit, because a measure spread over multiple benefits is too complex to manage. If a benefit cannot be measured then it is probably not a benefit but a capability or activity. For example, a 'standardized procurement process' is not a benefit but 'greater procurement productivity' would be.

Before assessing benefits it helps to compile a register of existing performance measures and group these by strategic objectives or outcomes. In some cases measures may be decomposed, for example by function, location, process or customer. Another example would be an overall savings target which is broken down by business unit, department and operating unit.

Tracking and reporting measures is complex with multiple types of analytics possible from simple measurement data. For example, if you had procurement savings as a measure and you report monthly, you could track the actual performance for this month against last month, the actual financial year performance to date versus target (amount and percentage), the trend since last month, the forecast versus the target to year end, and the level of exception taking measure tolerance into account. Benefit measures should also relate back to operational measures, to provide a line-of-sight from the strategy to benefits realization and value creation.

Realization planning

Benefit realization plans are defined in business cases, benefit profiles and work plans. Business cases tend to elaborate and explain the background and justification of the programme with details of work activities, resources and costs, and the overall steps required to achieve financial and non-financial benefit outcomes. Benefit profiles are either programme or non-programme specific and detail how each benefit will be realized including:

- benefit measures and their associated targets profiled by year, quarter or month;
- the capabilities and changes required, with their relative contributions to the benefit's achievement;
- quick wins that can be undertaken by the relevant beneficiaries without a major capability investment;
- related or dependent benefits that contribute to the benefit's achievement;
- relevant risks that qualify the likelihood of benefit achievement and their mitigating actions;
- specific actions to minimize related disbenefits;
- stakeholder engagement plans to ensure that beneficiaries or those affected by the change are engaged in the right way.

Initial iterations of realization plans detail the capabilities and changes needed, the required timelines and the priorities in terms of benefit achievement. Delivery priorities can be used to scope work plans so that the more value-adding activities are undertaken. As more detailed work plans are produced, resources allocated and delivery commitments are made, so the benefit realization plans will be updated.

Conclusion

Managing programme benefits is arguably the most fundamental and critical discipline in programme management. Programmes that adopt and apply benefits management practices will deliver more tangible results and successful outcomes than those that do not. Benefits management as a practice is complex and challenging and touches all parts of an organization as well as external stakeholders (customers and suppliers for example). It can be used to shape a more tangible and executable strategy, drive performance improvement within teams and ensure that the programme delivers capabilities that are beneficial to the organization.

Over time it is easy to foresee a convergence of management practices where benefits (or value) management is at the heart of a connected set of management disciplines including strategy, risk, performance, change, project and programme management. Benefits management may also merge or align with other disciplines such as Agile and Six Sigma.

Where an organization has no approach to benefits management it might be incumbent on the programme management to establish one. That could lead to a more strategic and fulfilling role for the programme office or benefits team. Individuals with experience in leading and coaching the practice of benefits management will be in considerable demand. Leaders who champion and adopt benefits management practices will be more successful at executing their strategy, with more motivated and engaged teams.

References and further reading

Bradley, G. (2006), *Benefit Realisation Management: A Practical Guide to Achieving Benefits through Change*, Farnham: Gower.

Jenner, S. (2014), *Managing Benefits: Optimizing the Return from Investments*, 2nd edn., High Wycombe: APMG International.

Kaplan, R. S. and Norton, D. (1996), *The Balanced Scorecard*, Cambridge, MA: Harvard Business School Press.

Lock, D. (2013), *Project Management*, 10th edn., Farnham: Gower.

National Audit Office, UK (n.d.), *Over-Optimism in Government Projects*. <www.nao.org.uk>.

Sapountzis, S., Harris, K. and Kagioglou, M. (2008), *Benefits Management and Benefits Realisation: A Literature Review*, Working Paper, University of Salford.

Thorp, J. (1998), *The Information Paradox: Realising the Business Benefits of Information Technology*, Toronto: McGraw-Hill.

Ward, J. and Daniel, E. (2006), *Benefits Management: Delivering Value from IS and IT Investments*, Chichester: John Wiley.

Ward, J. and Maylor, H. (2013), *ICPM – Beating the Odds: The Secrets of Successful Programmes*, Cranfield University.

Chapter 30

Managing Complexity in Programmes

Stephen Hayes

When dealing with complex programmes the reality is that, while they remain important, traditional project management methods and tools are not sufficient. The complexity of multiparty collaborations in ambiguous and uncertain environments means that traditional tools and methods, with their probabilistic and linear assumptions, are not sufficient to return the benefits expected of public or private sector investments.

Introduction

There has been significant debate in the international community about complexity in programmes. Earlier debate suggested that there was no such thing as complexity and that some projects were simply more complicated than others. A strong suggestion was that all programmes could be deconstructed in a linear fashion from the outset. However, in an environment of broader application of traditional project management methods and tools, plus experience in increasingly intricate projects, up-to-date research has found that worldwide only 40 per cent of programmes are delivered on time and within budget (IBM, 2008).

Healthy debate and dialogue have led to a global acceptance and understanding that complexity adds an extra – orthogonal – dimension to projects. Although significant progress has already been made as exemplified in the discussion of Second Order Project Management (Cavanagh, 2012), much work is still needed to address further the 'conspiracy of optimism, inappropriate contracting models, the application of methods and tools capable of dealing with complexity, and the need for creative, inspirational and adhocratic leadership'. New tools and enhanced skills are required through significant research investment in the science of project management to support programme management in the twenty-first century.

This chapter will begin by examining the characteristics of complexity to provide an understanding of what constitutes a complex programme. The reasons for programme failure associated with complexity will then be explored. Guidance will be provided on ways of measuring complexity. Using the work of Remington and Pollack (Remington and Pollack, 2007) the chapter will provide one framework for the different types of complexity and some approaches for dealing with them. With a focus on systems thinking (Jackson, 2003) and the work of Remington and Pollack (2007) the chapter will examine what tools and new education are available to help programme managers deal with complexity. The chapter will conclude with a new capability developed to support complex programmes. The capability, Think2Impact™ (Think2Impact, 2015), is a new global systems thinking platform.

The terms *projects* and *programmes*, as referred to in this chapter, should be seen as being somewhat interchangeable and their individual reference reflects more the scale of the activities involved, but the issues discussed in this chapter apply equally to both.

Characteristics of complexity

The Commonwealth Scientific and Industrial Research Organisation (CSIRO) (CSIRO, 2012), Australia's national science and research agency, identifies two properties that set a complex system apart from one that is merely complicated:

- emergence – the appearance of behaviour that could not be anticipated from a knowledge of the parts of the systems alone;
- self-organization – where no external controller or planner is engineering the appearance of the emergent features.

A 2007 international workshop of senior programme managers (Hayes *et al.*, 2007) developed a series of characteristics to inform the complexity discussion. These include programmes that:

- exhibit uncertainty, emergence, non-linearity, ambiguity, dynamic interfaces, and significant political or external influences;
- run over a period which exceeds the cycle time of the technologies involved or where significant integration issues exist;
- can be defined by effect, but not by solution at the time of inception.

Before globalization, complex programmes were more easily defined. They were generally big ticket, capital-intensive activities undertaken for defence, aerospace, resource, energy and infrastructure customers. However, in the twenty-first century, with the increasingly uncertain and globally interconnected environment, many more government and corporate activities or investments should be considered complex projects or programmes.

Failures in complex programmes

The starting point for improving the success of complex programmes is to understand why they fail, or indeed why they might fail. Although there is no simple answer, a global roundtable of some of the world's leading programme managers provided a level of consensus for the primary reasons for complex programme failure (Hayes *et al.*, 2009):

- Unaccommodated or misaligned stakeholder views of success – a failure to align expectations and programme knowledge of powerful programme stakeholders can slow down or derail even the best efforts of programme teams.

A key element here is also the lack of readiness for change and attention to the impact of change.

- Tension between product success and project success – paradoxically, project outcomes like Boston's 'Big Dig' tunnel and Sydney's Opera House are considered successful. However, in hindsight they were both behind schedule and grossly over budget. Success is not always just about delivering on time, to cost, to scope and with an agreed level of quality. Governments and corporations are increasingly making capital investments with a much bigger picture in mind. The United Kingdom's High Speed 2 (HS2) rail link between major cities, for example, moves well beyond being just a new transport system to being a programme about national and regional growth. Therefore the true success (or otherwise) of HS2 may not be known for many years after the infrastructure has been delivered.
- Programmes bending to political and public relations pressure – political and public influence often have profound and sometimes negative effects on programmes. In the worst cases, it can result in distraction of external direction resulting in programme inefficiencies and less effective outcomes. Lack of awareness and planning for events in the external social, political, technological and environmental influences of a complex programme can result in delays, rework costs and possible cancellation.
- Lack of understanding or acknowledgement of non-technical risk – current programme risk tools and techniques are focused on technical risks. But many programme risks actually result from non-technical leadership, organizational behavior and human factor issues. Programme leaders often lack the depth of experience, education or perhaps behavioural characteristics to comprehend the non-technical issues that can derail a programme.
- Use of competition as a weapon – in a competitive environment with few bidders, winner-take-all competitions can threaten the very survival of the losers, driving undesirable behaviours like underbidding to win. This is particularly prevalent in monopolistic environments exemplified by the government as a sole customer. Customers and suppliers therefore bear a responsibility to understand and disclose the true cost of the capability being sought.
- Institutionalized procurement practices – rigid, one-size-fits-all, often combative procurement practices limit agility and flexibility in complex programmes to respond to risks and opportunities. Linear processes and methodologies may be well suited for programmes in which uncertainty and emergence are less prevalent. However, unquestioned or ill-considered adherence to linear processes and methodologies in a highly complex environment can, in the worst case, drive a programme to failure.
- Capability of project managers to be project delivery leaders – effective complex project managers must be trained and experienced leaders in a wide variety of disciplines (such as engineering, law, economics and human resources). They must also be chosen from those leaders who have the personality to deal effectively with the inherent uncertainty and volatility of complex projects. There is a need for greater recognition of the importance of multidisciplinary education to develop leaders who are better equipped to think creatively in ambiguous and complex environments.

- Lack of opportunity for engagement between government and industry – government and corporate procurement guidelines often mean that the pre-award protocols are rigid and not well suited to fully understand the risks and alignment of outcomes and mutual benefits (goals) of the programme.
- Future capabilities are predicated on obtaining rational estimates – commercial pressures and incentives often drive unconstrained requirements coupled with unrealistically low cost/schedule estimates, leading to an unaffordable and unachievable portfolio.
- Current tools and decision processes are unsuitable for analysing uncertainty – although existing tools and decision processes remain important, new tools and techniques are needed for managing complex projects and programmes.
- There is an inevitability of scope creep, especially if the project is contracted too early. Programmes dependent upon scientific or engineering breakthroughs for success are all too prevalent in some portfolios. Where programmes are dependent on new or emerging technologies, greater investment is required to understand risk and integration issues before executing contracts. Additionally, austerity-driven 'efficiency savings' can undermine the fundamental assumptions on which initial scope is based.

These primary reasons for failure clearly point to the need for new tools and education required to improve complex programme delivery. They also point to the need to improve organizational preparedness for the inevitable change associated with complex programmes.

Assessing complexity in programmes

An often-asked question is how to determine the complexity of a programme. This is a subjective issue that is informed by the individual and organizational lens. For example, those involved in the global development of a new fighter bomber aircraft would have a very different view of complexity compared to those in the health community attempting to control or eradicate AIDS. There are a number of practical examples of complexity analysis frameworks including the Acquisition Categorisation (ACAT) framework developed by the Australian Department of Defence (Commonwealth of Australia, Department of Defence, 2012a), the Helmsman Complexity Scale (Helmsman Institute) and the Complex Programme Maturity Model (CPMM) (Murray, 2015).

The Australian Department of Defence has been using their ACAT framework for categorizing programmes since 2004. The framework has four categories, the most complex being categorized as ACAT I and the least demanding programmes as ACAT IV. The ACAT level provides a useful description of the scale, complexity and risks in the project with a score based on six attributes:

- Acquisition cost, includes the cost of the materiel system (mission system plus support system), as well as the facilities costs. This does not include ongoing sustainment budgets. This is based on the current 'dollar out-turn' (total budget) for the project.
- Project management complexity, which highlights complexity beyond that associated with traditional project management knowledge areas. These are

characterized by a project execution environment which is novel and uncertain, with high-level political interaction.

- Schedule, which recognizes the complexity brought about by schedule pressures on the project that need the application of varying levels of sophistication in schedule management.
- Technical difficulty, which describes the inherent complexities which are associated with technical undertakings of design and development, assembly, integration, test and acceptance.
- Operation and support, which highlights the complexity associated with the readiness of the organization and the environment in which the system will be operated and supported.
- Commercial, which recognizes the capability of industry to deliver and support the required system, and the complexity of the commercial arrangements being managed, including the number and level of interdependencies of commercial arrangements managed by the Department of Defence.

The Helmsman scale ranges from 1 to 10, and is designed to mimic the Richter earthquake scale in terms of numerical significance. Projects are evaluated against criteria in five areas:

- Context complexity – which looks at the complexity of the leadership and political environment the project is facing.
- People complexity – evaluates how deep the sociological change will be for the recipients of the project.
- Ambiguity – which is measured across two key areas, namely approach uncertainty and design uncertainly.
- Technical challenge – technical complexity is measured by examining the definition, history of development, and number of core subsystems expected in the final solution as well as previous experience in subsystem integration.
- Project management challenge – the areas being evaluated include contract complexity, risk sharing, schedule and project structure, supplier complexity and external project interdependencies.

The CPMM (see Figure 30.1) was developed to enable organizations to understand the capabilities that they need to undertake a complex change programme (addressing one of the previously identified primary causes of complex programme failure) (Hayes *et al.*, 2009). The model spans organizational boundaries to assess the existing level of capability that an organization has to undertake complex change. The model applies a maturity assessment similar in concept to the Carnegie Mellon Software Maturity Model (Paulk *et al.*, 1993). The CPPM assesses an organization's maturity against 20 CPMM domains of criteria including leadership, process, business readiness, systems thinking and competency. The CPMM maturity levels range from 'initial' at the lowest, to 'optimizing' at the highest. Importantly, if the target organization or change programme exhibits insufficient maturity, the model enables analysis and development of recommendations for achieving the required level of maturity.

The Variability Index

LEVEL 1

Single products/services. Limited customer impacts, limited supplier input. Contained within small project team within a department

LEVEL 2

Multiple products/services. Limited customer impacts, may require external suppliers. Contained within on project team with representation from technology and business

LEVEL 3

Inter-departmental, multiple products/services may impact customers, may require external suppliers. Outsourcing.Some moving parts and stakeholders. Employees impacted

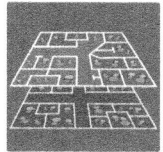

LEVEL 4

Multiple departments, products/services may impact customers, requires external suppliers. Outsourcing. Many moving parts and stakeholders, employee impacted

LEVEL 5

Cross organisation/ services/products. Impacts customers/suppliers and requires external suppliers. Outsourcing. Acquisition and mergers. Many moving parts and stakeholders

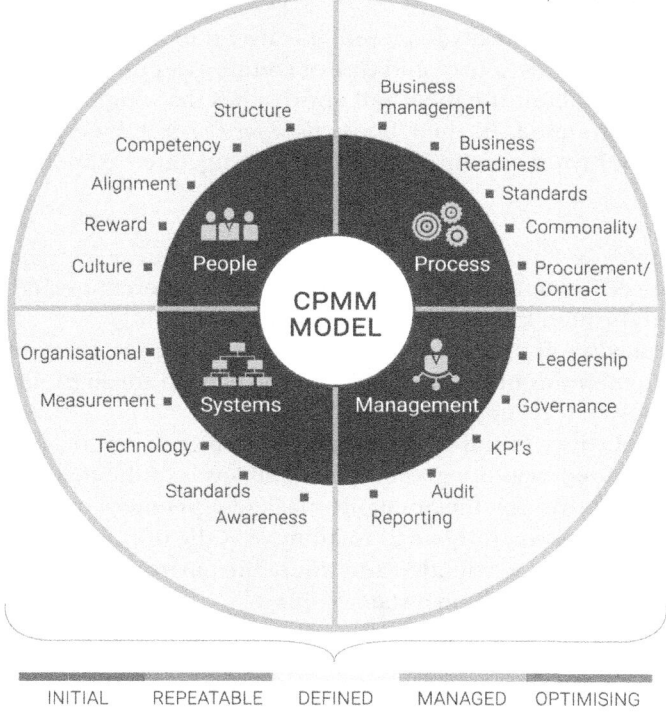

Figure 30.1 **Complex programme maturity model and variability index**

The CPMM includes an assessment framework called the *variability index*. This determines the complexity of change associated with the programme being undertaken using five categories varying from the least complex at level 1 to the most complex at level 5. Level 1 assumes a degree of complexity that can be corralled under one leader, a limited number of stakeholders and minimal impact to users/customers where a similar change has been undertaken many times. An example would be a 20 person department undergoing reorganization.

Conversely, a change programme at level 5 would have many 'unknown' unknowns and uncertainties in achieving (or even defining) the outcomes. This programme would also have a significant amount of unknowns or undefined detail, and it would be attempting to implement or undertake significant change for the first time. Examples would include deploying leading-edge technology associated with a new aircraft or merging two large companies.

Ultimately the organizational suitability of complexity analysis frameworks depends on the specific situation or context. Given their subjective nature, it might be necessary to use more than one framework or adapt existing frameworks to develop an optimum organizational complexity analysis framework.

A framework for assessing different types of complexity in programmes

Once the overall level of complexity is agreed, it is useful to understand the type of complexity. Understanding the source and type of complexity guides the practitioner in direction and choices about the tools and approaches that might be appropriate for managing the programme. In their book *Tools for Complex Projects* (Remington and Pollack, 2007), four types of complexity have been suggested as useful categories (Zolin *et al.*, 2009):

1. Structural complexity – that stems from potential non-linear, emergent behaviour which can occur from interactions between many interconnected tasks and can be analysed through the number of dependencies.
2. Technical complexity – found in projects with design characteristics or technical aspects that are unknown or untried and can be analysed through the potential impact of unresolved technical/design issues.
3. Directional complexity – found in projects where the goals or goal-paths for the projects are not understood or agreed upon at all levels of the project hierarchy and can be analysed through the ambiguity/lack of agreement on goals.
4. Temporal complexity – which refers to volatility over the duration of the project, where project durations are extended and where the environment (market, technical, political or regulatory) is in a state of flux.

These are illustrated in Figure 30.2. All can affect the project direction and can be analysed through expected time delays at key project stages. Importantly, the framework provides a shared language for managers, teams and other stakeholders to discuss factors that might stimulate complex and potentially unmanageable programme outcomes.

Large programmes and many smaller projects can exhibit one or more types and levels (*severity*) of complexity (Zolin *et al.*, 2009). Complexity will drive aspects of the

Think2Impact

Components and relationship with
Evolutionary learning Labs

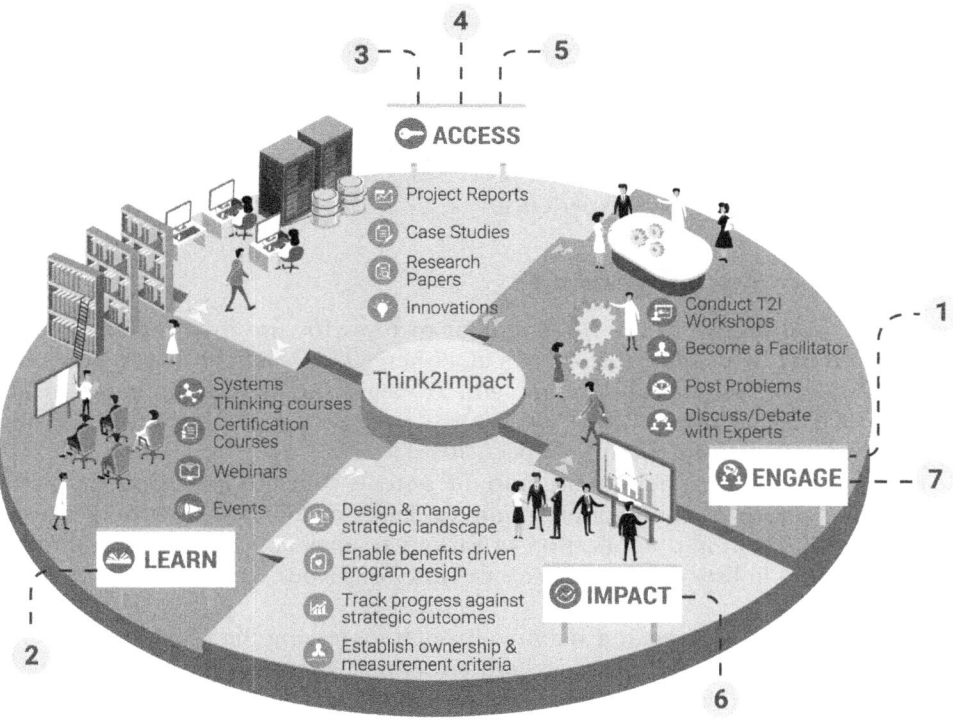

The ELLabs Framework

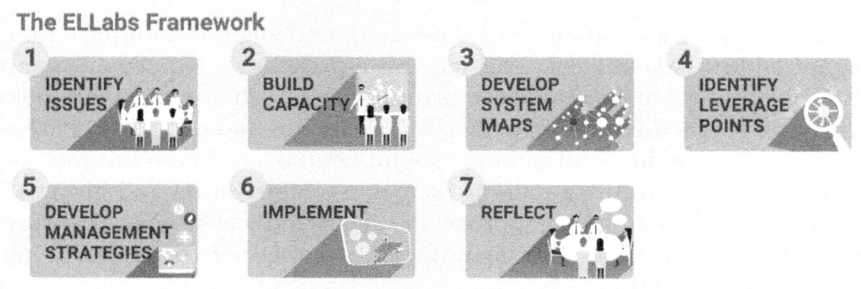

Figure 30.2 Remington and Pollack's four types of complexity

project from lifecycle, resource selection and governance organizational structure through to the type of contract and procurement arrangements (Remington and Pollack, 2007). The perceived severity of the four types of complexity depends upon the following factors (Zolin *et al.*, 2009):

- the breadth and depth of experience and capability of key personnel;
- the project organizational structure, and its interfaces with key participating organizations, with respect to communication and governance;
- existing cultural norms and work practices within and between participating organizations, including project culture;
- appropriateness of organizational processes, such as procurement practices, to the type(s) of complexity experienced.

Tools for complex programmes

Many have contributed to the development of tools for use in complex projects and it would not be possible to cover them all here. This is a field that requires significantly more research and development. To begin the journey we have already identified CPMM as a useful tool and the last part of this chapter introduces the Think2Impact™ platform (Think2Impact, 2015).

For those who wish to delve more into the systems concepts and applied systems thinking in support of complex programmes, Jackson (2003) is a useful resource for the identification and application of various systems approaches. In summary, Jackson classifies holistic systems approaches into four types:

1. Improving goal seeking and viability through increasing the efficiency and efficacy of organizational processes and structures. Systems approaches such as 'hard systems thinking', 'systems dynamics – the fifth discipline', 'organizational cybernetics' and 'complexity theory' are all useful for focusing on organizational performance in terms of how well tasks are done and the response to environmental changes.
2. Exploring purposes and ensuring agreement and alignment of purpose by the organization's stakeholders. The systems approaches – 'strategic assumptions surfacing and testing', 'interactive planning' and 'soft systems methodology' – are useful for focusing on evaluating different aims and objectives, establishing mutual understanding and gaining commitment to a common purpose.
3. Ensuring fairness in organizations focuses on empowering and giving a voice to all groups. Systems-based approaches such as 'critical systems heuristics' and 'team syntegrity' are useful for focusing on empowerment of groups to improve organizational performance.
4. Promoting diversity looks for exceptions and engaging people's emotions when seeking change. 'Postmodern systems thinking' focuses on challenging the normality and routine, celebrating difference and workplace fun to encourage open participation.

Because multiple different types of complexity can exist in any one programme, it is not possible to suggest one specific tool. Nor is it possible to suggest how and in what order sets of tools should be used. However, having identified a range of existing tools, Remington and Pollack (2007) have usefully shown what type of complexity these tools might help address. Programme managers need to be able to analyse what type of complexity exists and what tools could be deployed throughout the project lifecycle.

Remington and Pollack (2007) describe a number of non-standard tools and approaches that have been used and adapted by practitioners to deal with different types of complexity in programmes. The tools and approaches range from simple, short-hand ways of discerning the nature and source of complexity present or expected in the programme, to more elaborate methods that inform the whole management approach. The tools described by Remington and Pollack (2007) were drawn from conscious and intuitive experience of practitioners working in sectors ranging from international telecommunications roll-outs to transnational multiple infrastructure programmes. Most programmes from which these tools and approaches were drawn were very large.

However, the authors stress that complexity is not necessarily a product of size. Small projects can exhibit emergent behaviour that can be very difficult to manage and control. On the other hand, large programmes will always be complicated with high levels of interconnectedness and multiple interdependencies. In many cases interdependencies can be defined and managed, allowing outcomes to be predicted within an acceptable range. For these very complicated programmes the critical element that leads to complexity is associated with duration. In Remington and Pollack's (2007) framework this is described as Temporal Complexity.

Many of the tools for managing Directional Complexity have their origins in Soft Systems Thinking and cognitive psychology and most of the tools for managing structural complexity can trace their origins to cybernetics. Tools and approaches for managing technical complexity are informed by design theory and management in the performing arts sector. However, the tools and approaches for managing Temporal Complexity are drawn directly from practitioner experience of working in volatile environments that change unpredictably over time, such as politically sensitive contexts.

It is apparent that a significant range of tools already exist to support more successful delivery of complex programmes. However, key to their use is a better understanding of complexity through education and training.

Education

With growing international populations and finite resources, complex programmes must be sustainable in concept, design, development, delivery and disposal (ICCPM and GAP, 2011). No organization can keep pace with the changing demands of technology, customers and world markets by simply adhering to existing approaches to dealing with complexity. Education is today commonly acknowledged as a key to ensuring capability of organizations to manage complexity better. It should never be mistaken for or confused with training. Training teaches how to do one thing. Education deals with anything and everything from as wide (and often ostensibly unconnected) a knowledge set as possible.

One attempt to deal with this issue is the development of the Complex Project Manager Competency Standards (Commonwealth of Australia, Department of

Defence, 2012b) by a group of senior government and industry leaders from across the globe. This provides a model for the formation of knowledge for leaders to manage complex programmes. Special attention is given to the soft skills critical to successful adaptive leadership, and emphasizing the catalytic role of leadership in the delivery of sustainable business outcomes for the organization. Such programme leadership has a vital role to play in aligning programmes with an organization's strategic vision and ensuring that it remains competitive and effective over the long term.

The role universities can play in developing partnerships with governments and industry is critical to the acceleration of knowledge development and capacity building. Where it is not already the case, future approaches should consider the elements described in the Complex Project Manager Competency Standards, including systems thinking and integration; strategy; business planning, lifecycle management, reporting and performance measurement; change; innovation and creativity; organizational architecture; leadership and communication; culture; probity and governance.

At the behest of their respective governments or the private sector, a number of institutions have developed masters programmes and continuing professional development events aimed at improving programme leadership and complex programme delivery. These institutions include the Queensland University of Technology's (QUT) Graduate School of Business, the University of Sydney's John Grill Centre for Project Leadership, the University of Oxford's Said Business School and the University of Ottawa's Telfer School of Management. One criticism often levelled at new programmes is the lack of measurement of impact of the investment.

The QUT Executive Master of Business (Complex Programme Leadership) (Hatcher and O'Connor, 2009) also included a longitudinal research study (Pisarski *et al.*, 2013) sponsored by the Australian Department of Defence (and the Australian Research Council) to gauge in part the value of their education investment. This study found that emotional intelligence, cognitive flexibility and systemic thinking play a critical role in successful project delivery and that QUT executive masters graduates demonstrate that they are better equipped and feel more confident about their ability to lead complex projects than when they entered the programme.

The Evolutionary Learning Laboratory and Think2Impact™

This section describes a comprehensive systems thinking approach, embedded in a cyclic Evolutionary Learning Laboratory (ELLab) framework. This framework is designed to deal effectively with complex issues in a variety of contexts (Bosch *et al.*, 2014; Bosch and Nguyen, 2015).

Research and documentation of systems thinking abounds in the literature and research journals. However, its practical implementation and tracking of discernible impact is at best unclear, disjointed and highly variable (Bosch and Nguyen, 2015). The ELLab framework recognizes these deficiencies in the practical application of systems thinking. It encompasses the multidimensional nature of the broad environmental parameters and creates a practical approach to the engagement with stakeholders, and the identification, analysis and synthesis of complex issues.

The ELLab is not a physical place, but a concept that promotes a new way of thinking by individuals coming together to work towards consensus. It involves all

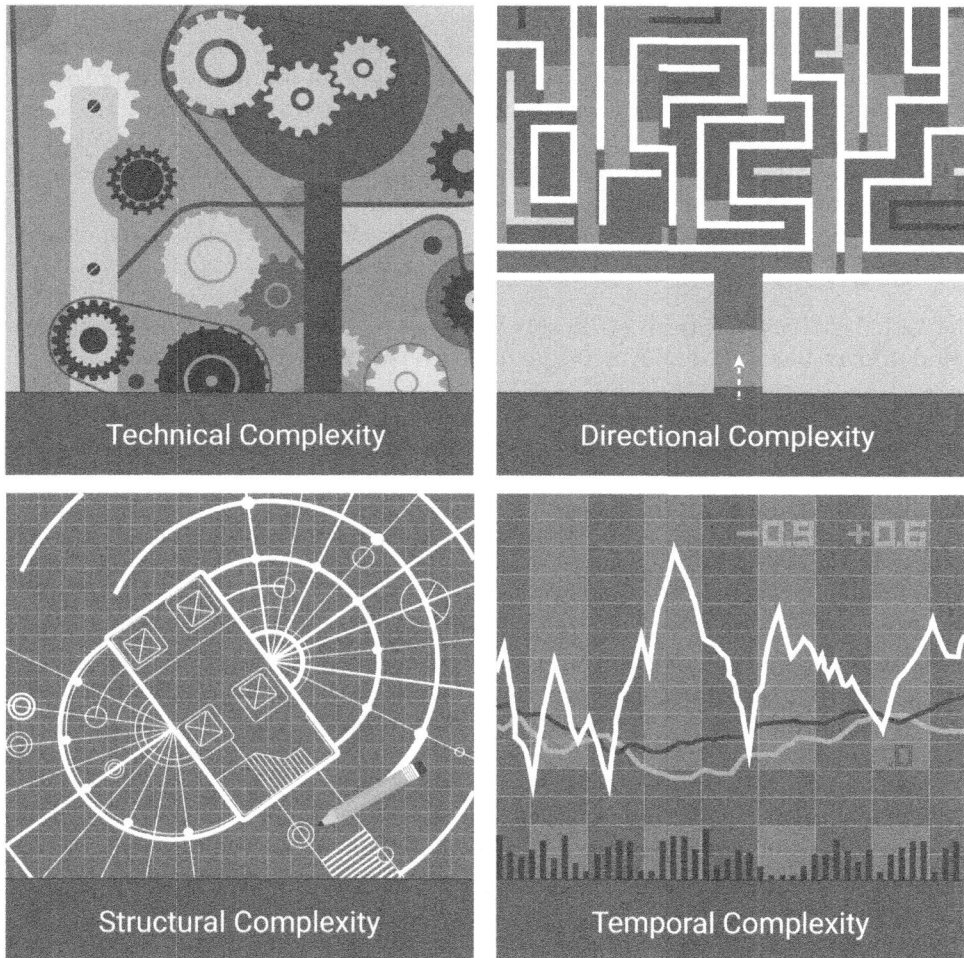

Figure 30.3 Relationship between the ELLab and the Think2Impact platforms

stakeholders in developing a deep understanding of the system, a shared vision and skills for identifying systemic solutions, continuous adaption, innovation and improvement (Bosch and Nguyen, 2015).

The ELLab (Figure 30.3) is a unique seven-step process and methodology of systems and interconnected thinking for integrated cross-sectorial decision-making, planning and collaboration in dealing with complex multi-stakeholder problems (Bosch et al., 2014). The ELLab provides processes and mechanisms for decision-makers, managers and stakeholders to:

- come together to develop a shared understanding of complex issues (Step 1);
- learn about (Step 2) how to integrate the mental models of different stakeholders into a systems structure or model (Step 3);

- explore patterns and relationships to identify leverage points in the system (Step 4);
- identify systemic interventions to achieve the desired outcomes for each leverage point and to create innovative, systemic long-term solutions that are socially responsible, economically viable, environmentally friendly and culturally sensitive (Step 5);
- implement the systemic interventions and determine monitoring criteria for tracking the impact of the interventions (Step 6);
- reflect and co-learn from the experiences to develop new levels of performance (Step 7).

The ELLab process has been effectively deployed in a variety of contexts with profound impact. Selected deployments include diverse examples such as:

- the sustainable development of the UNESCO Cat Ba Biosphere, Vietnam;
- integrated systemic governance of Haiphong City (Province), Vietnam;
- improving child safety in Japan;
- labour saving innovations in sub-Saharan Africa and South East Asia for the Bill and Melinda Gates Foundation.

Think2Impact takes the ELLabs framework and (by using online technologies) integrates it with traditional learning and management methods. In turn it takes systems thinking to a wider global audience through a scalable online global platform (Bosch and Nguyen, 2015). Through its collaborative and community driven approach, it aims at:

- identifying and addressing the right problem;
- using the combined intelligence of a cross-disciplinary panel of experts and the global audience (with experiential knowledge) to advise and facilitate solution building;
- building a big picture defining dependencies and multi-causal relationships within the complex problem under consideration;
- enabling forecasting of impact to avoid unforeseen or unintended consequences;
- iterating quickly and repeatedly to focus on moving targets;
- evolving innovative solutions that are people and sustainability focused;
- tracking and analysing impact of interventions.

Functionally, the Think2Impact™ framework is made up of four complementary parts. These allow users to:

1. **Access** an extensive repertoire of curated systems-related knowledge and case studies.
2. **Learn** about theories and practical application of systems thinking as well as test its application.

3. **Engage** and collaborate with the community to start and conduct projects to create sustainable solutions.
4. Track and analyse the **Impact** of the interventions and solutions in the long term.

Think2Impact™ addresses two of the most important needs of the knowledge economy – 'creation of knowledge' by bringing together people to work on projects that lead to solutions and strategies, and 'dissemination of knowledge' by allowing others to tap into this source of knowledge. The collaborative nature of the platform means that everything is co-created. So governments, organizations, aid agencies, universities and members of the community can all work together towards a common solution that takes all relevant viewpoints into account. This collaboration, development of shared understandings of each other's mental models and involvement in the analysis leads to stakeholders taking ownership of the solutions and creating willingness for implementation.

Conclusion

Regardless of how complex a programme might be, traditional project management methods and tools remain relevant and have their place within the programme.

However, those who seriously consider the need for additional tools and approaches to deal with aspects of complexity in programmes have cast the net much wider. Tools and approaches now being recommended for practitioners have been informed by disciplines ranging from cybernetics, soft systems thinking, cognitive psychology and design science through to the performing arts coupled with research across the natural sciences.

There is a need for better understanding of complexity, the reasons why complex programmes fail, what new tools and approaches could be used, and the investment required for complex programme change or transformation. Thus continued investment in education and research are key elements for improving complex programme performance in both the private and public sector.

One final word of caution, however. Useful (and indeed essential) as any tools and methods might be, their slavish, unthinking application can never, alone, automatically deliver the desired outcome. They must always be treated as guidelines, to be adapted according to the unique aspects of the programme and its relations and dependencies with the external environment. In systems terms, this environment – with its ever-changing political, technological, sociological and economic drivers – is the supersystem of the programme-at-hand. The more complex the programme, changes in that supersystem must always be monitored, considered and accommodated, irrespective of their inconvenience.

In the world of complexity, flexibility wins. Always.

References and further reading

Bosch, O. and Nguyen, N. (2015), *Systems Thinking for Everyone: The Journey from Theory to Making an Impact,* Canberra: Think2Impact Press.

Bosch, O., Krishnamurthi, K. and Nguyen, N. (2014), 'The Evolutionary Learning Laboratory (ELLab): A Better Way to Analyse and Overcome Complex Problems', in *EMCSR 2014 Book of Abstracts,* EMCSR.

Cavanagh, M. (2012), *Second Order Project Management,* Farnham: Gower.

Commonwealth of Australia, Department of Defence (2012a), *Defence Capability Plan Public Version – Department of Defence.* Retrieved 10 February 2015 from <www.defence.gov.au/publications/capabilityplan2012.pdf>.

Commonwealth of Australia, Department of Defence (2012b), Complex Project Manager Competency Standards, Defence Materiel Organisation & International Centre for Complex Project Management.

CSIRO (2012), *Complex or Complicated: What is a Complex System?* Retrieved 13 February 2015 from <www.csiro.au/resources/About-Complex-Systems>.

Hatcher, C. A. and O'Connor, B. (2009), 'High Impact Training: Achieving Synergies between Program Management Education and Workplace Practice', presented at the *BT Conference: Educating Programme Managers for the 21st Century, 22–23 June,* University of Oxford.

Hayes, S. S., Worley, J. and Burbage, T. (2007), *Complexity Characteristics Workshop,* Washington, DC: International Centre for Complex Project Management.

Hayes, S. S., Payne, F. and Cavanagh, M. (2009), *The Conspiracy of Optimism: Why Mega Projects Fail,* Canberra: ICCPM.

Helmsman Institute (n.d.), 'Helmsman International'. Retrieved 10 February 2015 from <www.helmsman-institute.com/sites/institute/PDF/HelmsmanDefenceProjectComplexityReport.pdf>.

IBM (2008), *Making Change Work,* Somers: IBM Global Business Services.

ICCPM and GAP (2011), *Complex Project Management – Global Perspectives and the Strategic Agenda to 2025 – The Task Force Report,* Canberra: International Centre for Complex Project Management & Global Access Partners.

Jackson, M. C. (2003), *Systems Thinking: Creative Holism for Managers,* Chichester: John Wiley.

Murray, D. (2015), 'The Complexity Program Maturity Model', 15 February.

Paulk, M. C., Curtis, B., Chrissis, M. B. and Weber, C. V. (1993), *Capability Maturity Model for Software, Version 1.1,* Pittsburgh, PA: Software Engineering Institute, Carnegie Mellon University.

Pisarski, A., Hatcher, C., Chang, A., Zolin, R., Ashkanasy, N. and Jordan, P. (2013), *Management and Leadership of Large Projects,* Brisbane: Queensland University of Technology.

Remington, K. and Pollack, K. J. (2007), *Tools for Complex Projects,* Aldershot: Gower.

StrategyDotZero (2015), <www.strategydotzero.com/>.

Think2Impact (2015), 'About Us: Think2Impact'. Retrieved February 2015 from <www.think2impact.org/app/#/home>.

Zolin, R., Turner, R. J. and Remington, K. (2009), '*A Model of Project Complexity: Distinguishing Dimensions of Complexity from Severity*', presented at the 9th International Research Network of Project Management Conference, 11–13 October, Berlin.

Chapter 31

Managing Uncertainties in Programmes

Motoh Shimizu

A programme is intended to create new value for its stakeholders and the organization but there are always negative uncertainties that can waste a large amount of investment in money, talented human resources and time if the programme fails.

Introduction

There are three stages in managing programme uncertainties. Stage one defines the programme and its goals. Often starting from rather ambiguous concepts, the goals are defined as a set of critical success factors (CSFs). Complexities and ambiguities derived from the complicated relationships among the elements relating to the programme are the main source of negative uncertainties. Reduction of such complexities and ambiguities is the primary effort of programme management at this stage. A programme will fail if the targeted CSFs are not appropriate for the customer's needs or intentions or if the CFSs are excessively ambitious. The organization will lose competitive edge in the market if marginal CSFs are selected. This first stage of programme uncertainty management is carried out concurrently with the programme's basic design process.

The second stage is the process of designing individual projects and the relationships among them. This is the stage for designing the detailed programme architecture (consisting of projects to be integrated but to be nearly independent and executable in an autonomous-decentralized manner). In this process, the programme architecture is designed to accept only allowable uncertainties for the final execution phase. Thus excessive uncertainties are eliminated and countermeasures are prepared against the possible remaining uncertainties.

Exposed uncertainty events are dealt with in the final stage of programme execution. These uncertainty events include deviations from project plans and changes in the internal and the external business environment.

Explanation of programme uncertainty

Decision-making is the most essential task in business management. It is impossible to know results precisely at the point of decision, because the activities arising from the decision require time to manifest their results. In this context, uncertainties are common in business management, and these can be significant in non-repetitive project management. In the practice of project management the plan for a single project is treated typically as if it is a complete set of processes without problems. Uncertainties are treated as deviations from the ideal result of the plan. Programmes are clearly more complicated than single projects and uncertainties are inherent in their nature.

Whether intended to create a new business market, to construct a huge industrial infrastructure or to restructure business processes, a programme aims to create new values for the business organization. If I can put that another way, a programme aims to disrupt the current balance in the market or society and establish a new balance that is more profitable. The accumulation of such efforts by numerous market actors is the concept of market competition. Is it possible to realize the desirable change as planned in the complex and highly competitive market environment? Also, the long duration of a typical programme increases exposure to these influences. In this context uncertainties are unavoidable in change programmes. The results might be good or bad for the organization executing the programme.

Some economists call the statistically predictable events risks and use the word uncertainties for the numerically unpredictable results. For the programme management practitioners, every possible event is estimated or assessed somehow, and such differentiation is not very important. Thus I shall use the words risk and uncertainty synonymously in this chapter.

Strategy and uncertainty

In many cases the strategy of business and public organizations is implemented by the processes of a programme. Strategy can be said to be an investment of money or other resources for the future or long-term success of the organization.

A typical organization has internal hierarchical structures for corporate top management, business management, functional management, programme implementation, project implementation and so on. Each such organization has its own hierarchical strategy. In many cases, a programme is a set of activities pursuing the accomplishment of strategic goals of the corporate or business level organization, while the programme also has its own implementation strategy.

Today, all organizations (including companies, public institutions, universities and research establishments) are facing large social and industrial changes. Strategic actions of change or innovation are required to tackle such external changes, which take the form of programmes integrating a number of unique and non-routine project-type activities.

The nature of today's change is derived from the digital revolution and globalization. 'Moore's Law' stating that the number of transistors integrated on a semiconductor chip doubles every two years was delivered in the 1960s and that law has remained effective for last five decades. At first it was an empirical rule. Then it started to push related industries to develop products with four times better performance every four years. As a result this became a driving force, compelling the progress of social 'digitalization' very strongly and steadily.

In the beginning, manufacturing companies of semiconductor manufacturing systems lost the business when they failed to meet this timetable. Such relationships have been steadily expanded to the industries of computer and peripheral equipment, software development, telecommunication and network systems, TV, video, audio and gaming equipment for consumers, control systems and related service industries. Countless thousands of highly capable researchers and engineers across the world have been challenged to make their highest efforts to avoid their employing organizations falling behind the competition. Robotics technology surpasses some areas of human capabilities today. This is seen for example in automotive industries in the form of robotic (driverless) cars and humanoid robots.

Socially, this trend makes us afraid of causing severe industrial competition and even serious problems of unemployment. Business organizations are required to adapt to the rapid changes of the market environment by formulating and implementing strategies to create new industries and markets. A large problem is that the specific future for each organization is ambiguous, although the macro trend is clear. It is very important to deal appropriately with the future uncertainties by way of programmes that set and realize the strategic goals.

Generally speaking, the strategic value represented by the strategic goals and the certainty of the programme to realize them are in a trade-off relationship. If the goals are more ambitious, the certainty of achieving them will decrease. On the other hand, if the goals are set too low, there will be another type of risk, which is to lose competitive market edge. From another standpoint, the time factor is also important for market competition. Whether programme management aims to pile up rather small successes repeatedly in a short period, or to create a larger framework for a big success over a longer time range, the certainty will change depending on individual circumstances.

From the initial concept to the design phase of a programme, the management of uncertainty has to be treated implicitly within the definition process of the strategic goal. High uncertainties have to be eliminated where necessary by changing the strategic goals, so that the programme is designed with an acceptable range of uncertainties. In the programme design phase, the execution strategy must also be examined so that the design configuration and related issues reduce the uncertainties. Then uncertainties have to be managed as an explicit part of the execution processes.

Uncertainty management processes

The basic processes of uncertainty management in a programme are illustrated in Figure 31.1. As with projects, programmes are executed by making detailed plans and organizing workforces to execute those plans. Many programmes aim to accomplish a mission or a somewhat abstract outcome such as 'business success' where the criteria might not be obvious at the beginning. Conversely, the objectives of projects are usually more certain and well-defined.

At first, a programme has a number of possible goals to be achieved. In the initial phases of mission definition and scenario development, the most appropriate combination of goals is chosen by analysis and investigation, which includes uncertainty management.

In the subsequent design phase, programme details are designed as an integrated architecture of projects. Individual project goals are defined at the same time. In the planning and design phases a programme concept that is highly effective and with sufficient certainty is conceived and designed, while less effective and less certain alternatives are discarded.

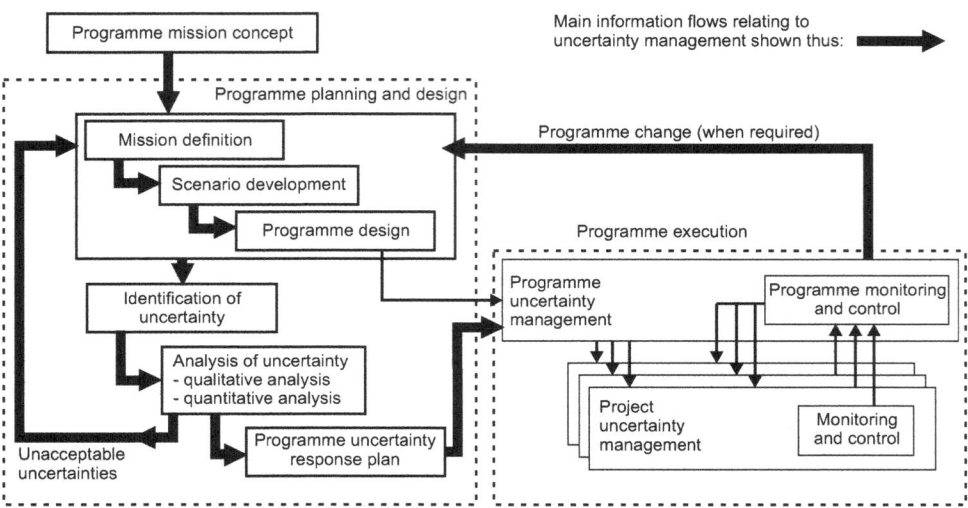

Figure 31.1 Basic processes of programme uncertainty management

Accordingly for execution phase tasks the uncertainties are restricted to those that are assessed as controllable or allowable in principle. In practice, unexpected large and small uncertain events will occur and management must deal with them. Although the nature of the causes and the scale of influence might be different for individual projects and the programme, the response procedures are similar.

Mission definition and scenario development phases

The initial phase of a programme lifecycle is for defining the programme mission. The objectives will be attained by a combination of strategic goals. There is 'multiplicity of meaning', which means a diverse mixture of possibilities of goals to achieve in the initial programme mission concept. As stated earlier, some goals may be found very difficult to achieve. Some easier goals may not be effective in achieving good business performance. Mission definition defines the CSFs of the essential goals for mission success. The combination of the defined goals must be the most promising outcome with a reasonable level of certainty.

The next step determines the programme execution scenario. In many cases, each programme goal is accomplished by way of one or more projects. The execution scenario is conducted by analysing how to integrate such projects to accomplish the defined set of goals conceptually. In this process, the programme uncertainties are identified and qualitative and quantitative analyses are made to confirm or improve the certainties. Unacceptably uncertain elements are discarded or reconsidered. In practice, the previous mission definition process is referred back to when an uncertainty problem is not closed in this phase. Though these two phases are logically sequential they are very closely alike and are sometimes subphases of a phase called 'mission profiling'.

Design phase

In the design phase, the architecture of the programme and its constituent projects is designed according to the scenario developed in the previous phase. Each project is assigned its respective programme goal as the project mission and its basic design is developed. More specific uncertainties are revealed as the design progresses. At this stage, the certainty of the projects and the total programme is assessed. Unacceptable uncertainty elements are eliminated to improve the probability of programme success. These processes are reiterated to remove all unacceptable elements of uncertainty and create confidence of success.

Execution phase

When the programme design is completed with sufficient confidence, the programme proceeds to the execution phase described in the right hand side of Figure 31.1. Now the tasks for each project are carried out to accomplish the assigned mission.

Provided the projects are properly designed the programme goals should be accomplished, but it is common for various miscalculations and incidental errors to occur. In many cases individual mishaps create only minor problems but the potential number of mishaps can be huge. After-the-fact countermeasures are used because that is far less expensive than preparing for all possible uncertainties. One common safeguard is to adopt good implementation methodology by selecting capable partners or subcontractors and having reserve allowances of time and money.

In managing the uncertainties, individual projects are monitored and controlled, in addition to gathering information (including the external environmental information) for the entire programme. It might be necessary to re-examine the programme change, going back to the programme planning and design processes. Significant changes in the programme environment (including major changes of the market, competitors' unpredictable movement and so forth) are also dealt with in this phase by adjustments, partial changes or even overall redesign of the projects and/or the programme.

As a general rule, project managers have a responsibility for managing the uncertainties of individual projects. However, when unacceptable impact is found on the achievement of the overall programme objectives, the programme manager is responsible for taking action to cope with the problem. That could include following a process to change the programme architecture or the organizational framework.

Combined phases

A perfect programme plan can be made if all the necessary information is obtained at the initial stage, but that does not happen often. The market environment and the intentions or behaviour of competitors will change with time. Also the internal resources and capabilities of the organization can change or will be found insufficient as the programme proceeds. Countermeasures against these issues must be prepared in the initial mission definition, the scenario development or the design phases. Modification or addition of such countermeasures is also required in the execution phase. For example, an optional plan to make a programme change during

Area of uncertainty causal elements	Major corresponding phases dealing with causal elements		
	Mission definition and scenario development	**Programme design**	**Execution phase**
Programme internal causal elements	• Objectives and goals of programmes (multiple meaning or ambiguity of objectives, complexity of programmes).	• Uncertainties of projects • Resource capabilities.	• Uncertainties in execution (inadequate capabilities, mis-estimation, incidental events).
Programme external causal elements	• Environmental change, complexity (market environment, economic environment and so on) • Intentions of competitors and collaborators.		• Unexpected cataclysmic incidents (cataclysmic changes of external environment).

Figure 31.2 Causal elements and corresponding phases

implementation can be formulated according to predetermined criteria on the possible impacts of uncertainties.

Area of uncertainty: causal elements

Programme uncertainties must be managed in the appropriate phase. Areas of uncertainty, causal elements and major corresponding phases dealing with the elements are classified in Figure 31.2. Composites of these elements also commonly have a large influence on the programme outcome. When a problem breaks out in the execution phase, it must be dealt with in that phase even though some activities in previous phases were its root causes. But, in many cases, the effect will be limited because the front-end planning has a large influence on the result.

Each specific problem will have suitable countermeasures and some of those measures are commonly appropriate for several types of problems. In the next section, explanations are given for such measures and management policies for the specific type of problems and some problems in common.

Categorized causal elements of programme uncertainties

Figure 31.3 shows a list of major causal elements of uncertainties and typical examples of their countermeasures. In the right column, the countermeasures printed in italics are of particular importance in each listed category and are generally effective also for the cases of other categories.

Major causal elements and countermeasures

Programme goals (multiple meaning and complexity)

Programme objectives are expressed as a programme mission in general. At the initial stage the mission starts as a form of rather abstract and qualitative concept or desire, such as development of a new market or enhancement of competitiveness.

Phases	Major causal elements	Examples of typical countermeasures
Mission definition, scenario development and design phase	**Programme goals** (multiple meaning, complexity) • Inappropriate goals/insufficient clarification • Goals too ambitious.	• *Establishment of programme governance* • *Mission definition (scrutiny or redefinition)* • Programme design (scrutiny)
	Complexity and change of environments (market, economic environment and so on) • Uncertainties of market size, growth rate and so forth • Complexity (interaction of products, market and technical innovations) • Rapid change in market and environment • Product lifecycle.	• *Environmental scenarios and execution scenario* • *Flexibility of programme (option); real option method* • *Short response cycle (lean), agile project management* • Establishment of business in niche market.
	Intention of competitors or collaborators • Porter's five forces from competitors • Disruptive innovation • Opportunism of collaborators (hold up problem).	• Individual competitive strategy • Responses fitting to the market position • Measures to individual threats • Measures by contract type (complete contract, successive contract, spot contrac:, long-term relationship and so on). Ownership of business.
	Deficiency of organizational capabilities • Planning and design.	Organizational capability improvement • *Resource acquisition (recruiting, R&D, M&A, alliance, outsourcing, public support)* • *Bottleneck countermeasures* • *Early information gathering and response* • *Lessons learned*
Execution phase	**Uncertainties in execution process** (deficiency of capabilities and resources, mis-estimation, incidental events) • Human resources (such as engineering or management capabilities) • Physical resources (such as facilities or materials) • Limit of predictive capability • Bankruptcy of collaborator.	
	Unexpected cataclysmic incidents (cataclysmic change of external environment) • Economic crisis, international conflicts • Huge natural disasters, accidents.	• Damage localization (preventing spread) • Situation holding and strategy restructuring • Financial response.

Countermeasures printed in italics are of particular importance in their exhibited category and can also be generally effective for cases in other categories.

Figure 31.3 Causal elements by category, and major examples of countermeasures

Supposing a strategic objective to develop a very new market, there might be many specific goals. These could include, for example:

• development of new products having particular functions and performances;
• development of core technology for the products;
• setting up the production facilities;
• production engineering;

- procurement of new materials or parts;
- building the sales network;
- training sales personnel;
- developing the sales campaign, and much more.

There might be various possibilities for fulfilling the strategic mission. It might not be necessary to fulfil all the goals: some specific selection of goals might be sufficient. Even for identical objectives, the selection for success could differ depending largely on the situation of the implementing organizations.

Ambiguity and multiplicity of meaning in the programme mission in the initial phase will decrease as analysis of issues and strategic planning proceed. Meanwhile the complexities of the tasks increase, or more precisely, hidden complexities will be revealed as the number of relating elements increases. The appearance of a programme starts from conceptual ambiguity at the initial stage, then turns to multiplicity of meaning as the analysis and the examination progress. Complexity increases as the planning progresses to detailed implementation. Probability of programme success is strongly affected by how correctly the increasing complexity is interpreted and handled.

Mission definition and programme goal scrutiny

It is most important to define the programme mission as a set of goals that clarify the essential outcome. Also, it is necessary to consider and scrutinize all the possibilities. It might be impossible to survive in a severe competition without big vision. On the other hand, a vaguely planned acquisitive strategy can be the cause of costly failure. The programme goals must be achievable by the available resources – otherwise success will be far from certain. Simplicity is encouraged because a simple programme is preferable in a competitive environment where speed of implementation and lower costs are essential.

When defining the programme mission and designing the strategy it is important to focus on something particular and decide what should be discarded. Those decisions are very important. To deal with the contradictory requirements of a big objective and the certainty of its accomplishment it is most important to define the truly essential goals for success. That can mean critical re-examination of the mission definition. Also, it is important to minimize the complexity of programme design as far as possible.

Programme governance

It is very difficult to make sound judgement objectively from a higher viewpoint, even for experienced managers. But that higher viewpoint is required for programme management, in making the definition of programme goals and other decisions that link directly to the higher level of the business strategy. Sometimes it can be difficult for an executing organization to make sound decisions on important programme problems (including the definition or change of programme goals and other programme policies) because conflicts of interest can occur among stakeholders.

Higher organizations or top management are required to review the plan and programme status at relevant times and give appropriate directives on implementation when necessary. Establishment of such programme governance is very important to ensure that implementation accords with the desired business strategy.

Complexity and change of programme environments

The programme environment can have many positive and negative influences on uncertainties. Because the environment includes complicated and changing relationships among various factors it can be difficult to make good judgement and cope well. The changing environment itself creates another complex situation that can have a big impact on the uncertainties. It is impossible or very difficult to alter external environmental factors towards a favourable condition for the programme. It is important to take these characteristics into account when dealing with uncertainties.

Environment and execution scenarios

When the business environment is badly predicted or develops unexpectedly, the programme may not achieve the expected outcome even it was executed completely as planned.

In the scenario development, it is necessary to analyse an execution scenario (manifesting the execution plan) and a separate environmental scenario (to describe possible environmental changes). The programme organization can carry out the execution scenario as planned with some level of certainty, if necessary making adjustments to the plan or its activities. But the external environment (which can include social, economic, market, international and cross-cultural environment and natural disasters) cannot be controlled and over time can show unpredictable change. There is no way other than to accept each environmental change and that is a major causal element of uncertainties.

The general approach for managing such environmental uncertainties is to base the execution scenario on the most possible environmental scenario. Preparation of a backup execution scenario is prudent, choosing from the other possible environmental scenarios one which has low possibility but large potential impact.

Flexible strategy

Many businesses have the possibility of big success combined with uncertainties that could lead to failure. In a highly uncertain environment, it is a basic precaution to have flexibility at the start of a programme, without committing the full investment. Then it can be decided whether to continue and make additional investment or not depending on the result of the initial investment. To expand a production facility according to the market trend and to test a new product in a limited area are two typical examples.

Programme flexibility is one of the fundamental procedures for coping with uncertainties. Flexibility includes providing programme execution options to continue, change, expand, reduce or cancel as information about higher certainty or greater risk is obtained at intermediate stages.

> [Editorial comment: Several other contributors in this Handbook offer similar advice in the process known as stage-gating. DL]

Flexibility allows us to make more accurate decisions as more reliable data are gathered with the passage of time. But that should not allow ambiguous decision-making or taking rash postponement or cancellation action. Thorough examination of decision-making criteria for cancelling, delaying or continuing a programme is important for allowing clear decisions.

Short response cycle and agile project management

With intense competition, it is very important to be able to respond quickly to change in the business environment. Suppose, for example, that Company A can complete a task in 50 days and Company B would need 100 days to do the same thing. Company A is clearly more efficient but it can execute the task more accurately with fresh and reliable information. In a changing competitive environment it is important to be able to react to change faster than competitors. Then a company can maintain sufficient competitive advantage (not necessarily following the environmental change itself exactly).

Speed or the capability of quick operational change is very important for every aspect of business from corporate management to programme and project management including R&D and product development. We can see good examples in business management of the lean production system, and quick replacement capabilities of goods on shelves and in large retail store chains.

The concept of agile software project management which has become popular recently may provide a useful reference for strategic programme management. In agile software development functional software package components are developed one by one in short durations (of one or two weeks for example), and each function is confirmed as fulfilling the requirements. The performance of the entire system evolves as the number of proven functions increases. Unlike the conventional 'waterfall' project management processes, development will be terminated when the overall objectives are substantially satisfied, even if some of the functions assumed in the initial phase are not completed. This might be a practical and efficient approach because perfect prediction and achieving value are difficult in a changing environment. However, the agile method is suitable for highly capable teams with relatively few members and not necessarily suitable for large complex projects.

Speed of action is most important to capture an emerging new market for example. The most important strategy is to put out new products of limited performance quickly to capture the new market. Then expansion follows, increasing market share by adding required or attractive new functions one after another. That is a strategic programme method for transforming an uncertain market into a prosperous business. Looking back to the past, the audio and video businesses developed by Japanese manufacturers such as Sony in the 1970s, PC software industries including Microsoft in the 1990s and Apple's iPod business programme in the 2000s were very good examples of such strategy.

Competitors' or collaborators' intentions

Programmes are often executed to implement competitive strategies. This may be a threat for the competitors and they will plan their own programme to implement their counter-strategy. The total sum of the strategic activities by all the market participants forms the market environment at this point. However, it may happen that intentional activity of a specific competitor is more influential for the uncertainties of one's own strategic programme in the macro market environment. For example, the strategy of the company carrying out the programme (the leader company) impacts directly on the other companies in an oligopoly market. On the other hand, a disruptive innovation by a follower company may become a serious threat even for the leader company.

While many companies and other organizations participate in a programme by contracts or other relationships, it is common that the short-term and long-term interests are different among the stakeholders. Sometimes a contractor or a business partner becomes a cause of uncertainty in a programme, for example when it has a hold-up or otherwise causes a delay.

Individual competitive strategy

Strategic programmes are measures for handling business uncertainties derived from competition. They are based on various frameworks of business strategy including 'the five forces' theory of M. Porter and 'the resource based view of the firm' theory of J. B. Barney and others. The above discussions headed 'Programme goals (multiple meaning and complexity)' and 'Complexity and change of programme environments' are premised on such knowledge of business strategy.

For a practical strategy, in addition to the above, it is necessary to add counter-measures against the competitor's strategic intention. As the situation is specific to the individual case and there is no generic methodology, it is important to include the considerations of one's own position in the competitive environment, the competitor's action and the factor of time. Sometimes approaches using gaming theories may be effective in this area.

Dealing with opportunism

Opportunism is a behaviour that utilizes the encountered situation in a self-interest manner – even to the extent of using unethical measures. When a programme depends on contracts with other organizations, there are possibilities of hold-up problems associated with opportunism. To avoid such uncertainties, it is necessary to make provisions including adoption of an appropriate contract method (such as complete contract, long-term contract, sequential contract and spot contract) and other means such as formation of a joint enterprise or transformation to an internal transaction by means of a business buy-out.

Uncertainties in the execution process

The successful accomplishment of a total programme will be in doubt if each planned task is not completed in the execution process even though the original plan was excellent. Causal elements in this category include estimating errors in the planned details such as schedules, costs of material procurement and workers' capabilities. Also included are inadequate resource capabilities and the incidental events of errors, delays and accidents.

Improving organizational capability

Organizational capability is the power of execution contained in various organizational resources including the human resources of experienced personnel and skills of managers, the knowledge resources accumulated in the organization, infrastructures and other physical resources and the financial resources. To avoid failing the tasks of the programme plan, well-planned and consistent effort to improve the execution capabilities of people is vital in today's ever changing business world.

High competence bottlenecks

The progression of a complex business pursuit can be constrained by bottlenecks as explained by Goldratt (1984) in his theory of constraints. The whole business will become stagnant unless each bottleneck is resolved, no matter how many resources are scooped up. There are two aspects to be noted for such bottleneck problems in programme and project management.

First, the case of a bottleneck appearing in the critical path is well known in project management. The second aspect is the bottleneck of high competence. Efforts for dealing with uncertainties are always non-routine exceptional work. The more serious the problem is, the more tasks devolve to the small number of competent managers or experts, and it very difficult to increase the number of such capable people. It is important to mitigate the load of such bottlenecks by diverting some part of the difficult tasks or the more routine tasks to others, thus freeing up the experts.

Early information gathering and response

Monitoring will reveal unsuccessful progress. Early correct response is essential for every such revealed variance. The earlier corrective action is taken, the better. That means being aware of possible problems and having countermeasures in place. Electronic and human information gathering networks are important to enable this process, and a process should be in place to identify and highlight problems.

[Editorial comment: the preferred method is to identify deviations from the plan as early as possible. These deviations are often called variances or exceptions. Management attention has to be concentrated on these exceptions, which includes limiting reports to higher management to minimize routine information and highlight exceptions. DL]

Unexpected cataclysmic incidents

Occasionally programmes are seriously affected by unexpected cataclysmic incidents, including economic crisis, demise of a regime, natural disasters and human-induced accidents. It is clear from the word 'unexpected' that countermeasures are not usually prepared beforehand. Even when precautions are taken, they might not be effective because the timing and the scale of the incident cannot be predicted. In such cases, a response plan has to be made and executed urgently as the situation progresses. The basic procedure is to localize and to prevent expansion of the damage at first, and then to grasp the situation of the damage and gather available resources. Then a revised or completely new plan has to be made to restructure the strategy. A financial response plan will also be required.

It should be a matter of course to include a contingency response plan and other countermeasures in the original plan for the predictable incidents.

> [Editorial comment: This can involve appointing a risk manager and establishing a risk log. The process is explained in Chapter 7 of Lock (2013). DL]

Conclusion

Programme uncertainties can be minimized or dealt with in various ways, including measures described in the sections above. It sometimes happens that situations became very difficult to deal with using the original programme plan, in which case that plan has to be revisited and improved or, in the last resort, the programme will have to be abandoned.

The primary strategic objectives may become difficult to accomplish owing to external environmental situations, or because of progress problems or other difficulties in the constituent projects. In those cases, significant changes will have to be made to

> • Change of customer's strategy or requirements
> • Change of organization (merger and acquisition, for example)
> • Change of top management
> • Change of strategy from one or more major stakeholders
> • Cash flow or other financing difficulty
> • Abrupt market shrinkage (commodity prices, economic crisis)
> • Emergence of strong competitors
> • Dissemination of new technology
> • Significant change of application technology
> • Change of laws and regulations
> • Economic crisis
> • Wars or insurrections
> • Huge natural disasters
> • Programme goals revealed as inappropriate
> • Significant difficulties in achieving programme goals
> • Organizational capabilities found to be inadequate
> • Programme interrupted or terminated
> • Programme objectives redefined
> • Programme architecture changed as a result of changes to one more of the constituent projects,

Figure 31.4 Some causes and effects of programme change

the original programme plan, which might include changing the programme architecture. Some typical causal elements and contents of changes are summarized in Figure 31.4. The effectiveness of programme governance must be safeguarded and assured when a change is made by following formally stipulated procedures.

References and further reading

Goldratt, E. M. (1984), *The Goal*, Great Barrington, MA: North River Press.

Lock, D. (2013), *Project Management*, 10th edn., Farnham: Gower.

Shimizu, M. (2010a), 'On Strategy and Risk Management in P2M' (Japanese literature), *Journal of the International Association of Project and Programme Management* (Japan), 5(1).

Shimizu, M. (2010b), *Jissen Project and Programme Management (Project and Programme Management in Practice)* (in Japanese), Tokyo: JMA Management Center.

Shimizu, M. (2011), 'Risk Management in Strategic Programme Management' (Japanese literature), *Journal of the Society of Project Management* (Japan), 13(4).

Shimizu, M. (2012), *Fundamentals of Programme Management*, Newtown Square, PA: Project Management Institute.

Chapter 32

Managing Programme Resources

Dennis Lock

The success of every project and every programme depends in part in having the appropriate resources in place. This important subject is somewhat neglected in the literature, so this chapter should go a little way towards putting that right.

Introduction

Resource management includes making sure that the organization has enough resources available to conduct its business and, in the context of this chapter, to carry out its projects and programmes. So first I need to define what is meant by 'resources'. To some extent that will depend on whether or not we are discussing commercial and industrial projects and programmes or change programmes. For the most part the methods for resource management are shared between all kinds of programmes, but change programmes bring in requirements for additional resources that are not always immediately obvious from the outset.

Resource management can mean several things. It can mean directing and motivating people to perform for the benefit of the organization. It can also mean scheduling people and other assets so that resources for project and programme tasks are available when they are needed. The management and motivation of people in programmes has been touched upon in other chapters but for a more comprehensive reference work on this aspect of resource management see Lock and Scott (2013).

The main body of this chapter will deal with methods for ensuring that resources are scheduled and available across projects, or multiple projects, or programmes so that progress is never delayed through lack of resources.

Resource categories

When asked to name the most important resource which needs to be managed, most would say 'People' – which means people with the appropriate skills and experience. Companies that regularly carry out programmes will accumulate people with good skills, establish project and programme management methods, have at least one permanent PMO, and know how to manage their human and other resources through experience and lessons learned over time.

But before discussing these aspects further, what about considering time as a resource? Time is a very special resource because it cannot be replaced or augmented. Once a deadline has passed it has gone for ever. So I would include time as a very important programme resource – so important and central to other resource management that this must be discussed in the next main section of this chapter.

Materials can also be considered as resources. They can be managed to some extent using the same methods used for skilled people. Indeed any resource that can be quantified in simple numbers can be scheduled using project or programme scheduling tools.

Cash is a vital resource. Not only the amounts of cash needed, but also the timing of cash flows are important and need managing. So cash management must form part of this chapter.

Accommodation and other space is another resource that must be managed in programmes. In change programmes that can pose huge problems when people and centres of operation are changed while having to continue operations to serve the organization's customers or clients.

Managing the resource of time

In order to manage work and events against time, it is usually necessary to define target dates for various tasks and, from those dates, establish priorities. The appropriate tool for that since the 1950s has been some form of critical path analysis. That process begins by listing all the tasks needed to complete each project and the programme. Forgetting to include any task from the list risks not only delays but also forgotten (and thus unbudgeted) costs. Check-lists and brainstorming sessions are two ways of helping to ensure that no task is forgotten. The act of drawing a critical path network, especially when done with team leaders present, is another way of ensuring that no important task is left out.

First shot critical path analysis, without at this stage considering resources, should produce a schedule that includes the following essential data for each task (this list is a mix of information provided initially by project management and subsequent data from the computations):

- task identifier code;
- task name or description (usually abbreviated because of limitations in the software and column space in the reports);
- earliest possible start date;
- latest permissible start date;
- earliest possible finish date;
- latest permissible finish date;
- total float;
- the manager responsible for the task and its resources (allocating each manager a departmental sort code is usually the method for arranging that in the database).

Additional, optional data might include:

- designation of the task as a milestone;
- a target or fixed start or finish date (particularly for tasks that come at the beginning or end of a project or programme).

All these data can be used later by the software for deciding priorities and allocating various resources to tasks. But if we consider time as a resource that has to be managed, here are some important points to consider:

1. Any project or programme that runs late will probably also exceed its budgets – if only because the fixed overhead costs have to be borne for longer than planned. In the case of change programmes, any delay in the programme clearly will mean delays in realizing the intended benefits.

2. Using methods such as earned value analysis (EVA) can predict whether or not your programme will finish on time or exceed its budgets. But EVA is an expensive process that takes up time from the PMO, requires regular input from senior programme and project staff, and by no means always yields accurate predictions. Be careful about using methods that add costs to your programme without adding value.

3. Progress (and thus time) is best managed by concentrating effort on tasks that are critical or in danger of running late. That applies the concept of management by exception. Unbudgeted money spent on additional resources or special measures to bring critical tasks back on schedule will often be repaid many times over by preventing delays to the entire programme.

4. Control changes. All but essential changes should be killed at birth. That means establishing an authority such as a change board to consider any proposed change. By a 'change' I mean any additional work or change of policy that would cause something to happen which was not part of the original business case. Changes can cause work already done to be scrapped. They can also lead to 'scope creep', which means you finish up trying to do far more work than was envisaged in the business case. Another point to consider is that changes made late in a programme are likely to be more expensive and disruptive than changes made at the beginning, because late changes can cause work done to be scrapped (with consequent loss of the sunk costs), delayed programme completion, distress and demotivation among programme staff and delays in achieving the intended programme benefits.

Scheduling resources

The main departments within the organization with responsibility for providing resources are HRM (where additional people have to be brought in permanently or temporarily), the purchasing department for materials and the finance department for cash (I shall discuss cash scheduling later in the chapter).

The PMO should coordinate resource needs across the programme, all its projects, and any other programmes and projects taking place at the same time in the organization. In every case the PMO has the responsibility to keep all the departmental and individual project managers informed as far in advance as possible of predicted resource needs and to warn of forecast shortfalls.

Project or programme management software

Resource scheduling used to be carried out on adjustable wallboards. That was difficult even for small single projects. Even if a practical schedule could be charted in that way, it would be rendered unusable as soon as the first change or performance default occurred. So of course this section assumes the use of competent project management software that can schedule resources and reschedule them whenever necessary.

The best computer programs can deal with simultaneous or overlapping projects as one model, which means that they can handle multiprojects and programmes. The computer model will amass considerable amounts of data, and so it must never be corrupted. The best way to ensure that is to have the multiproject or programme model controlled by competent staff within the PMO. By the way, in this chapter I am using the abbreviation PMO for programme management office (not project management office).

Good project management software will be able to allocate human resources to tasks according to their skill description and/or their functional department. That can be done for single projects or for multiple projects and programmes. 'Good' software by no means describes the most popular software available and a bad choice can make life very difficult for those in the PMO. I have known cases where higher management have forced the use of unsuitable software, with inevitable and unfortunate results. Remember also that if you choose software that fails to perform as you need, you will incur additional time and costs when you later have to input all the data again into replacement software.

Here are some tips on choosing appropriate software. First you must decide what you need your project or programme management software to do. Then compile a check-list in the form of a questionnaire. Then (but only then) approach the software companies with your questionnaire to see what they have to offer. There is an example of such a check-list in Chapter 18 of Lock (2013). As a consultant I advised a client to go through that process a few years ago and we sent out our questionnaire to around 18 companies. Most replied. One most popular software company failed to respond. Some, with creditable honesty, declared themselves unable to fulfil our requirements. Four were shortlisted. One was chosen and has since given good service.

Setting up the programme resource usage model

The programme manager (or the manager's delegate) must first decide which resources need to be scheduled. In this section we are considering only people, but the same questions must be asked later about other resources.

There will be many people in the organization who carry out routine or support roles who do not have to be allocated to specific programme tasks and therefore can be left out of the resource scheduling calculations. Clearly you do not have to schedule secretaries, cleaners, maintenance staff, other indirect workers or even the project managers and the programme manager. For each resource category that *does* need to be scheduled, the following data must usually be specified:

- The name of the particular human skill, considering the skill domain and the skill level.
- A short code which will identify that skill in the database.

- A unit cost rate (per person per day is recommended). It is to be hoped and expected that standard cost rates are available for each category – not for individually named people.
- The number of people in each category available for work generally on the entire programme. It is best to keep back (hide) about 15 per cent of the total availability to allow for people spending time on things that cannot be scheduled, such as unforeseen tasks, absences from the office and so on.
- A department code, identifying the manager responsible for each particular skill group. That will be useful later for filtering reports so that departmental managers get work-to-do lists and other reports listing only tasks for which they are responsible.
- Some programs will always assume rate-constant resource usage over a task, while others will allow the PMO to specify a variable rate (this principle is explained in Figure 32.1). My strong advice is to keep the data simple and always choose the rate-constant option. In a large programme to do otherwise would only add complication and is entirely unnecessary because such small details will be smoothed out over all the tasks in the programme.

It is unwise to attempt scheduling in very fine detail (say down to time units of hours) in a programme that will last for several months or longer. That is unnecessary and unrealistic. The large volume of resource data in a programme spread over several projects will even out daily fluctuations. Keep it simple.

The computer program will expect start and finish dates to be specified for the period when each resource is going to be available. That facility also allows the PMO to specify different availability levels to cope with planned changes in resource levels

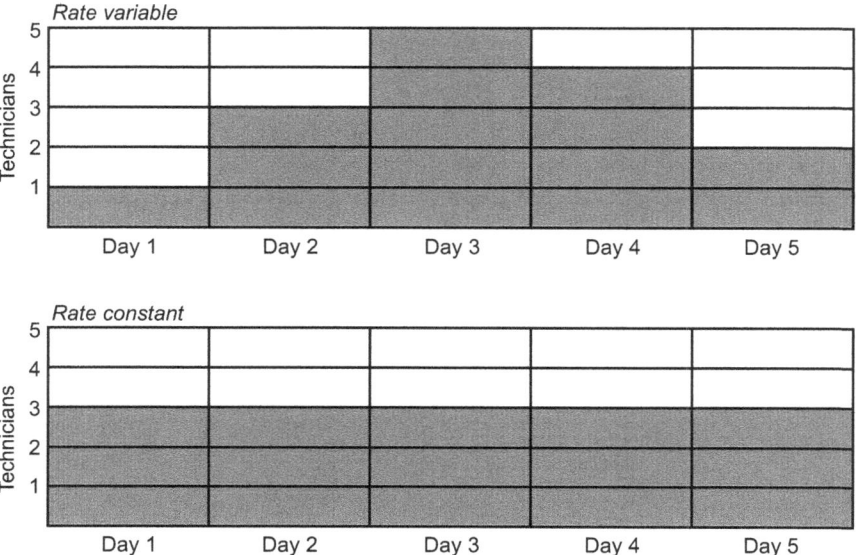

Figure 32.1 Rate variable and rate constant resource patterns for a single task

during the programme's lifecycle. Such predictable fluctuations can occur through pre-planned recruitment or staff reductions.

The resource scheduling process

Every project within the programme should be given a target start date and a target finish date or, alternatively (and preferably), its start and finish tasks should be interfaced with a main enveloping programme network that itself has simply one programme start date and one programme finish date. That might sound difficult and can result in large volumes of data, but should be well within the competence of an experienced PMO team.

Other projects in the organization using the same resources will have to be taken into account – so their demands will also be satisfied. In that case the resource model will include a mix of programme and project portfolio resources.

That method will produce time analysis data for every task in the programme, all with reference to the programme's required start and finish dates. In other words, the priority of every task (and its claim on specified resources) will be established for the benefit of the entire programme and other projects extant in the organization.

The background data should come from a critical path network, as outlined earlier in this chapter. The computer will attempt to allocate people of the specified skills to tasks. If insufficient resources are available on any day to carry out a particular task, the computer will decide on one of several options according to scheduling rules decided in advance by the PMO as follows:

1. Delay the task within the float available until resources are scheduled to be available.
2. Interrupt one or more tasks, to resume them later when resources are available. But I never recommend allowing tasks to be split in this way because it is very disruptive for the people engaged on the tasks. So ideally all tasks should be specified as 'non-splittable'.
3. For critical tasks, allow the level of resources scheduled to exceed the declared maximum availability to achieve completion on time. The resulting schedule will be known as 'time-limited' and the PMO or relevant manager will have to come up with some way of finding the additional people. Reports from the computer resource scheduling process will give the responsible manager advance warning of these overloads. Such extra resources are sometimes called 'threshold resources', and they will usually have higher cost rates.
4. Allow the final programme date to be delayed, so that resources are never overloaded. That will result in a 'resource-limited' schedule.

The principle of choosing between time-limited and resource-limited schedules is shown in Figure 32.2.

The process can and should be simplified greatly if constituent projects (or parts of projects) which are to be subcontracted can simply be shown on the programme network diagram as single tasks – allocation and management of those resources will become the responsibility of the subcontractors.

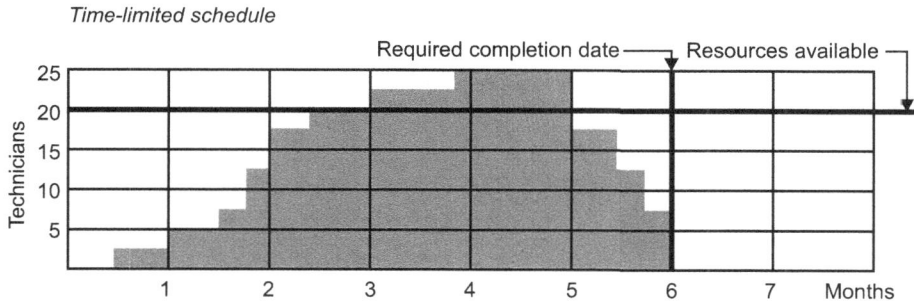

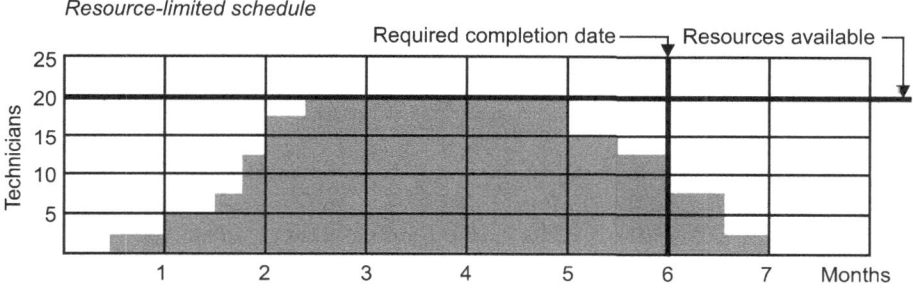

Figure 32.2 Resource-limited and time-limited resource usage plans

Earlier I listed data available for each task after a time analysis calculation. After resource scheduling, two additional dates will be available for each task. These are:

* scheduled start date;
* scheduled finish date.

These *scheduled* dates should govern the allocation of tasks to people. That should ensure the availability of human resources at all times throughout the programme.

Managing the resource model for the programme

So we have a picture of a master programme schedule, managed and updated by the PMO, with subcontractors responsible for managing their own resources to conform to that schedule. Now consider what would happen if any individual within the programme or one of its projects were to enter contradictory or incorrect data into the computer model. Chaos, a corrupted database and debased schedules would result. Clearly that cannot be allowed to happen.

Figure 32.3 illustrates how a PMO can manage the resource model. All regular progress reports from departmental and other responsible managers will be used to update the master model controlled by the PMO. The PMO will also alter the model

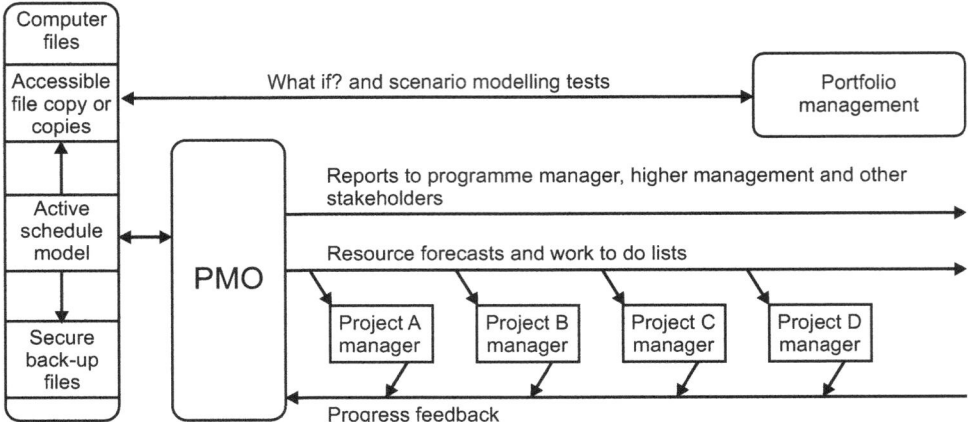

Figure 32.3 The PMO as guardian of the programme resource schedule model

as necessary so that it is kept up to date with any authorized changes. But copies of the model can be made available to others for experimentation with scenario analysis and 'what-if' trials, and it matters not if any or all of those models are corrupted because the PMO remains in expert control of the master schedule and its secure back-up files.

Risk management and programme resources

Every programme and every significant project within the programme should be subjected to risk assessment. The chapter assumes that a risk manager exists somewhere in the programme organization, either within the PMO or in some other department. Risk managers are not always fully engaged in risk management and their duties might be combined with some other role.

Lack of programme resources at any time can pose a threat to the programme and therefore that constitutes a risk. The risk log should contain recommendations for risk mitigation in the event that lack of suitable resources at any time jeopardizes programme success. I wonder how many risk logs do take lack of resources into account as a potential risk? Mitigating steps depend on how much time is available. Solutions can include recruiting new staff, drafting in existing staff not currently engaged in the programme (who might be from other companies in the group), engaging temporary agency staff or outsourcing tasks to a specialist company or consultant.

Now consider this scenario. Both your CEO and the programme manager are friends who enjoy the occasional weekend round of golf. These people are key resources in the organization. But both have undisclosed health issues involving high blood pressure and heart abnormalities. The golf course is on high ground where lightning strikes are fairly common (the electrical kind, not those initiated by trade unions). I think you would agree that I have identified some possible risks here. One possible mitigating action for this would be KPI.

In other chapters you will find frequent references to KPIs, which are key performance indicators. But KPI also refers to *key person insurance*. So to some extent you can compensate for losses caused by the unexpected and unscheduled incapacity of a key person in the programme. This will not usually prevent a programme overrun but can offset financial losses caused through delays in achieving the programme benefits.

Managing supplies and materials

Supplies and materials do not always feature largely when considering the cost aspects of change programmes, but in fact they can contribute over half the costs of some commercial and industrial projects and programmes. In some cases materials and bought services account for 80 per cent of total costs. Clearly supplies, materials and bought services have to be considered as programme resources.

This is not the place to describe materials management and procurement in depth (for more on that see, for example, Ward, 2008). But readers should be aware of the need to take special action if a project or programme is threatened with delays or worse through the absence of any vital component, equipment or service provision.

The purchasing manager and purchasing staff in a large organization will process a large number of orders for goods and services. To them the absence of a piece of equipment, the receipt of an incorrect good or the delayed provision of a bought item or service are fairly routine happenings which they deal with using customary and routine expediting procedures. The frustrated programme or project manager awaiting delayed purchases will take a different and more personal interest.

It is usually recommended that all purchases for goods and services and contractual discussions must be routed through the commercial or purchasing department for a variety of very sound reasons (with which I strongly agree). However, I believe it is justified for a programme or project manager to act directly with an outside agent or supplier if the usual expediting methods fail to produce the goods and services when they are needed. I have acted in that way myself in the past on two occasions, each time getting goods delivered almost immediately. Rules occasionally do need to be broken if that is the only way to obtain vital goods and services to support the programme.

One procedure that I learned and have exploited myself on rare occasions is the use of immediate action orders (IAOs). These authorize extraordinary steps to obtain goods or services pretty much regardless of any additional cost, which is a recognition that delay in receiving those goods or services would cause loss of money to the programme far in excess of the immediate action expenses. Of course this powerful tool has to be used with discretion and must never override quality and safety requirements. IAOs can be very disruptive to normal daily routines, causing shock and awe to those who receive them for action. So they should only be used on rare occasions and must be issued with the sanction and signature of a high manager, such as the managing director. Another rule is never to allow two such orders to be in operation at the same time.

Managing cash as a resource

An original programme's business case should include one or more cash flow schedules, showing the predicted net cash position of the programme at regular intervals. Cash outflows during a programme are inevitable. Inflows are not always so inevitable.

In a programme conducted under a commercial contract for external customers, the methods for ensuring adequacy of cash are well established. A vital condition in the contract terms of payment usually requires the customer to make a downpayment (deposit) when the contract is signed, and to make periodical stage or progress payments to the project or programme contractor as work proceeds. Thus the contractor does not have to find cash to tie up in work-in-progress.

Change programmes are completely different. The organization planning to change itself has no external customer to provide funding. All cash resources have to come from the organization's accumulated profits or must be found from some other source (among which might be a line of credit from a bank, sale and leaseback of assets or a new share issue).

Change programmes attract many unusual costs, particularly payments to displaced or released staff and (possibly) the recruitment of new staff for new roles created by the programme. These programmes are usually authorized with the ultimate expectation of cash and other benefits but those benefits might not be realized until a long time after programme completion and the outlay of much cash.

Figures 32.4 and 32.5 set out two imaginary cash flow schedules allowing comparison between two different kinds of projects – a construction project or programme carried out for a fixed price and an internal change programme carried out and funded by the organization itself. For simplicity I have not discounted any cash items in these two examples. All figures are for illustration only and are not based on actual cases.

Case 1: a construction programme or project

The first case, shown in Figure 32.4, is for the sole contractor of a modest construction project priced at just under £4 million. The table and graph in the illustration show contractor's cash flow patterns that would be typical for this kind of project. They could be scaled up to represent a larger programme and should show a similar pattern. The contractor is able to claim an advance payment on signing the contract plus substantial stage payments as various progress milestones are passed. Although the cash position reaches a negative peak of £655,000 the outcome is well assured and a profit of about 17 per cent results. The total contract span is three years, by the end of which everything is finished.

Case 2: an office relocation programme

The schedule in Figure 32.5 shows the completely different cash pattern that could result from a change programme. Here a London-based company (employing about 300 staff) has decided to research a programme to change its organization and relocate its headquarters to a provincial town. This programme kicks off with exploratory visits to possible new locations. A self-funded study ends with the presentation of a viable business case to the company's board of directors.

In this case the board has approved the move. The company has no real estate assets and its existing London lease will have to be terminated and a new lease negotiated when suitable office premises are found at the new location. The schedule here assumes this to be possible without penalty for ending the outgoing lease, but there

	Quarterly periods - all figures £'000s											
	1	2	3	4	5	6	7	8	9	10	11	12
Cash inflows												
Client's deposit	315											
Client's stage payments			100	260	420	480	500	650	600	500		
Final retention payment												100
Cash outflows												
Fees payable	35	35										
Construction costs	10	230	400	450	460	510	600	400	85	35	2	
Net cash flows												
Quarterly	270	(265)	(300)	(190)	(40)	(30)	(100)	250	515	465	(2)	100
Cumulative.	270	5	(295)	(485)	(525)	(555)	(655)	(405)	110	575	573	673

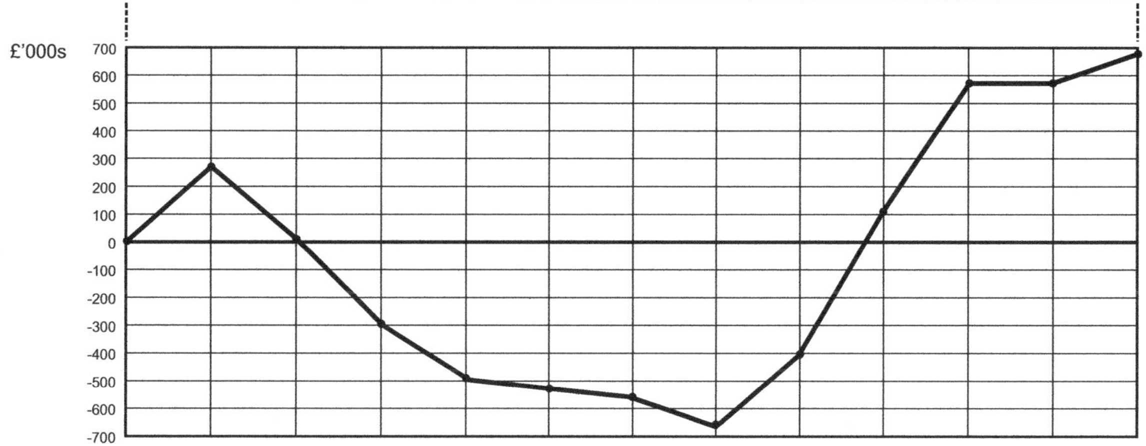

Figure 32.4 Possible cash flow for the contractor of a construction project

Quarterly periods - all figures £'000s

	1	2	3	4	5	6	7	8	9	10	11	12
Cash inflows (benefits)												
Staff cost savings							220	220	220	220	220	220
Office cost savings							200	200	200	200	200	200
Cash outflows												
Business case prep.	10	22	23									
Find new premises			5	45								
Outgoing lease costs					60							
Equip new premises					250	100						
Costs of removals						50						
Staff payments						2,600						
Recruit + train new staff						40	10					
Net cash flows												
Quarterly	(10)	(22)	(28)	(45)	(310)	(2790)	410	420	420	420	420	420
Cumulative	(10)	(32)	(60)	(105)	(415)	(3205)	(2795)	(2375)	(1955)	(1535)	(1115)	(695)

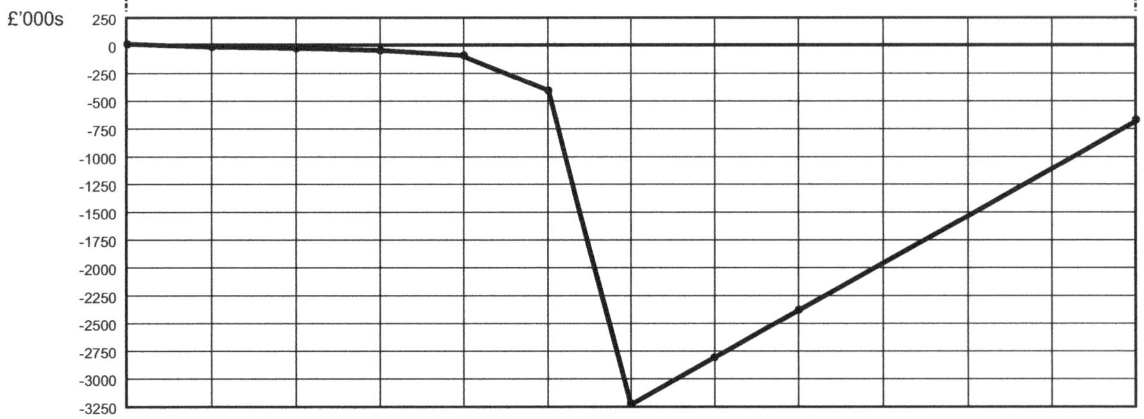

Figure 32.5 Possible cash flow for a change programme (office relocation)

will be a £60,000 charge for 'dilapidations' (a notional sum payable to the London landlord for restoring the property to its original condition).

The new premises will have to be found and equipped before they can be occupied, so that for six months the company will have two office premises to fund (although landlords for new commercial leases sometimes offer very useful initial rent-free periods as an incentive).

The item 'staff payments' will include statutory redundancy payments for those who choose not to move or otherwise will be required to leave, plus assistance with relocation expenses for those who do want to move. Other significant staff costs will include recruiting and training new staff, and some retraining of existing staff who move to the new offices. Some will have to assume new roles and learn to use new equipment. Other staff costs can be expected from lost productive time during moving and resettlement.

Unlike many industrial and commercial programmes, change programmes such as this will not begin to realize their full benefits until the change has been completed and the changed organization is fully operational. Those future benefits will be somewhat less than they first appear if they are discounted to their net present value (not done in this case).

So this company has to find cash resources that approach £3.25 million before the benefits begin to show. But the company has reduced its overheads and become more efficient, so that within four years of the programme being conceived the organization should have cleared the programme costs and be operating with increased profits. This chapter was written during a time when very low bank rates were operating and the outlook for this programme would have been somewhat worse if the cost of borrowing capital had been higher.

Case 3: a rebranding programme

The two cases outlined above were fairly 'safe' programmes because the benefits could be predicted with some certainty. Not all change programmes enjoy that amount of freedom from risk. Benefits expected some time into the future, perhaps even having to look ahead for several years, can be at risk through market changes or other unpredictable circumstances.

Some kinds of change programmes carry higher risks than others. Consider a large retail group with falling sales and revenues that decides to change its brand image in the hope of reviving sales. Already facing annual losses that are eating into cash reserves, the group is now embarking on an expensive programme that begins with hiring marketing consultants to create the new image. This is purely a rebranding programme with no corresponding change in the services and products offered for sale.

So this group will adopt a shorter, more attractive name for its high street and online sales. A new logo must be designed. Window displays and signage inside and out the stores must all comply with the new company image. All company vehicles will have to be repainted. New stationery will be needed. Staff who are in contact with customers (shop supervisors and sales assistants) will all need new uniforms. An expensive advertising campaign in the media will announce this 'exciting change'. The total expenditure could be enormous, creating another drain on strained cash resources. But markets are fickle and there is no guarantee that the programme will result in any benefits at all.

Here is a case where a change programme spelled death for the group because:

- the business case was flawed and the programme could never have delivered the expected benefits;
- cash resources were insufficient to cover the programme costs.

General

Funding for any programme should be planned as part of the business case but cash difficulties will arise if the programme fails to proceed as planned or suffers changes. So good progress management and the avoidance of changes will contribute to the total process of managing cash.

Should a programme be heading inevitably for financial trouble one option that must always be considered (provided it is not too late) is to 'pull the plug' and cancel or postpone the programme. Clearly it is important to keep all the stakeholders informed should any such difficulty be foreseen.

Within this topic of cash management I want to mention a case that I witnessed of very efficient cash control by a large service group. One of its hotels was undergoing refurbishment in an area that was about to stage an international event. The smell of new paint was everywhere when I took a one-week vacation at this hotel. My room was at the far end of a very long straight corridor, which was divided into three sections by self-closing smoke screen fire doors. When I arrived, evidence of new project activity was strong, with contractors' vans occupying some of the car park. All rooms in the first section of the corridor were being renovated. The carpets were protected with canvass covers, the walls were newly painted and men could be seen carrying pipes, bathtubs and other equipment into the rooms. After only three days, work had moved to the central corridor section and new guests were already occupying the renovated rooms in the first section. When I checked out at the end of the week, the second section was also ready for occupation and the corridor in my section was being painted. So this hotel maintained most of its revenues from guests as the work proceeded and thus safeguarded its cash inflows.

Managing office accommodation space

Accommodation can mean many things, from warehousing to factories, shipyards and so on. However, in the context of organization and other change programmes I have to limit this discussion to the effect of changes on office accommodation.

Change programmes can create transient accommodation requirements and difficulties. It can be necessary to arrange for temporary, secure and safe space where people can be provided with facilities that allow them to work and maintain continuity of company operations while their usual workplace is undergoing change (which could be anything from a local change to relocation to other premises). Companies using hot desking should find this less of a problem. In other cases disruption can often be minimized by making layout and equipment changes during weekends or on other non-working days.

You will find little mention in other chapters of the role of the organization's facil-ities manager (or administration manager) – the person in many companies whose role includes ensuring that people can have space in which to work in reasonab~e comfort and safety. In the United Kingdom those requirements have been governed for some time by the Offices, Shops and Railway Premises Act (1963) and the Health and Safety at Work Act (1974). Change programmes can create considerable but temporary accommodation difficulties. So the programme manager will need to ccl-laborate closely with the facilities manager, who might even need to be co-opted into the programme management team.

References and further reading

Lock, D. (2013), *Project Management*, 10th edn., Farnham: Gower.

Lock, D. and Scott, L. (2013), *Handbook of People in Project Management*, Farnham: Gower.

Ward, G. (2008), *The Project Manager's Guide to Purchasing: Connecting to Goods and Services*, Farnham: Gower.

Chapter 33

Managing People in Programmes

Dennis Lock and Alan Fowler, with Keiko Moebus

Many people can engage in or be affected by programmes, from the top stakeholders down to the organization's most junior employees. In programmes that comprise a number of projects to create something new where nothing previously existed, the people can usually be motivated relatively easily because they will look forward to the day when the results of their efforts are unveiled and they can share in collective pride. Change programmes, intended to alter an existing organization in one way or another, are a different case. Change programmes affect people personally, so the way in which *their* people are motivated is different and can be difficult, making or breaking ultimate success. So this chapter is principally about motivating (and not demotivating) people in change programmes.

Introduction

Change programmes are carried out with the intention of realizing benefits for their organization. It is universally acknowledged that the success of any such venture depends on the people involved. But motivational problems differ, depending on where people sit in the organization.

We should assume that the principal stakeholders and top management are motivated by the prospects of benefits for the organization. So their motivation should begin from the promises contained in the business case.

The programme manager, project managers and everyone working directly for them should not be too difficult to motivate because people are always excited by the prospect of taking a constructive part in a new venture. Of course individual rivalries and conflicts can arise. Irresolute or confused leadership can be a great demotivator. Also the organizational structure can influence the motivation of these people, with (generally speaking) dedicated teams and task forces being more conducive to personal motivation than matrix structures. For more on the advantages and disadvantages of different organizational structures see Chapter 9 in Lock (2013b).

The principal motivational difficulties in change programmes usually arise among the regular employees of the organization who:

- might be apprehensive about their very survival in the organization;
- wonder, if they are to survive, how they will be able to cope with the change;
- hear rumours and gossip, often unfounded, about the extent and nature of the forthcoming change.

The next section of this chapter will examine some of the theoretical aspects of motivating people in organizations. Then we shall give more specific recommendations on how to (and how not to) encourage people in the organization to accept and support the changes intended in the programme's business case.

The contribution of early management theorists towards our understanding of people in the workplace

When faced with difficult decisions, or having project managers struggling to deliver the results, the last thing a programme needs is having to deal with people who are difficult, hard to understand, emotional, unreliable and so on. But people are the main drivers who will make the key contribution to the programme's success (or failure). Regardless of how good the strategic planning is or how sound are the methods for governance, without people who are motivated to deliver the change the programme cannot succeed. One challenge for programme managers, therefore, is how well they understand the science of human behaviour and how effectively they can apply those theories in real life.

Examples from management theorists

Studies of how people think, decide and behave in organizations and how people can be affected and influenced by their peers and surroundings (such as culture, local customs and habits) can be absorbing. Beginning particularly around the year 1900 management theorists began to take a great interest in understanding fundamental human behaviour at the workplace and in organizations. Some of that early work is summarized in Lock (2013a).

Elton Mayo and the Hawthorne experiments

We should mention here the work of Elton Mayo, whose studies of workers at the Hawthorne Plant of the Western Electric Company near Chicago produced the observation that workers' productivity (and thus their motivation) improved when various changes in their work environment were made. So, productivity went up when, for example, lighting levels were improved. But, surprisingly, productivity improved even further when some of those changes were reversed.

The key fact here is that the workers responded positively because someone was taking a personal interest in what they did. That lesson applies generally, and people will always work better if they know that their supervisors and managers take a genuine interest in their work. Managers should never be slow to encourage people and praise them for jobs that are well done.

Maslow's hierarchy of human needs

The work of Abraham Maslow (1908–70) on the motivational needs of people is very well known. His 'hierarchy of needs' pyramid is shown in Figure 33.1 (another version appeared earlier in Figure 17.5).

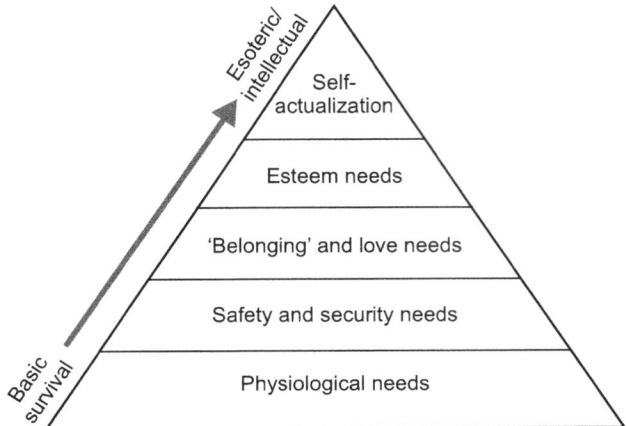

Figure 33.1 Abraham Maslow's hierarchy of human needs

Maslow's theory asserts that all people are motivated to satisfy five human needs, beginning at the bottom level of the pyramid with the very basic needs for survival (such as food and clean drinking water). These human needs are universal regardless of race, background, education or gender. Contrary to some popular thinking, money is not always the principal motivator.

Maslow's work can still serve programme and project managers as a useful reminder, helping us to understand individuals' motives. However, the needs of a particular individual will clearly be affected by personal factors such as length of employment, level of experience and skills, current function and responsibilities, family pressures, age and so on. These are not just idle wants or desires but profound needs that motivate every choice we make, whether consciously or subconsciously.

Kurt Lewin

Kurt Lewin (1890–1947) hypothesized that human behaviour is a function of the person and the environment. He produced a model known as the 'SOBC sequence'. This shows how to consider and review individual human behaviour systematically in organizations with relevance to the four SOBC factors, which occur in the following sequence:

1. **Stimulus.** This refers to stimuli from the work situation such as light, sounds, job demands, supervisors, co-workers' characteristics and equipment.
2. **Organism.** Characteristics of the person, including personality, needs, attitudes, values and intentions.
3. **Behaviour.** Behaviour and actions of the person in the situation under consideration.
4. **Consequences** or outcomes associated with the behavioural responses.

Now, of course, the question arises 'How can a programme manager or project manager apply this SOBC theory in real life?'

One can differentiate and monitor various individual performances (in the B for behaviour category) according to numerous factors, some of which you might be able to control. So the programme or project manager can change stimuli (S) to things like creating new goals (which does not mean setting impossible performance targets but spelling out the outcomes that are needed), setting up incentive schemes and identifying employees who need training.

Next, one can attempt to modify the human organism, for example by performing a trial run based on newly created work requirements. Once that task is completed it demonstrates the individual's behaviour (B), and then you can review, recognize and reward the consequent performance (C). If all that sounds somewhat complicated and unclear, here is a simple example to demonstrate the practical use of this theory.

Jack, a senior project manager, is 50 years old and has been with his company for 25 years since obtaining his electrical engineering degree. Jack has seen many strategic initiatives fail after being handled by new managers. Those unsuccessful managers have left the company. Now Jack has become pessimistic about everything and has a tendency to distrust management decisions, new managers and every new strategic initiative.

Now suppose that you are Jack's newly appointed programme manager. How might you use Lewin's SOBC model to motivate Jack to perform well in his project?

First you must find new stimuli that will fit Jack's individuality. As things stand, he is not really motivated to accept another person's ideas or initiatives. Would giving Jack a new title, promotion or incentives work? That would benefit Jack in the short term, but most likely he will eventually come back and complain that things are not working out.

Matching Jack's needs and ideas to your programme vision and goal should work. But before you even start sharing your programme vision and goals with him, you must allow time and listen to his stories about past company successes and failures and the lessons that might be learned from them. That dialogue will help you to begin building trust with Jack. It should also benefit you, as the new programme manager, to have a better idea of the 'devils in the detail' that the programme must address. Once Jack knows that you are listening to him seriously, and that you want to find a better way to meet his objections, he can begin to help you with ideas of how to do it.

Understanding how people can react to change

To understand how people react to change, you must first know yourself and your possible responses as the senior manager who will be partly or wholly responsible for implementing a change programme. Figure 33.2 (adapted from the work of Elisabeth Kübler Ross [1926–2004]) illustrates the sequence of responses that you might experience. This is a *controllable* change – you will be in control and be expected to implement the change yourself. Being aware of these possibilities will help you to overcome negativity and possibly also understand and deal with the responses of those who report to you.

Figure 33.2 is explained as follows:

1. *Uninformed optimism.* Knowing little about the change, you are optimistic and make positive assumptions. You might pass this optimism on to your juniors. You might even be tempted to give them assurances that you subsequently have to retract.

2. *Informed pessimism.* As you learn more you realize that your initial optimism was unfounded. You begin to question some or all of the changes. You must remain positive to your staff but you are developing a different (hidden) agenda.

3. *Checking out.* You probe and ask challenging questions about the change. You cannot believe that the proposals are true. If they seem to be irrational, you suspect that you might not have the whole agenda. You might begin to deny that the changes will happen, at least not in their proposed form. You might even be tempted to share these doubts with your staff, declaring 'There are some silly ideas in these changes but they are misguided and certainly they will not happen. In any case, I shall not let them happen.'

4. *Informed realism (OR) or opt-out.* You realize that the changes will happen and that you will have to face up to the situation. It is possible at this stage that you could elect to rebel and refuse to implement the changes. You might try to use your authority and your sponsor to block the project. That could end in your dismissal or dismal departure from the organization. But you might learn more of the hidden agenda and begin to accept the change. Now you must decide to change your position in relation to your staff. Can you share the whole agenda with them? If not, you might have to risk becoming a turncoat and having to accept loss of loyalty and criticism from your staff.

5. *Affirmed realism.* You convert to the new agenda and begin to see the advantages of the changes. Now you start to help make the change happen. You guide your staff in the right direction. That will not be easy. Making change happen effectively often means wiping out the old visions and throwing out deeply rooted traditions. Not easy. The process of rooting out bad traditions is very important.

Now consider a different situation, where you are not a senior manager but are a junior and vulnerable member of staff. You hear about the new programme and some of the proposed changes. You believe that you will have no control over the changes

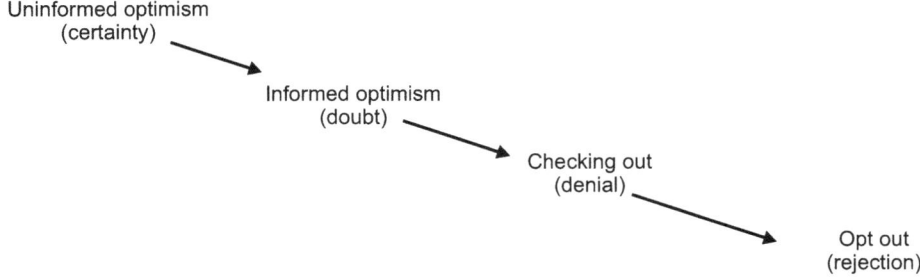

Figure 33.2 Typical human responses to a controllable change

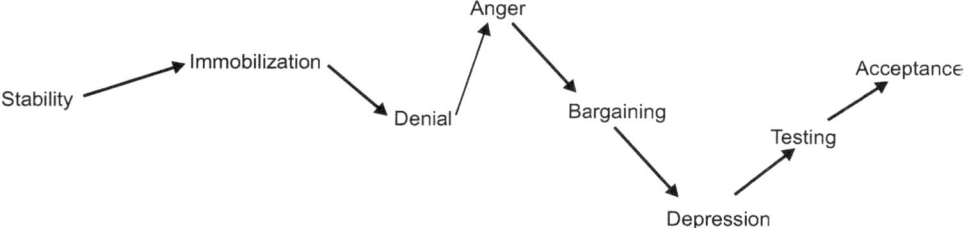

Figure 33.3 Typical human responses to uncontrollable change

and so will lose control over your future in the organization. You will probably go through the stages shown in Figure 33.3 (again adapted from the work of Elisabeth Kübler Ross), as follows:

1. *Stability.* You carry on as usual, not wanting to believe that the change will happen. You hear only what you want to hear.
2. *Immobilization.* You eventually 'get the message' and realize that the change will inevitably affect you. Metaphorically you freeze. This is like the moment of awful lucidity that happens when you are gravely injured. You know that you are about to feel pain, but right now it's painless and you can think clearly.
3. *Denial.* The news is so bad that you decide it cannot be true. You are likely to tell other people that it is not true, and that it cannot be going to happen. 'This can't happen to me (or us) because . . .'. Both this and the previous immobilization stage could possibly contribute to the natural selection process in nature, giving the threatened organism longer to think and postponing emotions that might cloud judgement about the best course of action. This state has allowed severely injured people to remain conscious and struggle over considerable distances to seek help.
4. *Anger.* In a surge of emotion you attack the idea of the change. When you are managing a project or a programme never underestimate the anger that impending change can create in some people. Two of us (DL and AF) have both witnessed scenes where such anger has erupted into actual physical violence.
5. *Bargaining.* When anger proves futile the emotion subsides and is replaced by attempts to make a deal or plead your way out of the change. 'OK. I realize that I shall have to make time for retraining but couldn't we put that off until . . .?' Or perhaps 'Fine. I know that the change is necessary, but my department could carry on if we just made this (and this) adjustment. We shouldn't throw the baby out with the bathwater should we? Just give me a little more time, that's all I ask.'
6. *Depression.* When anger and bargaining are in vain, you accept defeat and become depressed. People in this state might try to escape from the situation entirely. They contemplate leaving their job, and might actually do so.
7. *Testing.* If you cannot decide, or simply do not get round to getting out, you are likely to start to explore what the change will actually mean. You will test to see if there is any way in which you could make it acceptable. Maybe your future

new boss could be tolerated. Perhaps you could move house to that new location after all. Perhaps the children could withstand a change of schools. Maybe it's worth hanging on just for the job. These reactions are possible whenever there is a chance (no matter how small) to turn the change to your personal advantage.

8. *Acceptance*. Inevitably you will accept the change if you persevere. Sooner or later it will just become your new way of life. Perhaps it will turn out to be not as bad as you feared. Perhaps there are ways in which you will be able to make it tolerable or even turn it to your own advantage.

The important thing to know, remember, plan for and manage as a project or programme manager is that no matter how trivially *you* think the change will affect other people, you cannot know exactly what they imagine or what the change is going to mean to them. They will all go through one of the above change response cycles. Planning and managing their responses is as much part of your programme as the IT and other work. Consider how they can be mentored through their decision about whether to stay or leave. Failure to take account of people's reactions to the changes expected of them is a fundamental cause of lost return on investment.

The remainder of this chapter gives practical advice on ensuring that people will be motivated to accept forthcoming changes. The complement of that is to ensure that people will not be demotivated or frightened by forthcoming changes (or by unfounded rumours about changes under consideration).

The ways in which people in organizations will respond to impending changes depend very greatly on how information about those changes is imparted to them. Information needs to be managed, just as much as any other aspect of a change initiative.

Rumours and unfounded gossip

It has been known for a long time that one way to induce rumours and even panic among people in a large office is to have two strangers wearing grey suits and carrying clipboards appear in their midst carrying tape measures. They might be there simply to carry out an insurance valuation, but the people in the office will not know that. Instead they will suspect that the men with tape measures herald an unknown change, and they will of course believe that change can only be for the worse. Then rumours can spread through an entire organizing, gaining strength in the process.

Now suppose that you are a member of the top management in an organization, and you are contemplating a number of alternative business cases for a possible strategic change programme. It could be a merger or an acquisition or a complete change in all the company's IT systems. For this argument, suppose that your company is considering the idea of relocating away from the centre of London. Nothing has yet been decided.

One of us (DL) was once involved as a middle manager in a company that was going through this process. Senior managers visited towns and cities in various parts of England to research such things as living conditions, communications, schools, availability of skilled people and so on. This was only a study. Yet news leaked out to the general workforce. Rumours spread. People could be observed standing in little groups discussing what might happen, with some declaring that the new location would be this town or that. Productivity dropped like a stone, with people focusing their attention not on their daily tasks but on what they suspected was their uncertain future.

In the event, although the company had chosen and reserved a building plot in Newbury, the business case did not support the move and the organization remained in its existing London offices.

The lesson learned from this real case is that all initial schemes for any intended change programme must be considered in private, and not divulged to the workforce. This is not deception. It is simply a sensible way of preventing damaging rumours and unnecessary gloom and despondency. So until a business case has been established and approved for a major change, complete confidentiality is important.

This confidentiality will probably be easier to arrange when external consultants are doing the initial investigations and preparing the business case. If the work is to be done in-house, then a small dedicated team can be formed, but they should do their work quietly and privately, if necessary away from the company's main offices.

Of course, when a business case has been approved and the change will go ahead, senior management must arrange for open communication and discussions with staff, prevent rumours, spread the truth, and begin to encourage everyone's cooperation in making the future change work.

Communicating for programme success

The fallacy of setting financial targets

The Scottish-based company Isochron recognizes positive results from a change programme when the accounts or other performance figures reveal significant improvements in a business organization. Isochron calls each positive result a 'value flashpoint' in the programme. But although clearly important and highlighting benefits from the programme, these are deliberately *not* set as targets for people to achieve: rather they are outcomes resulting from improvements in the organization caused by the change programme.

Setting targets will not necessarily improve personal or organizational performance and can actually have a negative effect. That is often apparent, for example, when a national government or one of its departments sets targets for improvement. Those targets and the good intentions behind them might appeal to the electorate but in practice target-setting by itself will most often produce unwanted behaviours and effects.

So, if target-setting cannot be recommended, what is the alternative? People need to be given a mental picture of the future, showing them how the forthcoming changes will affect their working lives for the better in one way or another. Just as the organization has *its* vision, so the individual people in it need *theirs*. They can then decide for themselves whether they want to be a part of that future with all its upsides and downsides, or to risk changing to a different job.

Managing the mindsets

Organizations grow legends (stories based on past truths) and myths (untrue stories) about themselves. When people join an organization they are relatively free from all these stories. But as they settle to their new jobs they learn about these legends and myths and eventually become influenced by them.

One of us, when lecturing to management students, asked for reasons why their projects failed. Many reasons were given, filling flipchart sheets. Then the same students were asked to give reasons why their projects succeeded. Far fewer answers were forthcoming. From some groups no answers came at all. Their acquired myth was that their projects usually fail, and they had no reason to report success. They had learned to repeat failure.

Fortunately it is possible to demonstrate the reverse. If a story of success can be created, actual success will begin to happen. Some years ago one of us (AF) was working on an analysis of past successful projects in a government ministry. It became clear that a small number of large projects were widely regarded as being particularly successful. In each of these successful cases the project manager was regarded as a maverick – someone who did things radically differently and had the 'brass neck' to override customary procedures. When these managers were put in charge of programmes and projects, success was expected and failure was not an option. So success resulted. Unfortunately, 'different' behaviour is not always appreciated and that organization selectively removed its mavericks.

When managing change we have to create a detailed picture of what success will look like, and we must then communicate that picture widely and thoroughly. That will begin to harness the power of all those people who will be affected by the change programme in some way. It is often forgotten that people find it just as hard to forget things as to remember them. A vision of the successful future, represented in this case by achievement of all the programme objectives, can be unforgettable. Once heard (and remembered), that vision works away in the minds of everyone involved, guiding countless micro-decisions taken during people's day-to-day work.

The programme manager has to nurse this vision of success to make sure that powerfully entrenched failure legends and myths do not rise up and overwhelm the vision. Apart from being a positive and inspiring leader radiating certainty about the successful outcome, the programme manager can work out the 'show-me' outcomes (Isochron calls these 'recognition events') and positive measures of the vision (called 'value flashpoints' in Isochron's technology) and cement these into the programme plan. Taken together, these help to spell out the benefits of the programme in a real and personal way. Tasks will then grow on and around the recognition events and so align them with the successful outcome.

Experience-related performance

The results that people achieve in their daily work are directly related to the way they behave in response to events. In turn, the way they behave is directly related to how they feel and believe about events. Two examples follow to illustrate this point.

Example 1: pessimism and a negative outlook

Suppose that a person learns that, as a result of a change programme, his or her post is to be made redundant. Suppose further that this person had experienced a previous, past, painful redundancy, with a period of nine difficult months spent seeking a new job. Self-esteem and confidence had collapsed, with the person's family suffering financial distress, gloom and despondency. People who have endured such an experience fear that the same thing could happen again. So they feel both angry and depressed when they learn of a new change. They behave irritably and spread their depression to their co-workers.

Such a person might seek a meeting with his manager to express critical feelings about the company and demand better treatment. The manager in such a case, who is engaged in trying to make the change programme a success, will be upset and perhaps even retaliate with annoyance and strong words. As the aggrieved employee leaves the room the irritated manager might make a firm mental note to arrange dismissal as soon as the opportunity arises, arranging for the minimum deal the company can afford. The employee's pessimism, a product of his painful past experience, has contributed to his own fate in a clear case of a self-fulfilling prophecy.

Example 2: optimism and a positive outlook

In the same company as the previous example, imagine that another employee in similar circumstance to the person just described learns that her post will no longer exist when the change programme ends. But this person, although having been made redundant once before, was able to secure a better job almost immediately. So, with this new job and most of the allowances from the previous redundancy still in the bank, the first redundancy was one of the best things to happen to her financially. It has even been possible to describe those events to family and friends as a personal success. Consequently, she will be less upset by prospects of a new redundancy, knowing the possibility that the successful outcome of the previous event will be repeated.

Now imagine what might happen when this person's manager calls her in for interview. The employee exudes confidence and is cooperative. This positive and constructive attitude towards the change programme and the future will impress the manager. When she leaves the room the manager will make a mental note to try to support her, perhaps by arranging for career guidance and assisting her in finding a better role.

So, if we can help people affected by a change programme to have positive beliefs about the future, a positive outcome will be far more likely. Of course that can never be certain. But even the lack of certainty can be turned to advantage by opportunity analysis and preparing contingency plans. It need not be allowed to become a self-fulfilling prophecy of failure.

The induction of commitment to a successful outcome and positive beliefs about the future will be noticed by observers as a change in attitude. Following from the above argument, changes of attitude are based on communicating new and up-to-date facts. How often have you heard people say 'If only I had known (those facts that I now know) I would have behaved differently.' Different behaviour is what we

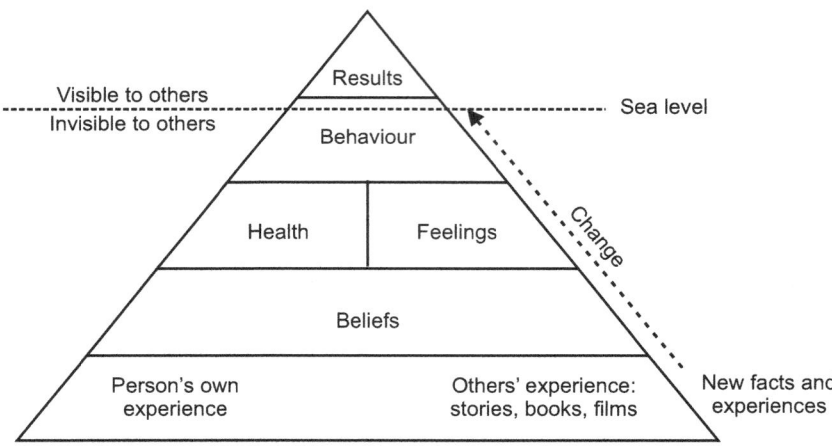

Figure 33.4 Understanding where people are coming from (the iceberg)

want, so sharing facts is a tool for change. These facts, in turn, influence beliefs, and so feelings, and thence behaviours and results (see Figure 33.4).

Ways of making change happen

At one time in the 1970s the public in Scotland were faced with no fewer than six proposals for policy changes in education at the same time. Now, it is possible for voters to lobby their Members of Parliament to object to one change, with a small chance that they will succeed in blocking it. But if the voters attempted to resist two change proposals they would have less chance of success. Try to oppose all six changes and, short of outright rebellion, they would stand no chance. The lesson from this for programme managers is that if you need to drive a change programme it is more effective to have a broad agenda to drive all its changes at once.

Using force alone

Most programmes operate by forcing change on to people. The executive board decides that change is necessary and decrees that it shall happen. Senior management implement it with gritted teeth and a message 'Get on with it or get out!' This common approach has two disadvantages:

1. It requires enormous effort and organization to set up and deliver the broad agenda.
2. It is confrontational. Pushing people to change will polarize attitudes and maximize resistance.

Although some people enjoy fighting and winning, most are uncomfortable about imposing their will on others too conspicuously. We tend to prefer a democratic approach based on persuasion and presentation of facts.

The carrot and stick approach

A modification of the forceful (or push) approach to change just described is to use the 'carrot and stick'. We can change people's perceptions so they believe their current situation is, or is about to become, intolerable. 'If we do not make these changes, the company will have to close all its UK factories and make all of you redundant. So, you see, you must accept these changes and new working conditions. You really have no alternative.'

Equally, at the same time, the organization can make people perceive that the alternative future is bright and irresistibly pleasurable – the carrot! 'These new terms and conditions will give those who remain higher consolidated basic pay. Overtime hours will disappear without financial loss, so you will have more leisure and family time. Imagine the improved working conditions. There will be opportunities for you to learn new skills. With the new streamlined organization you can expect opportunities for promotion to really exciting and rewarding jobs.'

However, the iron fist of compulsion still underlies the change programme in this 'carrot and stick' approach, giving the victim of change no option other than to comply.

Alternatives to the use of force

Force (push) is a temptingly simple way of making change happen. But even setting aside any moral scruples it is economically inefficient – that is to say expensive. So we need to find alternatives. Two case examples follow.

Case 1

One of us (AF) was required to make fundamental changes in an organization of 7,000 people working in 35 offices. The time allowed was five months and no special budget was allowed. A challenge indeed.

The first thought was, 'If I use the traditional programme approach this will be impossible. But if I perceive myself as having 7,000 people to do the project with, then it becomes feasible.' This change programme was achieved successfully by taking the following radical steps:

1. Designing the future state of the company in detail.
2. Describing practical, personal vignettes of how the future would be recognized when it happened.
3. Communicating the future state to everyone who was going to be affected (which meant all of the 7,000 people).
4. Setting up a communication network that would help people to achieve the change.
5. Implementing changes to the people's work environment (accommodation, procedures and eventually, although it was not on the critical path, the technology).

Certainly an element of force was used. A relatively small (but significant) number of new posts were created and some old posts were removed. A small number of people were promoted into more senior posts and a number of senior people moved. The main task, however, was to communicate the vision of the future and then provide the help that people need to change to meet it. That is the exact opposite of the traditional method using force.

With this approach, people have the future described to them in personal terms until they reach the future state today in their minds. They are then helped to pull their current state towards the future state, while the environment changes around them.

Case 2

Being the 'victim' of change in a non-forceful (pull) programme is quite different from being in a forceful (push) programme. To get an idea of this, consider the following case.

The organization involved in Case 1 had earlier decided to change the working methods in one of its units. It commissioned a professionally made training video to demonstrate the required changes. Actors in the video performed tasks in the new ways, but the scene was set in the office environment familiar to the real workers.

During one sequence in the video the actors spoke to each other in Spanish, without any subtitles. 'That's right', said the management to those watching the video. 'We shall need you to be able to speak with our clients in Spanish, because that is the language of over half our business world.' That had desired effect of getting the people watching the video to ask 'Where can I get my training in Spanish?' This was in stark contrast to the reaction that would have resulted from push methods, with disgruntled people saying 'I don't have time to go on any training – let me get on with my day job.'

Lessons learned from cases 1 and 2

These two cases exploited the human brain's capacity to imagine itself in a future state. When we watch a film or a video, especially when it uses a storyline, music and visual cues that involve us emotionally, we actually change our personality a little for an hour or so afterwards. It is if we had lived in a short while in the world shown in the film and we had shared some of the emotional experiences. Capitalizing on this effect can accelerate and simplify change when we use the non-forceful 'pull' option rather than the forceful 'push' tactics.

However, most (perhaps 90 per cent) of the changed perceptions are short-lived. In a change programme it is necessary not only to prolong these changed perceptions, but also to make the change permanent. We can do that by telling the people concerned that the most senior managers will be coming back later to look for (and recognize and reward) the changes that have been so vividly predicted and imagined.

Inspecting and measuring change

It is a principle of change management that 'whatsoever we measure we get'. Isochron's 'pull' approach to change programmes is not trying in the first instance to measure numerical targets so much as to inspect and recognize matters of fact. These are the 'recognition events' (show-me outcomes that clearly signal achievements of the programme's end goals) and 'value flashpoints' (when financial or other performance figures can be seen to improve clearly as a direct result of the programme).

Conclusion

Programme managers need to appreciate that the workforce is not so much an obstacle, but a force for change if its day-to-day efforts can be redirected to the new goals. Human beings are complex individuals. Motivating them towards any desired business outcome is not always straightforward. We have the work of past management theorists to help us in that understanding.

Success in change programmes cannot happen without the willing cooperation of all the people involved. Good communications are essential, which means not only imparting positive information about the programme at the right time, but also not allowing false information (rumours) to spread through the organization to demotivate everyone and make the possibility of obtaining the intended benefits far more difficult.

Much of this chapter outlines some of the practices developed by Isochron and tested and applied in its clients' change programmes (although here to give only a short summary of those methods).

It is commonly accepted that every company should have its vision of the future for success. But the message in this chapter is that the organization will perform better and manage its change programmes far more effectively if all its employees are moving towards a clear, personal, tangible 'show-me' vision of the future rather than being beaten over the head with targets or threatened with 'change or get out'.

Acknowledgement

We are very grateful to Alan Fowler's company Isochron for granting us permission to describe just a few techniques of the Isochron 'D4' methods in this chapter and for allowing us to quote extensively from Fowler and Lock (2006).

References and further reading

Fowler, A. and Lock, D. (2006), *Accelerating Business and IT Change: Transforming Project Delivery*, Farnham: Gower.

Johnson, S. (2000), *Who Moved My Cheese?*, London: Vermillion (Ebury Press).

Lock, D. (2013a), 'Management Theorists of the Twentieth Century', in D. Lock and L. Scott (eds.), *Handbook of People in Project Management*, Farnham: Gower.

Lock, D. (2013b), *Project Management*, 10th edn., Fanham: Gower.

Wong, Z. (2007), *Human Factors in Project Management*, San Francisco: John Wiley.

Chapter 34

Managing Partners in Programmes

Hubertus C. Tuczek and Jürgen Frank

Larger programmes are typically promoted by partners who share resources, funding and risks and are directly involved in the programme. On the one hand they are defining and regulating the work and on the other hand they are also contributing directly to programmes. Hence they influence the definition, planning and outcomes of most programmes. Main partners in programmes are usually market participants in customer and supplier relationships. Non-profit organizations or authorities can also be involved. By defining requirements, delivering know-how and products, or approving and releasing programme deliverables, partners play a crucial role for the success of programmes.

Introduction

To ensure a prosperous partnership, programmes have to manage the following dimensions:

1. Strategy/motivation: aligned understanding of strategic objectives and benefits of the partner cooperation as well as the programme responsible persons.
2. Relationship: defined scope of expectations, committed resources, defined roles and responsibilities, agreed ways of communication and decision-making.
3. Cooperation: contractual agreements, programme management guidelines including reporting and control standards, organizational processes, procedures and systems.

The main tools to organize cooperation with partners in programmes are:

- Detailed communication plan that includes frequency of meetings, definition and description of interfaces and agreement on management of these interfaces.
- Transparent and realistic planning in regards to timing, committed scope of delivery and agreed form of progress tracking and completion control.
- Committed controlling of deliverables like maturity of products and process results.
- Clear definition of change / claim management including contact persons, documentation and agreed and committed response time.
- Regular synchronization meetings to share information on status and progress openly in order to identify deviations in early stages and define collective measures.

For the successful delivery of programme objectives in a partnership, it is essential to perform on the highest level in all three dimensions of motivation, relationship and cooperation. Typically, you are faced with institutions with their own interests and agendas. They need to be aligned for a common goal by making sure that a clear commitment on the expected outcome is given from the beginning to the end. You will be faced with many conflicting situations along the programme work. The decision-makers of the involved partners need to be identified – those who will be able to help the programme over the hurdles without delay. The relationships between these decision-makers need to be built at the beginning of the programme, so that in a crisis a common understanding is possible. The level of formal documentation depends on the nature of the programme, but here as well the argument of early and transparent clarification is valid. A programme team with a joint spirit will assure the expected result.

In general, no company or institution can afford to work on larger programmes just on its own in these days of global cooperation. Today, companies share the different tasks of the value chain with other companies around the globe. Even though sometimes large distances have to be overcome, cooperation along the value chain is typically more efficient than one company covering all the tasks.

This of course increases the dependencies between the partners and creates high demand for an intense exchange of information and close cooperation. The management of such cross-company collaboration challenges has become an extremely important strategic success factor for the competitive ability of an organization in all branches.

Many different topics have to be dealt with. Besides clarifying the technical dimension, legal questions have to be thoroughly investigated. How do you set up a contract between partners? How do you exchange sensible information that used to be treated as a business secret? How do you deal with the breach of such agreements?

One key element for successful collaboration lies in the building of a true partnership between foreign organizations. How do you organize trust, when companies have their own strategies and agendas? How do you cope with different management concepts and processes? Cultural differences between the partners increase the complexity of involved management challenges. To help us discuss successful approaches for the management of partners in programmes we introduce the three-level model shown in Figure 34.1.

The strategic level of the involved institutions and authorities influences the motivation of the partners for a common programme. Potential strategic conflicts need to be understood and clarified. Individual people (as well as organizations) have to cooperate for the execution of a programme. The management and the respective decision-makers play a crucial role for success. The cooperation level consists of the programme and project teams and their processes for smooth execution. A high level of competence is needed for complex programme work with challenging targets.

Strategic level

When we talk about partners being market participants in customer and supplier relationships, non-profit organizations or authorities, we need to consider and understand the driving forces behind the motivation for these independent

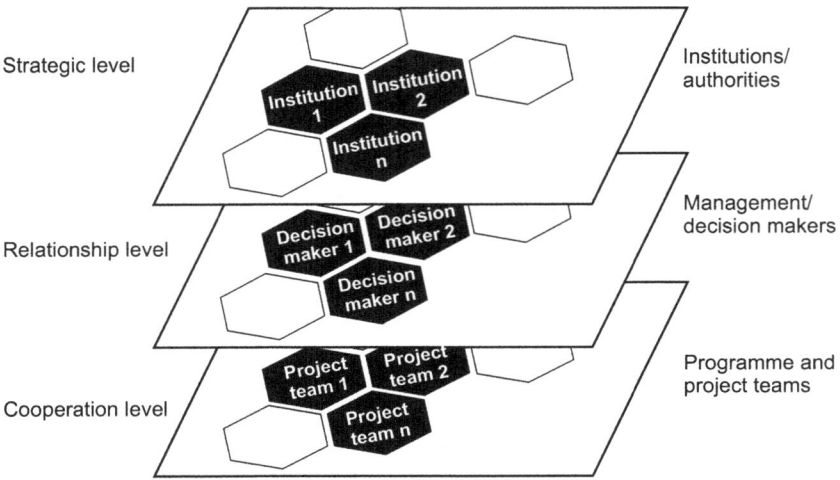

Figure 34.1 Three-level concept for the management of partners in programmes

organizations to engage in a common programme. This happens on a strategic level because every organization has its own strategy and goals. The motivation of every partner in the cooperation needs to lead to an aligned understanding of strategic objectives and benefits of the joint programme. This has to be assured in the early stage of programme definition, when strategic objectives still can be formed. Successful programme execution needs a win-win situation for the various business models of the partners.

Strategy formation and alignment

Strategy defines the direction and scope of an organization over the long term. It is supposed to lead to advantages over competitors in a given market environment. The corresponding configuration of resources and competencies is the key success factor. The individual strategies of the partner organizations come together when a common programme is formed. Each partner is motivated by concrete objectives derived from his or her own strategy to participate in a joint approach with joint goals.

Typically, partners in a programme operate in the same market. This can lead to overlapping or even conflicting strategies that must be clearly sorted out before the start of a common programme. Otherwise, these conflicts will infect the programme and cause failure.

Change of strategies and surrounding conditions

The dynamics of global markets and the global environment in general lead to fast-changing surrounding conditions for the participating institutions. As a consequence, strategies have to be reviewed on a regular basis and adapted if necessary. This also changes the environment for a programme. There are two choices:

1. The programme continues as agreed upon at the beginning.
2. The change in surrounding strategies is reflected within the programme objectives.

Both of these approaches result in additional challenges for the programme. This becomes very obvious in large public programmes. They are derived from a long-term strategy, political constellations and technical opportunities. The cost for these programmes is high. Changes can even double the cost. Involved authorities and companies are still learning to cope better with these challenges.

Executing the strategy

Various hurdles have to be overcome to execute a strategy successfully. Empirical investigations have revealed that over one third of the performance of an organization is lost by shortfalls in the planning and execution process (Mankins and Steele, 2005). One main difficulty can arise from inadequate or unavailable resources. Others are:

*   poor communication of the strategy;
*   actions required for execution not clearly defined;
*   unclear accountabilities;
*   organizational silos and culture blocking execution;
*   inadequate performance monitoring;
*   inadequate consequences for failures;
*   inadequate rewards for success;
*   poor and uncommitted leadership.

All these aspects are relevant for successful execution of a programme. Especially when different partners with individual cultures are involved, the strategic alignment as well as the quality of the planning and execution process form the foundation for successful programme work.

Relationship level

Decisions drive business and programmes. Decisions are based on communication. At the beginning of a programme the agreed ways of communication and decision-making need to be defined. This is relevant for the programme leaders and the programme teams. Also the decision-makers in the hierarchy of the involved organizations need to be clearly identified.

The decision-makers have to be aligned to a common goal by making sure that a clear commitment on the expected outcome is given from the beginning to the end. As you will be faced with many conflicting situations along the programme work, the decision-makers have to be prepared to help the programme over these hurdles without time delay. The relationships between these decision-makers need to be built at the beginning of the programme so that in a crisis mode a common understanding is found.

The culture and personality as well as the individual interests of the decision-makers will influence the programme work. Stakeholder analysis is a helpful tool for the project manager to understand the programme environment.

Stakeholder management

Stakeholder management is a very important part of project and programme management. There are many tools and templates available that discuss the analysis and handling of stakeholders. Stakeholder management is mainly focused on influencing people or organizations towards positive support of a project or programme.

Management of partners has a different, more interwoven approach. Partners have mutual interests. They cooperate to advance their common goals. But cooperating companies also have conflicting interests. Hence it is essential for the success of a programme to understand and manage these common goals and conflicting interests.

One should expect that the attitude of the involved partners towards the programme will generally be positive. However, the various partners may have different views about the strategic importance of an individual programme, and priorities can change over time. That has a direct impact on the committed resources and should be monitored closely. Partners with a high level of influence need to push the programme and the other involved partners to fulfil the committed objectives. On the other hand, the programme team must ensure that the stakeholder expectations are met, and that continuous support is provided.

In Figure 34.2, the left-hand side shows how stakeholders can be identified in the different areas of the internal organization, and with others who have interests in the programme (such as society, government and customers). The right-hand side shows how to classify the individual stakeholders (named here as A to I) in a two-dimensional matrix. Their levels of influence are ranked from 1 to 5, and the

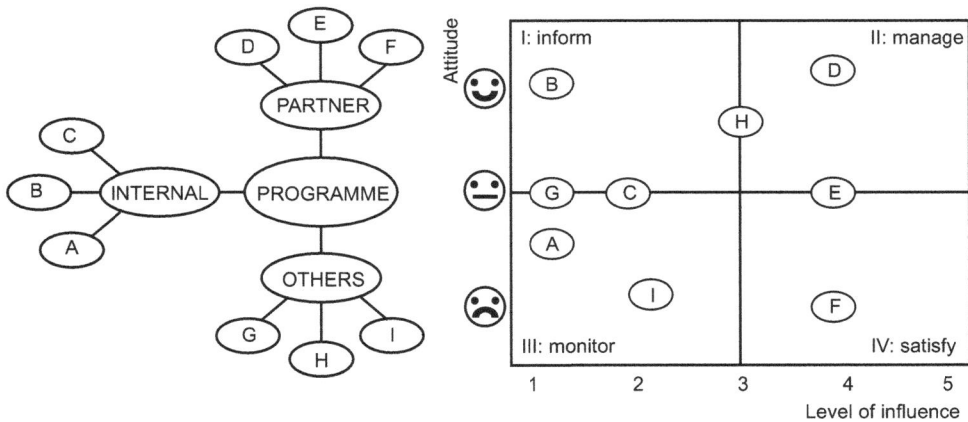

Figure 34.2 Concept for stakeholder analysis

little face images indicate their attitude towards the project (positive, neutral, negative). The relevant quadrant then indicates the recommended strategy.

Setting up communication

As a prerequisite for a smooth cooperation between partners, the defined scope of expectations, the committed resources and the roles and responsibilities need to be agreed in detail. To ensure good collaboration between the persons involved at every partner and every level of the different operational programmes, the following main processes have to be defined and understood between the responsible persons of all partners:

- programme management;
- data creation and release;
- prototype creation and release;
- product/service creation and release;
- change and claim management.

All important activities (including the achievement of milestones or deviation from planned accomplishments in a programme) initiate an interaction chain involving different people and roles from every partner. To identify these persons, a cooperation matrix indicating the required roles should be established along the lines of that shown in Figure 34.3.

Roles/ main tasks	Programme/company		Partner 1	Partner 2	Meetings
Role 1					**Meeting 1**
Task 1	Name representative	Form of coordination	Name representative	Name representative	Agenda/content
Task 2	*Function*	*Meeting*	*Function*	*Function*	Coordinator
Task 3	*Phone*	*Issues list*	*Phone*	*Phone*	Participants
Task 4	*Email*		*Email*	*Email*	When
and so on					Duration
Role 2					**Meeting 2**
Task 1	Name representative	Form of coordination	Name representative	Name representative	Agenda/content
Task 2	*Function*	*Meeting*	*Function*	*Function*	Coordinator
Task 3	*Phone*	*Issues list*	*Phone*	*Phone*	Participants
Task 4	*Email*		*Email*	*Email*	When
and so on					Duration
Role n					**Meeting n**
Task 1	Name representative	Form of coordination	Name representative	Name representative	Agenda/content
Task 2	*Function*	*Meeting*	*Function*	*Function*	Coordinator
Task 3	*Phone*	*Issues list*	*Phone*	*Phone*	Participants
Task 4	*Email*		*Email*	*Email*	When
and so on					Duration

Core team meeting
Agenda/content
Coordinator
Participants
When
Duration

Figure 34.3 Cooperation matrix with meeting planner

Project:		Status			Board	Number
		Red	Amber	Green		

Picture:	Situation:	Distribution:
Supporting picture or screen shot.	*Detailed description of the situation.*	*Names and job titles of the addressees.*
		Follow up: Date:

Root cause analysis:

Note: for root cause determination the 'Five Whys' method can be used here.

Measures:	Impact:
Description of proposed measures.	*Time. cost, scope and so on.*

Decision/ recommendation: *For example, change approved, follow up in one month.*

Figure 34.4 An escalation and decision template

To ensure accurate and fast decision-making, escalation has to be planned. Besides defining the roles during escalation in the cooperation matrix, part of this planning is to clarify criteria, procedure, rules and applicable documentation for escalation. Escalation without proper documentation does not solve issues, but shows only problems. Proper preparation and documentation of an escalation is necessary in order to reach and record decisions. This includes root cause analysis, prioritization, measure definition and evaluation as well as the decision proposal. The example in Figure 34.4 shows how to incorporate all necessary information into one escalation and decision document.

Contract management

A joint programme of partners is a declaration of the will to work together. Contracts build the framework and define the rules for cooperation. They create the base for a common understanding of the future programme work and therefore should be developed alongside the beginning of the definition of a programme. The contract management process is outlined in Figure 34.5.

Neglect of contract management is a common source of trouble in programme management. Contracts are not solely the responsibility of the legal department.

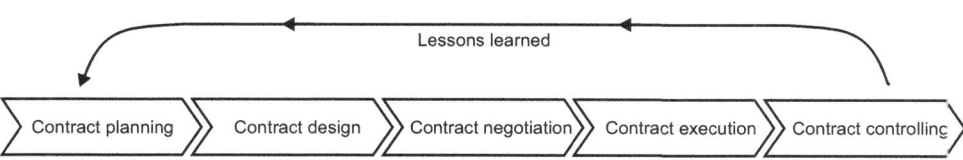

Figure 34.5 The process of contract management

They require a joint effort of all involved functions and departments, led by the programme leader. The necessary contracts and their contents have to be planned well in advance, so that they do not generate a bottleneck in the critical phase of programme agreement.

In the global context of contract management the first step is to identify the applicable law. The Anglo-Saxon part of the world is home to a common law (case law), which differs significantly from the civil law applied in most parts of Europe. The continental European legal logic has a long tradition and roots back to the Roman law of ancient times. Therefore, the developed general law system builds a strong foundation for individual contracts. Contents defined by the general civil law follow a pattern and do not have to be formulated in a contract again. Contracts in an Anglo-American environment typically cover legal aspects in more detail, which makes the contracts longer. In Asia, there is no such tradition for legal systems, which also results in a different attitude towards contracts.

One option in the membership states of the convention is the application of the international UN sales law CISG (CISG – United Nations Convention on Contracts for the International Sale of Goods). The UN sales law has existed since 1980 and is now widespread. The prerequisite for application would be, though, that the CISG law can be enforced in the home country of the business partner. In some emerging countries the knowledge of judges at the local courts for this international law is not sufficiently developed. The practical alternative is to choose an arbitration court. For example, this might be the CIETAC – the arbitration court in Shanghai for China.

Contract management covers all activities of planning and organizing a contract over the whole programme lifecycle. It is a holistic task – the contract manager needs to oversee all aspects associated with creating and realizing the contract with all involved parties.

The planning phase is most important. All the facts of the case must be collected and the contract objectives have to be defined. Further tasks are identifying contract risks, considering expert opinions, agreeing on persons in charge and timing. Contract design will determine the contract structure and draft wording. Subsequently the processes for review and release of the documents are arranged.

Negotiation can take place during this preparation, for which a defined negotiation strategy is advisable. Management of claims will have high priority during programme execution. The handling of changes often makes or breaks a successful programme. A professional approach that also takes care of potential disruptions in the programme is absolutely key.

Control includes tracking of the most important contract contents (cancellation period, scope of work, invoicing and so on) and the periodical revision of the contract work. Implementing a 'lessons learned' process guarantees continuous risk reduction and assist smooth execution of the contract management.

Cultural issues between international partners

International contract management in programmes can greatly increase complexity. Partners from different countries will have different perspectives on handling programmes and on the world in general. These cultural aspects are reflected on all three levels of strategy, relationship and cooperation and directly influence the functioning of the programme teams. Coping with these diverse cultures means that a profound understanding of the specific characteristics of every partner is essential. With in-depth knowledge of the cultural interplay, this challenge can be transformed into a benefit for cooperation within a programme.

An open mind and curiosity are good starting points for effective handling of intercultural interaction. According to Trompenaars and Hampden-Turner (1997) our culture is defined by explicit and implicit dimensions which are connected by norms and values (Figure 34.6). The outside view of a culture (explicit) is represented by the obvious realities of language, food, clothes, buildings, products, behaviours and so on.

While communities of people have developed in different geographic regions of the world they have formed diverse basic assumptions, which were originally driven by the impulse for survival. They are the result of each group's effort to overcome the imposed challenges. From these basic assumptions norms and values were derived. They define what is good and bad for the society and give a guideline on how to behave for the benefit of the community. As foreigners, we see the explicit expressions of these historically evolved norms and values and sometimes wonder when people react unexpectedly.

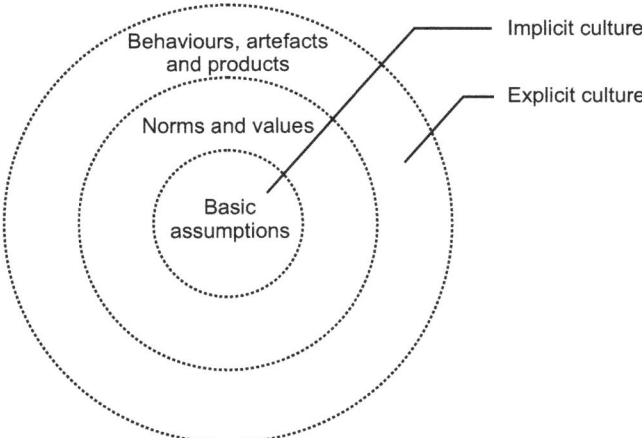

Figure 34.6 Explicit and implicit culture: Trompenaars' culture model

In the context of managing partners in programmes we have to consider the specific level of interaction that we are dealing with. At the strategic level we have to understand that different cultures have different approaches in seeing the future. In the German culture for example you find a strong need to avoid uncertainty, which leads to precise planning for the future and involved strategies.

Chinese people would generally consider the future as unpredictable. They would tend to work on details of product planning at a later stage and be prepared to change their strategies (and any related contracts) as necessary.

Different attitudes like this have to be understood when entering into a partnership for a programme.

The importance of relationship building has already been mentioned. At this level we find the most famous misunderstanding between Americans and Germans which is described as the 'peach and coconut' phenomenon. The public and private spheres are symbolized respectively by the outer and the inner parts of the fruit. The German (coconut) has a hard and thin outer shell (giving a rather reserved appearance). The public sphere of an American (peach) is softer and wider, which in the perception of the German already addresses the private sphere (Come and see me sometime!). The German then is surprised to find out that this is not a private commitment at all and thus thinks the American is superficial. The American on the other side is confused, as the conservative German suddenly is trying to intrude in his private sphere and the overall irritation takes its course.

Relationship building is crucial in Asian cultures and is absolutely essential for business success. Formal aspects have to be followed in showing respect for a business partner (such as handing over business cards with two hands) as well as protecting an overall harmony (never make someone lose face!).

At the cooperation level we can observe different ways of time management. An American would see time as a finite source (time is money) which needs to be closely managed. A Chinese instead would tend to work on different tasks in parallel and be more flexible with the overall time management, which might lead to slipping of agreed milestones in a programme. Because the quality of communication is most important for the work in a programme, the different approaches for direct and indirect communication need to be understood. Some cultures feel uncomfortable with a direct way of communication, and the programme team need to react with the partners accordingly.

Overall, it is very advisable to make sure that cultural differences are understood at the beginning of a programme and – where applicable – rules for cooperation are specified.

Cooperation level

Benefits of partnership management

The general benefits of an integrated, cooperative approach can be found in the dimensions of the magic triangle (costs, quality and time).

Cost savings are achieved through avoidance of misrouted or wrongly addressed communication. The goal is to avoid incomplete or unaligned programme information, and duplicated, replicated or overlapping documentation.

Improved quality is achieved through well-aligned goals, objectives and product/ service requirements. Also expectations of all partners involved are clarified and documented. Therefore key documents must be defined and shared among the partners in advance.

Time is saved by improved understanding and use of common processes and by streamlined and integrated programme management procedures, including reporting and control standards, organizational processes, procedures and systems. Time consuming identification of correct addressees is avoided by identifying and announcing the names of responsible persons and their roles, and by upfront coordination.

A programme as a temporary organization

Partners in programmes can be seen as a form of supply chain. The contract from the initiating organization acts as the starting point of the relationship between two companies, organizations or authorities. Once the collaboration is decided, the organization of a contracted company commissions the programme to execute the order. Hence the programme is the operational outcome of a contractual relationship and as a temporary organization performs as the contractor to the partner organization (for example customer, NGO or public authority). From this point on the temporary organization 'programme' takes over the direct, programme-related cooperation and communication with the external partner organization. The programme realizes the ordered service or product.

Going along the supply chain, in its role as the temporary (though operative) organization the programme also functions as the interface to sub-suppliers or authorities. In this relationship it becomes customer to other companies.

Sourcing products and services has to be seen as a joint effort between the programme and its company and is based on the company's strategy and processes. This approach is necessary to secure the company's interests and to protect it from risks.

Distributed and global cooperation leads to an increased amount of interdependencies. The different programmes of partner organizations have their individual goals and interests. A crucial factor in partnership management is to be aware of conflicting goals and interests.

Especially in product- and service-related programmes, numerous programmes exist on every stage of the supply chain. Depending on the type of business, they can be linked to each other (Figure 34.7).

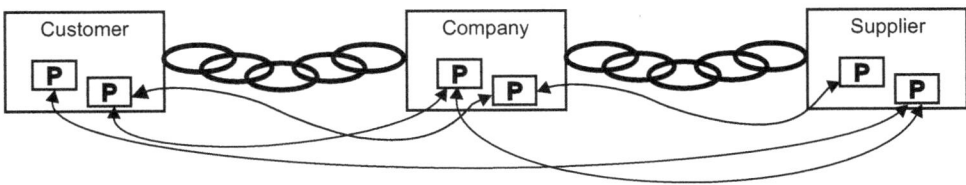

Figure 34.7 Linked programmes along the supply chain

The automotive industry provides an example. The car manufacturer OEM often has a direct contractual agreement with certain tier 2 and sub-suppliers and mandates components (including specifications and contractual conditions) to a tier 1 supplier. On the other hand, the tier 1 and tier 2 suppliers can be competitors in other commodities or market segments. And to make things even more complicated, companies that are tier 1 and tier 2 in one car production line can have opposite roles as customer and supplier on another car production line.

In addition to contractual agreements between two cooperating organizations an activity interface matrix (Figure 34.8) can be used to define roles and responsibilities between the individual programmes. This matrix can be also expanded to additional levels if substructures exist. A so called multiparty agreement is imperative if the customer has direct relationships with subsuppliers.

A jointly agreed activity interface matrix addresses the main aspects of programme management responsibilities such as timing updates, communication, documentation and change management duties as well as detailed operational responsibilities like data creation and release or prototype product or service creation and release. It can identify duties originated from contractual agreements, like risk transfer and complaint and claim management. It can also function as a guideline indicating processes or from sheets to be used.

In Figure 34.8 the structure of the activity interface matrix is shown in the form of a responsibility assignment matrix. While listing the processes and describing the main tasks on the left side, applicable phases can be referenced. There are various possibilities for compiling a responsibility assignment matrix.

Task description	Phase				Responsible			Date	Reference process	Reference formsheet	Remark feedback
	1	2	3	4	Customer	Supplier	Sub-supp.				
Programme management											
Timing	x	x	x	x	R						
Documentation		x	x			A					
Communication	x	x	x	x			C				
and so on.							I				
Processes											
Development	x				R						
Product release		x				A					
Prototype release			x				C				
Complaint management				x			I				
and so on.											
Deliverables											
Data	x				R						
Prototypes		x				A					
Product		x					C				
Documentation			x				I				
and so on.											
Support											
Data	x				R						
Prototypes		x				A					
Product		x					C				
Documentation			x				I				
and so on.											

Figure 34.8 Example of an activity interface matrix

In programmes with partner organizations interactions should focus on decision-making processes and therefore the responsibility of each partner. The executing roles should be expressed as follows:

- R (responsible);
- A (approves);
- C (must be consulted);
- I (must be informed).

For obvious reasons this assignment matrix is also known as a RACI chart.

Managing programme timing

One of the key instruments in the programme planning phase is an integrated timing schedule (Figure 34.9). That will provide a high-level overview of key dates (milestones) and deliverables in the programme. Timing includes the definition of overall phases and gates.

Although the first overview is usually issued by one of the partners, the focus in partnership programmes lies on the integration of the timing, which means that main milestones, key processes and expected deliverables are planned jointly between the partners. This integration process ensures that interfaces and responsibility transitions (especially those on the critical path) are understood between the

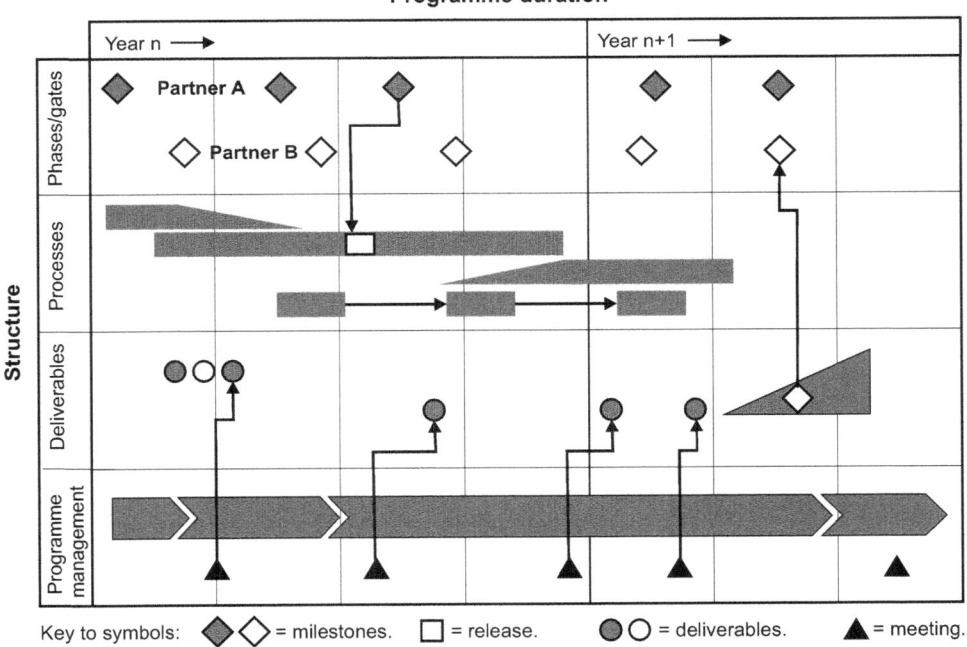

Figure 34.9 Integrated view of programme control over time

involved persons. Also expectations (dates, content and supporting documentation) on deliverables are agreed between partners. The integrated timing schedule serves the following purposes:

- understanding of programme phases and gates;
- reference of vital processes (such as change management);
- clarification of expectations (such as product delivery dates);
- visualization of interfaces and critical path;
- basis for scope and capacity planning (such as offer phase);
- possibility for all partners to plan detailed activities;
- documentation of timing changes (such as delays);
- glossary of terms used in the programme.

To exploit the potential of integrated timing schedules fully the following points should be considered:

- the schedule should be process orientated;
- colour and different shapes will visually highlight interfaces and responsibilities;
- use only one timing plan, not incorporated in other documents (but it can be a stand-alone appendix);
- use an easy and commonly available file format;
- name responsible contact person(s);
- list the document status and release or revision date;
- provide a key or index to explain important terms.

The meetings and process needed to draw up this jointly developed timing schedule is as important as the document itself. Detailed planning does not just clarify overall expectations on timing and deliverables but also enables the individual teams to understand company and programme-specific goals and interests, terms and processes as well as risks and chances. It also helps to identify the key people of each partner and understand their roles and responsibilities. This can also serve as a comprehensive team building process.

Programme control

In programme monitoring and controlling the actual status and progress is recorded and compared with the planning. This continuous process establishes a relationship to all programme targets and defines corrective measures to achieve these targets and also minimize risks.

Deviations from planning (costs, maturity or timing) result in additional or altered risks. The information necessary to evaluate risks and prepare educated decisions along the supply chain involves all partners. Solution of delays and definition of measures require a clear interaction chain and well as established escalation paths.

In order to define a clear escalation path the roles and members of respective committees, panels and boards at all partners have to be defined and known within the programme. That identification should be part of the stakeholder analysis. Also, criteria regarding of the nature of the issue as well as the criticality of the problem have to be defined in order for it to be addressed to the right decision-makers.

Gate and maturity reviews

Based on the programme planning, gates between the different phases act as synchronization points between all partners involved. The process of releasing defined work packages together with the review of major deliverables in the respective phase is valuable for synchronizing activities and establishing the programme maturity level.

The release of work packages and product or service deliverables needs to be a joint and planned activity, referenced in the timing overview. Expectations on these synchronization points must be aligned in the beginning of the programme. We recommend defining not only when these reviews should happen but also who will organize the event, which programme, product or service deliverable is needed in advance (for example, measurement or laboratory reports) and how the results of each review will be documented and distributed.

It is very helpful to agree a format for recording the outcome of the review meeting, including next activities and deliverables with expected dates and the person responsible. Gates used as review and synchronization points create a detailed overview of the work done so far and provide an action list for the next phase. In order to ensure maximum utilization the following points should be addressed:

- determination of programme content (analysis of work packages and deliverables that were not finished on time or had to be adjusted due to changed requirements);
- definition of recovery actions (agreement on measures to close gaps; prioritization of short-term and long=-term actions);
- revision of programme planning (removing of obsolete items and replanning of upcoming topics and tasks; evaluation of new and existing risks;
- development of prognosis (for example, evaluation of change management requirements; evaluation of claim management impacts);
- information to management (preparing decisions and approvals; presentation of impact on resources – time, cost, quality);
- analysis of root causes;
- checking of influences and risks to other programmes or processes;
- documenting and applying lessons learned.

Interface management

Product or service creation in a programme is based on partnership between multiple institutions or authorities along the supply chain and more and more a result of cooperation from various experts with different knowledge, backgrounds and goals.

The amount of information handled in a programme environment increases with the cross-linked involvement of different organizations (such as customers, suppliers, authorities). Hierarchical systems are not fast enough to comprehend information needed for good decisions and it is nearly impossible for single persons to overlook and capture all necessary information within a programme.

A possibility for streamlining this information flow that could support clear communication is interface management (see Figure 34.10). For each subproject, work package or key deliverable the main task of the interface manager is to meet regularly with programme leaders, subproject leaders and process owners from various partners to:

- clarify programme requirements, goals and strategies;
- describe the content and expected output of work packages and deliverables;
- identify interfaces between adjacent work packages and deliverables;
- establish a progress overview of work packages and deliverables;
- collect and track defined measures for recovery;
- record, distribute and inform involved parties including programme management.

Managing changes and claims

Owing to high market demands on quick product or service availability and the possibilities of IT based development and communication, complexity and pace of programme work is steadily increasing. In this environment change and claim management becomes a vital process in product or service-related programmes. Reasons for changes can be:

- technical (changes to the product or service and its functional testing);
- programme management changes (changes to timing, programme set-up, goals or strategies);
- organizational changes (people joining or leaving the programme and change roles of persons in the programme).

If we think about the supply chain the steps are moving from initiation to change request reception, from offer to approval, from execution to release. With these

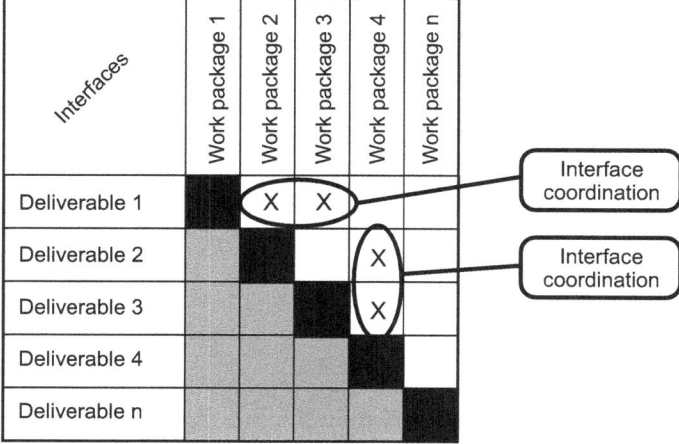

Figure 34.10 Interface matrix for deliverables and work packages

| Programme: |
| Release date: |
| Distribution to: |

No.	Work package	Topic	Description	Source	Responsible (role)	Responsible (role)	Deadline	Status
1	Change management	Timing adjusted	Milestone moved	Review meeting				Open
2								
3								
4								
n								

Figure 34.11 An issue list

steps the roles and responsibility of the programme at customer, company and supplier levels are changing. To accommodate a quick and reliable change and claim management process and to make everyone involved aware of these changing roles, the interaction chain including specified documents has to be defined among the partners. Also general rules for timeframes in which changes can be processed should be established. Last but not least the description of an escalation scenario is advised.

The basic procedure in change and claim management consists of the following points:

- initiation: fill out a change request form;
- definition: clarify the change content, scope and impact (timing, costs and so on);
- agreement: accept a claim or release a change document (authorizing and implementing the change) and inform partners of the decision;
- implementation: carry out the change and update documentation accordingly;
- closing: review execution to planning, close change issue, update issue list.

An issue list (Figure 34.11) is used to monitor deviations, changes and activities affecting all partners. It needs to be jointly updated on a regular basis as part of the cooperation and review meetings process. Part of the common overall issue list can be used by each partner individually to track implementation.

If programmes have to deal with many changes, separate and regular change management meetings are advised. The attendees at such meetings comprise committees that some organizations call change boards.

Programme closure

Every programme needs to be formally closed on completion or cancellation. Closure will terminate authority for work and spending on the programme, other than clearing up problems. Part of project closure is to compare the programmed detailed in the original business plan with the facts, checking for example its originally planned scope and comparing that with the final achievement. Now the programme team can be disbanded.

From programmes with cooperating organizations, institutions or authorities we know that partnerships grow over time. All important programme experiences, both positive and negative, need to lead to an increased understanding between the involved partners. Compiled lessons learned serve to avoid errors in subsequent programmes, to minimize project risks and to achieve continuous improvement (not only in processes but also in mutual understanding). The benefits from lessons learned can extend to parallel or adjacent programmes.

At least at the end of the programme a retrospective view is advised, and if such a closing workshop is conducted with participation of all partners, some rules apply. Lessons learned must not be turned into a 'finger pointing' contest. Nothing is ever easy in a complex and comprehensive programme. Decisions can turn out to be wrong and have to be viewed with the lapse of time. In the end everyone knows better, but many steps are necessary to reach goals together and a closing workshop needs to make use of this fact. Success needs to be celebrated and failure has to be analysed critically and turned into a new chance with the next venture. A good end takes care of an even better beginning the next time.

References and further reading

Heussen, B. and Pischel, G. (eds.) (2014), *Handbuch Vertragsverhandlung und Vertragsmanagement, Planung, Verhandlung, Design und Durchführung von Verträgen*, Köln: Verlag Dr Otto Schmidt.

House, R. J., Hanges, P. J., Javidan, M., Dorfmann, P. W. and Gupta, V. (2004), *Culture, Leadership, and Organizations: The Globe Study of 62 Societies*, Thousand Oaks, CA: Sage.

Malik, F. (2011), *Corporate Policy and Governance*, vol. 2 of the series *Management: Mastering Complexity*, Frankfurt am Main: Campus.

Mankins, M. C. and Steele, R. (2005), 'Turning Great Strategy into Great Performance', *Harvard Business Review*, July–August.

ProSTEP iViP (Hrsg.) (2010), Collaborative Project Management (CPM), Reference Model, PSI 1-1, Version 3.0, February.

Trompenaars, F. and Hampden-Turner, C. (1997), *Riding the Waves of Culture: Understanding Cultural Diversity in Business*, New York: McGraw Hill.

Tuczek, H. (2005), *Die 4 C des Projektmanagements bei der Dräxlmaier Group*, PMaktuell – Heft, March.

Chapter 35

Managing Contracts in Programmes

Tim Cummins

No manager wants to be associated with failure. Through a combination of skills, training, judgement and luck, you hope for consistently successful outcomes. But many programmes fail to deliver their expected results. In some cases better contracts and contract management could have prevented those failures.

Introduction

Imagine for a moment that you are in remote countryside on a dark, moonless night. You have to reach your destination as soon as possible and cannot wait for dawn. The good news is that there is a road and a car. The bad news is that the car has no headlights and the road is full of potholes. You can choose between two drivers. As a smart project manager, you realize it will be a good idea to speak with them both before you make a choice. You discover that one is an excellent mechanic and likes to drive really fast. The other is a much slower driver and prides herself on her research and planning skills. So which driver would you choose? This chapter explores the role and the purpose of contracts and their management. In particular, the focus will be on the way that good contract management can illuminate your journey and ensure safe arrival at your destination.

Far too many programmes do not arrive safely. For example, on average, megaprojects are delivered two years late and 80 per cent over budget (the European Union has defined a megaproject as any project requiring funding of more than 500 million euros; a working group has been exploring typical success rates and factors that cause them to fail or under-perform). Around 35 per cent of more standard programmes experience a substantial shortfall against plan – with technology projects particularly susceptible to problems. This chapter offers insights and solutions to the most common pitfalls in contracts and their management.

From this point on, think of the contract as a tool for better project management. Recognize that it defines what the project must deliver, who it is that will undertake that delivery, the responsibilities of the participants, the way that performance will be overseen and measured and (finally) the consequences if anyone fails to perform or the objectives are not achieved. Many project teams think of contracts only in the context of 'what happens when things go wrong'. As a result, they consign the contract to the drawer or to their document repository – and in so doing they immediately place the outcome of their project in jeopardy.

How many programmes fail to deliver their expected benefits? Precise numbers are hard to pin down, but it is clear that greater complexity and relative levels of uncertainty are major influences. IT and software projects commonly attract media headlines. For example, *Information Week* published an article in 2013 which said: 'Depending on which consultancy you ask . . . the failure rate for technology projects is anywhere from 37 per cent to 75 per cent.' The European Commission, based on research led by a group of academics, puts the failure rate for 'megaprojects' at 65 per cent, with 19 per cent resulting in no tangible benefits. As we know from the newspapers, public sector IT contracts appear to be especially vulnerable.

So while failure may not be the overall norm, it is far more frequent than anyone would like it to be – and the most common causes appear to be commercial, rather than technical. Given that project managers tend to come from a technical background, we could debate cause and effect. But whatever the underlying reason, it is clear that today's programmes demand far greater attention to contract and commercial issues.

Things that can go wrong

Contracts can be relatively complex instruments. Compiling one can almost be a project itself. There are multiple stakeholders, people and institutions with an interest in the content of a contract. A contract is driven by a host of policies, procedures and regulations, as well as the practical considerations of feasibility and risk. Complex agreements typically take months to assemble, simply because of the difficulty in undertaking review and approval and reaching consensus.

Unfortunately, there also tends to be confusion over the purpose of contracts. Are they legal instruments, dealing with matters of law? Are they economic instruments, dealing with matters of finance? Are they business instruments, dealing with matters of performance and governance? Or perhaps marketing instruments, dealing with brand and reputation? The answer is that they should be all of these things, but frequently are not. Many contracts – in the words of one expert – are 'written by lawyers, for lawyers, in the expectation of litigation'. This tendency is often exacerbated by lack of interest from around the business. Its effect is to reduce the usefulness of contracts and, as I shall explain later – contribute to problems with performance.

The international Association for Contract and Commercial Management (IACCM) undertakes regular research to understand the typical causes of poor performance. Not surprisingly, none of these causes is linked to legal issues. Figure 35.1 shows an example of the IACCM findings. It reflects a worldwide study undertaken with the UK's National Audit Office as part of that institution's efforts to improve the results of public sector projects. However, this chart still represents symptoms rather than the underlying causes, so IACCM's work has focused on better understanding why things go wrong and how they can be avoided. In 2014, this resulted in the publication of reports outlining 'the ten pitfalls of contract management', which I shall now outline.

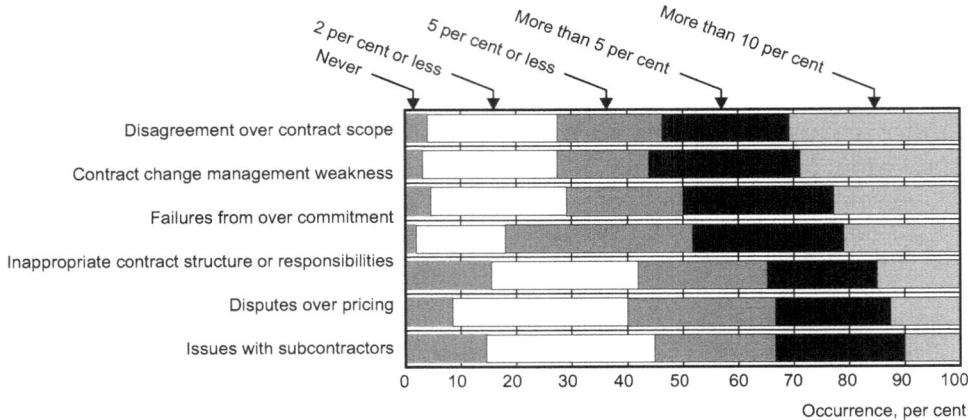

Figure 35.1 Major causes of value erosion

Pitfall 1: lack of clear scope and goals

Research shows that this is the most frequent source of claims, disputes and disrupted relationships, impacting around 40 per cent of projects. It results from poor communications, unclear responsibilities and failure to update business requirements. IACCM is not alone in recognizing this problem; failure to define fully, agree or prioritize requirements is consistently cited as the main cause of troubled projects. So what might a project manager do to avoid this problem?

First, it is important to recognize that many stakeholders contribute to this problem. Procurement wants to minimize the price, so might be selective in the requirements it discusses with the supplier. Sales organizations want to win the business: they are not really concerned about the quality or requirements, especially since prolonged discussion could derail the deal. And executive management are often the worst culprits – they just want to get moving and cannot understand the delay. Further, as identified by the International Centre for Complex Project Management (ICCPM), top executives are frequently guilty of a 'conspiracy of optimism' which is often hostile to truth or reality.

Suggested actions

At whatever point you first become involved, test whether both parties have a common view of goals and the related scope of the project. Ask questions about who was involved in setting and validating requirements and find out if key stakeholders were either not included, or their views were discounted.

Following contract signature, ensure there is a joint planning workshop and use this to facilitate team discussions that confirm alignment of scope and goals. If you identify mismatches, tackle them before work starts.

Some projects by their nature face uncertainty. This may be because there is legitimate uncertainty over the ability to achieve the outcome, or because there are factors – such as new technologies – that will almost inevitably lead to change. In these circumstances, ensure there are robust mechanisms for ongoing performance review and milestone management. Ensure clear escalation procedures for people with decision-making authority.

Pitfall 2: the commercial team is involved too late

Project managers are not alone in complaining that they are often not involved early enough. Commercial staff suffer a similar problem (sometimes because of the project manager) since there is a common belief that early involvement will cause delays and problems. Research shows the opposite: early engagement cuts cycle time to a signed contract by around 20 per cent and results in around 25 per cent fewer claims or disputes. Yet internal management and measurement systems often work against inclusive behaviour, resulting in poorly defined relationships and the wrong commercial structure or terms. Indeed, the work of the EU working group on megaprojects has identified that use of the wrong relationship structure is the number one contributor to failure. Good examples of this might be use of a standard 'time is of the essence', fixed price contract when actually the right model would be an agile contract. Also, key terms for supporting proper governance or performance oversight will often be missing since late involvement of the commercial team will often force them to focus exclusively on protective terms.

Suggested actions

If you are involved at early stages of the project, ensure that commercial advice is sought from the outset (just as you would not exclude technical experts from engaging). If you are involved at a later stage, talk with commercial staff – especially those responsible for developing the contract – and establish when they were consulted and the extent to which they contributed to defining the relationship model being used for this project. If they were involved late, or had no influence, try to validate whether or not the type of agreement you are using is actually suited to the nature of the project.

Even if the contract is signed, there is nothing to prevent you seeking to review the performance and governance terms. Consider running a 'relational workshop', in which both (or all) parties to the contract sign up to detailed commitments on issues like communication, reporting, joint working, problem solving and change procedures. Ensure these are fully documented and distributed; and that the teams are committed to periodic workshops to review whether the governance procedures are working.

Pitfall 3: failure to engage stakeholders

Wharton Business School organized a conference to discuss major infrastructure projects. It drew academics and industry experts from around the world – and there was widespread agreement that stakeholder analysis and management is perhaps the most critical aspect of successful programme management. The challenge is growing because of our increasingly networked world, creating not only increased transparency, but also providing every voice with an opportunity to be heard.

A recent example from Gloucestershire County Council in the United Kingdom concerned a decision to build a £500 million waste incinerator. Such projects inevitably create public concern and attract the attention of NGOs and others. Whatever consultation process the County Council went through, they soon discovered it was not enough. Having signed a contract with a £100 million penalty clause for termination, they found themselves facing an Internet campaign driven by local residents. The campaign rapidly gathered support – and this was exacerbated when someone discovered that a similar project in Australia had chosen a different incinerator because of environmental concerns with the model selected for Gloucestershire.

There are no secrets; even the smallest voice can now be heard; research and information flows globally. You fail to engage stakeholders at your peril.

Suggested actions

Assemble a team to brainstorm and create a comprehensive stakeholder list – that is, anyone who is affected by the programme or might have an interest in it. Review similar programmes to test your list.

Divide stakeholders into categories (see the stakeholder analysis method shown in Figure 35.2). Assess those who are natural supporters, those who can potentially be turned into supporters and those who are inevitable opponents. Accept that not everyone will like what you are trying to achieve – so your job is to find ways to prevent them delaying or derailing your programme. Develop a detailed engagement plan and monitor progress against it.

Pitfall 4: adversarial approach to negotiations

Programmes are often the victims of poor collaboration. This might be because negotiation planning typically starts with powerful internal stakeholders promoting specific rules and policies. These are frequently reflected in rigid contract templates that are difficult to change and may be contrary to the required relationship. This often creates an adversarial environment, undermining the collaboration needed for innovation and trust.

As a project manager, you must be objective in the assessment of your behaviour, the behaviour of your organization, the behaviour of your counter-party and adjust your approach accordingly. As with all human relationships, an overt absence of trust

High power, important:	Keep satisfied	Manage closely
Lower power, less important:	Monitor (minimum effort)	Keep informed

Figure 35.2 A framework for stakeholder analysis

and failure to engage in open and honest communication generates a defensive reaction. This is often the case with negotiations, both internal and external.

Suggested actions

Make an honest appraisal of the attitudes that have influenced or will influence negotiation. Assess how this is impacting behaviour and what you can do to address the challenges this creates. Seek areas where collaboration might be possible, so that greater cooperation can be achieved. Without this, your project is in jeopardy. Consider, for example, sharing project elements so that people feel included, or holding meetings where it is clear that all views and opinions are respected.

If the problem is a rigid and adversarial contract template take time to talk with the template owner and explain why it could have a negative impact. Propose alternatives or solicit the help of the template owner in developing alternatives.

Pitfall 5: negotiations focus on risk allocation

Successful projects depend on identifying and managing risks. There is a tendency in many organizations to believe that the best approach to risk mitigation is to shift it to counter-parties. Such attitudes frequently reflect a very narrow focus on protecting assets and on driving performance through negative incentives. This often results in negotiations which are dominated by issues such as indemnities, liabilities, liquidated damages and intellectual property rights.

'The most frequently negotiated terms' is an annual survey undertaken by IACCM, to which thousands of negotiators contribute (see Figure 35.3). It illustrates the overwhelming focus in most negotiations on legal and financial issues, often at the expense of clarity of purpose (such as scope, service levels) or of key operational tools (like change management, communications and reporting, business continuity). As a result, the likelihood of risks occurring and being poorly managed is increased.

Concentration on protecting assets and avoiding loss creates an adversarial environment in which battles over risk allocation undermine the creativity and openness that support innovation and value. These defensive behaviours result in failure to tackle the sources of greatest risk and undermine cooperation between the parties. As a result, the real risks are often overlooked or ignored and the contract lacks mechanisms that support their ongoing identification and management.

Suggested actions

Investigate the risk appetite of major parties and stakeholders, so that you understand the environment in which you are operating. Review actual or proposed contracts to gain a sense of balance and fairness and also to identify the mechanisms they offer for future management of risks.

Ensure that risk registers are established and maintained. Align these with the contract and explore the ways that contract terms will or can influence risk management and mitigation. Encourage sharing of identified risks between the parties to the contract, ideally establishing full transparency and shared risk registers. Establish forums or mechanisms through which risks will be discussed and managed. In particular,

	The top 30 terms, 2013/14	↓↑	2012	2011	2010	2009	2008	2007
1	Limitation of liability	–	1	1	1	1	1	1
2	Price/charge/price changes	↑	3	3	3	3	3	4
3	Indemnification	↓	2	2	2	2	2	2
4	Service levels and warranties	↑	8	11	7	6	7	11
5	Payment	↑	6	5	6	8	8	9
6	Service withdrawal or termination	↑	20	14	13	12	5	5
7	Warranty	↑	9	12	10	11	13	14
8	Intellectual property	↓	7	4	4	4	4	3
9	Performance/guarantees/undertakings	↑	16	7	18	-	15	15
10	Delivery/acceptance	↑	12	8	8	7	9	8
11	Liquidated damages	↓	5	6	9	9	11	10
12	Scope and goals	↓	4	16	12	14	-	-
13	Responsibilities of the parties	↓	11	17	15	13	-	-
14	Invoices/late payment	↑	17	19	16	19	14	19
15	Confidential information/non-disclosure	↓	14	10	5	5	10	7
16	Insurance	↓	10	13	11	15	12	12
17	Data protection/security	↑	18	15	5	5	10	7
18	Security	↑	34	-	-	-	-	-
19	Rights of use	↓	13	23	22	22	18	15
20	Dispute resolution	↓	15	21	19	16	16	17
21	Change management	↓	19	18	17	17	-	-
22	Information access and management	–	22	30	29	29	-	-
23	Audits/benchmarking	↑	29	20	20	18	17	18
24	Force majeure	↑	25	24	24	26	22	27
25	Communications and reporting	↓	24	28	26	24	-	-
26	Applicable law/jurisdiction	↑	30	9	14	10	6	6
27	Assignment/transfer	↓	26	22	21	20	19	16
28	Freight/shipping	–	28	25	28	23	21	21
29	Business continuity/disaster recovery	↑	33	26	23	-	-	-
30	Product substitution	↓	27	-	-	-	-	-

Figure 35.3 The most frequently negotiated terms and conditions

consider ways that problems and issues will be highlighted and resolved. Hidden risks are the ones most likely to derail your project.

Pitfall 6: relationships lack flexibility and governance

Change management is one of the most contentious areas of contracting. It is the area where issues around scope, price, value and innovation all come together and create a potentially vitriolic mix. Many buyers seek to constrain change because they know that it leads to price increases; many suppliers seek to maximize change as a route to margin improvement. But this is a simplistic view which assumes change is primarily due to issues around specification.

Each year, the speed of change and market volatility increase (IACCM research shows that the frequency of contract changes and amendments has grown by more than 30 per cent over a recent five-year period). Yet more than 80 per cent of trading relationships remain traditional in their terms and structure. At senior levels, management encourages more collaborative, performance-based relationships, yet commercial practices are struggling to adapt. As a result, organizations are not effective in anticipating or enabling change, and operational teams lack tools for managing performance. 'Weaknesses in contract change management' is identified as the second most important cause of value erosion (see Figure 35.1). Experienced project managers frequently highlight the challenge of 'staying on top of change'.

Sources of change are diverse and examples include new technology or materials, regulation, geopolitical factors, environment, shifts in market expectations or needs and alterations to business ownership or strategy. Contract change procedures need to include practical methods of dealing with the frequency and nature of change. They should include:

- practical methods of communication;
- defined forums in which change requirements can be discussed and evaluated;
- clear procedures for resolution, including paths of escalation;
- shared recording systems for agreed changes.

Without practical mechanisms, changes are either frustrated or they are handled informally (with inadequate records). Both situations threaten project success and often result in delays, claims and potential disputes.

Suggested actions

Presume that the only certainty for your project is uncertainty. Your contract must facilitate dealing with that uncertainty. Check that you have the right form of agreement: for example, does it contain appropriate milestones and review points? Should it be defining an input or an outcome? Is the pricing mechanism flexible to your likely needs?

Work with your commercial staff to ensure that the mechanisms for change management are practical and efficient. For example, enable electronic communications and ensure a clear path for escalations. Monitor change procedures throughout the life of your contract and adapt as necessary to provide acceptable speed of resolution and continued control. If necessary, highlight the need for renegotiation of terms. Use your contract as an instrument for project management, not as a weapon.

Pitfall 7: contracts that are difficult to use or understand

Many people see contracts as having relevance only when there are problems. Yet in a world of longer-term service and solution delivery, contracts contain critical rights, obligations and performance criteria. Complexity in their structure and language is not only unnecessary – it is a source of risk.

More than 90 per cent of business people admit that they find contracts hard to understand and have difficulty in finding relevant information. Many times, we deviate from a contract unintentionally – just because it is not easy to use. Two main factors contribute to this problem:

1. Contracts are often designed by lawyers, to serve the purpose of lawyers in anticipation of possible litigation.
2. Different sections of the contract are often assembled and negotiated by different groups or stakeholders, then put together at the last minute into a single document.

Your ability to influence either of these factors may be limited (though if you can influence them, do so!). But that does not mean you are helpless in dealing with them.

Suggested actions

Always read your contract and seek explanations on any points you find unclear. The fact that it is complex is not an acceptable excuse for ignorance of the terms. Request support in converting the contract to summaries that can be distributed to the implementation team. Alternatively, have the various sections marked up for the different groups or functions that will be using the contract, so it is easy for them to find and extract relevant information. Ensure you have the support resources you need to manage the contract. Don't accept responsibility for something you do not have the skills or resources to undertake.

Pitfall 8: poor handover to implementation

Over 60 per cent of project managers and implementation teams complain about the problems caused by handover from the bid team to the post-award execution team. Lack of engagement, communication and appropriate software tools often results in missed commitments or obligations. Frequently, there is no transition plan that engages personnel from both supplier and customer to ensure shared understanding. As a project manager, this phase is under your control.

Who is responsible for extracting data from the contract and communicating it to the business? What checks are there for accuracy and completeness? By what methods will communication occur? How shall we ensure that our version of events and responsibilities aligns with that of our counter-party? What happened during negotiation that might influence attitudes or behaviours? What issues were discussed that may not be evident in the contract, but might be material to the way it is performed? Questions like these are fundamental to the transition period.

Suggested actions

Insist on clear documentation and data extraction that sets out the key goals, obligations and agreed mechanisms for their management.

Ensure at least two workshops. One should be the internal handover of the signed contract, with background information being supplied to the implementation team. This must include not only what is written in the contract, but also the experiences during negotiation. The other should be a joint meeting of the implementation teams from both/all contracting parties.

Maintain links back to the original negotiation team to address future questions, clarifications or disagreements.

Pitfall 9: limited use of contract technology

If you are fortunate, you will have software tools or systems available to assist your contract management. However, contract management is one of the least automated processes: over 60 per cent of organizations lack a coherent application or have the wrong software. This results in inefficiency and weaknesses in performance oversight. It also results in a lack of management reporting and information.

Many contracts today contain – quite literally – several thousand obligations. Extracting these from the contract is itself a major task (though potentially made easier by automation). Once extracted, they need to be allocated to responsible individuals, communicated and monitored. How will this critical task be undertaken? Even when everything is purely manual, project teams today will be using at least some technology, even if only Excel spreadsheets and Outlook calendars. Complexity drives a need for use of technology and when it comes to the contract, you may need to set the example.

Suggested actions

Before implementation, establish what technology exists in your organization to support contract management. You may discover systems being used in certain departments, or discover techniques that have been deployed by other teams. Develop a communications and reporting plan for contract management, covering all stakeholders. Define the reports you need, together with their frequency, to monitor contract performance, change requests, improvement opportunities and stakeholder issues/satisfaction.

Pitfall 10: weak post-award process governance

Given the range of issues discussed so far, it is really no surprise that post-award governance is often a source of weakness. But it doesn't have to be that way. Top performing organizations suffer contract value erosion of less than 4 per cent. A distinguishing feature in all of these organizations is the investment they have made in post-award contract management capability. Through a combination of rigorous process, clearly defined roles, development of skills and supporting tools, they are eliminating repetitive issues and errors – and have made themselves more attractive and reliable trading partners.

If you have a dedicated contract management function or tools at your disposal, make sure you use them. Also, investigate what approach your counter-party will take to contract management and ensure alignment. Such enquiries might reveal critical insights. For example, if one of your major interfaces from the supplier is a 'claim manager', you should probably take this as a warning of what to expect.

Suggested actions

Confirm contract management tools and resources both internal and external. Check their motivations/measurements and seek to align them. Review the elements of relational governance and establish whether these are defined and enabled adequately through the contract. Where there are gaps in these elements, work with your counter-party (and internal stakeholders) to define methods and mechanisms that will be adopted.

Ensure there are regular meetings to review the effectiveness of the governance procedures and adjust or supplement as necessary.

Achieving better results

At this point, we have explored some of the most frequent causes of project failure and highlighted aspects of contracting that contribute to improving results. However, it is important to recognize that this transition is not painless. It involves significant shifts in attitude and behavior. This has implications for all the parties involved and may significantly impact your selection criteria for those you work with.

Figures 35.4 and 35.5 reflect research that IACCM undertook with Newcastle University Business School (UK) and the University of Paderborn (Germany). The study explored corporate experience in moving towards more collaborative, outcome-based contracts. Figure 35.4 indicates the benefits that are typically

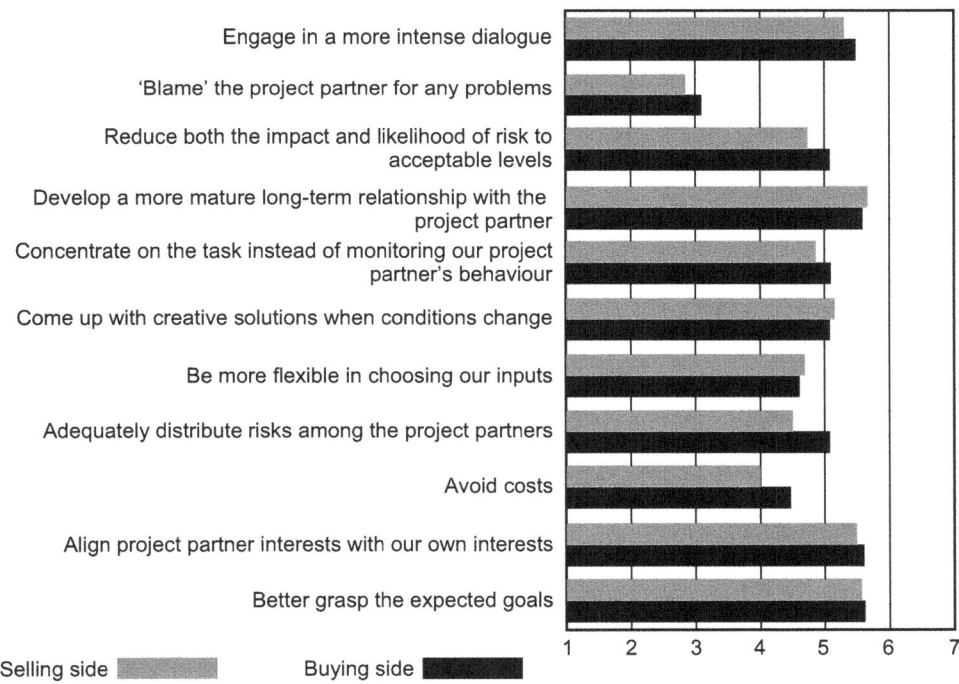

Figure 35.4 Benefits typically achieved moving towards more collaborative, outcome-based contracts

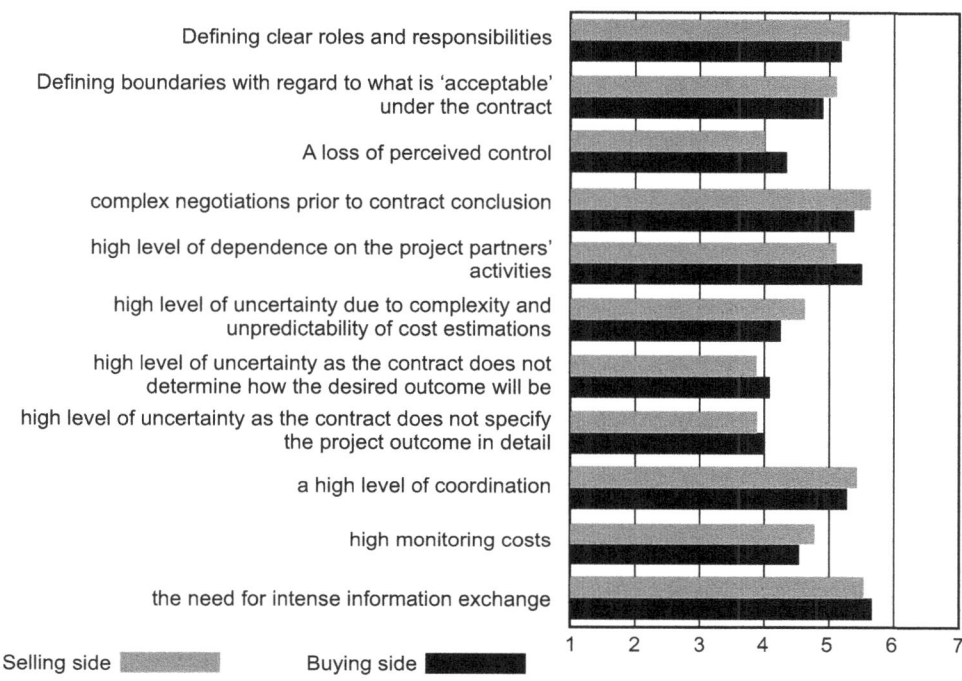

Figure 35.5 Challenges expected when moving towards more collaborative, outcome-based contracts

achieved and Figure 35.5 illustrates the challenges that the project team must expect to encounter.

Conclusion

The contract is a critical tool for programme or project success. It establishes what is to be done, who will do it, how success will be measured and the consequences if things go wrong. Contracts must be actively managed – not only for what they say now, but also because they must be adapted to new or changing circumstances.

As this chapter has indicated, there are many places in which poor contracting can undermine a programme or project. The first step in improved performance is to be aware of those risks; but the real differentiator is to ensure their active management.

Referring back to this chapter's introduction, many projects are driven at high speed and whenever they hit a pothole, remedial action is undertaken. Indeed, the project and contract specialists take great pride in their ability to 'fix things' (or blame someone else) when they go wrong. Over time, this approach can cause significant delay and cost overruns; it might even result in damage that puts the project beyond repair.

There are other cases where it is recognized that perhaps a slower pace, accompanied by someone who has a torch and is experienced in the terrain, can yield a far better result. This approach is anticipatory, adaptive, encourages teamwork and uses the various tools and techniques that are available. It might not be so exciting, but it is precisely what good contract management is about.

References and further reading

Scriven, J. and Pritchard, N. (2011), *EPC Contracts and Major Projects: A Guide to Construction and Other Project Contracts*, London: Sweet & Maxwell.

Turner, J. R. (2003), *Contracting for Project Management*, Farnham: Gower.

Chapter 36

Creating Knowledge Services for Modern Technical Project Organizations: The REAL Knowledge Approach

Edward J. Hoffman and Jon Boyle

This chapter centres on a descriptive, project practitioner-centred framework called the Rapid Engagement for Accelerated Learning (REAL) model, derived from experience in developing knowledge services (KS) in complex technical project organizations

Introduction

Consider this uneasy but familiar situation that is common to many organizations. A project is undergoing a design review. During the review, questions are raised about engineering mishaps. The discussion centres on methods for addressing the mishaps and how effectively the programme captured the lessons and shared them in order to mitigate future risks. The project team members talk with great excitement about their commitment and approach to knowledge capture and lessons learned. Then a review team member asks, 'What is being done to ensure that these lessons are being formally and systematically captured and made accessible across the whole organization?' Silence envelops the room. Finally, the team realizes that there is no system that effectively captures, shares and allows other projects to benefit from these critical lessons.

This opens the door to a wide range of questions for project organizations. Where does your workforce go to find out what they need to know in order to succeed? Can such lessons be found immediately after five years, ten years? Can stored knowledge be infused into the broader organization? Can experience and innovations be captured from current and retiring practitioners for reuse in future projects? Can project practitioners be taught to value knowledge sharing to benefit the wider organization while in the midst of requirements, complexity and deadlines?

These questions pose fundamental challenges for organizations attempting to manage project knowledge – even in the best organizations possessing mature, integrated knowledge management (KM) systems. A complex technical project organization might be totally committed to identifying and sharing critical knowledge and lessons, but could find that increasingly hard to accomplish across systems that cross project and portfolio boundaries. These organizations may intuitively grasp the power of sharing and learning, but can falter when knowledge stumbles across these larger boundaries. In an increasingly complex and interconnected world, this integration and awareness can spell the difference between success and failure.

The REAL model described in this chapter derived from experience in developing KS in complex technical project organizations. It evolved from organizational knowledge systems perspectives that better negotiate rapid change and accelerated learning in data-rich complex project environments. We shall discuss the modern project environment in terms of strategic imperatives that guide the design and development of a KS model for individuals, teams and organizations. The operational components of knowledge capture and retention, sharing and application, and discovery and creation are specified as core processes with individual and organizational inputs of capabilities and expectations.

We shall also discuss considerations for the design of KS, including governance, approach, knowledge mapping, biases and heuristics, and practitioner capabilities. Examples are described based on the presented strategic imperatives and model, and our chapter closes with a summary and recommendations for future research in this area. Being a descriptive model, the REAL knowledge model allows organizations to validate and add imperatives within their context to design better KS for diverse challenges and opportunities.

The project knowledge environment

How can organizations and practitioners best use project knowledge and KS to get things done in the modern complex project environment?

Based on research, experiences and conversations across public, private, government, industry, academia and professional organizations, practitioners say it is increasingly difficult to bring ideas to fruition and projects to completion. This difficulty is reflected through several facets of recent research. One study finds only 56 per cent of strategic initiatives meet original goals and business intent in surveyed project organizations, and also reports that 48 per cent of projects that are not highly aligned to organizational strategy succeed (PMI, 2014). Another study by *Aviation Week* and industry leaders, the second annual Young Professionals Study, discovered that the top frustration of the under-35 workforce was bureaucracy and politics, and that there is no time to innovate and create (Anselmo and Hedden, 2011).

Significant improvements can be gained through a focus on the capture and flow of project knowledge in terms of organizational, individual and team project factors within an organizational systems perspective. In many organizations, knowledge involves unique requirements, solutions and expertise shared across individuals, teams, projects, programmes and the broader organization that are often defined as 'codified knowledge' (scientific knowledge, engineering and technical knowledge, and business processes) and 'know-how' (individual and team experience, techniques, processes, procedures and craftsmanship), presenting the classic dichotomy of explicit and tacit knowledge – where Polanyi (1966) first says of tacit knowledge, 'we can know more than we can tell'.

In a non-traditional sense, other types of knowledge play a significant role in projects, such as the social dimension of knowledge that allows individuals and groups to achieve success within the organizational context. In one example, Neffinger and Kohut (2013) emphasize the importance of perceptions of strength and warmth in interpersonal and team environments and how an optimal balance of these characteristics informs social situations. A better understanding of the social context of

project knowledge can serve as a basis for improved prioritization and a more pragmatic approach to problem solving. Organizational disregard for this type of knowledge can lead to project failures such as those described by Hoffman and Boyle
(2013) regarding the NASA Challenger and Columbia Shuttle disasters, where the
technical root causes were investigated but the underlying causes were poor team
communications and lack of organizational learning.

Complexity often works against organizational focus on achieving goals and outcomes. But what do we mean by complexity? It can take many forms:

- Confusing, vague, poorly defined priorities, strategies, lines of authority, governance, policies, roles and responsibilities and support, characterized by iterative
reorganizations, constant budget changes, constant resource level adjustments, a
proliferation of administrative burdens and endless requirements.
- A proliferation of customers, stakeholders and strategic partner interfaces at
multiple levels of interest, involvement and responsibility.
- Technical complexity and system integration issues within and across multiple
disciplines and multiple systems.
- Increased data and information amount and availability for process input,
throughput and output.
- Multiple overlapping, conflicting, outdated processes and procedures that
involve multiple points of contact distributed across multiple organizational levels and across multiple oversight and advisory entities, characterized by competing priorities, strategies, lines of authority, governance, policies, roles and
responsibilities and support requirements.

Complexity in turn drives a rapid pace of change that affects organizational social,
technical, strategic and administrative systems. Davenport and Prusak (1998) recognized this when they defined future success in terms of organizations that know how
to do new things well and quickly. The shelf-life of products and services is increasingly shortened, requiring a management methodology that is flexible and adaptable
across the operational and strategic contexts to accommodate change, yet rigorous
enough to ensure that progress continues towards goals and objectives in the most
efficient and effective way possible.

Project management is a discipline often applied to achieve this flexibility and
adaptability. Thus handling the knowledge requirements for projects to perform better under these increased burdens makes sense. For many modern complex project
organizations, a project knowledge systems perspective best addresses handling complexity within an environment of increasingly constrained resources.

As mentioned, one form of complexity is the sheer amount of available data and
information. According to the independent research organization SINTEF (Dragland,
2013), 90 per cent of the data in the world have been generated over the past two
years, an incredible statistic that reinforces a claim by former Google chief executive
officer Eric Schmidt at a recent Techonomy Conference (2010) that human beings
currently create as much information in two days as we did from the dawn of man
through to the year 2003. That is an accelerating revolution of data, information and
knowledge which demands effectiveness and efficiency in the core processes of how
it is captured and retained, shared and applied, and enables discovery and creation.

Change is accelerated by this expansion of data and information and requires organizations to address strategy and decisions better. Learning is alternately enabled and hindered by the rapid development and implementation of technological tools accompanying this relentless pace of change and churn. On the one hand, it ensures data and information availability 24 hours a day, seven days a week. On the other hand, the capability to process the data and information into usable and actionable knowledge and wisdom, and to focus organizations and practitioners on implementing solutions suffers. This wealth of data and information interferes with focusing, prioritizing and moving confidently into the future because planning often suffers when new data and information obscure the original intent. The inductive process of building a list of good ideas is worthless without the deductive prioritization of what is truly important in terms of context, urgency and relevance, the magic that is delivered through good leadership.

This burden of change is ultimately placed squarely on the shoulders of what is termed the 'technical workforce' – practitioners possessing specialized skills that contribute to engineering efforts involving the disciplines of maths, science and technology. Over the years, their responsibility has shifted from a focus on the operational project objectives of scope, technical performance, quality, schedule and cost to a more encompassing responsibility of functional activities that includes business management, commercialization, new technology identification and development, strategy development and often much more.

What is the nature of these barriers and complications originating from multiple sources on the path to achievement? Some are political. Others are related to competence at the organizational, team and individual levels. Some concern leadership capability accompanied by poor communications up, down or laterally in the organization. Perhaps there are incorrect, ill-defined expectations and a lack of strategic alignment in the project or across the larger organization. Others may reflect significant external market or business change. Regardless, they conspire in the dark corners of organizations to create a lack of focus and mission, a fragmenting of common purpose into special interests and personal agendas, and ultimately stasis in a volatile competitive world.

A strategic knowledge systems perspective is essential to uncover and define project relationships and the risks inherent in project knowledge interfaces. This is critical, since it provides insight into the nature of the realities in which others live. Unless this is analysed and contingencies are planned for, the risk of failure increases. Fortunately the message is getting through to senior executives. In a Conference Board (Hackett, 2000) research report on KM, 80 per cent of surveyed organizations had KM activities under way, 60 per cent expected an enterprise-wide KM system within the next five years, and 25 per cent had a chief knowledge officer or chief learning officer in place. Capturing and effectively relating the journey to achieve outcomes is a story that each individual and team creates and shares. Relating this context helps in understanding where particular organizations are today and how these shared lessons can inform their progress in using project knowledge.

Knowledge services governance

Any KM approach needs to be adaptable and flexible to accommodate the diverse requirements and cultural characteristics of various organizational components.

In reviewing KM efforts and initiatives in other organizations, one realization was that many knowledge practitioners have tried to manage all the knowledge in their organizations, and failed in that these management efforts at best did not achieve full potential. The KM approach needs to be adaptable and flexible enough to accommodate the varied requirements and cultural characteristics of each organizational component. A federated approach can be a good fit, defining knowledge practitioners as facilitators and champions for KS, not overseers and direct managers. It strikes a balance between autonomy and responsibility, where organizational components are free to determine the approach that best fits their particular needs, but are also held responsible to share the knowledge that benefits the overall organization.

This approach ensures that the organization manages knowledge resources in a way to best execute projects, programmes and portfolios with the highest likelihood of success, emphasizing a KS integrated strategic framework. It also defines expectations in terms of roles and responsibilities for knowledge professionals across the organization. This addresses a set of KS priorities that clarifies organizational objectives for project knowledge and emphasizes the development and implementation of future knowledge initiatives, measures and metrics (Figure 36.1):

- In terms of people, sustain and expand the use of intellectual capital across the organization through better networks, alliances and communities of practice.
- In terms of people, increase collaboration across organizational barriers through promotion of a culture of openness.
- In terms of systems, support the technical workforce in executing projects and programmes efficiently and effectively through lessons learned, case studies and promulgation of best practices.
- In terms of systems, create an integrated infrastructure of knowledge that identifies the value of information and aligns practitioner and organizational imperatives through accessible information and user-friendly services.

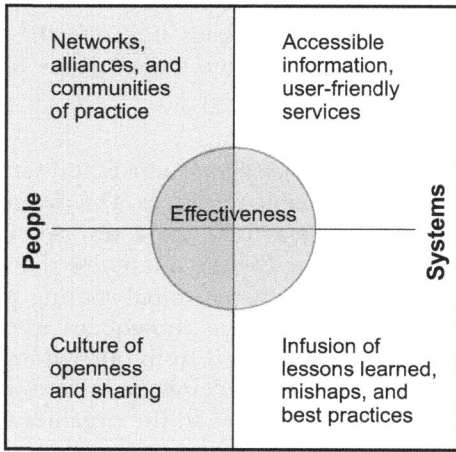

Figure 36.1 Knowledge services strategic framework

Once focused on the status of knowledge, one of the striking things most organizations discover is the depth and breadth of formal and informal knowledge activity that may already be under way. Some occurs through self-service, such as typing a query into a search box and getting answers that point in the right direction, involving one person at a time, and works best with explicit knowledge that does not require a lot of context or personal judgement. At the other extreme, the transmission of tacit knowledge that is dependent on context, experience and personal judgement can be occurring through social interaction at meetings and through storytelling mechanisms and events.

A simple initial set of knowledge categories may address most of the activities taking place across an organization, and can serve as a baseline for creating a knowledge map such as the example from NASA shown in Figure 36.2:

- Online tools include but are not limited to: portals, document repositories, collaboration and sharing sites, video libraries.
- Search/tag/taxonomy tools such as dedicated search engines for knowledge (for example Google Search Appliance) and any initiatives related to meta tagging or taxonomy,
- Case studies/publications such as original documents or multimedia case studies that capture project stories and associated lessons learned or best practices.
- Lessons learned/knowledge processes covering any defined processes that an organization uses to identify or capture knowledge, lessons learned, or best practices, including: lessons learned, organization-specific lessons and learned processes, benchmarking, cases, knowledge sharing recognition programmes, knowledge product validation processes, communications about expectations related to knowledge sharing.
- Knowledge networks consisting of defined knowledge networks, such as: communities of practice, expert locators, mass collaboration activities, workspaces specifically designed to enable exchanges and collaboration.
- Social exchanges consisting of any activities that bring people together in person to share knowledge (such as forums, workshops, brown bags and so forth). The reach of these activities can be multiplied through online tools such as videos and virtual dialogues.

Once completed, a knowledge map links identified knowledge products and services to the map and can mature to create active links to available resources. The categories might not be a perfect fit for every type of knowledge activity across diverse organizations and multiple disciplines, but the hurdle cleared is the awareness that 'the *perfect* is the enemy of the *good*'. These categories serve as an initial starting point that can be institutionalized, modified and clarified during subsequent iterative reviews. Furthermore, there are valuable lessons to be learned from other domestic and international organizations in government, industry, academia and professional organizations that can be used to improve and add resources to the organizational knowledge map.

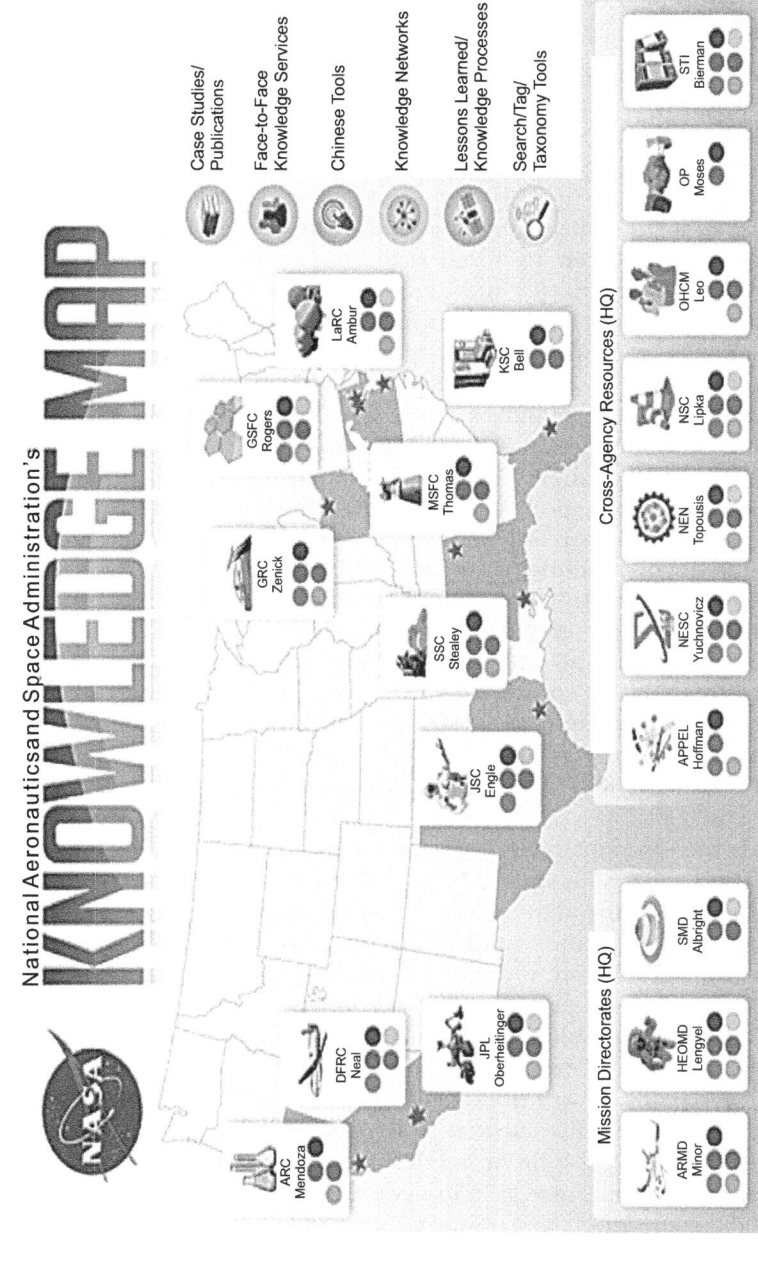

Figure 36.2 Example NASA knowledge map

Strategic imperatives in the modern project knowledge environment

What emerges as potential driving strategic imperatives that inform the development of KS for complex technical project organizations? There are 12 current mutually reinforcing strategic imperatives that have emerged to guide the design, implementation and evaluation of KS for organizations. These are discussed below in no particular order of priority.

One critical strategic imperative is *leadership*, where one of the more fragmented disciplines provides valuable answers for the application of KS in organizations. Without effective leadership, KS and its results are at best serendipitous, at worst fail. The essence of leadership occurs with an insight that things should change, but also a profound realization that the reasons for change may be clear to leaders themselves but not necessarily to the rest of the organization. There exists an external stakeholder community as well as a core internal project team to lead, and both should be understood and managed. Additionally, good leaders align projects with organizational strategy, mission and goals, admittedly easier said than done in the modern project environment of information overload and change. Successful implementation happens with a carefully articulated vision, leadership focus on that vision, and attention to detail on implementation.

It is a *project world*. Diverse organizations worldwide require a methodology allowing for rigour in managing temporary, unique initiatives towards the achievement of defined requirements and project goals and outcomes that are aligned to organizational strategy in an era of constrained resources. In this context, project management is uniquely positioned as an adaptable discipline that fits these requirements and can maximize the use of knowledge and learning to promote efficiency and effectiveness. The alignment of project goals to organizational strategy through good leadership is critical.

Knowledge is the essential element for the creation of successful physical and virtual products and services. It should be viewed as an organized set of content, skills and capabilities gained through experience as well as through formal and informal learning that both organizations and practitioners apply to make sense of new and existing data and information. It can also exist as previously analysed and formatted lessons and stories that are already adaptable to new situations. The ascendance of leaders who can validate the realities to which projects are able to apply knowledge (and base decisions on) is key.

Talent management deals with the specification, identification, nurturing, transfer, maintenance and competitive advantage expansion of practitioner expertise and competence. It encompasses the broad definition of diversity that goes beyond the classic categories of colour, race, religion and national origin to domestic and international variables important to geographically dispersed multicultural teams, such as multi-generational, cross-discipline and cross-experiential variables. This allows diverse groups to bring a diversity of experience, attitudes, knowledge, focus and interests to the table, strengthening both inductive and deductive problem solving approaches and nurturing innovation. Good leaders link talent management with executive sponsorship, organizational strategy and the core work of the organization. They also achieve operational efficiencies by learning, working and collaborating together at a distance independent of time and geography and leverage smart networks that provide content, access and connection to project data, information and knowledge. Talent management is best represented as the variables of abilities, assignments, attitudes and alliances (see Figure 36.4 later in this chapter).

Portfolio management integrates projects with strategies and creates an organizing framework and focus that drives organizational purpose and activities. It provides a centralized function that promulgates a systems view of knowledge, where stove-piped disciplines and activities can transcend boundaries and discover and apply cross-disciplinary knowledge to increase competitive advantage and achieve better results. Organizational expectations can also be tested against reality at this level and adjusted and communicated accordingly to eliminate or mitigate errors and achieve better decisions.

Certification establishes objective, validated standards and functions to benchmark achievement in defined categories of practitioner performance and capability. It also provides organizations and practitioners with a way to establish trust with superiors, peers, team members, customers and stakeholders, and provides a framework for adapting to change as well as a method to address emerging performance requirements. For practitioners, it provides a roadmap for individual development and serves to link organizational performance and individual capability (Duarte *et al.*, 1995). Certification allows for objective definitions of the four Talent Management variables of Abilities, Assignments, Attitudes and Alliances. An example of a discipline standard is the Project Management Body of Knowledge (PMI, 2013) that specifies the ten knowledge areas that currently define the framework of the discipline.

Transparency is an important consideration as the network of organizational portfolio sponsors, project team members, customers, stakeholders, strategic partners, suppliers and other interested parties tie into organizational strategy and project operations through information and communication technology tools. In this environment, nothing is hidden for long and errors travel at the speed of light. Communications with each interface should be carefully defined across intensity and frequency dimensions, for example where external stakeholder communities may expect to be informed about progress at a higher level, but not as frequently or as in-depth as internal leadership. Transparency that is formally built into the strategic business process encourages innovation, translating economies of scale and a breadth of experiential lessons into innovation and flexibility.

Frugal innovation, highlighted by *The Economist* (2010), is a mindset that views constraints in an era of restricted and diminished resources as opportunities, leveraging sustainability and a focus on organizational core competencies to reduce complexity and increase the probability of better outcomes. Sustainability in particular has gained momentum as the cost to the planet and availability of resources increasingly affect business decisions. Organizational core competencies for a product or service involve what it must do in depth rather than what it can do in breadth, ensuring that organizational capacity in areas such as technological, social, political, economic and learning dimensions are part of the frugal innovation process. In a mutually reinforcing perspective, imperatives such as transparency allow the broader team to share knowledge and experience to improve and innovate in terms of products and services, supporting the frugal innovation effort. Knowledge-sharing activities, modern learning strategies, social media processes and tools, and cross-discipline knowledge feed into the broadest possible view of learning for an organization. The operational knowledge process is closely linked to key internal and external knowledge sources and serves to clarify organizational expectations to optimize knowledge searchability, findability and adaptability.

A *problem-centric approach* emphasizes a non-partisan, non-biased, non-judgemental and pragmatic orientation towards problems and solutions, keeping the focus on achievement, improvement and innovation. Organizational expectations for projects are kept pragmatic and constructive when a problem-centric approach is encouraged and expected. At the end of the day, it is about problems, communications, power and building a community of support focused on credible challenges. This orientation serves as the fuel for change while addressing competing agendas and administrative barriers, and directly addresses the issue of bias and heuristics that may introduce error in decisions.

Governance, business management and operations provide for governance, pragmatic alignment, oversight, approvals and implementation of project operations and establish rigour and processes. In an era of frugal innovation, management of the budget and clarity of funding requirements that supports the overall effort must be visible and valued by the leadership and the workforce. Nothing brings trouble faster than mismanagement of resources and a lack of focus on resource flow, so the oversight, tracking and implementation of project activities require definition. Defined governance deals with the issue of 'siloed implementation' and raises executive awareness as well as encouraging and formalizing successful, localized, grassroots knowledge efforts.

Digital technology makes it possible to examine new frontiers of potential knowledge and access multiple sources of data and information, but simultaneously causes organizations to be increasingly buried in data and information and have less time for focus and reflection. Technology is necessary but not sufficient for KS. However, wonderful things can result from the application of technology such as open, social network-centric, non-proprietary, adaptable and flexible frameworks that accelerate learning processes to deliver the right knowledge at the right time for particular needs while respecting context. The proper application of technology helps achieve learning results and better decisions at a lower cost.

The REAL model

With the project environment, the strategic knowledge imperatives, and defining events serving as a framework, there is a critical need for a project KS model that describes the interfaces, variables and components. Alternatively, the last thing needed is a normative model prescribing knowledge methods specific to siloed processes and tools as opposed to broader integrated approaches that are able to accommodate complex organizational strategies.

What analogy can another discipline provide in terms of a systems approach in better understanding the role of knowledge and learning in organizations? The entanglement principle of quantum theory suggests that the measurement of the state of a qubit (a unit of quantum information) determines the potential states of other qubits to which it is linked regardless of distance, but itself is only definitively defined when observed, prompting Einstein's famous description of 'spooky action at a distance' (Bell, 1987). In extending this analogy, information can be understood when local knowledge is applied, but can be misunderstood if the information exists across levels of organization and time that lack context and drives interpretations coloured by assumptions, biases, politics, personal agendas and emotions. In this analogy, leaders applying an incorrect measure in defining the data and information could corrupt the original meaning and extract the wrong lessons, just as applying the wrong measure in physics would corrupt the hypothesis being tested. Retaining and learning not only the lesson but also the context allows practitioners the potential to adapt lessons to diverse project environments.

According to the Conference Board (Hackett, 2000), executives may not be familiar with or possess experience in the KM discipline, resulting in a lack of specific knowledge objectives and goals that can be integrated, measured and managed, thus leading to the potential extraction of the wrong lessons. KS suggests a facilitative approach that not only addresses the topic of knowledge, but also emphasizes learning as an organization and ties the importance of knowledge as a resource across operational and strategic imperatives, reinstating the critical context of the information.

The REAL knowledge model (Figure 36.3) can promote the capabilities to define a problem more comprehensively and accurately, encourage a pragmatic orientation that informs better decision-making, and help to address the issues of bias, ego, special interests and personal agendas. At the core of the REAL knowledge model is the operational KM cycle activities of capture, share and discover, but with a potential effectiveness measure paired with the knowledge activity.

For example: capturing knowledge is the action and retaining is the measure; sharing knowledge is the action and applying is the measure; and discovering is the action and creating outcomes is the measure. Surrounding the REAL knowledge core activities are the individual/team knowledge factors and the organizational/societal

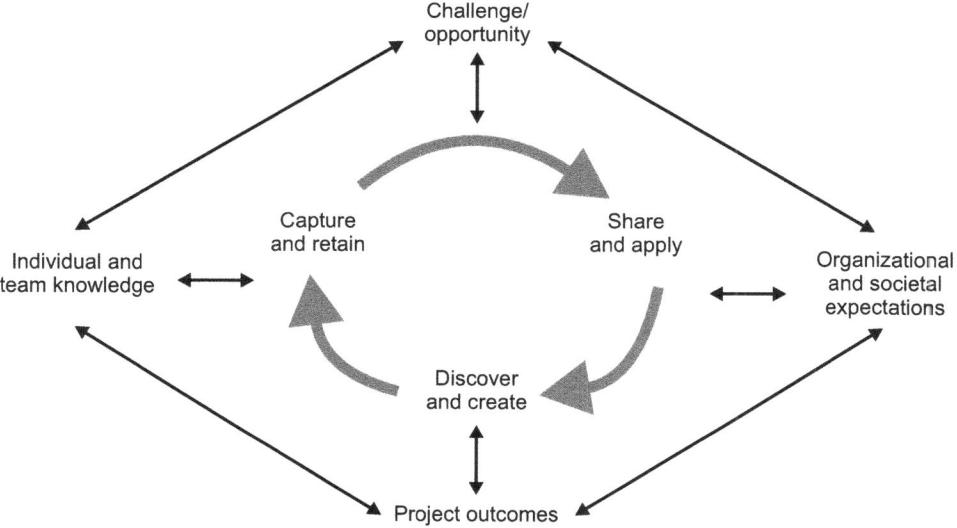

Figure 36.3 The REAL knowledge model

expectations that facilitate the journey of the organizational challenge/opportunity from inception through the knowledge cycle to successful project and programme outcomes. Note that the process arrows are bi-directional in terms of influence and input, addressing continuous change, learning and adaptation.

In describing the REAL knowledge model, the following top-level generic flow serves to illustrate a potential progression of knowledge activity:

- A challenge/opportunity is selected and prioritized (characterized by leadership, knowledge, project world, portfolio and problem-centric imperatives).
- A learning project plan that complements the project charter and project plan is initiated (characterized by knowledge, accelerated learning, frugal innovation and governance, business management and operations imperative).
- The functional communities of practice are recruited with points of contact identified (characterized by leadership, project world, knowledge and talent management imperatives).
- The core operational KM cycle is supported by specific KS learning strategies, methods, models and technology tools to better define the opportunity; aggregate the data, information and knowledge; populate the alternatives for project decisions; provide appropriate online and traditional environments to spur and support innovation through discovery and creation; and support implementation through progressive and iterative knowledge support as the project proceeds through the lifecycle (characterized by knowledge, technology, frugal innovation and accelerated learning imperatives).
- Individual and team knowledge is exploited, encouraged, supported and enhanced through KS activities (characterized by knowledge, talent management, accelerated learning, transparency, frugal innovation and certification imperatives)
- External environment expectations in terms of the organization and broader society are identified and operationalized into objective definitions of performance over time and space (characterized by leadership, knowledge, transparency, frugal innovation, accelerated learning, technology and governance, business management and operations imperatives).
- Project outcomes are achieved in terms of improvement and innovation, and the activity proceeds through closeout to capture and retaining lessons for upcoming projects (characterized by knowledge, portfolio management, transparency, accelerated learning, governance, business management and operations, and digital technology).

The REAL knowledge model component definitions are provided along with associated keywords and concepts to aid potential future research in taxonomies and ontologies related to the narrower model and to the broader knowledge and learning disciplines:

- The Challenge/Opportunity is a problem-centred issue in terms of a product or service that presents a potential for action towards defined outcomes. Possible keywords and concepts include: vision and possibilities; requirements; and organizational capacity in technological, social, political, economic and learning.

- Individual and Team Knowledge are formal and informal individual and collect-ive education, professional development, and lessons from direct and indirect experience applied to a challenge/opportunity. Possible keywords and concepts include: assignments; abilities; formal education; professional development; and mentoring.
- Attitudes and values are the predispositions based on learning, experience and the challenge/opportunity to evaluate the environment in particular ways. Possible keywords and concepts include: personality and inclination; resilience; open-mindedness; curiosity and scepticism; and tempered optimism. Note that these attitudes and values may also be collectively reflected in organizational and societal expectations.
- Heuristics and biases are cognitive shortcuts and simplifications by individuals, teams and organizations used to reduce complexity. Possible keywords and con-cepts include: normalization of deviance; problem-solving and decision-making; fundamental attribution error; and culture of silence. These may be reflected collectively in organizational and societal expectations.
- Abilities and talent are learned or natural patterns of action for both individ-uals and teams that possess potential to achieve goals. Possible keywords and concepts include: critical thinking and creative thinking; problem solving and decision-making; creating alliances; and leadership and persuasion. These may be collectively reflected in organizational and societal expectations.
- Project knowledge is the sum of the formal and informal individual and team knowledge (as previously discussed) within the project context that is applied to existing and new data and information to a challenge/opportunity to gain effi-ciency and effectiveness towards project outcomes. Possible keywords and con-cepts include: success stories and failure stories; learning through analogies; and organizational learning. These may be collectively reflected and applied through organizational and societal expectations.
- Expectations are assumptions on probability of event occurrence for individuals, groups, organizations and societies based on learning and experience. Possible keywords and concepts include: adaptation to change; reputation; executive communications; and past performance.
- Organizational culture comprises common sets of values and assumptions that guide behaviour in organizations that inform problem-solving and decision-making activity. Possible keywords and concepts include: organ-izational norms and mores; environmental context; and performance management.
- Knowledge capture and retention is a core knowledge step involving the identification and storage of relevant content and skills. Possible keywords and concepts include: alliances, communities and networks; cases and pub-lications; risk records, mishap reports, organizational communications; and stories.
- Knowledge sharing and application is a core knowledge step involving the representation, promulgation and utilization of searchable and findable relevant content and skills. Possible keywords and concepts include: digital technology tools; informal learning; and best and emerging practices.

- Knowledge discovery and creation is a core knowledge step that covers original content and skills derived and developed from previous relevant content and skills that result in project outcomes. Possible keywords and concepts include: searchability and findability; taxonomies; and innovation.
- Project outcomes are the achievement of original or improved products or services as defined by the project charter and validated by organizational expectations. Possible keywords and concepts include: value; improvement; innovation; and learning, knowledge and growth.
- One of the components in the REAL knowledge model – organizational and societal expectations – needs to be discussed due to its importance when addressing the topic of complexity. Human cognition, whether individual or group, is coloured by inherent hard-wired preferences in thinking and in shortcuts that accompany decision-making processes, a product of choices and evolution. Biases and heuristics serve to reduce the amount of complexity, but also may introduce error. Additionally, these predispositions may differ across cultures. For example, a complex technical project organization may consist of several divergent domestic and international cultures with different perceptions. Understanding these perceptions is important for success.

Biases and heuristics are not just cognitive distortions that affect decisions, but also are social biases that affect individual and organizational behaviour as well as learning and memory tendencies that affect perceptions and explanations of the world. Daniel Kahneman, in his recent *New York Times* bestseller *Thinking, Fast and Slow* (2013), clarifies how humans address increasing levels of complexity in the project environment through heuristics that can introduce errors into decisions, a veritable catalogue of fundamental predispositions that characterize human cognition. System 1 thinking is fast, instinctive and emotional, while System 2 thinking is slower, more deliberative and more logical. Kahneman delineates cognitive biases associated with each type of thinking, starting with his own research on loss aversion, the unsettling tendency of people and organizations to continue funding a project that has already consumed a tremendous amount of resources but is likely to fail, simply to avoid regret. From framing choices to substitution, the book highlights several decades of academic research to suggest that people may place too much confidence in human judgement, resulting in different outcomes even given the same information input.

Biases and heuristics should be viewed not exclusively in a negative context, but one where these distortions and shortcuts can also provide positive outcomes. Many projects would not be started if executives waited until all the data and information were available to make a rational decision. Biases and heuristics serve a purpose in creating an environment where possibilities and vision can drive an idea towards reality. Busenitz and Barney (1997) found that there is a fundamental difference in the way that entrepreneurs and managers in large organizations make decisions, and that biases and heuristics drive entrepreneurial decisions and are used to reduce complexity in the project environment, simplifying decision-making and preventing data and information from overwhelming programmes and projects, as well as serving to achieve buy-in and motivating practitioners. This often morphs into a tremendous disadvantage as projects mature from start-up activities to implementation and sustainability requirements. A brief set of examples from an extensive catalogue of common biases and heuristics are:

- Availability: making judgements on the probability of events by how easy it is to think of examples and their consequences.
- Substitution: substituting a simple question for a more difficult one.
- Optimism and loss aversion: generating the illusion of control over events and fearing losses more than we value gains.
- Framing: choosing the more attractive alternative if the context in which it is presented is more appealing.
- Sunk-cost: throwing additional money at failing projects that have already consumed large amounts of resources in order to avoid regret.
- Mental filter: focusing on one feature of something that influences all subsequent decisions.
- Fundamental attribution error: the tendency to overemphasize personality-based causes of behaviour and underemphasize situational-based causes of behaviour.
- Egocentric bias: recalling prior events in a favourable light to one's self rather than an accurate objective analysis.

Another important facet of the REAL knowledge model is termed as the 4 A's – Ability, Attitude, Assignments and Alliances – the dimensions that were first developed from original research in workforce development at NASA (Duarte *et al.*, 1995). These components of the model are extracted from interpersonal and team knowledge, attitudes and values, abilities and talent, knowledge capture and retention, and knowledge sharing and application components. They are represented in Figure 36.4 in the 4A word cloud across a personal and interpersonal dimension of effectiveness.

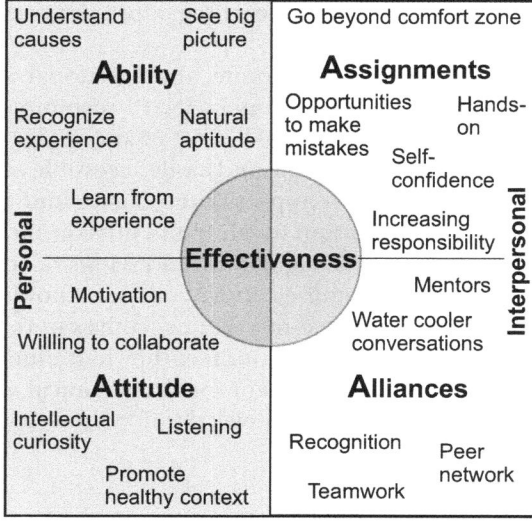

Figure 36.4 The 4A word cloud

REAL knowledge services examples at NASA

The problems that NASA projects seek to solve are often novel in nature, firsts or one-of-a-kind, that increasingly demand the application of strategic imperatives such as frugal innovation, findable and searchable knowledge, and accelerated learning. REAL knowledge services derived from the model are designed to promote excellence in project management and engineering by building a community of practitioners who understand the knowledge flow framework of the organization and are reflective and geared towards sharing. By facilitating and integrating agency-wide KS through interviews, forums, conferences, publications, research and digital offerings, the NASA CKO Office helps to ensure that critical lessons and knowledge remain searchable, findable and adaptable. The CKO knowledge network extends beyond NASA as well, to include expert practitioners from industry, academia, other government agencies, research and professional organizations, and international space agencies. Here we cover three examples of REAL KS activities at NASA.

NASA example 1: critical knowledge activity

This is based on discussions with NASA senior leaders and is conducted by the NASA CKO Office to identify and understand high priority lessons-learned from the executive point of view that have significant impact on programmatic and engineering mission success for the overall agency. The intention is to identify an executive most-critical lessons list and ensure that list is appropriately captured in agency-level policies, standards and learning and development programmes. The REAL knowledge framework represents this as executive knowledge that creates organizational expectations for ongoing and future projects as well as informing all three of the central operational knowledge process elements and activities. Note that these lessons are heavily informed by previous programme and project outcomes. This effort is driven primarily by the strategic knowledge imperatives of leadership, knowledge, portfolio management, transparency, accelerated learning, a problem-centric approach and technology.

This activity was initiated across centres, mission directorate, and functional office leadership in response to an Aerospace Safety Advisory Panel (ASAP) recommendation for a continuous, risk-informed, prioritized and formal effort in knowledge capture and lessons learned that will make them highly visible and easily accessible across NASA, supplemented by formal incorporation into appropriate policies and technical standards of those lessons that are most important to safety and mission success.

To achieve buy-in at executive level, the process begins with interviews of senior leaders designed to promote a discussion that identifies critical mission knowledge and high priority lessons learned. For NASA, it turned out that executives were very enthusiastic to share their views on these lessons but did not feel they had time or a process to ensure retention, sharing and discovery of them for the technical workforce. Examples of sources for data, information and knowledge for these lessons were identified as:

- programme and project reviews;
- NESC technical reports;

- mishap findings,
- Lessons-Learned Information System (LLIS) submissions;
- ASAP recommendations;
- interviews;
- knowledge-sharing forums;
- other technical findings as appropriate.

This activity addresses a factor in the original question of managing projects in an increasingly complex project environment. Examples of complex environments abound: the management of the London Olympics; the development of new pharmaceuticals; the engineering of new airliners like the Boeing 787; and the development of new weapons systems such as the Joint Strike Fighter. The multidisciplinary aspect of integrating the discipline technologies required for these systems is daunting, and requires project managers to juggle several balls in terms of which choices will result in the best outcomes for their project.

The more disciplines that are involved, the deeper and faster is the data and information stream. Managing teams in this environment is another facet of complexity, as well as managing all of the other project interfaces in the broader environment so that the expectations of customers and stakeholders remain reasonable.

Finally, since rarely does a plan remain immutable, changes of all magnitudes and bandwidth must be factored into the project equation. Critical KS at the front end of the process helps to set and promulgate organizational expectations as well as identify and leverage existing and potential digital channels of distribution and engagement. It also functions to identify critical biases and heuristics at the executive level that can potentially be mitigated or translated into improved project measures and metrics.

As the critical knowledge activity progresses, the characteristics of appropriate agency lessons are defined in coordination with executives and the ASAP. To qualify as critical knowledge within this framework, the lessons would need to fit the following criteria:

- possess broad applicability across the agency that does not only refer to narrow information and knowledge essential only to a specified discipline community;
- represent the top 5 per cent of updatable knowledge that is most important for programmatic and engineering missions to learn and implement;
- involve knowledge that keeps evolving towards new applications and missions within a cost-constrained organizational environment;
- lend themselves to a formal process under current and future NASA KS for formal incorporation into appropriate policies and technical standards as well as to technical workforce learning and development products and activities to prevent skills dissipating over time.

Once the interviews were completed and analysed, the NASA CKO and Deputy CKO reported the results back to NASA executives and presented a proposal for the 'knowledge referee process' that would determine lesson applicability, importance, evolution and integration (Figure 36.5). This process is envisaged to occur bi-annually at

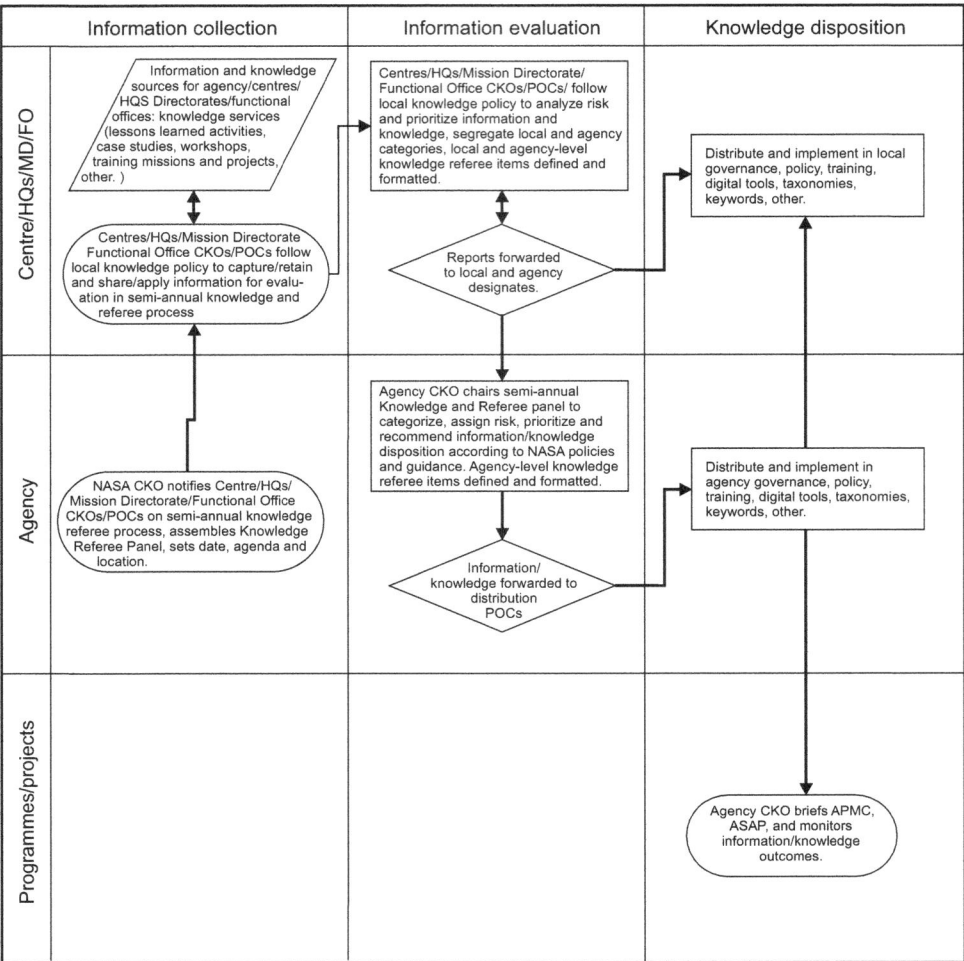

Figure 36.5 The NASA knowledge referee process

NASA headquarters and iteratively briefed to the NASA Deputy Administrator and the ASAP as well as centres, mission directorates and functional offices.

NASA example 2: knowledge forums

Communication about the effective use of knowledge is central to all leadership and management challenges and is critical to the success of NASA's missions and the organization's long-term sustainability. The complexity of NASA's programmes and projects demands an open, vigorous culture where communication is continuous, empowering individuals and teams at all levels to ask questions, share information and raise concerns.

One form of KS that particularly lends itself to multiple requirements and formats is the knowledge forum. This format is particularly adaptable across organizational constituencies and is cooperatively designed to promote open communications through a number of channels about best practices, lessons learned and new developments at NASA and throughout the world. These forums range from small, engaging one-day events at centres to agency-wide synchronous and asynchronous discussions with leading practitioners that are captured digitally and modularized through multiple distribution channels such as NASA TV. The forum service is driven primarily by the strategic knowledge imperatives of leadership, knowledge, talent management, portfolio management, transparency, frugal innovation, a problem-centric approach, accelerated learning and technology.

Each customized forum features leading experts and practitioners selected by the particular organizational entity and involves relevant knowledge-related challenges, relevant case studies, formal and informal discussions, and networking in order to accelerate learning and cultivate a vibrant knowledge network that can benefit NASA and its partners, customers and stakeholders. Attendance is both virtual and physical, and forums leverage social media for concurrent and follow-on engagements.

Just months before the retirement of the Space Shuttle, a forum entitled Passing the Torch provided an opportunity for master practitioners from the Space Shuttle and Constellation programmes to reflect on some of the lessons learned from the formulation, development and operations of their programmes and to look forward to and anticipate future space transportation systems requirements. As with most KS activities, it was a collaborative effort across the Academy and the Public Affairs Offices of the Kennedy Space Centre and NASA headquarters. The programme included several panel discussions, including one dedicated to young professionals from various NASA centres and academia.

A final forum example was the Principal Investigator (PI) Team Forum, an iterative collaborative effort between the NASA CKO and the Science Mission Directorate (SMD) that brought together teams from the Discovery mission Announcement of Opportunity (AO) process and the Mars 2016 Trace Gas Orbiter mission to gain a better understanding of the role of a Principal Investigator (PI) at NASA. Expert practitioners from past science missions shared stories, perspectives, lessons learned and best practices with their colleagues. The proceedings from the forum were published in a multimedia wiki that keeps the knowledge updated and relevant. SMD currently views this activity as critical and it is a mandatory event for new NASA PIs.

NASA example 3: hands-on project experience

An example of an agency-wide knowledge priority that focused on talent development as a priority was a cooperative workforce development programme sponsored with the SMD called Project HOPE (Hands-On Project Experience). Project HOPE was driven primarily by the strategic knowledge imperatives of leadership; project world; knowledge; talent management; frugal innovation; a problem-centric approach; accelerated learning; governance, business management and operations; and technology.

This KS was designed to provide an opportunity for a team of early-entry NASA managers and engineers to propose, design, develop, build and launch an actual sub-orbital flight project over the course of 18 months, enabling practitioners in the early stage of their careers to gain the knowledge and skills necessary to manage NASA's real future flight projects. All of the organization's governance, business management, and operations policies, procedures, standards and sources of knowledge were applied to the project, yielding critical lessons within a real world context.

One example project was the joint Ames Research Centre (ARC) and Langley Research Centre (LaRC) Radiation Dosimetry Experiment (RaD-X) that was designed to obtain the first-ever, high-altitude dosimetric measurements of cosmic ray interaction in the upper atmosphere, while combining LaRC's unique capabilities in space weather applications, radiation effects on air transportation, and microsatellite development to create a low-risk, high-fidelity mission that addressed agency programmatic goals. Public and private entities currently use the NASA Nowcast of Atmospheric Ionizing Radiation for Aviation Safety (NAIRAS) model for informed decision-making about radiation exposure safety for flight crews, the general public, and commercial space operations. RaD-X improves NAIRAS by obtaining data to perform verification and validation activities that enhance this capability.

The project also strengthens microsatellite development at LaRC. The RaD-X microsatellite structure developed at LaRC flies on a scientific research balloon for 24 hours at approximately 36 km (approximately 120,000 feet). It validates low-cost sensors for future missions and provides data to improve the health and safety of all future commercial and military aircrews who transit the poles.

The High Energy Replicated Optics to Explore the Sun (HEROES) project was a joint effort by Goddard Space Flight Centre (GSFC) and Marshall Space Flight Centre (MSFC). It involved a balloon-borne hard X-ray telescope observing solar flares with 100 times better sensitivity and 50 times more dynamic range than the best solar observations to date. The instrument provided new views (improved angular resolution and sensitivity) of hard X-ray astrophysical targets. The HEROES team modified and flew the HEROES telescope to perform solar observations while taking advantage of nighttime for astrophysical observations. The project built on previous knowledge from past flight projects at MSFC and previous GSFC experience in developing instrumentation for solar observations and performing quality solar data analysis. It paved the way for future generations of both solar and astrophysics space-borne hard X-ray imager missions and the scientists and engineers to support them.

The Development and Evaluation of Satellite Validation Tools by Experimenters (DEVOTE) project was flown by LaRC. This project successfully achieved its science goals of:

- enabling evaluation of next-generation satellite retrievals focusing on the ACE Decadal Survey Mission;
- developing an *in situ* measurement platform that would be available for frequent and relatively low cost flights;
- developing advanced instruments and comparing measurements to satellite and ground-based instruments.

At the project's end, the DEVOTE team had:

* successfully completed all planned modifications to the aircraft, enabling both *in situ* and remote sensing platforms;
* flown 12 science flights for over 69 hours;
* successfully completed all of its science and training objectives.

The Coastal and Ocean Airborne Science Testbed (COAST) project was flown by ARC over Monterey Bay, California. The team integrated and simultaneously flew three instruments in the testbed: a sun photometer, an imaging spectrometer and radiometers. The instrument suite obtained data during the mission coincident with measurements from existing satellite sensors, measurements from a research vessel, and a small set of ground calibration sites.

A final example is the Terrain-Relative Navigation and Employee Development (TRaiNED) project by the Jet Propulsion Laboratory. In 2006, an initial development test was conducted onboard a sounding rocket flight that collected analogue ground imagery during the descent portion of the rocket trajectory and positional data from launch to landing. These data were then used to further develop and test Terrain-Relative Navigation (TRN) computer algorithms. The TRaiNED project was the next step in the development of this new technology. As a second developmental test flight, the TRaiNED project advanced the first flight results by expanding the dataset to include exo-atmospheric imagery in addition to descent imagery. Key members from the initial project acted as mentors for the TRaiNED team and assisted with the design, fabrication and testing of the payload.

Summary and future research

How can organizations and practitioners best use project knowledge and KS to get things done in today's complex project environment?

Effective KS is often a steady progression of maturity influenced by the requirements of specific requirements over time. A particular organization as it exists today is not the same one that existed previously. For example, individual practitioner capability can fit the organization at the beginning, but that soon can morph into a team-based approach driven by diverse project and programme requirements as the purpose of the organization changes over the years.

The complexity of the project environment forces KS to adjust to the new realities of knowledge findability, searchability and adaptability, highlighting the need for accelerated learning within a systems perspective and revealing the synergy between the disciplines of KM and organizational learning, often driving a need to take advantage of opportunities for greater coordination and collaboration across the organization.

The strategic imperatives that guide the development of KS are a product of their times, addressing the realities and requirements for planning and action concerning leadership, complexity, limited resources, communication, knowledge, individual and organizational capability, and process. These imperatives can take different forms depending on specific organizational characteristics and needs at the strategic, operational and tactical levels.

The federated approach allows for an effective balance of autonomy and responsibility. With this approach, the knowledge community generates common definitions and purpose and develops reinforcing products and services that address both local and broader organizational knowledge considerations, to potentially include desired outcomes such as a new knowledge policy, a knowledge map, and improved communications with customers and stakeholders.

We presented the REAL knowledge model as a description of how knowledge flow and KS can work in an organization. It allows organizations to formulate KS activities that address identified strategic knowledge imperatives, achieve buy-in across diverse communities, and accelerate learning to reduce complexity and ensure risks based on knowledge are identified and mitigated or eliminated.

Future research can advance the understanding of the components of this model to achieve normative assumptions, definitions and standards that promote effective and efficient knowledge practices that reduce complexity and accelerate learning to achieve successful outcomes. Accordingly, the following future research initiatives should advance understanding and yield practical benefits for project organizations:

1. What are the characteristics of challenges and opportunities that achieve organizational and individual commitment, align individual and organizational agendas, and promote effective project management?
2. How should organizations systematically address talent development in terms of abilities, attitudes, assignments and alliances?
3. What are the metrics and measures that best capture effectiveness and efficiency in the knowledge processes and outcomes of capturing and retaining, sharing and applying, and discovering and creating?
4. Can biases and heuristics that drive organizational and societal expectations be identified and addressed to inform how organizations can make better decisions and design better measures for the challenge/opportunity, the core knowledge processes and project outcomes?
5. What are the operational definitions and certification parameters of knowledge behaviours for project practitioners and how do these affect talent development and capability requirements?
6. How can the characteristics that make data and information searchable and findable and result in adaptable knowledge in a systems approach to organizational knowledge and learning be operationalized to effective requirements and behaviours?
7. What is the nature of the relationship between KS, accelerated learning and reducing complexity?

In closing this chapter, there is much work and research needed for examining how organizations and practitioners can best make use of project knowledge and KS to get things done in the modern complex project environment. The potential mitigating and complicating variables that reduce the power of knowledge and learning are too numerous to list, but from an organizational systems perspective the REAL knowledge descriptive model can serve as a framework to ensure that the breadth of relevant components are identified and operationalized, as well as serving as a map for future research towards informing a normative project knowledge model.

References and further reading

Anselmo, J. and Hedden, C. (2011), 'Up and Down: A Workforce in Transition – Commercial Companies Hire as Defense and Space Pare Down', *Aviation Week and Space Technology*, 22 August, 44–53.

Bell, J. S. (1987), *Speakable and Unspeakable in Quantum Mechanics*, Cambridge: Cambridge University Press.

Busenitz, L. W. and Barney, J. B. (1997), 'Differences between Entrepreneurs and Managers in Large Organizations: Biases and Heuristics in Strategic Decision-Making', *Journal of Business Venturing*, 12: 9–30.

Davenport, T. and Prusak, L. (1998), *Working Knowledge*. Boston, MA: Harvard Business School Press.

Dragland, A. (2013), 'Big Data – for Better or Worse'. <www.sintef.no/home/corporate-news/Big-Data–for-better-or-worse/>.

Duarte, D., Lewis, A., Crossman, D. and Hoffman, E. (1995), 'A Career Development Model for Project Management Workforces', *Journal of Career Development*, 22(1): 149–64.

Economist (2010), 'First Break all the Rules: The Charms of Frugal Innovation',15 April.

Hackett, B. (2000), *Beyond Knowledge Management: New Ways to Work and Learn. Research Report 1262-00-RR*, New York: The Conference Board.

Hoffman, E. and Boyle, J. (2013), 'Tapping Agency Culture to Advance Knowledge Services at NASA', *The Public Manager*, Fall: 42–3.

Kahneman, D. (2013), *Thinking, Fast and Slow*. New York: Farrar, Straus & Giroux.

Kirkpatrick, M. (2010), 'Google, Privacy and the New Explosion of Data', Web log post, 4 August. <http://techonomy.typepad.com/blog/2010/08/google-privacy-and-the-new-explosion-of-data.html>.

Neffinger, J. and Kohut, M. (2013), *Compelling People: The Hidden Qualities that Make Us Influential*, New York: Hudson Street Press.

PMI (2013), *A Guide to the Project Management Body of Knowledge: PMBOK Guide*, 5th edn., Newtown Square, PA: Project Management Institute.

PMI (2014), *Pulse of the Profession In-Depth Report: The High Cost of Low Performance*, Newtown Square, PA: Project Management Institute.

Polanyi, M. (1966), *The Tacit Dimension*, Chicago: University of Chicago Press.

Part V

Developing Maturity in Programme Management

Introducing Programme Management into an Organization

Marcus Paulus

Programmes have become an indispensable part of many organizations. This chapter is about establishing programmes in organizations that have little or no previous programme management experience.

Introduction: the nature of programmes

Programmes are undertaken to achieve long-term strategic goals, which usually means an outcome that produces measurable benefits for the organization. A programme comprises various projects, each with its own set of individual project deliverables, all contributing to the eventual benefits.

A programme organization has to be established above any existing dedicated project organization. This new organization brings together all the individual projects and provides an additional management framework that is necessary to reach the intended benefits for the organization. In projects we customarily speak about achieving 'deliverables' but 'benefits realization' has largely prevailed in the context of programmes. In the context of programme management the focus is on developing new skills for the organization and dealing with change management challenges and achieving the strategic goals of the organization.

In addition to dealing with programmes and their internal management, organizations are faced with external influencing factors. Of course there are usually external stakeholders. Also, an organization might be involved in the programmes of a parent organization (such as a holding company). Another possibility is that the organization is contributing work to the programme of another organization (for example, in a project that belongs to a particular project or programme of another company). Thus it is possible that there will be internal and external drivers and factors for any organization that has to organize and manage a programme.

We have to assume, as a prerequisite, that an 'enterprise programme management office' (EPMO) is established that can take care of the governance and guidelines for project management. The EPMO has to ensure that every programme and its management fit into the organization's governance model. The EPMO has to be prepared in an appropriate manner, so that a suitable answer is available whenever there is a need to deal with programmes.

At the beginning it is advisable to develop a roadmap for the organization which shows how it will develop programme management skills and competence. This roadmap (specific for the organization) should demonstrate what must be done to

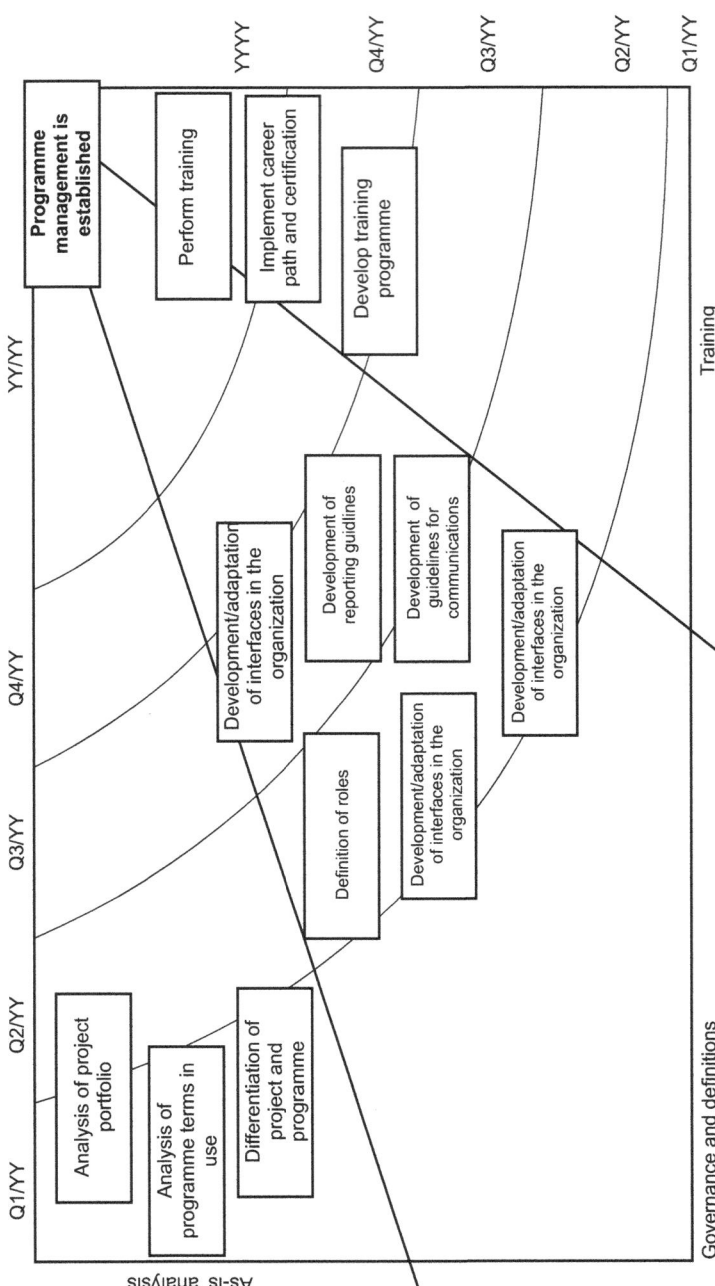

Figure 37.1 Development roadmap of programme management in an organization

support any programme in addition to the existing professional support for project management. The roadmap should show how the management of programmes will differ from the management of projects in the organization (see Figure 37.1).

There is much confusion in many organizations about the term 'programme'. Compared to the definition of a project, there are entirely different and a greater number of explanations for a programme. Examples are investment programme, reorganization programme, strategic programme, education programme, energy efficiency programme, funding programme and development programme. In recent years definitions have emerged from organizations like IPMA, OGC and PMI. Nevertheless, the term 'programme' as understood in the project management discipline is not used accordingly by many organizations and it is not yet well established.

The IPMA describes in ICB 3.0 (International Competence Baseline) both projects and programmes and distinguishes these roughly as follows: 'The goal of a project is to produce deliverables' and 'The goal of a programme is to achieve strategic change' (IPMA, 2006).

OGC published the first edition of the standard *Managing Successful Programmes* (MSP) in 2003. OGC defines a programme as a temporary organization, created to coordinate, direct and oversee the implementation of a set of related projects and activities in order to deliver outcomes and benefits related to the organization's strategic objectives (OGC, 2007).

In 2006 PMI published the *Standard for Program Management* (PMI, 2013). PMI defines a programme as a group of related projects, subprogrammes and programme activities that are managed in a coordinated way to obtain benefits not available from managing them individually.

Since 2011 the institution GAAPS has published *GAAPS Program Manager: A Framework for Performance Based Competency Standards for Program Managers* (GAPPS, 2011). GAPPS does not publish its own definition but rather gives different examples of definitions and compares and comments on these.

Programme governance in the context of portfolio, programme and project management

Governance is conducted very differently in different countries around the world and there is more variation in the different organizations in these countries. However, it should be apparent that programme governance must match and be well coordinated with the existing project governance of a company.

An organization has to decide for itself how to use and handle the entire topic of governance in the context of portfolio, programme and project management. Even among experts there is considerable debate about how deep in detail the governance of portfolio, programme and project management should go. In other words, how far should the governance extend into the depth of the project or programme itself, or how much freedom and independence must be preserved to the project, or the programme? How much autonomy should be left to the programme owner and the programme manager in order to take into account the individual needs of the programme?

Practice has shown that the implementation of programme management in any case leads to a review of the previously developed governance for project management. A wide-ranging, generally valid statement about how to integrate programme management into existing project management governance cannot be made. Each organization should make a decision after a careful consideration of its specific requirements. An organization that defines only very superficial governance for project management should make sure that it can be more rigorous when it introduces programme management. A good governance framework will support the set-up of deliverable-orientated initiatives in the form of projects and also the set-up of benefits-orientated initiatives in the form of programmes.

Now we have to ask 'What subjects or key principles should be addressed in any case regarding programme governance?' Here is a check-list:

- Define and explain terms for programme management in the context of the organization concerned.
- Distinguish between portfolio management, programme management and project management and provide descriptions of the differences with simple and clear statements. Important here is to produce good and relevant reference for the company concerned, which can be done by using examples from company practice and history.
- Visualize possible forms of programme organization and describe roles and responsibilities. Describe how the organization of a project will be integrated into the programme organization.
- Clear processes for initiating, planning and control of programmes should be in place. Established processes for project management may change because of the introduction of programme management. In particular these potential changes should be addressed.
- Ensure integration into the recognized communication and reporting structures, especially from the programme to the portfolio management and from programme to the programme's projects. Attention to communication within the programme and externally has to be considered. Thus all change management aspects must be considered.
- Describe how new projects will be integrated into the programme and how completed projects throughout the programme lifecycle will be released from the programme.

Creating clarity in the terminology

It soon becomes obvious that an organization needs to provide clarity in the use of the term 'programme' and that the term must be defined clearly within the organization. In most organizations the company's EPMO takes the responsibility for this task. The EPMO should be responsible for ensuring that there are rules and instructions for the application of the terms project, programme and portfolio management within the organization. The EPMO communicates the key performance indicators (KPIs) which are necessary for the control of the portfolios.

The programme management office (PMO) is responsible for the definition of guidelines and governance for project management. It is assumed that the PMO has been guided by one of the common international project management standards since project management was introduced in the organization concerned. These standards usually provide a good basis for defining the term 'programme' and give guidelines for the implementation of programme management. Each organization needs to elaborate its specific definitions for itself. As one of the first steps, a PMO manager should investigate how the term 'programme' is currently used within the organization and then question whether the current definition can be applied to the management of programmes in general.

The PMO needs to enquire and ensure whether or not a formal definition of the term 'programme' already exists in all parts of the organization (see Figure 37.2) and then examine whether this definition supports the view of PMO, or whether the existing definition would prevent the application of the concept from the viewpoint of the PMO. Any kind of definition that has arisen in the context of project management would be called *supportive*. Any kind of definition that originates from other sources or concepts unrelated to project management could be mentioned as the *preventing* definitions.

Where an organization operates multiple programmes, including programmes within programmes, it might be helpful for the organization to differentiate between different types of programmes. That might not apply in the beginning of a company's programme development but the PMO should map different programme types for possible use in the future. A distinction between different types of programmes could be made, for example, where programmes are initiated to support the achievement of several strategic lines of attack.

Examples of different strategic approaches could be new product development, mergers and acquisitions or the introduction of new technology. Not all programmes are based on strategic objectives. Drivers for such exceptions could, for example, be conforming to external regulations or legislation from a government or regulatory authority.

Definitions that distinguish between different types of programmes must be approved at a very high level. That should guarantee that there are no subsequent

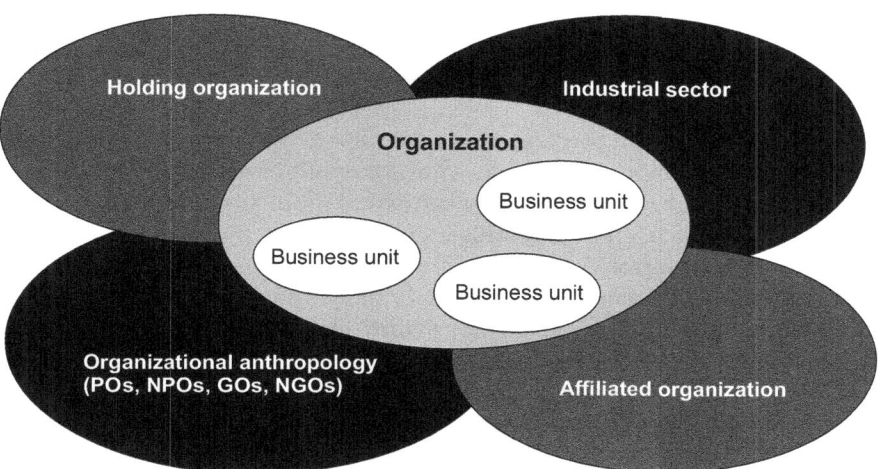

Figure 37.2 Internal and external environment for analysing usage of the term 'programme'

contradictions or restrictions between the types of programmes and the types of projects assigned to the programme.

Creating distinction between projects and programmes

When introducing programme management into an organization it must be ensured that there is good definition and delineation between projects and programmes from the beginning. In any case, an already clean definition of project represents a good foundation. The distinction between projects and programmes can be illustrated with some striking examples from the relevant organization.

The higher the level of project management maturity in the organization, the more likely the introduction of programme management will succeed. If a company already follows a standard for project management and this standard also takes into account a generic definition of programmes, that definition is clearly a good start and a good basis for the organization-specific definition of programmes. It is sometimes necessary to redefine the term 'project' so that there is a clear and unambiguous understanding of these two terms. A sharp and unambiguous separation of the terms project and programme is not always easy.

It is recommended to make the distinction depending on various parameters which together make up a particular picture. It is necessary to ensure that the distinction is explainable and does not end up being a pseudo-scientific consideration. For example, the parameter 'degree of strategic importance', viewed by itself, cannot be used to distinguish between programme and project. In a single case, if a clear strategic goal is available and accountable to a specific intention, the project form of organization will most likely lead to a success.

At a generic level it is not easy to set distinguishing features, such as the duration, the number of involved units or the number of employees in a project or a programme as a differentiator. However, for a specific organization the distinguishing features are relatively easy to specify. If an organization on average employs 30 to 50 participants from three to five different organizational units in a project, then the organization is able to draw a line between project and programme, based on the number of involved employees and organizational units involved. Also, criteria such as project duration or project budget can serve as a guide for the organization concerned.

A good way to detect distinctive features is the after-action review of completed projects or the review of the current project portfolio and to examine whether the settlement as a programme would have been better and more advantageous. If somebody chooses this approach, simultaneously a good basis for the definition of programmes on the basis of various examples from their own organization is created. Following this practice, the focus should take place in investigating historical data on projects in the context of change. These are mainly projects where strategic initiatives of the company were undertaken and projects where attention was paid to winning new skills for the organization.

IT projects are typically a good source within an organization. IT projects are very often started in order to introduce a new software solution on a large scale in organizations. Often hundreds of employees are affected and processes and responsibilities within the company are changed dramatically. It is in the nature of things that the managers of IT projects often focus on implementing the software solution and completely ignore the corresponding organizational change. If IT projects are implemented as programmes there is a high probability of achieving a much better result because the relatively high complexity level can be managed better in a programme.

Mergers and acquisitions (M&A) are a similarly interesting source for research. The complexity and diversity of the projects initiated within a merger suggests implementation in the form of a programme. M&A projects have short-, medium- and long-term perspectives. They can be better planned, better managed and controlled if they are initiated as programmes.

Big relocation projects are typical candidates for managing as programmes. For example, when the different locations of an organization are consolidated and centralized, that is first and foremost a relocation project. The organization will run a lot of projects in parallel, which are very closely linked to this project. The construction of the new headquarters is a project itself. There might also be changes in the organization structure. In order to prevent losing the strategic goals to realize the benefits of concentrating activities and know-how in one location, it is reasonable to perform the entire initiative in the form of a programme.

Distinguishing between portfolio management and programme management

Organizations which introduce programme management will also have to have well-founded project portfolio management. Organizations with a relatively high project management maturity level can do this more easily. The distinction between the management of projects and the management of a portfolio is simple. In portfolio management we are talking of a variety of individually managed and independently performed projects, which were launched to achieve or support the strategic objectives of an organization. A project portfolio is formed when several independent projects exist in parallel to achieve the strategic objectives of an organization. The management of a project portfolio is to be understood as a permanent body and is usually not limited in time, as is the case with projects and programmes.

Projects or programmes will be prioritized in a portfolio in terms of their support or their contribution to strategy in order to assist the achievement of the organization's overall strategy. An example could be an energy supplier whose strategic goal is to generate 150 MW of electricity from wind power over the next 12 years. Therefore eight projects are initiated. These projects are combined in the subportfolio of wind energy. Should one of the projects for any reason be proven as commercially unviable, another opportunity will be launched as a project so that the overall strategic goal of 150 MW can be reached.

In contrast to a project portfolio, the projects of a programme are in a stronger relationship and are interdependent. In order to achieve the programme's objectives, all projects in the programme need to be successfully completed. Only then is it guaranteed that the programme benefits can be reached. In addition there is other related work at the level of the programme that is necessary to achieve the benefits of the programme.

There may be occasions when subportfolios are called programmes (for example, when an organization performs certain similar projects at the same time). Particular importance should therefore be attached to this different interpretation before the implementation of programme management is started.

It is important for the organization to understand the above differentiations between portfolio management and programme management. This will affect the allocation of roles, which is dealt with in the next section. Programme and portfolio managers will have less to do with the details of individual projects or problems, than with issues that are superior or across projects and therefore have to be addressed at the programme level or portfolio level.

Roles, responsibilities and duties

Organizations that have already achieved a good overall maturity level of project management should already have good role descriptions and regulations for managing projects. These descriptions will need to be examined, and almost certainly revised and expanded to include the roles and functions of programme management. Established international project management standards offer a good generic base that can be adapted to the organization's specific requirements.

As is well known from the description of roles and responsibilities of project management, there are also no uniform definitions of roles and responsibilities in programme management. Every organization has to develop its own definitions. The importance of project management in an organization, or how strongly the organization is dominated by the line function, depends on the respective organization. Depending on that, the organization has to handle carefully the necessary adaptation of project management roles and the definition of programme management roles.

The organization has to make sure that there is no duplication of roles or overlapping areas of responsibility. It is recommended to offer models, where possible forms of organization for the programme are presented on the basis of the identified types of programmes. These scenarios provide on one hand the possible forms of programme organization and explain on the other hand how the project organization has to be integrated into the programme organization.

Usually a programme organization includes a PMO. Among other things the PMO is responsible for tasks such as consolidating and aggregating the project plans from the various projects of the programme. In addition, the PMO should document and observe the dependencies and interactions within the projects and between the projects of the programme. Another role that can be transferred to PMO is the coordination of additional components that cannot be accommodated in any of the projects of the programme (but are necessary to achieve programme benefits). Overall, it is recommended that the PMO has more of a tactical scope of duties rather than operational or administrative tasks.

The programme sponsor has the highest authority in the programme organization. Consequently, the programme sponsor should also have the authority to initiate or end projects in the programme because of his/her overall responsibility for the programme's success. Depending on the governance of a particular organization it has to be decided whether that authority can be given to a programme sponsor. Sufficient thought must be given when deciding on how to work with this single authority, when the usual way to initiate or start a project is done by a portfolio group or a project board.

In the opposite case the organization has to think about how a programme sponsor can take over the responsibility for a programme, if he/she is subject to the same rules for initiating a project as the rest of the organization. This question must be considered very carefully and in great detail and answered unambiguously. In some organizations it is not possible to establish an authority outside the existing rules, for example when parent companies are involved. Also to be considered are the specified signatories and rules for making and approving decisions. The introduction of programme roles and programme authorities has to be aligned with the well-established decision-making hierarchy.

Another very important governance issue is the relationship between programme sponsors and project sponsors. Depending on the type of programme, it might make sense that the programme sponsor is also nominated as a sponsor for each project within the programme. If the sponsorship for the programme project is at the same level, the programme can run largely without conflict and be result-orientated. If the programme sponsor and the project sponsors are different, a higher potential for conflict can be expected. On the other hand, it might make more sense for certain types of programmes that the project sponsors are chosen differently for each project. In such cases, it is even more important that the responsibilities and authority of the programme and the responsibilities and authority of the project are described and designated clearly.

Roles and responsibilities that must be defined in all cases

In an organization that wants to implement programme management a clear definition of roles is essential. Roles must be defined by the PMO and implemented after good coordination at all levels of the organization. This cannot be done by training alone. Management awareness is necessary and all relevant interfaces of the organization need to be aligned accordingly.

The OGC defines four key roles for the programme organization: the Senior Responsible Owner, the Programme Manager, the Business Change Managers and the Programme Office (OGC, 2011)

PMI defined as roles the Program Sponsor, the Program Governance Board Members, the Program Manager, Project Manager and the Program Team Members (PMI, 2013).

In an organization where project management is already well established, it should be investigated on which hierarchical level a project sponsor is typically placed. For example, if the project sponsor is settled in middle management, then the programme authority can come from a higher hierarchical level (from the senior management). If this is the current situation in an organization it is not expected that the introduction of programme management will lead to a conflict. In many organizations the project sponsor is settled already in top management and then it will not be easy to explain the differences between the role of a programme sponsor and the role of a project sponsor.

Programme initiation, planning, control and closing

Just as with projects, a programme needs to be initiated, planned, conducted, controlled and closed. If an organization decides to introduce programme management, the processes for programmes must be defined too and the existing processes for projects will have to be adjusted.

It is usually expected that a new change initiative will be conducted from the beginning as a programme. However, programme initiation does not always run to an ideal pattern. Initiatives are often launched as projects when it is later realized that these would have been better handled as programmes. Sometimes it is necessary to integrate projects that were initially launched independently in a programme organization. Conversely, there might be a request to detach a project from a programme and continue with it as an independent project. When introducing programme management it is necessary to be aware of these possibilities and provide ways to deal with them.

With the introduction of programme management there must be a mechanism in place that considers the transfer of changed conditions and requirements from the programme level into the project level. Conversely it must be ensured that planning and other data from each project can be fed into the programme. In the programme, all components must be taken into consideration which includes the interrelated project components as well as the work coming from programme level. Other factors could include (for example):

- central communication to the external environment and stakeholders at programme level;
- collective and coordinated procurement to exploit economies of scale;
- joint logistics, warehousing and materials management;
- joint recruitment of project resources.

The new programme management has to elaborate rules, such as how to integrate projects that will be launched at a later date in the programme. The organization must answer the question of how much guidance on programme governance is to be supplied from the organization and how much freedom should be left to programme management responsibility.

An organization should not underestimate the necessity of a well-considered and transparent process for introducing new projects into the programme. The faster a new project and its project team can be integrated, the faster this project will be able to work, the fewer friction losses will occur and there will be less risk.

Just as in project management, programme management has to monitor the progress, the issues, the risks, the results and benefits of a programme and take appropriate control and corrective actions. These actions can be generated at the level of the projects in the programme (bottom-up), or from the programme level (top-down). Suitable complementary structures have to be established at programme and project levels which involve the appropriate management. The programme manager appointment must be considered more carefully than a project manager appointment, A good programme manager must ensure that the components are able to achieve their intended results and that the dependencies of the components are managed in a coordinated way.

Closedown procedures

Another component that needs to be observed during the implementation of programme management is the closedown procedure. First, the closing of each project completed during the programme lifecycle needs to be considered. As the projects in a programme have strong interdependencies, management of relationships and dependencies must be ensured. When projects follow each other in the programme, adequate transfer time has to be allowed between projects or phases for the successor to receive the results from the predecessor. Thus, 'friction losses' in the handover of project results or project subresults can be kept low. Something that needs clarification here is the extent to which a project in its closing phase needs to be involved in the start-up phase of its successor project.

Initial programme closedown is of course not the end of the story. Following internationally established standards, one of the key differentiators between projects and programmes is that projects provide deliverables and programmes achieve benefits. Benefits realization is an important subject in itself – see for example Bradley (2010). Fowler and Lock (2006) also deal with this subject. Benefits realization depends on aligning all the constituent project results to a common programme objective.

Three fundamental indicators

Three fundamental indicators should be considered before introducing programme management in an organization. These indicators derive from the organization's project portfolio and are as follows:

- Project chain: several projects that were initiated in sequence to achieve a particular end state or result.
- Accumulation and parallelisms in the projects: a number of projects which are attributable to a particular strategic objective, or projects running simultaneously on similar topics.
- Projects with high contributions to strategic potentials: top-down initiated projects which can make a significant strategic contribution, or projects that are assigned to the same strategic goal and were started in different units of the organization.

Project chains

Projects chains have their justification in a portfolio. It can happen that several attempts to find a solution for unclear objectives or a very complex project goal are hidden behind a project chain. Such a sequential approach can lead to a more laborious situation with inferior results compared with the more holistic approach in the organizational form of a programme. What needs to be examined in this context is whether the cost of developing and delivering a programme organization will pay off. Managing the projects and their dependencies on programme level and processing the projects in overlap (or even in parallel) should lead to better and faster results and additional benefits for the organization.

Cumulative or parallel projects

Cumulative or parallel projects in a portfolio can arise from different triggers. A typical trigger is for example to achieve a specific strategic objective of the organization. To achieve this specific strategic objective, numbers of projects are initiated in the organization. Despite the fact of a clear top-down approach, each project follows its specific project goals. By spreading the overall target over a number of projects, focus on the strategic objective is lost. A high level of coordination (as typically exists in programme management) can solve this. The strategic objectives and the expected benefits for the organization can be better managed and achieved more successfully using a programme.

Examples of other types of cumulative projects can be found in product development, multidisciplinary engineering projects and IT. Each project has defined objectives and must deliver the agreed results. The overall objectives such as the technological leadership or the achievement of synergies in product development can often only be realized if these projects are combined and managed in a programme.

In the above-mentioned examples the necessary top-down approach is often missing. By analysing the project portfolio and viewing the dependencies of parallel projects, it is quite easy for an organization to consider if a higher-level programme organization and programme control could help to achieve the expected benefits. In addition, a programme organization can help to identify synergies between the various projects. Then risks of double working can be detected and avoided earlier.

Projects with potentially high strategic contributions

The most promising projects in the project portfolio are those that contribute to achieving high-level strategic goals (such as mergers and acquisitions or other organizational changes). In general, establishment as a project might not be wrong and could produce good results. However, the organization should consider whether setting up a programme would increase the chances of achieving all the desired benefits. Combining projects in a programme and controlling their interdependencies and results raises the probability of realizing the benefits. Applying programme management when implementing a major organizational change puts the programme manager in a better position to coordinate the issues and challenges across the entire organization.

Integration of programmes in the total portfolio

A plan must be developed showing how programmes can be included in the total portfolio. The organization has to check and adjust existing rules for allocating projects to subportfolios. One of these already defined rules could be, for example, that projects are assigned to the organizational units that bear most responsibility for project implementation – so departments are made responsible for relevant projects.

Owing to their typically greater importance and value, programmes and their management will typically be allocated to higher levels in the organization (such as a division or business unit). In organizations with a strong hierarchy the project portfolio is usually also structured hierarchically: then programme management can be implemented relatively straightforwardly.

Programme management must not be mixed with subportfolios, as these are typically found in hierarchical organizations. From their very nature, programmes are not portfolios but must be considered as components of a portfolio. Suppose that the portfolio of the organization is always divided according to the hierarchy of the organization. The first level of the organization covers the entire portfolio. Based on the hierarchy of the organization, the portfolio divides further downwards. In the example shown in Figure 37.3, the organization's portfolio is followed by the division or business units. The smallest subportfolio of the organization is represented at the department level.

Organizations usually have rules for assigning projects to organizational units. Basically, if a project is assigned to a department, this project is also visible as a project in the portfolio of the hierarchical level above. If the organization introduces programme management now, it must be worked out on which portfolio level the programme will be presented and at what level the component project of a programme should be visible.

It is not uncommon for programmes to be initiated that go beyond the hierarchical boundaries of organizations. Then it must be ensured that a constituent project which is performed in a specific organizational unit can be reported at the subportfolio level, independent of the organizational level at which the programme is allocated. This change in the reporting requirements needs to be considered very well through the implementation process of programme management in the relevant organization.

The mostly common hierarchical ways of looking at a portfolio (for example, departmental or business unit level) must be disregarded in order to make the

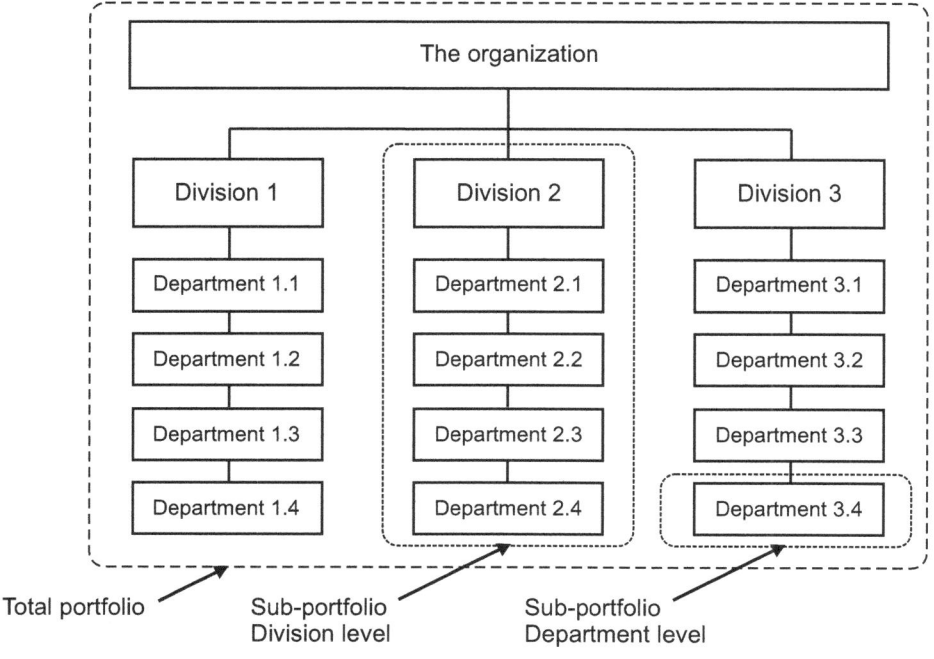

Figure 37.3 Principles of a hierarchical project portfolio

programme visible over the hierarchical boundaries. This particularly can lead to serious challenges in already implemented software solutions for portfolio management.

Another challenge is that during the initialization of a programme it is quite often not known that projects already in progress must be assigned to the programme in arrears. Decisions can be taken that an existing project should be integrated in a programme or, conversely, that a project assigned to a programme should be removed from the programme and performed as a stand-alone project.

Revising existing project management reporting and communication structures

When introducing the programme management, the entire existing reporting and the reporting levels have to be reconsidered and revised. It needs to be clarified and defined what information needs to appear for which component (programmes and projects) on which level of portfolio. Rules and guidelines have to be worked out between PMO and portfolio management in order to avoid double work and misunderstandings in the reporting. If a relatively high project management maturity exists, the structures for reporting within the project should already be developed, with established standards available for project portfolio management.

Projects of a programme are characterized by their dependencies and their strong interrelationships. At the portfolio level it might be necessary to view the projects of a programme in certain subportfolios as a project, and at defined levels of the portfolio as a programme. Projects of a programme are displayed at subportfolio level as projects but shown consolidated as a programme within the entire portfolio. By doing that, the requirements for managing subportfolios are taken into account, since the display is on an individual project level.

In a higher-level portfolio or in the overall portfolio of the organization only the aggregated views of programmes are presented. This avoids representing resource consumption twice and prevents falsification of key portfolio figures. This different perspective allows a correct representation of the projects at the level of subportfolios, while the correct figure of the programme with aggregated information about the included projects in the programme is shown at the level of the overall portfolio.

The established project management communication structures in an organization must be adapted to the requirements of programme management. Besides good and controlled reporting from the projects in the programme, it is necessary to take care that an information flow from the programme through defined channels into the projects is provided and that the flows back to the programme are not restricted. In addition, a way must be found to communicate the overall objectives and the expected benefits from the programme to each project in an appropriate form.

Target-orientated communications from the programme to the projects should contain the programme objectives and the expected organizational benefits from the programme. Then project managers and their teams will understand decisions that are made at programme level.

Impact of programme management introduction on interfaces within the organization

In organizations with a well-developed project management maturity level, interfaces from projects to the various supporting areas of the organization are usually established. Support functions (such as purchasing, controlling, contract management and so on) will be well accustomed to project management and will already have developed basic understanding. Apart from that, when programme management is implemented all the interfaces have to be verified and adjusted.

When programme management is implemented it is necessary to decide how its constituent projects will be initiated. Assume that the organization typically starts projects when they are authorized by a project committee or by group portfolio. Often there is quarrelling for budget and resources.

In addition to the organizational aspects of the interfaces, the IT technical interfaces as they are typically built into enterprise resource planning (ERP) systems must be considered. Let us assume that these structures are initially strong on all types of projects in the organization. There are interfaces in the area of procurement for those units of the organization which deal more with investment projects. These interfaces, organizational processes and procedures are set out as processes supported by IT systems that handle (for example) requests, approvals and verification routines.

Interfaces for units that mainly process orders for external customers in the form of projects are mainly affected by the organization's procedures and processes of tenders and contracting, materials management, logistics and financial reporting.

When introducing programme management the organization needs to examine whether these processes should be reviewed and be subject to adjustments. The programme will create a new entity that, for example, needs to be aggregated on the budget. The programme itself will normally lead its own budget. If the organization needs to consider the process of adding and/or removing a project from a programme, the consideration of these circumstances can already lead to massive changes in existing structures.

Training and recruitment

The introduction of programme management must be integrated into the training programmes of the organization. Suppose that the organization has already established a standardized approach for the training of project managers and project staff. Further suppose that there exists also training for project owners, so that they are aware of their roles, duties and responsibilities in projects.

In training sessions the different roles and their differentiation in project, programme and portfolio management must be made clear. Explaining the differences is not a single act and does not end with the training. It must be ensured that a continuous discussion takes place and that the distinctions are clear for all areas of the organization.

Recruited project managers should be able to demonstrate competence through suitable education, preferably backed up by certification in project management. This is particularly important for the recruitment of programme managers. Programme managers must have good experience in the management of programmes (or at least in the management of complex and long-term projects). It is not advisable to appoint a programme manager whose experience lies outside the domain of the organization's projects.

When developing a recruitment and selection process it is essential to work closely together with the organization's HR department. A job profile and specification should be developed. The engagement of an experienced external consultant who is experienced in programme and project management can strengthen recruitment and selection

References and further reading

Bradley, G. (2010), *Benefit Realisation Management: A Practical Guide to Achieving Benefits Through Change*, 2nd edn., Farnham: Gower.

Fowler, A. and Lock, D. (2006), *Accelerating Business and IT Change: Transforming Project Delivery*, Farnham: Gower.

GAPPS (2011), *A Framework for Performance Based Competency Standards for Program Managers*, Sydney: Global Alliance for Project Performance Standards.

IPMA (2006), ICB – International Competence Baseline.

OGC (2007), *Managing Successful Programmes*, 3rd edn., Norwich: The Stationery Office.

OGC (2011), *Managing Successful Programmes*, 4th edn., Norwich: The Stationery Office.

PMI (2013), *The Standard for Program Management*, 3rd edn., Newtown Square, PA: Project Management Institute

Chapter 38

Assessing and Improving Programme Management Maturity

Matti Haukka and Mirrka Lyytikäinen

This chapter contains a series of checks that can you can use to assess the level of maturity your organization has reached in managing and implementing projects and programmes. Identifying weaknesses is one important step on the road to making improvements.

Introduction

We identify three different approaches to programme management as follows:

1. Reactive programme management, where an organization realizes that or two or more projects in its portfolio are aiming at the same strategic objective and thus can be managed as a programme. Hence the organization starts reactively using some programme management methods.
2. Managing a single change programme, where an organization recognizes that a programme management approach is necessary for implementing a single important change in the organization. In this case the organization needs to organize the programme as an independent programme, meaning that there is a strong programme organization with clear responsibilities, budget and authority to implement the single change.
3. Using a programme management approach to implement the organization's strategic objectives as a part of the governance system. Programme management is then part of the organization's normal management procedures when implementing strategic objectives.

This chapter deals mainly with the last of these three approaches, where programmes are an integral part of implementing strategic changes. Our discussion also focuses on improving programme management maturity on a continuous basis. In addition we shall describe how the maturity of a single programme can be assessed with the help of benefits management, programme governance and programme stakeholder management.

Prerequisites for programme management maturity

Programme management maturity depends heavily on the organizational environment. In other words, an organization's prerequisites for mature programme management are defined by many underlying issues related to its organization structure and background. Here we describe the prerequisites that affect the programme management maturity of an organization.

Figures 38.1 and 38.2 present the prerequisites according to a six-level maturity model (levels from zero to five). The maturity levels have been adapted and modified from the Capability Maturity Model Integration (CMMI) framework (Wikipedia, 2014), which divides processes according to their maturity levels. Our approach in this chapter is to use these maturity levels as a basis and describe the prerequisites for programme management maturity accordingly.

These figures show the programme management maturity prerequisites in two different areas, namely prerequisites related to organization management culture and structures and prerequisites related to project management (PM) and project portfolio management (PPM) capability (described in more detail in the following sections).

Prerequisites related to organization management culture and structures

Figure 38.1 presents four features that affect the maturity of an organization regarding organization management culture and structures, as follows:

- *Connection with strategic processes* indicates how well the organization strategy and programmes are aligned with each other. In higher levels of maturity the strategic and programme management processes have been optimized to support each other.
- *Project management office (PMO) or its equivalent* indicates what kind of functions or structures the organization has to support the project management and programme management approach. In higher levels of maturity this usually means that the organization has established an organization level project management office (PMO) to support the project, programme and project portfolio management processes in the organization.
- *Organization structure (line and project relationship)* indicates how the project/ programme related work is organized and how much authority and power the projects/programmes have over the budget and resources. On higher levels of maturity the organization structure is projectized and projects/programmes have more control over their budget and resources than on the lower levels.
- *Management understanding and involvement* indicates how well the project management issues are in the 'radar' of the senior management of the organization. In other words, how actively the management is involved in the decision-making of projects. In higher levels of maturity the management team (or equivalent) actively monitors and steers the project portfolio of the organization.

Prerequisites related to project management and project portfolio management capability

Because programmes consist of projects and actually form project portfolios of their own, many principles of project management and project portfolio management apply also in programme management. In order for an organization to be successful

General project management maturity level (CMMI)	Connection with strategic processes	PMO	Organization structure (line and project relationship)	Management understanding and involvement
Level 5: optimized.	Strategic and programme management processes have been optimized to support each other and are continuously developed.	Corporate level, strategic project office (or other body) is established and the PMO director is part of the organization's management team.		Management team or equivalent regularly monitors actual against forecast progress data for all ongoing projects. They actively steer the project portfolio to reach the organization's strategic objectives.
Level 4: managed and measurable.	Realization of strategies is measured against how programme objectives can be achieved.	There is an established formal body (such as a PMO) responsible for project management methodology through the organization.	Projectized. Almost all work is organized in projects/programmes. Very low hierarchical organization structure. Project/programme managers have full control over budget and resources.	Management team or equivalent actively monitors the set of ongoing projects based on the progress data. Management may take actions and make decisions based on the project status information.
Level 3: defined.	The strategy process describes how programmes should be initiated in order to achieve strategic objectives.	A formal body (such as a PMO) has responsibility for project management development and standardizing project management practices. Formal bodies exist in individual business units/departments (for example Corporate IT) but not company wide.	Strong matrix. All appropriate work is organized as projects/programmes. Full time project managers are nominated to the work and they have full control over project budgets and resources.	Management has a general view of ongoing projects (for example, a project list) and it monitors the status of the more significant projects.
Level 2: repeatable but intuitive.	Some programmes have been initiated to implement some specific strategic objectives.	There are more or less formal organizational functions with responsibility or interest in project management development, but not necessarily with the associated resources or budget.	Balanced matrix. Some work is organized as projects or programmes. Full time project managers nominated for important projects but without control over budgets/resources.	Management monitors the status of the most significant projects. However, management lacks a general view of all ongoing projects.
Level 1: initial/ad hoc.	Strategic plans have some objectives that can be used as the basis for initiating programmes.	Project management development depends on the activity of individuals. A person might be named but his/her resources are not really allocated to project management development.	Weak matrix. Some work is organized as projects or programmes. Project managers might be nominated but work full-time with no authority over project budgets and resources.	Management is occasionally interested in individual projects but management involvement in monitoring projects is random.
Level 0: non-existent.	There is no connection between programmes and strategy/there are no programmes.	No organizational body or individual is responsible for (or interested in) developing or standardizing project management practices.	Functional organization. Projects and programmes are executed as part of normal, routine line work.	Management is not interested in projects and does not monitor project activities.

Figure 38.1 Prerequisites related to organization management and structures

General project management maturity level (CMMI)	PPM process	PM process	Project owners' and steering groups' competence	Project managers' competence
Level 5: optimized.	The PPM process is continuously developed based on the experiences and measured project business benefits.	A standard project management model/ process is defined and used in all projects. This process has already demonstrated its functionality but is being improved continuously based on user experiences.	All persons acting as owner and steering group members know their roles and responsibilities in project management and act accordingly.	All project managers (PMs) can verify that they have the experience and knowledge to manage their projects relevant to the projects' size and difficulty (for example IPMA or PMI certification)
Level 4: managed and measurable.	Project prioritization and selection is systematic and based on current resource allocation.	A standard project management model/ process has been defined and is used in all projects.	Most persons acting as owner and steering group members know their roles and responsibilities in project management and act accordingly.	At least those PMs responsible for complex/important projects can verify that they have the experience and knowledge to manage their projects (for example IPMA or PMI certification). There is a described career path for PMs.
Level 3: defined.	Resource load of project portfolio is known (current projects/tasks plus reservations are known).	A standard project management model/ process has been defined but is not used systematically in all projects.	Owners' and steering groups' tasks defined but only a few people acting as owner and steering group members know their roles and responsibilities in project management and act accordingly.	Only competent PMs with prior experience and good competence in project management techniques are chosen for complex/important projects. Some PMs are certified (for example IPMA C or PMP).
Level 2: repeatable but intuitive.	There is a common process for project progress reporting which produces status and balance information for PPM.	Some instructions and guidelines are available for project management (for example an experienced PM instructs others) but there is no organization-wide project management model/ process.	Persons acting as owner and steering group members do not usually know their roles and responsibilities in project management. Some owners have competence (for example as project managers).	All PMs have basic information about PM methods, have attended a PM training course or received other project management training. PMs with prior project management experience are chosen for the most important/ complex projects.
Level 1: initial/ad hoc.	A list of ongoing projects is available and there is a process for updating the list.	There are no instructions or guidelines available for project management, but there is some kind of shared conception of how projects should be carried out.	Persons nominated as project owners and steering group members have no ensured competence.	Usually a person with no relevant project management experience (such as a technical expert of a line manager) is held responsible for a project.
Level 0: non-existent.	No one knows what projects are going on in the organization.	There are no instructions or guidelines for project management.	There are no named project owners or steering groups.	There are no project managers.

Figure 38.2 Prerequisites related to project and portfolio management (PPM) capability

in programme management, it needs to have certain project management and project portfolio management practices in place. The more mature an organization is in terms of PM and PPM, the better prerequisites it has to succeed also in programme management.

Figure 38.2 presents four features that affect the PM and PPM capability in an organization, namely the PPM process, PM process, competence of the project owners and steering groups and finally the project managers' competence.

PPM process indicates how competent the organization is in terms of its project portfolio management process. On higher levels of maturity the organization has a well-functioning project portfolio management process with systematic project prioritization and selection in place.

PM process indicates how competent the organization is in terms of its project management process. On higher levels of maturity the organization has a standardized project management process/model that has been adapted and is systematically being applied throughout the organization.

Project owners' and steering groups' competence indicates how competent the people acting in projects as project owners or steering group members are. Project owners and steering groups have an essential role in ensuring that the projects reach their business objectives. Thus the competence of the project owners and the steering group members highly affects how successful the organization is in reaching the business benefits of its projects. In higher levels of maturity the persons acting as project owners and steering group members know their roles and responsibilities in projects and act accordingly.

Project managers' competence indicates how competent the project managers are. The project manager is responsible for ensuring that the project deliverables are realized according to agreed end results (scope and quality), time and budget. These are the implementation objectives. Thus the project manager's competence highly affects how successful the organization is in reaching the project implementation objectives. In higher maturity level organizations it is therefore ensured that the project managers have (and can verify that they have) the necessary experience and knowledge the projects allocated to them. Project managers' experience and knowledge can vary according to the difficulty/complexity level of the project. Thus, with a mix of complex and simpler projects in the portfolio or programme, not all project managers in the organization need to be on the same competence level.

The organization's capability (or readiness) for change

Some of the factors affecting an organization's readiness for change programme implementation are not included in Figures 38.1 and 38.2. However, this is an important point of view affecting not only the organization's ability to apply programme management in change programmes, but also its ability to change the whole organizational culture towards a project and programme orientated approach.

Hoverfält (2012) divides the indicators of readiness for change programme implementation into three categories, as follows:

1. *Intent.* A visible need and pressure for change and a sustained momentum. There is a clear and shared vision, sense of direction and commonly accepted goal,

based on a shared understanding of what needs to be changed and why. There are sufficient plans to realize the intended changes.

2. *Ensuring resources*, meaning that there are sufficient resources for realizing the intent. This means skilful and charismatic leaders, including the programme owner and programme manager, and dedicated programme teams, with explicitly motivated members and visible senior management support and involvement. There must be a receptive environment in terms of prepared recipients of change.

3. *Autonomy*, which means that the programme has a legitimate position in the organization and there is sufficient authority to use the resources and realize the intended changes.

Even though most of the mentioned success factors are somehow considered in the prerequisites presented here, it would be useful to use this approach in addition to those prerequisites each time a new change programme is initiated.

If considering an organization's readiness for change on a continuous basis (not only the readiness for change programme implementation), there are six relevant categories of factors. This approach is originally presented also by Hoverfält (2012) and adapted and further developed in the training material of Project Institute Finland (2014). According to this adapted version, the categories and related factors affecting organization's readiness for change are as follows:

1. Historical background:
   (a) organization's history;
   (b) organizational structure;
   (c) work rhythm and cycles;
   (d) experiences from successful and unsuccessful changes.
2. Governance and management culture:
   (a) strategy process and clearance of strategy;
   (b) decision-making structures;
   (c) leadership culture;
   (d) trust between management and employees.
3. Management processes and control:
   (a) project management practices;
   (b) infrastructure;
   (c) controlling procedures;
   (d) learning mechanisms and rewarding systems.
4. Communication culture:
   (a) communication infrastructure;
   (b) communication networks;
   (c) transparency of communication;
   (d) feedback culture.
5. Economic resilience:
   (a) status and scenarios of economic stability;
   (b) ability to tolerate uncertainties.

6.   Human capital:
     (a) organizational competencies;
     (b) the spirit and processes of innovation;
     (c) sensitivity to weak signals;
     (d) way of dealing with failures and well-being.

This is an additional point of view which is recommended to be considered when assessing and improving the ability to apply programme management in an organization. A 'quick and dirty' assessment of all these factors can be made in a simple way using levels good (2 points), medium (1 point) and poor (0 points). Getting more than 30 (from the maximum possible 44) proves that the organization's change capability is at least fairly good.

Assessing programme management maturity in a single programme

In addition to the prerequisites for programme management maturity described above, there are three themes that can be used to describe the programme management maturity in a single programme. The themes have been adapted and modified from MSP's *Managing Successful Programmes* (Axelos, 2011). The three themes are:

1.   Benefits management.
2.   Programme governance.
3.   Stakeholder management.

Benefits management relates to how well the programme organization ensures that the business benefits of the programme are being realized. In higher levels of maturity the programme management is continuously following the business environment where the programme is implemented and ensures that the business benefits of the whole programme are being realized.

Governance indicates how well the programme's governance model has been created to support programme management. Governance means the structure of how the programme is managed throughout its lifecycle. It includes among others the programme organization, decision-making and reporting structures, and procedures for programme risk, issue, time, cost, resource and quality management. On higher levels of maturity the functionality of the programme governance model is continuously being followed up, and it is ensured that it supports the programme management at any given time/stage of the programme.

Stakeholder management indicates how well the programme stakeholders are taken into consideration in managing the programme. In strategic change programmes the change caused by the programme in the organization is usually both extensive (affects an extensive amount of people) and deep (affects several different areas including processes, organization structures, competencies and so on). Thus there is a vast amount of stakeholders affected by the programme. That is why stakeholder management is an essential part of programme management maturity. On higher levels of maturity the stakeholder environment is being monitored

General project management maturity level (CMMI)	Programme management practices		
	Benefits management	**Governance**	**Stakeholder management**
Level 5: optimized.	Programme management continuously follows and tracks evolvement of the business and organizational environments and to ensure that the programme benefits are still valid (and makes the necessary adjustments).	Programme management is continuously following and tracking changes needed in the programme governance model and updates the agreed governance model and procedures accordingly.	The stakeholder environment is continuously being followed and the stakeholders' attitudes are being monitored. The stakeholder management plan is updated accordingly.
Level 4: managed and measurable.	Realization of the programme's business objects is followed continuously through the programme's projects (realization of the benefits map is followed). Programme managers can forecast continuously how the programme's benefits will be achieved.	Decision-making works efficiently. Programme reporting and communication is appropriate and adjusted according to the purpose. There are necessary procedures in place, for example for risk, issues, time, cost, resource and quality management.	The stakeholder management plan is continuously followed and stakeholder management actions are being made accordingly.
Level 3: defined.	The programme content is planned based on the approved programme benefit objectives. There are plans showing how projects in the programme help to achieve the programme's benefit objectives (for example with the help of a benefits map).	The decision making and reporting structures have been defined. There is a defined responsibility matrix and all people in the programme know their responsibilities. A programme management office coordinates and supports the programme.	A stakeholder management plan is being created, where the stakeholders have been identified, analyzed and prioritized and an engagement plan has been created.
Level 2: repeatable but intuitive.	Business cases of the programme's projects are being followed and the projects' business case realization can be measured.	There are some guidelines and documented plans showing how programme decision making and reporting is being handled. Most people know their responsibilities.	There are some guidelines for stakeholder management that include the identified stakeholders and actions for each stakeholder.
Level 1: initial/ad hoc.	The programme's benefits objectives are recognized.	There is a named programme organization but roles and responsibilities are not clear.	Identification of programme stakeholders has been made.
Level 0: non-existent.	The programme's benefits objectives are not known.	No programme governance structure.	Programme stakeholders not identified.

Figure 38.3 Indicators of readiness for change programme implementation

continuously and actions towards stakeholders are taken accordingly. Figure 38.3 describes the themes of programme management maturity of a single programme in more detail.

Summary and conclusions

In the case where an organization is applying programme management for a single programme as a one-time effort, it may be possible to assess and improve the programme management maturity using the factors presented above. However, this is possible only if the programme in question is organized very independently.

When an organization is managing several programmes simultaneously and on a continuous basis, all the programmes in the organization cannot be organized as independent programmes without tight association with the organization's other governance processes. In this case all the prerequisites for programme maturity described above become very relevant.

As the variety of factors affecting the maturity is very large, it is not reasonable to assess the total maturity level of an organization. If this has to be attempted, one approach to do this is to use the principle of the 'weakest link', meaning that all the criteria given in Figures 38.1, 38.2 and 38.3 are assessed, and the total programme management maturity level of the organization is determined by the weakest link of the assessment criteria. However, this approach may be too harsh. The most important thing when using the maturity model defined in this chapter is first to find the weakest links and start the improvement actions from those. Following this principle the organization can use this model as a concrete tool to find out the major weaknesses to be improved, if the aim is to develop the organization towards programme and project orientated organization.

In conclusion, the first requirement for an organization is that it ensures that the maturity of its project management practices is on a high enough level. This enables the organization to develop the maturity of its project portfolio management practices towards the higher levels. When the PM and PPM practices are on a high enough level, the organization is able to apply programme management effectively and reach the highest levels of programme management maturity.

References and further reading

Axelos (formerly OGC) (2011), *Managing Successful Programmes*, 4th edn., Norwich: The Stationery Office.

Hoverfält, P. (2012), 'Boundary Activities and Readiness for Change during Change Programme Initiation', PhD thesis, Aalto University publication series, Doctoral dissertations 70/2012

Project Institute Finland (2014), PM Master Training Programme for PMO Managers.

Wikipedia (2014), *Capability Maturity Model Integration*. <http://en.wikipedia.org/wiki/Capability_Maturity_Model_Integration>.

Chapter 39

Developing Competencies of People in Programmes

Michael Young

The development of competence is one of the key challenges facing individuals and organizations. Much has been written on this subject but the concept of competence remains one of the most diffuse terms in the organizational and occupational literature

Introduction

Much has been written about the competencies of project managers and literature is emerging in relation to portfolio management competencies. However, to date very little has been written about the competencies of programme managers. This chapter examines the notions of programme management competence and will identify a number of approaches for developing, improving and assessing competence. It will discuss potential barriers to competence development. The chapter will also examine current and emerging competence standards that have been developed to articulate the expected performance of programme managers in industry.

Defining competence

The concept of competence remains one of the most diffuse terms in the organizational and occupational literature (Robotham and Jubb, 1996). The simple meaning of the word 'competence' is 'the ability to do something well or successfully' (Gale, 2007). However, more accurately it is defined as an 'underlying characteristic of a person in that it may be a motive, trait, skill, aspect of one's self-image or social role or a body of knowledge which he or she uses' (Boyatzis, 1982). Competence is a normative concept rather than descriptive. It requires the integration of many aspects of practice and is often regarded as a psychological construct (Gale, 2007).

The competence of individuals derives from their possessing a set of attributes (such as knowledge, skills, values and attitudes), which they use to undertake occupational tasks (Gonczi, 1996). A competent person, therefore, is one who possesses the attributes necessary for job performance.

Researchers and practitioners in the human resources management (HRM) field have been devoting an increasing interest in managerial competence models. Crawford (2000) provides a detailed examination of the primary research on project management competence that began in the 1970s, citing the work of Gemmill (1974), Thamhain and Gemmill (1974), Thamhain and Wilemon (1977, 1979), Posner (1987), Cleland and King (1988), Gadeken (1991), Pettersen (1991), Ford and McLaughlin (1992), Spencer and Spencer (1993), Zimmerer and Yasin (1998) and Morris (2000).

Project management competencies have become the subject of much literature and debate. Much has been written in project management texts, magazine and journal articles about what it takes to be an effective project manager, 'culminating in Frame's work on project management competence published in 1999' (Crawford, 2000). More recent research has resulted in the development of competencies for programme managers (Partington et al., 2005), for operations managers (Bouraard, 2008) and portfolio managers (Young and Conboy, 2013).

Heywood, Gonzczi and Hager indicate that performance-based or occupational competency standards, on the other hand, specify 'what people have to be able to do, the level of performance required and the circumstances in which that level of performance is to be demonstrated' (Crawford and Pollock, 2008) with the emphasis being on demonstrating performance to the standards required of employment in a work context (Knasel and Meed, 1994). In a project management context, a performance-based competency standard indicates what a project manager is expected to do in their working roles, as well as the knowledge and understanding of their occupation that is required (Crawford, 2000). The emphasis is on the threshold rather than high performance or differentiating competencies (Crawford and Pollack, 2008).

Performance-based competency standards are specifically designed for assessment and recognition of current competence. Glassie (2003) suggests that this is assessed independently from how that competence has been achieved (Crawford and Pollack, 2008). They also encourage self-assessment, reflection and personal development in order to provide evidence of competence against the specified performance criteria (Crawford, 2007). The advantage of assessment in a performance-based competency standard context is that an individual is assessed with a binary result being provided: either as person is 'competent' at the time of assessment, or 'not yet competent' (Crawford, 2007).

Current and emerging competence standards for programme managers

Competence standards have been developed by industry bodies for project managers (Australian Institute of Project Management, 2010; Association for Project Management, 2006) to codify the minimum performance requirements for project managers. However, such standards are not used only for assessment or certification purposes, but are also used by individuals to self-assess their current skills, knowledge or experience levels, or as part of their own personal development planning. HRM professionals also use competence standards as a normative reference when developing job descriptions and career hierarchies within organizations. Those who design and develop training programmes also link back to such standards to ensure that each course covers all expected knowledge and skills areas.

Development of competency standards is a largely qualitative approach, based on the collective opinion of experienced practitioners as to what project personnel need to know and what they need to be able to do in order to be considered competent (Crawford, 2004). Creating new standards by consensus is a difficult process, where it is arguable as to whether there is any such thing as a 'best' solution. Rather, as Crawford and Pollack (2008, p. 72)(2008) suggest, 'standards that reach the marketplace are often the product of lengthy political negotiation and act as accommodated positions between the different professional associations'. Given these challenges new approaches to competency development have emerged. Partington *et al.* (2005) have taken an interpretive approach to studying human competence, known as phenomenography. This approach is based on the idea that, for any aspect of reality, there is a hierarchy of conceptions of that reality in relation to some phenomenon.

While there are many performance-based or attribute-based competency standards covering the project management domain, there are relatively few standards for programme managers. A number of authors and bodies have developed performance-based competency standards in programme management, including the International Project Management Association and the Global Alliance of Project Performance Standards.

International Project Management Association (IPMA)

The International Project Management Association (IPMA) has published an Individual Competence Baseline, which is currently in its third edition. At the time of writing, the fourth edition (ICB4) was under development and due for release in September 2015. ICB4 will examine project management, programme management and portfolio management, identifying the technical, contextual and personal and social competencies required for individuals operating in these domains. This standard (ICB4) has been developed through a consensus process. It gathered input from over 150 academic and industry experts from more than 55 countries through surveys, workshops, research, poster presentations and literature reviews over a four-year period. IPMA offers a four-level certification programme based on the ICB.

To be recognized as fully competent, a project manager must prove competence in each of these three dimensions. Their relative importance changes with the different roles in projects. IPMA has recently introduced an organization competence baseline (OCB) for setting the baseline for organizational competencies in management by projects, which uses ICB for individual development, but also adds the project and organizational competence level.

Global Alliance for Project Performance Standards (GAPPS)

GAPPS has developed a performance-based competency standard for programme managers. GAPPS is a volunteer organization working to create frameworks and associated standards by providing a forum for stakeholders from different systems, backgrounds and operating contexts to work together to address the needs of the global project and programme management community. The GAPPS standard takes a detailed approach to differentiating three levels of programme manager based upon:

- programme management complexity;
- eight units of performance-based competency standards for the role of programme management;
- description of six types of programme manager based on which of the eight units apply.

The eight units of the GAPPS standard are as follows:

1. Provide leadership for the programme.
2. Facilitate stakeholder engagement.
3. Craft the programme.
4. Orchestrate the attainment of benefits.
5. Sustain programme progress.
6. Manage organizational change.
7. Direct the management of contract.
8. Engage in collaborative alliances.

Other sources

A number of other authors have identified a range of competencies for programme managers, although they have not been published in the format and structure of a standard. Thiry (2010), for example, details the range of skills required of programme managers at each of the five stages that he describes as the programme lifecycle in his book.

In their 2005 paper, Partington *et al.* 17 key attributes of programme management work at four levels in a hierarchy of competence, grouped as follows:

- Relationship between self and work:
  - granularity of focus;
  - emotional attachment;
  - disposition for action;
  - approach to role plurality.
- Relationship between self and others:
  - relationship with team;
  - approach to conflict and divergence;
  - education and support;
  - use of questions;
  - expectations of others.
- Relationship between self and programme environment:
  - adaptive intent;
  - awareness of organizational capabilities;
  - approach to risk;
  - approach to face-to-face communications;
  - approach to governance;

- attitude to scope;
- attitude to time;
- attitude to funding.

While they acknowledge that programme management as a homogeneous concept is difficult to pin down, they have suggested that a staged approach better articulates how programme management is enacted than a single-level, rationalistic model.

Competence assessment

Competence assessment is often undertaken on the completion of a training course or when an individual believes they possess the competencies described by the competence standard. While the approach to assessment and some of the mechanics (such as the number of assessors) vary between countries and cultures, most competency-based assessments are undertaken in a similar manner.

As the name suggests, competence assessment involves the assessment of an individual's competence. This assessment often takes the form of an interview, plus the candidate providing a portfolio of workplace documents as evidence of having demonstrated specific competencies in the recent past. On some occasions assessment methods may be used in addition to an interview, as follows:

- an assessment workshop (to see how an individual works with others);
- an examination (to test knowledge);
- skills tests (to test underlying skills) or a third party report (to understand how individuals apply their skills and knowledge in the workplace.

The assessor examines evidence provided by the candidate and makes a judgement as to whether the candidate has met the competencies described in the standard. If all competencies are met, then the person is deemed competent. If there are gaps in their competencies, the candidate is assessed as 'not yet competent' and often is asked provide additional evidence in order to substantiate the claim for competence.

Quite often some form of qualification or certification is provided upon being deemed competent against all aspects of the specified standard.

Other uses of competence standards

Competence standards are often thought of as benchmarks against which an individual can be assessed. While many professional bodies and government-supported qualification frameworks around the world do so, competence standards can be useful in many other ways. Competence standards can be used by professional people for the reasons listed below:

- Individual practitioners:
    - developing a baseline for personal development;
    - identifying potential career paths;
    - identifying potential gaps in current skills and knowledge.

- Educators and trainers:
  - as a curriculum document for input into course design;
  - to develop course content and assessments;
  - as a basis for developing new training products.
- Consultants:
  - as a basis for developing new consulting products or services;
  - as an international benchmark to reference on consulting assignments.
- Human resource practitioners:
  - as the basis for job descriptions;
  - to design pay scales and career hierarchies;
  - as a benchmark to use when recruiting staff;
  - as the basis for staff development programmes.

Developing competence

There has been much discussion and debate over time as to how competence is developed. Some authors argue that individuals learn and develop their knowledge, skills and attitudes through traditional learning pathways, whereas others do so on-the-job over a period of time. These approaches interact with each other resulting in a situation where competence development is highly dependent upon individual factors such as a person's background, personal and employment circumstances, personal motivations, past and current job roles and the extent to which they commit time and effort to pursuing self-improvement.

There are various approaches to the development of individual competencies. These depend on factors such as the preferences of the individual or the organization in which they work (or volunteer), the situation and the availability of resources, and which approach fits the individual's circumstances and preferences. The tendency when discussing competence development is that an individual needs to undertake work-specific activities through which they gain experience, learn new things or apply existing knowledge in new contexts. Other approaches to developing competence follow.

Self-development

Self-development involves the person reading books, standards, case studies and relevant industry or academic articles to increase individual knowledge. This might also take the form of reflective practice, where an individual reflects on the application of specific knowledge in practical situations and derives learning from that. Other ways of self-development are studying, experimenting, trying things out or learning by doing. The last of these helps a person to gain experience in a certain context or to develop certain skills.

Peer development

Peer development means interacting and reflecting with colleagues on how things are going, requesting feedback on their own performance and asking for suggestions as to how to improve it.

[Editorial comment: In many industries it has always been customary to put people with little experience next to skilled people in a process that we affectionately call 'sitting next to Nellie'. On a more professional level, interaction with colleagues, not necessarily even from the same organization, brings mutual benefits. These associations can be informal or formal and are known as 'communities of practice'. Chapter 39 in Lock and Scott (2013) gives more on this subject. DL]

Volunteering

Volunteering can often provide an excellent opportunity for learning new skills or to demonstrate competence in a new discipline. Examples include moving from project management to programme management, learning about a different kind of organization and gaining experience of another industry.

[Editorial comment: Many people, including some of my own colleagues, have become better people by volunteering to do hands-on charitable work. That can produce a benefit for the way in which those volunteers interact with people in the programme management workplace. DL]

Education and training

Formal education and training are clearly important for gaining the qualifications needed by people to obtain their first jobs in an organization. That process usually results in a recognized qualification in a vocational or professional field. But continued education and training are necessary for skills development and for keeping pace with technological advancements. That can involve attending seminars, refresher courses, lectures and training programmes delivered by industry experts. The methods used include presentations, interactions between participants and the trainer, case studies, group exercises and simulation games.

Coaching and mentoring

This approach involves receiving feedback, advice and support from a coach, leader or mentor while the trainee performs certain activities or strives to develop specific competencies. Typically, a coach, leader or mentor is an experienced person who challenges individuals by asking questions that draw the trainee's attention to certain aspects and requires them, not the trainer, to find adequate answers.

Simulation and games

This practice is intended to develop competencies through case-based simulation games, reflecting on interactions and behaviours of individuals which become apparent during the process. Simulation games and other forms of game-based learning are often a mix of approaches, such as enabling self-development combined with peer-development and coaching (all conducted in a training environment). These approaches are not always used singularly or independently of each other. It is possible to combine some of them to create more structured competence development programmes, with custom designed approaches used for specific stages of the development process.

Barriers to competence development

In some instances people might meet barriers on the path of their competence development. Such barriers can prevent or limit the development of individual competence. They might result in individuals having gaps in their skills which prevent them from being assessed as competent. Or possibly they might be deprived of possessing the range of skills needed for them to move into specified roles. At a macro level. the challenge is that one needs to gain experience in order to demonstrate competence. The following factors are among those that can result in this paradox.

Internal politics

Internal politics in some organizations can prevent a person from being able to apply for a particular role (and thus having the opportunity to develop experience and competencies). Such prejudice can even prevent an individual from having the opportunity to be assessed by an external assessor against an industry or professional benchmark. These circumstances can result in a senior manager being embarrassed or looking less qualified. Individuals can be strongly discouraged or even told not to pursue such endeavours.

Pigeonholing

In a number of organizations, individuals often get stuck in a particular job or role, with limited opportunity to learn new things or try different kinds of work. They are seen by their peers and superiors as being perfectly suited to their current work, without any thought being given to the latent talent that could be unlocked by providing suitable subjects with a greater challenge.

Different industries

Managers often can see the transferable skills which individuals might bring from their experiences in other industries. But different industries can be insular, and then only those individuals with a long track-record in their existing industry get the opportunities to move into programme management roles.

Issues of evidence or proof

A critical limiting factor for competence recognition is the inability to provide workplace evidence to support an individual's assertion of competence during an assessment. While by all accounts the individual has the competence, sufficient evidence of that cannot be provided to the satisfaction of an assessor. This lack of evidence often occurs because the individual has moved from one company to another. In such cases a security classification or confidentially provisions in the individual's former contract of employment can prevent evidence of competence from being seen by the assessor.

Insufficient investment in professional development

Employers often want to hire individuals who already have the appropriate skills for the job. So they tend to limit funding to develop the skills and competence of their staff. Without opportunities for developing new skills through training and professional development, job rotations or working on projects, employees (including programme managers) will not be able to develop the competencies that would, in the end, benefit the employing organization.

Conclusion

This chapter has explored a number of themes in relation to the development and assessment of competence for those working on programmes.

Competence standards have been developed by industry, professional and government bodies to give benchmarks against which individuals can be formally assessed and recognized with a qualification or certification. Such standards are also used by other groups such as human resource professionals and educators and trainers. Development of competencies in programme management is not always straightforward, however, as there are numerous barriers to competence development.

There are only a limited number of competence standards that clearly articulate the performance expected of programme managers. With the release of ICB4 by IPMA, recognition of the skills, knowledge and competencies of those working in programme management should be made more visible.

References and further reading

Association for Project Management (2006), *APM Body of Knowledge*, 5th edn., Princes Risborough: Association for Project Management.

Australian Institute of Project Management (2010), *About APIM Standards*. <http://aipm.com.au/html/pcspm/cfm>.

Bouraad, F. (2008), 'IT Project Portfolio Governance: The Emerging Operation Manager', *Project Management Journal*, 41(5): 74–86.

Boyatzis, R. E. (1982), *The Competent Manager*, New York: John Wiley.

Cleland, D. I. and King, W. R. (1988), *Project Management Handbook*, 2nd edn., New York: Van Nostrand Reinhold.

Crawford, L. (2000), *Profiling the Competent Project Manager*, Paris: Project Management Institute.

Crawford, L. (2004), *Senior Management Perceptions of Project Management Competence*, Newtown Square, PA: Project Management Institute.

Crawford, L. (2007), 'Global Body of Project Management Knowledge and Standards', in P. W. G. Morris and J. K. Pinto (eds.), *The Wiley Guide to Project Organization and Project Management Competencies*, Hoboken, NJ: John Wiley.

Crawford, L. and Pollack, J. (2008), 'Developing a Basis for Global Reciprocity: Negotiating Between the Many Standards for Project Management', *International Journal of IT Standards and Standardization Research*, 6(1): 21–8.

Ford, R. C. and McLaughlin, F. S. (1992), '10 Questions and Answers on Managing MIS Projects', *Project Management Journal*, 23(3): 21–8.

Gadeken, O. C. (1991), *Competencies of Project Managers in the DOD Procurement Executive*, Shrivenham: Royal Military College of Science.

Gale, A. (2007), 'Competencies: Organisational and Personal', in P. W. G. Morris and J. K. Pinto (eds.), *The Wiley Guide to Project Organization and Project Management Competencies*, Hoboken, NJ: John Wiley.

Gemmill, G. R. (1974), 'The Effectiveness of Different Power Styles of Project Managers in Gaining Project Support', *Project Management Quarterly*, 5(1).

Glassie, J. (2003), 'Certification Programs as a Reflection of Competency', *Association Management*, 55(6): 17–18.

Gonczi, A. (1996), *Reconceptualising Competency-Based Education and Training: With Particular Reference to Education for Occupants in Australia*, Sydney: University of Technology.

Heywood, L., Gonczi, A. and Hager, P. (1992), *A Guide to Development of Competency Standards for Professions*, Canberra: Australian Government Publishing Service.

Knasel, E. and Meed, J. (1994), *Becoming Competent: Effective Learning for Occupational Competence*, Sheffield: Employment Department and Learning Methods Branch.

Lock, D. and Scott, L. (eds.) (2013), *Gower Handbook of People in Project Management*, Farnham: Gower.

Morris, P. W. G. (2000), *Benchmarking Project Management Bodies of Knowledge*, Sydney: University of Technology.

Partington, D., Pellegrinelli, S. and Young, M. (2005), 'Attributes and Levels of Programme Management Competence: An Interpretive Study', *International Journal of Project Management*, 23(2): 87–95.

Pettersen, N. (1991), 'Selecting Project Managers: An Integrated List of Predictors', *Project Management Journal*, 22(2): 21–5.

Posner, B. Z. (1987), 'What it Takes to be a Good Project Manager', *Project Management Journal*, 18(1): 51–4.

Robotham, D. and Jubb, R. (1996), 'Competencies: Measuring the Immeasurable', *Management Development Review*, 9(5): 25–9.

Spencer, L. M. and Spencer, S. M. (1993), *Competence at Work*, New York: John Wiley.

Thamhain, H. J. and Gemmill, G. R. (1974), 'Influencing Styles of Project Managers: Some Project Performance Correlates', *Academy of Management Journal*, 17(2): 216–24.

Thamhain, H. J. and Wilemon, D. (1977), Leadership Effectiveness in Programme Management', *Project Management Quarterly*, 6: 25–31.

Thamhain, H. J. and Wilemon, D. (1979), 'Skill Requirements of Engineering Programme Managers', *Professional Engineer*, 49(2): 25–6.

Thiry, M. (2010), *Programme Management*, Farnham: Gower.

Young, M. and Conboy, K. (2013), 'Contemporary Project Portfolio Management: Reflections on the Development of an Australian Competency Standard for Project Portfolio Management', *International Journal of Project Management*, 31(8): 1089–1100.

Zimmerer, T. W. and Yasin, M. M. (1998), 'A Leadership Profile of American Project Managers', *Project Management Journal*, 29(1): 31–8.

Index

Accra Agenda for Action 175–6
ACDC table *see* Aitken-Carnegie-Duncan
   Complexity table
Activity interface matrix 511
Aerospace Safety Advisory Panel
   (ASAP) 548–50
After market management 90
Agile 233, 242–3, 277–9, 306, 356, 359, 364,
   368, 422, 429, 433, 468; *see also* Waterfall
   versus agile
Airbus 61, 66, 82–4, 88–9, 292
Aitken-Carnegie-Duncan Complexity
   table 20
Ames Research Centre 552
Antares space launcher 58
APM *see* Association for Project Management
Apollo programme 5, 41, 60–61
APQP product development process 98–104
Architecture for programme management
   359–63, 459, 463
Ariane space launchers 58, 60–81
ASAP *see* Aerospace Safety Advisory Panel
Association for Project Management (APM)
   6, 168, 277, 279–81, 360–61, 371; Body of
   Knowledge 6, 22, 273, 275; Programme
   Management Special Interest Group 30
Atlas space launcher 58
Audits *and* auditing 31–2, 64, 68, 126–8, 141,
   143, 146, 278, 283, 368, 370, 405
Australian Transport Safety Bureau 88
Automotive industry 92–116
Aviation industry 117–31
AXELOS: Management of Risk 219;
   Management of Value 219; Standard
   on Portfolio, Programme and Project
   Offices 24–5; *see also* Managing Successful
   Programmes (MSP) *and* Office of
   Government Commerce

BCM *see* Business change manager
Benchmarking 260, 279–81, 346
Benefit manager 437–8
Benefit mapping 440–41

Benefit owner 437
Benefits lifecycle 341–4, 433–7
Benefits management 202–3, 371, 439–41
Benefits management practice leader 438–9
Benefits measurement 167, 441–3
Benefits of partnership management 511–12
Benefits realization 8, 10, 14, 215, 330,
   344, 420
Benefits realization management/planning/
   strategy 187, 202, 207, 210, 317, 389,
   393, 436
Body of knowledge 5, 6, 16, 22–3, 273, 273, 275
Boeing 82, 85, 89
Bombardier test and certification
   programme 85
British Standards Institution (BSI) 245
British standards: BS 6079 361; BS 11000
   245–7, 250–57
Budgets 47, 96, 122, 135, 209, 222, 296, 308,
   316–17, 392, 404, 411–12, 419, 422, 441,
   447, 475
Build schedules *see* Configuration
   management
Business case 13, 22, 25, 39, 83–6, 90, 97,
   100, 110, 177, 181, 186, 200, 209, 215–16,
   251, 275–6, 280, 313, 322, 324, 326, 341–8,
   353, 355, 357, 366, 374–83, 391–2, 404,
   406–7, 411, 419–21, 434, 438–9, 441–2,
   475, 481–2, 486, 488–9, 494–5
Business change manager (BCM) 420–21
Business process reengineering 260

C & E *see* Construction and engineering
   programmes
Cascade from corporate strategy to
   projects 34–5
Cash flow 441, 481–6
Categorization of programmes *see*
   Programme categorization
CCI (in space sector programmes)
   controlled configuration item 73
Central Computer and Telecommunications
   Agency 31

Certification (in aerospace industry) 87
Challenges and concepts for programme
    management 8
Challenges and trends for future PMOs 326–8
Change management (organization and
    systems changes) 218, 229, 231–2, 323, 325,
    331–6, 364, 369–72, 414, 500, 513, 515,
    525; *see also* Managing changes (changes
    to the business case or programme details)
    and osb international model
Change Management Institute 371–2
Change programmes 22, 36, 51, 54, 201, 204,
    232–43, 575, 579, 580–3
Closing down the PMO 325–6
CMO *see* Current mode of operation
CNES *see* French National Space Agency
Collaborative working 245–8; *see also*
    Communities of practice
Common parts management 106–7
Communication 13, 15, 27, 61, 63, 67–8,
    119–22, 128, 135–7, 202, 238–42, 249–50,
    297, 310, 327–8, 336, 348, 385, 418, 495–6,
    505, 507, 511–13, 522–3, 525–9, 535–6,
    538, 541–2, 545, 550–51, 553–4, 560, 562,
    568, 572, 580, 582, 587
Communications management 24, 94,
    362, 368–9
Communications plan 146, 212, 388,
    399–400, 408–9, 502
Communications strategy 190, 388, 399
Communications systems technology and
    telecommunications 54–5, 61, 81, 133,
    195, 201–27, 291, 293, 426, 453, 460
Communities of practice (CoP) 330, 332–3,
    537–8, 544, 590
Company PMO *see* Enterprise programme
    management office
Competence assessment 588
Competence bottlenecks 470, 479
Competence development 589–92
Competence standards 18–20, 584–5, 588, 592
Competence, definition of 584–5
Competencies *see* Developing competencies
    of people in programmes
Competency mapping 140
Complexity: coping with/managing 7,
    444–57; in humanitarian and development
    projects 177–8; in planning 223–4, 226–7
Concurrency (of programme tasks) 86
Configuration management (or version
    control) 62, 76, 87–9, 362, 369, 374
Construction and engineering programmes:
    best practices 137–41; definitions and
    characteristics 132–3; governance and
    organization 135–7; relevance of 133–4;
    role of government 134

Contract management 508–10, 520–32;
    changes and claims 517–18; improving
    results 530–31; things that can go
    wrong 521–30
Control cycles 415–17
Controlled configuration item (space sector
    programmes) 73
Cooperation matrix 507
Cost breakdown structure (CBS) 70, 418
Cost control/cost management 79,
    316–17, 419
Costain Group 254–5
Cost–benefit analysis 301
Cost–time relationship 345
CRAFT methodology 246–7
Critical path 5, 60, 79, 159, 163, 314–16,
    396, 418, 470, 474, 478, 499, 514–15; *see
    also* PERT
Critical success factors (CSFs) 175, 259, 323,
    330, 459
Culture of excellence 61
Culture(s): business partners 505; company,
    corporate, organization 427, 454, 537,
    545–6, 576–80; national 489, 510–11;
    programme culture 330–37; Trompenaars'
    model 510
Cumulative or parallel projects 569–70
Current mode of operation (CMO)
    379–80; *see also* Future mode of
    operation (FMO)
Cyclic delivery from programmes 36–7; *see
    also* Programme lifecyles

De Bono, Edward, six thinking hats 335–6
Defoe, Daniel 3
Delta space launcher 58
Department for International Development
    (DFID) 181, 184, 186
Department of Defense (US) 5
Design-to-cost management 79–80
Developing a high performance programme
    management team 140–41
Developing competencies of people in
    programmes 584–93
Development roadmap of programme
    management 560–60; *see also* Programme
    roadmap *and* Strategic roadmap
DEVOTE project 552–3
DFID *see* Department for International
    Development
DFMEA, design failure mode and effect
    analysis *see* FMEA
Documentation 88, 372–4
Domain experience of the programme
    manager 574
Double loop control cycle 416–17

Earned value management (EVM) 345,
 397, 475
Earned value measurement (EVM) 68, 83,
 119, 308, 404
EMA *see* European Medicines Agency
EMCOR UK 251
Enabling projects 353
Engaging people in changes 261–3
Enterprise (i.e. the company) programme
 management office (EPMO) 113, 559, 562
European Aviation Safety Agency (EASA) 87
European Cooperation for Space
 Standardization (ECSS) 81
European Medicines Agency (EMA) 166
European Space Agency 61
Exceptions *and* exception reporting 11, 412,
 438, 470
Explorative projects 352–3
Eye of competence 19

Failure mode and effect analysis (FMEA) 77,
 101, 103, 400
Failures in complex programmes 445–7
Fast systems development 412–13
FDA *see* US Food and Drug Administration
Federal Aviation Administration (FAA) 87
Fitness for purpose 87, 272, 370–71
Flight data review (FDR) in space sector
 programmes) 74
Flight readiness review (FRR) in space sector
 programmes 74
FMO *see* Future mode of operation
Ford, Henry and Fordism 92–4
French National Space Agency (CNES)
 65, 79–80
Frugal innovation 541–2
Functional specification (FS) in space sector
 programmes) 74
Future mode of operation (FMO) 377–81;
 see also Current mode of operation (CMO)

GAPPS *see* Global Alliance of Project
 Performance Standards
Gated processes *see* Stage gates
General Electric 82
General Motors 92
German Project Management Association 6
Global Alliance of Project Performance
 Standards (GAPPS) 20–21, 561, 586–7
Globalization effects (automotive industry) 108
Goals *see* Objectives
Google 156, 535, 538
Governance *see* Programme governance and
 Project governance
GPM *see* German Project Management
 Association

GPO *see* Programme management group
Haiti earthquake relief programme 188–92
Herkules programme 221–8
History of project and programme
 management 3–6, 29–31
HOPE (acronym for hands on project
 experience) 551–2
House style (for documents and
 websites) 373
Human Development Index (HDI) 174–5
Human Development Reports (HDR) 176–7
Human reaction to change 491–500
Humanitarian and development
 projects 174–93

ICT (information and communication
 technology) programmes 221–8
ICW *see* Institute for Collaborative Working
Identifying the programme 364
Importance of contractual and commercial
 issues 521
IMS *see* Integrated master schedule
Industrial architect (in space sector
 programmes) 72
Industrial Revolution 5
Information flow 365; *see also*
 Communication *and* Communications
 management
Inspecting and measuring change 500–501
Institute for Collaborative Working (ICW) 245
Integrated master schedule (IMS)
 68, 390–99
Integrating programmes in the total
 portfolio 570–72
Interfaces between partners 516–17
Internal rate of return (IRR) 100, 409, 411,
 433, 441
International Project Management
 Association (IPMA) 6, 14; Individual
 Competence Baseline (IPMA ICB) 6,
 19–20, 586; Organizational Competence
 Baseline 6, 25; Organizational
 Project Management Maturity Model
 (OPM3) 26–7
International standards 18–37; *see also*
 ISO standards *and* Project Management
 Institute
International Standards Organization (ISO)
 81; *see also* ISO standards
Interrelationship management 227
Interrelationships between projects 8,
 159–60, 572
Interrelationships between risks 402
Introducing programme management into
 an organization 559–74

Investment portfolio 38
IPMA *see* International Project Management Association
IRR *see* Internal rate of return
ISO standards: ISO 9000, Quality management 361; ISO 11000 245; ISO 14300 Space systems – Programme Management 18; ISO 21500 Guidance on project management 21, 361; ISO 21503 Guidance on programme management 21; ISO 21505 Project, programme and portfolio management – Guidance on governance 25–6; ISO 27026 Space systems – Programme management – Breakdown of project management structures 18; ISO 31000, Risk management 361
Isochron D4 method 364
Issue(s) list (list of exceptions or problems) 518

Japanese Pharmaceuticals and Medical Devices Agency (PMDA) 166
Jargon 13–14
Just-in-time (JIT) 93, 109
Justification file (JF in space sector programmes) 72

Key competence indicators (KCIs) 20
Key performance indicators (KPIs) 10–11, 97, 100, 110, 261, 277, 407, 411–12, 416, 420–23, 562
Key person insurance (KPI) 480–81
Knowledge management 531–55
Knowledge services strategic framework 537
KPI *see* Key performance indicator *and* Key person insurance
KS (knowledge services) *see* Knowledge management

Langley Research Centre 552–3
Leadership 6, 36, 120–21, 200, 204, 236, 242, 247, 250–52, 262, 264–5, 282–3, 288, 354, 356, 428–9, 444, 446, 448, 454, 488, 536, 540–42, 544–5, 548, 551, 553, 570
Lessons learned 89, 122, 140, 178, 180, 192, 255, 282, 288, 310–11, 324–5, 352, 368, 385, 400, 421, 510, 519, 533, 548, 551
Lewin, Kurt 490–91
Lifecycles: Mine project 154; Pharmaceutical programmes 165–8; PMO 322–4; Product development 109; Programme benefits 341–4, 433–7; Projects 154, 208, 215–16, 256, 278–9; Programme 117, 241–3, 246–7, 317, 321, 341–52
LIFT (Livelihoods and Food Security Trust Fund) report 181–8

LLIS (lessons learned information systems) *see* Lessons learned
Lockheed Martin 252
LogFrame model 179–82
Long-term outcomes 8, 10, 179
LRR, launcher readiness review (in space sector programmes) 74

Maintenance, repair and overhaul organization (MRO) 83
Make-or-buy decisions 89
Making people accept change 498–500
Management by exception 475
Managing change programmes 229–44
Managing changes (change control) 419–20; *see also* Change management (organization and systems changes) *and* Scope creep, checks and management
Managing changes and claims (contractual) 517–18
Managing complexity in programmes 444–58
Managing contracts *see* Contract management
Managing interdependencies 317–18
Managing interfaces between partners 514–16
Managing interrelationships 227; In the PMO 324–5
Managing partners in programmes 502–19
Managing programme benefits 430–43
Managing programme delivery 367; *see also* Benefits realization
Managing programme resources 405, 473–87
Managing programme timing 514–15
Managing risk *see* Risk management
Managing Successful Programmes (MSP) 21–4, 175, 182, 184, 186, 200, 273, 277, 355, 360–61, 363, 366, 377, 378
Managing uncertainties in programmes 459–72; *see also* Risk management
Market (in the aircraft industry) 82–4
Market environment 463, 469, 504
Market environmental changes 461, 463
Maslow's hierarchy of motivational needs 250, 489–90
Mastering integration in programme management 290–311
Mayo, Elton 489
Megaprojects 20, 36, 38, 262, 520–21, 523
Microsoft 327, 468; Excel 320; Project 200, 226, 320, 327; SharePoint 320; Yammer 327
Milestones 68, 72–3, 75–6, 79, 84, 123–4, 143–7, 219, 226–7, 241, 311, 318, 324, 328, 348, 378–9, 397, 474, 507, 511, 514, 523, 527

Mining industry 149–62
Mission definition 466
Mission statement 300
Monte Carlo simulation 396, 400
Morris, Jonathan 235
Morris, Peter 5
MSP *see* Managing Successful Programmes
Multilevel intervention design 242–3
Multiprogramme management 107–8
Multiprojects 5, 29–32
Myanmar programme 181–8

NAO *see* National Audit Office
NASA *see* National Aeronautics and Space
  Administration
National Aeronautics and Space
  Administration (NASA) 60–61, 535,
  539, 547–52
National Audit Office (NAO) 271
Nature of programmes 14, 29–40, 560–62
Net present value (NPV) 100, 345, 409–11,
  433, 441
Network Rail 246, 256
NPV *see* Net present value

Objectives (goals) 10
OECD framework 273
OEM *see* Original equipment manufacturer
Office of Government Commerce 31–4, 54,
  175, 182, 186, 203, 241–2, 300, 360, 373,
  377–8, 561, 567; *see also* AXELOS
OGC *see* Office of Government Commerce
  and AXELOS
Olympic Games *or* Olympics 8, 263, 549
Operational programme manager 238
OPM3 *see under* International Project
  Management Association
Organization's readiness for change 579–81
Organizational capabilities, categories and
  structures: aircraft production 84–5;
  categorizations for organizations that
  manage programmes 44–8; Chinese
  bridge building battalion 4; high
  performing (table) 249; improving
  capability 479; matrix 12, 84, 113;
  organization breakdown structure (OBS)
  418; project based 33; project orientated
  33–4; temporary 12, 34–5, 512–14
Organizational knowledge map 539
Original equipment manufacturer (OEM)
  83, 94–8, 106, 108–9, 513
Orion spacecraft 61
osb international model of change types 230
Outsourcing: supplies and services 89, 98,
  108–9, 113, 137, 172, 197, 391, 480; the
  PMO 322

Panama Canal Expansion
  Programme 139–41
Partnership Sourcing Ltd *see* Institute for
  Collaborative Working (ICW)
PDCA *see* plan-do-check-act cycle
PDP *see* Product development process
PERT *see* Programme evaluation and review
  technique; *see also* Critical path
PFMEA, process failure mode and effects
  analysis *see* FMEA
PFO *see* Portfolio management office
Pharmaceutical programmes 163–73
Plan, do, check, act (PDCA) cycle 98, 333–4,
  337, 416
PMDA *see* Japanese Pharmaceuticals and
  Medical Devices Agency
PMI *see* Project Management Institute
PMO *see* Portfolio management office,
  Programme management office *and*
  Project management office
Polaris 60
Portfolio (definition of) 32–3
Portfolio management 105–6, 168, 265,
  272–4, 325, 361, 363–4, 367, 416, 423
Portfolio management office (PFO *or* PMO)
  411, 415–16, 418–20, 423
Portfolios, programmes and projects –
  relationships and comparisons 9
PPAP (Production part approval
  process) 102
Pratt and Whitney 82, 84
Prince2 *or* PRINCE2 195, 200, 273, 361,
  363, 378
Product development process (PDP) 96
Production part approval process
  (PPAP) 102
Professionalization 7
Programme (definition and nature of) 32,
  35–8, 559–61
Programme and project differences 35–8
Programme and project portfolio
  interactions 345
Programme categorization 43–57;
  capability-related purposes 47–8; collation
  of programme types 51–6; uses by external
  entities 49–50; interfaces between
  component projects 45–7; organizational
  uses and purposes 45, 48–9; strategic
  alignment 47
Programme closure 367–8, 421–2
Programme culture 330–37; *see also*
  Cultures
Programme definition document 347–8; *see
  also* Business case
Programme director 20, 84, 132, 135–7,
  285, 305

Programme Evaluation and Review
    Technique (PERT) 5, 396
Programme governance 84, 109–13, 271–89,
    466–8, 520, 561–2; case studies 284–8;
    key players 283; mastering integration
    290–311; ten golden rules 277–83
Programme initiation 366, 375–84
Programme lifecycles 117, 241–3, 246–7,
    317, 321, 341–52
Programme management and control:
    applications in the automotive industry
    94–6; control against schedule 515–17;
    evolution in the automotive industry
    94; in construction and engineering
    132–48; introducing into an organization
    559–74; parallel programmes 105; process
    overview 355–74; specialist processes
    368; supporting processes 368; typical
    processes and control methods 363, 369;
    using modern technologies 424–9; with
    suppliers in the automotive industry 95
Programme management challenges 8–14
Programme management gates see Stage gates
Programme management group (GPO) in
    the aviation industry 121–8
Programme management maturity 575–93
Programme management office (PMO) 5,
    7, 24–5, 85, 107, 110, 112–13, 132, 135,
    140–41, 143, 147, 199–202, 305, 312–29,
    354, 382, 415, 419, 473–80, 562–3,
    566–7, 572
Programme management sectors: aerospace
    41–81; aircraft industry 82–91; automotive
    industry 92–116; aviation industry 117–31;
    construction and engineering 132–48;
    humanitarian and development projects
    174–93; information and communications
    technology (ICT) 221–8; mining 149–62;
    pharmaceuticals 163–73; police 194–204;
    transport 205–20
Programme management standards see
    AXELOS, International standards and ISO
    standards
Programme management support 382–3
Programme manager(s) 109–12, 163,
    170–71, 217, 224, 236, 238–9, 247, 252–3,
    262, 299, 323, 326, 347, 352, 354, 366–70,
    388, 390, 397, 404, 412, 419–22, 453, 463,
    476, 487–9, 496, 501, 561, 568, 585–7
Programme mandate 377
Programme plan (or programme schedule)
    155–8, 170, 186, 305, 318, 321, 365–6,
    379–83, 470–72
Programme planning 21, 72, 113, 168,
    190–92, 385–405, 462–3, 514, 616;
    preparation phase 348
Programme reviews 88, 103, 199–200

Programme risk management see Risk
    management
Programme roadmap 241, 306–7, 347
Programme sponsor 438
Programme tailoring 372
Programme types 43–57
Programmes, projects and portfolios
    (distinctions between) 564–6
Progress checks 96; see also Schedule control
Progress management see Schedule control
Progress reports 210, 287, 270, 418–19, 479
Project (definition of) 31
Project and programme differences 35
Project and programme portfolio
    interactions 345
Project chains 569
Project governance 223, 279, 283, 561; see
    also Programme governance
Project interrelationships 8, 159–60
Project knowledge 545; see also Knowledge
    management
Project lifecycles 154, 208, 215–16,
    256, 278–9
Project management body of knowledge 5, 6,
    16, 22–3, 273, 273, 275
Project Management Institute (PMI) 6, 16,
    31, 168, 259, 262; Standard for Program
    Management 23–4
Project management office (PMO) 576–7
Project orientated organization 7, 33–4
Project portfolio management 364, 565,
    572, 576, 579, 583; see also Portfolio
    management
Project-based organization 33
Projectification 6

Qantas Flight QF32 damage 88
Quality assurance and management 76–9,
    136, 141–2, 146, 319, 348, 361, 370, 382,
    404, 422, 581
Quality gates 364
Quality in C&E programmes 141–3
Quality management plan and processes 367
Quality planning 97–8, 142, 404

RAMS (Reliability, availability,
    maintainability and safety) 77–8
Raytheon Systems Limited 257
REAL knowledge management see
    Knowledge management
Recognition events (in Isochron D4
    technology) 364, 496, 501
Relationship between engineering and
    programme management 85
Relationship of programmes/projects/
    portfolios/operations 38–9
Reporting lines see also Communication

Reporting of costs and/or progress 79; *see also* Exception reporting
Resource scheduling (or resource management) 315–16
RESPECT model (Midas Projects Limited) 248
Return on investment (ROI) 45, 433–4, 494; *see also* Internal rate of return (IRR)
Return on sales (RoS) 100
Rhythm of change 242
Right first time 61
Risk 76; associated with concurrency 86
Risk management 11, 24, 26, 69, 85–6, 104, 137, 147, 170, 219, 225, 335, 345, 356, 361, 369, 385, 394, 398–403, 434, 480–81, 525; *see also* Managing uncertainties in programmes
Roles *and* role definitions 415–6, 437–9, 566–7
RoS *see* Return on sales
Rosetta space mission 61

Safety criticality (aircraft) 87
Safran 61
SCDR, system critical design review (in space sector programmes) 74
Schedule control 79
Scope checks, creep and management, 13, 24, 216, 388–9, 391–2, 419, 447, 475
Scott's three principles of observation 335
Scottish police reform programme 194–204
SCRUM *or* Scrum technology 233, 242, 422
SDFR, system definition review (in space sector programmes) 74
SDSR, system design review (in space sector programmes) 74
SGQR, system ground qualification review (in space sector programmes) 74
Shao, Jingting 36
Silo thinking 129
Six Sigma 230, 353, 364, 443
Skanska Civil Engineering 253
Skills and organizational enablers 248
Sloan, Alfred P. 92–3
SMART objectives 36
SME *see* Subject matter expert; *also* widely used to signify a small or medium enterprise
SOP *see* Start of production (automotive industry)
Soyuz space launcher 58
Space sector programmes 58–81; cost breakdown structure (CBS) 70; configuration management 76; development process 72–70; history of programmes 60–62; main characteristics 58–61; programme governance, organization and communication 63–8; programme management specifications 62–3; relationships between programme planning phases and technical states 74–5; reviews 74–6; risk 59–60
SPM *see* Strategic programme manager
Sponsor *see* Programme sponsor
Stage gates and gated processes 85, 96, 98, 186, 210, 212–23, 216, 225, 241–2, 278–9. 282, 287, 308, 311, 345, 348, 364, 378, 393, 420, 514–16
Stakeholders 5; access to progress monitoring and reports 143, 147, 281, 365, 367; agreement by/ alignment with 8, 58, 60, 100, 170, 194, 201–2, 215, 277, 295, 347, 378, 452; analysis 299, 379, 506, 515, 524; benefits 47; coaching and training 12; communication 137, 239, 323, 390, 399, 412, 489, 568; complex problems with 455; conflict of interests 466; description of in programme definition 378; different interests of 332, 336; disagreements 216; duty of care towards 272; engagement and involvement of 6, 13, 22–3, 27, 126, 146, 202, 218–19, 271, 275, 284–5, 366, 398, 421, 436, 440, 456–7, 488, 522; external community of 540; failure to engage 523–4; identifying 216; in programme evaluation 422; internal 202; involvement of 347, 382, 385, 405; issues/satisfaction 529; listing 524; managing 136–7, 146, 198, 217, 354, 506, 578, 581–3; motivation of 488; needs, interests, satisfaction of 39, 240, 366, 378, 406; PMO 315; relationships 20, 204, 323; responsibilities of 407; rights of 26; risk sharing 59; sharing lessons learned 413; support for strategic objectives 346; three levels 190; viewpoint of 381, 445
Standards for programme management 20–25; *see also* Axelos, International standards, *and* ISO standards
Start of production (SOP in automotive industry) 96, 101–3
Strategic alignment matrix 439
Strategic portfolio board 407, 415
Strategic programme manager (SPM) 238
Strategic roadmap 276–7, 284, 286
Succession planning 141
Suppliers, capability of 89
Supply chain 89–90, 92, 94, 108–10, 112, 114, 118, 206, 251, 253–6, 385, 388, 391, 403, 512, 515–17; *see also* Outsourcing

Talent management 260, 281, 540–41, 544, 546, 551

Taylor, Frederick Winslow and Taylorism 5, 92
TBP *see* Triangle of Belief Polarities
Technical specification (TS in space sector programmes) 74
Telecommunications and communications systems technology 54–5, 61, 81, 133, 195, 201–27, 291, 293, 426, 453, 460
Ten golden rules of programme governance 277–83
TfL *see* Transport for London
Three organizations involved in the management of projects 34–5
Tichy's TPC matrix 332
Time as a programme resource 473–4
Time-limited resource schedule 478–9
Timesheets 316–17
Timespan of programmes 10; *see also* Programme lifecycles
Time-to-market 82, 93, 107
Total quality management (TQM) 93
Toyota production system (TPS)
Training and recruitment 573–4
Transformational flow 22
Transition projects 353
Transport for London (TfL) programme management: context 206–8; product matrix 209–13; roles and core functions 213–19
Triangle of Belief Polarities (TBP) 240

Triangle of constraints 92; *see also* Triangle of objectives
Triangle of objectives (Martin Barnes), 92, 417–18
Trompenaars' culture model 510

UFQR, unmanned flight qualification review (in space sector programmes) 74
UK Corporate Governance Code 273–4
United Nations Development Programme (UNDP) 189–90
Units of measurement (UOM) 143–5
US Food and Drug Administration (FDA) 166, 172

Value flashpoints 364, 495–6, 501
Version control *see* Configuration management
Volatility, uncertainty, complexity and ambiguity (VUCA) 229

Waterfall versus agile 242
WBS *see* Work breakdown structure
Work breakdown structure (WBS) 68–71, 96, 144, 263, 392–3, 401, 404
Work package (WP) 68, 70–71, 79, 84–5, 96, 110, 112, 142–4, 146, 328, 360–63, 366, 373, 393, 516–18
Wren, Sir Christopher 5